CHARITIES
An Industry Accounting and Auditing Guide

Fifth edition

CHARITIES

An Industry Accounting and Auditing Guide

Fifth edition
Anthony Epton BA FCA CTA FCIE

a Wolters Kluwer business

Wolters Kluwer (UK) Ltd
145 London Road
Kingston upon Thames
Surrey KT2 6SR
Tel: 0844 561 8166
Fax: 020 8547 2638
E-mail: customerservices@cch.co.uk
website: www.cch.co.uk

Disclaimer

This publication is sold with the understanding that neither the publisher nor the authors, with regard to this publication, are engaged in rendering legal or professional services. The material contained in this publication neither purports, nor is intended to be, advice on any particular matter.

Although this publication incorporates a considerable degree of standardisation, subjective judgment by the user, based on individual circumstances, is indispensable. This publication is an 'aid' and cannot be expected to replace such judgment.

Neither the publisher nor the authors can accept any responsibility or liability to any person, whether a purchaser of this publication or not, in respect of anything done or omitted to be done by any such person in reliance, whether sole or partial, upon the whole or any part of the contents of this publication.

Telephone Helpline Disclaimer Notice

Where purchasers of this publication also have access to any Telephone Helpline Service operated by Wolters Kluwer (UK), then Wolters Kluwer's total liability to contract, tort (including negligence, or breach of statutory duty) misrepresentation, restitution or otherwise with respect to any claim arising out of its acts or alleged omissions in the provision of the Helpline Service shall be limited to the yearly subscription fee paid by the Claimant.

© 2009 Wolters Kluwer (UK) Ltd

ISBN 978-1-84798-201-8

All rights reserved. No part of this publication may be reproduced, stored in a retrieval system, or transmitted in any form or by any means, electronic, mechanical, photocopying, recording or otherwise, without the prior permission of Wolters Kluwer (UK) Limited or the original copyright holder.

No responsibility for loss occasioned to any person acting or refraining from action as a result of any material in this publication can be accepted by the author or publisher.

Material is contained in this publication for which copyright is acknowledged. Permission to reproduce such material cannot be granted by the publisher and application must be made to the copyright holder.

Crown copyright is reproduced with the permission of the Controller of Her Majesty's Stationery Office.

British Library Cataloguing-in-Publication Data.

A catalogue record for this book is available from the British Library.

Throughout this book the male pronoun has been used to cover references to both the male and female.

Typeset by Kerrypress Typesetters Limited, Luton, Bedfordshire
Printed in the UK by Hobbs the Printers Ltd.

Contents

		Page
Preface and acknowledgements		xv
List of abbreviations		xix

Chapter 1 – History and definition — 1
1.1	Introduction	1
1.2	The history of charity	2
1.3	Definition of a charity	3
1.4	Registration	8
1.5	Declaration of status	9
1.6	Charity names	11

Chapter 2 – Trustees, duties, liabilities and insurance — 13
2.1	Introduction	13
2.2	Who is a 'charity trustee'?	13
2.3	Who may not be a charity trustee?	14
2.4	What are the trustees' duties?	15
2.5	Responsibility for preparing the report and accounts	16
2.6	Other financial responsibilities	18
2.7	Risk	20
2.8	Investment of charitable funds	20
2.9	Liabilities and insurance	21

Chapter 3 – The regulatory framework — 23
3.1	Introduction	23
3.2	The 1960 Act	24
3.3	The impetus for reform	24
3.4	The 1993 Act	25
3.5	Further changes	39

Chapter 4 – The Charities Act 2006 — 41
4.1	Introduction	41
4.2	Implementation timetable	42
4.3	New definition of charitable purposes	46
4.4	Providing public benefit	48
4.5	New thresholds for registration	54
4.6	Exempt charities	54
4.7	Excepted charities	55
4.8	Greater flexibility for smaller charities	58
4.9	Charitable incorporated organisation (CIO)	58
4.10	Audit and accounts	60

4.11	Charity Tribunal	66
4.12	Duty and protection for whistle blowers	68
4.13	Other measures	69
4.14	Office of the Third Sector (OTS) thresholds consultation	76

Annex 1 Regulatory framework comparisons	80
Annex 2 Public benefit – the Charity Commission	88
Annex 3 Group accounts flow chart	94

Chapter 5 – Fundraising regulations 95

5.1	Summary	95
5.2	Definitions	95
5.3	Agreements with fundraisers and participators	96
5.4	Availability of books, documents and other records	96
5.5	Transmission of money or property	96
5.6	Indications of benefits and remuneration	97
5.7	Cancellation of payments	97
5.8	Unauthorised fundraising and false statements	97
5.9	Street collections	98
5.10	House-to-house collections	98
5.11	Revised guidance on professional charity fundraising	99

Chapter 6 – SORP 2005 101

6.1	Introduction	101
6.2	Background, overview and main changes	102
6.3	The key features	107
6.4	Practical considerations	127

Annex 1 Summary of formats	131
Annex 2 Accounting for smaller charities	134
Annex 3 A list of appendices and tables in the SORP	136

Chapter 7 – Trustees' annual report 137

7.1	Introduction	137
7.2	Changes in SORP 2005	137
7.3	Preparing the Trustees' Annual Report	139
7.4	Structure and components	140
7.5	Reference and administrative information	140
7.6	Structure, governance and management	141
7.7	Objectives and activities	142
7.8	Achievements and performance	143
7.9	Financial review	144
7.10	Plans for future periods	145
7.11	Funds held as custodian trustee on behalf of others	145

Annex 1 Comprehensive example – Training For Life	146

Chapter 8 – Reserves 165
- 8.1 Introduction 165
- 8.2 Charity reserves 165
- 8.3 Examples of reserves policy 169
- 8.4 Revaluation reserve 172

Chapter 9 – The Statement of Financial Activities 173
- 9.1 Introduction 173
- 9.2 Changes in SORP 2000 173
- 9.3 Changes in SORP 2005 174
- 9.4 The form and content of the SOFA 175
- 9.5 Incoming resources 178
- 9.6 Voluntary income 184
- 9.7 Gifts in kind 187
- 9.8 Donated services and facilities 188
- 9.9 Activities for generating funds 190
- 9.10 Investment income 191
- 9.11 Incoming resources from charitable activities 192
- 9.12 Other incoming resources 194
- 9.13 Expenditure and costs 194
- 9.14 Allocation of costs 198
- 9.15 Resources expended 200
- 9.16 Costs of generating funds 200
- 9.17 Charitable activities 202
- 9.18 Grant making 204
- 9.19 Governance costs 208
- 9.20 Transfers 209
- 9.21 Gains and losses on fixed assets 209
- 9.22 Gains and losses on investment assets 210
- 9.23 Actuarial gains or losses on defined benefit pension schemes 210

Chapter 10 – Balance sheet 211
- 10.1 Introduction 211
- 10.2 Presentation 211
- 10.3 Fixed assets 213
- 10.4 Investment assets 223
- 10.5 Programme-related investments 227
- 10.6 Current assets 228
- 10.7 Current liabilities and long-term creditors 229
- 10.8 Provisions for liabilities and charges 230
- 10.9 Defined benefit pension scheme asset or liability 232
- 10.10 Share capital 232
- 10.11 Revaluation reserve 233
- 10.12 Pension reserve 233
- 10.13 Guarantees 233
- 10.14 Contingent assets and liabilities 233

Contents

    10.15 Loan liabilities   234

Chapter 11 – Accounting for separate funds   237
    11.1 Introduction   237
    11.2 What is a 'fund'?   237
    11.3 Fund structure   239
    11.4 Reconciliation and analysis of funds   240
    11.5 Transfers between funds   241
    11.6 Overhead costs   241
    11.7 Disclosures – particulars of individual funds and notes to the accounts   241
    11.8 Total return   247

Chapter 12 – Cash flow statements   249
    12.1 Introduction   249
    12.2 Exemption   249
    12.3 Format of cash flow statements   249
    12.4 Major non-cash transactions   254
    12.5 Reconciliation with balance sheet figures   254
    12.6 Comparatives   254
    12.7 Disclosure examples   255

Chapter 13 – Accounting policies   259
    13.1 Introduction   259
    13.2 FRS 18 Accounting policies   259
    13.3 Disclosure of accounting policies   260
    13.4 Specific policies   262
    13.5 Incoming resources policy notes   262
    13.6 Resources expended policy notes   264
    13.7 Assets policy notes   265
    13.8 Funds structure policy notes   267
    13.9 Other policy notes   268
    13.10 Full example   268
    13.11 Small charity example   271

Chapter 14 – Other matters to be covered in the notes to the accounts   273
    14.1 Introduction   273
    14.2 Related party transactions   273
    14.3 Trustees' remuneration and benefits   276
    14.4 Trustees' expenses   277
    14.5 Staff costs and emoluments   278
    14.6 Cost of audit, independent examination and other financial services   280
    14.7 *Ex gratia* payments   281
    14.8 Analysis of the net movement in funds   281

Chapter 15 – Accounting for retirement benefits — 283
15.1 Introduction — 283
15.2 Defined contribution schemes — 283
15.3 Defined benefit schemes — 283
15.4 Allocation of retirement benefit costs and gains — 284
15.5 Restricted funds — 285
15.6 Consideration of going concern — 286
15.7 Reserves policy — 286
15.8 Disclosures — 287

Chapter 16 – Application of accounting standards — 289
16.1 Statements of Standard Accounting Practice (SSAPs) — 289
16.2 Financial Reporting Standards (FRSs) — 291
16.3 Urgent Issues Task Force (UITF) Abstracts — 301

Chapter 17 – Consolidated accounts — 307
17.1 Introduction — 307
17.2 Changes made by SORP 2000 — 307
17.3 How are parent and subsidiary undertakings defined? — 307
17.4 What are the requirements governing the preparation of consolidated accounts? — 309
17.5 Method of consolidation — 311
17.6 Disclosures — 312
17.7 Approval and filing of consolidated accounts — 314
17.8 Accounting for associates, joint ventures and joint arrangements — 315

Chapter 18 – Company charities — 321
18.1 Introduction — 321
18.2 Accounts and reports — 321
18.3 The Statement of Financial Activities and the summary income and expenditure account — 322
18.4 Presentation of the summary income and expenditure account — 322
18.5 The balance sheet format — 323
18.6 Revaluation reserve — 324
18.7 Summary financial information — 324
18.8 Disclosure examples — 324

Chapter 19 – Accounting for branches — 329
19.1 Introduction — 329
19.2 What is a branch? — 329
19.3 Accounting requirements — 331
19.4 Further considerations — 332
19.5 Connected charities — 334

Contents

Chapter 20 – Summary financial information and statements 335
  20.1 Introduction 335
  20.2 What are the requirements relating to summary financial information and statements? 336

Chapter 21 – Small charities 339
  21.1 Introduction 339
  21.2 The Charities Act 2006 340
  21.3 The Charities 1993 Act versus the Companies 2006 Act 343
  21.4 Preparing accounts on the receipts and payments basis 344
  21.5 Accruals accounting for the smaller charity 352
  21.6 The application of the Financial Reporting Standard for Smaller Entities (FRSSE) 352
  21.7 Charities with gross income not exceeding £500,000 (England and Wales) 353

Chapter 22 – Risk management 357
  22.1 Introduction 357
  22.2 Why risk management? 357
  22.3 Charity objectives 358
  22.4 Critical risk register 358
  22.5 Collate, prioritise and categorise 359
  22.6 Controls 360
  22.7 Continuity and change 360
  22.8 Commitment and responsibility 361
  22.9 Communication 361
  22.10 Creativity 362
  22.11 Costs 362
  22.12 Culture 362
  22.13 How can risk be managed? 363
  22.14 What type of risks do charities face? 363
  22.15 Identifying and managing risk 364
  22.16 Conclusion 365

  Annex – Case study – risk assessment letter 366

Chapter 23 – Audit of charities 369
  23.1 Introduction 369
  23.2 Adoption of International Standards on Auditing (UK and Ireland) 370
  23.3 The special audit features of charities 371
  23.4 Reporting requirements 373
  23.5 Terms of audit engagement 374
  23.6 Audit planning 377
  23.7 Materiality 380
  23.8 Consideration of laws and regulations 381
  23.9 Audit risk 384

23.10	Audit evidence	398
23.11	Audit completion	403
23.12	Audit reports	411
23.13	Reporting to the Charity Commission	419
23.14	Adding value	423
23.15	Ethical Standards	427
23.16	Recent auditing issues	430
	Annex 1 Bank report requests	437

Chapter 24 – Independent examination — 439

24.1	Introduction	439
24.2	What is an 'independent examination'?	439
24.3	Who is an independent examiner?	440
24.4	Who is an 'independent person'?	441
24.5	Which persons would have the 'requisite ability'?	441
24.6	What is 'practical experience'?	441
24.7	Selection procedures	442
24.8	The Charity Commission's Directions	442
24.9	Reporting on summarised accounts	468

Annex 1 Guidance on the selection of an examiner Charity Commission guidance under section 43(7)(a) of the Charities Act 1993	469
Annex 2 Examples of independent examiner's reports	472
Annex 3 Examples of deliberate or reckless misconduct	477

Chapter 25 – Trading income — 479

25.1	Main statutory exemption	479
25.2	What is a trade?	479
25.3	Statutory exemption from tax	481
25.4	Trading activities of charities	481
25.5	Primary purpose trades	484
25.6	Chargeable periods beginning on or after 22 March 2006	491
25.7	Extra-statutory concession relief for fundraising activities	492
25.8	Calculating the profits of the trade	495
25.9	Using a trading company	495
25.10	Financing the trading company	496
25.11	Business rates	497
25.12	Stamp duty land tax (SDLT)	497
25.13	Stamp duty reserve tax (SDRT)	498
	Annex Trading by charity – flowchart	500

Chapter 26 – Employment taxes — 501

26.1	Introduction	501
26.2	Casual, temporary and volunteer workers	501
26.3	Is somebody an employee or self-employed?	502

Contents

26.4	Tax advantages for charities	508
26.5	Schedule E liability of beneficiaries of charities	509
26.6	National Insurance Contributions (NICs)	509

Chapter 27 – VAT — 511

27.1	Introduction	511
27.2	How VAT applies to charities	511
27.3	The meaning of business	512
27.4	VAT recovery for VAT-registered charities	514
27.5	The treatment of grants	515
27.6	Donations	516
27.7	Examples of business and non-business activities	516
27.8	Business membership and supporters' subscriptions	517
27.9	VAT reliefs that apply to all charities	517
27.10	Donated goods	519
27.11	Goods used by charities to collect donations	519
27.12	Reliefs for medical goods	520
27.13	Charity buildings	520
27.14	VAT reliefs that apply to VAT-registered charities only	521
27.15	Recent developments	523

Chapter 28 – Giving to charities — 527

28.1	Introduction	527
28.2	Gift aid	527
28.3	Deeds of covenant	534
28.4	Benefits received by donors	535
28.5	Payroll giving (GAYE – give as you earn)	544
28.6	Giving through the tax return	544
28.7	Legacies	545
28.8	Gifting shares and securities	545
28.9	Gifting land and buildings	548
28.10	Giving to charity by businesses	548
28.11	Recent changes	549
28.12	List of statutory references	555

Chapter 29 – Charities in Scotland, Northern Ireland and the Republic of Ireland — 557

29.1	Scope of SORP 2005	557
29.2	Scotland	557
29.3	Northern Ireland	559
29.4	Republic of Ireland	572

Chapter 30 – The Companies Act 2006 — 575

30.1	Introduction	575
30.2	Objectives	575
30.3	Directors' duties	577
30.4	Community interest companies	581

30.5	Senior Statutory Auditor (SSA)	583
30.6	Filing dates	585
30.7	Late filing penalties	585
30.8	Small companies	586
30.9	Auditors limiting their liability	590
30.10	Auditors' rights to information	590
30.11	Other measures (affecting company charities)	591

Chapter 31 – Recent developments in SORP 2005 — 595

31.1	Scope of the SORP	595
31.2	SORP 2005 – Information Sheet 1	595
31.3	Charities accounts survey	600
31.4	Updated Financial Reporting Standard For Smaller Entities (FRSSE)	601
31.5	Small charity disclosures	601
31.6	SORP 2005 – Information Sheet 2	602
31.7	Financial Reporting Exposure Draft (FRED) 42 – Heritage Assets	604
31.8	Trustees' Annual Report	605
31.9	Standard information return (SIR)	607
31.10	SORP for the future	608

Chapter 32 – Managing in a downturn — 611

32.1	Recent survey	611
32.2	Key points	611
32.3	Conclusion	614
	Annex – Performance management	616

Appendix 1 – The Charities (Accounts and Reports) Regulations 2008 — 619

Appendix 2 – Extract from Charities Act 2006: Chapter 6 Audit or Examination of Accounts where Charity is not a Company and Chapter 7 Charitable Companies — 665

Appendix 3 – Section 505 of the Income and Corporation Taxes Act 1988 — 671

Appendix 4 – Section 256 of the Taxation of Chargeable Gains Act 1992 — 675

Appendix 5 – Model Gift Aid declarations — 677

Appendix 6 – Charity reserves and defined benefit pension schemes — 679

Index — 699

Preface and acknowledgements

The preface to the fourth edition of *Charities: An Industry Accounting and Auditing Guide* stated that it appeared 'at a time of major regulatory change'. The very same is true for this fifth edition.

Nearly four years have passed since the fourth edition was written. In that time, the following have been published:

- Charities Act 2006;
- Companies Act 2006;
- Charities (Accounts and Reports) 2008 Regulations;
- Charities and Trustee Investment (Scotland) Act 2005;
- Charities Accounts (Scotland) Regulations 2006;
- Charities SORP 2005 2nd edition – May 2008, and
- The APB's Practice Note 11 "The Audit of Charities in the United Kingdom" (Revised) December 2008.

This edition of *Charities: An Industry Accounting and Auditing Guide* concentrates on all the major developments affecting charity accounting and auditing that have occurred during the past four years. The first two items listed above are the most significant, and a whole chapter has been devoted to each.

Chapter 4 deals with the Charities Act 2006, which has proved to be one of the most historic pieces of legislation affecting the charity sector in that it has revised the definition of what a charity is – something that had not been achieved for over 400 years. Chapter 30 covers the extensive changes brought in by the Companies Act 2006.

As for the SORP, the fourth edition of this book had to deal with how SORP 2005 revised its predecessor SORP 2000. I have had a less onerous task in this area, as the May 2008 update of SORP 2005 has not introduced any major new material. Nonetheless, in addition to the Charities Act and Companies Act, numerous other important documents have been published in the interim, and these have been fully reflected in this book. I have also added a brand-new chapter on the impact of the ongoing economic recession, suggesting how charities can turn the situation to their advantage.

In terms of the general and background information on the charity sector, the majority of this information has been retained from previous editions.

I would like to express my thanks and appreciation to my two partners at Goldwins, Stephen Goodwin and Anthony Benosiglio, who have both supported

Preface and acknowledgements

me throughout this project. Simon Levine, Goldwins' VAT consultant, provided the necessary technical input to Chapter 27 on VAT, and Harvey Freeman offered his usual incisive comments throughout the book.

I would also like to thank all those at CCH for enabling this book to be published.

My dear wife, Lara, has also been a source of inspiration and encouragement to me. Finally, I am particularly indebted to Adrian Randall, who is now Chief Executive Officer of the Heart & Stroke Foundation of Barbados. It was Adrian who first introduced me to the world of charity accounting and gave me the opportunity to succeed, without which I would not have been able embark on this rewrite.

I am also grateful to the Charity Commission for allowing me to reproduce extensively from their various publications.

I particularly acknowledge the invaluable contributions made by the authors of the previous editions of this book, Nick Morgan and David Chitty.

I sincerely hope that all readers of this book will find it of value to them in their respective charitable pursuits.

Anthony Epton BA, FCA, CTA, FCIE

June 2009

For Ariel and Shira ……. may they always act charitably.

List of abbreviations

Professional and regulatory bodies

ACCA	Association of Chartered Certified Accountants
APB	Auditing Practices Board
ASB	Accounting Standards Board
ASC	Accounting Standards Committee
BERR	Department for Business Enterprise & Regulatory Reform
CCAB	Consultative Committee of Accountancy Bodies
CIPFA	Chartered Institute of Public Finance and Accountancy
DTI	Department of Trade and Industry
FRC	Financial Reporting Council
ICAEW	Institute of Chartered Accountants in England and Wales
ICAI	Institute of Chartered Accountants in Ireland
ICAS	Institute of Chartered Accountants of Scotland
NCVO	National Council for Voluntary Organisations
OSCR	Office of the Scottish Charity Regulator
Registrar	Registrar of Companies
UITF	Urgent Issues Task Force

Accounting and statutory terms

1960 Act	Charities Act 1960
1985 Act	Companies Act 1985
1989 Act	Companies Act 1989
1992 Act	Charities Act 1992
1993 Act	Charities Act 1993
ED	Exposure Draft
FRAG	Financial Reporting and Auditing Group
FRED	Financial Reporting Exposure Draft
FRS	Financial Reporting Standard
IAS	International Accounting Standard
IFRS	International Financial Reporting Standard
ICTA	Income and Corporation Taxes Act
IHTA	Inheritance Tax Act
ISA	International Standard on Auditing
para.	paragraph
paras	paragraphs
Reg.	regulation
s.	section
SAS	Statement of Auditing Standards
Sch.	Schedule

List of abbreviations

1960 Act	Charities Act 1960
ss.	sections
SI	Statutory Instrument
SOFA	Statement of Financial Activities
SORP	Accounting and Reporting by Charities: Statement of Recommended Practice Charities SORP 2005 (2nd edition – May 2008)
SSAP	Statement of Standard Accounting Practice
SSRA	Statement of Standards for Reporting Accountants
TCGA	Taxation of Chargeable Gains Act
The Regulations	The Charities (Accounts and Reports) Regulations 2008
TR	Technical Release

Chapter 1 – History and definition

1.1 Introduction

The word 'charity' comes from the Latin 'caritas' meaning 'affection', 'love' or 'dearness'. It denotes benevolent goodwill towards, or love of, humanity. A kindly attitude towards people is represented by charity. There is a well-known idea that the world rests on three pillars, one of which is charity.

Charities nowadays represent a variety of causes. A recent Charity Commission survey found charities to operate in the following areas:

- culture and recreation   23 per cent;
- education   23 per cent;
- social welfare   22 per cent;
- health   11 per cent;
- religion   9 per cent;
- general   9 per cent;
- environment   2 per cent, and
- housing   1 per cent.

The charity sector is often known as the voluntary or 'third' sector. This can best be understood through the diagram below, which illustrates the various sectors.

Figure 1.1 Model of the three sectors

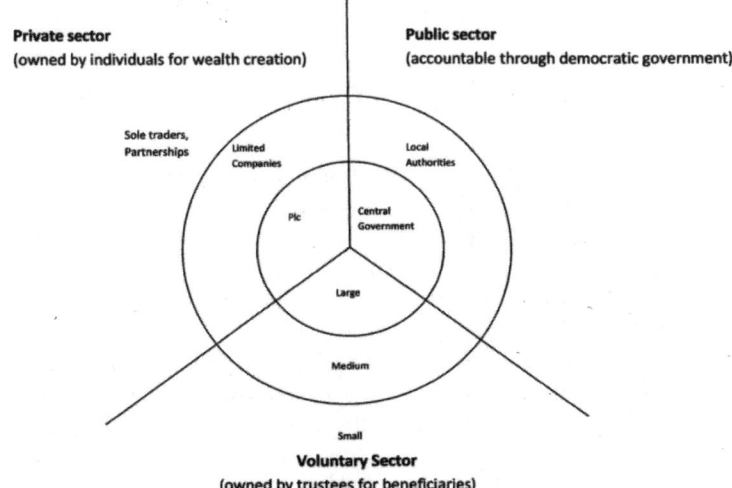

1

History and definition

1.2 The history of charity

Charities date back nearly 900 years. One of the earliest is the Hospital of St Cross in Winchester, which was founded in 1136 by a grandson of William the Conqueror. The hospital still looks after old people and provides bread and ale to passing travellers.

Charity has been a virtue recognised and fostered by religion throughout human history. In medieval Europe, the Church bore the responsibility for organising and promoting poor relief and it was not until the 16th century that the State began to take over this responsibility. In England, the first statutory measures to alleviate poverty were enacted in the late Tudor period. Relief, however, was directed not at the population at large but at the poor and disabled. The method employed was to place responsibility on the parishes, which were helped by a property tax known as the 'poor rate'. However, even in that period, there was a resurgence of private charity and a resentment of state paternalism.

This paternalism did produce generalised relief in the form of the poor laws, but these were no more acceptable to the merchants than indiscriminate monastic almsgiving had been. Philanthropic merchants contributed more than half of the vast sums of money provided for private charities, which were, in the long run, probably more effective than the State aid for the poor.

The philosophy of these enlightened merchants was that people should be helped to help themselves. They poured money into the comprehensive remodelling of the English education system. The middle-class work ethic called for dedication to work, honesty, thrift and charity. It was fundamentally opposed to the corruption and paternalism associated with the institutionalised Church and State.

Towards the end of the 18th century, there was a great revival of interest in charities. Many organisers and supporters felt that it was a Christian duty for the rich to help the poor. It was coupled with a belief that philanthropic action by the richer classes could make a real difference to the lives of the poor, both directly in the provision of donations and also through practical guidance and help. All these charities depended for funds largely on support from subscriptions and donations. The charities varied greatly in size and function. The largest were national institutions, such as the RSPCA, which by the end of the 19th century had nearly 150 branches and over a thousand local auxiliaries.

Until the 19th century, charities were largely established as the result of bequests made in the wills of rich merchants, and of others who were charitably minded. As a result, many towns still have almshouses housing elderly men and women. Many schools were also established as the result of charitable bequests. These charities grew up indiscriminately. The City of London as well as cathedral and markets towns were often well provided for. The new industrial towns of

Lancashire and Yorkshire, though, had very few parochial charities. By the mid-19th century, these charities were largely an anachronism, even if they remained important sources of assistance to the poor.

By the end of the 19th century, around 500,000 women regularly took part in some form of voluntary activity each week, and another 20,000 were engaged in paid work with one charity or another. Disaster funds were frequently opened to help widows and survivors of mining and shipping accidents, including the loss of the *Titanic* in 1912. Until the 20th century, welfare continued to be characterised by its focus on the genuinely poor or disadvantaged through a localised system of distribution, with the emphasis on private duty to help one's fellow man.

By the outbreak of World War I, it had largely been agreed that the State should play a greater role in helping the poor, whether by slum clearance or by paying a pension to all old people. However, the two world wars acted as catalysts to this process by making governments believe that, in the situation of war, society needed to be organised and provided for by central management. After World War II, the Government found these arrangements totally conducive to its philosophy and proceeded to entrench the system permanently. Until World War II, charities had an additional responsibility of caring for hundreds of thousands of poor people – functions which have now been largely absorbed into the welfare state.

For many centuries the provision of welfare services to the needy was primarily the responsibility of private citizens and voluntary agencies, with the State acting as a supplier of last resort. The emergence in the late 20th century of a rights-based, universal welfare state has posed a dilemma for parts of the voluntary sector. The 'contract culture' of the 1980s has resulted in some charities becoming Government sub-contractors, charging fees to provide services. These charities need to guard against losing some of their independence and capacity to be innovative.

The voluntary sector in the early 21st century is still strong and dynamic, and is held in high esteem by the public at large. Charities need to keep demonstrating how they promote public benefit to maintain and, preferably, enhance their reputation still further.

1.3 Definition of a charity

Towards the end of the 20th century, the Charity Commission was faced with a dilemma. The Register of Charities was first established in 1961 under the Charities Act 1960. There are now nearly 170,000 main charities on the Register. There are also thousands of other charities which are not registered with the Charity Commission but are nevertheless fully fledged charities.

History and definition

The dilemma faced by the Charity Commission was that, when dealing with applications for charity registration, it had to consider legal questions as to the legitimacy of charitable status. However, the Charity Commission could only work within the confines of precedents laid down by case law and current statutory definitions. The statutory definition of a charity was contained in s. 96 of the Charities Act 1993, and merely stated that 'charity means any institution, corporate or not, which is established for charitable purposes and is subject to the control of the High Court in the exercise of the court's jurisdiction with respect to charities'.

Under s. 97 of the Act, the expression 'charitable purposes' is defined as meaning merely 'purposes which are exclusively charitable according to the law of England and Wales'. The statutory definition itself begs the crucial question as to which purposes are charitable and which are not.

Case law, on which charitable definition is based, is drawn from a list of charitable purposes contained in the Preamble to the Charitable Uses Act of 1601. The Preamble provides an early legal definition of charity. This list of charitable purposes included 'relief of aged, impotent and poor people, repair of bridges, ports, havens, causeways, churches, seabanks and highways'. This list reflected the Tudor nature of the times and, although not intended to be exhaustive, has nevertheless set a precedent for the legal principles in which charitable status can be conferred. Although the legislation itself has since been repealed, the Courts, through case law, have interpreted its 'spirit and intendment' in order to be able to determine charitable status.

In the case of *Income Tax Special Purposes Commissioners v Pemsel* (1891 AC 531 at 583), Lord Macnaghten updated the principles of the 1601 Preamble by stating that charity in its legal sense comprises four divisions, as follows:

- trusts for the relief of poverty;
- trusts for the advancement of education;
- trusts for the advancement of religion, and
- trusts for other purposes beneficial to the community, not falling under any of the preceding heads.

The Charity Commission was faced with the unenviable task that it had to interpret charitable status based on principles laid down hundreds of years ago. This led it to conclude that there were charities on its Register that some people would not now regard as charitable; and, similarly, other organisations not on its Register that other people would regard as charitable.

In March 1999, the Charity Commission published *Review of the Register of Charities* (RR1) in which it outlined its strategy for reviewing the Register. The Charity Commission wanted to update and modernise the definition of charities

Definition of a charity

within the legal framework. In doing this, it published guidance *The Essential Characteristics of Charity*, in which it laid down the principles by which it undertook the review.

This dilemma faced by the Charity Commission is crystallised by the changes occurring in the society in which charities operate. To illustrate this, the Deakin Report (1996) stated that 'there is a fundamental reconsideration now taking place in most western democratic countries of the role of the State, the health of civil society and about the rights and responsibilities of their citizens. This rethinking has fundamental implications for the future of voluntary action'.

The Deakin Report also outlined basic principles to help gauge how the modern charity sector should operate. They were as follows:

- public policy must recognise the unique qualities of the sector and provide the right context for it to flourish;
- successful partnership is partnership negotiated between equals;
- the role of users is crucial to the sectors future;
- voluntary bodies must be free to be advocates even where they are also partners;
- the sector must learn to manage professionally and not to allow professionalism to dominate its agenda, and
- diversity of funding sources is one of the best guarantees of continued independence.

The social climate in which the Charity Commission has to operate is further highlighted by the contract culture which evolved in the 1980s. This saw charities entering into legally binding agreements to provide services on behalf of public bodies. The Charity Commission has also to consider the extent to which these charities are acting both independently and for the public benefit. In November 1998, the Government produced a compact which set out principles for the relationship between the Government and the voluntary sector. This laid down the codes of practice for certain key areas of funding. Similarly, the Better Regulation Task Force published a review which set out best principles to produce a virtuous circle of good funding practice. It can clearly be seen that the wider social context for charities has fundamentally changed. In considering how charities operate, the goalposts have moved. As RR1 acknowledges, 'the Courts develop charity law to keep the law's view of what is charitable reasonably in line with modern social needs and conditions. Thus, the legal concept of charity alters; and its evolution is influenced by ideas about social values'.

In order to be able to evaluate the usefulness of the legal definition of a charity prior to the Charities Act 2006 and to suggest any reforms, it is necessary to understand the legal situation as set down in the Pemsel case. In order to be considered charitable, not only must the activity fall within the four heads of the

Pemsel case but the activity must be wholly and exclusively charitable and must also be of a public benefit, unless it is for the relief of poverty.

These four headings can now be looked at in more detail.

1. The relief of poverty

Charities for the aged will relieve not only the physical disabilities of old age by the provision of appropriate accommodation, facilities and services, but also its loneliness by the provision of regular visiting and the organisation of outings. The category of 'impotent' includes both the physically and mentally ill; those permanently or temporarily incapacitated; those in need of convalescence or rest; and children who by reason of their circumstances are in need of special care and protection. In charity law the term 'poor' is a relative term. It includes not only those who are destitute but equally those who are in reduced circumstances. Therefore, charities may relieve beneficiaries by providing housing and other such services as well as by making grants and loans.

The Courts have held that the public benefit requirement can be relaxed for charities under this first head, so that a relationship between the benefactor and the beneficiary (such as a familial or employment relationship) does not deny charitable status.

2. The advancement of education

Charity law interprets the provision of education widely – that is, to society as a whole and it is not restricted to young people. Universities, colleges of further and higher education may even charge fees. However, public schools such as Eton and Winchester are also considered charitable. The promotion of new hobbies and pastimes will tend not to be charitable. Research into any recognised branch of study will be charitable, provided that all the results of such research are made available to the public at large.

3. The advancement of religion

Charity law does not restrict religion to the Christian religion. Provided that there is an acknowledgement and worship of a supreme being, the Courts will tend to find a religion as being for charitable purposes. For example, the Freemasons and more recently the Church of Scientology failed in their applications for charitable status as they were deemed to have a lack of the prerequisite conditions as interpreted for religious observance. Although there is still a requirement for there to be a public benefit in the advancement of religion, the Charity Commission has interpreted this public benefit in various ways.

4. Other purposes beneficial to the community

Although this fourth head is very wide-ranging, any purpose which can be shown to be beneficial to the community must do so within the 'spirit and intendment' of the Preamble to the Act of 1601. However, society has changed and public perception of activities has also changed. This is illustrated by the case of *the National Anti-Vivisection Society v IRC* (1948AC 31, 42), which highlights how an activity may cease to be charitable as social circumstances change. The National Anti-Vivisection Society's main object was the abolition of vivisection, and in 1895 this was found to be charitable as it was considered to be a benefit to the community at large. However, by 1948 the House of Lords reversed this decision as it felt that to **withhold** the practice of vivisection would be detrimental to the public at large as there would be a significant loss of medical science and research. This change in interpretation of what a charity is, necessitated that the Charity Commission undertake its review of the Register.

Put in this context, it is clear to see that that the Charities Act 2006 is the most important piece of charity legislation since Elizabethan times. Chapter 4 lists the 21st century charitable purposes and describes how the Charity Commission will gauge what constitutes and what does not constitute 'public benefit'.

1.3.1 The six 'hallmarks'

To assist in considering the definition of a charity, the Charity Commission revised CC10 'Hallmarks of an Effective Charity' in July 2008. The Charity Commission sets out what it considers to be the six main characteristics (or 'hallmarks') of a well-run charity, which are described below.

Hallmark 1: Clear about its purposes and direction

An effective charity is clear about its purposes, mission and values and uses them to direct all aspects of its work.

Hallmark 2: A strong board

An effective charity is run by a clearly identifiable Board or trustee body that has the right balance of skills and experience, acts in the best interests of the charity and its beneficiaries, understands its responsibilities and has systems in place to exercise them properly.

Hallmark 3: Fit for purpose

The structure, policies and procedures of an effective charity enable it to achieve its purposes and mission and deliver its services efficiently.

Hallmark 4: Learning and improving

An effective charity is always seeking to improve its performance and efficiency, and to learn new and better ways of delivering its purposes. A charity's assessment of its performance, and of the impact and outcomes of its work, will feed into its planning processes and will influence its future direction.

Hallmark 5: Financially sound and prudent

An effective charity has the financial and other resources needed to deliver its purposes and mission, and controls and uses them so as to achieve its potential.

Hallmark 6: Accountable and transparent

An effective charity is accountable to the public and others with an interest in the charity (stakeholders) in a way that is transparent and understandable.

There is also some new vocabulary for describing charities. Charitable companies are now more accurately called company charities. Unincorporated charities and Charitable Incorporated Organisations, or CIOs (see section **4.9**), are now more accurately called non-company charities. This distinction has arisen because CIOs are non-company charities but are still incorporated.

1.4 Registration

A system of registration was introduced by the 1960 Act, continued with amendments by the 1992 Act and, through consolidation, by the 1993 Act.

Section 9 of the Charities Act 2006 now requires every charity to register unless the charity is:

a) exempt;
b) excepted and has gross income below £100,000, or
c) one whose gross income is below £5,000.

1.4.1 Exempt charities

Section 3(5)(a) of the 1993 Act excludes 'exempt charities' from the requirement to register. These institutions generally have some other form of supervision approved by Parliament and, insofar as they are charities, they include (as amended by s. 11 of the Charities Act 2006):

- the universities of Oxford, Cambridge, London, Durham and Newcastle, including the colleges and halls in the universities of Oxford, Cambridge, Durham and Newcastle, and Queen Mary and Westfield College in the University of London;
- grant maintained schools;
- the trustees of the British Museum and the British Library and also various other specified museums and galleries, and
- any registered friendly or industrial and provident society which is also registered in the registrar of social landlords under Part 1 of the Housing Act 1996.

Schedule 2 to the 1993 Act provides a complete list of exempt charities.

Declaration of status

Under s. 4(2) of the 1960 Act, exempt charities were permitted to register voluntarily. This is no longer possible, since ss. 2(3) and (8) of the 1992 Act effected two changes: firstly, the possibility of registering on a voluntary basis was removed; and, secondly, registration of any exempt charity ceased to have effect. These changes were brought into force on 1 September 1992 by The Charities Act 1992 (Commencement No. 1 and Transitional Provisions) Order 1992 (SI 1992 No 1900).

1.4.2 Excepted charities

Section 9 of the Charities Act 2006 excludes from the registration requirement certain charities excepted by regulation or order. The following charities have been excepted by regulation:

(a) by the Charities (Exception of Voluntary Schools from Registration) Regulations 1960 (SI 1960 No 2366), all voluntary schools which have no permanent endowment other than the premises of, or connected with, the school;
(b) by the Charities (Exception of Certain Boy Scouts and Girl Guides from Registration) Regulations 1961 (SI 1961 No 1044) funds, not permanent endowments, accumulated for the purpose of local units of the Boy Scouts Association or the Girl Guides Association and which produce an income of more than £15 a year;
(c) by the Charities (Exception from Registration) Regulations 1996 (SI 1996 No 180), certain religious charities connected with certain bodies (this exception was temporary and expired on 1 March 2001) and trusts conditional upon the upkeep of graves. (**Note:** The Charities (Exception from Registration and Accounts) Regulations 1963 (SI 1963 No 2074) and the Charities (Exception from Registration and Accounts) Regulations 1964 (SI 1964 No 1825) are revoked);
(d) by the Charities (Exemption from Registration and Accounts) Regulations 1965 (SI 1965 No 1056), charities generally concerned with the promotion of the efficiency of any of the armed forces of the Crown; and
(e) by the Charities (Exception of Universities from Registration) Regulations 1966 (SI 1966 No 965), every university which is not an exempt charity.

In the case of the Roman Catholic Church and the Church of Wales, the Charity Commission has dealt with the charities vested in diocesan trustees by order, excepting the charities individually.

1.5 Declaration of status

Under s. 5(2) of the 1993 Act (previously s. 3 of the 1992 Act), registered charities with a *gross income* in their previous financial year greater than £10,000

History and definition

are required to state the fact that they are registered on certain specified business documents. (**Note**: the limit of £10,000 was raised, from £5,000, by The Charities Act 1993 (Substitution of Sums) Order 1995 (SI 1995 No 2696) as a result of a recommendation of the 8th Deregulation Task Force and took effect on 1 December 1995.)

Section 5(2) applies to the following documents:

(a) notices, advertisements and other documents issued by or on behalf of the charity and soliciting money or other property for the benefit of the charity;
(b) bills of exchange, promissory notes, endorsements, cheques and orders for money or goods purporting to be signed on behalf of the charity, and
(c) bills rendered by it and invoices, receipts and letters of credit.

It is regarded as good practice to include the statement on letterheads as well.

The purpose of the provision is to alert the public to the fact that it is dealing with a registered charity (which is subject to the Charity Commission's jurisdiction and about which information and accounts may be obtained) and not with a private individual or commercial organisation.

Excepted charities which have registered voluntarily will have to comply with these requirements.

The statement may be in a language as well as, but not instead of, English. It must be clear and easy to read, but otherwise may be printed, rubber-stamped or handwritten. In its booklet *A trustees' guide to the Charities Act 1992*, the Charity Commission suggested that the following examples would satisfy the requirement: 'A Registered Charity'; 'Registered Charity No', followed by the number; 'Registered as a Charity'; or 'Registered with the Charity Commission'.

There is no requirement to give the charity registered number, although charities may do so if they wish.

While s. 68 of the 1993 Act is similar to s. 5, it is not identical. Section 68 requires that where a company is a charity and its name does not include the word 'charity' or the word 'charitable', the fact that the company is a charity must be stated in English (in legible characters) on certain documents. The documents are very similar to those in s. 5 but, unlike that section, they include, for example, business letters. Section 68 applies to all company charities, whether or not registered. Because it is concerned with charitable status, rather than registered charity status, it seems that company charities will need to ensure that their documents comply with both sections.

Under s. 5(4), trustees and staff of charities who issue any document falling within (a) or (c) above and do not include this statement will be committing an offence and liable, on summary conviction, to a fine. Section 5(5) imposes a similar penalty on any person who signs a document, falling within (b) above, without the necessary statement.

Section 5(6) confers powers on the Secretary of State to amend the applicable gross income limit, now of £10,000.

1.6 Charity names

Prior to the 1992 Act, the Charity Commission could not refuse registration on the grounds that the charity had a name similar to, or even the same as, an existing charity.

With effect from 1 September 1992, ss. 4 and 5 of the 1992 Act (now ss. 6 and 7 of the 1993 Act) give powers to the Charity Commission to give directions requiring a charity to change its name in certain specified circumstances. These are if:

(a) at the time that the name is entered in the register, the registered name is the same as, or is too like that of, another charity (whether or not registered);
(b) the name of the charity is likely to mislead the public as to the true nature of the purposes or activities of the charity;
(c) the name of the charity includes any word or expression specified in regulations made by the Secretary of State which is likely to mislead the public as to its status;
(d) the name of the charity is likely to give the impression that it is connected in some way with the Government, or any local authority, or with any body of persons or any individual, when it is not so connected, or
(e) the name of the charity is offensive.

While any direction in respect of (a) must be given within 12 months of registration, there are no time limits for (b) to (e). The powers apply to all charities, whether or not registered (although (a) is specifically concerned with changing the registered name of a registered charity), other than exempt charities that are excluded by s. 6(9).

Chapter 2 – Trustees, duties, liabilities and insurance

2.1 Introduction

There has been a significant growth in the charity sector with the need for increased accountability. The requirements for charity accounts, increased controls over fundraising and the strengthened powers of the Charity Commission are part of a general initiative to upgrade the regulatory framework within which charities operate. The Charities Act 2006 has seen further changes to the duties and responsibilities of trustees, while there are also other aspects of the law (for example, the Companies Act 2006), to which charities may generally be subject and which are constantly evolving. As a result, trustees may be unsure whether or not they are acting within the law.

2.2 Who is a 'charity trustee'?

The Charities Act 2006 confirms that 'charity trustees' has the same meaning as s. 97(1) of the 1993 Act, which defines 'charity trustees' as 'the persons having the general control and management of the administration of a charity'. Paragraph 7 of Appendix 1 of the SORP states that 'the status of a charity trustee is defined in terms of the function to be performed, and not by reference to the title given to any office, or membership of any committee or committees'. Thus, regardless of the constitutional form of a charity, the group of individuals who have responsibility for the overall management and administration (for example, members of the board of directors, or management or executive committee or similar description) will be the charity trustees.

Where a non-charitable body corporate acts as a trustee of the charity, as in the case of the NHS charities, it and not its directors will be the charity trustee. Persons elected to manage a branch, where it is an integral part of the whole charity, may not be charity trustees. Conversely, some national charities have a structure where their local groups are constituted as independent registered charities; in these circumstances, those in charge will be charity trustees. 'Custodian' (or 'holding') trustees are not included within either of the above definitions, as they do not actively involve themselves in the management and administration. Rather, their responsibilities are limited to holding the assets of the charity for safe-keeping and in carrying out the instructions of the charity trustees.

2.3 Who may not be a charity trustee?

Sections 72 and 73 of the 1993 Act implemented the recommendation of the earlier Woodfield Report but widened the grounds for disqualification.

Under s.72(1), a person is disqualified from acting as a charity trustee if he:

(a) has been convicted of any offence involving dishonesty or deception (including theft, forgery or fraud)
(b) has been adjudged bankrupt or sequestration of his estate has been awarded and (in either case) he has not been discharged
(c) has made a composition or arrangement with, or granted a trust deed for, his creditors and has not been discharged in respect of it
(d) has been removed from the office of charity trustee by order of the Charity Commission or by the High Court on the grounds of any misconduct or mismanagement in the charity's administration for which he was responsible or to which he was privy, or which he by his conduct contributed or facilitated
(e) has been removed under s. 7 of the Law Reform (Miscellaneous Provisions) (Scotland) Act 1990 (powers of Court of Sessions to deal with management of charities) from being concerned in the management or control of any body; or
(f) is subject to a disqualification order under the Company Directors Disqualification Act 1986 or an order made under s. 429(2)(b) of the Insolvency Act 1986 (failure to pay under county court administration order)

Disqualification is, generally, automatic. Disqualified trustees, who may have been appointed lawfully, do not have to take steps to resign or be removed from trusteeship. They should immediately cease to take any further part in the charity's affairs. Under s. 73(4), the Charity Commission may even require the return to the charity of the value of any benefits trustees may have received from the charity while disqualified. However, acts done for a charity while disqualified will not be invalid by reason only of the disqualification (s. 73(3)).

Section 72(4) allows the Charity Commission to waive disqualification either generally or in respect of a particular charity or a particular class of charities, for example in the case of charities working with ex-offenders. However, a waiver may not be granted in relation to any company charity if the person is disqualified under the Company Directors Disqualification Act 1986 and has not been granted permission under that Act to act as director of any other company.

Section 73 imposes penalties (either a term of imprisonment or a fine, or both) for acting as a trustee while disqualified. This does not apply to a trustee disqualified on the grounds of (b) or (f) above, as those offences will be dealt with under company law.

Section 72(7) requires the Charity Commission to keep a register, which is open to the public, of all persons removed from office by them.

2.4 What are the trustees' duties ?

It is important that trustees not only know that they are trustees but, also, have an awareness of their duties in order that they may effectively discharge them.

In February 2008, the Charity Commission updated their leaflet CC3 (*The Essential Trustee – what you need to know*), which defines charities as 'organisations set up for the benefit of the community'. It states that 'charity trustees are the people who serve on the governing body of a charity'.

Trustees' duties are as follows:

1. accept ultimate responsibility for directing the affairs of the charity, and ensuring that it is solvent, well-run, and delivering the charitable outcomes for which it has been set up;

Duty of compliance – trustees must:

1. ensure that the charity complies with charity law, and with the requirements of the Charity Commission as regulator; in particular ensure that the charity prepares reports, annual returns and accounts as required by law;
2. ensure that the charity does not breach any of the requirements or rules set out in its Governing Document and that it remains true to the charitable purpose and objects set out there;
3. comply with the requirements of other legislation and other regulators which govern the activities of the charity, and
4. act with integrity, and avoid any personal conflicts of interest or misuse of charity funds or assets;

Duty of prudence – trustees must:

1. ensure that the charity is and will remain solvent;
2. use charitable funds and assets wisely, and only in furtherance of the charity's objects;
3. avoid undertaking activities that might place the charity's endowment, funds, assets or reputation at undue risk, and
4. take special care when investing the funds of the charity or borrowing funds for it to use;

Duty of care – trustees must:

1. use reasonable care and skill in their work as trustees, using their personal skills and experience as needed to ensure that the charity is well-run and efficient, and

2. consider getting external professional advice on all matters where there may be material risk to the charity, or where the trustees may be in breach of their duties.

2.5 Responsibility for preparing the report and accounts

The accounts should include an adequate description of the trustees' relevant responsibilities. The matters to be included will reflect the specific requirements of the reporting entity. The APB Practice Note No. 11 *The audit of charities in the United Kingdom (Revised) December 2008* Appendix 4 gives an illustrative wording of a description which may be included in a charity's accounts. Two examples of the wording are reproduced below dealing for both company and non-company charities.

Example 1 *Non-company charity*

Trustees' responsibilities in relation to the financial statements

The trustees are responsible for preparing the Trustees' Annual Report and the financial statements in accordance with applicable law and United Kingdom Accounting Standards (United Kingdom Generally Accepted Accounting Practice).

The law applicable to charities in England and Wales requires the trustees to prepare financial statements for each financial year which give a true and fair view of the state of affairs of the charity and of its incoming resources and application of resources of the charity for that period. In preparing these financial statements, the trustees are required to:

- select suitable accounting policies and then apply them consistently;
- observe the methods and principles in the Charities SORP;
- make judgements and estimates that are reasonable and prudent;
- state whether applicable accounting standards have been followed, subject to any material departures disclosed and explained in the financial statements,
- prepare the financial statements on the going concern basis unless it is inappropriate to presume that the charity will continue in business.

The trustees are responsible for keeping proper accounting records that disclose with reasonable accuracy at any time the financial position of the charity and enable them to ensure that the financial statements comply with the Charities Act 1993 and the Charity (Accounts and Reports) Regulations 2008. They are

Responsibility for preparing the report and accounts

also responsible for safeguarding the assets of the charity and hence for taking reasonable steps for the prevention and detection of fraud and other irregularities.

Example 2 *Company charity*

Trustees' responsibilities in relation to the financial statements

The trustees (who are also the directors of the charity for the purposes of company law) are responsible for preparing the Trustees' Annual Report and the financial statements in accordance with applicable law and United Kingdom Accounting Standards (United Kingdom Generally Accepted Accounting Practice).

Company law requires the trustees to prepare financial statements for each financial year which give a true and fair view of the state of affairs of the charitable company and of its incoming resources and application of resources, including its income and expenditure, for that period. In preparing these financial statements, the trustees are required to:

- select suitable accounting policies and then apply them consistently;
- observe the methods and principles in the Charities SORP;
- make judgements and estimates that are reasonable and prudent;
- state whether applicable UK Accounting Standards have been followed, subject to any material departures disclosed and explained in the financial statements, and
- prepare the financial statements on the going concern basis unless it is inappropriate to presume that the charity will continue in business.

The trustees are responsible for keeping proper accounting records that disclose with reasonable accuracy at any time the financial position of the charity and enable them to ensure that the financial statements comply with the Companies Act 2006. They are also responsible for safeguarding the assets of the charitable company and hence for taking reasonable steps for the prevention and detection of fraud and other irregularities.

If there is an audit, add

In so far as the trustees are aware:

- there is no relevant audit information of which the charity's auditor is unaware, and
- the trustees have taken all steps that they ought to have taken to make themselves aware of any relevant audit information and to establish that the auditor is aware of that information.

(See section **30.10**).

If the accounts are included on the charity's website, add

The trustees are responsible for the maintenance and integrity of the charity and financial information included on the charity's website. Legislation in the United Kingdom governing the preparation and dissemination of financial statements may differ from legislation in other jurisdictions.

The trustees are responsible for the preparation of the annual report and accounts. Paragraph 25 of the SORP recommends that both documents are approved by the trustees as a body, in accordance with their usual procedure (for example, at a quorate trustees' meeting).

2.6 Other financial responsibilities

Trustees are accountable for the solvency and continuing effectiveness of the charity and the preservation of its endowments. They must exercise overall control over its financial affairs. They should ensure that the way in which the charity is administered is not open to abuse by unscrupulous associates or employees, and that their systems of control are rigorous and constantly maintained.

In practice, this statement can be broken down into of the following components:

- internal controls;
- investment of surplus funds;
- budgeting;
- borrowing, and
- fundraising.

2.6.1 Internal controls

Should trustees fail to act prudently, lawfully and in accordance with their governing document they may be in breach of trust and personally liable to meet any resulting call on the charity's property or to make good any loss to the charity. Furthermore, since trustees of non-company charities must act jointly in administering a charity, they will be responsible jointly for any liability incurred by them or on their behalf.

It follows that while trustees should exercise appropriate care when entering into transactions or contracts on behalf of the charity, their responsibilities extend to careful oversight of the activities of others. Key to this is the establishment, monitoring and updating of appropriate internal controls. As emphasised repeatedly in Charity Commission inquiry reports, delegation of these duties to a chief executive or senior management team is not appropriate unless the trustees then exercise appropriate scrutiny in respect of the activities of that chief executive or team.

2.6.2 Investment of surplus funds

Whatever the agreed level of reserves maintained by a charity, it is good practice to invest any funds not needed for immediate expenditure.

Trustees are responsible for taking appropriate advice and ensuring that any investment is suitable in terms of its duration, risk and rate of return. They are responsible also for constant monitoring of the performance and continuing suitability of the investments chosen. From the point of view of internal controls, it is advisable that no single trustee should be in a position to control a particular investment or policy generally.

2.6.3 Budgeting

It is essential that trustees make proper estimates about expected income and expenditure in order to plan ahead effectively.

Budgeting, cash-flow forecasts and financial planning generally should form a central part of a charity's financial controls and this area should be subject to regular reporting to and monitoring by the trustees as a body. The charity should have in place effective mechanisms to obtain the necessary level of information at an appropriate frequency. Variances against budget should be questioned and, if deemed necessary, the underlying causes addressed.

2.6.4 Borrowing

Before borrowing any sum, trustees should consider whether appropriate powers are present in their governing document. If there is any doubt, the Charity Commission should be consulted. If suitable powers exist, the trustees should obtain advice from a person of appropriate experience who has no interest in the proposed loan. This advice should cover whether the loan is necessary, whether the terms are reasonable and whether the charity will be able to repay the loan on those terms.

2.6.5 Fundraising

Trustees are responsible for ensuring that any fundraising activity is properly undertaken and that all funds raised are properly accounted for.

Where trustees allow others to undertake fundraising on their behalf, they should ensure that all sums are paid into a bank account in the charity's name before deduction of expenses. Trustees should ensure that all fundraising methods are subject to their approval and, where external fundraisers are employed, should arrange for a proper contract to be drawn up.

Finally, it should be noted that trustees should not benefit financially or otherwise from the charity either directly or indirectly. In the absence of an express provision in the governing document or specific authority from the Charity Commission, trustees are not entitled to receive any payment out of the charity's property beyond the reimbursement of reasonable expenses (and these should only be paid when supported by appropriate documentation). Any other payments, borrowing, contracts or other business with the charity may constitute a breach of trust. In such cases, the trustee may be required to make good to the charity any loss that results or to account for any profit made (see section **4.13.16** of Chapter 4).

2.7 Risk

Under SORP 2005 the trustees are required to include a statement in their annual report confirming that the major risks to which the charity is exposed, as identified by the trustees, have been reviewed and systems established to manage those risks. Risk management is covered more fully in Chapter 22.

2.8 Investment of charitable funds

Following the Trustee Act 2000, which came into effect on 1 February 2001, the Charity Commission produced guidance dealing with its effects and much of this is CC14 (*Investment of Charitable Funds: Basic Principles*).

The guidance (which does not apply to the corporate property of company charities and of other charities incorporated by or under legislation or to trustees of common investment funds (other than pooling schemes) or common deposit funds), should be followed when investments are being made. In particular it refers to:

- the statutory duty of care;
- trustees' investment powers;
- employing agents and delegating functions;
- appointing nominees and custodians;
- trustee responsibility for review;
- effects of trustees exceeding their powers, and
- investing in land.

2.9 Liabilities and insurance

In the case of liability to third parties in contract, a company charity will enter into contracts, sue and be sued in its own name. In contrast, for non-company charities, creditors contract with the trustees and it will be them from whom creditors may seek redress.

Whether or not a charity is a company, all trustees will be personally liable for all acts and omissions where a duty of care is owed to third parties. This will be so where there has been a breach of trust – for example, where the charity has purchased investments not authorised by its constitution or under the Trustee Act 2000, where funds have been spent on unauthorised activities, or where the trustees have acted outside of the objects of the charity. Thus, any perception that charity trustees of an incorporated charity are protected from personal liability is misguided.

The Companies Act offers a measure of protection for officers in cases where they may be liable in respect of negligence, default, breach of trust or breach of duty, but have acted honestly and reasonably and where, having regard to all the circumstances of the case, they ought fairly to be excused. Section 61 of the Trustee Act 1925 offers similar protection.

(See sections **4.13.19** and **4.13.20** of Chapter 4.)

Chapter 3 – The regulatory framework

3.1 Introduction

Sections 41–49 of the 1993 Charities Act, and the Regulations, heralded a new statutory regime for charities. The Charities Act 2006 Act further developed the framework. Revised regulations were issued in 2008 as The Charities (Accounts and Reports) Regulations 2008 (SI 2008 No 629). These Regulations replace SI 2005 No 572, SI 2000 No 2868 and SI 1995 No 2724.

The requirements apply in different ways to charities that are registered, those that are exempt and those that are excepted from registration. In general, charities have to maintain proper accounting records and submit accounts, a report and return annually to the Charity Commission. The 1993 Act introduced, for the first time in charity law, the requirement for most accounts to show a true and fair view and to be audited or subject to some degree of independent scrutiny. This chapter contains a commentary on the evolution of the regulatory framework of charities.

3.1.1 2008 Regulations

The 2008 Regulations do not make significant changes to the requirements of the 1995, 2000 and 2005 Regulations.

The accounting requirements of the Regulations make provision for the form and content, methods and principles and notes to the accounts.

The objective of the Regulations is to ensure the accounting requirements continue to provide a framework relevant to charities' reporting needs and to maintain appropriate accountability to charities' stakeholders and the wider public for the resources they control. There is a need for greater consistency in financial reporting to enable the application of UK Generally Accepted Accounting Practice (UK GAAP) in a manner consistent with charity sector financial reporting needs and the particular transactions undertaken within the charity sector. In particular the Regulations are updated to adopt the methods and principles of the proposed revision of the *Statement of Recommended Practice: Accounting and Reporting by Charities* (the Charities SORP).

The Regulations provide for a review of the activities of the charities with an objective of enabling the reader to interpret better the financial information provided within the accounts as well as providing other information relating to the charity, its trustees or officers. The objective of these changes is to ensure this framework remains relevant to the reporting needs of charities and users of the Trustees' Annual Report.

3.2 The 1960 Act

Section 32 required trustees of all charities, whether or not registered, to:

(a) keep proper books of account;
(b) prepare consecutive statements of account, consisting of an income and expenditure account, relating to a period of not more than 15 months' duration, and a balance sheet relating to the end of that period, and
(c) preserve books and statements of account for at least seven years.

There was no general requirement to submit statements of account to the Charity Commission. Trustees were required to submit statements of account to the Charity Commission on request, however, and trustees of permanently endowed charities, unless excepted, were required to send a statement of account relating to the permanent endowment without any request.

Although the Act contained no general requirement for the accounts of charities to be audited, some trustees were under an obligation, imposed by the governing document, to have the accounts audited. Under s. 8, the Charity Commission was entitled to order an audit of a charity's accounts (other than those of an exempt charity), but the costs were to be borne by them.

3.3 The impetus for reform

Both the Woodfield Report and that of the Public Accounts Committee (*Monitoring and control of charities*), published in 1988, highlighted charity accounts as a key area of weakness. These reports found that, in spite of the importance of good financial information for supervision and accountability, the requirements for submitting annual accounts to the Charity Commission were being 'widely ignored'; only a limited number of accounts were examined each year, and only a small proportion of accounts were professionally audited.

Both the Government and the Charity Commission fully accepted that the arrangements for submitting and examining accounts needed to be considerably strengthened. Accordingly, the White Paper, published in May 1989, identified, *inter alia*, the regular provision of good quality financial information by charities as an essential element in their public accountability and an important means for their supervision.

Among the White Paper's proposals were:

(a) a requirement that, in future, all registered charities should submit, annually, statements of account to the Charity Commission. Such charities would be required to supplement their statement of account with a trustees' report, modelled on SORP 2, and to provide legal and administrative details of the kind recommended by that SORP;
(b) the introduction of graduated requirements governing the content and audit of accounts, and
(c) a requirement for trustees to make copies of their charity's accounts available to the public on request.

The White Paper was followed by the Charities Bill, which was introduced by the Government in 1991 and received the Royal Assent on 16 March 1992.

3.4 The 1993 Act

3.4.1 Overview

To which charities does the regulatory framework apply?

The framework applies to different charities in different ways. The following identifies the principal categories of charity, but does not address every possible situation:

(A) NHS charitable trusts

NHS charitable trusts are subject to the 1993 Act, as well as to NHS legislation governing the activities of the Health Service bodies administering them. A detailed manual, *NHS Charitable Funds: A Guide*, has been produced.

(B) Friendly and industrial and provident societies

Friendly and Industrial and Provident Societies which are charities and registered with the Registrar of Friendly Societies are exempt charities (Sch. 2 to the 1993 Charities Act). The exemption does not extend to a charity administered by such a registered industrial and provident or friendly society, nor to a charity simply because it has a subsidiary which is an exempt society.

(C) Registered housing associations

Housing associations that are charities and registered with the Housing Corporation (and which are not registered industrial and provident societies and, therefore, exempt) are subject to Regulation 7.

(D) Higher and further education institutions

Most universities and higher education colleges are exempt. For the few which are not, the accounts they prepare for the relevant funding council will satisfy the requirements of Regulation 7, which makes special provision for them.

(E) Charitable companies

Charities which are companies are subject to the CO Act 2006. They are, however, also subject to charity law. Unless they are excepted from registration with the Charity Commission and have chosen not to register, they must file an annual report and their own statutory accounts with the Charity Commission if their income or expenditure exceeds £10,000, or they are requested to do so by the Charity Commission in other cases.

(F) Exempt charities

Charities listed in Sch. 2 to the 1993 Act are exempt from registration with the Charity Commission. They are required to keep proper accounting records and prepare statements of account under ss. 46(1) and (2) of the 1993 Charities Act, unless they are subject to an alternative statutory regime (for example, industrial and provident societies). Section 47(2) of the 1993 Charities Act provides that members of the public may have access to these charities' accounts on request.

(G) Excepted charities

Certain charities are excepted from registration with the Charity Commission. Such charities may choose to register, but, if they do, are treated like any other registered charity.

3.4.2 Accounting

Accounting records

Section 41 of the 1993 Charities Act requires charity trustees to ensure that accounting records are maintained which are sufficient to:

(a) show and explain all the charity's transactions;
(b) disclose, at any time, with reasonable accuracy, the financial position of the charity at that time;
(c) enable the trustees to ensure that any statements of account required by s. 42(1)1993 Charities Act comply with the requirements of the Regulations;

and, in particular, contain:

The 1993 Act

(d) entries showing, from day to day, all sums of money received and expended by the charity, and the matters in respect of which the receipt and expenditure takes place, and

(e) a record of the assets and liabilities of the charity.

Accounting records are to be preserved for a minimum of six years from the end of the financial year to which they relate, although s. 41(4) of the 1993 Charities Act permits the Charity Commission to agree, in writing, to the records being destroyed or otherwise disposed of should a charity cease to exist. Interestingly, the requirement to keep accounting records for a charity that is not a charitable company appears onerous. Under s. 386 of the Companies Act 2006 (previously s. 221 of the 1985 Act), while a public company must retain its accounting records for six years, a private company, which would include charitable companies, needs only to preserve them for three years. Although s. 41 does not apply to charitable companies, by virtue of their being required to comply with the requirements in the Companies 2006 Act, such companies would be well advised to retain their accounting records for the longer period.

The section does not apply to exempt charities. Such charities must comply with ss. 46(1) and (2) of the 1993 Charities Act, which requires the charity trustees to keep proper books of account with respect to the charity's affairs and to retain them, together with statements of account, for a minimum period of six years unless the charity ceases to exist and the Charity Commission consents, in writing, to their being destroyed or otherwise disposed of.

This section does, however, apply to all excepted charities, whether or not registered.

Duty to prepare accounts

Section 42 of the 1993 Charities Act introduced provisions relating to the preparation of annual accounts.

Trustees of charities with a gross income which, in any financial year, does not exceed £100,000 may elect to prepare a simpler form of accounts on the receipts and payments basis comprising a receipts and payments account and a statement of assets and liabilities.

The trustees of charities whose gross income in any financial year exceeds £100,000 must prepare a 'statement of accounts', the detailed requirements relating to which are laid down in the Regulations. In circumstances where a charity is trading, committed to substantial capital expenditure or has significant investment assets, the trustees are advised to prepare their accounts on the accruals basis.

Section 42 does not apply to company charities, by virtue of their being required to comply with the requirements in the Companies Act 2006.

The regulatory framework

Exempt charities are excluded from this provision (s. 46(1) of the 1993 Charities Act) but, if not required by another statutory regime (for example, industrial and provident societies are bound to comply with the Friendly and Industrial and Provident Societies Act 1968 to prepare periodic statements of account), are required to prepare consecutive statements of account consisting of an income and expenditure account of not more than 15 months' duration, and a balance sheet relating to the end of that period.

The section does, however, apply to all excepted charities, whether or not registered.

Statements of accounts – Introduction

Sections 42(1) and (2) of the 1993 Charities Act requires statements of accounts to comply with such requirements as to their form and content as prescribed by the Regulations made by the Secretary of State.

The Regulations make provision as to the form and content of the statements of accounts, including the methods and principles to be used, and information to be provided by way of notes. They also make provision with respect to the financial years of charities, the requirements relating to audit, or examination, of their accounts and the annual reports of charity trustees.

Regulation 8 prescribes the form and content of statements of accounts prepared by charity trustees under s. 42(1) of the 1993 Charities Act, including the information to be provided by way of notes to the accounts and the methods and principles applicable.

The statement of accounts must comprise:

(a) 'a SOFA, which satisfies the requirements of reg. 8 (3)(a);
(b) a balance sheet, which satisfies the requirements of reg. 8 (3)(b); and
(c) by way of notes to the accounts, the information specified in reg. 8 (10) and Sch. 2 to the Regulations.

Statements of accounts – Methods and principles

Regulation 8 (5) requires the statement of accounts to be prepared in accordance with the methods and principles specified in the SORP.

Regulations 8 (4) a and b require both the SOFA and the balance sheet to give a true and fair view of, respectively, the incoming resources and application of those resources of the charity in, and the state of affairs of the charity at the end of, the financial year in respect of which the statement of accounts is prepared.

Where compliance with the Regulations would not be sufficient for the statement of accounts to give a true and fair view, Regulation 8 (4)(c) requires the necessary additional information to be given either in the accounts or in a note to them. If, in special circumstances, compliance with any of those provisions would be inconsistent with the requirement to give a true and fair view, reg. 8 (4)(d) requires the charity trustees to depart from that provision to the extent necessary to give a true and fair view, and to give particulars of the departure, the reasons for it and its effect in a note to the accounts. The provisions regarding use of, and disclosures relating to, the true and fair override for charity trustees are the same as those for directors of companies, as set out in s. 396 of the Companies Act 2006 (previously ss. 226(4) and (5) of the 1985 Act). The interpretation of those disclosure requirements by FRS 18.

As regards measurement, reg. 8 (5) requires the values of the assets and liabilities of the charity to be determined in accordance with the methods and principles for their inclusion in the balance sheet set out in the SORP.

The comparative total figure must be given for each heading in the SOFA, but there is no requirement to show comparatives for each of the principal funds. Comparatives are required for all balance sheet headings (reg. 8 (6)).

If not comparable, the corresponding figure must be adjusted and particulars of the adjustment disclosed in the notes to the accounts (reg. 8 (8)).

Paragraph 1 (v) of Schedule 2 to the Regulations requires the notes to the accounts to give a statement as to whether or not the accounts have been prepared in accordance with applicable accounting standards and statements of recommended practice and particulars of any material departure from those standards and practices and the reasons for such departure. Compliance with the SORP is, thus, not mandatory, but charity trustees will be expected to follow its recommendations, which are consistent with accounting and reporting standards.

Statements of accounts – Special cases

Regulations 6 (1) to (8) and Schedule 1 of the Regulations prescribe the form and content of statements of accounts of common investment funds, and common deposit funds and reg. 8 prescribes the form and content of statements of account of registered housing associations and charities conducting higher and further education institutions. The regulatory framework relating to these charities is not dealt with further in this book.

Financial years – How are these determined?

Section 42(2) of the 1993 Charities Act allows the Secretary of State to make provisions with respect to the determination of a charity's financial year. (Note: These will not apply to charitable companies, as they are subject to s. 390 of the Companies Act 2006 (previously s. 223 of the 1985 Act). Regulation 3 of the Regulations sets out these provisions.

The regulatory framework

Financial years are determined by reference to periods, which are calendar based, and end on the charity's accounting reference date. In order to allow for the use of 52/53-week years, the period can vary by up to seven days either side of that date.

The first financial year of a charity will begin on the day on which the charity is established and end with its accounting reference date (reg. 3 (2)).

Subsequent financial years run from the previous financial year end to the next accounting reference date, plus or minus seven days (reg. 3 (3)).

For the purposes of this regulation, the accounting reference date of a charity shall be:

- in the first financial year of a charity such date, not less than six months nor more than 18 months after the date on which the charity was established, as the charity trustees may determine, and
- in any subsequent financial year of a charity, the date 12 months after the previous accounting reference date of the charity or such other date, not less than six months nor more than 18 months after the previous accounting reference date of the charity as the trustees may determine reg. 3 (4) b.

As regards (b), there are provisions to restrict the frequency with which accounting reference dates may be changed. Such dates cannot be changed unless the two financial years immediately preceding were each of 12 months' duration. Regulation 6 (7) permits trustees to change the accounting reference date only where they are satisfied that there are exceptional reasons (which are not defined), which must be disclosed in the notes to the accounts.

What is 'gross income' and 'total expenditure'?

'Gross income' is defined in s. 97(1) of 1993 Charities Act as 'gross recorded income from all sources, including special trusts'. All incoming resources of a charity are income unless they are permanent or expendable endowment (permanent endowment is capital which may not be expended as income; expendable endowment may be so expended, at the trustees' discretion). Trading income, donated income, transfers from capital to income, income from investments including property, and asset disposal gains are to be included, but revaluation gains are to be excluded. Total expenditure includes depreciation of fixed assets for use by the charity and asset disposal losses.

Appendix 1 of the Charity Commission's publication CC32 (*Independent examination of Charity Accounts*) states that gross income 'is the total recorded income of the charity in all unrestricted and restricted funds, but not resources received as capital (endowment) funds'. Therefore, donations made to permanent endowment (including property to be retained as endowment) do not count as gross income.

Using this approach, income, which should be calculated before deduction of any costs or expenses, includes:

- donations, grants, gifts, legacies, and subscriptions;
- tax refunds;
- investment income (including interest receivable, dividends and rents);
- money received from the sale of goods or services in furtherance of the charity's objectives;
- gross proceeds from fundraising, and
- other income. When trustees decide to spend expendable capital, they should include the amount spent as 'other income'. This is because capital receipts are not included as income when they first come into the charity.

Income excludes:

- the receipt of a loan by, and loan repayments to, the charity;
- the proceeds of sale of investment assets and tangible assets for use by the charity;
- gains or profits on disposal of investment assets and tangible assets for use by the charity, and
- donations, etc. that the donor expects will, or may, be retained for investment by the charity and other capital donations (for example, gifts of land and buildings to be retained and used for a particular charitable purpose).

Expenditure will include:

- expenditure relating to the objects of the charity including grants, donations, cost of services provided and support costs;
- management and administration costs of the charity;
- fundraising and publicity costs;
- interest payable, and
- when the accounts are prepared on an accruals basis, depreciation or amortisation of the assets.

Expenditure excludes:

- the granting or repayment of a loan;
- the purchase of investment assets and tangible assets for use by the charity, and
- losses on disposal of investment assets and tangible assets for use by the charity.

Where accruals accounts are prepared, gross income will be the total of the figures entered in the SOFA under para. 118 of SORP 2005 (excluding any amount included under para. 147 which represents gains on the disposal of tangible assets for use by the charity). Total expenditure will be that entered under para. 177 of SORP 2005 after omitting any amount relating to losses on disposal of tangible assets for use by the charity.

It should be noted that s. 96(4) of the 1993 Act empowers the Charity Commission to determine the amount of a charity's income from all sources and makes its decision final and binding. If any unrecorded income is discovered, it is advised that it should be taken into account in determining gross income.

The current limits for all registered charities are:

Annual gross income	Type of accounts	Type of review
Below £10,000	Receipts and payments	None
Above £10,000 but below £100,000	Receipts and payments	Independent examination
Above £100,000 but below £500,000	Accruals	Independent examination
Above £500,000	Accruals	Audit

3.4.3 Auditing

Audit or independent examination?

Section 43 of the 1993 Charities Act requires the annual accounts of a charity generally to be audited or independently examined.

For accounting periods beginning before 27 February 2007, if the gross income, or total expenditure, exceeded £250,000 in the year for which the accounts are being prepared, or in the immediately preceding two years, the accounts must be audited by a person who is:

(a) eligible to act as a company auditor under s. 25 of the 1989 Act (that is, a registered auditor), or
(b) a member of a body specified under regulations made by the Secretary of State and, under the rules of that body, is eligible for appointment as auditor of the charity.

For accounting periods beginning on or after 27 February 2007 the audit requirement will apply where income exceeds £500,000, or alternatively where income exceeds £100,000 and gross assets exceed £2.8 million

Where a charity's governing document requires an audit to be carried out, consideration should be given to the intention at the time it was drawn up. The governing document may contain more rigorous provisions than the Regulations. For example, if a charity's governing document requires the accounts to be audited, but the charity trustees wish to elect (assuming that they are able so to do) for an independent examination to be carried out, they may have the power to vary the governing document themselves or they may be able to make the change. If not, the trustees are advised to obtain Charity Commission approval to an amendment to the document.

A lack of clarity in the provisions of the governing document may highlight other practical problems – for example, not only in relation to the level of scrutiny required, but by whom that scrutiny should be carried out. It is often the case that governing documents were drawn up many years ago, when the term 'audit' had a different interpretation, given the regulatory framework applicable then. Accordingly, if an audit is required, governing documents may not state by whom that audit should be carried out (for example,, by a registered auditor). It is recommended that all governing documents (and letters of engagement, for that matter) are revisited and, where necessary, amended to reflect actual requirements of the new regulatory frameworks that are in place.

A further issue which may raise practical problems is the threshold of £500,000 and its attendant provisions, particularly for any charity that receives large or unexpected donations late in its accounting year or for a charity undertaking a major project likely to generate substantial funds and expenditure, possibly over a limited period of time. **Charities now need to consider their income only, not expenditure, and then only on an annual basis.**

What are the duties of an auditor?

Section 44(1)(b) of the 1993 Charities Act allows for the Secretary of State to make provisions with respect to the duties of an auditor, including provisions with respect to the form of report (either on the statement of accounts or the account and statement.)

(A) The auditor's report under s. 42(1) of the 1993 Charities Act – Statement of accounts

Where a statement of accounts has been prepared for a financial year, the auditor must make a report on that statement to the charity trustees. The report must:

(a) state:
  (i) the name of the charity, and
  (ii) his name and address (reg. 24 (a));
(b) be signed by him and state that he is a registered auditor (reg. 24 (b and c));
(c) be dated and specify the financial year in respect of which the accounts to which the report relates have been prepared (reg. 24 (d));
(d) specify that it is a report in respect of an audit carried out under s. 43 and in accordance with the Regulations (reg.24 (e)), and
(e) state whether, in his opinion, the statement of accounts complies with the requirements of reg. 8 (or, as the case may be, reg. 6 or 7) and, in particular,

gives a true and fair view of the state of affairs of the charity at the end of the financial year and of the incoming resources and application of the resources of the charity in that year (reg. 24 (f)).

If the auditor is of the opinion that:

(a) accounting records have not been kept in accordance with s. 41;
(b) the statement of accounts is not in agreement with those records;
(c) any information contained in the statement of accounts is inconsistent in any material respect with the annual report for the financial year, or
(d) any information or explanation to which he is entitled under reg. 33 has not been afforded to him,

reg. 24 (g) requires his report to contain a statement of, and of his grounds for forming, that opinion.

(B) The auditor's report under Part 16 of the Companies Act 2006 (previously Part 7 of 1985 Companies Act) – Statement of accounts

Where a statement of accounts has been prepared for a financial year, the auditor must make a report on that statement to the charity trustees. The report must:

(a) state:
 (i) the name of the charity, and
 (ii) the auditor's name and address (reg. 25 (a));
(b) be signed by him and state that he is a registered auditor (reg .25 (b and c));
(c) be dated and specify the financial year in respect of which the accounts to which the report relates have been prepared (reg. 25 (d)), and
(d) specify that it is a report in respect of an audit carried out under s. 43 of the 1993 Charities Act and in accordance with the Regulations (reg. 25 (e)).

If the auditor is of the opinion that:

(a) accounting records have not been kept in accordance with s. 386 of the Companies Act 2006 (previously s. 221 of the 1985 Companies Act);
(b) the statement of accounts is not in agreement with those records;
(c) any information contained in the statement of accounts is inconsistent in any material respect with the annual report for the financial year; or
(d) any information or explanation to which he is entitled under reg. 33 has not been afforded to him,

reg. 25 (h) requires his report to contain a statement of, and of his grounds for forming, that opinion.

What form does an independent examiner's report take?

The 1993 Act

Section 44(1)(c) of the 1993 Charities Act enables the Secretary of State to make provision with respect to the form of report of the independent examiner. This is set out in Regulation 31.

An independent examiner who has carried out an examination of the accounts in accordance with s. 43 must make a report to the charity trustees. The report must:

(a) state:
  (i) the name of the charity, and
  (ii) the examiner's name and address (reg. 31 (a));
(b) be signed by the examiner and specify any relevant professional qualifications or professional body of which he is a member (reg. 31(b));
(c) be dated and specify the financial year in respect of which the accounts to which it relates have been prepared (reg. 31 (c));
(d) specify that it is a report in respect of an examination carried out under s. 43 and in accordance with any directions given by the Charity Commission under s. 43(7)(b) of the 1993 Charities Act that are applicable (reg. 31 (g));
(e) state whether or not any matter has come to the examiner's attention in connection with the examination which gives him reasonable cause to believe that in any material respect:
  (i) accounting records have not been kept in accordance with s.41 of the 1993 Charities Act
  (ii) the accounts are not in agreement with those records, or
  (iii) in the case of an examination of a statement of accounts, that statement does not comply with any of the requirements of reg. 8, and
(f) state whether or not any matter has come to his attention in connection with the examination to which, in his opinion, attention should be drawn in order for a proper understanding of the accounts to be given (reg. 31 (h)).

Where:

- any material expenditure or action appears not to be in accordance with the trusts of the charity;
- any information or explanation to which he is entitled under reg. 31 has not been afforded to him, or
- in the case of an examination of a statement of accounts prepared under s. 42(1) of the 1993 Charities Act any information contained in that statement is inconsistent in any material respect with the annual report of the charity trustees,

reg. 31 (j) requires his report to contain a statement to that effect.

The regulatory framework

What are the auditor's and independent examiner's rights?

Sections 44(1)(d) and (e) of the 1993 Charities Act enable the Secretary of State to make provision conferring on the auditor, or independent examiner, a right of access to books, documents and other records (however kept) that relate to the charity.

Regulation 33 (1) provides that an auditor or independent examiner has a right of access to any books, documents and other records (however kept) which relate to the charity concerned and which the auditor, or examiner, considers necessary to inspect for the purposes of carrying out the audit, or examination.

Regulation 33 (2) provides that the auditor, or independent examiner, is entitled to require such information and explanations from past or present charity trustees or trustees for the charity, or from past or present officers or employees of the charity, as he considers necessary for the purposes of carrying out the audit, or examination.

Charity Commission's powers to require an audit

Where the statutory requirements for the accounts to be audited, or independently examined, have not been complied with within 10 months of the end of the relevant financial year, s. 43(4)(a) 1993 Charities Act confers upon the Charity Commission a power to require an audit of the accounts. In these circumstances, the auditor will be appointed by the Charity Commission and the trustees will be personally liable, jointly and severally, for his costs. Only if it appears to the Charity Commission that it would not be practical to seek recovery of the costs of the audit from the trustees, will the costs be met from the funds of the charity.

Section 43(4)(b) of the 1993 Charities Act confers on the Charity Commission a power to require an audit of the accounts of any charity to which the section applies in circumstances where, although the requirement for an audit does not apply, it appears to the Commission that one would be desirable. In these circumstances, the trustees may appoint the auditors and, provided the trustees comply with the Charity Commission's order, the costs of the audit will be met from the charity's funds.

Dispensation from audit or independent examination requirements in certain circumstances

Section 44(1)(f) of the 1993 Charities Act allows the Secretary of State to make provision enabling the Charity Commission, in certain circumstances, to dispense with an audit or independent examination, for a particular charity or any particular financial year of a charity where an adequate scrutiny of the accounts is otherwise carried out. Those circumstances, which are set out in reg. 34, are where the Charity Commission:

(a) is satisfied that the accounts of the charity are required to be audited in accordance with any statutory provision contained in or having effect under an Act of Parliament which, in its opinion, imposes requirements which are sufficiently similar to the requirements of s. 43(2) of the 1993 Charities Act for those requirements to be dispensed with;
(b) is satisfied that the accounts of the charity have been audited by the Comptroller and Auditor General
(c) are satisfied that the accounts of the charity for the financial year have been audited or examined in accordance with requirements or arrangements which, in its opinion, are sufficiently similar to the relevant requirements of s. 43 of the 1993 Charities Act applicable to that financial year for those requirements to be dispensed with;
(d) is satisfied that, in the financial year in question, there has been no transaction which would be required to be shown and explained in the accounting records; or
(e) considers that, although the financial year of a charity is one to which s. 43(2) of the 1993 Charities Act applies, there are exceptional circumstances which justify the examination of the accounts by an independent examiner rather than an audit in accordance with that subsection and the accounts have been so examined, and where the charity trustees have supplied to the Charity Commission any report made to it with respect to the accounts of that charity for the financial year that the Charity Commission has requested.

Exclusions

These provisions do not apply to:

- charitable companies, although s. 69 retains the powers of the Charity Commission, under what was ss. 8(3) and (6) of the 1960 Act, to require the accounts of such a charity to be investigated and audited, but at the cost to the Charity Commission;
- (exempt charities, and
- excepted charities that have neither a permanent endowment nor the use or occupation of any land and whose income is not greater than £1,000 a year and which are not registered (s. 46(3) of the 1993 Charities Act). If they register voluntarily, the provisions apply. The provisions do apply, however, to other excepted charities.

3.4.4 Annual reports

Section 45 of the 1993 Charities Act requires trustees to prepare an annual report for each financial year. This is an important document in its own right and will contain a report on the activities of the charity during the year and such other information relating to the charity, or to its trustees or officers, as is prescribed by the Regulations.

The regulatory framework

Unless a charity's gross income and total expenditure amount to less than £10,000 in a financial year, trustees must submit the annual report, together with the statement of accounts, or account and statement, together with the auditors', or independent examiner's, report within 10 months of the year end. The Charity Commission may grant a longer period where there are special reasons (s. 45(3)(b) 1993 of the Charities Act). Other excepted charities that are not registered on a voluntary basis are also excluded, unless the Charity Commission specifically request them to prepare and submit an annual report (ss. 46(5) and (6) of the 1993 Charities Act). In these circumstances, the annual accounts and the report of the auditors, or independent examiner, should be attached.

3.4.5 Public inspection of accounts

Section 47 of the 1993 Charities Act provides for all annual reports kept by the Charity Commission to be open to public inspection at all reasonable times. This will ensure that the public has access to information about registered charities.

Where a person requests, in writing, the trustees of any charity to provide him or her with a copy of that charity's accounts and pays them a reasonable fee to comply with the request, the trustees must comply with the request within two months of receiving it. This provision applies to all charities, including exempt charities. Thus, the accounts of any charity may be obtained by a member of the public which, hitherto, may have been difficult to obtain.

3.4.6 Annual return

The 1993 Act provides for more active supervision of the charity sector by the Charity Commission through the process of annual monitoring.

Subject to the exclusions set out in (a) and (b) below, s. 48(1) requires the trustees of all registered charities to complete an annual return in the form prescribed by regulations made by the Charity Commission and submit it to the Commission within 10 months of the year end.

1. Section 48(3) provides for the Charity Commission to dispense with the need to prepare an annual return in the case of a particular charity or particular class of charities, or in the case of a particular financial year of a charity or of any class of charities.
2. Section 48(1A), as inserted by s. 30(3) of the Deregulation and Contracting Out Act 1994, states that these requirements do not apply to registered charities whose gross income and total expenditure do not exceed £10,000 in a financial year. This implemented a further recommendation of the eighth Deregulation Task Force.

The Secretary of State may amend the figure of £10,000 by substituting a different amount, at any time (s. 48(4), as inserted by s. 30(4) of the Deregulation and Contracting Out Act 1994).

3.4.7 Penalties for non-compliance

Under section 49 of the 1993 Charities Act, charity trustees will commit an offence if persistently in default, without reasonable excuse, in:

(a) preparing and submitting annual reports and accounts to the Charity Commission;
(b) making the accounts available to the public, or
(c) preparing and submitting an annual return.

Such a person will be liable, on summary conviction, to a fine. Persistent failure to supply this information would be evidence of mismanagement and the Charity Commission could then institute enquiries.

3.5 Further changes

The significant changes implemented under the Charities Act 2006 and the Companies Act 2006 are considered in greater detail in Chapters 4 and 30 respectively.

Chapter 4 – The Charities Act 2006

4.1 Introduction

In July 2001, the Prime Minister commissioned a review of the law and regulation of charities and other not-for-profit organisations. The review was carried out by the Prime Minister's Strategy Unit and its recommendations were published as 'Private Action, Public Benefit' in September 2002. The Government sought views on these recommendations through public consultation, which ran to January 2003. In July 2003, the Government published 'Charities and Not-for-Profit: a Modern Legal Framework' which summarised the results of the public consultation on the Strategy Unit's recommendations and stated the Government's acceptance of almost all of the recommendations.

The proposals for revising charity legislation were first published as a Draft Bill in May 2004. Following pre-legislative debate and scrutiny, the Charities Bill itself was introduced into Parliament in December 2004, only to be timed out by the May 2005 general election. The Bill was reintroduced following the general election and completed its passage through the Lords in November 2005 and through the Commons in October 2006. Its final debate was in the Lords on 7 November 2006.

The table below charts the Bill's passage through Parliament.

Table 4.1 The passage of the Charities Bill through Parliament

House of Lords	Date
First Reading	19 May 2005
Second Reading	7 June 2005
Committee Stage	28 June and 12 July 2005
Report Stage	12 October 2005
Report Stage (day 2)	18 October 2005
Third Reading	8 November 2005
House of Commons	
First Reading	9 November 2005
Second Reading	26 June 2006
Committee Stage	4, 6, 11 and 13 July 2006
Report and Third Reading	25 October 2006
House of Lords	
Consideration of Commons Amendments	7 November 2006

The Act makes amendments to the Charities Act 1993 (for non-company charities) and to the Companies Act 2006 (for company charities). It reflects both the changes in society generally and in the charity sector in particular. The Act releases charities from some of the previous regulatory requirements, enabling them to adapt to the ever-changing needs in society and also to adopt more effective ways of working.

In addition to the primary pieces of legislation, the following regulations and Commencement Orders have also been implemented:

- The Charities Act 2006 (Commencement No. 1, Transitional Provisions and Savings) Order 2007 [SI 2007/309];
- The Charities Act 2006 (Commencement No. 2, Transitional Provisions and Savings) Order 2007 [SI 2007/3286];
- The Charities Act 2006 (Commencement No. 3, Transitional Provisions and Savings) Order 2007 [SI 2008/751];
- The Charities Act 2006 (Commencement No. 4, Transitional Provisions and Savings) Order [SI 2008/945];
- The Charities Act 2006 (Commencement No.5, Transitional and Transitory Provisions and Savings) Order [SI 2008/3267];
- The Charities Act 2006 (Charitable Companies Audit and Group Accounts Provision) Order 2008 [SI 2008/527]l
- The Charities (Accounts and Reports) Regulations 2008 [SI 2008/629]; and
- The Companies Act 2006 (Commencement No. 6, Saving and Commencement Nos. 3 and 5 (Amendment)) Order 2008.

In an attempt to make the legislation more accessible to users, The Office of the Third Sector (OTS) has made an informal consolidation of Part 6 of and Sch 5A to the Charities Act 1993 to reflect the changes made to it on 1 April 2008.

4.2 Implementation timetable

4.2.1 Introduction

The implementation of the Act has been led by the OTS in the Cabinet Office, working with the Charity Commission. Parts of the Act came into force in February 2007 and subsequent provisions were implemented over the following two years. The Act's provisions were due to be introduced with four Commencement Orders (although it is now clear that at least six will be needed). A future consolidating Act following the Charities Act 2006 is likely to take place sometime in the future.

4.2.2 First Commencement Order

The first Commencement Order (SI 2007/309) was made in Parliament on 31 January 2007 and brings into force the specific sections covered by the Order, with an effective date of 27 February 2007 subject to transitional provisions as set out in the Order. The main changes are:

- increases to the financial thresholds above which charities are required to have a professional audit (ss. 28 and 32);
- relaxation of the publicity requirement for schemes (s. 22);
- participation of Scottish and Northern Ireland charities in Common Investment Schemes (s. 23);
- power for non-company charities to modify powers or procedures (s. 42);
- reserve power to control fundraising by charitable institutions (s. 69);
- powers for Secretaries of State and the Minister for the Cabinet Office to give financial assistance to charitable, philanthropic or benevolent organisations (s. 70);
- waiver of trustees' disqualification (s. 35);
- measures giving the Charity Commission powers to relieve trustees and auditors of personal liability where they have acted honestly and reasonably (s. 38);
- measures to enable trustees to purchase indemnity insurance with the charity's money (s. 39);
- changes to the restrictions on mortgaging charity property (s. 27);
- changes to the registration limits, increasing them to £5,000 (s. 10), and
- removal of the need for charities to consider their expenditure in determining whether or not they are required to submit an Annual Return to the Charity Commission.

In addition to the above measures, the following provisions relating to the constitution, powers and independence of the Charity Commission were commenced at the same time.

1. The Charity Commission's current constitution is over 45 years old. The Act modernises it to establish the Charity Commission as a body corporate, with new statutory objectives, functions and duties. The Charity Commission's independence is preserved, as it remains a non-ministerial department, outside the direction or control of ministers. The number of board members is increased to nine, to reflect the diversity of the sector. The Charity Commission is required annually to report direct to Parliament, and to hold an open AGM (ss. 6 and 7, and Schedules 1 and 2).
2. A large number of amendments to other Acts are consequential on the establishment of the Charity Commission replacing references to the 'Charity Commissioners' with references to the 'Charity Commission' (many paragraphs of Schedule 8).

3. One of the Charity Commission's new objectives is to promote awareness and understanding of the requirement that the purposes of charities must be for the public benefit. The Act requires the Charity Commission to consult and publish guidance on the public benefit test (s. 4).
4. There is a new requirement for the Charity Commission to send a copy of any Order it makes under its protective powers under s. 18 of the Charities Act 1993, along with the reasons for the making of the Order. This must be done as soon as possible after the Order is made, although the Charity Commission can suspend the requirement for as long as it believes that complying would prejudice any inquiry or investigation or would not otherwise be in the interests of the charity (para. 113 of Sch. 8).
5. The Charity Commission's power to give formal advice is updated (s. 24).
6. The provisions that govern disclosure of information to the Charity Commission and disclosure of information by the Charity Commission are modernised. In particular, there are tighter controls on the disclosure of HM Revenue & Customs (HMRC) information. An order-making power to prescribe a similar information-sharing regime for the proposed regulator of charities in Northern Ireland is provided in the Act (para. 104 of Sch. 8, s. 72).
7. Power is given to the Charity Commission to determine membership of a charity and also to enter premises and seize documents under a warrant (ss 25 and 26).

The enabling legislation was made under The Charities Act 2006 (Commencement No. 1, Transitional Provisions and Savings) Order SI 2007/309.

4.2.3 Second Commencement Order

The second Commencement Order was made on 21 November 2007 and brings into force the following:

- provisions to facilitate charity mergers (s. 44). These provisions came into force on 28 November 2007.
- changes to the requirements in the Charities Act 1992 relating to solicitation statements of professional fundraisers and commercial participators and a new requirement for those involved in running a charity – its trustees and employees – to make a simple statement when being paid to collect in public (ss 67 and 68). These provisions came into force on 1 April 2008.

The enabling legislation was made under The Charities Act 2006 (Commencement No.2, Transitional Provisions and Savings) Order SI 2007/3286.

4.2.4 Third Commencement Order

The third Commencement Order was made on 15 March 2008, bringing a number of provisions into force on 18 March 2008.

Implementation timetable

- the Charity Tribunal (s. 8 and Sch. 3 and 4);
- changes to the law of cy-près (s. 18);
- new powers for the Charity Commission – to remove or suspend trustees from membership of a charity, to give specific directions for the protection of charity property, to direct the application of charity property, and to give advice and guidance (ss. 19, 20, 21 and 24);
- remuneration of trustees providing services to a charity (ss. 36 and 37), and
- powers for non-company charities to transfer all their property and to replace purposes or to spend capital (ss. 40, 41 and 43).

The enabling legislation was made under the Charities Act 2006 (Commencement No.3, Transitional Provisions and Savings) Order SI 2008/751.

4.2.5 Fourth Commencement Order

The fourth Commencement Order has been made, bringing the following provisions into force on 1 April 2008:

- the statutory definition of 'charity', including the list of headings of charitable purposes and the public benefit requirement (ss 1, 2 and 5);
- the removal of the presumption of public benefit for charities established for the advancement of education, the relief of poverty or the advancement of religion (s. 3);
- the requirement for trustees to have regard to the Charity Commission's guidance on public benefit, when exercising powers or duties to which the guidance is relevant (s. 4);
- provisions relating to audit and accounting for group accounts and provisions clarifying the whistle blowing duties of auditors or independent examiners (ss. 30 and 33 and an order under s. 77, and Sch. 6);
- changes for 'excepted' charities (parts of s. 9), and
- provisions relating to Miners' Welfare Trusts and Community Amateur Sports Clubs (ss 5(3) to (5) of the Act) effective from 1 April 2009.

The enabling legislation was made under The Charities Act 2006 (Commencement No.4, Transitional Provisions and Savings) Order SI 2008/945.

4.2.6 Fifth Commencement Order

The fifth Commencement Order has been made, bringing several provisions into force on 31 January 2009. The provisions commenced are:

- the requirement for charities that are currently excepted from the requirement to register with the Charity Commission to be registered if their gross income exceeds £100,000;

- the removal of exempt charity status from formerly specified educational institutions (that is, foundation and voluntary-aided schools) but preserving the benefits of exempt status until 1 October 2009, and
- the requirement for an evaluation and report on the operation of the Charities Act 2006 to begin before 5 April 2011.

The enabling legislation was made under the Charities Act 2006 (Commencement No.5, Transitional and Transitory Provisions and Savings) Order SI 2008/3267.

4.2.7 Ongoing commitments

The OTS is committed to undertake the following reviews:

- current financial thresholds – this took place, as planned within a year of Royal Assent. The aim of the review was to consider whether there was scope to raise or simplify existing thresholds (see section **4.14** below);
- Charities Acts 1992 and 1993 – to simplify existing secondary legislation;
- the impact of public benefit reporting by 1 April 2011, and
- the overall impact of the Charities Act 2006 within five years of Royal Assent.

4.3 New definition of charitable purposes

4.3.1 Definition of charity

The Charities Act 2006 represented the biggest overhaul of charity law in the UK for 400 years. One of the most fundamental changes was that charities would no longer be presumed to provide public benefit, but would have to prove that they do so in order to retain their charitable status and accompanying tax breaks.

Previous requirements

Prior to the Act, in order to be classified as a charity, an organisation had to have purposes which were exclusively charitable and were for the public benefit. The charitable purposes were:

- relief of poverty;
- advancement of education;
- advancement of religion, and
- a purpose beneficial to the community.

Until 1 April 2008, any organisation under one of the first three 'heads' (as they were called) was automatically assumed to be for the public benefit. This is no longer the case and a number of charities, especially fee-charging ones, will have to carefully monitor the implementation of these new rules. Those under the fourth head were required to provide evidence that they were for the public benefit.

New requirements

The existing four heads used to determine charitable status have been expanded to 13 purposes. The Act defines a charity as an institution which is established for charitable purposes only (s. 1). Charitable purposes are then defined in section 2 as:

- falling within the list below, and
- being for the public benefit.

This list covers the majority of purposes which are already charitable. The last purpose means that everything that is currently charitable is included.

To satisfy the requirement for charitable purposes, the organisation will need to demonstrate that its activities are within the new purposes and are for the public benefit. The new purposes are:

1. the prevention or relief of poverty;
2. the advancement of education;
3. the advancement of religion;
4. the advancement of health or the saving of lives;
5. the advancement of citizenship or community development;
6. the advancement of the arts, culture, heritage or science;
7. the advancement of amateur sport;
8. the advancement of human rights, conflict resolution or reconciliation, or the promotion of religious or racial harmony, or equality and diversity;
9. the advancement of environmental protection or improvement;
10. the advancement of animal welfare;
11. the relief of those in need, by reason of youth, age, ill-health, disability, financial hardship or other disadvantage;
12. the promotion of the efficiency of the armed forces of the Crown, or of the efficiency of the police, fire and rescue services or ambulance services, and
13. any other purposes within section (s. 4).

Section 4 allows for any purposes not included in the above list if they would be 'recognised as charitable purposes under existing charity law'. This means any other purposes currently recognised as charitable and any new charitable purposes which are similar to another charitable purpose.

There is no definition of 'public benefit'. The term is not automatically linked to any of the above purposes. What is and what is not for the public benefit will be allowed to evolve over time. The Charity Commission has issued guidance in respect of the term 'public benefit'. Trustees are required to have regard to this guidance.

Recreational charities and sports clubs

For a recreational charity or sports club to be considered a charity, it must exist in the interests of social welfare. In order to do this, it must satisfy basic conditions. The facilities must be provided with the object of improving conditions of life for persons and

- the persons need the facilities by reason of youth, age, infirmity or disability, poverty, or social/economic circumstances, or
- the facilities are available to members of the public at large.

Registered sports clubs under Sch. 18 of Finance Act 2002 cannot be charities.

4.4 Providing public benefit

The Act underlines the requirement that all charities must exist for the public benefit, and the Charity Commission has a new objective to promote understanding and awareness of this public benefit requirement. General guidance has been developed to help understand what this requirement means (see **Annex 2**).

4.4.1 Reporting on the charity's public benefit

The Charity Commission will assess whether the aims of all organisations applying to register as charities are for the public benefit. Charities that are already registered have to continue to meet the public benefit requirement. The Charity Commission performs this assessment by carrying out research studies on the extent to which different types of charity are meeting the requirement and by working with representative professional and umbrella bodies and with users of those charities.

Trustees have a new duty to report in their Trustees' Annual Report how their charity fulfils a public benefit. This will take effect for accounting periods beginning on or after 1 April 2008. The level of detail required will depend on whether the charity is above or below the audit threshold. An audit is required when a charity's gross income in the year exceeds £500,000, or where income exceeds £100,000 and the aggregate value of its assets exceeds £2.8 million.

Most charities already explain their activities in their Trustees' Annual Report and so this information now needs to be set in the context of the charity's aims, to show how in practice the aims have been carried out for the public benefit.

Trustees will also need to confirm that they have had regard to public benefit guidance where relevant. Trustees of all charities must state in their annual report that they have 'complied with the duty in s. 4 of the Charities Act 2006 to have due regard to guidance published by the Charity Commission'.

Smaller charities (below the audit threshold) must include a brief summary in the Trustees' Annual Report setting out 'the main activities undertaken by the charity to further its charitable purposes for the public benefit'.

For larger charities (above the audit threshold), trustees are required to provide a fuller explanation in the Trustees' Annual Report both of the significant activities undertaken in order to carry out the charity's aims for the public benefit, as well as of their aims and strategies. They are required to explain the charity's achievements, measured by reference to the charity's aims and objectives as set by the trustees. These charities must provide a 'review of the significant activities undertaken by the charity during the year to further its charitable purposes for the public benefit'.

It is for the trustees to decide how much detail they want to provide to illustrate clearly what their charity has done in the reporting year to meet the requirement. The Charity Commission will not be prescriptive about the number of words or pages needed. However, a charity that said nothing on public benefit in its Trustees' Annual Report, or produced only the briefest statement with no detail, would be in breach of the public benefit reporting requirement.

Trustees should have read the Charity Commission's general guidance on public benefit. Sub-sector guidance (for charities in the areas of advancement of education, relief of poverty, advancement of religion and fee-charging), published in December 2008, should also be read.

The new duties should be taken as a positive opportunity to explain public benefit in a rounded way, by telling the reader about the charity's activities and who benefits and how. Charities that already explain the outcome or impact of their work will be well placed to explain how their activities further their charitable purposes for the public benefit. The public benefit focus should therefore involve little extra work.

There is now a distinct focus on public benefit and this should be reflected in the style, tone and coverage of the Trustees' Annual Report. Focusing on how public benefit criteria are used to inform the strategy or activities undertaken and on how the charity's activities and outcomes assist beneficiaries is key.

The Charity Commission's website has example reports for public benefit reporting. These demonstrate how charities that are already following the SORP can adapt to the new requirement with minimal change to the structure of their annual reports.

Public benefit reporting should not be treated with a dismissive single sentence. Minimalist reporting is not a good advertisement for the charity and possibly indicates that trustees are unaware of their new duties or are not abiding by them.

A good Trustees' Annual Report will enable the reader to understand better the activities undertaken and the benefits they bring to beneficiaries. A review of activities that fails to provide this information in a meaningful way is a missed opportunity.

4.4.2 Sub-sector guidance

In December 2008 the Charity Commission published final versions of its public benefit sub-sector guidance. This guidance has been published following consultation by the Charity Commission on draft versions issued in March 2008. Trustees must now make sure that they are aware of how the final guidance impacts on their particular charity, in terms of both their planning for the future and fulfilling the requirement to report each year on how the charity has delivered public benefit.

There are four sets of guidance, as follows:

- charities for the relief of poverty;
- charities for the advancement of religion;
- charities for the advancement of education, and
- fee-charging charities.

1 Charities for the relief of poverty

The Charity Commission has accepted the view that there is a difference between relief of poverty and relief of financial hardship. It recognises that it may, in some circumstances, be charitable to relieve the needs of people who are asset rich but temporarily in hardship.

A great deal of concern was raised by occupational benevolent funds concerning a contentious interpretation in the draft guidance of the rules relating to restricted classes of beneficiary. The Charity Commission has moved back from its initial position on that and now accepts that occupational benevolent funds may exist for purposes other than the prevention and relief of poverty.

2 Charities for the advancement of religion

Religious charities will be pleased to see there is now clarity that they have the same liberty to be involved in political campaigning as other charities. The guidance for religious charities also makes clear that, whilst the Charity

Commission will have regard to objective and informed public opinion, any argument that an organisation advancing religion causes detrimental harm must be supported by clear factual evidence.

3   Charities for the advancement of education

The Charity Commission's guidance provides the following examples of ways in which charities might advance education:

- formally in institutions and informally in community groups;
- in highly structured formats or, conversely, with very little formal process, and
- by making materials, or objects capable of educating, available to the public, such as in libraries or on databases.

Specifically, charities might advance education by:

(a)   **providing services** through:
 - running a school;
 - providing online education via the web or other new media, publications, television or radio programmes;
 - running classes in particular subjects for retired people;
 - providing after-school clubs in specific subjects;
 - providing school breakfast clubs for students;
 - lessons, seminars, conferences and lectures;
 - visits to the theatre and other arts facilities;
 - motivational learning;
 - teaching illiterate or innumerate adults to read, write or understand mathematics;
 - providing schoolbooks, either domestically or overseas, and
 - displaying works of art or of historic or scientific interest for people to see;

(b)   **providing support** through:
 - mentoring and coaching;
 - supporting schools overseas, including building or maintaining schools and supporting teacher training for schools overseas;
 - employing youth workers to promote social inclusion and increase attendance at the local school;
 - helping children with learning difficulties, such as dyslexia, to enable them to be taught in mainstream classes if they wish;
 - providing student welfare or student accommodation;
 - supporting parents to engage more with their children's education or encouraging greater parental involvement, and
 - providing support for students with behavioural problems;

(c) **promoting knowledge and raising standards** through:
- undertaking academic research and publishing the results online;
- publishing articles in journals which are peer-reviewed;
- maintaining an academic library with access for academics and students;
- independent accreditation of courses or course providers;
- setting examination and qualification standards;
- marking examinations;
- conducting research that is made generally available, including publishing the useful results of that research, and
- running courses for local teachers who want to improve their teaching skills;

(d) **providing grants of money** to:
- fund individual students' education or providing bursary funding;
- endow a Chair at a university or a department at a school, and
- enable students to buy books, computers or school uniforms.

4 Fee-charging charities

The Charity Commission has maintained its policy that those in poverty must not be excluded. It is left to the discretion of trustees as to what opportunities they provide to people who cannot afford fees. The guidance is clear that direct access to the service provided is not the only way of demonstrating public benefit. Other significant opportunities to benefit can be equally valid. It remains a question throughout as to what the Charity Commission will decide is 'sufficient' in each case. Schools charging high fees might have to 'think about other ways in which people who cannot afford those fees can benefit'. The Charity Commission suggests that working in partnership with a local state school might be one way.

A new feature of the guidance is the statement that, in its assessment, the Charity Commission can consider any evidence of significant detriment or harm caused by a charity in carrying out its activities.

Previously, the Charity Commission provided guidance listed as items (1) to (10) below to help organisations to provide benefits to people who are unable to pay the fees.

1. Providing concessions, subsidised or free places – for example, in the case of schools, by offering bursaries or assisted places; or, in the case of theatres or concert halls, by offering concessionary tickets.
2. The existence of accessible insurance or other benefit schemes – for example, medical insurance schemes. This would depend, though, on the cost of such schemes and what sorts of services people are entitled to receive under them.
3. The existence of other reliable sources of funding that are specifically made available to beneficiaries, or as a funding arrangement between an

independent school and a separate, but linked, grant-making body, or funding offered by a local authority to pay for a place in a care home.
4. Providing wider access to charitable facilities or services. Some charities may provide additional facilities or services for people who would otherwise be excluded because they are unable to pay the fees. Some charities may lend equipment or staff out to other charities or groups that provide the same facilities or services to people who are unable to pay the fees – for example, a charitable independent school allowing a state-maintained school to use its educational facilities.
5. The educational benefits to state school pupils who are able to attend certain lessons or other educational events at independent schools.
6. The educational benefits to pupils in state schools arising from collaboration and partnerships between state schools and independent schools.
7. The benefits of free access to specialised medical equipment not available in the local NHS hospital, or through a number of beds in the charitable hospital being made freely available to NHS patients.
8. The increased appreciation of literary or artistic performances gained by people who are unable to pay the fees who are able to attend musical concerts or theatre performances through concessionary tickets.
9. In addition to offering concessions on ticket prices, a local theatre might also have an exhibition space for local people to view works of art and an amateur dramatic society that local people can join.
10. Providing medical training to nurses or doctors at an NHS hospital which benefits the non-fee-paying patients at that hospital.

The Odstock case

A case in 2007 provided an example of how the Charity Commission will actually interpret case law on public benefit for fee-charging charities. The Charity Commission's decision on the recent application for a charitable registration by Odstock Private Care Limited demonstrates that the Charity Commission will follow existing case law. Odstock was established by Salisbury NHS Foundation Trust to undertake private healthcare work in Salisbury District Hospital. There is a statutory limit on the capacity of foundation trusts to benefit from private healthcare work.

The hospital sought to earn more than the statutory limit through the establishment of a separate charitable company. It was intended that Odstock would enter into agreements with patients and insurance companies for the provision of private care, and contract with the foundation trust for the provision of staff facilities. The arrangement was partly designed to satisfy the desire of consultants for private patient work. The Charity Commission rejected the application and that decision was then appealed for review by three Board members of the Charity Commission.

Odstock was established so that its income would be derived from private patients who received the benefit of medical insurance. It appeared that Odstock

The Charities Act 2006

was not in a position to accept poor patients for whom no fee was payable. Perhaps more importantly in this case, there was no evidence produced that through medical insurance plans, some poor persons were able to obtain benefit. The reviewers considered the Privy Council case of Re: Resch where, in an analogous situation relating to a public hospital and its associated charity, public benefit was found in that the poor were not excluded.

This decision of the Charity Commission is helpful since it has simply applied the case law as it stands. If better evidence had been produced, then it is likely that Odstock might have been deemed charitable. For example, employer-paid medical insurance could have enabled poor people to use the facilities of Odstock, or some charitable bursary fund could have been offered by Odstock for private care.

4.5 New thresholds for registration

For would-be registered charities, the new income level for registration will be £5,000. This took effect from 23 April 2007. Previously, small charities that had an annual income of £1,000 or less did not have to register unless they had a permanent endowment or the use, or occupation, of land.

The Act removes the permanent endowment or land requirement and raises the income threshold to £5,000. Therefore, if any organisation is charitable and has an annual income of £5,000, it must be registered with the Charity Commission. Approximately 30,000 charities will have the registration requirement removed through this measure.

Charities below this threshold will be able to register voluntarily. Existing charities below this threshold will be able to ask to be removed from the register, but they will remain charities and have to abide by charity law. These requirements will not apply to Charitable Incorporated Organisations, which must be registered regardless of their income.

4.6 Exempt charities

Exempt charities were those listed in Schedule 2 of the Charities Act 1993. The list included some educational institutions, and most universities and national museums. Some changes have been made to the list of exempt charities in Schedule 2. The Church Commissioners and institutions administered by them have been removed from the list. Industrial and Provident Societies and Friendly Societies are also removed with the exception of those Industrial and Provident Societies that are also registered in the register of social landlords. There may be changes to other exempt charities as well, but this is dependent on consultation with other regulators. However, this will only initially affect those with an annual income over £100,000.

From 1 October 2009, exempt charities that are not subject to any other principal regulator will need to apply to the Charity Commission for registration if they have an annual income over £100,000.

Exempt charities have not previously been allowed to register with the Charity Commission because it has been assumed that they were adequately regulated by other public bodies, such as the Financial Services Authority or the Housing Corporation. The Act now ensures that these charities are also monitored for their compliance with charity law.

The Act puts previously exempt charities into two categories:

(a) Those already regulated by a body (other than the Charity Commission) which has agreed to take responsibility for ensuring they meet charity law. These charities will continue to be exempt and will be regulated by their current regulator, now known as a 'principal regulator'. The Charity Commission will be able to investigate any of these charities if the charity's principal regulator asks it to.
(b) If no suitable regulator exists, then a previously exempt charity will stop being exempt and will have to register with the Charity Commission. To ease the transition, only those charities with an annual income of over £100,000 will have to register.

The £100,000 threshold for registration is an interim level and may be reduced in the future, but this will not happen before 2011, when there will be a review of the Act.

The proposed timescale will enable those charities, the proposed principal regulators of exempt charities, and the Charity Commission to prepare for the changes (parts of s. 9, ss. 11 to 14, and Sch. 5). The Office of the Third Sector (OTS) is working with principal regulators to agree how the new arrangements will work and to make sure that it has the powers needed for this role.

4.7 Excepted charities

Excepted charities always have, and continue to be, fully under the supervision of the Charity Commission. They are called excepted charities because they have been excepted from the requirement to register with the Charity Commission. This exception has been given them either by legislation or by an Order of the Charity Commission. Such charities include some religious charities, the Boy Scout and Girl Guide charities and some armed forces charities.

The Act requires some of these charities to register with the Charity Commission. Initially, only excepted charities with an annual income of £100,000 or over will have to register. Those under the £100,000 threshold will not have to register but will still come under the Charity Commission's jurisdiction. This £100,000 threshold is an interim level and may be reduced in the future, but this also will not happen until the review of the Act in 2011.

The main provisions were introduced in January 2009, rather than October 2008, in order to give some excepted charities that are affected more time to prepare for registration with the Charity Commission and to put in place measures to minimise the regulatory impact of the Charities Act 2006 on the governing bodies of foundation and voluntary-aided schools in England and Wales. However the registration programme for church and armed forces charities started, as planned, in October 2008. The vast majority of these registrations must be completed by 1 October 2009.

The necessary excepting regulations have been extended until 2012. This is to allow time for the review of the Act to take place and for recommendations arising from it to be considered. It is anticipated that ultimately the income level triggering the requirement to register will be the same for all charities.

4.7.1 Excepted church charity programme

Local church charities associated with the bodies listed below *and* established wholly or mainly for the purpose of public religious worship, are excepted from the requirement to register as charities by The Charities (Exception from Registration) Regulations 1996 as amended.

This means that although the law recognises them as charities, they do not have to have a registered charity number.

Church charities not required to register as charities

- Baptist Union
- Church in Wales
- Church of England
- Congregational Federation
- Evangelical Fellowship of Congregational Churches
- Fellowship of Independent Evangelical Churches (FIEC)
- General Assembly of Unitarian and Free Christian Churches
- Grace Baptist Trust Corporation
- Methodist Conference
- Presbyterian Church in Wales (also known as Calvinistic Methodist Church)
- Religious Society of Friends
- Strict and Particular Baptists
- Union of Welsh Independents
- United Reform Church

When the relevant part of the Act is enacted, then such charities with an annual income over £100,000 will have to apply for registration unless the Charity Commission issues a written determination to the contrary.

There will be a review of the Charities Act 2006 in 2011. This may result in the income threshold being reduced. However, until then, church charities with an annual income below £100,000 will continue to be excepted from the requirement to register and so will not have a registered charity number.

4.7.2 Registered places of worship

The Charities Act 1993 introduced the requirement for all charities with an income in excess of £1,000 a year to apply for registration. Therefore, a registered place of worship that did not specifically have its working funds included within the property trust should have applied to register its working funds as a charity.

The Charities Act 2006 (Interim changes in the threshold for registration of small charities) Order 2007, which came into force on 23 April 2007, raised the general threshold for registration to £5,000 and removed the requirement to register that previously applied to charities having the use or occupation of land or ownership of property that is a permanent endowment. This effectively removed the exception in respect of registered places of worship.

This means that the following have a duty to apply for registration if their funds exceed the normal registration threshold of £5,000 income per year:

- charities connected with all groups of churches not specifically excepted from registration by the 1960 or 1996 excepting legislation, and
- all wholly independent church charities.

4.7.3 The armed services

Those charities concerned with promoting the efficiency of the armed forces and affected by the changes in charity law will be registered on a phased basis over 18 months. Registration of Royal Navy, Royal Marines and British Army charitable service funds with annual income of £100,000 or more started from October 2008. Registration of RAF service funds with annual income of £100,000 or more started in 2009.

While the Charity Commission is registering the large numbers of formerly excepted and exempt charities that it now has to register, the current law which enables the Charity Commission to exercise its discretion in relation to applications for voluntary registration will continue in force. Once those excepted and exempt charities that are required to register have been registered, the provision in the Act requiring the Charity Commission to register charities that apply for voluntary registration will be commenced.

It is estimated that between 4,000 to 5,000 charities are currently excepted.

4.8 Greater flexibility for smaller charities

Under previous legislation, charities could make changes to their purposes through resolutions agreed with the Charity Commission. The new Act liberalises and extends these powers.

It allows smaller non-company charities with income of less than £10,000 a year to take certain actions without having to obtain permission from the Charity Commission. The Charity Commission will still require copies of the resolutions passed by the trustees to make these changes.

4.8.1 Transferring assets

Trustees of these charities can transfer the charity's assets to other charities whose objects are consistent with their own (s. 40).

4.8.2 Changing a charity's purposes

Trustees can also replace their charity's purposes with new purposes that make more sense in today's society, as long as the changes are consistent with what the charity was set up to do. For example, a charity set up to relieve sickness can update its purposes to participate in a health promotion scheme to encourage healthy living (s. 41).

4.9 Charitable incorporated organisation (CIO)

CIOs were first mentioned in the Department for Trade and Industry (DTI) 2001 Company Law Review. Establishing a new corporate form designed specifically for charities was then recommended by the Strategy Unit, a recommendation the Government accepted. Provision was made for the CIO in the Charities Act 2006. The CIO is the first incorporated legal form designed specifically with the needs of charities in mind. It will be available only to charities and will add to the existing range of forms that charities can use.

The Act creates a new vehicle for a charity to exist. A CIO will have the advantages of a corporate structure, such as reduced personal liability for trustees, without the burden of dual regulation as CIOs will only have to report to the Charity Commission. It is anticipated that CIOs will not be available until Spring 2010.

The features of a CIO are:

- limited liability;
- the choice of membership structure;
- explicit duty of care for trustees and members;
- ease of conversion;
- charitable status;
- registered with the Charity Commission;
- principal office in England or Wales, and
- name and disclosure requirements.

Two forms of model constitution have been produced. The first is a *foundation model*, where the only members of the CIO are its trustees. The second is *an association model*, where the CIO will have a separate body of members other than the trustees. All CIOs will be required to have a constitution. The constitution will be required to include the following:

- name;
- purpose;
- who is eligible for membership;
- appointment of trustees, and
- application of property if the CIO is dissolved.

Existing company charities will be able to convert to CIOs. This will not be possible though if the company has shares which are not fully paid up or if it is an exempt charity.

Charities which want a corporate structure currently have to register both as charities and as companies, which means they have to meet the regulatory burdens of both the Charity Commission and Companies House.

A CIO with gross annual income of less than £100,000 (£250,000 for accounting periods ending on or after 1 April 2009) will be able to choose receipts and payments accounts – which is not the case for all other limited companies, which must prepare accruals accounts however small they are.

A joint consultation by the OTS (which is part of the Cabinet Office) and the Charity Commission on the secondary legislation that is needed to complete the legal framework for the CIO was concluded in December 2008. The consultation is aimed at balancing the need for CIOs to be simple and attractive for charities with the need for a legal framework that is robust enough for business purposes. A further hurdle to overcome is that directors of CIOs need to be afforded the same protection that directors of company charities receive under company law. Under charity law (which will govern CIOs) directors of CIOs will only be under Charity Commission jurisdiction.

Questions raised in the consultation were:

- the minimum age for a trustee of a CIO;
- the duty of care expected of a trustee of a CIO;
- the accounting regime which should apply to CIOs;
- the requirements for a CIO's constitution, and
- the requirement for a CIO to maintain a register of trustees and members, and making this and certain other information available to members of the public on request.

Whilst the CIO will bring advantages for some, it will also bring new obligations for others and will not be the right option for all charities. The Charity Commission estimates there are approximately 26,000 registered charities established as companies limited by guarantee that would potentially be eligible to convert.

4.10 Audit and accounts

The Charities Act 2006 is not a consolidating act, so in this change to the thresholds, the external scrutiny requirements are still enshrined in the Charities Act 1993. The new Charities Act does, however, amend the existing audit exemption thresholds, but it does so by amending previous legislation.

4.10.1 Non-company charities

The criteria that determine whether or not an audit is required will be based on income only, the reference to expenditure being removed together with the reference to the two previous years.

The audit requirement will apply where the income exceeds £500,000, or income exceeds £100,000 and gross assets exceed £2.8 million.

Independent examination will continue to apply at £10,000, but there will be changes to the requirements in respect of the independent examiner. Independent examiners of charities with incomes up to £250,000 will not be required to hold a qualification. Independent examiners of charities with income between £250,000 and £500,000 will need to be members of a professional accountancy body.

The independent examiner must be a member of one of the following bodies:

- Association of Accounting Technicians;
- Association of Authorised Public Accountants;
- Association of Charity Independent Examiners
- Association of Chartered Certified Accountants;

Audit and accounts

- Association of International Accountants;
- Chartered Institute of Management Accountants;
- Chartered Institute of Public Finance and Accountancy;
- Institute of Chartered Accountants in England and Wales;
- Institute of Chartered Accountants in Ireland;
- Institute of Chartered Accountants in Scotland, or
- Institute of Chartered Secretaries and Administrator.

If the non-company charity's annual income is below £250,000, the independent examiner does not need to have an appropriate qualification but will need to be independent and appropriately experienced.

For accounting periods beginning on or after 27 February 2007, the position for **non-company** charities is as detailed in Table 4.2 (see also section **4.14**).

Table 4.2 Auditing requirements placed on non-company charities for accounting periods beginning after 27 February 2007

Gross income	Up to £1,000	£1,001 – £10,000	£10,001 – £100,000	£100,001 – £500,000	Over £500,000
Accounting Records	Not regulated	Must be kept	Must be kept	Must be kept	Must be kept
Type of Accounts	Not regulated	Receipts and payments	Receipts and payments	Full, on accruals basis	Full, on accruals basis
Type of examination	Not regulated	Not required	Independent examination	Independent examination	Full audit
Examiner or auditor qualified?	Not regulated	Not required	Need not be	Qualified independent examiner if over £250,000	Registered auditor
Accounts sent to Charity Commission	Not regulated	Only if requested	Compulsory	Compulsory	Compulsory
Annual Return sent to Charity Commission	Not regulated	Not required	Compulsory	Compulsory	Compulsory

4.10.2 Company charities

For accounting periods beginning on or after 27 February 2007, company charities with an annual income between £90,000 and £500,000 and assets of £2.8 million or less are not required to have their accounts audited if they

61

provide an accountant's report. For company charities with annual income of £90,000 or less, neither a professional audit nor an accountant's report is required unless its assets are over £2.8 million.

Therefore, company charities accounts will only have to be professionally audited if the company charity has:

- gross annual income over £500,000, or
- a balance sheet total (aggregate assets) over £2.8 million regardless of income.

The higher thresholds apply on or after 27 February 2007. However, Sch. 10 of the Act states, in relation to these provisions, that they apply for financial periods starting on or after 27 February 2007 – that is, 31 March 2008 year end.

For company charities, the equivalent of an independent examination is a Reporting Accountant's report. The upper limit for this increases to £500,000 annual income. Those company charities with, say, 31 March 2008 or 31 December 2008 year ends will still use the £90,000 to £500,000 income threshold. The harmonisation rules will then apply for accounting periods beginning on or after 1 April 2008. So, for accounting periods beginning on or after 1 April 2008 (that is, year ending 31 March 2009, or later), company charities have the same rules as non-company charities (see **Annex 1**).

4.10.3 Harmonisation of thresholds

For 31 March 2009 year ends onwards, the harmonisation of company and non-company charities takes effect, and the Reporting Accountant's report is replaced by an Independent Examination for company charities with annual incomes between £10,000 and £500,000. This creates a level playing field for company and non-company charities. Charity law audit and independent examination arrangements now apply to small company charities. The result brings company charities into line with non-company charities (that is, independent examinations instead of audits for any charity with annual income of between £10,000 and £500,000).

Following the implementation of the Commencement Order No.6, the Companies Act 2006 will no longer set out different audit thresholds for charities. An audit will only be required under the Companies Act 2006 if the charity exceeds the thresholds for small companies (s. 382 (3) of the Companies Act 2006). Small company charities are therefore those company charities that are not required to have their accounts audited under company law.

Instead, the practical audit thresholds will be determined by the Charities Act 1993 (as amended by the Charities Act 2006). The specific amendments were introduced by the Charities Act 2006 (Charitable Companies Audit and Group

Accounts Provisions) Order 2008/SI 527, which is accompanied by an Explanatory Memorandum and Impact Assessment. The Companies Act 2006 (Commencement No 6. Saving and Commencement Nos. 3 and 5 (Amendment)) Order 2008 disapplied the special company law accounts scrutiny provisions to small charitable companies. This was dealt with under s. 1175 and Sch. 9 of the Companies Act 2006 and s. 77 Order, bringing small company charities into the external scrutiny regime of Part 6 of 1993 Charities Act.

The Companies Act 2006 only switches the external scrutiny thresholds for company charities, as the bookkeeping, format and content of their Accounts still remain under the Companies Act. This means that the external scrutiny thresholds for company charities are now determined by the 1993 Charities Act, as amended by Charities Act 2006, but the bookkeeping, format and content of their Accounts will refer to the Companies Act 2006.

4.10.4 Group accounts

The Charities SORP has long recommended the preparation of group accounts where a charity has one or more material subsidiary undertakings. When it was first published, SORP 2005 specifically recommended the preparation of group accounts where the income of the group, after consolidation adjustments, exceeded the charity audit threshold set by the Charities Act 1993.

Until the implementation of new group accounts provisions introduced by the Charities Act 2006, there was no legal requirement placed on **non-company charities** to prepare group accounts. Moreover, parent company charities were only required by company law to prepare group accounts where the threshold for a large group set by the Companies Act 1985 was exceeded. Subsequently, the Companies Act 2006 requires group accounts where the threshold for the small companies' regime is exceeded.

There is now a new requirement for a certain parent charities to prepare group accounts. A new Schedule is included which:

- defines a parent undertaking, and
- requires the parent to prepare group accounts unless excepted from doing so and where the only exceptions are:
    - the parent charity is also a subsidiary of another charity, or
    - the gross income of a group is below the threshold.

An audit of the group accounts is required if thresholds are exceeded. The thresholds for both the preparation and audit of group accounts are included in the Regulations.

The new legal requirements apply for accounting years beginning on or after 1 April 2008. They effectively mirror the SORP's recommendations for the preparation of group accounts. The effect of these changes is that all parent charities, whether companies or not, will need to prepare group accounts. The levels set are equivalent to those set out in the SORP 2005; namely, gross income in the financial period of less than £600,000 and net income less than £500,000. Groups will need to be audited at the same levels. There will therefore never be a situation in which group accounts must be prepared but only need an independent examination.

Non-company parent charities

Previously, for non-company charities in a group, the requirement was generally that the parent and each of its subsidiaries should prepare accounts relating to itself alone, although the SORP required consolidated accounts in most cases. A new s. 49A and Sch 5A are inserted into Charities Act 1993 to provide the requirement for a parent charity to prepare group (that is, consolidated) accounts. Group accounts do not need to be prepared by a parent charity that is also itself a subsidiary of a charity.

Where the parent charity is not a company, the group accounts will be prepared and audited under charity law. The Charities Act 2006 amends the Charities Act 1993 and provides a framework for the preparation and audit of group accounts by inserting Sch 5A into it. The Charities (Accounts and Reports) Regulations 2008 set out the requirements for:

- the calculation of aggregate gross income of a charity group;
- the form and content of charity group accounts and required notes;
- the content of an annual report for a charity group, and
- the matters to be included in the auditor's report on the group.

Those already preparing group accounts as recommended by the SORP are unlikely to find any major surprises in the form and content requirements for charity group accounts. The 'group accounts package' filed with the Charity Commission should, as at present, also contain the primary statements of the parent charity and relevant notes.

Company parent charities

Where the parent charity is a company, group accounts will be required if the aggregate gross income of the group exceeds £500,000. However, the group accounts of a parent company charity are prepared under the Charities Act 1993, where the parent charity is not required by law to prepare group accounts under Companies Act provisions. The directors' report must meet the requirements of company law and the requirements of the Trustees' Annual Report can be included as part of a combined directors' report.

If the parent company charity has a legal obligation to prepare group accounts under company law provisions, then the charity must do so. The provisions of charity law do not apply to the form and content of those accounts, although the methods and principles of SORP still apply to their preparation. Where there is a company law requirement to prepare group accounts, those group accounts will also be audited under company law provisions.

Table 4.3 *References in the Companies Act 2006 applicable from 6 April 2008*

2006 Companies Act provision	Relevant 1985 Companies Act provision
Section 399 (duty to prepare group accounts)	Sections 227 and 248
Section 479 (availability of small companies exemption in case of group company)	Section 249(B)
Section 398 (option to prepare group accounts)	Section 248 and 248(A)
Section 404 (Companies Act group accounts)	Section 227
Section 475 (requirement for audited accounts)	Section 249(B)

However, where the size of the group is such that there is no legal requirement to prepare group accounts under company law, then a requirement will arise for group accounts to be prepared under charity law requirements where the aggregate gross income of the group exceeds £500,000.

Where group accounts are prepared under charity law, the framework is provided by Sch. 5A of the Charities Act 1993 and the Charities (Accounts and Reports) Regulations 2008. Where group accounts are prepared under charity law requirements, they must also be audited under charity law. The 2008 Regulations and the Charities Act 1993 set out the reporting duties of the auditor of a charity group.

The charity law requirements for group accounts draw heavily on and are compatible with company law. However, where the trustees of a parent company charity wish to use their group accounts as part of their statutory accounts for company law purposes (for example, filing with Companies House), care will need to be taken that the group accounts meet the requirements of both charity and company law. Trustees are also reminded that for a company's statutory accounts to be exempt from a Companies Act audit, a statement must be provided on the face of the balance sheet of the parent company confirming entitlement to audit exemption (see s. 475 of the Companies Act 2006).

The parent charity is legally required to prepare its own entity accounts but there is no legal basis for preparing group accounts. The new Act enables a parent charity to provide group accounts which include its subsidiaries.

The Charities Act 2006

Legal references

1. Part 39, s. 1175 and s. 9 of the Companies Act 2006 provided for the removal of the special provisions about accounts and audit of company charities. These provisions came into effect on 1 April 2008 and were enacted by The Companies Act 2006 (Commencement No 6, Saving and Commencement Nos. 3 and 5 (Amendment)) Order 2008, SI 674.
2. Section 77 of the Charities Act 2006 provided a power for amendments to be made to company law. Using this power, The Charities Act 2006 (Charitable Companies and Group Accounts Provisions) Order 2008, SI 527 extended the Charities Act regime to small company charities that are not subject to audit under company law.
3. The Small Companies and Groups (Accounts and Directors' Report) Regulations 2008, No 409 apply for financial years beginning on or after 6 April 2008.
4. The Charities (Accounts and Reports) Regulations 2008, SI 629 apply for the financial years of charities beginning on or after 1 April 2008.

4.11 Charity Tribunal

4.11.1 Introduction

The Government first raised the idea of the tribunal in 2003 and legislated for it in the Charities Act 2006. Section 8 of the Charities 2006 sets out the arrangements for the new Charity Tribunal. The tribunal is to act as the 'court of first instance' for appeals and applications in respect of certain Charity Commission decisions. The Act has created a new tribunal to deal with appeals against, and reviews of, legal decisions by the Charity Commission. Establishing the tribunal is the responsibility of the Department for Constitutional Affairs.

Sometimes charities, and others affected by a legal decision the Charity Commission has made, believe that the decision is wrong and want to challenge it. In order to appeal against a decision by the Charity Commission, the case previously had to be taken to the High Court, which was difficult and expensive.

The Charity Tribunal will also take referrals from the Charity Commission or the Attorney General that involve the operation or application of charity law. It opened after a short delay on 18 March 2008. The tribunal will not deal with customer service complaints, which will continue to be dealt with by the Charity Commission's internal complaints system and the Independent Complaints Reviewer.

Alison McKenna was appointed president for the tribunal in February 2008 and took up the post in June 2008. The tribunal is seen as an inexpensive way for charities to challenge Charity Commission decisions. There is no charge for bringing cases and those who do so can get free legal help from a pool of *pro bono* lawyers. The tribunal could also become a battleground for some of the most contentious issues of charity law, perhaps including the public benefit test.

The tribunal is resourced on the basis of 50 cases a year. Most attention has focused on how the tribunal could save charities a fortune on High Court appeals against the regulator's judgements.

All five legal members and seven lay members have been appointed on daily rates of £450 and £255 respectively. Nagendram Seevaratnam, who was removed from his post as trustee of a London Hindu charity called Sivayogam, brought the first case. By June 2009, the tribunal was considering its third case – a challenge by two Dartford residents over the Commission's decision on a land sale.

4.11.2 How the Charity Tribunal works

The Charity Tribunal has unusual powers that have not been conferred on most of the other 31 tribunals in the Tribunals Service, an executive agency of the Ministry of Justice. Most notably, it can consider points of law referred to it by the Attorney General or the Charity Commission without a case being brought. It might not therefore be left to individual charities to challenge rulings on issues with sector-wide importance, such as public benefit or political campaigning.

The Cabinet Office says that the tribunal's enhanced powers will help it develop case law that has not always kept pace with changes in society and the charity sector. The tribunal aims to complete 75 per cent of cases within 30 weeks. Three of the 12 tribunal members will sit in judgement and few hearings are expected to last beyond a day. The tribunal will be part of the general regulatory chamber, which also includes the Gambling Appeals Tribunal and the Consumer Credit Appeals Tribunal.

As part of this new arrangement, tribunal members will no longer sit on only one tribunal. However, the eligibility criteria for the Charity Tribunal state that members must have 'experience and expertise in relation to charities', so mobility will be restricted. The tribunal's performance will be assessed as part of the review of the Charities Act in 2011.

4.11.3 How the appeal process works

The appeal process follows these steps:

1. Charity Commission issues its final decision on a charity.
2. The charity has 42 days from notification of the Charity Commission's final decision to appeal to the Charity Tribunal.
3. The tribunal considers whether the appeal falls within its jurisdiction.

4. The tribunal sends the appeal application to the Charity Commission and informs it of the grounds for appeal.
5. The Charity Commission has 28 days to file a response to the appeal.
6. The charity has the right to reply to any response raised by the Commission.
7. The Charity Commission files any previously undisclosed evidence.
8. A 'directions hearing' takes place, at which the two parties agree a timetable for submitting documents to members of the Charity Tribunal, as well as agreeing a hearing date and a list of witnesses.
9. Tribunal hearing takes place.

4.12 Duty and protection for whistle blowers

The whistle-blowing provisions have been extended to auditors and reporting accountants of company charities. Auditors may well be able to identify abuse or significant breaches of trust during the audit process. The Charities Act 2006 provides that auditors of charity accounts will be protected from the risk of action for breach of confidence or defamation when they communicate relevant information to the Charity Commission. Independent examiners of charity accounts will also be protected.

Section 33 of the Charities Act 2006 makes an amendment to the Companies Act 1985 and introduces, for both auditors and reporting accountants, the same reporting responsibilities and protections as exist for the auditors and independent examiners of non-company charities. The Charity Commission has issued guidance on the circumstances in which it would expect the auditor or examiner to report to it.

The Act takes up the provisions in previous Regulations regarding the duty to make a written report to the Charity Commission where the activities or affairs of a charity would be likely to be of 'material significance for the exercise by the Charity Commission of its functions under sections 8 or 18 of the Charities Act 1993' (power to institute inquiries, and power to act for the protection of charities).

The Act ensures that auditors of charity accounts will be protected from the risk of action for breach of confidence or defamation when they pass on relevant information to the Commission. Independent examiners of charity accounts will also be protected. These provisions were effective from 1 April 2008 (see section **23.8.2** of Chapter 23).

4.13 Other measures

4.13.1 Suspending or removing trustees and others from membership of charities

When the Charity Commission has serious causes for concern about a charity and opens an inquiry, occasionally a trustee, employee or other agent of the charity threatens the property or continued administration of the charity. This happens rarely, but it can make it more difficult to conclude the inquiry as quickly as the Charity Commission would like and can damage the charity's reputation.

There are times in formal inquiries when the Charity Commission has to suspend or remove a person from his or her position as trustee, officer, agent or employee. The Act allows the Charity Commission to make an order to suspend or remove the person from membership of the charity and so prevent that person from seeking re-election to his or her former position.

This power is unlikely to be used often, but it will be helpful in those rare instances when a member of a charity under investigation threatens its effective running.

4.13.2 Specific directions for protecting a charity

The Act allows the Charity Commission to direct trustees, officers, employees of a charity organisation to take specific actions to protect a charity, when an inquiry is open.

This will be used in those rare circumstances where the Charity Commission has found that misconduct or mismanagement has occurred in the charity and the Charity Commission needs to ensure that actions are taken to protect the charity's property or make sure that it is used for the purposes for which it was intended.

4.13.3 Ensuring charity property is used correctly

On rare occasions, trustees are unwilling to apply charity property for its intended purposes. The Act enables the Charity Commission to deal with this by giving it a power to direct it to do so. The Charity Commission can use this power without opening a formal inquiry.

4.13.4 Deciding a charity's membership

The Act gives the Charity Commission the power to decide a charity's membership, either if the charity applies to the Charity Commission to do so or if the Charity Commission needs to find out during the course of an inquiry. The power also allows the Charity Commission to appoint someone else to do this – for example, the person who is appointed to undertake the inquiry.

4.13.5 Entering premises and obtaining documents

There are occasions when documents are deliberately destroyed by those involved in a charity when the Charity Commission tells them that an inquiry is being opened. Where the Charity Commission has reason to believe this might happen, the Act gives it the power to get a warrant from a Justice of the Peace to enter and search premises and take away specified material, including electronic material.

It also gives the Charity Commission the power to prevent interference with, or the destruction of, specified documents, and to make copies of them and get information from the charity about what, and where, such documents are.

These powers can only be used as part of an inquiry and the Charity Commission will have to satisfy the Justice of the Peace that it has strong reason to believe the documents are at risk before he or she will grant a warrant.

4.13.6 Fundraising solicitation statements

Currently, professional fundraisers and commercial participators fundraising for charities must have a written agreement with the charity. They must also make a statement telling potential donors that they are getting paid when they ask for money. This is so that potential donors can make an informed choice about giving.

The Act makes two main changes to these 'solicitation statements':

- they will have to include the amount the professional fundraiser or commercial participator will be paid for fundraising for the appeal, or
- if the specific amount is not known, they will have to give a reasonably accurate estimate of what the fundraiser will receive.

Slightly different statements will also have to be made by employees, officers and trustees of charities who act as collectors. This statement does not apply to volunteers.

4.13.7 Public charitable collections

The Act provides for a new system for licensing charitable collections in public. It applies to all such collections, including face-to-face fundraising which may involve requests for direct debit authorisation.

There is a new role for the Charity Commission in checking whether charities and other organisations are fit and proper to carry out public collections. The Charity Commission will be responsible for issuing public collections certificates, which will be valid for up to five years. The Charity Commission will need to develop the regulations and guidance required for this new role although it is not expected to take it on for some years.

4.13.8 Collections in public places

Previous legislation referred to 'street' collections. The Act extends this to collections in 'public places' which includes some privately owned land, railway station ticket halls and supermarket forecourts. Once a charity has a public collections certificate, it will be able to apply to a local authority for a permit to hold collections at certain times in certain places in that local authority area.

Local authorities will need to ensure that there are not too many collections taking place at the same time, in the same place.

4.13.9 Door-to-door collections

Previous legislation referred to 'house-to-house' collections. The Act refers instead to 'door-to-door' collections, to make clear that this also includes business premises.

A charity with a public collections certificate will be able to conduct door-to-door collections without permission from a local authority, but it must inform the local authority that the collection is taking place (see section **5.10** of Chapter 5).

4.13.10 Local, short-term collections

Some collections will be exempt from licensing and will not require either a certificate or permit, but organisers will have to notify the local authority that the collection is taking place; so small-scale activities should not be disproportionately affected.

4.13.11 Amending administrative rules

The Charities Act 2006 gives the trustees of all non-company charities power to pass a resolution to alter the parts of their charity's governing document which set out how they administer their charity (for example, the number of trustees needed to form a quorum at meetings). The trustees will only need to use this power if it is not already included in the charity's governing document.

4.13.12 Flexibility for transferring the assets of 'failed' appeals or trusts

Charities occasionally run appeals that fail to get enough money to meet their original aim, and funds can exist for which there are no longer any beneficiaries. The 'cy-pres' (literally 'near to') doctrine has previously restricted the Charity Commission's and the Court's ability to allow charities to use these 'failed' funds in flexible ways.

The Act now allows the Charity Commission and the Courts to take into account current social and economic circumstances when approached by charities seeking more freedom in how they can use donated money when they cannot use it as originally planned. The spirit in which the original donation was made will also need to be taken into account.

4.13.13 Effective use of permanent endowments

Permanent endowments can be either charitable funds or property, such as land or a building, which a charity cannot spend or sell in its entirety. Trustees of permanently endowed charities can use the income generated by permanent endowment but, except for very small charities, they cannot usually spend the capital.

The Act now allows a wider range of smaller charities to spend the capital and, for larger charities, power to do the same in certain circumstances.

4.13.14 Company charities

Company charities must ask the Charity Commission for prior consent if they want to make changes to their Memorandum and Articles of Association. The Act reduces the occasions where they will have to seek the Charity Commission's permission before making these changes, helping these charities make amendments more quickly and easily.

4.13.15 Merger relaxations

One of the obstacles to charity mergers can be uncertainties about what will happen to legacies and donations which were left to those charities which 'disappear' as the result of a merger.

The Charity Commission will now keep a public register of charity mergers. Registering a merger will be voluntary. When a merger is registered, gifts and legacies to the previously separate charities will automatically be transferred to the new merged charity. This will reassure both charities and the donating public that the spirit of legacies will be honoured if a charity merges.

4.13.16 Payment of trustees

The Act does not allow trustees to be paid for being trustees. Voluntary trusteeship still remains a key principle of charity law.

The Act does, however, allow trustees to pay an individual trustee for providing an additional service to the charity – if they think it is in the best interest of the charity – without having to come to the Charity Commission for authorisation to do so.

There are several important points:

- the number of trustees receiving payment in this way must be a minority;
- the amount paid must be reasonable and set out in a written agreement between the trustee and the charity, and
- the governing document must not contain any specific provision forbidding this type of payment.

An example of this situation could be a trustee who is a plumber providing plumbing services to the charity as long as the trustees agree that it is in the charity's best interest – for example, because the trustee is charging a better price or in some way giving a service that the trustees could not get elsewhere.

4.13.17 Publicity requirements for schemes

When the Charity Commission proposed to make a scheme to allow a charity to do things that will affect the way it carries out its purposes or the way it is run, the charity previously had to advertise this at least one month in advance, usually in local papers. This gave charities an additional administrative burden and was often disproportionate to the change proposed. The Act gives the Charity Commission discretion to decide whether publicity for a scheme is needed or not, with a default that it will not be needed unless absolutely necessary.

Even if the Charity Commission believes publicity is needed, it can choose the length of notice period and whether publicity must occur in the local area of the charity. This will have the practical effect of fewer instances where publicity is needed and also shorter notice periods.

4.13.18 Waiver of trustees' disqualification

Trustees who are disqualified because they have been removed by the Charity Commission or by the Court will be able to apply the Charity Commission for their disqualification to be waived after five years. The presumption will be that the disqualification should be waived, unless there are special reasons for not doing so. The waiver cannot apply in certain circumstances, such as where the disqualified trustee is disqualified from acting as a company director.

However, the Charity Commission cannot grant a waiver if the trustee is still disqualified as a company director, is an undischarged bankrupt or has defaulted under a County Court administration order.

4.13.19 Relief from personal liability for trustees

Recruiting new trustees can be difficult if potential recruits are worried that they may be personally liable for mistakes they make which put the charity's assets at risk. Two small but important changes have been introduced with the Charities Act 2006, as follows:

(a) if trustees act prudently, lawfully and in accordance with their governing document, then any liabilities they incur as trustees can be met out of the charity's resources, and
(b) charities can now take out professional indemnity insurance to cover such circumstances where the charity has insufficient funds to cover such a cost.

Charities may, however, still be in breach of trust and personally responsible for liabilities incurred by or on behalf of the charity, or for making good any loss to the charity, where they do not act prudently or lawfully. Since trustees are acting collectively in administering a charity, they will be responsible 'jointly and severally' to meet any liabilities to third parties which has been incurred by them or on their behalf. The Charity Commission is able to take proceedings in court for the recovery, from trustees personally, of funds lost to a charity as a result of a breach of trust by the trustees.

In some respects different rules apply to the directors of company charities. There are a variety of reasons for obtaining limited liability status by registering as a company. Employing staff, taking up a lease and owning property are common prompts to seek limited liability. In principle, it automatically limits the liability of company directors.

However, they are still liable for negligent conduct. In terms of liability, the difference between limited company directors and non-company trustees is a legal distinction, but an important one. It occurs where a charity incurs losses in the course of operations for which the charity lacks sufficient funds to indemnify the loss (and for which no insurance had been taken). Limited liability company directors or trustees will not be held personally liable for the losses unless it can be demonstrated that there was gross misconduct or negligence.

The trustees of a non-company charity, in the same situation, up until the recent change in the law would have needed to seek relief from personal liability in court. They would gain such relief by demonstrating that they acted in good faith and in accordance with the governing document. The Charities Act 2006 amends the law by now enabling the Charity Commission to grant such a relief. This will make the process swifter and easier. This obviously applies only to circumstances where mistakes have been made honestly. The Charity Commission and the Courts will still take deliberate breaches of trust by trustees very seriously.

4.13.20 Trustee indemnity insurance

Trustees can insure themselves – out of the funds of the charity – against personal liability to third parties arising from acts properly undertaken in the administration of the charity, where the assets of the charity are insufficient to enable them to indemnify themselves out of those assets. They can now do this without the Charity Commission's permission, as long as there is no provision in the governing document which specifically forbids it. If there is a specific prohibition in the charity's governing document, then trustees will need to approach the Charity Commission so that the Charity Commission can amend it before they can buy trustee indemnity insurance.

This protection will only work as long as the mistake was made honestly and not the result of wilful misconduct. When deciding whether insurance is justified, trustees need to consider the nature of the charity's activities, the degree of risk of personal liability to which the trustees are exposed, the number of trustees, the value of indemnity required and the cost to the charity of paying the premiums.

Insurance against personal liability in other circumstances is a trustee benefit and, until now, explicit authority, granted by either the governing document or the Charity Commission, has been required for payments to be made by the charity for such insurance. Such payments can, in any case, only be made by the charity if that is in the interests of the charity rather than of the trustees personally. Trustees have always been entitled to pay privately for their own indemnity insurance if they so wish.

4.13.21 Mortgaging charity property

One power that no longer rests with the Courts and the Charity Commission is in relation to the mortgaging of charity property. Trustees no longer need the consent of the Courts or the Charity Commission before they mortgage land that they own. As a safeguard, the trustees must obtain and consider proper advice on whether it is in the charity's best interests to embark on such a course of action. This change became effective on 27 February 2007.

4.13.22 Authority of the Charity Commission

The Charities Act 2006 establishes the Charity Commission as a body corporate (previously, what was referred to as the functions of the Charity Commission were held by Charity Commissioners personally). The Charity Commission has been granted more independence from central government and more powers to intervene in the running of charities. Such powers, which will only be exercised in exceptional circumstances, include:

- suspending or removing trustees and others from membership;
- directing trustees to take specific actions to protect a charity;
- ensuring charity property is used correctly, and
- entering premises and obtaining documents.

4.13.23 Objectives of the Charity Commission

The Act gave the Charity Commission the following five objectives

1. **public confidence** – to increase public trust and confidence in charities;
2. **public benefit** – to promote awareness and understanding of the operation of the public benefit requirement;
3. **compliance** – to promote compliance by charity trustees with their legal obligations in exercising control and management of the administration of their charities;
4. **charitable resources** – to promote the effective use of charitable resources, and
5. **accountability** – to enhance the accountability of charities to donors, beneficiaries and the general public.

4.13.24 Grant making disclosure exemption

Paragraph 133 of Schedule 8 provides a statutory exemption for accounts disclosure for institutional grants made by trusts in the lifetime of the founder, spouse or civil partner. This measure is aimed at protecting wealthy philanthropists.

4.14 Office of the Third Sector (OTS) thresholds consultation

The OTS and the Charity Commission jointly carried out a consultation entitled 'Financial Thresholds in the Charities Acts – Proposals for Change', which closed for responses on 31 March 2008. The very next day saw many of the changes of the Charities Act 2006 become effective. These further changes affected 31 March 2009 year ends onwards. The first changes of the Charities Act 2006 had already affected 31 March 2008 year ends.

The Statutory Instrument (SI) needed to implement the threshold changes recommended to the OTS by the Charity Commission in 2008, after public consultation (The Charities Acts 1992 and 1993 (Substitution of Sums) Order 2009), was laid before Parliament on 11 March 2009 to take effect for accounting periods **ending** on or after 1 April 2009.

These are the revised thresholds relating to charity accounts:

- the entry threshold for mandatory accruals accounting for non-company charities rises from £100,000 to £250,000 annual income – that is, the option of receipts and payments accounts becomes available for charities with annual income of up to £250,000. This will reduce burdens for around 12,000 charities, which will now be able to prepare accounts on a receipts and payments basis. Receipts and payments accounts do not necessarily show a true and fair view of the charity's affairs. There is therefore a concern in some circles that this could possibly be a backward step in terms of charity accountability and stewardship;
- the requirement to have an external scrutiny of a charity's accounts (that is, the entry threshold for independent examination) rises from annual income of £10,000 to £25,000, which means that around 37,000 charities will no longer be required to have their accounts externally examined;
- the requirement to submit both a Trustees' Annual Return and Annual Accounts to the Charity Commission rises from annual income of £10,000 to £25,000, which will affect around 23,000 charities, and
- the trigger for an assets test leading to a requirement for audit is amended as follows:
  - annual income rises from £100,000 to £250,000; and
  - assets rise from £2.8 to £3.26 million (this is in line with company legislation).

There are also a small number of other specialist provisions.

Several proposed changes have not been taken forward, or will be reviewed as part of the five-year review of the Charities Act, due in 2011. These include:

- the requirement to produce a Trustees' Annual Report (a continued requirement for *all* charities);
- the income-only audit threshold of £500,000 (however, see assets test above);
- the £250,000 threshold at which an Independent Examiner is required to be qualified;
- the £5,000 threshold at which registered charities must be registered, and
- the £10,000 threshold at which registered charities must state that they are registered on certain documents.

The Charities Act 2006

The changes are summarised in the table below.

Table 4.4 Summary of changes in the financial thresholds affecting charities

Level of income above which a charity:	Current threshold	Consultation proposal	Government response
must file accounts at the Charity Commission.	£10,000	£25,000	£25,000
must have some form of external scrutiny of its accounts (that is, an independent examination).	£10,000	£25,000	£25,000
is not allowed to prepare receipts and payments accounts.	£100,000	£250,000	£250,000
must have a full audit of its accounts.	£500,000	£1,000,000	£500,000*

The audit asset trigger requirement for charities with income over £250,000 (currently £100,000) and with assets of more than £3.26 million (currently £2.8 million) has changed.

This change to the external scrutiny thresholds will have the following affect for company charities:

Example 1

Year end	Gross Income	External scrutiny
31 March 2008	£18,000	1. None
31 March 2009	£18,000	2. Independent examination
31 March 2010	£18,000	3. None

1. As income is less than £90,000, no Reporting Accountant's Report is required.
2. Following harmonisation of rules, company charities follow Charities Act requirements.
3. The external scrutiny threshold increases from £10,000 to £25,000 gross income.

Example 2

Year end	Income	External scrutiny
31 December 2007	£400,000	Audit
31 December 2008	£400,000	Reporting accountants' report
31 December 2009	£400,000	Independent examination

Annex 1 Regulatory framework comparisons

Table A1.1: *Charities with financial years beginning on or after 27 February 2007*

Type	Income level	Accounts	External scrutiny	Trustees' Annual Report	Information to be sent to the Charity Commission
Non-company charities	Gross income is £10,000 or less.	Receipts and Payments or accruals based on SORP and 2005 Regulations.	No requirement (unless required by Governing Document).	Only if registered must a report be prepared but it may be simplified.	Annual Information Return only.
	Gross income exceeds £10,000 but does not exceed £100,000.	Receipts and payments or accruals based on SORP and 2005 Regulations.	Trustees may choose either independent examination or audit by registered auditor, unless one or other is stipulated in charity's governing document.	Must be prepared but may be simplified.	Annual Return, Annual Report and Accounts must be sent to the Charity Commission within 10 months of year end.
	Gross income exceeds £100,000 but does not exceed £500,000, and gross assets do not exceed £2,800,000.	Accruals basis in accordance with SORP and 2005 Regulations	Trustees may choose either independent examination or audit by registered auditor, unless one or other is stipulated in charity's governing document. If gross income exceeds £250,000 and independent examination is chosen, examiner must belong to a body specified in the 2006 Act.	Must be prepared but may be simplified	Annual Return, Annual Report and Accounts must be sent to the Charity Commission within 10 months of year end.

Annex 1 Regulatory framework comparisons

Type	Income level	Accounts	External scrutiny	Trustees' Annual Report	Information to be sent to the Charity Commission
	Gross income exceeds £500,000, or gross assets exceed £2,800,000 and gross income exceeds £100,000.	Accruals basis in accordance with SORP and 2005 Regulations.	A statutory audit is required and audit must be carried out by a registered auditor.	Full Annual Report must be prepared.	Annual Return, Annual Report and Accounts must be sent to the Charity Commission within 10 months of year end. Charities with a gross income exceeding £1million must also complete a Summary Information Return.

Table A1.2: *Charities with financial years beginning on or after 27 February 2007*

Company charities	SORP also applies to company charities. Trustees must prepare a directors' report and accounts under the Companies Act, and file them with Companies House. Requirement for Trustees' Annual Report as for non-companies with Annual Report requirements set out in 2005 Regulations. If income is greater than £10,000, then trustees must send us a Trustees' Annual Report (or suitably modified directors' report). Annual Return requirements are as for non-companies with an Annual Information Return where gross income or total expenditure is £10,000 or less.

Type	Income level	Accounts	External scrutiny	Trustees' Annual Report	Information to be sent to the Charity Commission
	Gross income exceeds £500,000 or gross assets exceed £2,800,000 (regardless of income).	Accruals based on SORP.	Accounts must be audited by a registered auditor.	Full Annual Report or a suitably modified directors' report must be prepared.	Annual Return, Accounts and Annual Report to be sent to the Charity Commission within 10 months of year end. Charities with a gross income exceeding £1million must also complete a Summary Information Return.

81

Annex 1 Regulatory framework comparisons

Type	Income level	Accounts	External scrutiny	Trustees' Annual Report	Information to be sent to the Charity Commission
	Gross income exceeds £90,000 but does not exceed £500,000 and gross assets do not exceed £2,800,000.	Accruals based on SORP.	A Reporting Accountant's report (or audit exemption report) may be prepared.	Must be prepared but may be simplified or suitably modified directors' report.	Annual Return, Accounts and Annual Report to be sent to the Charity Commission within 10 months of year end.
	Gross assets do not exceed £2,800,000 and gross income does not exceed £90,000.	Accruals based on SORP.	No external scrutiny required.	Must be prepared but may be simplified or suitably modified directors' report.	Annual Return, Accounts and Annual Report to be sent to the Charity Commission within 10 months of financial year end where gross income (or total expenditure) exceeds £10,000
Excepted charities	If registered voluntarily, accounting and reporting requirement are as for any registered charity. If not registered, they must produce annual accounts in the same way as an equivalent type of registered charity (company or non-company). Copies of accounts must be provided to the public on request, but not sent to the Charity Commission unless it asks. Although not required by law to produce an Annual Report, it is good practice to do so, and the Charity Commission may require one to be produced in exceptional circumstances.				

Annex 1 Regulatory framework comparisons

Table A1.3: *Charities with financial years beginning on or after 1 April 2008 (common external scrutiny thresholds)*

Type	Income level	Accounts	External scrutiny	Trustees' Annual Report	Information to be sent to the Charity Commission
Non-company charities	Gross income is £10,000 or less.	Receipts and payments or accruals accounts in accordance with SORP and 2008 Regulations.	No requirement (unless required by Governing Document).	Only if registered, must a report be prepared but it may be simplified.	Annual Information Return only.
	Gross income exceeds £10,000 but does not exceed £100,000.	Receipts and payments or accruals accounts in accordance with SORP and 2008 Regulations.	Accounts must have external scrutiny but trustees may choose independent examination or audit by a registered auditor, unless the governing document stipulates one or the other.	Must be prepared but may be simplified.	Annual Return (online or paper form). Annual Report and Accounts must be sent to the Charity Commission within 10 months of year end.
	Gross income exceeds £100,000 but does not exceed £500,000 and gross assets do not exceed £2,800,000.	Accruals basis in accordance with SORP and 2008 Regulations.	Accounts must have external scrutiny but trustees may choose independent examination or audit by a registered auditor, unless the governing document stipulates one or the other. If independent examination is chosen and gross income exceeds £250,000, then independent examiner must belong to a body specified in the 2006 Act.	A full Annual Report must be prepared.	Annual Return (online or paper form), Annual Report and Accounts must be sent to the Charity Commission within 10 months of year end.

Annex 1 Regulatory framework comparisons

Type	Income level	Accounts	External scrutiny	Trustees' Annual Report	Information to be sent to the Charity Commission
	Gross income exceeds £500,000 or gross income exceeds £100,000 and gross assets exceed £2,800,000.	Accruals basis in accordance with SORP and 2008 Regulations.	Statutory audit carried out by a registered auditor.	A full Annual Report must be prepared.	Annual Return, Annual Report and Accounts must be sent to the Charity Commission within 10 months of year end. Charities with a gross income exceeding £1million must also complete a Summary Information Return.
	Where the charity has either charitable or non-charitable subsidiaries and the income of the group exceeds £500,000.	Accruals basis in accordance with SORP and 2008 Regulations.	Statutory audit carried out by a registered auditor.	Accruals based on SORP.	The parent charity completes the Annual Return and Summary Information Return on a group basis. Annual Report and Accounts must be sent to the Charity Commission within 10 months of year end. Charity groups with a gross income exceeding £1million must also complete a Summary Information Return.

Annex 1 Regulatory framework comparisons

Table A1.4: *Charities with financial years beginning on or after 1 April 2008 (common external scrutiny thresholds)*

Company charities	Trustees must prepare directors' report and accounts under the Companies Acts and file these at Companies House. Trustees must comply with Annual Report requirements set out in 2008 Regulations. In practice, the directors' report is expanded to include information required in the Annual Report. Annual return requirements are as for non-companies with an Annual Information Return where gross income or total expenditure is £10,000 or less.				
Type	**Income level**	**Accounts**	**External scrutiny**	**Trustees' Annual Report**	**Information to be sent to the Charity Commission**
	Gross income is £10,000 or less.	Accruals accounts in accordance with SORP.	No requirement unless governing documents stipulates it.	Must be prepared but may be simplified, or a suitably modified directors' report.	Annual Information Return.
	Gross income exceeds £10,000 but does not exceed £500,000, and where gross income exceeds £100,000, the charity's gross assets do not exceed £2,800,000.	Accruals accounts in accordance with SORP.	May have independent examination or audit, unless Articles of Association stipulate an audit.	Annual Report (which may be simplified if gross income does not exceed £500,000) or a suitably modified directors' report.	Annual Return, Annual Report and Accounts must be sent to the Charity Commission within 10 months of year end.

Annex 1 Regulatory framework comparisons

Type	Income level	Accounts	External scrutiny	Trustees' Annual Report	Information to be sent to the Charity Commission
	Gross income exceeds £500,000 or gross assets exceed £2,800,000 and gross income exceeds £100,000.	Accruals accounts in accordance with SORP.	Statutory audit carried out by a registered auditor.	Full Annual Report (which may be a suitably modified directors' report).	Annual Return, Annual Report and Accounts must be sent to the Charity Commission within 10 months of year end. Charities with a gross income exceeding £1million must also complete a Summary Information Return
	Where the charity has either charitable or non-charitable subsidiaries and the income of the group exceeds £500,000.	Accruals basis in accordance with SORP and 2008 Regulations regarding group accounts.	Statutory audit carried out by a registered auditor.	A full Annual Report must be prepared, together with the additional disclosures about the activities of subsidiaries required by the SORP.	The parent charity completes the Annual Return and Summary Information Return on a group basis. Annual Report and Accounts must be sent to the Charity Commission within 10 months of year end.

Annex 1 Regulatory framework comparisons

Type	Income level	Accounts	External scrutiny	Trustees' Annual Report	Information to be sent to the Charity Commission
	Where either the company is not small or the group is not a small group, as defined by the Companies Act 2006.	Accruals basis in accordance with SORP.	Statutory audit under the Companies Act carried out by a registered auditor.	A full Annual Report must be prepared, (which may be a suitably modified directors' report) together with additional business review disclosures required by company law.	Annual Return, Annual Report and Accounts must be sent to the Charity Commission within 10 months of year end. (The parent charity completes the Annual Return and Summary Information Return on a group basis). Charity groups with a gross income exceeding £1million must also complete a Summary Information Return.
Excepted charities	If registered voluntarily, accounting and reporting requirements are as for any registered charity. If not registered they must produce annual accounts in the same way as an equivalent type of registered charity (company or non-company). Copies of accounts must be provided to the public on request, but not sent to the Charity Commission unless asked for. Although not required by law to produce an Annual Report it is good practice to do so, and the Charity Commission may require one to be produced in exceptional circumstances.				
Exempt charities	Must keep proper accounting records and prepare accounts. Where having to prepare accounts giving a true and fair view, they should follow SORP 2005, unless a specialised SORP applies. Must provide copies of accounts to the public on request. Audit requirements depend on how charity is constituted and the regulatory regime under which it operates.				

Annex 2 Public benefit – the Charity Commission

A2.1 Introduction

All charities must have charitable purposes or 'aims' that are for the public benefit. This is known as the 'public benefit requirement'. Although all charities already have to meet this requirement, the Charities Act 2006 highlights it by explicitly including public benefit in the definition of a charitable purpose. These changes take effect from 1 April 2008. From that date, all organisations wishing to be recognised as charities must demonstrate that their aims are for the public benefit.

Previously, the law presumed this to be the case for charities that advance education or religion or relieve poverty. The Charity Commission has to ensure that all charities meet the public benefit requirement and provide guidance on what the requirement means. Trustees will be required to have regard to the Charity Commission's public benefit guidance and to report on their charity's public benefit. For the public benefit test, charities need to consider potential current beneficiaries and also future ones.

The emphasis on justifying a charity's public benefit will need to demonstrate a change in the public perception of a public benefit. For example, what previously may have been acceptable in terms of medical research will now need to overcome animal welfare issues.

Charities and public benefit: The Charity's Commission's General Guidance on Public Benefit (January 2008) – extract

Public benefit

There are two key principles of public benefit, both of which must be met in order to show that an organisation's aims are for the public benefit. Within each principle there are some important factors that must be considered in all cases.

The principles of public benefit

Principle 1: There must be an identifiable benefit or benefits

- Principle 1a: It must be clear what the benefits are.
- Principle 1b: The benefits must be related to the aims.

Annex 2 Public benefit – the Charity Commission

- Principle 1c: Benefits must be balanced against any detriment or harm.

Principle 2: Benefit must be to the public, or a section of the public

- Principle 2a: The beneficiaries must be appropriate to the aims.
- Principle 2b: Where benefit is to a section of the public, the opportunity to benefit must not be unreasonably restricted:
    - by geographical or other restrictions, or
    - by ability to pay any fees charged.
- Principle 2c: People in poverty must not be excluded from the opportunity to benefit.
- Principle 2d: Any private benefits must be incidental.

The principles of public benefit apply to all charities, whatever their aims. Each charity must be able to demonstrate that its aims are for the public benefit. Public benefit decisions are about whether an individual organisation is a charity and not about whether particular types of charity or groups of charities, as a whole, are for the public benefit.

Principles of public benefit

Principle 1: There must be an identifiable benefit or benefits

Principle 1a: It must be clear what the benefits are

It must be clear what benefits to the public arise from carrying out a charity's aims. Examples of different sorts of benefit include providing housing for the homeless or giving medical care to the sick. It should be possible to identify and describe the benefits provided, but that does not mean they must be able to be quantified or measured; non-quantifiable benefits will be taken into account as long as it is clear what they are.

Most benefits are self-evident but sometimes the Charity Commission may need evidence depending on the type of benefit provided. Sometimes benefit can be shown by a consensus of objective and informed opinion. In some cases, we may ask for evidence of independent, expert opinion from someone suitably qualified. It will usually be for the trustees to provide evidence that their organisation's aims are for the public benefit but the Charity Commission may sometimes need to check evidence from other sources.

Principle 1b: Benefits must be related to the aims

Benefits must be related to the charity's aims, so benefits which arise from the charity's work that are not related to its aims will not be taken into account. Where a charity has more than one aim, each of those aims has to meet the public benefit requirement. It will not be enough if only some do.

Principle 1c: Benefits must be balanced against any detriment or harm

Finally, benefits must be balanced against any detriment or harm which arises. Examples of detriment or harm could include something that is damaging to the environment or mental or physical health or encourages hatred towards others. In judging whether this detriment occurs, the Charity Commission would need to see real evidence; it will not just assume it. Where there is more detriment than benefit, or where the organisation has aims that are illegal or is a sham, it would not be charitable.

Principle 2: Benefit must be to the public, or a section of the pubic

Principle 2a: The beneficiaries must be appropriate to the aims

While this sounds like a statement of the obvious, who constitutes the 'public' or 'a section of the public' varies according to the charitable aims. Sometimes a charity's aims are intended to benefit the public generally, sometimes a specific section of it. Who benefits, and how, will depend on the organisation's aims. Considering who the charity's aims are mainly intended to benefit is important when deciding whether the public benefit requirement is met.

It is not a simple matter of numbers, but the number of people who can potentially benefit must not be insignificant. The 'class' of people who can benefit must be sufficiently large or open, given the charitable aim being carried out. The actual number of people who can benefit at any one time can be quite small as long as anyone who could qualify for the benefit is eligible. So, for example, it is fine to offer only a small number of rooms in a care home as long as anyone who is eligible to apply can be considered for those limited places.

It is important that the opportunity to benefit is not unreasonably restricted given the nature of the charity's aims and the resources it has. If the benefit is to a 'section of the public', rather than the public generally, then the restrictions must be reasonable and relevant to the charity's aims. If they are not, this will affect public benefit.

Principle 2b: Where benefit is to a section of the public, the opportunity to benefit must not be unreasonably restricted by geographical or other restrictions, or by ability to pay any fees charged

Ways in which restrictions might apply to the 'class' of people who can benefit include geographical restrictions, those involving charitable need, such as poverty, age or ill-health, and those involving personal characteristics, such as gender, race or religion, for example. The Charity Commission will consider the circumstances in each case when deciding whether that restriction is reasonable.

At the extreme, charities must not be seen as 'exclusive clubs' that only a few can join. So, where the aims of a charity are more closed, inward looking and exclusive, greater justification for the restriction may need to be provided.

Many different sorts of charities can, and do, charge for their services or facilities. Charities can charge fees that more than cover the cost of those services or facilities, provided that the charges are reasonable and necessary to carry out the charity's aims – for example, in maintaining or developing the service provided. However, where, in practice, the charging restricts the benefits only to people who can afford to pay the fees charged, this may result in the benefits not being available to a sufficient section of the public.

Principle 2c: People in poverty must not be excluded from the opportunity to benefit

The fact that the services will be charged for and therefore provided mainly to people who can afford to pay does not necessarily mean the organisation's aims are not for the public benefit. However, if an organisation excluded people from the opportunity to benefit because they could not pay the fees, then its aims would not be for the public benefit. In particular, people in poverty must not be excluded from the opportunity to benefit. So it would not, for example, be enough to reduce very high fees slightly to enable more 'middle income' people to benefit, if people in poverty were still excluded from the opportunity to benefit.

In general, the lower the fees that are charged, the greater the opportunity there is for most people to have the opportunity to benefit. But where the fees charged are, of necessity perhaps, very high, then trustees of those charities will have to think about other ways in which people who cannot afford those fees can benefit in some material way related to their charity's aims. This does not mean charities have to offer services for free, or offer concessions on fees, although clearly that would help. There could be other ways of benefiting people who cannot afford the fees in a way that is related to the aims. For example, one way of doing this might be an independent school working in partnership with a local state school, or an arts charity might broadcast concerts or operatic performances via TV or radio to a wider audience. What matters is that people unable to pay are not excluded from the opportunity to benefit, whether or not they actually choose to take up the opportunity.

Principle 2d: Any private benefits must be incidental

Where people or organisations benefit from a charity, other than as a beneficiary, then those sorts of 'private' benefits must be incidental, which means they are a necessary result, or by-product, of carrying out the charity's aims. Where private benefits are more than incidental this might mean the organisation is set up for private, rather than public, benefit and so might not be charitable.

Annex 2 Public benefit – the Charity Commission

Reporting on the charity's public benefit

Charity trustees have a new duty to report in their Trustees' Annual Report on their charity's public benefit. The level of detail you will need to provide in your public benefit report will depend on whether the charity is above or below the audit threshold. An audit is required when a charity's gross income in the year exceeds £500,000, or where the income exceeds £100,000 and the aggregate value of its assets exceeds £2.8 million. Most charities already explain their activities in their Trustees' Annual Report and so this information now needs to be set in the context of the charity's aims to show how in practice the aims have been carried out for the public benefit.

Trustees will also need to confirm that they have had regard to our public benefit guidance where relevant.

For smaller charities, below the audit threshold, trustees are required to include a brief summary in their Trustees' Annual Report of the main activities undertaken in order to carry out the charity's aims for the public benefit. Trustees can, of course, provide fuller public benefit statements if they wish.

For larger charities, above the audit threshold, trustees are required to provide a fuller explanation in their Trustees' Annual Report of the significant activities undertaken in order to carry out the charity's aims for the public benefit, as well as their aims and strategies. They are required to explain the charity's achievements, measured by reference to the charity's aims and to the objectives set by the trustees.

It is up to the trustees to decide how much detail they want to provide so as to illustrate clearly what their charity has done in the reporting year to meet the requirement. The Charity Commission will not be prescriptive about the number of words or pages needed. A charity that said nothing on public benefit in its Trustees' Annual Report, or produced only the briefest statement with no detail, would, however, be in breach of the public benefit reporting requirement.

Assessing public benefit

The Charity Commission will assess whether the aims of all organisations applying to register as charities are for the public benefit. Charities that are already registered have to continue to meet the public benefit requirement. The Charity Commission will do this by carrying out research studies on the extent to which different types of charity are meeting the requirement and by working with representative professional and umbrella bodies and with users of those charities.

In some cases, the Charity Commission may need to carry out detailed assessment of individual charities. Where that needs to happen, the Charity

Commission will advise the trustees on what needs to change in order to meet the public benefit requirement, and give clear reasons and advice on what happens next where it is not possible for the organisation to meet the requirement. No charity will be expected to make changes overnight and the Charity Commission will take reasonable account of how much time and resources might be needed by a charity that needs to make changes in order to meet the requirement. A charity, or anyone affected by one of the Charity Commission's public benefit decisions, can seek a review of that decision using the Charity Commission's internal decision review procedures. If considered necessary, a further appeal to the new Charity Tribunal (see section **4.11** of chapter 4) and, ultimately, to the Courts, can be made. However, by working constructively with trustees and undertaking extensive public consultation on public benefit guidance, it is hoped that such circumstances would be rare.

Annex 3 Group accounts flow chart

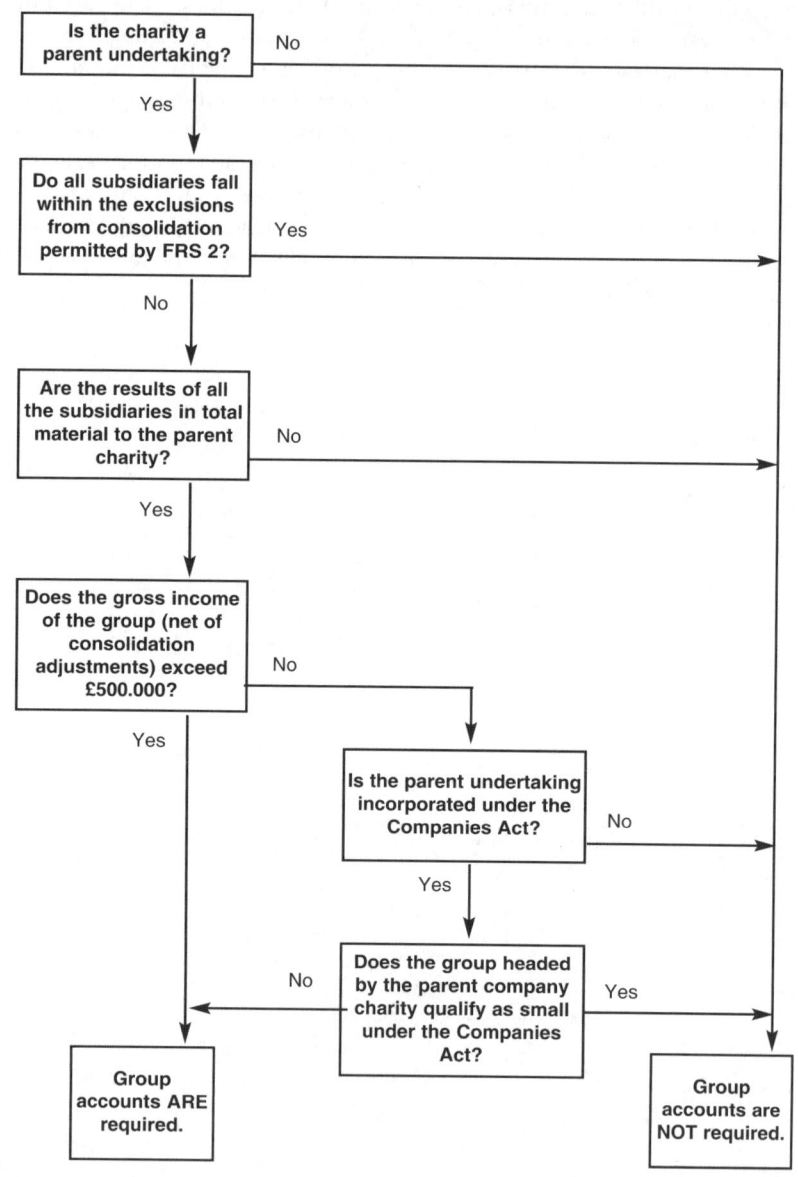

Chapter 5 – Fundraising regulations

The Charitable Institutions (Fund Raising) Regulations 1994, SI 1994 No 3024 brought controls on fundraising for charities into force on 1 March 1995. They implemented Part II of the Charities Act 1992.

5.1 Summary

Professional fundraisers are required to give an indication of the institutions benefiting and the arrangements for remuneration. Charities have a right to prevent unauthorised fundraising and there is a new crime – the coupling of solicitation of money with a false representation that the institution concerned is a registered charity – although there is a defence of belief on reasonable grounds that the institution was so registered. There is a right for donors to request the repayment of donations made by credit or debit card following radio or TV appeals by fundraisers acting for reward, and to request repayment or a cooling-off period where there has been a telephone appeal, provided at least £50 is involved.

Professional fundraisers may not solicit money or property for a charity, and no person engaged in a promotional venture for reward may represent that contributions are to be given or applied for the benefit of the charity except in accordance with an agreement with the charity which satisfies prescribed requirements.

If these rules are contravened, the charity can apply to the High Court or a County Court for an injunction and offending agreements are only enforceable to the extent allowed by court order.

5.2 Definitions

Section 58 of the Act defines two distinct categories of commercial organisation:

1. *The professional fundraiser* – a person who carries on a fundraising business or who, for reward, solicits money or other property for the benefit of a charity otherwise than in the course of carrying on a fundraising business as such. There are a number of exclusions in s. 58 – for example, a charity itself or a company connected with it (an associate trading company, celebrities fronting a radio or television appeal, and so on). Collectors are also

excluded unless they can be regarded as promoters of the collection. Commercial participators are excluded too, but are controlled under their own definition (see below).

2. *The commercial participator* – a person who carries on, for gain, a business other than a fundraising business, but in the course of that business engages in promotional ventures in the course of which it is represented that charitable contributions are to be given to or applied for the benefit of a charitable institution. This could be a bank or building society that issues a credit card on the basis that a percentage of the customer's monthly debits will be donated to a particular charity or charities.

5.3 Agreements with fundraisers and participators

Section 59 of the Act prohibits fundraisers or participators from soliciting money or other property for a charity, or representing that charitable contributions will be made except in accordance with an agreement. Regulations 2 and 3 prescribe the requirements and state that agreements must specify:

- the names and addresses of the parties;
- the date of signature by the parties;
- the duration of the agreement;
- any provision relating to earlier termination;
- any terms relating to variation;
- the principal objectives and methods to be used to achieve them;
- the charitable institutions to benefit and their shares;
- the method of determining the proportion of consideration, proceeds or donations, and
- what they will receive from participators, or the remuneration payable to fundraisers.

5.4 Availability of books, documents and other records

Under Regulation 5, fundraisers and participators must, on request and at all reasonable times, make available to any charity that is party to a relevant agreement any books, documents or other records (however kept) that relate to the charity and are kept for the purposes of the agreement.

5.5 Transmission of money or property

Under Regulation 6, any monies or other property due to a charity are to be transmitted by the fundraiser or participator to the charity as soon as is practicable, and in any case not later than 28 days from receipt or such other period as may be agreed.

5.6 Indications of benefits and remuneration

Section 60 of the Act provides that a fundraiser soliciting money or other property for a charity must draw up an accompanying statement that identifies the benefiting charity or charities and indicates, in general terms, the methods of calculating the fundraiser's remuneration. The section also covers participators who represent that 'charitable contributions' will be given to or applied for a charity or charities. They must identify the benefiting charity or charities and, in general terms, the method of determining:

- what proportion of the consideration given for goods sold or for services the participator supplies, or of any proceeds of promotional ventures he or she has undertaken, will be given to or applied for the charity or charities concerned; and
- what sums by way of the participator's donations as a result of the sale or supply of any goods or services are to be given or applied, as the case may require. Failure to comply with s. 60 is a criminal offence punishable by a fine not exceeding £5,000.

Regulation 7 contains similar provisions where funds are raised for charitable purposes otherwise than by professional fundraisers or commercial participators. Persons involved are those who carry on, for gain, a business other than a fundraising business, and are not participators, but who on occasion carry out promotional ventures for charities. There is no requirement of reward.

5.7 Cancellation of payments

Section 61 of the Act provides a right of repayment for charitable donations made by credit or debit card in response to a television or radio broadcast or a telephone appeal. Because of the need to balance the interests of donors and charities, repayment is restricted to payments over £50. Notice must be served on the relevant fundraiser within seven days of the solicitation, and the charity may deduct administrative expenses. Relevant donors must be given notice of these repayment rights.

5.8 Unauthorised fundraising and false statements

Sections 62 and 63 introduce powerful safeguards under which a charity may obtain an injunction against any person raising funds for it if the charity objects to the method being used or does not wish to be associated with a promotional venture. In addition, persons making false representations that an institution is a registered charity when it is not are guilty of a criminal offence punishable by a

Fundraising regulations

fine of up to £5,000. Section 26 of the Deregulation and Contracting Out Act 1994 adds a defence of belief on reasonable grounds that the institution concerned was a registered charity.

Failure to comply with the requirements could lead to difficulty in enforcing agreements with charities and a criminal prosecution leading to a fine.

Fundraisers and participators will need to review their arrangements with charities since the provisions described above apply from 1 March 1995 to both new and existing arrangements.

See section **4.13.6** of Chapter 4 for changes introduced by the Charities Act 2006.

5.9 Street collections

Raising money or selling goods for charity in streets or public places usually requires a permit or licence from either the appropriate local authority or if the collection takes place in London, the police or the Common Council of the City of London.

Legislation allows local regulations to be made. These deal with such matters as the obstruction and hindrance caused to traffic by events, and the conditions under which, persons may collect money or sell articles for charitable and other purposes.

See section **4.13.8** of Chapter 4 for changes introduced by the Charities Act 2006.

5.10 House-to-house collections

House-to-house collections must have a licence or an exemption from a licence. Licences are issued by local authorities or in London by the police or the Common Council of the City of London. Exemptions may be granted by the Home Office for collections covering a wide area or the police for a local collection being held over a short period of time.

Regulations exist governing the conduct of collections on doorsteps, in public houses and at places of work. The regulations cover collections of both money and other property.

(See section **4.13.9** of Chapter 4 for changes introduced by the Charities Act 2006.

5.11 Revised guidance on professional charity fundraising

Since the early 1990s, certain types of businesses involved with charity fundraising have had to make statements to disclose either the method by which they were being paid or the method by which they would donate money to a charity. Since 1 April 2008, there has been a change in that the 'notifiable amount' must now be included in the statement.

In December 2008, the Office of the Third Sector (OTS) published its guidance on fundraising statements to be made by professional fundraisers and commercial participators under the Charities Act 1992. The aim of the guidance is to help charities, professional fundraisers and commercial participators involved in fundraising ventures to comply with changes that have been made to legal requirements. The revised guidance highlights the key provisions that came into force on 1 April 2008 and provides some examples of fundraising statements that satisfy the new requirements.

Fundraisers who are paid to raise money are required to tell potential donors up front how much of each donation goes to charity and what proportion goes towards their own wages. Similarly, shops that donate a portion of the sale price on particular items to charity are required to state explicitly the extent to which a charity will benefit. The OTS guidance does not have the force of law but is likely to be looked at by any court asked to decide if a particular statement complies with the law.

Where a commercial participator is giving an amount or percentage of a product price to a charity, there is no obligation for the commercial participator to state, in addition, the total amount it expects to pay. Simply soliciting a person's details (sometimes known as prospecting) does not trigger the requirement to make a fundraising statement under Part II of the 1992 Act.

The guidance includes an example of a compliant statement for payroll-giving agencies. The statement describes the method by which the agencies payment is calculated and gives an estimate of the overall amount it expects to be paid in total by all the charities over the course of a year.

However, there is neither guidance nor examples of how a statement should be worded where a charity structures a payment from a commercial participator via the charity's trading subsidiary. There is also still a recommendation that charities and their trading subsidiaries (which were specifically exempted from the legislation) should make equivalent statements as part of their fundraising.

All charities working with professional fundraisers or commercial participators should now review promotional material for existing and future fundraising campaigns to make sure that it complies with the guidance.

Chapter 6 – SORP 2005

6.1. Introduction

The updated Statement of Recommended Practice *Accounting and Reporting by Charities* (SORP 2005) was issued in March 2005. A second edition of SORP 2005 was published in May 2008. This chapter aims to familiarise readers with the main changes from the SORP issued in October 2000 and to summarise some of the other key features which are likely to affect most charities. This chapter will 'signpost' readers to the relevant sections of the SORP depending on the particular characteristics of their charity, and provide them with a reminder of the principal features of charity reports and accounts.

6.1.1 Scope

The accounting recommendations of SORP 2005 apply (except in specific and exceptional circumstances) to all charities in the United Kingdom that prepare accounts on the accruals basis to give a true and fair view of their activities and financial position, regardless of their size, constitution, or complexity. Each accounting recommendation should be considered in the context of what is considered to be 'material' to the charity concerned. In England and Wales, accompanying information to the financial statements is often provided through a Trustees' Annual Report. Best practice recommendations for the form and content of such information, contained in the SORP, is underpinned by law.

Whilst the SORP is intended to apply in Scotland to all charity financial statements which are required to give a true and fair view, its status may be amended by further Regulations. In Scotland and in Northern Ireland, the recommendations relating to the form and content of the accompanying information, such as a Trustees' Annual Report, are consistent with applicable law – they should therefore be regarded as voluntary best practice recommendations.

Charities in the Republic of Ireland do not fall within the scope of SORP 2005, but they may wish to comply with its recommendations – in which case, they are encouraged to disclose this fact.

SORP 2005 contains a summary of the legislative framework for charity accounts in the United Kingdom in its Table 1. Certain classes of charities (for example, Registered Social Landlords, and Further and Higher Education Institutes) may be subject to a separate (non-charity) SORP, and charity trustees should adhere to that SORP and any additional reporting requirements placed upon them by charity law. This chapter does not therefore necessarily cover the full requirements in respect of those charities.

The accounting recommendations of SORP 2005 do not apply to charities preparing cash-based receipts and payments accounts, although such charities are encouraged to adopt the activity approach featured in the SORP. Additionally, smaller charities which prepare accruals accounts may decide to take advantage of certain concessions contained within the SORP (see **Annex 2** of this chapter, and Appendix 5 of the SORP).

6.1.2 Charity Commission guidance

Guidance, including example accounts and reports packs, has been provided for charities that prepare cash-based receipts and payments accounts. According to the Charity Commission, this guidance will be comprehensive enough to remove the need for such charities to refer to the SORP itself.

SORP 2005 can be downloaded from the Charity Commission's website. In addition to the SORP, in April 2005 the Charity Commission issued the publication *SORP 2005: What has Changed?*, which provides an overview of the main changes. Also available is a copy of SORP 2005 that shows the changes in more detail as 'tracked changes' from the previous SORP. These documents should not, however, be used as substitutes for reading the relevant sections of the full SORP. The Charity Commission has also produced a series of example accounts.

The Charity Commission produces many other publications which are designed to assist those involved in charity management, governance and accounting, and their professional advisers.

6.2. Background, overview and main changes

6.2.1 Background

Considerable emphasis has been placed on the SORP as a mechanism to improve the overall quality, consistency and transparency of reporting and accounting in the charity sector. It is widely recognised that the provision of better quality information, such as that portrayed in the annual reports and accounts of charities, plays a significant role in enhancing public confidence in individual charities, as well as improving the understanding of the role and achievements of the sector in general. The SORP has a key role to play in this process by assisting charities to provide quality financial information of interest to their many stakeholders, whilst complying with legal requirements, and best practice, to ensure that such accounts give a 'true and fair' view.

Sector involvement has been a central part of producing SORP 2005. Research, input and feedback provided by the sector and the Charities SORP Committee has informed each stage of its development. Whilst the principles underlying SORP 2005 are broadly unchanged, it seeks to create a new focus for charity reporting, by better reflecting the continually changing dynamics of the environment in which charities operate. The Charity Commission states that the updated SORP 'provides a framework that enables charities to explain what they do, how they go about it and what they achieve…in a way that pulls together narrative and financial reporting into a coherent package focused on the activities undertaken'.

In particular, SORP 2005 focuses on the need for clearer reporting of objectives, activities undertaken, achievements, outcomes and impact – both discursively through the Trustees' Annual Report, and numerically through a restructuring of the Statement of Financial Activities (SOFA). SORP 2005 also reflects the impact of accounting standards issued or withdrawn since the last revision of the SORP in October 2000.

6.2.2 Overview

The SORP reflects how accounting standards, charity law, relevant company law and best practice impact on the preparation of charity reports and accounts. SORP 2005 is supported by the updated Charities (Accounts and Reports) Regulations 2008, issued by the Home Office in a Statutory Instrument (2008 No. 629). Thus the Regulations are the legal requirements conferred by the Charities Act; the SORP states how those requirements and other matters should be reflected in charity reports and accounts. It also provides an interpretation of accounting standards and principles for the charity sector, and clarifies the accounting treatment for sector-specific transactions.

SORP 2005 is longer than its predecessor, although this is largely due to expanded explanations and examples, many in the form of more user-friendly tables and charts. A full list of tables is given in the SORP's contents page, and is reproduced in this chapter as **Annex 3**. The need to address the increasing number of accounting standards in issue has also contributed to its length. The main text of the updated SORP deals with normal accounting practice for those charities producing accruals accounts – thus assisting preparers of such accounts to fulfil their legal and other reporting duties in ensuring that the accounts show a true and fair view. Trustees must ensure that any other specific requirements are also addressed, where these exceed those dealt with by the SORP.

Although the SORP has been rewritten and the sequence of paragraphs changed in order to introduce some new concepts and eliminate inconsistencies, there are no major changes to the overall structure of the accounts and no new requirements that the Charity Commission regards as onerous. There is,

SORP 2005

however, increasing concern by many users of the SORP that it has become overly complex, particularly for smaller charities. This problem may be exacerbated by the removal of the 'AA' ('Applicable to All') paragraphs introduced in SORP 2000. Concessions for smaller charities, applicable at the date of publication of the SORP, are summarised in Appendix 5 to the SORP, and in **Annex 2** to this chapter.

Accounting disclosure requirements are separately identified throughout the SORP. The SORP emphasises that only 'material' items need to be reported – although certain items will always be material. Materiality needs to be judged in the context of a particular disclosure; the SORP therefore moves away from arbitrary thresholds such as 'five per cent of total resources expended'.

The requirements for the Trustees' Annual Report have been substantially rewritten and, though much of the detail is unchanged, these are best read as a new section. SORP 2005 seeks to provide a more structured approach to annual reporting and gives prominence to the Trustees' Annual Report as the medium to explain the link between objectives, strategies, activities and resulting achievements. It also introduces a new section entitled 'Structure, Governance and Management' to enable charities to better explain such processes and arrangements. Disclosure of the recruitment, induction and training processes for trustees should also now be included.

Appendix 1 of the SORP comprises an updated glossary to reflect the new definitions and concepts introduced in the main body of the SORP. Several existing definitions have been clarified and refined. Some definitions replace terms introduced by the previous SORP – for example, 'intangible income' has been replaced by 'donated services and facilities'. The SORP continues to allow the recognition of donated services within the SOFA where a demonstrable cost is borne by the donor, and a current value to the recipient charity can be measured. However, following careful consideration and much debate within the sector, it does not propose to include the valuation of the contribution of volunteers within the SOFA. Instead, it encourages more informative disclosure of the contribution made by volunteers within the Trustees' Annual Report.

The SORP has been updated for Financial Reporting Standards (FRS) and Urgent Issue Task Force (UITF) Abstracts issued, amended or withdrawn by the UK's Accounting Standards Board up to 31 December 2004. Charities will need to ensure that they comply with subsequent relevant accounting pronouncements. Appendix 2 of the SORP summarises the accounting standards and UITFs in issue at the time of revision of the SORP with comments on their applicability, or not, to charities.

The option of adopting International Financial Reporting Standards (IFRS) is not available to charities. Charities should therefore continue to adopt UK accounting standards, although the convergence of these with IFRS over the next few years will mean that changes will occur as UK standards are replaced by their IFRS equivalent. The SORP Committee is committed under the ASB's code of practice to review the SORP annually to ensure that it remains relevant and consistent, particularly in the light of the changes arising from the accounting standards convergence process.

6.2.3 Second edition of SORP 2005

A second edition of SORP 2005 was published in May 2008 largely to bring the SORP's references into line with the new Charities Act 2006 and with the Companies Act 2006. A new introduction has also been included to provide further guidance specifically aimed at small charities. The introduction refers to the need for a charity's report and accounts to be open and transparent. Charities need to demonstrate where their money came from and what was done with it. If a non-company charity's annual income is less than £100,000, it can choose to prepare a receipts and payments account with the SORP not being applicable. For company charities, accruals accounts always have to be prepared and need to include 'primary' financial statements that include a SOFA, balance sheet and notes. For small charities (that is, below the audit threshold), a simplified Trustees' Annual Report is required, as detailed in Table 11 of Appendix 5 of the SORP

6.2.4 The main changes

The main changes in SORP 2005 may be summarised as follows:

- restructuring of the Trustees' Annual Report using seven key sections, with some additional disclosures included within these sections;
- emphasis on performance information to enable the reader to assess progress against the charity's stated aims and objectives, and to understand the charity's future plans, and
- the structure of the SOFA has been changed to encourage charities to establish a clearer correlation between incoming resources and related resources expended.

The headings should highlight the activities being undertaken by the charity rather than merely describe the nature of the income stream, or the method by which resources are expended. The SOFA *pro forma* is reproduced as **Annex 1** to this chapter.

1. The sections dealing with recognition of incoming resources, and of resources expended, have been substantially rewritten and expanded to provide more specific and tailored guidance for charities, especially in relation to grants and contracts.

SORP 2005

2. There is greater emphasis on the analysis and disclosure of grant-making activities by purpose and objective, rather than by the type of funding provided to the grant recipient. The split by type of funding should be included in the notes to the accounts.
3. There are some minor changes to institutional grant disclosure, particularly where non-disclosure may be justified. Trustees no longer have to inform the Charity Commission of proposed cases of non-disclosure prior to the approval of the accounts.
4. Support costs are no longer shown as a separate category on the face of the SOFA, but instead should be allocated to, and analysed as a component of, each category of expenditure in the notes to the accounts.
5. A new heading 'Governance Costs' replaces SORP 2000's 'Managing and administering the charity' category. Governance costs are more narrowly defined.
6. More detailed recommendations are provided on attributing costs between the activity categories on the SOFA, with further guidance on the bases that can be adopted. The basis and method of cost allocation to each category should be disclosed.
7. Clarification of the treatment of costs incurred on multipurpose activities (such as those which may be intended as both fundraising and educational).
8. The requirement to disclose the cost of trustees' indemnity insurance has been removed.
9. The £10,000 bandings provided for the analysis of emoluments of higher-paid staff should start at £60,000 (not £50,000).
10. The term 'heritage assets' replaces 'historic and inalienable assets' in the previous SORP.
11. There are specific recommendations in relation to 'programme-related investments' and 'pooling schemes'.
12. Following the introduction of FRS 17: Accounting for Retirement Benefits, a new section has been added to the SORP which will primarily impact charities that operate a defined benefit pension scheme.
13. If a charity makes use of financial derivative products, there are now requirements relating to information to be given in the notes to the accounts.
14. The reserves definition in the SORP's glossary has been changed. Designated funds are not automatically excluded from 'reserves', so charities can be more flexible when calculating and defining 'reserves'.
15. The section dealing with consolidated accounts has been rewritten to reflect changes in FRS 2: Accounting for Subsidiary Undertakings in relation to dominant influence, and to clarify the meaning of 'control'. The SORP also explains when consolidation is not required.
16. There is greater clarification regarding the recognition and measurement of Gift Aid payments from a trading subsidiary, and the production and scrutiny of summarised accounts and information.

17. SORP 2005 has a table of contents at the front in the order of the paragraphs appearing in the SORP.

The above changes, together with some other relevant matters which are likely to affect most charities, are dealt with in more detail below, in the order of the SORP.

6.3. The key features

6.3.1 Trustees' Annual Report

The SORP encourages a more structured and focused approach to annual reporting and emphasises the importance of the Trustees' Annual Report as a mechanism for the charity to explain the link between its objectives, strategies, activities and achievements. The more detailed narrative information should include, or have attached to it, a statement containing reference and administrative details of the charity, its trustees and advisers.

Paragraph 36 states that the Report 'should be a coherent document that meets the requirements of law and regulation and provides a fair review of the charity's structure, aims, objectives, activities and performance'. Generally, the Report should explain what the charity is trying to do and how it is going about it, and should show whether the charity has achieved its objectives during the year and explain its plans for the future. By also explaining the governance and management structure it should 'enable the reader to understand how the numerical part of the accounts relates to the organisational structure and activities of the charity'.

Whilst accepting that charities may use other means of providing further information about themselves (for example, through an Annual Review, newsletters, websites, etc.) paragraph 39 emphasises that such sources 'should not be seen as a substitute for good statutory annual reporting'.

The SORP uses the following seven headings to provide the required information. Under each heading are brief details of the main matters to include, particularly where these are additional to, or different from the 2000 SORP. Those marked * are new disclosures introduced by SORP 2005.

The SORP encourages all charities to make full disclosure of their requirements as a matter of good practice. However, it does allow smaller charities (being those below the statutory audit threshold) to limit their disclosures to only a few paragraphs: these are shown in **bold** below.

SORP 2005

Reference and administrative details of the charity, its trustees and advisers

Registered name (including any other name by which the charity is known) and registered charity and, if applicable, company numbers.

Principal and registered office addresses.

The names of trustees at the date of approval of the Report as well as those who served during the financial year.

- The name of any Chief Executive Officer or other senior staff to whom the trustees delegate day-to-day management.*
- Names and addresses of relevant organisations or people (for example, auditors, bankers, solicitors).

Structure, governance and management

Nature of the governing document and how the charity is constituted.

Methods adopted for the recruitment and appointment of new trustees.

If applicable, details of those outside the charity who can appoint the trustees.

- Policies and procedures for the induction and training of trustees.*
- Organisational structure and decision making process.
- Details of related parties and wider networks in which the charity is involved.
- Risk management statement.

Objectives and activities

Summary of the objects of the charity, together with a summary of significant activities undertaken in relation to those objects.

- Explanation of the charity's aims and objectives for the year together with its strategies for achieving those objectives.
- Details of significant activities (as identified in the SOFA).
- Where applicable and material, policies regarding:
- Grant making.
- Selection of social or programme related investments.*
- Details regarding the role and contribution (but not financial value) of volunteers.

Achievements and performance

Summary of the main achievements during the year.

- In connection with charitable activities, an explanation of performance achieved against objectives set, together with relevant qualitative or quantitative information – for the charity and its subsidiary undertakings.
- Similar information regarding fundraising activities but with additional comments on significant expenditure for future income generation (including its effect on fundraising returns).
- Investment performance achieved against investment objectives.
- Comments on other factors which are relevant to the achievement of its objectives (for example, relationship with stakeholders and the charity's position in the wider community).

Financial review

Reserves policy including relevant details of designated funds.

Details of any fund materially in deficit, the circumstances giving rise to the deficit and details of steps being taken to eliminate the deficit.

- A brief review of the financial position of the charity and its subsidiaries at the year end.
- Statement of the principal financial management policies adopted in the year.
- Principal funding sources.*
- How expenditure during the year has supported the key objectives of the charity.
- Investment policy and objectives, including any ethical policy* adopted in the selection of investments.

Plans for future periods

- Plans for the future including aims and key objectives together with any activities planned to achieve them.

Funds held as custodian trustee on behalf of others

Description of such assets.

Name and objects of the charity whose assets are held and how this activity falls within their own objects.

Details of arrangements for the segregation and safe custody of such assets from their own assets.

6.3.2 General accounting principles

The underlying accounting principles of the SORP are unchanged in the new version. Compliance with UK accounting standards, charity law, and the need for fund accounting remain central themes of SORP 2005.

Accounts intending to show a true and fair view must be prepared on the going concern assumption and using the accruals concept, and provide information that is relevant, reliable, comparable and understandable. UK accounting standards provide the financial reporting framework under which the SORP has been developed; hence, accounts should also follow applicable accounting standards and principles.

6.3.3 Fund accounting

The requirements for charities to account properly for the funds under their control have not changed. Appendix 3 to the SORP explains the legal position as regards the various funds of a charity and the implications of this for the way in which the funds are accounted for. The main funds are normally:

Unrestricted income funds

- General
- Designated.

Restricted funds and special trusts

- Income
- Endowment (capital)
  - Expendable
  - Permanent.

The SOFA should reflect the principal movements between the opening and closing balances on all of the charity's funds. The notes to the accounts should provide information on the structure of the charity's funds, so as to disclose the fund balances and the reasons for them (analysed by type of fund, above). In particular, the following information should be given:

- analysis of assets and liabilities representing each type of fund (unless shown on the balance sheet itself);
- brief description of the origin and purpose of each fund, including any restrictions imposed;
- separate disclosure of funds in deficit, together with an explanation in the Trustees' Annual Report;
- disclosure of material transfers between different funds, and allocations to designated funds, including explanations; and

The key features

- disclosures in relation to permanent endowment where a 'total return approach' has been adopted.

An explanation of the total return approach, and how this should be accounted for, is provided in the SORP, primarily in Appendix 3.

In the light of previous studies of charities' reserves, the SORP encourages more disclosure of the designated funds of the charity, and their role in relation to the reserves policy of the charity. The reserves definition in the glossary has been changed so that designated funds are not automatically excluded from 'reserves'. Therefore, charities can be more flexible when calculating and defining 'reserves'.

Following the introduction of FRS 21: *Post Balance Sheet Events*, the SORP suggests that amounts allocated to designated funds before the year end may be amended post-year end if more accurate information becomes available which enables the designation to be calculated with greater accuracy.

Depending on the complexity of the funds structure of the charity, separate statements may be produced for each major fund, linked to an overall summary. An example is given in the SORP (Table 2).

6.3.4 Branches

Before preparing accounts, trustees must be quite clear as to the legal structure of the charity, and the resulting accounting treatments. Whilst there are no major changes, charities with branches should be familiar with paragraphs 77–81 of the SORP. The definition of branches is clearly stated in the SORP's glossary.

6.3.5 Statement of financial activities (SOFA)

Overview

The SOFA is a single accounting statement with the objective of showing the reader of the accounts where the charity's resources came from, and how they were used during the year – in relation to all of the charity's funds. The SOFA is structured to show whether there has been a net inflow or outflow of resources, including capital gains and losses on assets. It should provide a reconciliation of all movements in the charity's funds.

The SOFA should clearly show the activities undertaken by the charity. As far as possible, the terminology used for analysing the components of resources expended should mirror that reflected within the analysis of incoming resources. The categories for both incoming and outgoing resources have been altered and linked under the following three activity categories:

- generation of funds, (that is, fundraising);
- charitable activities, and
- other

In addition, resources expended include a further heading dealing with governance costs. Grant expenditure and support costs are not activities in themselves and should no longer appear as headings on the SOFA. However, an analysis of such costs should be provided in the notes to the accounts.

The format still requires, for the current year, a columnar split between funds with a total column, together with a total column for the previous year. Table 3 within the SORP, and **Annex 1** to this chapter, summarises the revised format of the SOFA. Charities can expand this structure, where necessary using notes. The SORP emphasises that 'the SOFA may be adapted to give a true and fair view, but disclosure requirements should always be met and the underlying structure should not be changed' (para. 86). In addition, the following should be noted:

- the order in which the activity categories are presented may be varied according to the 'presentational needs' of the charity;
- category headings can be omitted if there is nothing to report in both the current or preceding periods;
- if the categories change from those used in the previous year (for example, due to changes in the activities in the year), comparative figures must be restated accordingly;
- additional subtotals may also be included if this is felt to benefit the reader of the accounts, and
- the trustees may wish to add additional columns to the SOFA where funds are of particular importance or significance (otherwise this information must be shown in the notes to the accounts).

Smaller charities may adopt an alternative approach to the analysis within the SOFA. The structure and format of the SOFA are covered in paras 83–243 of the SORP – these paragraphs also confirm the recognition principles for certain types of income and expenditure in more detail than SORP 2000, and also cover other presentation matters which should be included in the notes to the accounts. We have highlighted the following.

Incoming resources

Recognition

- Incoming resources should be recognised in the SOFA when the effect of a transaction, or other event, results in an increase in the charity's assets. This is likely to be only when the conditions for receipt have been met and there is reasonable assurance of receipt.
- Recognition will depend on the three factors of entitlement, certainty of receipt, and reliability of measurement being met.

The key features

- Guidance is provided on accounting for the spectrum of different arrangements and transactions which the charity may encounter, in the light of general accounting standards and principles. For each source of funds, the following should be determined:
- the legal arrangements involved, including settlement of disputes;
- whether the funding is dependent on specific performance achievements or outcomes, and
- whether the funds can be used for any purposes of the charity, or are restricted for specific uses.
- The SORP details the specific accounting treatment required for income generated through the contractual provision of goods or services (paras 98–103); income received in the form of grants and donations (paras 104–111); and resources raised by, or for, a third party (paras 112 and 113).
- There is also clarification (para. 116) on the distinction between incoming resources which are subject to restrictions (on their use by the charity), and those which are subject to conditions (prior to entitlement by the charity).
- In general, contracts and grants with specific performance conditions attached should be recognised as the specified goods or services are supplied.
- Grants with conditions that are not performance related should be recognised when the conditions for receipt are met, or fall within the control of the grant recipient. Grants that are not subject to conditions should be recognised when receivable.

Incoming resources from generated funds

This section of the SOFA identifies those resources which have been generated (for example, through fundraising) for use on charitable activities. This category should include the following, where applicable.

Voluntary income

1. Gifts, donations and legacies.
2. Grants which provide core funding or are of a general nature, or are in response to an appeal (but not those given specifically for the performance of a service or activity).
3. Membership subscriptions.
4. Gifts in kind and donated goods and services.
5. Further detail is provided in relation to the recognition of legacies (paras 123–128), building on the guidance contained in SORP 2000, and the conditions of certainty, entitlement and measurement. Where material, the accounting policy notes should distinguish between the accounting treatment for different types of legacies (pecuniary, residuary, and those subject to a life interest held by another party).
6. Gifts in kind should be included in the SOFA on the basis of;

(a) either a reasonable estimate of their gross value to the charity (likely to be the amount that the charity estimates it would have to pay on the open market for an equivalent item), or

(b) the amount actually realised when subsequently sold.

1. Donated facilities and services, which replaces the term 'intangible income', should be included in the SOFA where quantifiable and measurable, and on the basis of the gross value to the charity (again, with reference to the open market had the charity not received the services or facility). An equivalent amount should be included as expenditure under the appropriate heading.
2. The value of the contribution of unpaid volunteers should *not* be included in the SOFA. However, the contribution of volunteers should be referred to in the Trustees' Annual Report, along with any other donated services not included in the SOFA.

Activities for generating funds

- Fundraising events
- Sponsorships and social lotteries which are not regarded as pure donations
- Shop income from selling donated and/or bought in goods
- Provision of goods and services which are not for the benefit of the charity's beneficiaries

Certain letting and licensing arrangements of the charity's property

This category encompasses the trading and other fundraising activities carried out primarily to raise funds which will then be used to undertake charitable activities. The activities included will generally involve an element of 'exchange' of income, in return for provision of goods, services, or entry to an event.

The tax consequences and treatment of these sources of funds should be reviewed carefully, although this should not ultimately affect their disclosure in the SOFA.

Investment income

- Dividends, interest and rental income from investment assets.
- In the parent charity's SOFA – payments to the charity by its subsidiary undertakings where these are not in respect of the provision of goods and services, typically Gift Aid.
- The SORP clarifies the recognition and measurement of Gift Aid payments from a trading subsidiary, in the light of FRS 21: Post Balance Sheet Events, particularly where the amount of a Gift Aid payment is recalculated with greater accuracy after the year end.

Incoming resources from charitable activities

This category comprises incoming resources received by the charity as payment for provision of goods and services for its beneficiaries.

- Primary purpose trading – the sale of goods or services as part of the direct charitable activities of the charity.
- The sale of goods or services made or provided by the charity's beneficiaries.
- Contractual payments from government or public authorities received in the normal course of trading under the above.
- Grants specifically for the provision of goods and services to beneficiaries (as part of the direct charitable activity), including service level agreements.
- Ancillary trades connected to primary purpose trading in the above.

An analysis of incoming resources from charitable activities should be given in the notes to the accounts, to supplement that provided on the face of the SOFA. This should enable the reader to understand the main charitable activities undertaken by the charity, and the income generated from each. This analysis should link into that provided for resources expended on charitable activities.

Other incoming resources

Most charities should not need to use this category as it is expected that they should be able to analyse resources received using one of the above specified headings.

This category may, however, include a gain on the disposal of a fixed asset held for the charity's own use, and a gain on the disposal of a programme related investment.

Resources expended

Recognition

The SORP seeks to interpret more clearly the requirements of FRS 12: *Provisions, Contingent Liabilities and Contingent Assets* in relation to the particular circumstances of charities. Explanations have been improved and more examples provided, especially in relation to multi-year grants.

Expenditure should be recognised when, and to the extent that, a liability is incurred or increased without a corresponding increase in assets, or a reduction in liabilities.

A liability will arise when the charity is obliged to make a 'transfer of value' to a third party, as a result of past transactions or events.

A legal or constructive obligation which commits the charity to a certain course of expenditure will generally result in the recognition of a liability, and the corresponding expenditure.

The SORP seeks to provide guidance on accounting for the spectrum of different arrangements and transactions which the charity may encounter when

SORP 2005

expending its resources. Again, judgement will be required in deciding how any particular transaction fits into the framework provided by accounting standards and principles.

The key is to identify whether, and when, the grant-giving charity has a legal or constructive obligation, and hence should recognise a liability in its accounts. This will also be influenced by the extent to which a 'valid expectation' has been raised in the mind of the recipient, and the extent to which any conditions remain in the control of the grant-giving charity.

SORP 2005 provides guidance on accounting for contractual arrangements, such as service level agreements with conditions for payment based on certain performance criteria.

The glossary includes a definition of 'performance-related grants', and para. 151 proposes that such grants are recognised as resources expended to the extent that the recipient of the grant has indeed provided the specified services or goods.

Care should be taken to distinguish between arrangements based around *performance* criteria, and a grant given for a particular *purpose* (that is, restricted), as the recognition point may differ in the grant-giving charity's accounts.

Entitlement will only arise on performance-related grants as the performance conditions are met.

Costs of generating funds

This section of the SOFA identifies the costs of generating incoming resources from all sources other than undertaking charitable activities, and should include the following, where applicable.

Costs of generating voluntary income

- All fundraising costs.
- Agents' costs where fundraising agents are used.
- Additional disclosure may be required in the notes where the activities comprising costs of generating voluntary income are material, or where the start-up costs of a new fundraising activity are material in the context of the charity's overall fundraising profile.

Fundraising trading

- Costs of goods sold or services provided.
- The costs related to the licensing of a charity logo.

Investment management costs

- Where investment managers deduct their fees from investment income, amounts should be grossed-up and disclosed accordingly in both income and expenditure.
- Investment management costs associated with endowment fund investments should generally be charged to the endowment fund in the SOFA.

Charitable activities

This category comprises all resources applied by the charity in undertaking its work to meet its charitable objectives. It will include the cost of delivery of services, the provision of goods for charitable purpose, programme and project work, and should include direct expenditure as well as allocated support costs. The following should be noted.

1. An analysis of resources expended on charitable activities should be provided on the face of the SOFA or in the notes to the accounts; a breakdown of the cost components for each material category, activity, programme or project should be provided in the notes to the accounts (as proposed in Table 5 of the SORP).
2. The total cost of each charitable activity will comprise costs incurred directly by the charity, as well as any funding provided to third parties through grant making activities. Hence, grant expenditure should no longer be a separate category on the face of the SOFA.
3. The SORP provides specific guidance as to the treatment and disclosure of grant making activities in paras 195–209. Table 6 in the SORP illustrates how grant information may be presented.
4. The disclosure requirements for grants made to institutions have been reorganised, and suggestions as to what is 'material' have been removed in order to increase flexibility through the use of judgement.

Governance costs

Governance costs are defined in the SORP's glossary, and comprise a narrower category than SORP 2000's 'management and administration' costs.

This category should comprise both direct costs and related support costs associated with the governance arrangements of the charity, as opposed to general management costs.

The accounting policy notes should define the nature of the costs allocated to this category; an analysis of the main components of this category may be provided in the notes to the accounts where this is deemed to provide useful information to the reader of the accounts.

Other resources expended

This category will include any other resources expended which cannot be analysed within the other three main categories.

Transfers between funds

All transfers between the different categories of funds should be shown on the transfer row of the SOFA, and para. 214 of the SORP illustrates the types of transfers that may occur.

Material transfers should not be netted off, but be shown on the face of the SOFA. The notes should then explain the nature of each material transfer between funds.

Other recognised gains and losses

The SORP provides guidance as to the treatment and disclosure of gains and losses on fixed assets, including investment assets, in paras 217–219.

For unincorporated charities, realised and unrealised gains and losses on investment assets may be included in a single line on the face of the SOFA. For charitable companies, these will need to be split in order to comply with Companies Act requirements.

Actuarial gains or losses on defined benefit pension schemes should be separately disclosed in the gains and losses section of the SOFA. The SORP provides more detail on the application of FRS 17: Accounting for Retirement Benefits in a special section (paras 430–448 of the SORP).

Other SOFA matters

Support costs

Support costs should no longer be disclosed as a separate category on the face of the SOFA as they do not, in themselves, constitute a distinct activity of the charity. They should therefore be allocated to their respective activity cost categories so that the total cost of that activity is shown on the face of the SOFA.

The notes to the accounts should show the breakdown of support costs by activity; the method of allocation and apportionment should also be clearly stated in the accounting policy notes.

Allocation and apportionment of costs

Costs should be allocated directly to a cost category wherever possible. Where costs are shared between cost categories, they should be apportioned on a basis which is 'appropriate, reasonable, justifiable, and consistent' and this should be disclosed in the notes to the accounts, along with any estimation techniques employed.

Charities should balance the need for a reliable and consistent approach to the allocation of support costs, with the cost of preparing such information, and the ultimate benefit to the reader of the accounts.

The basis adopted for apportionment will normally be consistent between accounting periods.

A distinction may need to be drawn, and disclosed, between 'multi-purpose activities' where, for example, information about the charity's work is provided in the context of fundraising literature. The SORP provides guidance as to the criteria which should be used to assess the basis of the allocation of such costs between SOFA activity categories (paras 172–174).

6.3.6 Related notes

Related party transactions

Related parties are defined in the glossary to the SORP. Paragraphs 221–229 highlight the importance of transparency and detail the required disclosures (as well as those which are not required).

Trustees' remuneration and benefits

The SORP emphasises the fact that, due to the nature of trusteeship, it is not normal practice for charity trustees, or people connected with them, to receive remuneration or benefits from the charity for which they are responsible.

Should such transactions occur, they should always be regarded as material; each type of related party transaction should be separately disclosed.

Where there are no such transactions, this fact should be stated.

Trustees' expenses

The SORP clarifies the criteria for disclosure of trustee expenses – whether met by the charity on behalf of the trustee by payment to a third party, or through reimbursement to the trustee.

There is no need to disclose routine expenditure which is collectively attributable to the services provided by the trustees, such as the hire of a room for meetings or the provision of 'reasonable refreshment' at trustee meetings.

Where trustees have received no such expenses, this should be stated.

Trustees' indemnity insurance

The requirement to disclose the cost of this indemnity insurance has been removed.

Staff Costs and emoluments

The £10,000 bandings provided for the analysis of emoluments of higher-paid staff should start at £60,000 (not £50,000). Where there are no employees with emoluments over £60,000, this should be stated.

The disclosures in relation to staff costs and emoluments have otherwise remained largely unchanged from the previous SORP, although there is clarification on the disclosures in relation to part-time staff.

Staff costs disclosed should include those payments made to third parties and connected companies in relation to the provision of staff, as well as the direct expenditure incurred by the charity for the staff it employs.

Ex gratia payments

These should be treated in accordance with additional guidance contained in CC7: Ex Gratia Payments by Charities.

Payments which the trustees reasonably consider to be in the interests of the charity, and which constitute more than a moral obligation (but are not a legal obligation) should *not* be treated as *ex gratia* payments.

Analysis of net movement in funds

This represents the increase or decrease in the resources available to the charity to deploy in undertaking future activities. Whilst information on certain charitable applications and sources of funding can be extracted from the charity's cash flow statement (if prepared), para. 243 of the SORP proposes additional information which may be useful to readers of the accounts in interpreting net movement of funds.

6.3.7 Balance sheet

Although the SORP prescribes a more detailed structure, many charities will in fact notice little difference to the format of their balance sheet. Those that will are charities with heritage assets, programme-related investments or defined benefit pension schemes.

1. **Heritage assets**, which replace those defined in the previous SORP as 'inalienable and historic fixed assets', are defined in the glossary as 'assets of historical, artistic or scientific importance that are held to advance preservation, conservation and educational objectives of charities and through public access contribute to the nation's culture and education either at a national or local level'.
2. The glossary gives examples of such assets, which paras 279–294 enlarge upon. These paragraphs also make it clear whether or not such assets should be included in the balance sheet, how they should be valued and how they should be disclosed.

3. In summary, in order to reflect the underlying principles of FRS 15: Tangible Fixed Assets, heritage assets should be capitalised unless:
   (a) there is no reliable cost information available; or
   (b) valuation methods would not be sufficiently reliable, or
   (c) the costs in producing a valuation would outweigh its benefits.

This approach caused much concern from respondents during the SORP consultation process, and issues raised are being considered further by the ASB.

1. **Programme-related investments** are a new concept and such investments need to be disclosed separately from those investments intended primarily to generate a return to the charity. Programme-related investments (also known as social investments) are those made directly for charitable purposes and the primary purpose for making them is not financial. They will include loans to beneficiaries or to other charities.
2. The SORP (paras 308–312) prescribes the amounts that should be included, together with the treatment of impairment or gains.
3. There is an entirely new section in the SORP dealing with **retirement benefits**, as a result of the requirements of FRS 17.
4. When a charity has a **defined benefit pension scheme** the balance sheet will need to include the asset or liability relating to that scheme, together with any relevant pension reserve (as part of the funds of the charity).

Insofar as the balance sheet is concerned the other main changes or points worth noting are as follows:

- table 7, which follows para. 251, sets out the **structure** of the balance sheet (as shown in Annex 1 of this chapter);
- there is now an option to prepare the balance sheet using a **columnar format** to differentiate between the main types of funds. This is an alternative to the equivalent summarised analysis being given in the notes to the accounts;
- table 8 in para. 274 shows how changes to **tangible fixed assets** should be reflected, and
- table 9 in para. 302 shows how the **movements in investments** should be analysed. Further details should also be provided of any particular investments considered to be material in the context of the charity's investment portfolio (the 'five per cent' threshold having been dropped).

Negative balances on restricted funds (if material) should be shown separately and not netted off against positive balances.

There are new short sections dealing with charities which have **share capital** (par. 333) or **revaluation reserves** (para. 334).

If a charity makes use of **financial derivative products** there are now requirements relating to information to be given in the notes to the accounts (paras 337 and 338). This guidance is based on FRS 13: *Derivatives and Other Financial Instruments* although any charities which make significant use of such products will need to be mindful of further disclosures that may be required by standards such as FRS 25 and FRS 26 which also relate to financial instruments.

6.3.8 Cash flow statement

There are no changes in the requirements to prepare a cash flow statement and this must therefore continue to be prepared in accordance with FRS 1: *Cash Flow Statements* if the statement is required.

The starting point for a cash flow statement will normally be the figure on the SOFA against 'Net incoming/outgoing resources before other recognised gains and losses'.

Movements in endowments should not be included in cash flows from 'operating activities' but should be treated as increases or decreases in the 'financing' section. Details of how this is achieved and other information on the cash flow statement is in paragraphs 351–355.

6.3.9 Disclosure of accounting policies

This section of the SORP draws on the principles of FRS 18: Accounting Policies which explains how accounting policies should be determined. Accounts are normally prepared on the basis that the charity is a going concern, and must also include relevant, reliable, comparable and understandable information. It is essential that accounts are accompanied by an explanation of the basis and estimation techniques on which they have been prepared.

Paragraph 356 states 'charity accounts should include notes on the accounting policies chosen. These should be the most appropriate in the particular circumstances of each charity for the purpose of giving a true and fair view. The policies should be consistent with this SORP, Accounting Standards and relevant legislation'. All charities should therefore include policies which explain:

- the basis of the preparation of the accounts;
- any departures from the SORP and Accounting Standards;
- the reasons for any omissions of branches from the accounts;
- paragraphs 361–370 deal with disclosure of policies for specific items, and provide examples of matters for which accounting policies may be required – although this depends on the materiality of the matter concerned, and the relevance to the charity.

Explanations need only be brief but they should be clear, fair and accurate. Any changes to policies resulting in a material adjustment to prior periods must be disclosed. Other policies which should be stated, where items are relevant and material, include the following.

1. Incoming resources – basis of recognition of each type of material incoming resource, such as legacies, grants receivable, gifts in kind and donated services and facilities.
2. Resources expended – the policy for including items within each activity category in the SOFA, and the methods and principles for the allocation and apportionment of costs between the categories.
3. The policy for recognition of liabilities, particularly in relation to grants payable.
4. Fixed assets for use by the charity – including the policy and threshold for capitalisation, the rates of depreciation used, and the policy with respect to impairment reviews of fixed assets.
5. Investments – normally shown at market value, but explanations should be given for any departures from this. The basis of including gains and losses in the SOFA should be stated.
6. Funds structure – including a brief description of the different types of funds held by the charity, the policy for any transfers between those funds, and the policy for determining each designated fund.
7. Other policy notes – examples are given in paragraph 370.

6.3.10 Summarised financial statements and summary financial information

SORP 2005 does not change the requirements but it does make clearer the distinction between summarised financial statements (or accounts) and summary financial information. It includes a table (reproduced below) showing this distinction.

Table 6.1 Contrasting characteristics of summarised financial statements and summary financial information

Characteristics of summarised financial statements	Characteristics of summary financial information
Includes a summary of the Statement of Financial Activities and Balance Sheet of the accounts	Draws information from only parts
The summary is derived from statutory accounts	May be based on interim accounts or other financial information as well as statutory accounts

Characteristics of summarised financial statements	Characteristics of summary financial information
A financial statement that purports to be a Statement of Financial Activities or Balance Sheet or summary thereof	Makes no reference to either of these primary statements
Represents the entire finances of a charity or a charity group	Represents analysis – for example, of a particular activity or region

The information which must accompany **summarised financial statements** generally remains unchanged. As a reminder, the specimen statement given below satisfies the requirements of the SORP.

> 'These summarised accounts are not the statutory accounts but are a summary of information extracted from both the Statement of Financial Activities and the Balance Sheet for the year ended (date). For further information a copy of the full audited accounts, which were approved on (date) and on which the auditors have given an unqualified report, [Note: if the report was qualified sufficient details should be provided] together with a copy of the reports of the trustees and auditors, can be obtained from (address). Copies of the annual report and accounts have been submitted to the Charity Commission (and Registrar of Companies).'

A statement from the auditors or other external scrutineer should also be attached confirming whether or not the summarised financial statements are consistent with the full accounts.

If only branch accounts are produced, it must be stated that the summarised accounts are for the branch only and have been extracted from the full accounts of the reporting charity (showing also the name of that charity).

Summary financial information, in whatever form, must be accompanied by a statement signed on behalf of the trustees regarding:

- the purpose of the information;
- whether or not it is from the full annual accounts;
- whether or not the full accounts have been externally scrutinised, and
- details of how copies of the full accounts and related reports can be obtained.

There is no requirement to present a statement from the external scrutineer together with the summary.

6.3.11 The special sections of the SORP

SORP 2000 contained four 'special sections'; SORP 2005 retains the first three of these, which deal with consolidation of subsidiary undertakings; associates and joint ventures and joint arrangements; and charitable companies. Two new special sections have been added, on:

The key features

- Accounting for Retirement Benefits; and
- Common Investment Funds and Investment Pooling Schemes.

The section dealing with smaller charities in SORP 2000 is now incorporated as Appendix 5 to the updated SORP, a summary of which is included as **Annex 2** to this chapter. Where the sections apply to your charity, we recommend that you read them in detail. We summarise some of the more fundamental matters below.

Consolidation of Subsidiary Undertakings

Consolidation should be in line with FRS 2: Accounting for Subsidiary Undertakings and on a line-by-line basis. There is, however, additional information in the SORP relating to exclusions and the definition of 'control' and dominant influence when considering whether or not consolidation is necessary.

In particular, it is not necessary to consolidate if the gross income of the group is no more than the charity audit threshold or if the results of the subsidiary are not material to the group.

Although technically there should be a SOFA for both the group and the parent, that for the parent is often omitted. The Charity Commission is prepared to accept such accounts provided that gross income or turnover and results of the parent charity are clearly disclosed in the notes. The Group accounts must still include the parent charity's own balance sheet. However, the Commission retains the power to require a charity SOFA and the public has a legal right to request it.

Funds or reserves of subsidiaries, other than those funds used for carrying out the charity's objects, should be shown separately on the consolidated balance sheet.

Paragraphs 381–406 provide further detail in respect of consolidation matters.

Associates, joint ventures and joint arrangements

In accordance with FRS 9: Associates and Joint Ventures, associates should be included in the accounts based on the net equity method and joint ventures on the gross equity method.

Where there is a joint arrangement, the charity's gross share of the incoming resources and resources expended, and the assets and liabilities, should be included in the same way as for a branch. Guidance is provided on the treatment of an obligation where, under the arrangement, the charity is jointly and severally liable.

There are detailed disclosure requirements contained in paras 417 and 418.

SORP 2005

The SORP in relation to charitable companies in the UK

Charitable companies must comply with the Companies Act 2006 with respect to the form and content of their accounts.

Companies House will normally accept the Trustees' Annual Report as also fulfilling the purpose of the Directors' Report provided that it contains all of the necessary additional information required. In practice we recommend that this is made clear in the title and content of the report.

Company law requires an income and expenditure account to be prepared. However, this may not always be necessary for charitable companies provided that:

- the title makes it clear that the SOFA includes the income and expenditure account;
- there are no movements on endowment (capital) funds, and
- there are no unrealised gains or losses or if there are, then these are below the line entitled 'Net income/(expenditure) for the year', which replaces or is in addition to 'Net incoming/(outgoing) resources for the year'. However, realised gains/(losses) will need to be included before arriving at the above sub-total, (that is, realised and unrealised gains/(losses) will need to be separately shown for charitable companies).

If a separate (summary) income and expenditure account is prepared it should be derived from, and cross-referenced to, the corresponding figures in the SOFA.

Where there is an upward revaluation of fixed assets, a revaluation reserve will arise and this should be separately shown on the balance sheet of charitable companies.

6.3.12 Accounting for retirement benefits

Following the introduction of FRS 17: Accounting for Retirement Benefits, a new section has been added to the SORP which incorporates guidance previously provided in Update Bulletin 1 issued in 2003. This will primarily impact charities that operate a defined benefit pension scheme.

New categories have been added to the SOFA and balance sheet *pro formas* to cater for the information required by FRS 17.

Appropriate comment should also be made in the Trustees' Annual Report in respect of any significant pension assets or liabilities now included within the funds of the charity.

The updated glossary also includes definitions in respect of terms central to FRS 17.

Paragraphs 430–448 should be read in detail by those charities particularly affected by FRS 17.

6.3.13 Common investment funds and investment pooling schemes

A short section has been added (paras 449–451) to highlight the accounting implications of the above, particularly in the light of the Trustee Act 2000 which made it easier for charities in England and Wales to use such schemes.

6.4. Practical considerations

The overriding emphasis of SORP 2005 is to enhance the messages portrayed in the Trustees' Annual Report, and to ensure that the numbers in the accounts clearly support these messages through presenting the performance and activities of the charity in a straightforward, logical, and consistent way.

Of course, the accounts (those showing a 'true and fair view') must also comply with relevant legislation, accounting standards and pronouncements – this should have been happening long before the introduction of SORP 2005. All that SORP 2005 does is to interpret more recent developments into a more user-friendly and logical format for charitable organisations. Hence, the adoption of SORP 2005 should bear few surprises in terms of material changes in accounting treatment of transactions, or significant new disclosures.

Smaller charities should familiarise themselves with the concessions highlighted in the SORP in order to be able to take advantage of the opportunities these provide for simplified reporting and accounting procedures (see **Annex 2** of this chapter).

What are the main areas you should be focusing on, and the questions you should be asking? Highlighted below are some 'old chestnuts', as well as some new questions raised by SORP 2005, which it is recommended are considered by trustees and charity executives – preferably, long before these questions appear on our audit planning meeting agendas!

Enhancing the words

As a trustee:

- To what extent do you consider the Trustees' Annual Report to be exactly that – **your report?**
- Do you and your fellow trustees take **joint responsibility** to ensure that the Report fairly reflects the structure, aims, activities, achievements and performance of the charity – and that the opportunities to do this are maximised?

SORP 2005

- How do you ensure that the information contained within the Report is **clear, complete, accurate and consistent** with fact and with the accounts?
- Is there scope (or need) for additional or more **informative explanation** of performance, trends, ratios or other matters highlighted later in the accounts?
- Does the Report engage the reader so that he/she can understand the **future plans** and proposed direction of the charity?
- **Who will actually read this report?** With the demands of so many 'stakeholders' to fill (let alone the requirements of the SORP), how successful are you in ensuring that the Report strikes the right balance between formality and examples; overview and detail; strategy and operational matters; successes and struggles?
- Apart from discharging your responsibilities in respect of good statutory annual reporting, what part does the Trustees' Report play in the **overall communication strategy** of the charity?
- If your charity has income of over £1million, how will you link the information presented in this Report with that required in the **Summary Information Return** (SIR)?
- Could your charity benefit from producing a separate **Annual Review** in addition to the statutory Report – perhaps including summary financial statements, or summary information? Have you asked the auditors to confirm and report on the consistency of summarised financial statements, if presented?
- Consider the **'new' information** proposed by SORP 2005 – for example, policies and procedures for the induction and training of trustees; details of social, programme-related, or ethical investments. Even if these do not feature in your charity now, should these matters be addressed, and then disclosed, in the future?
- Consider and discuss (well in advance of the approval date) the **key policies and statements** required – how can you make them meaningful, and not merely just 'boilerplate' statements?
- In particular, consider the charity's **reserves policy**, particularly in the light of the actual results, and the charity's future plans. Define what is meant by 'reserves' in your charity – note the increased flexibility provided by the SORP's revised definition of 'reserves' which does not automatically exclude designated funds.
- Can you justify and explain the **level of reserves** held, through a process which is an integral part of the charity's financial management?
- How have you utilised **designated funds** in the year? Should the level and nature of your designated funds be reviewed in the light of post-balance sheet events?
- **Utilise opportunities** to explain why reserves may be too high or too low compared to your policy – don't be defensive. Are you investing for the future? Or do you need to appeal for additional funding (particularly unrestricted funds)?

Practical considerations

- Can you explain why funds are in **deficit**, and the steps being taken to address this ?
- Can you describe the charity's **principal funding sources?** How do these link with the charity's overall risk management profile and strategy?
- What evidence is there to support the **risk management statement** – and to show that you and your fellow trustees regularly monitor and manage risk?
- If your charity operates a **defined benefit pension scheme**, are you able to explain the effect of a material pension liability (or asset) on the funds and the reserves policy of the charity – and the impact on the charity's future plans, its services to beneficiaries, and its obligations to staff?

In summary, how will the information in the Trustees' Annual Report 'stack up' when compared to the actual numbers presented in the accounts? Do the words and numbers complement each other – or confuse or conflict?

Presenting the numbers

As a Trustee, Chief Executive or Finance Manager:

- How should your charity's **SOFA** be structured to ensure that the reader will better understand the activities of the charity rather than just the nature of the income or expenditure stream?
- Can you further improve the **link** between the charity's income streams and the related costs of the activity?
- How will you **allocate support and indirect costs** to each activity category, in order to best portray the cost profile of the charity's work?
- Is your **basis and method of cost allocation** and apportionment practical to implement, logical and consistent? How will you describe this in the notes to the accounts?
- To what extent will you need to restate **previous year comparative figures?** Can this be done well in advance of the first year of adoption to minimise surprises (information not readily to hand; inconsistent ratios, trends or patterns emerging) – are further explanations required?
- Have you got consistent and compliant **accounting policies** in place for all material items? Are these policies clearly explained in the notes to the accounts?
- Are you clear about the **recognition points** for all material income streams – have you analysed these in relation to the factors of 'certainty', 'entitlement' and 'measurement'?
- Have you reviewed, for example, the nature of **donation, grant and contract income?** Are there restrictions on the use of the income? Are there any performance-related conditions? At what point do you consider that these have been met?
- Do you have any **gifts in kind, or donated goods and services?** How do you capture these – and then attribute a value for the purposes of the accounts?

- For expenditure, particularly **grant expenditure**, when do you recognise the liability in your accounts? At what point is a valid expectation created and communicated to the recipient? To what extent are conditions attached – and when do these fall outside your control? What discretion do you ultimately have in relation to making the payment?
- Are you able to **analyse grants** made to institutions and individuals (and also by the nature or type of project or activity being supported) in the detail recommended by the SORP? How will you allocate and disclose the support or monitoring costs related to grant making activities?
- Has your charity got any assets which now fall under the new definition of **'heritage' assets**? Is it possible to attribute a reliable cost or valuation to these for inclusion in the accounts? If not, what disclosures are required to give the reader an accurate picture of the situation and the nature of stewardship of these assets?
- Does your charity operate a **defined benefit pension scheme?** If so, are you able to extract the figures required for insertion in the SOFA and the balance sheet – and are you able to explain the impact of these to the readers of the accounts?
- Are you clear about the **legal structure** of your charity and its activities – particularly where it operates through branches (local, national or overseas), subsidiaries, or other arrangements perhaps involving joint working, joint ventures or partnerships?
- Have you considered the extent of **control or influence** your charity has over these activities or entities? How will you therefore need to account for these activities?

Annex 1: Summary of formats

STATEMENT OF FINANCIAL ACTIVITIES (SOFA) £

Incoming resources

Incoming resources from generated funds

Voluntary income

Activities for generating funds

Investment income

Incoming resources from charitable activities

Other incoming resources

Total incoming resources

Resources expended

Costs of generating funds

Charitable activities

Governance costs

Other resources expended

Total resources expended

Net incoming/outgoing resources before transfers

Transfers between funds

Net incoming resources before other recognised gains and losses

Other recognised gains/losses

Gains on revaluation of fixed assets for the charity's own use

Gains/losses on investment assets

Actuarial gains/losses on defined benefit pension schemes

Annex 1: Summary of formats

Net movement in funds

Reconciliation of funds

Total funds brought forward

Total funds carried forward

Notes to SOFA Format:

1. There is scope to change the order of the headings in the SOFA and to insert additional sub-totals, within reason, to better suit a charity's circumstances.
2. For those charities not subject to a statutory audit, the SOFA need not contain an analysis of either incoming resources or resources expended by categories of activity. Instead, resource classifications relevant to their circumstances may be chosen.
3. From this point, charitable companies will need to modify the presentation of the SOFA if it is also to be used as an income and expenditure account.
4. A columnar analysis of funds is required for the current year, with a total funds comparative shown for the previous year.

BALANCE SHEET £

Fixed assets

Intangible assets

Tangible assets

Heritage assets

Investments

Investments

Programme-related investments

Total fixed assets

Annex 1: Summary of formats

Current assets

Stocks and work-in-progress

Debtors

Investments

Cash at bank and in hand

Total current assets

Liabilities

Creditors: Amounts falling due within one year

Net current assets or liabilities

Total assets less current liabilities

Creditors: Amounts falling due after more than one year

Provisions for liabilities and charges

Net assets or liabilities excluding pension asset or liability

Defined benefit pension scheme asset or liability

Net assets or liabilities including pension asset or liability

The funds of the charity

Endowment funds

Restricted income funds

Unrestricted income funds

Share capital

Unrestricted income funds

Revaluation reserve

Unrestricted income funds excluding pension asset or liability

Pension reserve

Total unrestricted funds
Total charity funds

Annex 2: Accounting for smaller charities

Appendix 5 of SORP 2005 lists certain concessions that are available to smaller charities, (that is, those defined by size) and some relevant thresholds are given in the SORP's Appendix 4. It is important to note that all thresholds are as at May 2008 and may change from time to time. The main concessions are as follows.

Receipts and Payments Accounts

- Unincorporated charities with a gross income not exceeding £100,000 may prepare accounts on this basis, which should be based on guidance given by the Charity Commission.
- Small company charities must always prepare accruals accounts and are therefore not subject to this concession.

The Financial Reporting Standard for Smaller Entities (FRSSE)

- Any charity below certain thresholds (see below) can follow the FRSSE, except where it conflicts with the SORP in which case the SORP must be followed and in particular:
- The accounts must include a SOFA in place of a profit and loss account and statement of total recognised gains and losses.
- The principles of fund accounting, including all relevant disclosures, must be followed.
- Investments must be included at market value.
- Foreign exchange gains and losses and exceptional items must be included in the SOFA.
- The thresholds effective for accounting periods begining on or after 6 April 2008, of which at least two out of three conditions must be met are:
  (i) annual gross income: not exceeding £6.5 million (previously £5.6 million);
  (ii) balance sheet total: not exceeding £3.26 million (previously £2.8 million), and
  (iii) average number of employees: not exceeding 50.

Trustees' Annual Reports

For those charities not subject to a statutory audit:

- An abbreviated trustees' report may be prepared based on the paragraphs shown in bold in section **6.3.1** above.
- The minimum content is also given in Table 11 of the SORP (para. 5.4.2 of Appendix 5). However, those charities which are incorporated will still need to either prepare, or include, the relevant paragraphs relating to a Directors' Report.

Financial Statements of Smaller Charities

For those charities not subject to a statutory audit:

- The SOFA need not contain an analysis of either incoming resources or resources expended by categories of activity. Instead, resource classifications relevant to their circumstances may be chosen.
- Where these alternative classifications are adopted certain note disclosures may no longer be necessary. Details are given in para. 5.3.1(b) of Appendix 5.
- In addition, there is no requirement to give details of staff emoluments in bands, although if there are no employees with emoluments above £60,000 this fact should still be stated.

Annex 3: List of appendices and tables in the SORP

A3.1 Appendices

Appendix 1 Glossary

Appendix 2 Application of Accounting Standards

Appendix 3 The Funds of a Charity

Appendix 4 Thresholds

Appendix 5 Accounting for Smaller Charities

Appendix 6 The Charity Accounting Review Committee (2003/5)

A3.2 Tables

Table 1 Legislative Framework for Charity Accounts in the United Kingdom

Table 2 Outline Summary of Funds Movements

Table 3 Statement of Financial Activities

Table 4 Example of Support Cost Breakdown by Activity

Table 5 Breakdown of Costs of Charitable Activity

Table 6 Analysis of Grants

Table 7 Balance Sheet

Table 8 Analysis of Movement of Fixed Assets

Table 9 Analysis of Movement of Investments

Table 10 Contrasting Characteristics of Summarised Financial Statements and Information

Table 11 Contents of the Trustees' Annual Report for a Smaller Charity

Chapter 7 – Trustees' annual report

7.1 Introduction

Like directors' reports of commercial organisations, the Trustees' Annual Report forms the main narrative section accompanying the accounts. Unlike commercial organisations, however, many features of a charity's operations, particularly those in respect of voluntary help, donations-in-kind and other intangible income, can be difficult to measure in financial terms. Accordingly, both in terms of accountability and in order to complement the remainder of the accounts, the trustees' annual report should measure the achievement of the charity's objectives not only in quantitative, but also in qualitative, terms, as imaginatively and openly as possible.

The report's completeness and transparency are, thus, prerequisites if the charity's operations and accounts are to be properly understood and appreciated.

The Charity Commission now attach greater importance to the report than before and this increased emphasis on reporting is reflected in the title of the SORP: *'Accounting and Reporting by Charities'*; the 1995 SORP did not include the words 'and Reporting'. The Commission have been quoted as stating:

> 'Annual Reports provide charities with a wonderful opportunity to tell their story, but they can often be presented in dull and outdated prose and be unimaginatively structured. We would like to see every charity's report become a key document, explaining why and how the charity does its work and adding to the stock of accountability by charities.'

7.2 Changes in SORP 2005

The Trustees' Annual Report has played a major role in charity accountability since the issue of SORP 1995. In SORP 2005 the reasons why the Trustees' Annual Report is such a key document are clarified. Whilst most of the detailed content of the report was requested in previous SORPs, SORP 2005 builds on these past recommendations by adding a number of additional disclosures to the report, including:

- the name of the chief executive (or senior staff);
- the induction and training provided for new trustees;
- details of any social or programme-related investments;
- principal funding sources, and

- details of any social, environmental and ethical concerns taken account of in investment policy.

SORP 2005 also presents the recommendations for the report in a more structured way using the following six sections:

- reference and administrative details;
- structure, governance and management;
- objectives and activities;
- achievements and performance;
- financial review, and
- plans for future periods.

Reference and administrative details of the charity, its trustees and advisers

Disclosure recommendations are expanded to include the name of any Chief Executive Officer or other senior staff members to whom day-to-day management of the charity is delegated.

Structure, governance and management

SORP 2005 pulls together existing recommendations concerning governance and structure into one section of the report and includes the statement about risks first introduced by SORP 2000. An additional disclosure is added to this section that sets out the policies and procedures adopted by the charity for the induction and training of its trustees.

Objectives and activities

This new section creates a stronger and more focused structure than past SORP recommendations. It is designed to help the reader understand the aims and objectives set by the charity, and the short and long-term strategies and activities undertaken to achieve them.

SORP 2005 confirms that the valuation and inclusion of volunteers' contribution to charity activities is not required within the SOFA; however the SORP encourages trustees to provide readers with sufficient information to understand the role and contribution of volunteers. SORP 2005 also recognises that charities may provide funding through the use of social or programme-related investment, and in such cases the charity's policy for making such investments should now also be explained.

Achievements and performance

Again, this new section provides greater clarity as to disclosure expected about the achievements and performance of the charity and its subsidiary undertakings in the year. A summary of any measures or indicators used by the charity to assess its achievements should be included in the report.

The recommendations of SORP 2000 to report on the effectiveness of fundraising activities have been expanded. In addition to providing details of fundraising performance any material expenditure for future income generation should be explained, together with the effect on both current and future income generation.

SORP 2005 also recognises that factors outside the control of the charity may impact on its ability to achieve the objectives set and, where relevant, details of such factors should be included within the report.

Financial review

SORP 2005 states: 'The report should contain a review of the financial position of the charity and its subsidiaries and a statement of the principal financial management policies adopted in the year'.

Reserves are also now reported as part of the financial review section. The definition of 'reserves' in the glossary has been changed so that designated funds are not automatically excluded from reserves, and flexibility has been introduced for charities to calculate reserves based on their specific circumstances.

This section now also includes details of the charity's principal funding sources and how expenditure has supported the key objectives of the charity. Also, where material investments are held, the report should include details of the extent to which social, environmental or ethical considerations are taken into account in setting investment policy.

Plans for the future

Although SORP 2000 recommended that plans for the future be disclosed in the report, SORP 2005 gives greater emphasis to this disclosure and recommends that future plans should include the aims and key objectives set for future periods and details of any activities planned to achieve them.

7.3 Preparing the Trustees' Annual Report

The trustees of all charities, including small charities, must prepare an annual report. The report should describe what the charity is trying to do and how it is going about it and, as part of the report or attached to it, there should also be a statement containing the legal and administrative details of the charity. Whilst the report is legally a separate document from the accounts, the two are normally presented together in the same publication.

Trustees' annual report

Where required, or requested to, company charities must send the annual report to the Charity Commission together with annual accounts prepared under the Companies Act 2006. The directors' report, as prepared under ss 415–419 of that Act, will not suffice as the Trustees' Annual Report. To be valid as a Trustees' Annual Report, and to avoid the preparation of two separate documents, the directors' report could be expanded to incorporate the additional information recommended by the SORP and the Regulations. In cases where the trustees' report and directors' report are combined as one document, it is recommended that this be made clear either at the beginning of the report and/or in the heading to the report.

7.4 Structure and components

SORP 2005 contains guidance on the presentation of information on the following matters in the trustees' report:

- reference and administrative information;
- structure, governance and management;
- objectives and activities;
- achievements and performance;
- financial review, and
- plans for future periods.

Legal requirements and the SORP do not limit the inclusion of other information within the Trustees' Annual Report or as additional information accompanying the accounts. Charity trustees may incorporate other material into their annual reporting – for example, a chairman's report, environment report, impact assessment or an operating and financial review.

Charities may also use other means of providing information, outside of the accounting and reporting framework, about who they are and what they do. Such information is often tailored to the needs of particular audiences and presented through annual reviews, newsletters and websites. Whilst charity trustees might usefully refer to these other sources of information within their Trustees' Annual Report, such additional information should not be seen as a substitute for good statutory annual reporting.

Company charities must also prepare a Directors' Report in order to meet the requirement of ss 415–419 of the Companies Act 2006. A separate Trustees' Annual Report is not required, provided that any statutory Directors' Report prepared also contains all the information required of the Trustees' Annual Report.

7.5 Reference and administrative information

The report should provide the following reference and administrative information about the charity, its trustees and advisers.

1. The name of the charity, which in the case of a registered charity means the name by which it is registered. Any other name by which a charity makes itself known should also be provided.
2. The charity registration number (in Scotland, the Scottish Charity Number) and, if applicable, the company registration number.
3. The address of the principal office of the charity and in the case of a charitable company the address of its registered office.
4. The names of all of those who were the charity's trustees (Glossary GL 7) or a trustee for the charity on the date the report was approved. Where there are more than 50 charity trustees, the names of at least 50 of those trustees (including all the officers of the charity, e.g., chair, treasurer, etc.) should be provided. Where any charity trustee disclosed is a body corporate, the names of the directors of the body corporate on that date.
5. The name of any other person who served as a charity trustee (Glossary GL 7) or as a trustee for the charity (Glossary GL 59) in the financial year in question.
6. The name of any Chief Executive Officer or other senior staff member(s) to whom day-to-day management of the charity is delegated by the charity trustees.
7. The names and addresses of any other relevant organisations or persons. This should include the names and addresses of those acting as bankers, solicitors, auditors (or independent examiner or reporting accountant) and investment or other principal advisers.

Where the disclosure of the names of any charity trustees, senior staff member, or persons with the power of appointment, or of the charity's principal address could lead to that person being placed in personal danger (for example., in the case of a women's refuge), the charity trustees may dispense with the disclosure provided that (for charities in England and Wales) the Charity Commission has given the trustees the authority to do so. It is recommended that the reasons for such non-disclosure should be given in the report. The directors of charitable companies should note that there is no corresponding dispensation in relation to the disclosure requirements for the statutory directors' report.

Charities that are not subject to a statutory audit requirement may omit the disclosures presented in italics above. However, the disclosure of these items is encouraged as a matter of good practice.

7.6 Structure, governance and management

The report should provide the reader with an understanding of how the charity is constituted, its organisational structure, how its trustees are appointed and trained, and assist the reader to better understand how the charity's decision-making processes operate. The level of detail provided in the report is

Trustees' annual report

likely to be dependent on the size and complexity of the charity and proportionate to the needs of the users of the report. In particular, the report should explain points 1–6 below.

1. The nature of the governing document (e.g. trust deed, Memorandum and Articles of Association, Charity Commission Scheme, Royal Charter, etc.) and how the charity is (or its trustees are) constituted (e.g. limited company, unincorporated association, trustees incorporated as a body, etc.).
2. The methods adopted for the recruitment and appointment of new trustees, including details of any constitutional provisions relating to appointments – for example, election to post. Where any other person or body external to the charity is entitled to appoint one or more of the charity trustees, this should be explained, together with the name of that person or body.
3. The policies and procedures adopted for the induction and training of trustees.
4. The organisational structure of the charity and how decisions are made. For example, which types of decisions are taken by the charity trustees and which are delegated to staff?
5. Where the charity is part of a wider network (for example, charities affiliated within an umbrella group), the relationship involved should be explained where this impacts on the operating policies adopted by the charity.
6. The relationships between the charity and related parties, including its subsidiaries (see paras 221–229 and Glossary GL 50) and with any other charities and organisations with which it cooperates in the pursuit of its charitable objectives.

A statement should be provided confirming that the major risks to which the charity is exposed, as identified by the trustees, have been reviewed and systems or procedures have been established to manage those risks.

Charities that are not subject to a statutory audit requirement may limit their disclosures within this section to those presented in italics above (para. 44). The additional disclosures of this section are encouraged as a matter of good practice.

7.7 Objectives and activities

The report should help the reader understand the aims and objectives set by the charity, and the strategies and activities undertaken to achieve them. The report may also, where relevant, explain how the objectives set for the year relate to longer term strategies and objectives set by the charity. Where significant activities are undertaken through subsidiary undertakings, these should be explained in the report. In particular, the report should provide:

Achievements and performance

(a) a summary of the objectives of the charity as set out in its governing document;
(b) an explanation of the charity's aims, including the changes or differences it seeks to make through its activities;
(c) an explanation of the charity's main objectives for the year;
(d) an explanation of the charity's strategies for achieving its stated objectives, and
(e) details of significant activities (including its main programmes, projects, or services provided) that contribute to the achievement of the stated objectives

The details of significant activities provided should focus on those activities that the charity trustees consider to be significant in the context of the charity as a whole. The details of activities should, as a minimum, explain the objectives, activities, projects or services identified within the analysis note accompanying charitable activities in the SOFA (see paras 191–194).

Where the charity conducts a material part of its activities through grant making, a statement should be provided setting out its grant-making policies.

Where social or programme-related investment (Glossary GL 47) activities are material in the context of charitable activities undertaken, the policies adopted in making such investments should be explained.

Where a charity makes significant use of volunteers in the course of undertaking its charitable or income-generating activities, this should be explained. Whilst measurement issues, including attributing an economic value to such unpaid voluntary contributions, prevent the inclusion of such contributions within the SOFA (see para. 133), it is nevertheless important for readers to be provided with sufficient information to understand the role and contribution of volunteers. Such information may, for example, explain the activities that volunteers help provide, quantify the contribution in terms of hours or staff equivalents, and may present an indicative value of this contribution.

7.8 Achievements and performance

The report should contain information that enables the reader to understand and assess the achievements of the charity and its subsidiary undertakings in the year. It should provide a review of its performance against objectives that have been set. The report is likely to provide both qualitative and quantitative information that helps to explain this. It will often be helpful to identify any indicators, milestones and benchmarks against which the achievement of objectives is assessed by the charity. In particular, the report should contain the following.

(a) A review of charitable activities undertaken that explains the performance achieved against objectives set. Where qualitative or quantitative information is used to assess the outcome of activities, a summary of the measures or indicators used to assess achievement should be included.
(b) Where material fundraising activities are undertaken, details of the performance achieved against fundraising objectives set, commenting on any material expenditure for future income generation and explaining the effect on the current period's fundraising return and anticipated income generation in future periods.
(c) Where material investments are held, details of the investment performance achieved against the investment objectives set.
(d) Comment on those factors within and outside the charity's control that are relevant to the achievement of its objectives; these might include relationships with employees, users, beneficiaries, funders and the charity's position in the wider community.

Charities that are not subject to a statutory audit requirement may limit their disclosures within this section to providing a summary of the main achievements of the charity during the year. The additional disclosures of this section are encouraged as a matter of good practice.

7.9 Financial review

The report should contain a review of the financial position of the charity and its subsidiaries and a statement of the principal financial management policies adopted in the year. In particular, the report should explain the following.

(a) The charity's policy on reserves (Glossary GL 51), stating the level of reserves held and why they are held. Where material funds have been designated, the reserves policy statement should quantify and explain the purpose of the designations and, where set aside for future expenditure, the likely timing of that expenditure.
(b) Where any fund is materially in deficit, the circumstances giving rise to the deficit and details of the steps being taken to eliminate the deficit.
(c) The charity's principal funding sources and how expenditure in the year under review has supported the key objectives of the charity.
(d) Where material investments are held, the investment policy and objectives, including the extent (if any) to which social, environmental or ethical considerations are taken into account.

7.10 Plans for future periods

The report should explain the charity's plans for the future including the aims and key objectives it has set for future periods, together with details of any activities planned to achieve them.

Charities that are not subject to a statutory audit requirement may omit this disclosure, although disclosure of this matter is encouraged as a matter of good practice.

7.11 Funds held as custodian trustee on behalf of others

Where a charity is, or its trustees are, acting as custodian trustees, the following matters should be disclosed in the report:

(a) a description of the assets which they hold in this capacity;
(b) the name and objects of the charity (or charities) on whose behalf the assets are held and how this activity falls within their own objects, and
(c) details of the arrangements for safe custody and segregation of such assets from the charity's own assets.

Annex 1 Comprehensive example – Training For Life

Company No: 02959580
Registered Charity Number: 1040422

Training For Life Limited
Report and Financial Statements for the year ended 31 December 2007

Contents

	Page
Trustees, officers and registered office	1
Report of the Trustees	2–14
Report of the independent auditors	15–16
Consolidated statement of financial activities	17
Consolidated and charity balance sheet	18
Notes to the financial statements	19–27

We are very grateful for support that we receive.

Corporate supporters include:

Adhoc pr	Goldman Sachs
Anchor Partnerships Limited	Goldwins Chartered Accountants
Argles Stoneham Burstows	Hilton Thompson Limited
Arq International	C Hoare & Co
ASB Travel Solutions	HBOS
B & W Group Limited	HSBC
Barclays Bank	Interserve (Defence) Limited
Bonhams	JP Morgan
Brewin, Leighton, Paisner	KPMG
Buro Happold	Liberty Wines
Burson Martseller	Lovells
Cisco Systems	Mazars
Charles Forte Foundation	Meridian Pure
Cobra Beer	More London Development
Compass Group	Natwest Bank
Conran Restaurants	Permira
Cormack Tancy	Pinfolds
Coutts Bank	SEI Investments
Credit Suisse	Slaughter and May
Deutsche Bank	Sodexho UK & Ireland
Dresdner Kleinwort Wasserstein	The Hilton Group
Dome Consulting	Thomas Miller & Co
Eugena Limited	Trust House Forte

Comprehensive example – Training for Life

Adhoc pr
Field Fisher Waterhouse
Gadespring
Gensler
Gerald Eve
Gilmore Hankey Kirke Limited
The Golden Bottle Trust

Goldman Sachs
UBS
Unilever
Virgin Airways
Vizards Tweedie
Whitbread
Zigfrid Limited

Many others provided their support through attendance at events

Government, Trusts, Foundations and Third Sector supporters include:

British Hospitality Association
Bridge House Trust
Brookes Charitable Trust
Centrepoint
City Parochial Foundation
Cleveland Education Limited
The Clothworkers' Foundation
Community Action Network
David & Elaine Potter Charitable Trust
Department for Communities and Local Government
Dollis Hill House Trust
Doncaster Borough Council

Downside Fisher Youth Club
East London e-Learning
The Forte Charitable Trust
Futurebuilders England
Hackney Community College
Hackney Works
HM Customs and Revenue
The Henry Smith Charity
The Housing Corporation
Garfield Weston Foundation

Government Office for London
The Ingham Trust
The Learning Trust
The Leathersellers' Company
Lewisham College
Lawrence Atwell's Charity
Learning and Skills Council
Learn Direct

London Borough of Lambeth
London Borough of Southwark
London Councils
London Development Agency
Marathon Trust
Mercer's Company
Ministry of Defence
People 1st

Persula Foundation

Places for People
The Rank Foundation
Renaisi
Royal Borough of Kensington and Chelsea
The Royal British Legion
The Salters' Company
Savoy Educational Trust
School for Social Entrepreneurs
Shoreditch Trust
Sir Oswald Stoll Foundation
Sport England
Social Enterprise London
South Hams District Council
Southwest Regional Development Agency
Spectrum Housing Group
StreetSmart
Thames Valley University
The 29th May 1961 Charitable Trust
University of Northampton
Westminster City Council
Wooden Spoon Society

Annex 1 Comprehensive example – Training For Life

British Hospitality Association
London Borough of Barking & Dagenham

London Borough of Brent

London Borough of Hackney
London Borough of Hammersmith & Fulham
London Borough of Islington

London Borough of Lambeth

The Worshipful Company of Cooks
The Worshipful Company of Haberdashers
The Worshipful Company of Innholders

Working Links
Venture Partnership Foundation
Youth Education Support Service

Training For Life Limited is a company limited by guarantee and is a registered charity (Registered number 1040422) and registered under the Companies Act 1985 (Co Number 2959580).

The liability of members in the event of the charity being wound up is limited to £1 each.

Registered office
37 Houndsditch
London
EC3A 7DB

Trustees
Rev Canon Peter Challen
Mr Keith Faulkner
Ms Jacqueline Henderson
Mr Alexander Hoare
Mr Niall O'Gara Resigned: 17 May 2007
Mr Ron Perry
Baroness Dorothea Glenys Thornton
Mr Simon Ward Resigned: 3 May 2007

Bankers
HSBC Bank Plc
123 Chancery Lane
London
WC2A 1QH

Solicitors
Vizards Tweedie
42 Bedford Row
London
WC1V 1QH

Auditors
Goldwins Limited
Chartered Accountants
75 Maygrove Road
West Hampstead
London
NW6 2EG

***Chief Executive* Gordon D'Silva**
***Company Secretary* Pat Haikin**

The trustees, who are directors of the company, present their annual report and the charity's financial statements for the year ended 31 December 2007.

Reference and Administrative Details of the Charity, its Trustees and Advisers

Details of the charity's addresses, its trustees and advisers are given on page 1.

Structure, Governance and Management

Training For Life Limited is a company limited by guarantee and is a registered charity (1040422) and registered under the Companies Act 1985 (2959580). The liability of members in the event of the charity being wound up is limited to £1 each.

Trustees who served during the year were as listed on page one. There is provision for a minimum number of six Trustees on the Board of Directors, each of whom is subject to annual re-election at the Annual General Meeting.

Trustees are recruited by a variety of methods including recommendations from existing Trustees or by members of the senior management team. Each individual who has been recommended is then interviewed by the Chairman and other Trustees as appropriate and then elected by the Board. New Trustees are provided with an induction pack and an induction session is conducted by the Chief Executive. Trustees are given regular presentations on the business of the charity at their meetings.

The Trustees elect a Chairman, a Vice Chairman and a Treasurer from their number. A Finance and General Purposes Committee has been established with its main terms of reference being to:

- review and monitor the accounting processes;
- oversee preparation of the financial accounts;
- advise on financial information requirements of the Board of Trustees; and
- advise on appointment of senior financial staff.

Annex 1 Comprehensive example – Training For Life

The Trustees are responsible for setting the strategic direction of the charity and day to day decisions are delegated to the Chief Executive.

During the year, Training For Life had two wholly owned subsidiaries:

- **Hoxton Apprentice Limited:** is a training restaurant that has developed its innovative Apprenticeship programme to prepare young people for employment. Further details are provided later in the report.
- **Meta Central Limited**: this company is dormant.

Training For Life also holds a 42 per cent interest in another entity, 16 Hoxton Square Limited. This company has a long-term lease on 16 Hoxton Square, that houses a Prospect Centre operated by Training For Life. Again, further details are provided later in the report.

Since the year end, Training for Life underwent a corporate restructure to separate the group's businesses into sectoral expertise and to minimise risk. This has resulted in the addition of two significant new subsidiaries, Dartmouth Apprentice Limited and Prospects for Life Limited.

Risk management

The trustees and management of Training For Life carried out a review of the charity's activities in order to identify the major opportunities available to the charity and the risks to which it is exposed. A risk management strategy has been finalised that comprises an annual review of the risks that the charity might face; the establishment of systems and procedures to mitigate those risks identified; and an implementation plan designed to minimise any potential impact on the charity should any of those risks materialise.

Objectives, activities and achievements

The objects of Training For Life, as set out in its governing document, is to 'provide and promote the education and training of people who are unemployed, in particular by the provision of advice and training in skills needed in employment to enable them to obtain gainful employment.'

Training For Life is an enterprising organisation that helps people who have faced difficulties make positive changes to their lives. It has developed its own entrepreneurial approach and methods of learning to help people make the move into lasting employment and economic self-sufficiency.

People who come to Training For Life want to change their lives for the better. They want to work, but they have obstacles to overcome. They will have gaps in their learning, they may have an unsettled lifestyle, or they might just have been out of work for some time and lost confidence and energy.

But, given the right support and the right opportunities, people who have experienced challenge in their lives can demonstrate qualities that are of enormous benefit to society: tenacity, determination and the resilience to overcome difficulties, empathy, enthusiasm and the imagination to solve problems.

We help people who are at most risk of social and economic exclusion in society. One fundamental indicator of inclusion is participation in the world of work. Training For Life is committed to taking people who want and need to work on a journey to improve their prospects. But we know that just addressing their vocational needs will not be enough for them to get and keep a job. So, we tailor programmes to take into account how the trainees feel about themselves and how they live their lives. We help people develop the skills that equip them for work through personal learning and work-based training and experience leading to vocational qualifications. We help them find a job and then the support to enable them to thrive.

To support our objectives, we deliver our activities through enterprising learning communities known as 'prospect centres'. Each prospect centre has a particular industry focus, with customised practical learning and vocational training in social enterprises that provide real work experience and support for our apprentices and income for the charity.

The charity has five key strategies to help deliver the objects:

- To create Prospect centres in areas of high unemployment that retain community buildings for community use; that combine regeneration priorities of training and social enterprise and, as regeneration projects, that create jobs for local people;
- To deliver a learning methodology that engages individuals who have not been able to take advantage of traditional learning opportunities;
- To create communities of learning and enterprises that train and employ beneficiaries in real business that are industry specific and industry led through corporate partnerships;
- To match skills to opportunities and opportunities to employer needs through employer compacts that have, in turn, the potential to complement a company's corporate social responsibility strategy;
- To create an online toolkit that supports the development of a licence and franchise model to build capability and capacity of local individuals and groups to deliver prospect centres against key quality standards and benchmarks.

Overview

Last year we consolidated two important areas of activity that underpin every aspect of how we work:

Annex 1 Comprehensive example – Training For Life

- We reviewed the content and delivery of our learning journey that provides a holistic response to the needs of unemployed people and captured this within an online resource available to staff and clients at any of our dispersed prospect centres;
- We also reviewed the methodology by which we run our prospect centres and social enterprises and captured that into a common framework, a 'toolkit', that has become an online resource to enable future prospect centres and social enterprises to be established on the basis of current best practice. The 'toolkit' provides for a two-way exchange of activity and intelligence, enabling the model to be dynamic, growing in effectiveness as new prospect centres feed into the 'toolkit' and contribute to its evolution.

We continued to consolidate the two major new initiatives launched in 2006:

- a prospect centre dedicated to providing services for disabled people at 42 Westbourne Park Road in Westminster;
- a prospect centred working specifically with homeless ex-service people at Westway Beacons in Hammersmith and Fulham.

We continued to focus on the development of future prospect centres and worked specifically on:

- the £2.4 million capital refurbishment in Southwark, in partnership with The Downside Settlement, of an existing centre to create a prospect centre with a health and fitness focus and to take over responsibility for a youth club for children and young people;
- the £3.0 million capital refurbishment of a redundant church in Dartmouth, Devon in partnership with Signpost Housing Association to develop 11 flats for homeless people and a social enterprise restaurant with linked training.

Since the year end, both these projects have been completed. The prospect centre in Southwark has opened but is not yet fully operational and the operation of the restaurant and flats in Dartmouth commenced in July 2008.

We responded to significant requests from local authorities and from other charities for support in adopting the Training For Life prospect centre model of regeneration, particularly where that model included social enterprise activity.

We reviewed the structure of the charity in order to arrive at a model that provided continuity and consistency for current service delivery, that released management time to take advantage of development potential and that took account of succession issues. This led to a corporate and management restructure that is now being implemented.

In terms of finance/funding, our overall budget has increased and the emphasis continues to be on attracting future core funding and on increasing work with clients to improve employment sustainability.

Comprehensive example – Training for Life

Programmes

In 2007, Training For Life worked with more than 1,500 people. Of these about 60 per cent were women and more than 70 per cent were from Black, Asian, Mixed Race or other ethnic groupings.

We ran over 20 different programmes in our prospect centres, ranging from one-day taster/engagement sessions to six- and ten-month Apprenticeships. All emphasised personal development in preparing trainees to make the transition into education, further training or employment.

Our established training programmes continued but with the major ESF-funded group of programmes that had been running over the last three years coming to an end during 2007. A break in the availability of new ESF funding resulted in some gaps in service delivery in the second half of the year as applications were made for the new ESF-supported programme beginning in 2008.

New programmes in 2007 included our 'In Touch' alumni support programme, continuing the investment we make in people, from when they graduate from our programmes and adjust to new working environments and perhaps a new home. Funded by Deutsche Bank, with support from Cisco Systems, the In Touch project provides targeted support when people need it, backed up by a developing alumni network to track and support graduates from our practical learning programmes. In Touch will use coaching and high levels of personal contact provided by Training For Life, backed up by a dedicated website and SMS text technology to check progress and effectively deal with and prevent trigger points that could otherwise result in unemployment or crisis.

London becoming an Olympic City has been an additional spur to our work on a hospitality pilot to broker job outcomes in the hospitality and catering industry for our trainees. Our hospitality brokerage was a new partnership with Hackney Council and local employers to help people to see hospitality and catering as a career rather than low-status stop-gap employment. The pilot is also helping to meet local business need by providing training for people where they need it.

To break the 'no home, no job' cycle, we have also developed a new HomeWork Apprentice programme that integrates personal development training, real work experience through the Apprenticeship programme and intensive and specific individual support to help our Hoxton Apprentices who have experienced or are at risk of homelessness to move into settled accommodation and a job.

During 2007 we delivered our programmes under a variety of contracts with a number of different funders including:

Annex 1 Comprehensive example – Training For Life

Funders and supporters	Programme and projects funded
Barclays Foundation	Financial awareness
Bridge House Trust	Core funding
British Telecom	Hoxton Apprentice
Cisco Systems	In Touch
City Parochial Foundation	Networking Women industry orientation
Community Action Network	Working capital
Compass Group	Hoxton Apprentice
Corporation of London	Capital works on Prospect Centres
Dartmouth & Kinswear Society	Capital works on Prospect Centres
Department for Communities and Local Government	Capital works on Prospect Centres The Phase Project
Deutsche Bank	In Touch
Downside Fisher Youth Club	Prospect Centres
European Social Fund, through Government Office for London, London Development Agency and London Councils	IT Link Prospect Centres Networking Women Women into IT
The Forte Charitable Trust	Hoxton Apprentices
Futurebuilders England	IT Systems and online toolkit
Garfield Weston Foundation	Capital works on Prospect Centres
Hackney Community College	HOST hospitality programme
Hackney Council	Gymtrain, feasibility study
Hackney Works	Hoxton Apprentices
HBOS	Hoxton Apprentices starter packs
Henry Smith Charity	Capital works on Prospect Centres
HM Revenue & Customs	Taxability
The Holliday Foundation	Hoxton Apprentices
Lawrence Atwell's Charity	Hoxton Apprentices
Learning and Skills Councils	Homework Apprentices Future Focus Sport Street Sport Westway On Line
Learn Direct	Learn Direct Project

Comprehensive example – Training for Life

Funders and supporters	Programme and projects funded
London Borough of Islington	Network Apprentices ICT/ILM EC1 Apprentices
London Borough of Lambeth	The Get Set Fund
London Borough of Southwark	Prospect Centre
London Councils	SETTLE: On line toolkit
London Development Agency	Women into IT
Marathon Trust	Capital works on Prospect Centres
Mercer's Company	Capital contribution for Prospect Centres
People 1st	Brokerage into Hospitality
Royal Borough of Kensington and Chelsea	Westminster Project
Savoy Educational Trust	Apprentice Sponsorship
Shoreditch Trust	Whitmore ESOL
Sir Oswald Stoll Foundation	StollNet
Sport England	Capital works on Prospect Centres
South Hams District Council	Capital works on Prospect Centres
Street Smart	Apprentice sponsorship
The Learning Trust	Project support
The Leathersellers Charitable Trust	Hoxton Apprentices
The Royal British Legion	Project Compass
The Venture Partnership Foundation	Core funding
Westminster City Council	Revenue funding for Westminster Prospect Centre
The Wooden Spoon Society	Capital works on Prospect Centres
Worshipful Company of Cooks	Homework Apprentices
Worshipful Company of Innholders	Hoxton Apprentices
Working Links	IT Link Accelerate Hoxton Apprentices Homework Apprentices
Youth Education Support Service	Apprentices

During the year, we also developed Social Enterprise income through property rental and services to other voluntary sector organisations, Networks for Life and through our wholly owned subsidiary, Hoxton Apprentice Limited.

Annex 1 Comprehensive example – Training For Life

Prospect Centres

Training For Life's practical learning programmes develop entrepreneurial skills across a range of industries and locations.

A summary of activity in each prospect centre is set out below.

Training For Life Westminster Centre for Independent Living

Training For Life was awarded a five-year contract by the City of Westminster to manage a centre providing for disabled people in the Borough of Westminster and began operations under the contract in October 2006.

The centre occupies a modern purpose built building at 42 Westbourne Park Road. Since its inception eight years ago, the centre has run as a day centre providing respite care for an average of thirty disabled people a day and outreach support to others in the community. A significant proportion of the clients is elderly and most have attended the centre for a considerable period of time. A range of activities is available to enhance well-being and stimulate interest but there has been limited interaction with mainstream activity and limited progression.

The orientation of the centre has shifted to become a Centre for Independent Living to enable many more disabled people in Westminster (particularly young people) to access support from the centre and to participate as actively as they want in society including in employment.

This necessitated a major shift in culture and operation within the centre and significant activity within the borough to attract new service users and to establish new provision. The centre will be run by disabled people for disabled people. Senior members of the charity received training from Harrow Association of Disabled People, to help Training For Life understand how best to implement practical learning programmes that are effective in helping people with disabilities to access the labour market.

The Centre has provided Training For Life with the opportunity to extend its expertise into working with disabled people and, thus, to ensure that they are properly represented in its existing and new prospect centres.

The Centre supported over 300 disabled people during 2007.

Training For Life Westway Beacons

The centre is part of a new housing complex in East Acton built by Threshold Housing Association in partnership with Sir Oswald Stoll Foundation. Training For Life has a 'learning zone' and a 'community zone' there that provide training and support for new residents, specifically for homeless ex-service people who have had trouble readjusting to civilian life.

Training For Life runs Project Compass from the centre, funded by the Royal British Legion and supported by the Ministry of Defence and KPMG. The project provides ex-service people with work-orientated coaching, skills training and work experience with a job brokerage service to help find the right jobs to lead them to financial independence.

The centre supported over 80 ex-service people in 2006.

Training For Life City

In 2006 and 2007, Training For Life started to reorientate the focus of its City Prospect Centre away from IT support and networking to enterprise and administration. A survey commissioned by Training For Life of nearly 800 Hackney and City companies indicated that the local labour market served by the prospect centre had changed. One of the main findings from the survey was that the market was already oversubscribed, resulting in reduced demand for IT graduates from our training programmes.

New training elements are being introduced to provide opportunities for the charity to investigate, develop and test solutions to generating enterprising behaviour that could lead to self-employment or increase capability in employment.

Many of the people accessing our practical learning programmes have limited financial acumen and often need specific financial advice and support to understand how to successfully manage their money and their lifestyles, so that they can access and keep a job and also their home. In 2006 and 2007 the Office of the Deputy Prime Minister funded Training For Life to develop the PHASE (Preventing Homelessness and Securing Employment) project. Strands of this programme help to develop the financial awareness of trainees and support the development of an interactive money management game.

During 2007, Training for Life worked with a number of partners on plans to use the centre as a incubator space and serviced accommodation for those wishing to start their own enterprises. However, these plans did not come to fruition and the accommodation remained underutilised for some of 2007. In 2008, a decision was made to let the space to reduce the burden of meeting the premises costs and the property was let in May 2008.

Our head office has been retained in the City.

16 Hoxton Square and the Hoxton Apprentice Restaurant

Our first prospect centre in Shoreditch opened in 2004 with an integral social enterprise, Hoxton Apprentice restaurant that focuses on opportunity within the hospitality industry and provides training and work experience in catering and hospitality. The 16 Hoxton Square Prospect Centre enabled over 300 people to benefit from training mainly related to the hospitality industry.

The restaurant has become a popular and successful venue, was voted one of the 320 best places to eat in the UK by Tatler's 2006 Restaurant Guide and is listed in the Michelin Guide. Its strategic corporate partner is Compass Group plc, which provides financial support, expertise, secondments and quality jobs for successful graduates in the catering and hospitality industry.

With an industry focus on catering and hospitality, Hoxton Apprentice has been consistently successful commercially and in the throughput of its apprentices into employment. Hoxton Apprentice also developed its innovative Homework Apprenticeship programmes, to prepare young homeless people for employment. In partnership with Places For People and Circle Anglia, Apprentices who are homeless were placed in settled accommodation upon graduation as part of the programme..

Since inception, Hoxton Apprentice social business restaurant has helped 60 apprentices to start earning a real wage with real work experience. Ninety per cent of those completing their apprenticeships have moved into full time employment, with 80% still in their jobs six months later.

The partnership with The Bob Breen Martial Arts Academy has also been consolidated and developed in 2007 to incorporate well-being and healthy lifestyles as an important element of the learning journey within 16 Hoxton Square.

Hoxton Apprentice also received recognition as a successful public/private/voluntary sector partnership, in the 2007 Business in the Community Awards for Excellence. Compass Group and the Hoxton Apprentice were Big Tick winners in the Power in Partnership Award.

In 2008, the restaurant continues its success in attracting significant publicity, high ratings for its food, and apprentices anxious to learn new skills and achieve qualifications.

Training For Life Lambeth

Established in 2000, the Met@lambeth gym has helped to improve the health, fitness and lifestyles of people living in the Stockwell area of Lambeth. The industry focus is on improving health and fitness and promoting training and employment options with in the sports and leisure industry.

In 2006, Training For Life Lambeth moved away from an individual membership base to group-participation programmes targeted at hard-to-reach groups such as young people involved in gangs, ex-prisoners, homeless people and those misusing drugs and alcohol.

We launched a 12-week Street Sport programme, working with young people aged 16-24 at risk of homelessness. The programme, which develops a range of personal effectiveness skills, helps trainees to achieve Community Sports Leaders Awards, an NVQ level 1 or 2 in literacy and numeracy as well as a recognised IT qualification.

This programme continued into 2007. With the advent of our new Training For Life Downside Prospect Centre in 2008 providing similar facilities, a decision was taken to close the Lambeth Centre during 2008.

Training For Life Whitmore

An IT-based family learning centre, Training For Life Whitmore operates adjacent to a local primary school in Hackney to help local people, particularly women with children, to improve their ICT skills and provides personal development, ESOL and vocational training for the local community.

The centre runs a Saturday School for local children and has developed a number of programmes to support and engage with the local Turkish community.

During 2007, the charity increased participation on programmes run at Whitmore by incorporating ESOL within elements of our Learning Journey. This change proved successful in helping more of the local community to engage with our learning programmes and develop their personal and vocational skills. We will use our understanding of what has worked by embedding ESOL training as part of our Learning Journey to improve access to our programmes across all of our prospect Ccentres. The centre is also used by trainees from other prospect centres, such Hoxton Square and Westway.

The centre benefited from being awarded Learndirect Centre status and has been able to offer Skills For Life online programmes as an additional resource at the centre.

Development work

Training For Life, Downside, Southwark

Working with The Downside Settlement, this prospect centre, in the London Borough of Southwark, opened in 2008 and is in the process of becoming fully operational. It will have an emphasis on well-being outcomes with a focus on exercise, fitness, diet, nutrition and healthy lifestyles. Based in Bermondsey, the centre is less than five miles from the Olympic 2012 site. The centre will house a gym, training room, dance studio, swimming pool, two indoor sports halls, crèche and healthy community café. Over £2 million has been raised and spent on totally refurbishing the building. The building will run the Downside Fisher

Annex 1 Comprehensive example – Training For Life

youth club that has run from the centre for 33 years and will also provide a range of personal development, health and lifestyle training and enterprise activity.

Training For Life Barnabas, Dartmouth

The charity, working in partnership with Signpost Care Partnership (a registered social landlord providing affordable housing in the South West), has completed the refurbishment of a redundant church in Dartmouth, Devon. The charity has been supported by South Hams District Council, Devon County Council, South West Regional Development Agency, the Department for Communities and Local Government and the Wooden Spoon Society to develop a Prospect Centre in Devon.

The £3 million refurbishment brings the dilapidated St Barnabas church in Dartmouth back into community use with 11 flats for people who have experienced homelessness and a range of social businesses, providing training and employment support for the local community, colleges and businesses. A café, bar and restaurant with retail and performance space opened in July 2008, providing local people with the opportunity to train in employment skills, to sell local produce, to exhibit works and to develop their own enterprises.

Financial review

Training For Life has an enviable track record in accessing funds to build new prospect centres and has created a significant capital base invested in fixed assets. The charity uses these assets to deliver its training and apprentice programmes, which are funded from a variety of sources. The increase in investment in assets and the delivery of training programmes have been achieved against a background of minimal reserves. In addition, the growth in the asset base of the charity has not been matched by a growth in working capital.

In reviewing the financial strategy, the charity considered the value of its fixed assets and concluded that the open-market value of its assets is considerably in excess of their book values. Therefore, the charity is seeking to generate sufficient working capital funds to underpin the charity's financial strategy by leveraging both the capital assets and the 'Apprentice' brand that has been created in its hospitality businesses and training programmes.

Turning to the year, the principal funding sources and their use is set out earlier in this report and in the financial statements. Training for Life had a successful 2007 with a reported surplus of £973,000. The surplus includes income from capital grants and the resulting investment in capital projects was over £2 million in the year.

The provision of a working capital of £175,000 by the CAN Breakthrough Programme and the working capital loan of £300,000 from Future Builders in

2006 assisted greatly, ensuring operational viability whilst allowing us to refocus our operational and training programmes.

However, the investment in fixed assets was considerably in excess of the capital grants made available and there were cost pressures arising from excess space available at the City Prospect Centre, mentioned earlier in this report. These factors led to cashflow pressures, which are being successfully managed.

In April 2008, the charity has assessed its financial position and reviewed its financial strategy with Trustees setting budgets and plans for the future. Key elements of the financial strategy are to diversify income to reduce dependence on statutory contracts, which can carry considerable risks, and to develop relationships with philanthropists and partner organisations to underpin the working capital of the charity and its subsidiaries.

Since the year end, the charity has made a significant investment, with the assistance of Futurebuilders, in an enterprise and resource planning system which is being developed to manage all back-of-house functions, including relationship management, human resources and finance. This has allowed robust financial procedures to be implemented, including weekly cashflow reviews, management reporting against budget to inform decision making and the development of longer-term forecasts.

All of these elements give confidence that the charity will be able to succeed in achieving the reserves policy noted in the section below.

Reserves Policy

Historically, the charity has attracted restricted funding for specific projects, while only a small part of the revenue has been available for the charity to spend freely as it wished. It is a feature of the restricted funding projects that there can be no surplus to pass to reserves on anything other than a short-term basis while anticipating an extension of an earlier contract.

It is the intention of the Trustees that the funding base and the activities of the charity be diversified in order to attract more unrestricted funding and to establish sufficient number of sources so as not to become over dependent upon any single source, thus reducing the overall financial risk to the charity.

The Trustees target level for free reserves is six months of expenditure.

Plans for future periods

Roll-out of Prospect Centres

Our Prospect Centre model is becoming widely recognised and we are increasingly coming under demand to roll out prospect centres in other parts of the country. There is significant demand by local councils to develop prospect centres in their locations, and we are in various stages of discussion with a range of different agencies. Our challenge, vision and desire is not to grow Training For Life, but to share our experience and expertise through a franchising model to locate developments in local communities, supported by an on ine toolkit. In order to do this, Training for Life:

- has developed a business model that is sustainable, based on a growing capital asset base and reinvestment of social enterprise surplus
- has developed an online business process toolkit to support the replication of the Prospect Centre model and
- is developing a significant working capital base to support growth and to ensure the long-term sustainability of the charity and our partners as we roll out the prospect centre model

Development of the Apprentice brand

Training for Life has built a significant social brand that assists individuals, who are homeless or jobless, by combining commercial realities and training support into an apprenticeship. The has many impacts, including:

- empowerment of the individual, making them employable in their chosen industry;
- reducing the burden on the state, where it is estimated that the cost of an unemployed or homeless individual over their lifetime is £1.2 million;
- the redevelopment of buildings into prospect centres, which contributes significantly to regeneration in communities;
- the creation of permanent commercial jobs in the businesses; and
- the repatriation of profits generated by the enterprises created into the charity for reinvestment in training.

Training for Life is seeking to further develop the brand by the development of partnerships with like-minded organisations to assist in the development of its plans for major hospitality and health-based operations.

Trustees' responsibilities

The Trustees are responsible for preparing the financial statements in accordance with applicable law and United Kingdom Generally Accepted Accounting Practice.

Company law requires the Trustees to prepare financial statements for each financial year, which give a true and fair view of the charitable company's financial activities during the year and of its financial position at the end of the year. In preparing those financial statements, the Trustees are required to:

- select suitable accounting policies and apply them consistently;

- make judgements and estimates that are reasonable and prudent;
- prepare the financial statements on the going concern basis unless it is inappropriate to presume that the charitable company will continue in business.

The trustees are responsible for keeping proper accounting records, which disclose with reasonable accuracy the financial position of the charity and which enable them to ascertain the financial position of the charity and which enable them to ensure that the financial statements comply with the Companies Act 1985. They are also responsible for safeguarding the assets of the charity and hence for taking reasonable steps for the prevention and detection of fraud and other irregularities.

Trustees' statement of disclosure to auditor

So far as the Trustees are aware, there is no relevant audit information of which the charity's auditors are unaware and they have taken all the necessary steps that they ought to have taken as trustees to make themselves aware of any relevant audit information and to establish that the charity's auditors are aware of that information.

Auditors

The auditors during the year were Goldwins Limited Chartered Accountants. A resolution will be proposed at the Annual General Meeting that Goldwins Limited be reappointed as auditors to the company for the ensuing year.

By order of the Trustees

Keith Faulkner
Chair of the Board of Trustees
27 October 2008

Chapter 8 – Reserves

8.1 Introduction

In the commercial world the term 'reserve' is used in a variety of ways and to describe many areas of business activities. The accounts of businesses normally include reserves in one form or another: for example, the accounts of trading companies are required to have a heading 'Capital and Reserves' on the face of the balance sheet and, at the very least, reserves will normally include the balance on the profit and loss account. Indeed, the definition of reserves given in the Glossary to the SORP begins by stating that such a term 'has a variety of technical and ordinary meanings, depending on the context in which it is used'.

In contrast to trading companies, however, the balance sheet of a charity is required to disclose its 'funds', split, as a minimum, between income funds (whether unrestricted or restricted) and endowment funds. Indeed, there is no reference to reserves within the SORP paragraphs dealing with the structure of the balance sheet. Although, in practice, the public may often consider the funds of a charity are its reserves, the term has no legal definition in relation to charities.

However, the Charity Commission quite clearly does regard a charity as having reserves and the Commission's guidance and requirements are extensive. This chapter deals with charity reserves as viewed by the Charity Commission. In addition, the Charity Commission has produced operational guidance (OG) on charity income reserves, which is available on the Charity Commission's website and, in particular, it describes why the issue is so important –, for example, by discussing the question of reserves that may be either too large or too small.

8.2 Charity reserves

8.2.1 Funds of a charity

Before discussing the level of reserves within a charity, it is important to understand the different funds that a charity may have, and these are dealt with both in Chapter 11 (*Accounting for separate funds*) and in Charity Commission guidance CC19 – 'Charities' reserves'. In summary, the funds of a charity may be divided as follows:

(a) unrestricted income funds, which may be
- general,
- designated;
(b) restricted income funds; and
(c) endowment capital funds, which may be:
- permanent, or
- expendable.

8.2.2 Reserves of a charity

SORP 2005 states: 'The report should contain a review of the financial position of the charity and its subsidiaries and a statement of the principal financial management policies adopted in the year'. Reserves are also now reported as part of the financial review section. The reserves definition in the glossary has been changed so that designated funds are not automatically excluded from reserves and flexibility has been introduced for charities to calculate reserves based on their specific circumstances.

In both the operational guidance and CC19, the Charity Commission uses the term 'reserves' to describe that part of a charity's income funds that are freely available for its general purposes after it has met its commitments and covered its other planned expenditure. These are therefore normally referred to as 'free reserves'.

The glossary to the SORP contains the following definition:

'The term "reserves" has a variety of technical and ordinary meanings, depending on the context in which it is used. In this SORP the term "reserves" (unless otherwise indicated) describes that part of a charity's income funds that is freely available.'

The greater flexibility of the definition is recognised by the following comment from the glossary:

'Individual charities may have more or less reserves available to them than this simple calculation suggests, for example:

- Expendable endowments may be readily available for spending or
- Unrestricted funds may be earmarked or designated for essential future spending and reduce the amount readily available.'

In fulfilling the requirement to disclose the charity's policies on reserves, the three key questions are:

- What is meant by reserves?
- What constitutes an acceptable reserves policy?
- How should this policy be disclosed?

The Charity Commission's CC19 guidance was revised in March 2008 and sets out help on the three questions above. Operational guidance (OG 43) gives practical examples of both acceptable and unacceptable reserves policies and their disclosure.

What is meant by reserves?

Reserves are defined as 'the resources that the charity has or can make available to spend, for any or all of the charity's purposes, once it has met its commitments and its other planned expenditure'.

More specifically, CC19 defines reserves as income which becomes available to the charity and is to be spent at the trustees' discretion in furtherance of any of the charity's objects (sometimes referred to as 'general purpose' income), but which is not yet spent, committed or designated (that is, is 'free').

This definition of reserves therefore excludes:

- permanent endowment;
- expendable endowment;
- restricted funds;
- designated funds, and
- income funds that could only be realised by disposing of fixed assets held for charity use

There is an argument for saying that expendable endowment and designated income funds ought to be counted as reserves. The argument is that in each case the trustees are free to regard the funds, if they so choose, as available for general purpose expenditure. There are no legal restrictions preventing trustees treating those two types of funds as free, general purpose funds. But there are practical reasons, why the funds should not normally be regarded as free, though there are exceptions. A charity will not be justified in creating, or transferring resources to, a designated fund where the main purpose of doing this is to allow the charity to show a reduced level of reserves. By contrast, restricted funds can never be regarded as general purpose funds.

Restricted income funds do not fall within the scope of reserves as the term is used in this SORP. Nevertheless, the legal principles on the retention of income apply to restricted income funds, as do the principles of justifying and explaining any retention.

For the purpose of applying the principles in this SORP, it is suggested that trustees treat each restricted income fund as if it were a separate charity. Thus, each restricted income fund could have its own 'reserve', which should be justified and, if practicable, explained in its own right.

8.2.3 Reserves policy

The Charity Commission first recommended that charities should have a formal reserves policy when CC19 was originally issued in May 1997. SORP 2005 and the 2000 Regulations formalised that recommendation into a requirement.

SORP 2005 made some changes to the disclosure requirements for reserves.

Following SORP 2005 and CC19, the trustees should:

- justify the holding of reserves;
- formally discuss, agree and record in writing the reserves policy based on a realistic assessment of their reserves needs, and
- report on the reserves policy and level of reserves in the annual report (see Chapter 7).

In general, the reserves policy should cover, as a minimum:

- policy on reserves stating the level of reserves held and why they are held;
- where material funds have been designated, the reserves policy statement should quantify these; and
- explain the purpose of the designations and, where set aside for future expenditure, the likely timing of that expenditure.

What constitutes an acceptable reserves policy?

A charity's reserves policy should be informed by:

- its forecasts for levels of income in future years, taking into account the reliability of each source of income and the prospects for opening up new sources;
- its forecasts for expenditure in future years on the basis of planned activity;
- its analysis of any future needs, opportunities, contingencies or risks the effects of which are not likely to be able to be met out of income if and when they arise, and
- its assessment, on the best evidence reasonably available, of the likelihood of each of those needs arising and the potential consequences for the charity of not being able to meet them.

How should the reserves policy be disclosed?

A charity's purpose in reporting on reserves is to disclose the level of its reserves and to explain convincingly why it needs that level of reserves. The policy should cover as a minimum:

- the reasons why the charity needs reserves;
- what level (or range) of reserves the trustees believe the charity needs;

- how the level or range stated in the policy compares to the year-end reserves;
- what steps the charity is going to take to establish or maintain reserves at the agreed level (or range), and
- arrangements for monitoring and reviewing the policy.

Where material funds have been designated, SORP 2005 sets out that the reserves policy statement should quantify and explain the purpose of the designations and, where set aside for future expenditure, the likely timing of that expenditure.

If a charity has more resources than it could reasonably need to fulfil all of its purposes, the trustees should contact the Charity Commission. The law requires that charitable resources are applied for charitable purposes, even if trustees cannot find a way of using those resources within their existing objects. The Commission has the power to enable the charity to alter its governing document to allow the charity to use its resources more widely than its existing objects permit. Trustees have a legal duty(under s. 13(5) of the Charities Act 1993) to apply for such a scheme where it is appropriate.

This section also includes details of the charity's principal funding sources and how expenditure has supported the key objectives of the charity. Also, where material investments are held, the report should include details of the extent to which social, environmental or ethical considerations are taken into account in setting investment policy.

8.3 Examples of reserves policy

The policies presented reflect the requirements of SORP 2005.

Example A   Arts Theatre Trust Limited

Reserves policy

The trustees have forecast the level of free reserves (that is those funds not tied up in fixed assets and restricted funds) the charity will require to sustain its operations over the period when it is anticipated that some of the income generating activities may be curtailed temporarily whilst the anticipated project will be carried out. The actual free reserves at the year end were £381,000. Whilst the current free level of reserves may prove sufficient, it is the trustees' view that it is prudent to ensure that there are sufficient free reserves to provide financial flexibility over the course of the forthcoming challenges.

The trustees have therefore planned a new fund-raising strategy concentrating on raising funds from our existing audiences and customers of our wholly owned

Reserves

trading subsidiary, HTC Limited, with a view to increasing our free reserves to the appropriate level. The trustees will closely monitor this initiative against the targets which have been set. As part of the feasibility study, we have shared our plans with our bankers, Cruffs Bank plc, which has indicated that it will provide support in order to see our planned developments come to fruition.

Example B   Dorsetshire Drugs Advice Centre

Reserves

At present the free reserves amount to £16,567. The management committee considers that this level is not sufficient and is considering ways in which additional unrestricted funds can be raised.

The management committee has established a policy whereby the unrestricted funds not invested in tangible fixed assets ('the free reserves') held by the charity should be between three and six months' worth of the resources expended, which equates to £60,000 to £120,000 in general funds. At this level, the management committee feels that it would be able to continue activities of the charity in the event of a significant drop in funding. It would obviously be necessary to consider how the funding would be replaced or activities changed.

Example C   The Rosanna Grant Trust

Reserves

It is the policy of the charity to maintain unrestricted funds, which are the free reserves of the charity, at a level which equates to approximately six months' unrestricted expenditure. This provides sufficient funds to cover management and administration and support costs and to respond to emergency applications for grants which arise from time to time. Unrestricted funds were maintained at this level throughout the year.

Example D   Aid Overseas

Reserves

The free reserves at 30 September consist of the general reserves of £2.7million, less financial commitments not accrued in the financial statements amounting to approximately £0.9million when secured funding is taken into account.

The trustees have examined the requirement for free reserves, which are those unrestricted funds not invested in fixed assets. The trustees consider that, given the nature of our work, this should be approximately £3million, which gives flexibility to cover temporary timing differences for grant claims, adequate working capital for our core costs, and will allow us to respond quickly to emergencies where immediate relief is needed. The trustees therefore plan to retain £0.5million each year until the target for unrestricted free reserves is reached.

Example E   The Edinburgh Educational Trust

Reserves

The free reserves represent the unrestricted funds arising from past operating results. The trustees are satisfied that the balance of free reserves of £311,109 approximates to the equivalent of two months' operating expenditure, which is satisfactory given the revenue funding secured with the Scottish Executive and local authorities, the contractual obligations to staff and the ongoing maintenance of those parts of the campus not affected by the current major building works. The trustees have examined the requirement to maintain free reserves and concluded that the most appropriate level is between two and three months of operational expenditure.

Example F   The Higher College Charity

Reserves

Unrestricted funds amounted to £9,261,000, but only £1,146,000 of this is freely available because the balance is invested in fixed assets or is designated for other purposes (see note 14). The Board has determined that the appropriate level of free reserves which are not invested in tangible fixed assets or designated for other purposes should be equivalent to 12 weeks' expenditure, approximately £2,000,000.

Our policy is, therefore, to continue building up reserves to that level by means of annual operating surpluses and judicious management of our investment assets, supplemented by general purpose appeals from time to time.

Example G   The ABC Charity

Reserves

During the year the charity's general reserve increased from £2,900,000 to £4,785,000 (see note 17).

The Trustees have reviewed the reserves of the charity. This review encompassed the nature of the income and expenditure streams, the need to match variable income with fixed commitments and the nature of the reserves. The review concluded that to allow the charity to be managed efficiently and to provide a buffer for uninterrupted services, a general reserve equivalent to £3,500,000 should be maintained. This equates to approximately seven months of unrestricted fund expenditure. The budget for the next two years has forecast deficits to reduce the general fund to the level agreed by the trustees.

8.4 Revaluation reserve

Where fixed assets (other than investments) are revalued, then, assuming the revaluing is upwards, a revaluation reserve will arise. However, since any such valuation is reflected within the Statement of Financial Activities (SOFA), it will automatically form part of the funds in which the revalued asset is held and is therefore not necessarily shown separately. Nor will it form part of the charity's free reserves, as these specifically exclude this class of fixed assets.

However, under the Companies Act 2006 there is a requirement to show separately the revaluation reserve. The SORP therefore recommends that charitable companies disclose revaluation reserves by way of a prominent inset on the face of the balance sheet.

Where there are impairment losses or downward reductions, these can be offset against the revaluation reserve.

Chapter 9 – The Statement of Financial Activities

9.1 Introduction

In terms of presentation, the main feature, and the most controversial change introduced by the 1995 SORP was the introduction of a new statement, the Statement of Financial Activities (SOFA). This is an omnibus statement which, by including all changes to all funds, takes fund accounting to its logical conclusion. Paragraph 69 of the 1995 SORP explained the reasoning behind its introduction:

> 'A traditional income and expenditure account with the distinction between revenue and capital does not always fully explain all the charity's activities, whose primary purpose must be the provision of benefit to its beneficiaries rather than the corporate pursuit of gain for the benefit of shareholders. Furthermore, since charities often receive significant amounts of restricted income which can affect the types and level of service they provide, it is important to consider changes in the amounts of all the resources of the charity. A single accounting statement is now proposed which will analyse all capital and income resources and expenditures and contain a reconciliation of all movements in the charity's funds. Such analysis will be provided by the Statement of Financial Activities, showing total movements on all funds with supporting analyses in the notes of the movements in individual funds.'

9.2 Changes in SORP 2000

SORP 2000 retained the SOFA as the most important primary statement issued by a charity. Although the fundamental approach of the SOFA did not alter several changes were made to the detailed layout to improve understanding and address problems which arose from the application of the 1995 version. Therefore the format continued to require, for the current year, a columnar split between unrestricted, restricted and endowment funds with a total column, together with a total column for the previous year.

The presentation of incoming resources and resources expended was altered to provide a more logical layout and fit in with the way in which charities handle their transactions and prepare their accounts. Incoming resources of a similar nature were grouped together and resources expended of a similar nature were

The Statement of Financial Activities

also be grouped together. Categories of income and expenditure under these two headings were consolidated on a line-by-line basis where there are subsidiary undertakings (instead of summarising the results of non-charitable trading activities of subsidiary undertakings on a one-line basis).

Charities with a gross income not exceeding the audit threshold do not have to use the standard expenditure headings and sub-headings but can choose expenditure classifications to suit their circumstances.

9.3 Changes in SORP 2005

SORP 2005 retains the overall concept of the SOFA as a primary reporting statement. However, changes have been made to the way that the SOFA is presented. In SORP 2005 the analysis of resources is based on 'activity', rather than 'function' as in the previous SORP. Three activity groups are used:

- charitable activity (achieving the charity's charitable objectives);
- fundraising activity (generating funds to expand on charitable objectives), and
- governance activity (overseeing the work of the charity).

Each of these groups could support a variety of individual activities. Support costs and grants made are not activities and so are not a focus for reporting in SORP 2005. However, charities will be able to report on the extent to which these costs are a part of activities in the notes to the accounts.

Consequently, under SORP 2005 the SOFA provides for the analysis of incoming resources by activity. Incoming resources from generating funds are broken down into the following categories which are matched by a similar breakdown of resources expended on generating funds:

- voluntary income
- activities for generating funds; and
- investment income

As a result of the focus on activities, support costs are no longer shown in the SOFA, as they do not represent a distinct activity of the charity. Support costs are therefore reported in the notes.

Similarly 'grants made' is not a separate activity, but part of grant making, which is one way of delivering a charitable activity. Therefore 'grants made' will normally be shown in the notes rather than the SOFA.

The Charity Commission's publication SORP 2005: *What has Changed?* also states:

> 'Though the main structure of the SOFA is fixed, charities may, within limits, adjust the statement to reflect their particular charity needs. SORP 2005 gives indications of when this may be done, for example by adding a second unrestricted fund column or by changing the order of incoming resources categories within incoming resources.'

9.4 The form and content of the SOFA

Paragraphs 82–220 set out the recommendations regarding the form and content of the SOFA. There are parallel requirements in Regulation 8 (SI 2008 No.679).

Paragraph 82 of SORP 2005 states:

> 'The Statement of Financial Activities is a single accounting statement with the objective of showing all incoming resources and resources expended by the charity in the year on all its funds. It is designed to show how the charity has used its resources in furtherance of its objects for the provision of benefit to its beneficiaries. It shows whether there has been a net inflow or outflow of resources, including capital gains and losses on assets, and provides a reconciliation of all movements in the charity's funds.'

The form of the SOFA is given in Table 3 of the SORP and reproduced below.

Table 9.1 *Table 3 of SORP 2005*

Description	Unrestricted funds	Restricted funds	Endowment funds	Total funds	Previous year total funds
Incoming resources Incoming resources from generated funds: Voluntary income Activities for generating funds Investment income Incoming resources from charitable activities Other incoming resources					
Total incoming resources	A	A	A	A	A

The Statement of Financial Activities

Description	Unrestricted funds	Restricted funds	Endowment funds	Total funds	Previous year total funds
Resources expended Costs of generating funds Costs of generating voluntary income Fundraising trading: costs of goods sold and other costs Investment management costs Charitable activities Governance costs					
Total resources expended	B	B	B	B	B
Net incoming resources before transfers = A–B	C	C	C	C	C
Transfers **Gross transfers between funds**	D	D	D	D	D
Net incoming resources before revaluations and investment asset disposals = C+D	E	E	E	E	E
Other recognised gains and losses					
Gains and losses on revaluations of fixed assets for the charity's own use	F	F	F	F	F
Gains and losses on investment assets	G	G	G	G	G
Actuarial gains/losses on defined benefit pension schemes	H	H	H	H	H
Net movement in funds = E+F+G+H	I	I	I	I	I
Reconciliation of funds					
Total funds brought forward	J	J	J	J	J
Total funds carried forward = I+J	K	K	K	K	K

Thus, as well as the total movements, the SOFA shows, in columnar format, for each prescribed heading, the movements in the principal types of fund (that is, unrestricted, restricted and endowment). This is the minimum segregation permitted on the face of the SOFA. There is nothing to prevent a further analysis (for example, of unrestricted funds, between general and designated funds), however, where space permits. Movements in all material underlying funds should be analysed in the notes, using the headings from, and reconciling with the figures in, the SOFA.

The SOFA should be prepared following the structure described in paras 83–93. Charities should expand the structure, where necessary using notes, in order to present a true and fair view and convey a proper understanding of the nature of all their activities. Charities should, where possible, have a clear link between the incoming and outgoing resources and in particular the functional analysis of activities. Two examples of this are:

(a) a charity running a care home could use the subheading 'Residential care fees' within incoming 'resources from charitable activities' and 'Residential care costs' within 'resources expended on charitable activities'; and
(b) a charity fundraising through a shop could use the subheading 'shops' within 'activities for generating funds' and also within 'costs of generating funds'.

Thus incoming resources and resources expended can be linked together by using similar or identical headings in different parts of the SOFA. A charity may also find it helpful to show extra columns, for instance, to highlight the financial impact of a particular activity.

Some charities may find it informative to their readers to insert additional sub-totals. For example, after 'other costs of generating funds', an additional sub-total 'net incoming resources available for charitable application' may be added.

Headings should be omitted where there is nothing to report for both the current and preceding financial years (para. 91).

Regulation 8 (3)a SI 2008 No.679 requires the SOFA to show the total incoming resources and their application, together with any other movements in the total resources during the financial year. Regulation 8 (7) requires that information to be analysed by reference to the type of fund to which it relates.

The Statement of Financial Activities

9.4.1 SOFA Example

Women's Health and Family Services
Statement of Financial Activities
for the year ended 31 March 2008

	Notes	Unrestricted Funds £	Restricted Funds £	Total 2008 £	Total 2007 £
Incoming resources					
Incoming resources from charitable activities					
Grants receivable	2	–	355,513	355,513	390,012
Fees for services and other sundry income		15,948	15,986	31,934	5,004
Incoming resources from generated funds					
Interest receivable		2,876		2,876	1,682
Total incoming resources		18,824	371,499	390,32	396,698
Less costs of generating funds		8,877	22,258	31,135	28,516
Incoming resources available for charitable application					
		9,947	349,241	359,188	368,182
Resources expended					
Charitable activities					
– Advocacy		–	124,703	124,703	116,073
– Advice and Information		–	100,000	100,000	91,566
– Education		–	119,716	119,716	129,814
Governance costs		2,439	–	2,439	4,224
TOTAL RESOURCES EXPENDED	3	2,439	344,419	346,858	341,677
Net incoming resources before transfers		7,508	4,822	12,330	26,505
Transfers between funds		(2,706)	2,706	–	–
		4,802	7,528	12,330	26,505
Reconciliation of funds					
Fund balances at 1 April		58,096	52,352	110,448	83,943
Fund balances at 31 March		62,898	59,880	122,778	110,448

9.5 Incoming resources

Paragraphs 94–147 of SORP 2005 set out the recommendations relating to incoming resources. Incoming resources should be analysed according to the activity that produced the resources. The analysis adopted should follow that given in Table 3 of SORP 2005 (Table 9.1 above), in particular grouping those resources generated by charitable activity separately from those activities aimed primarily at generating funds. The analysis is repeated below.

(a) Incoming resources from generated funds:
   (i) voluntary income;
   (ii) activities for generating funds, and
   (iii) investment income.
(b) Incoming resources from charitable activities
(c) Other incoming resources

9.5.1 Recognition of incoming resources

SORP 2005 contains a series of general rules on the recognition of incoming resources in paras 94–97. These general rules expand the guidance presented in SORP 2000 and take account of recent developments such as Application Note G to FRS 5.

Incoming resources – both for income and endowment funds – should be recognised in the SOFA when the effect of a transaction or other event results in an increase in the charity's assets. This will depend on the following three criteria being met:

(a) **entitlement** – normally arises when there is control over the rights or other access to the resource, enabling the charity to determine its future application;
(b) **certainty** – when it is virtually certain that the incoming resource will be received, and
(c) **measurement** – when the monetary value of the incoming resource can be measured with sufficient reliability.

Income therefore cannot be recognised until the trustees know that they have a right to receive some income, have a clear idea as to when that income will be received and have a reasonable understanding as to the amount that will be received.

All incoming resources should be reported gross whether raised by the charity or its agents. The SORP applies these general rules by commenting on the following sources of incoming resources:

- contractual arrangements;
- grants and donations receivable;
- funds received as agent, and
- incoming resources subject to restriction.

The Statement of Financial Activities

Contractual arrangements

Some charities earn income by providing goods and services in return for a fee as part of their charitable activities. Such contractual income is recognised in the SOFA to the extent that the charity has provided the service or goods. Where such incoming resources are received in advance then a charity may not have entitlement to those resources until the goods or services have been provided. In this situation incoming resources received in advance should be deferred until the charity becomes entitled to the resources. Certain grant funding arrangements may contain conditions that closely specify the service to be performed by the charity. The terms of such funding may be set out in a service level agreement where the conditions for payment are linked to the performance of a particular level of service or units of output delivered, for example number of meals provided or the opening hours of a facility used by beneficiaries. Entitlement to the incoming resources derived from such performance-related grants may be conditional upon the delivery of the specified level of service and in such circumstances should be recognised to the extent that the charity has provided the services or goods.

Where charities receive membership subscriptions, these may be in the nature of a gift, or they may effectively buy services or access to certain privileges. Where the substance of the subscription is that of a gift, the incoming resource should be recognised on the same basis as a donation. If the subscription purchases the right to services or benefits, the incoming resource should be recognised as the service or benefit is provided. If the subscriber receives rights to such benefits evenly over the period of membership then recognising such membership income on a *pro rata* basis for the period of time covered by the subscription may be an appropriate estimation technique for income recognition.

Charities may also, on occasions, undertake activities under a long-term contract. Owing to the length of time taken to complete such contracts, it is appropriate to take credit for ascertainable incoming resources and the cost of any resources expended while contracts are in progress in accordance with the guidance given in SSAP 9. Application Note G to FRS 5 provides specific guidance on revenue recognition under long-term contractual arrangements. A charity should recognise incoming resources in respect of its performance under a long-term contract when, and to the extent that, it obtains entitlement to consideration. This should be derived from an assessment of the fair value of the goods or services provided to its reporting date as a proportion of the total fair value of the contract.

Grants and donations receivable

A prerequisite for recognition of a promised grant or donation is evidence of entitlement. Evidence will normally exist when the grant is formally expressed in writing. Where entitlement is demonstrable, and no conditions are attached, such promises should be recognised once the criteria of certainty and measurability are met.

Charities often receive grants or donations with conditions attached that must be fulfilled before the entity has unconditional entitlement (control) of the resources. Meeting such conditions may be either within the recipient charity's control or reliant on external factors outside its control. Where meeting such conditions are within the charity's control and there is sufficient evidence that the conditions will be met, then the incoming resource should be recognised. Where uncertainty exists as to whether the recipient charity can meet conditions within its control, the incoming resource should not be recognised but deferred as a liability until certainty exists that the conditions imposed can be met. For example, a grant may be conditional on a charity obtaining matched funding, or subject to a successful planning consent.

Meeting the conditions attaching to such grants would not be either certain or wholly within the control of the recipient charity. The charity would not therefore have unconditional entitlement (control) of the incoming resource until these conditions were met. The incoming resource and corresponding asset should not be recognised until the conditions set have been met. Conditions such as the submission of accounts or certification of expenditure can be seen as simply an administrative requirement as opposed to a condition that might prevent the recognition of incoming resources. Incoming resources may also be subject to donor-imposed conditions that specify the time period in which the expenditure of resources can take place. Such a precondition for use limits the charity's ability to expend the resource until the time condition is met. For example, the receipt in advance of a grant for expenditure that must take place in a future accounting period should be accounted for as deferred income and recognised as a liability until the accounting period in which the recipient charity is allowed by the condition to expend the resource.

Where the existence of a condition prevents the recognition of an incoming resource, a contingent asset should be disclosed where it is probable (but not virtually certain) that the condition will be met in the future. Charities are normally entitled to incoming resources when they are receivable. Recognition of a grant or donation without preconditions should not be deferred even if the resources are received in advance of the performance of the activity funded by the grant or donation. In such cases the charity has entitlement to the resource with the timing of the expenditure being within the discretion of the charity. Incoming resources cannot be deferred simply because the related expenditure has not been incurred.

Where either incoming resources are given specifically to provide a fixed asset or a fixed asset is donated (a gift in kind), the charity will normally have entitlement to the incoming resources when they are receivable. At this point, all of the incoming resources should be recognised in the SOFA and not deferred over the life of the asset. The possibility of having to repay the incoming resources does not affect their recognition in the first instance. Once acquired, the use of the asset will either be restricted or unrestricted. If its use is unrestricted the trustees should consider creating a designated fund reflecting the book value of the asset. The relevant fund will then be reduced over the useful economic life of the asset in line with its depreciation. This treatment accords with the requirements under accounting standards for the recognition of assets and liabilities and provides the most appropriate interpretation of SSAP 4 for charities.

Funds received as agent

Some incoming resources do not belong to the charity, for instance where it receives the resources in circumstances where the trustees acting as agents (and not as custodian trustees) are legally bound to pay them over to a third party and have no responsibility for their ultimate application. In these circumstances the transaction is legally a transfer of resources from the original payer (who remains the principal) to the specified third party. If the original payer retains the legal responsibility for ensuring the charitable application of the funds, the intermediary charity should not recognise the resources in the SOFA or the balance sheet (para. 319).

However, in some cases an intermediary charity may control the use of resources prior to their transfer to a third party and its trustees will act as principal and have responsibility for their charitable application. For instance, where the trustees of the intermediary charity may have applied for the grant of the resources or are able to direct how the grant should be used by the third party or both. Other forms of funding arrangements involving intermediary charities may need their trustees to accept the legal responsibility for the transfer of the grant to the third party (and for its charitable application, where the third party is not a charity). In all of these circumstances the resources should then be included in the intermediary charity's SOFA and balance sheet (para. 320).

Incoming resources subject to restrictions

The fact that a grant or donation is for a restricted purpose does not affect the basis of its recognition within the SOFA. There is an important difference for accounting purposes between restrictions placed on the purposes for which a particular resource may be used and conditions which must be fulfilled prior to entitlement or use by the charity. The existence of a restriction does not prevent the recognition of the incoming resource as the charity has entitlement to (control of) the resource and is simply limited by the restriction as to the purposes to which the resource can be applied.

Funds received for the restricted purpose of providing fixed assets should be accounted for immediately as restricted funds. The treatment of the fixed assets provided with those funds will depend on the basis on which they are held. The terms on which the funds were received may either require the fixed asset acquired to be held in a restricted fund or the fixed asset's acquisition may discharge the restriction and the asset will be held in the unrestricted funds. There is no general rule and the treatment will depend upon the circumstance of each individual case. Where assets move from one fund to another, this should be reflected as a transfer between the relevant funds.

9.5.2 Disclosure

Where any incoming resources have been deferred the notes to the accounts should explain the reasons for the deferrals and analyse the movement on the deferred account between incoming resources deferred in the current year and amounts released from previous years. Incoming resources of a similar nature can be grouped together in the notes as appropriate.

Where a charity has held resources for a third party which have not been included in the SOFA, the notes to the accounts should analyse the movement of these resources during the year relating to each party or type of party where material. Where resources have been held for related parties the required disclosure of paras 227–228 should be given.

9.5.3 Examples

Several of the examples in this book are updated and amended examples previously issued by the Charity Commission for SORP 2005.

The disclosure of the movement in deferred income is illustrated by Example 1.

Example 1 *XYZ Limited*

14. Deferred income	**Group**	**Charity**
Balance at 1 April 2009	46	49
Amount released to incoming resources	(46)	(49)
Amount deferred in the year	55	46
Balance at 31 March 2010	**55**	**46**

Deferred income comprises admission fees received in advance and grants which the donor has specified must be used in future accounting periods.

Example 2 *School Charity*

(j) Statement of accounting policies – extract

The school offers parents the opportunity to pay for up to seven years tuition fees in advance in accordance with a written contract. The amount received is invested and interest is accrued to contracts. This is treated as deferred income

The Statement of Financial Activities

until the pupil joins the school whereupon the fee for each school term is charged against the remaining balance and taken to income. Any shortfall is treated as a deduction from school fee income and any excess accrued is treated as additional school income.

Notes to the financial statements – extract

13. Advance fees scheme

Parents may enter into a contract to pay to the school up to the equivalent of seven years' tuition fees in advance. The money may be returned subject to specific conditions on the receipt of one year's notice. Assuming pupils will remain in the school, advance fees will be applied as follows:

	2010 £'000	2009 £'000
After 5 years	**108**	129
Within 2 to 5 years	**1,316**	1,291
Within 1 to 2 years	**407**	438
	1,831	1,858
Within 1 year	**505**	630
	2,336	2,488

The balance represents the accrued liability under the contracts. The movements during the year were:

	£'000	£'000
Balance at 1 September 2009		2,488
New contracts		423
Amounts accrued to contracts		165
		3,076
Amounts utilised in payment of fees:		
To the school	(646)	
To other schools	(52)	
		(698)
Capital repaid		(42)
Balance at 31 August 2010		**2,336**

9.6 Voluntary income

Voluntary income includes incoming resources generated from the following sources:

- gifts and donations, including legacies given by the founders, patrons, supporters, the general public and businesses.

- grants which provide core funding or are of a general nature provided by government and charitable foundations, but will not include those grants which are specifically for the performance of a service or production of charitable goods, for instance a service agreement with a local authority.
- membership subscriptions and sponsorships where these are, in substance, in the form of donations rather than payment for goods or services, and
- gifts in kind and intangible income.

9.6.1 Disclosure

Where material, details of the types of activities undertaken to generate voluntary income should be provided either on the face of the SOFA or in the notes to the accounts. As far as possible the analysis categories provided here should match the detailed analysis provided for the costs of generating voluntary income.

9.6.2 Legacies

It is good practice to monitor a legacy from the time when notification is received to its final receipt. A charity should not, however, regard a legacy as receivable simply because it has been told about it. It should only do so when the legacy has been received or if, before receipt, there is sufficient evidence to provide the necessary certainty that the legacy will be received and the value of the incoming resources can be measured with sufficient reliability.

There will normally be sufficient certainty of receipt, for example, as soon as a charity receives a letter from the personal representatives of the estate advising that payment of the legacy will be made or that the property bequeathed will be transferred. It is likely that the value of the resource will also be measurable from this time. However, legacies which are not immediately payable should not be treated as receivable until the conditions associated with payment have been fulfilled (for example, the death of a life tenant).

It is unlikely in practice that the entitlement, certainty of receipt and measurability conditions will be satisfied before the receipt of a letter from the personal representatives advising of an intended payment or transfer. The amount which is available in the estate for distribution to the beneficiaries may not have been finalised and, even if it has, there may still be outstanding matters relating to the precise division of the amount. In these circumstances entitlement may be in doubt or it may not be possible to provide a reasonable estimate of the legacy receivable, in which case it should not be included in the SOFA.

Where a charity receives a payment on account of its interest in an estate or a letter advising that such a payment will be made, the payment, or intended payment, on account should be treated as receivable.

Similarly, where a payment is received or notified as receivable (by the personal representatives) after the accounting year end, but it is clear that it had been agreed by the personal representatives prior to the year end (hence providing evidence of a condition that existed at the balance sheet date), then it should be accrued in the SOFA and the balance sheet.

9.6.3 Disclosure

Where the charity has been notified of material legacies which have not been included in the SOFA (because the conditions for recognition have not been met), this fact and an estimate, where possible, of the amounts receivable should be disclosed in the notes to the accounts.

9.6.4 Accounting examples

Example 1

A charity with a year end of 31 December 2009 receives notification in November 2009 that it will receive payments from an estate of £20,000 in April 2010 and £25,000 in July 2010. There may be further advances but the representatives cannot determine the amount or timing. The financial statements prepared at 31 December 2009 should contain an incoming resource for this legacy of £45,000 together with a corresponding debtor of £45,000.

Eaxmple 2

The facts are similar. The charity has long been aware that it is a potential beneficiary from the estate but details of the amounts payable to the charity are received in January 2010, reporting a meeting of the personal representatives in December 2009. The accounting, involving the recognition of the incoming resource and the debtor at 31 December 2009, will be the same. This is because the receipt of the payment details in January 2010 is an adjusting post-balance sheet event.

9.6.5 Disclosure examples

The disclosure of legacies is illustrated below. The accounting policies explain the basis for recognising incoming resources, including legacies, and a note gives details of legacies which have not been recognised in the SOFA.

Example

Incoming resources

(d) All incoming resources are included in the SOFA when the charity is legally entitled to the income and the amount can be quantified with reasonable accuracy. For legacies, entitlement is the earlier of the charity being notified of an impending distribution or the legacy being received.

Gifts in kind donated for distribution are included at valuation and recognised as income when they are distributed to the projects. Gifts donated for resale are included as income when they are sold. Donated facilities are included at the value to the charity where this can be quantified and a third party is bearing the cost. No amounts are included in the financial statements for services donated by volunteers.

3. Legacies

The charity is the residuary beneficiary of a farm in Essex. This is occupied by a life tenant and has not been included in the financial statements. The existing unencumbered value of the farm is estimated at £200,000.

In addition, legacies with a probate value of £1,500,000 have not been included in the financial statements as no notification of impending distribution has been received.

9.7 Gifts in kind

Incoming resources in the form of gifts in kind should be included in the SOFA in the following ways:

(a) Assets given and held in stock for distribution by the charity should be recognised as incoming resources for the year within 'voluntary income' only when distributed.
(b) Assets given for use by the charity (for example, property for its own occupation) should be recognised as incoming resources when receivable.
(c) Where a gift has been made in kind but on trust for conversion into cash and subsequent application by the charity, the incoming resource should normally be recognised in the accounting period when receivable. However in certain cases this will not be practicable and the incoming resources should be included in the accounting period in which the gift is sold. The most common example is that of second-hand goods donated for resale, which, whilst regarded as a donation in legal terms, is in economic terms similar to trading and should be included within 'activities for generating funds'. In the case of second-hand goods donated for resale, prudence dictates that no cost should be recognised until the goods, which cost nothing, are subsequently sold.

In all cases the amount at which gifts in kind are brought into account should be either a reasonable estimate of their gross value to the charity or the amount actually realised.

The Statement of Financial Activities

The principles of materiality should, of course, be applied. In many cases gifts in kind may be of negligible value and will have no material impact upon the financial statements.

9.7.1 Disclosure

The basis of any valuation should be disclosed. Where material, an adjustment should be made to the original valuation upon subsequent realisation of the gift.

Referring to (a) above, where there are undistributed assets at the year end, a general description of the items involved and an estimate of their value should be given by way of a note to the accounts provided such value is material.

In the example below, gifts in kind are immaterial but are still disclosed in a note analysing the total of donations and gifts. This disclosure serves as an acknowledgement of the gift.

Example

2. Donations and gifts

	2010 £	2009 £
Individuals	**2,106**	1,678
Charitable foundations	**4,100**	3,500
Corporate donors	**1,100**	800
Gifts in kind	**24**	22
	7,330	6,000

Gifts in kind comprise free accommodation for the charity's childcare team in Highbury, which has kindly been provided by the Emet Foundation. A corresponding amount is included within childcare expenditure.

9.8 Donated services and facilities

A charity may receive assistance in the form of donated facilities, beneficial loan arrangements or donated services. Common examples in practice include occupying premises rent free or with a significant discount, or the charity receiving free or heavily discounted professional services.

Such incoming resources should be included in the SOFA where the benefit is quantifiable and measurable. The value placed on these resources should be the estimated value to the charity of the service or facility received: this will be the price the charity estimates it would pay in the open market for a service or facility of equivalent utility to the charity. Donated services and facilities recognised in financial statements would include those usually provided by an individual or entity as part of their trade or profession for a fee. In contrast, the contribution of volunteers should be excluded from the SOFA as the value of their contribution to the charity cannot be reasonably quantified in financial terms. Commercial discounts should not be recognised as incoming resource except where they clearly represent a donation.

Where donated services or facilities are recognised, an equivalent amount should be included as expenditure under the appropriate heading in the SOFA.

As an example a charity occupies premises rent free. The market rent is able to be determined and is estimated at £30,000 per annum. Therefore an incoming resource, together with a corresponding entry for deemed expenditure of £30,000 should be recognised in the SOFA. Recognition might not be necessary in a situation where the benefit is of nominal value. For example, where the market value of the rent is negligible because of the poor state of repair of the building or because the charity is occupying previously let space for the remainder of the period paid up by the former tenant.

The receipt of free or discounted professional services may be more difficult to account for, and more likely to be disclosed as help from volunteers. This is because the real market value of the support is difficult to determine because of its 'voluntary' nature and lack of information about charge-out rates and the amount of time recorded.

Again, the principles of materiality must be remembered as often even the cost borne by the third party is not material to the charity. For example, a charity with incoming resources of £1 million was allowed to occupy premises at a nominal rent. The market rent for the premises of £10,000 per annum is clearly immaterial.

9.8.1 Disclosure

The notes to the accounts should give an analysis of donated services or facilities included in the SOFA distinguishing appropriately between the different major items – for example, seconded staff, loaned assets, etc. The accounting policy notes should also indicate the basis of valuation used. Where donated services are received but not included in the SOFA (for example, volunteers) this should be disclosed in the Trustees' Annual Report if this information is necessary for the reader to gain a better understanding of the charity's activities.

Example AJWE Ltd has an accounting policy for intangible income and a note explaining why a donation in kind cannot be recognised.

The Statement of Financial Activities

Example AJWE Ltd

Donated services and facilities

Donated services and facilities are included in income at a valuation which is an estimate of the financial cost borne by the donor where such a cost is quantifiable and measurable. No income is recognised when there is no financial cost borne by a third party.

20. Related parties

The charity has a very close relationship with C Arts Trust, which is a charity, and AFC Borough Council, both of which nominate the majority of the trustees and provide funding to enable the charity to carry out its charitable objectives. The following is a summary of transactions with those entities.

Revenue funding	**2010**	**2009**
	£'000	**£'000**
C Arts Trust	405	501
AFC Borough Council	104	100
	509	**601**

All the above funding was received under contracts with the charity to provide services – for example, training in medical care, and has been included in the financial statements under the heading 'Incoming Resources: from charitable activities'.

The charity also received a donation in kind, from AFC Borough Council, for the rent of premises, the value of which could not be quantified and therefore has not been included in these financial statements.

9.9 Activities for generating funds

Activities for generating funds are the trading activities carried out by a charity to generate incoming resources which will be used to undertake its charitable activities. This category will include:

- fundraising events such as jumble sales, firework displays and concerts (which are legally considered to be trading activities);
- those sponsorships and social lotteries which cannot be considered as pure donations;
- shop income from selling donated goods and bought-in goods;
- providing services other than for the benefit of the charity's beneficiaries, and

- letting and licensing arrangements of property held primarily for functional use by the charity but temporarily surplus to operational requirements.

Whilst selling donated goods is legally considered to be the realisation of a donation in kind, in economic terms it is similar to a trading activity and should be included in this section. Therefore, sales by charity shops or catalogue operations should be included in this section. Ancillary trades where the principal aim (whilst still providing a service to the beneficiaries) is to generate incoming resources to support or contribute to the funding of other charitable activities, should also be included in this section.

It may be possible to segregate the incoming resources and resources expended for each different type of activity (this may have to be done for tax purposes) but often these will be viewed as contributing to a single economic activity. Charity trustees should consider the balance of the activities being undertaken to determine the most appropriate place to include the incoming resources from such enterprises but having done this the mix of incoming resources need not be segregated further. For example, a shop may mainly sell donated and bought-in goods, but it may also sell a small amount of goods made by its beneficiaries and incidentally provide information about the charity. It would be acceptable to class all the incoming resources from the shop as 'shop income' under 'activities for generating funds'.

9.10 Investment income

Investment income includes incoming resources from investment assets, including dividends, interest and rents but excluding realised and unrealised investment gains and losses.

9.10.1 Disclosure

The notes to the accounts should show the gross investment income arising from each category of investment in accordance with para. 303.

As a minimum this would normally include:

(a) investment properties;
(b) investments listed on a recognised stock exchange or ones valued by reference to such investments, such as common investment funds, open-ended investment companies, and unit trusts;
(c) investments in subsidiary or associated undertakings or in companies which are connected persons;
(d) other unlisted securities;
(e) cash and settlements pending held as part of the investment portfolio, and
(f) any other investments.

The Statement of Financial Activities

9.10.2 Example

Example **LTE Trust** illustrates this disclosure.

(b)   Investment income

Investment income is accounted for in the period in which the charity is entitled to receipt.

2.   Investment income

	2010 £'000	2009 £'000
Dividends – UK equities	431	385
Interest – UK fixed interest securities	287	276
Interest on cash deposits	19	19
	737	680

9.11   Incoming resources from charitable activities

This category includes any incoming resources received which are a payment for goods and services provided for the benefit of the charity's beneficiaries. It will include trading activities undertaken in furtherance of the charity's objects and those grants (although legally donations) which have conditions which make them similar in economic terms to trading income, such as service level agreements with local authorities.

This category will not include grants which are for core funding or do not have particular service requirements or are in response to an appeal. Such grants should be included in the section for voluntary income:

Incoming resources from charitable activities should include:

(a)   the sale of goods or services as part of the direct charitable activities of the charity (known as primary purpose trading);

(b)   the sale of goods or services made or provided by the beneficiaries of the charity;

(c)   the letting of non-investment property in furtherance of the charity's objects;

(d)   contractual payments from government or public authorities where these are received in the normal course of trading under (a) to (c) – for example, fees for respite care;

(e)   grants specifically for the provision of goods and services to be provided as part of charitable activities or services to beneficiaries, and

(f) ancillary trades connected to a primary purpose in (a) to (e) where the principal aim is to provide a service to the charity's beneficiaries.

9.11.1 Disclosure

An analysis of charitable activities should be given in the notes to the accounts to supplement the analysis on the face of the SOFA. It should be sufficiently detailed so that the reader of the accounts understands the main activities carried out by the charity and the main components of the gross incoming resources receivable from each material charitable activity. As far as possible, incoming resources should be analysed using the same analysis categories as used for resources expended on charitable activities.

9.11.2 Disclosure example

Example A **Arts Trust**

3. Incoming resources from operation of theatre and arts centre

	2010 £'000	2009 £'000
Admission fees	**614**	589
Public authority service agreements for operation of theatre	**409**	601
Service agreements with other charities for workshops	**154**	50
Other income	**23**	19
	1,200	1,259

4. Commercial trading operations and investment in trading subsidiary

The wholly owned trading subsidiary GT Limited, which is incorporated in the United Kingdom, pays all its profits to the charity by gift aid. GT Limited operates the snackbars and restaurants, all commercial trading operations carried on by GT Limited. The charity owns the entire issued share capital of 100 ordinary shares of £1 each. A summary of the trading results is shown below.

Summary profit and loss account	2010 £'000	2009 £'000
Turnover	**649**	295
Cost of sales and administrative expenses	**(437)**	(281)
Interest receivable	**2**	–
Net profit	**214**	14
Amount gifted to the charity	**(214)**	(14)
Retained in the subsidiary	**–**	–

Summary profit and loss account	2010 £'000	2009 £'000
The assets and liabilities of the subsidiary were:		
Current assets	156	1
Creditors: amounts falling due with one year	(155)	–
Total net assets	1	1
Aggregate share capital and reserves	1	1

9.12 Other incoming resources

Other incoming resources will include the receipt of any resources which the charity has not been able to analyse within the main expenditure categories. This will be a minority of incoming resources and most charities will not need to use this category.

The most common example is a gain on the disposal of a tangible fixed asset held for the charity's own use and a gain on the disposal of a programme-related investment.

9.13 Expenditure and costs

Expenditure should be recognised when and to the extent that a liability is incurred or increased without a commensurate increase in recognised assets or a reduction in liabilities. In accounts prepared on the accruals basis liabilities are recognised as soon as there is a legal or constructive obligation committing the charity to the expenditure as described in Financial Reporting Standards 5 and 12. A liability will arise when a charity is under an obligation to make a transfer of value to a third party as a result of past transactions or events.

The SORP provides a commentary on the recognition of liabilities and related expenses arising from contractual arrangements entered into by charities and particularly commitments relating to grants.

9.13.1 Contractual arrangements

Where a charity enters into a contract for the supply of goods or services, expenditure is recognised once the supplier of the goods or services has performed their part of the contract, for example, the delivery of goods or the provision of a service.

Certain grants made may contain conditions that closely specify a particular service to be performed by the recipient of the grant. The terms of such grants may be set out in a service level agreement where the conditions for payment are linked to the performance of a particular level of service or units of output delivered, for example number of meals provided or the opening hours of a facility used by beneficiaries. Often, in such cases, the grant maker will have negotiated the services to be provided to it or its beneficiaries. Expenditure on such performance-related grants should be recognised to the extent that the recipient of the grant has provided the specified service or goods.

A grant that is merely restricted to a particular purpose of the recipient does not create a performance-related grant unless specific performance terms are included that meet the criteria set out above.

9.13.2 Grants payable and constructive obligations

In the case of grants (other than performance-related) and certain other expenditure relating directly to charitable activities, an exchange for consideration does not arise. Such expenditure is incurred to further the charity's objectives but without creating a contractual or quasi-contractual relationship with the recipient of the grant or the charity's beneficiaries. Nevertheless, the charity may still have a liability which needs to be recognised.

Liabilities may arise from a constructive or a legal obligation. A constructive obligation arises under FRS12 where events have created a valid expectation in other parties that the charity will discharge its obligations. Determining whether a valid expectation has been created will be evidenced by the charity's current and past practice in discharging such obligations and the specific communication of a commitment to the recipient. A constructive obligation always involves a commitment to another party that has been communicated to those affected in a sufficiently specific manner to raise a valid expectation on the part of the recipient that the charity will discharge its obligations.

Charities may on occasion make general or policy statements of their future intentions – for example, of an intention or aim of relieving famine in a particular location or to improve the quality of care provided to a particular group of people. Such statements can be communicated in a variety of ways including mission statements, setting out future plans in a Trustees' Annual Report or simply by making a general policy statement. Statements such as these do not create a constructive obligation as discretion is retained by the charity as to their implementation.

A constructive obligation is likely to arise where:

- a specific commitment, or promise to provide goods, services or grant funding is given, and
- this is communicated directly to a beneficiary or grant recipient.

In such circumstances, the charity is unlikely to have a realistic alternative but to meet the obligation. However, the recognition of any resulting liability will be dependent on any conditions attaching to such commitments.

A charity may enter into commitments which are dependent upon explicit conditions being met either by itself or by the recipient before payment is made or upon future reviews. A liability, and hence expenditure, should be recognised once such conditions fall outside the control of the giving charity. If the conditions set remain within the control of the giving charity, then the charity retains the discretion to avoid the expenditure and therefore a liability should not be recognised.

By way of illustration, where a charity makes a specific commitment to grant-fund a project over a three-year period, the following situations may arise:

(a) If the multi-year grant obligation:
 (i) is conditional on an annual review of progress that determines whether future funding is provided, and
 (ii) discretion is retained by the giving charity to terminate the grant.
(b) then provided evidence exists (for example, from past review practice) that the discretion retained by the charity has substance, this amounts to a condition and an immediate liability arises only for the first year of the funding commitment.
(c) If the annual review process, although set out in the conditions of the grant, is not in practice used to determine whether funding is provided in the subsequent years of the commitment, then the review stipulation should not be interpreted as a condition and a liability for the full three years of the grant should be recognised.
(d) If there is no condition attaching to the grant that enables the charity to realistically avoid the commitment, the liability for the full three years of the funding should be recognised.

Commitments may contain conditions that are outside the control of the giving charity. For example, a charity may promise a grant payment on the condition that the recipient finds matching funding. As the condition falls outside the control of the giving charity, a liability arises and expenditure should be recognised.

9.13.3 General issues

Where a liability is not accrued, because conditions have not been met, such a commitment should normally be treated as a contingent liability. The balance sheet treatment for both outstanding commitments and contingent liabilities is given in paras 340–348.

Expenditure and costs

The trustees may wish to designate some of the charity's income funds to represent contingent liabilities and other planned expenditure which may not have created a liability.

Where later events make the recognition of a liability no longer appropriate, the liability should be cancelled by credit against the relevant expenditure heading in the Statement of Financial Activities. The credit should mirror the treatment originally used to recognise the expenditure for the liability and should be disclosed separately.

9.13.4 Support costs

In undertaking any activity there may be support costs incurred that, whilst necessary to deliver an activity, do not themselves produce or constitute the output of the charitable activity. Similarly, costs will be incurred in supporting income generation activities such as fundraising, and in supporting the governance of the charity. Support costs include the central or regional office functions such as general management, payroll administration, budgeting and accounting, information technology, human resources and financing.

Support costs do not in themselves constitute an activity; instead they enable output-creating activities to be undertaken. Support costs are therefore allocated to the relevant activity cost category they support on the bases set out in paras 168–174. This enables the total cost of an activity category to be disclosed in the SOFA and for the cost of the constituent sub-activities to be presented at a service, programme or project level within the notes to the accounts. There is nevertheless legitimate user interest in both the level of support costs incurred and the policies adopted for their allocation to the relevant activity cost categories that should be addressed through relevant note disclosures.

9.13.5 Disclosure

The notes to the accounts should provide details of the total support costs incurred and of main items or categories of expenditure included within support costs.

Where support costs are material, an explanation should be provided in the notes of how these costs have been allocated to each of the activity cost categories disclosed in the SOFA or the supporting notes to the accounts. The explanation may include percentages or amounts allocated, details of the methods of apportionment used or a table showing the detailed allocations such as that shown below in Table 4 of the SORP.

The Statement of Financial Activities

Table 9.2 *Table 4 of SORP 2005*

Support Cost (Examples)	Fund-raising	Activity 1	Activity 2	Activity 3	Activity 4	Activity 5	Basis of allocation
Management	£X	£X	£X	£X	£X	£X	Text describing method
Finance	£X	£X	£X	£X	£X	£X	Text describing method
Information Technology	£X	£X	£X	£X	£X	£X	Text describing method
Human Resources	£X	£X	£X	£X	£X	£X	Text describing method
Total	£X	£X	£X	£X	£X	£X	

9.14 Allocation of costs

In attributing costs between activity categories, the following principles should be applied.

1. Where appropriate, expenditure should be allocated directly to activity cost category.
2. Items of expenditure which contribute directly to the output of more than one activity cost category, for example, the cost of a staff member whose time is divided between a fundraising activity and working on a charitable project, should be apportioned on a reasonable, justifiable and consistent basis.
3. Depreciation, amortisation, impairment or losses on disposal of fixed assets should be allocated in accordance with the same principles.
4. Support costs may not be attributable to a single activity but rather provide the organisational infrastructure that enables output producing activities to take place. Such costs should therefore also be apportioned on a reasonable, justifiable and consistent basis to the activity cost categories being supported.

There are several bases for apportionment that may be applied. Examples include:

(a) usage – for example, on the same basis as expenditure incurred directly in undertaking an activity;
(b) *per capita* – that is, based on the number of people employed within an activity;

Allocation of costs

(c) on the basis of floor area occupied by an activity, and
(d) on the basis of time.

The bases for apportionment adopted by a charity should be appropriate to the cost concerned and to the charity's particular circumstances, selected to enable its accounts to give a true and fair view. The bases adopted for apportionment will normally be consistent between accounting periods.

Particular issues arise where a charity provides information about its activities in the context of a fundraising activity. Information about the aims, objectives and projects of a charity is frequently provided in the context of mailshots, collections and telephone fundraising. In determining whether a multi-purpose activity arises, and therefore a need to apportion costs, a distinction should be drawn between:

- publicity or information costs involved in raising the profile of a charity which is associated with fundraising (costs of generating funds); and
- publicity or information that is provided in an educational manner in furtherance of the charity's objectives (charitable expenditure).

In the context of a fundraising activity, for publicity or information to be regarded as charitable expenditure, it must be supplied in an educational manner. To achieve an educational purpose, information supplied would be:

(a) targeted at beneficiaries or others who can use the information to further the charity's objectives; and
(b) information or advice upon which the recipient can act in an informed manner to further the charity's objectives; and
(c) related to other educational activities or objectives undertaken by the charity.

Where information provided in conjunction with a fundraising activity does not meet these criteria, it should be regarded as targeted at potential donors and therefore relating wholly to the fundraising activity.

This could be contrasted with, for example, a health education charity that targeted high-risk beneficiary groups or the medical profession supplying information as to health risks or symptom recognition and advising on steps that should be taken. Such information would fall within charitable expenditure in that it is targeted at beneficiaries, advises on steps that can be taken and is likely to link to the charity's activities or objectives in health education. Therefore when such information is provided in the context of a fundraising activity, a joint cost would arise with costs apportioned between the fundraising and charitable activities.

9.14.1 Disclosure

The accounting policy notes should explain the policy adopted for the apportionment of costs between activities and any estimation technique(s) used to calculate their apportionment.

The Statement of Financial Activities

Where any fundraising activity is identified as meeting the criteria of a multi-purpose activity (see paras 172–174) and part of the costs of the multi-purpose activity are allocated to charitable activities then the policy for the identification of such multi-purpose costs should be explained in the accounting policy notes together with the basis on which any allocation to charitable activities is made.

9.15 Resources expended

The Statement of Financial Activities provides an analysis of the resources expended by a charity based on the nature of the activities undertaken. Resources expended are split into three main activity categories, being:

- the costs of generating funds (paras 178–187);
- the costs of charitable activities (paras 188–209); and
- the governance costs (paras 210–212).

The Statement of Financial Activities or the notes to the accounts should include an analysis of the sub-activities, services, programmes, projects or other initiatives that contribute to a particular activity category.

9.16 Costs of generating funds

These are the costs which are associated with generating incoming resources from all sources other than from undertaking charitable activities. The main components of costs within this category are:

(a) costs of generating voluntary income (Glossary GL 13 and see paras 180–184);
(b) costs of fundraising trading, including cost of goods sold and other associated costs (see paras 185–186), and
(c) costs of managing investments for both income generation and capital maintenance (see para 187).

Costs of generating funds should not include:

- costs associated with delivering or supporting the provision of goods and services in the furtherance of the charity's objects; nor
- the costs of negotiating the terms of a contract or performance-related grant relating to the provision of such services.

9.16.1 Costs of generating voluntary income

Costs of generating voluntary income are defined in the Glossary. All such fundraising costs, including agents' costs where fundraising agents are used, should be included within this category. In the case of consolidated accounts any such costs incurred by any subsidiary companies or other entities should be consolidated on a line-by-line basis.

Some fundraising costs may be incurred in starting up a new source of future income such as legacies, or in developing a supporter database.

(a) Start-up costs of a new fundraising activity should be dealt with in accordance with UITF 24: *Accounting for Start-up Costs*. In most cases, it will be inappropriate to carry forward start-up costs as prepayments or deferred expenditure as the future economic benefits that may be derived are usually not sufficiently certain.

(b) Data capture costs of internally developed databases may only be capitalised where future benefit can be demonstrated and the resulting database has a readily ascertainable value.

The start-up costs of a new fundraising activity may be material in the context of the overall fundraising activity and may, because of their exceptional size or incidence, require separate disclosure to explain performance.

9.16.2 Disclosure

Where the costs of generating voluntary income are material, details of the types of activity on which the costs were expended should be shown in the notes to the accounts. Types of activity could include collections (for example, street and house-to-house collections), sponsorship, legacies, membership and direct mail campaigns.

As far as possible the analysis provided here should match the detailed analysis of voluntary incoming resources (see paras 121–122).

Exceptional fundraising costs should not be presented on the face of the SOFA as a separate category of costs but, rather, should be disclosed as an exceptional item within the fundraising activity cost category. The amount of each exceptional item, either individually or as an aggregate of items of a similar type, should be disclosed within the fundraising activity note or on the face of the SOFA if that degree of prominence is necessary to give a true and fair view. An adequate description should be given to enable its nature to be understood.

9.16.3 Fundraising trading: cost of goods sold and other costs

This category should include all those costs that are incurred by trading for a fundraising purpose in either donated or bought-in goods or in providing non-charitable services to generate income. This includes:

The Statement of Financial Activities

(a) the cost of goods sold or services provided;
(b) other costs related to the trade, including staff costs, premises costs and other costs incurred in the activity including allocated support costs, and
(c) costs related to the licensing of a charity logo.

In consolidated accounts this category will include the costs incurred by both the charity and any subsidiaries or other entities consolidated on a line-by-line basis.

9.16.4 Disclosure

Where the costs associated with fundraising trading are material, details should be given in the notes to the accounts to distinguish the cost of separate trading activities in a way that matches the analysis of income.

9.16.5 Investment management costs

Investment management costs are defined in the Glossary (GL 29). As explained in Appendix 3, para 3(c), investment management costs associated with endowment fund investments should generally be charged to the endowment fund capital.

9.16.6 Example

The example below illustrates the presentation of costs of generated funds.

6. Costs of generating funds

	Unrestricted £'000	Restricted £'000	2010 Total £'000	2009 Total £'000
Staff costs	640	90	730	721
Consultancy costs	501	8	509	427
Brochures and material	264	2	266	249
Office costs and other overheads	241	5	246	187
	1,646	**105**	**1,751**	**1,584**

9.17 Charitable activities

Resources expended on charitable activities comprise all the resources applied by the charity in undertaking its work to meet its charitable objectives as opposed to the cost of raising the funds to finance these activities and governance costs. Charitable activities are all the resources expended by the charity in the delivery of goods and services, including its programme and project work that is directed at the achievement of its charitable aims and objectives. Such costs include the direct costs of the charitable activities together with those support costs incurred that enable these activities to be undertaken.

Charities may carry out their activities through a combination of direct service provision and grant funding of third parties to undertake work that contributes to the charity's objectives or programme of work. In such cases, the total cost of the activity involves both costs incurred directly by the charity and funding provided to third parties through grant-making activities.

Where incoming resources are received either under contract or by a restricted grant to provide a specified service, further analysis of charitable activities expenditure may be provided in the notes to the accounts to demonstrate the link between the incoming resource and the charitable activity that it funds.

An analysis should be provided to inform readers of the accounts how resources have been deployed between the charity's main areas of work. The activities disclosed should be consistent with those disclosed for incoming resources.

9.17.1 Disclosure

Resources expended on charitable activities should be analysed on the face of the SOFA or in a prominent note to the accounts. This analysis should provide an understanding of the nature of the activities undertaken and the resources expended on their provision. This analysis may, for example, set out the activity cost of the main services provided by the charity, or set out the resources expended on significant programmes or projects undertaken by the charity.

The note to the accounts should identify the amount of support costs allocated to charitable activities if not separately disclosed on the face of the SOFA.

Where activities are carried out through a combination of direct service or programme activity and grant funding of third parties, the notes to the accounts should identify the amount of grant-making expenditure using the note to explain the activity funded.

The disclosures required may, for example, be presented in a table, such as Table 5 from the SORP (with totals reconciling with the SOFA) and other notes as appropriate)

The Statement of Financial Activities

Table 9.3 *Table 5 of SORP 2005:*

Activity or Programme	Activities undertaken directly £	Grant funding of activities £	Support costs £	Total £
Activity 1				
Activity 2				
Activity 3				
Total				

9.18 Grant making

Costs associated with grant making activity include the grants actually made and the support costs associated with the activity. The term grant is defined in the Glossary (GL 29) and associated support costs are explained further at para. 196.

Grant-making charities may undertake their entire programme of work through grant making activities, whilst other charities may undertake their activities through a combination of direct service provision and grant funding of third parties. In either case, further analysis of grant making, where material, should be provided.

Grant making will be material if in any accounting year a charity makes grants totalling at least five per cent of its total resources expended in that year.

The analysis of grants payable should differentiate between grants made to individuals and those payable to institutions. An individual grant is one that is made for the direct benefit of the individual who receives it, for example, to relieve financial hardship. All other grants should be regarded as institutional. For example, a grant which is made to an individual to carry out a research project should be regarded as a grant to the institution with which the individual is connected rather than as a grant to the individual.

Support costs related to grant making will include:

(a) costs incurred before grants are made (pre-grant costs) as part of the decision-making process;
(b) post-grant costs – for example., monitoring of grants, and
(c) costs of any central or regional office functions such as general management, payroll administration, budgeting and accounting, information technology, human resources, and financing.

Grant making

9.18.1 Disclosure

The analysis and explanation should help the reader of the accounts understand how the grants made relate to the objects of the charity and the policy adopted by the trustees in pursuing these objects.

The notes to the accounts should identify the amount of support costs associated with grant making activities.

The analysis and explanation in the notes should provide details, with amounts that reconcile with the total of grants payable of:

(a) the total number and total amount of grants analysed between grants to individuals and grants to institutions, and
(b) an analysis of the grants by purpose.

This statement may, for example, be structured as follows, as illustrated by Table 6 to the SORP:

Table 9.4 *Table 6 of SORP 2005:*

Analysis	Grants to Institutions Total Amount £	Grants to Individuals Total Amount £
Activity or Project 1		
Activity or Project 2		
Activity or Project 3		
Total		

The analysis of grants by their purpose should relate to the charity's objectives – for example, categories may be social welfare, medical research, the performing arts, welfare of people in financial need, or help to people seeking to further their education, depending on the nature of the charity. Some charities may decide that it is appropriate to provide further or alternative levels of analysis, perhaps, for example, showing a geographical analysis of the number and value of grants made.

The trustees may give further analysis and explanation of the purposes for which grants were made as part of the Trustees' Annual Report or by means of a separate publication. Such further analysis does not excuse the trustees from providing sufficient detail in the notes to the accounts as is needed to provide a true and fair view.

If a charity has made grants to institutions, the charity should disclose details, as specified in para. 207, of a sufficient number of institutional grants to provide a reasonable understanding of the range of institutions it has supported. This information may be provided either in the notes to the accounts, as part of the

The Statement of Financial Activities

Trustees' Annual Report, or by means of a separate publication. Where the analysis is contained in a separate publication, it should be made available to the public in the same way as the accounts. The notes to the accounts should identify the publication and state how copies of it can be obtained.

The disclosure of institutional grants should give the name of the institution and the number and total value of grants made to that institution in the accounting year. Where grants have been made to a particular institution for different purposes, the number and total value of the grants made for each purpose should be disclosed. For example, a charity may have made grants to different officers or departments of a particular university for different projects. Such grants should be treated as having been made to the same institution with an analysis provided of the number and total value of grants made for each purpose (see section **4.13.24** of Chapter 4).

Very exceptionally, even though the grants to a particular institution are material, it is possible that the disclosure of the details of one or more of those grants could seriously prejudice the furtherance of the purposes either of the recipient institution or of the charity itself. Situations where serious prejudice is clearly indicated include those where disclosure could result in serious personal injury. Mere unwillingness to disclose grants or inconvenience or embarrassment to one or more trustees cannot be regarded as serious prejudice. Commercial disadvantage is not of itself seriously prejudicial.

Where the circumstances amount to serious prejudice, a charity may withhold details of the recipient of any institutional grant concerned but should in such circumstances:

(a) disclose in the notes to the accounts the total number, value and general purpose of those grants the details of which have not been disclosed
(b) give in writing to the charity's regulatory body:
  (i) the full details of any grants not disclosed; and
  (ii) a full explanation of the reasons why those details have not been disclosed in the accounts, and
(c) state in the notes to the accounts whether or not those details have been given to the charity's regulatory body

It is unlikely in practice that all the material institutional grants of a charity would fall within this exception.

9.18.2 Disclosure example

Example People's Trust

Grants payable are charged in the year when the offer is conveyed to the recipient except in those cases where the offer is conditional, such grants being

Grant making

recognised as expenditure when the conditions attaching are fulfilled. Grants offered subject to conditions which have not been met at the year end are noted as a commitment, but not accrued as expenditure.

4. Grants payable

	2010		2009	
	£'000	£'000	£'000	£'000

The amount payable in the year comprises:

Education and research
Manchester Institute of Technology
Four grants (2009 – four grants) as follows:

to fund educational post	51		36	
genetic research	31		31	
research into awareness of symptoms of Alzheimer's in general practitioners	20		20	
the impact of Alzheimer's on family and carers	21		21	
		123		108

University of Slough
Two grants to fund educational posts (2009 – one grant) | | 91 | | 57 |

University of Taunton
Two grants (2009 – three grants) as follows:

Research into drug therapies	51		49	
Research on nursing homes caring for patients with Alzheimer's	34		30	
compilation of registry of practitioners and hospitals specialising in Alzheimer's	–		24	
		85		103
Total Institutional grants		299		268
PhD scholarships – grants to 79 individuals (2009 – 52 individuals)		244		153
		543		421

Reconciliation of grants payable:

Commitments at 1 October 2009		545		281
Commitments made in the year	561		431	
Grants cancelled or recovered	(18)		(10)	

The Statement of Financial Activities

Grants payable for the year	543	421
Grants paid during the year	(929)	(157)
Commitments at 30 September 2010	159	545
Commitments at 30 September are payable as follows:		
Within one year (note 12)	84	375
After more than one year (note 13)	75	170
	159	545

Commitments

In addition to the amounts committed and accrued noted above, the trustees have also authorised certain grants which are subject to the recipient fulfilling certain conditions. The total amount authorised but not accrued as expenditure at 30 September 2010 was £184,000 (2009: £191,000).

9.19 Governance costs

These costs include the governance arrangements which relate to the general running of the charity as opposed to the direct management functions inherent in generating funds, service delivery and programme or project work. These activities provide the governance infrastructure which allows the charity to operate and to generate the information required for public accountability. They include the strategic planning processes that contribute to the future development of the charity.

Expenditure on the governance of the charity will normally include both direct and related support costs.

Direct costs will include such items as:

- internal and external audit;
- legal advice for trustees, and
- costs associated with constitutional and statutory requirements (for example, the cost of trustee meetings and preparing statutory accounts).

There should also be an apportionment of shared and indirect costs involved in supporting the governance activities (as distinct from supporting its charitable or income generation activities).

9.19.1 Disclosure

There should be a clear analysis of all the main items of expenditure on governance in the notes to the accounts.

9.20 Transfers

All transfers between the different categories of funds should be shown on the transfer row of the SOFA. The transfer row will be used for several purposes including:

(a) when capital funds are released to an income fund from expendable endowment;
(b) where a charity has authority to adopt a total return approach to investment (see Appendix 3 para. 3(g)) to record the release of funds to income from the unapplied total return fund held within the permanent endowment fund;
(c) to transfer assets from unrestricted income funds to finance a deficit on a restricted fund; and
(d) to transfer the value of fixed assets from restricted to unrestricted funds when the asset has been purchased from a restricted fund donation but the asset is held for a general and not a restricted purpose.

Material transfers should not be netted off but should be shown gross on the face of the SOFA.

9.20.1 Disclosure

The notes to the accounts should provide an explanation of the nature of each material transfer between funds.

9.21 Gains and losses on fixed assets

Gains and losses arising on disposal, revaluation or impairment of fixed assets – whether held for the charity's own use or for investment purposes – will form part of the particular fund in which the investment or other asset concerned is or was held at the time of disposal, revaluation or impairment.

Such gains and losses should be recognised as follows.

1. Impairment losses of assets held for the charity's own use, (that is, not investments) should be regarded as additional depreciation of the impaired asset and included appropriately in the resources expended section of the statement of financial activities.
2. Gains on the disposal of fixed assets for the charity's own use should be included under the heading 'other incoming resources'. Losses on disposal should be treated as additional depreciation and included appropriately in the resources expended section of the SOFA.

3. Revaluation gains or losses (which are not considered to be impairment losses) on assets held for the charity's own use should be included in the section on gains and losses on revaluations of fixed assets for the charity's own use.

9.22 Gains and losses on investment assets

Any gains and losses on investment assets (including property investments) should be included under the gains and losses on the revaluation and disposal of investment assets. Realised and unrealised gains and losses may be included in a single row on the SOFA. In particular this approach will be necessary where a charity adopts a 'marking to market' or continuous revaluation approach in relation to its investment portfolio.

9.23 Actuarial gains or losses on defined benefit pension schemes

Actuarial gains or losses on defined benefit pension schemes should be separately disclosed in the gains and losses section of the SOFA (See paras 430–448 – *Accounting for Retirement Benefits*).

Chapter 10 – Balance sheet

10.1 Introduction

The balance sheet provides a snapshot of the charity's assets and liabilities at the end of its accounting year and assets are split between the different types of funds. The balance sheet will not always include all of the assets and liabilities of a charity, nor attach an up-to-date valuation for all assets. Some heritage assets (paras 279–294), or contingent liabilities (paras 340–348) may be omitted. Where such assets or contingent liabilities exist and are not included in the balance sheet, details must be provided in the notes to the accounts.

The objective of the balance sheet is to show the resources available to the charity and whether these are freely available or have to be used for specific purposes because of legal restrictions on their use. It may also show which of the resources the trustees have designated for specific future use. It will normally be necessary to read the reserves policy and plans for the future in the Trustees' Annual Report to gain a full understanding of the availability and planned use of the charity's funds.

SORP 2005 has had little impact upon the general presentation of the balance sheet, with the exception of introducing the concept of 'heritage assets'.

10.2 Presentation

10.2.1 Structure of the balance sheet

The funds of a charity should be grouped together in the balance sheet according to the nature of the fund. The balance sheet should distinguish, as a minimum, between unrestricted income funds, restricted income funds and endowment funds. Distinctions between permanent and expendable endowment and designated funds can also be shown.

The balance sheet should show assets and liabilities under the following headings.

(a) **Fixed assets**, subdivided between:
    (i)   intangible assets;
    (ii) tangible assets, and
    (iii) heritage asset.

Balance sheet

(b) **Investments,** sub-divided between:
    (i)   investments, and
    (ii) programme-related investments.

(c) **Current assets,** subdivided between:
    (i)   stocks and work in progress;
    (ii)   debtors;
    (iii) investments, and
    (iv) cash at bank and in hand.
(Subtotals should be given for (a) and (c) above).

(d) **Creditors**: amounts falling due within one year.

(e) **Net current assets or liabilities** (that is, the amount in (c) less the amount in (d))

(f) **Total assets less current liabilities** (that is, the amount in (a) plus (or minus) the amount in (e)).

(g) **Creditors**: amounts falling due after more than one year.

(h) Provisions for liabilities and charges.

(i) **Net assets or liabilities** excluding pension asset or liability (that is, the amount in (f) less the amount in (g) and (h)).

(j) Defined benefit pension scheme asset or liability

(k) **Net assets or liabilities** including pension asset or liability (that is, the amount in (e) less the amounts in (f) and (g))

(l) **The funds of the charity**, divided between:
    (i)   endowment funds;
    (ii)   restricted income funds, and
    (iii) unrestricted income funds, divided between:
- share capital
- unrestricted income funds
- revaluation reserve:
  - unrestricted income funds excluding pension asset or liability
- pension reserve:
  - total unrestricted funds, and
  - total charity funds.

The balance sheet can be presented in one continuous vertical format, or it can be presented in columns appropriately divided between the three types of fund. A columnar presentation shows the asset and liability categories analysed in columns between each fund group in a similar way to the SOFA showing incoming resources and resources expended by type of fund. This presentation is not mandatory, but using it ensures that charities present the required analysis of assets and liabilities by category of fund. Where a charity does not have funds of a particular category, the column related to that category of fund is omitted. If the columnar presentation is not adopted, the assets and liabilities (for example, investments, fixed assets, net current assets) representing each category of fund should be summarised and analysed between those funds in the notes to the accounts.

In addition, the assets and liabilities should be analysed in a way that enables the reader to gain a proper appreciation of their spread and character. For example, long-term debtors should, where the total is material, be separately stated in the balance sheet – otherwise their total amounts by category should be disclosed in the notes to the accounts.

If there are no amounts for the current and previous year, no entries need to be made on the balance sheet and the headings can be omitted.

Expenditure may be incurred in anticipation of the receipt of restricted income, possibly leading to a negative balance on a specific fund. Where such balances are material, they should not simply be netted off against positive balances on the fund category in the balance sheet. This means that the balance sheet may need to separately identify positive and negative balances on restricted funds.

10.3 Fixed assets

10.3.1 Introduction

There have been significant developments in accounting for fixed assets by the charity sector and charities are now subject to the same standards as commercial companies. Before the appearance of the 1995 SORP the importance of fixed assets was recognised in a paper by a group of researchers (*Charity accounting standards: Issues for charity researchers* compiled by the NCVO) which stated:

> 'We know very little about the value ... of the assets held by the charity sector, and yet the proper application of assets is probably the longest-standing area of public concern about charities ... A more accurate accounting of their true worth would paint a wholly different picture of the charitable sector, and the standards of its asset management ...'.

Historically, the charity sector has accounted for expenditure on fixed assets in a variety of ways. However, the 1995 SORP recommended that, subject to the specified exceptions, all such expenditure is capitalised, meaning that the charity sector had to account for fixed assets in the same way as the commercial sector.

There were further developments in reporting in SORP 2000, mainly arising from the introduction of FRS 15 Tangible fixed assets. These developments particularly affected the treatment of inalienable and historic fixed assets. SORP 2005 introduced the concept of 'heritage assets' in place of 'inalienable and historic fixed assets'.

10.3.2 Intangible fixed assets

Intangible fixed assets should be included in the balance sheet in accordance with FRS 10 Goodwill and Intangible Assets.

Balance sheet

Goodwill arising from the acquisition of another entity will tend to be rare in the charity sector, but some charities may have intangible assets representing intellectual property arising from activities subject as research and development or publishing. The costs of acquiring the intangible asset should be capitalised and amortised over an expected life, which should not normally exceed 20 years.

10.3.3 Tangible fixed assets (other than investments)

Financial Reporting Standard 15 Tangible Fixed Assets requires that all fixed assets should be capitalised on initial acquisition and included in the balance sheet at cost or valuation. They may then be periodically revalued. Subsequent expenditure which enhances (rather than maintains) the performance of fixed assets should also be capitalised.

Within charities, tangible fixed assets (other than investments) fall into two categories – those held for charity use (including those used for the running and administration of the charity) and those classed as heritage assets. There may be some overlap in that some heritage assets may also be used in the functional activities of the charity.

10.3.4 General rules for the inclusion of tangible fixed assets

Tangible fixed assets should initially be included at their cost of acquisition including costs that are directly attributable to bringing the assets into working condition for their intended use.

This can include costs of interest on loans to finance the construction of such assets but only where the charity has adopted this as a policy for all tangible fixed assets, and capitalisation should cease when the asset is ready for use. This applies whether assets are bought outright or through hire purchase or finance leasing.

If a fixed asset is acquired in full or in part from the proceeds of a grant it should be included at its full acquisition cost (or in the case of a joint arrangement at the gross value of the charity's share in the asset) without netting off the grant proceeds.

Where functional fixed assets have been donated, they should be valued at the amount of the gift included as an incoming resource in the SOFA.

Similarly, where such assets are capitalised some time after being acquired – for example, as a result of a change in accounting policy – they should be included at original cost or at the value at which the gift was included in the SOFA, less an amount for depreciation. However, if neither of these amounts is ascertainable, a reasonable estimate of the asset's cost or current value to the charity should be used. Such a valuation will be regarded as the asset's initial carrying amount and will not be regarded as a revaluation.

Where the net book value of a fixed asset is higher than its recoverable amount, it will be impaired and should be written down to its recoverable amount.

10.3.5 Mixed use of fixed assets (functional and investment)

Where land and buildings are held for mixed purposes (that is, partly as functional property and partly as investment), the way in which they are capitalised depends upon the primary purpose for holding the asset and the extent to which they are separable. In general, the following rules should be followed.

(a) Assets held primarily for charity use of which a part is leased at a commercial rent can be regarded as functional fixed assets if:
 (i) only a small part of the asset is leased, or
 (ii) the lease is for a short period of time.
(b) Assets held primarily for investment purposes where a small part is used for functional purposes should be classed as investment assets.
(c) Assets that contain clearly distinguishable parts which are held for different purposes (that is, partly functional and partly investment) and which do not fall under (a) or (b) above should be split in the balance sheet between functional and investment assets.

10.3.6 Depreciation of tangible fixed assets (other than investments)

Most tangible fixed assets depreciate – that is, they wear out, are consumed or otherwise suffer a reduction in their useful life through use, the passing of time or obsolescence. Their value is thus gradually expended over their useful economic life. This expenditure should be recognised by means of annual depreciation charged in the SOFA and shown in the balance sheet as accumulated depreciation deducted from the value of the relevant fixed assets.

Fixed assets held for use by the charity which are included in the balance sheet should be depreciated at rates appropriate to their useful economic life in each case.

Exceptions to charging depreciation may only arise if any of the following three conditions apply.

Balance sheet

(a) the asset is freehold land that is considered to have an indefinitely long useful life
(b) the depreciation charge and accumulated depreciation are not material because:
  (i) the asset has a very long useful life, or
  (ii) the residual value (based on prices at the time of acquisition or subsequent revaluation) of the asset is not materially different from the carrying amount of the asset
(c) provided that the stringent conditions of paras 89–91 of FRS 15 are met and the asset is subject to an annual impairment review (except for charities under the threshold for following the FRSSE).
(d) the assets are heritage and have not been included in the balance sheet.

In general, the requirement to depreciate is clear and cannot be avoided. In particular, freehold and long leasehold buildings are subject to depreciation over the expected useful life of the building.

Where a fixed asset for charity use comprises two or more major components with substantially different useful lives, each component should be accounted for as a separate asset and depreciated over its individual useful life.

The useful economic lives and residual values of fixed assets should be reviewed at the end of the accounting period and, where there is a material change, the value of the asset should be depreciated over its remaining useful life.

10.3.7 Disclosure

Tangible fixed assets for use by the charity should be analysed in the notes to the accounts within the following five categories.

1. Freehold interest in land and buildings.
2. Leasehold and other interests in land and buildings.
3. Plant and machinery, including motor vehicles.
4. Fixtures, fittings and equipment.
5. Payments on account and assets in the course of construction..

These are broad categories and any charity may, within reason, split the headings or adopt other narrower classes that meet the definition of a class of tangible fixed assets and are appropriate to its operations.

The notes should summarise all material changes in the values of each class of functional fixed assets and reconcile the opening and closing balances. This should include, separately stated at the beginning and end of the period:

(a) cost, valuation or revalued amount;
(b) accumulated depreciation and impairment provisions;

(c) additions;
(d) disposals;
(e) revaluations;
(f) transfers, and
(g) impairment losses (or reversals).

Totals should be given for all classes of assets (including a combined total), separately identifying the depreciation charged for the period.

The methods of depreciation used and useful economic lives or depreciation rates should be disclosed in the accounting policy notes.

There is often a considerable difference between the carrying value and market value of interests in land and buildings not held as investments. Where the trustees consider this to be so significant that it needs to be drawn to the attention of the users of the accounts, then the difference should be included, with such precision as is practicable, in the notes to the accounts. If it is not practicable to quantify the difference, a written explanation will suffice.

10.3.8 Heritage assets

FRS 15 requires that all fixed assets should be capitalised in the balance sheet. In principle this includes fixed assets which are of historic, artistic or scientific importance that are held to advance presentation and conservation objectives of a charity.

The SORP defines 'heritage assets' as:

> '... assets of historical, artistic or scientific importance that are held to advance preservation, conservation and educational objectives of charities and through public access contribute to the nation's culture and education either at a national or local level. Such assets are central to the achievement of the purposes of such charities and include the land, buildings, structures, collections, exhibits or artefacts that are preserved or conserved and are central to the educational objectives of such charities.'

The SORP states that examples of these assets include:

> '(a) Charities with preservation objectives may hold specified or historic buildings or a complex of historic or architectural importance or a site where a building has been or where its remains can be seen.
> (b) Conservation charities may hold land relating to the habitat needs of species, or the environment generally, including areas of natural beauty or scientific interest.
> (c) Museums and art galleries hold collections and artefacts to educate the public and to promote the arts and sciences.'

Balance sheet

However, charities will not necessarily need to capitalise such heritage assets as were acquired in past accounting periods and omitted from previous balance sheets when the circumstances detailed below apply.

To fall within the definition of heritage assets, the charity must hold the relevant assets in pursuit of preservation or conservation objectives. The objective of the charity may be specifically of a preservation or conservation nature, or the heritage assets may be integral to a broader objective such as educating the public in history, the arts or science as in the case of museums and galleries.

Newly purchased heritage assets should be initially measured and recognised at their cost.

When heritage assets were acquired in past accounting periods and not capitalised, it may be difficult or costly to attribute a cost or value to them. In such cases these assets may only be excluded from the balance sheet if:

(a) reliable cost information is not available and conventional valuation approaches lack sufficient reliability, or
(b) significant costs are involved in the reconstruction or analysis of past accounting records or in valuation which are onerous compared with the additional benefit derived by users of the accounts in assessing the trustees' stewardship of the assets.

FRS 15 provides details of appropriate valuation bases. However, certain heritage buildings, structures or sites may present particular valuation issues. Whilst most specialised buildings can be valued using depreciated replacement cost (DRC), particular issues can arise in attempting to estimate the replacement cost of achieving the same service potential of certain historic buildings. The uniqueness of certain structures that are associated with particular locations, events, individuals or periods in history may be irreplaceable in terms of recreating the same service potential. The same service potential in terms of its heritage value or educational benefit to the public may only be achieved through the original structure or site.

Examples of heritage assets for which a cost or valuation may be difficult to attribute include:

(a) museum and gallery collections and other collections including the national archives, and
(b) medieval castles, archaeological sites, burial mounds, ruins, monuments and statues.

It may also be difficult or costly to attribute a cost or valuation to heritage assets which are donated where such assets are rarely sold on the open market. Where assets are purchased by a party who shortly afterwards donates the asset to the charity, the purchase price should be considered as reliable cost information and could be used as a reference point for the fair value of donations of similar assets. Where an asset is partly purchased by the charity and partly donated, it should be possible to make a reasonable estimate of its cost or value to the charity. Gifts on death or lifetime transfers of significant value may also carry valuations for inheritance tax purposes that may provide sufficient reliability.

Heritage assets should be included in a separate row in the balance sheet and can be further analysed, in the notes to the accounts, into classes appropriate to each charity – for example, collections, artefacts, and historic houses. An appropriate depreciation policy should be applied.

Certain heritage assets may have an indefinite useful life and a high residual value resulting in any depreciation charge being immaterial.

Where assets of historical, scientific or artistic importance are held by a charity but not for preservation or conservation purposes, they cannot be regarded as heritage assets. Examples of assets that do not fall within the heritage assets category include situations where a charity:

(a) holds and occupies an historic building as its administrative offices or as part of a property investment portfolio unrelated to any preservation or educational purpose;
(b) has in its possession works of art, or a collection of historic importance, antique furnishings within its boardroom, as a store of wealth, the retention of which is unrelated to any objectives of preservation or education, or
(c) occupies a functional property that is used to house or display a collection of heritage assets (unless the property itself is held for preservation or conservation purposes).

(See section **31.7** of Chapter 31.)

10.3.9 Inalienable assets

Charities may be required by trust law to retain an asset indefinitely for their own use or benefit and are effectively prohibited from its disposal without external consent. Such assets are termed inalienable.

Inalienability, of itself, does not preclude capitalisation of an asset.

Inalienable assets that do not fall within the definition of heritage assets should be capitalised and disclosed in the relevant categories of the balance sheet and in related notes. For example:

Balance sheet

(a) an investment property will be included as an investment within fixed assets, valued at open market value and disclosed as part of investment properties within the investment notes
(b) functional properties used by a charity in undertaking its activities are included within tangible fixed assets and are included at cost or valued on an existing use basis unless of a specialised nature, when a depreciated replacement cost valuation is adopted, and
(c) tangible fixed assets other than properties are included at cost or valued at open market value

Inalienable assets, by their nature, will belong to a charity's restricted funds, often being permanent endowment.

Abbeys, monasteries, cathedrals, historic churches and ancient centres of learning may not meet the heritage asset definition as the preservation of the buildings they occupy is unlikely to be the primary objective of the charity. Such assets might nevertheless be considered integral to the activities of the charity, and this may give rise to difficulties in ascertaining an estimate of the current cost of construction of an asset that has the same service potential as the existing one. For example, a new structure could recreate the floor area and seating capacity of a medieval cathedral but such a structure would not recreate the uniqueness of the original in terms of the religious and historical significance. In such cases a valuation of previously non-capitalised assets may be impractical and the notes should contain a statement to that effect explaining why conventional valuation techniques cannot be applied. Similar issues may arise in the context of artefacts contained within and associated with such structures – for example, religious artefacts contained within a cathedral or historic church.

10.3.10 Disclosure

Information on heritage assets (whether or not they have been capitalised) should be given in the notes to the accounts. The notes should contain:

(a) an analysis or narrative that enables the user to appreciate the age, scale and nature of the heritage assets held and the use made of them;
(b) either:
   (i) details of the cost (or value) of additions and disposals of heritage assets during the year; or
   (ii) where details of cost or value are not available (non-capitalisation in previous periods), a brief description of the nature of the assets acquired or disposed of, together with the sales proceeds of any disposals, and
(c) accounting policy notes explaining the charity's capitalisation policy in relation to heritage assets and the measurement bases adopted for their inclusion in the accounts.

10.3.11 Revaluation of tangible fixed assets (other than investments)

In accordance with FRS 15, tangible fixed assets (other than investment assets) do not need to be revalued unless the charity adopts a policy of revaluation. Where such a policy is adopted, whilst it need not be applied to all fixed assets, it must be applied to entire classes of fixed assets. Therefore, if an individual fixed asset is revalued, all other assets in that class must also be revalued. Classes of assets can be narrowly defined, within reason, according to the operations of the charity.

The initial valuation of an asset when it is donated or where it is capitalised as a result of the change in an accounting policy will not be regarded as a revaluation, and hence will not require the entire class of such assets to be revalued.

Where there is a policy to revalue such fixed assets their value must be updated on a regular basis. The trustees may use any reasonable approach to valuation at least every five years subject only to obtaining advice as to the possibility of any material movements between individual valuations. Where a charity has a number of such assets it will be acceptable for valuations to be carried out on a rolling basis over a five-year period. Independent formal professional valuations are not mandatory in the case of a charity, which instead can rely on the option of a suitably qualified person who could be a trustee or employee for this purpose.

In the case of assets other than properties, such as motor vehicles, there may be an active second-hand market for the asset, or appropriate indices may exist to allow a valuation to be made with reasonable certainty by an appropriate person (but not necessarily a qualified valuer) either internal or external to the charity. Where this method of valuation is used the assets' values must be updated annually. As an alternative to market value, such assets can be recorded at depreciated replacement cost.

10.3.12 Disclosure

Where any class of functional fixed assets of a charity has been revalued the notes to the accounts should give:

(a) the name and qualification of the valuer and whether they are a member of staff or a trustee or external to the charity;
(b) the basis or bases of valuation;
(c) where records are available, the historical cost less depreciation;
(d) date of the previous full valuation, and
(e) if the value has not been updated in the reporting period, a statement by the trustees that they are not aware of any material changes since the last valuation.

10.3.13 Impairment of fixed assets for use by the charity

On rare occasions a functional fixed asset may become impaired. This occurs if its net book value (at cost or valuation) is higher than its recoverable amount. In such a case, FRS 11 Impairment of tangible fixed assets would require it to be written down to its recoverable amount.

The recoverable amount is the higher of the net realisable value and the value in use. Value in use is normally the present value of the future cash flows obtainable as a result of an asset's continued use. If a fixed asset is not held for the main purpose of generating surplus cash flows, either by itself or in conjunction with other assets, it is not appropriate to measure the value in use of the asset at an amount based on expected future cash flows. In such cases, an alternative measure of its service potential may be more relevant, such as the intrinsic worth of the service delivery or the replacement cost of the asset. Each charity can determine its own measure of service delivery but this must be reasonable, justifiable and consistently operated.

Impairment reviews should only be carried out where this is some indication that the recoverable amount of a functional fixed asset is below its net book value. Such a review should, as far as possible, be carried out on individual assets. Where this is not possible, certain categories of assets can be grouped instead.

Events or changes which may indicate an impairment are:

(a) physical deterioration, change or obsolescence of the fixed asset;
(b) social, demographic or environmental changes resulting in a reduction of beneficiaries for a charity;
(c) changes in the law, other regulations or standards which adversely affect the activities of a charity;
(d) management commitments to undertake a significant reorganisation;
(e) a major loss of key employees associated with particular activities of a charity, and
(f) operating losses on activities using fixed assets primarily to generate incoming resources.

Where an impairment review is required, the charity should first determine the net realisable value of the asset. If this is lower than the net book value, the value in use will need to be considered. If the value in use is considered to be above the net book value, the asset should be valued at the net book value. If it is decided to sell the asset, it should be valued at its expected net realisable value.

Value in use calculations should not be used to manipulate the write-down of fixed assets. For instance when a new specialised asset is purchased, although it may have a low net realisable value, it is unlikely that it will suffer an impairment in service delivery within the first years after acquisition.

Where there is an impairment loss that needs to be recognised, charities should determine this in accordance with the requirements of FRS 11 (whilst being able to use alternative valuation methods for some assets). The loss should be treated as additional depreciation and included in the SOFA in accordance with para. 218 of the SORP. The revised carrying amount of the asset should be depreciated over its remaining useful economic life.

10.3.14 Disclosure

The methods used in the impairment review to determine net realisable value and value in use should be disclosed in the notes to the accounts.

10.4 Investment assets

10.4.1 Introduction

The extent of a charity's powers of investment will be set out in its governing document. These will generally be quite wide, giving freedom to invest more or less as an individual would in a range of investments and investment products, but subject to the overriding duties of trustees. However, a number of older non-incorporated charities (and a few incorporated bodies also) have historically been bound by the Trustee Investments Act 1961 – either through specific reference to this legislation or, in the absence of appropriate powers in the trust deed, by default.

The 1961 Act permitted a split of investments between two pools, the narrower range (consisting primarily of government stocks and other fixed interest securities) and the wider range (encompassing also those equities that satisfied certain conditions). The split was initially on a 50:50 basis, although this was relaxed in 1995 such that the wider range could be equal to up to three times the value of the narrower.

Because of the under-performance of gilts compared to equities, the terms of the Trustee Investment Act have undoubtedly been very costly for those charities subject to its restrictions. However, it had always been possible for trustees to apply to the Charity Commission for an extension of their investment powers and, in anticipation of new legislation, the Commission announced in December 1999 that it would be willing to agree to such applications more or less automatically.

The anticipated legislation came in the form of the Trustee Act 2000, which became effective from 1 February 2001 and extended to almost all charitable trusts the wide powers of investment that would be found in any modern trust deed (if trustees consider that they remain subject to restrictions that inhibit their work, the option of approaching the Charity Commission is still available). The

Balance sheet

Trustee Act 2000 does, however, impose two requirements that apply when unincorporated charities exercise any investment power:

- the trustees must take proper advice, and
- they must have regard to the 'standard investment criteria', (that is, relating to the suitability of the investment proposed and to the need for diversification).

The Act also imposes a new duty of care and a requirement that trustees, when delegating asset management functions, should prepare a written policy statement to guide their appointed agent.

Although strictly applicable only to unincorporated charities, the Trustee Act 2000 contains a good deal of guidance that should be regarded as 'best practice' when it comes to dealing with investment matters.

10.4.2 Presentation

In effect, the SORP takes a portfolio approach to the classification of investments. Because investment assets are generally held with the overall intention of retaining them long-term for the continuing benefit of the charity in the form of income and capital gains, an investment should be classified as a fixed asset, except where the intention is to realise the investment without reinvestment of the sale proceeds.

Investment assets (including investments and investment properties and cash held for investment purposes) should be classified as a separate category within fixed assets except where the intention is to realise the asset without reinvestment of the sale proceeds. In such a case, it should be reclassified as a current asset. The reason for this is that investment assets are generally held with the overall intention of retaining them long-term, (that is, as fixed assets) for the continuing benefit of the charity in the form of income and capital appreciation.

10.4.3 Valuation of investment assets

All investment assets should be shown in the balance sheet at market value or at the trustees' best estimate of market value, as described below. Market value best represents a true and fair view of the value of these assets to the charity, given the duty of the trustees to administer the portfolio of investment assets so as to obtain the best investment performance without undue risk. Investment assets should not be depreciated. All changes in value in the year, whether or not realised, should be reported in the 'gains and losses on investment assets' section of the SOFA.

Most freely tradable investments will have a readily available market price (for example, shares on a recognised stock exchange). For investment assets for which there is no readily identifiable market price, the trustees should adopt a reasonable approach: for instance, valuing shares in unlisted companies by reference to underlying net assets or earnings or the dividend record, as appropriate. Sometimes, where there is no readily available market value for an investment asset (such as a trading subsidiary), the cost of obtaining a valuation outweighs the benefit to the users of the accounts. In such a situation, the asset may be included in the accounts at cost.

For investment assets other than shares or securities, the trustees may use any reasonable approach to valuation, which must be done at least every five years subject only to obtaining advice as to the possibility of any material movements between individual valuations. If there is a material movement the assets must be revalued. Where a charity has a number of such assets, it will be acceptable for valuations to be carried out on a rolling basis over a five-year period.

10.4.4 Disclosure

Where values are determined other than by reference to readily available market prices, the notes to the accounts should disclose who has made the valuation giving their name, qualification and position (for example, trustee, employee, external valuer) and how the valuation has been carried out.

In the rare case where the size or nature of a holding of securities is such that the market is thought by the trustees not to be capable of absorbing the sale of the shareholding without a material effect on the quoted price, the trustees should summarise the position in the notes to the accounts. If they are able to do so, the trustees should give an opinion on how much the market price should be adjusted to take this fact into consideration.

The notes to the accounts should show all changes in values of investment assets and reconcile the opening and closing book values.

The notes should also show the total value of investment assets divided between distinct types. As a minimum this would normally include:

(a) investment properties;
(b) investments listed on a recognised stock exchange or ones valued by reference to such investments, such as unit trusts and common investment funds;
(c) investments in subsidiary or associated undertakings or in companies which are connected persons;
(d) other unlisted securities;

Balance sheet

(e) cash and settlements pending held as part of the investment portfolio, and
(f) any other investments.

Items in categories (a) to (f) above should be further differentiated between investment assets in the UK and investment assets outside the UK

The total value of shares or investment schemes (including unit trusts) relating to companies listed on a UK stock exchange or incorporated in the UK are treated as investment assets in the UK, and no further analysis is required of whether such entities invest their funds in the UK or outside the UK.

Further details should be given in the notes to the accounts to show how the portfolio is structured. This should indicate direct and indirect investment in listed securities (including unit trusts), details of any material investments and any material restrictions which might apply on the realisation of any such assets.

The notes to the accounts should indicate the value of investments held in each type of fund. This may be included in the overall analysis of assets held in the different type of funds.

10.4.5 Disclosure examples

Example 1 – David Trust

10. Investments

	2010 £'000	2009 £'000
Market value at 1 October 2009	**27,102**	27,501
Acquisitions at cost	**5,150**	4,013
Sales proceeds from disposals	**(5,720)**	(4,309)
Gain/(loss) in the year	**467**	(103)
Market value at 30 September 2010	**26,999**	27,102
Investments at market value comprised:		
UK equities	**18,897**	18,168
UK fixed interest securities	**8,102**	8,934
	26,999	27,102
Historical cost as at 30 September 2010	**14,303**	14,121

All investments are listed UK securities.

A more complex example, including investments held in unrestricted, restricted and endowment funds, as well as invested deferred income is presented in the following example.

Example 2 – Thierry Trust Fund

10. Investments

Group:	Unre-stricted £'000	Re-stricted £'000	Endow-ment £'000	Advance fees £'000	Total £'000
Balance at 1 September 2009	203	744	3,963	2,027	6,937
Additions	20	73	1,402	–	1,495
Disposals at book value	–	(33)	(1,605)	(41)	(1,679)
Revaluations	27	27	273	(47)	280
Balance at 31 August 2010	**250**	**811**	**4,033**	**1,939**	**7,033**
Listed on UK Stock Exchange (Historical cost: £6,150,000)	250	711	3,783	1,939	**6,683**
Cash deposits	–	100	250	–	**350**

Charity: as above	7,033
Investment in Subsidiary Company (see Note 3 and below)	7
	7,040

The assets and liabilities of the subsidiary were:	2010 £'000	2009 £'000
Tangible fixed assets	8	12
Current assets	162	215
	170	227
Creditors: amounts falling due within one year	(155)	(215)
	15	12
Representing:		
Share capital	7	7
Profit and loss account	8	5
	15	12

Details of the subsidiary's profit and loss account are given in note 3.

10.5 Programme-related investments

Programme related investments (also known as social investments) are made directly in pursuit of the organisation's charitable purposes. Although they can generate some financial return (funding may or may not be provided on commercial terms), the primary motivation for making them is not financial but to further the objects of the funding charity. Such investments could include

Balance sheet

loans to individual beneficiaries (for example, for housing deposits) or to other charities (for example, in relation to regeneration projects).

Such investments should be disclosed separately within the investment asset category from those investments intended primarily to generate a financial return for the charity.

Programme-related investments should generally be included in the balance sheet at the amount invested less any impairments (in the case of equity or loans) and any amounts repaid (in the case of loans). Impairments should be charged to resources expended on charitable activities. Similarly a loan subsequently converted to a grant would be charged to charitable activities.

Where a gain is made on the disposal of a programme-related investment, then the gain should either be set off against any prior impairment loss or included as a gain on disposal of fixed assets for the charity's own use and recorded under 'other incoming resources'.

10.5.1 Disclosure

Where the use of programme-related investments forms a material part of the work of the charity, or the amounts form a material part of the investment assets of the charity, the notes to the accounts should show all changes in carrying values of programme-related investments, including any impairment losses, and reconcile the opening and closing carrying values of such investments.

The notes should also analyse programme-related investments held between equity, loan and other investments and indicate the charitable objectives, programmes or projects the investment supports.

10.6 Current assets

Current assets (other than current asset investments) should normally be recognised at the lower of their cost and net realisable value.

10.6.1 Disclosure

Where there are debtors that do not fit into any of the following categories, the headings may be added to or adapted as appropriate to the type of debtor and nature of the charity.

Debtors should be analysed in the notes to the accounts between short-term and long-term (above one year) giving amounts for the following:

(a) trade debtors;
(b) amounts due from subsidiary and associated undertakings;
(c) other debtors;
(d) prepayments, and
(e) accrued income.

Where long-term debtors are material in the context of the total net current assets, they should be separately shown in the balance sheet.

Where investments are held as current assets, the same disclosure is required as for fixed asset investments.

10.7 Current liabilities and long-term creditors

Liabilities should normally be recognised at their settlement value. In the case of provisions, this will be the amount that an entity would rationally pay to settle the obligation at the balance-sheet date or to transfer it to a third party at that time and may therefore involve discounting.

10.7.1 Disclosure

Where there are creditors that do not fit into any of the following categories, the headings may be added to or adapted as appropriate to the type of creditor and nature of the charity.

The totals for both short-term and long-term creditors should each be separately analysed in the notes giving amounts for the following:

(a) loans and overdrafts;
(b) trade creditors;
(c) amounts due to subsidiary and associated undertakings;
(d) other creditors;
(e) accruals, and
(f) deferred income.

Where a charity is acting as an intermediary agent (as opposed to a custodian trustee) for another organisation (as described in para. 112 of the SORP), any assets held and the associated liabilities should be separately identified in the notes to the accounts but not included in the balance sheet. The notes to the accounts should provide sufficient detail to enable the reader of the accounts to understand the relationship and nature of the transactions between the charity, the funding organisation and the recipient of the funds.

Balance sheet

10.8 Provisions for liabilities and charges

Expenditure resulting from provisions that arise due to a legal or constructive obligation (as per FRS 12) should be recognised as expenditure in the SOFA. Such provisions should be appropriately split in the balance sheet between liabilities due within one year and those falling due after one year.

The amount recognised as a liability should be the best estimate of the expenditure required to settle the present obligation at the balance-sheet date or to transfer it to a third party at that time. When calculating this amount, consideration should be given to:

(a) the timing of the cash flows, and
(b) future events and uncertainties that may affect the amount required to settle the obligation.

Where provisions are accrued in the current financial year but are to be paid over several years, then future payments may have a reduced value in today's terms (current value). Where the effect is material, the outflow of resources required to settle the obligation at the balance-sheet date should be discounted to their present value. The discount rate used should reflect the current assessments of the time value of money and the risks specific to the provision. The interest rate either for the cost of borrowing or investment could be an appropriate discount rate.

The best estimate of the liability should be reviewed at the balance-sheet date and adjusted appropriately. If a transfer of resources is no longer needed to settle the obligation, then the amount of the liability no longer representing an obligation should be deducted from the expenditure category where it was originally charged in the SOFA.

Where a charity has earmarked part of its unrestricted funds for a particular future purpose, this intention to expend funds in the future is not recognised as a provision for a liability in the accounts. Such earmarked amounts may be recorded by setting up a designated fund.

10.8.1 Disclosure

Particulars of all material provisions for commitments accrued in the balance sheet as liabilities should be disclosed in the notes. Similarly particulars of all material commitments in respect of specific charitable projects should be disclosed if they have not been charged in the accounts.

Provisions for liabilities and charges

These particulars should include the amounts involved, when the commitments are likely to be met and the movements on commitments previously reported. Particulars of all other material binding commitments should also be disclosed (for example, operating leases).

The notes should distinguish between those commitments included on the balance sheet as liabilities and those that are intentions to spend and are not included; but in both cases, they should detail:

(a) the reason for the commitments, giving separate disclosure for material projects;
(b) the total amount of the commitments, including amounts already charged in the accounts;
(c) the amount of commitments outstanding at the start of the year;
(d) any amounts charged in the SOFA for the year;
(e) any amounts released during the year due to a change in the value in the commitments, and
(f) the amount of commitments outstanding at the end of the year and an indication as to how much is payable within one year and over one year.

Any designated funds should be separately disclosed as part of the unrestricted funds of the charity and appropriately described in the notes. The purpose of the disclosure is to identify that portion of the unrestricted funds that has been set aside to meet the commitments. Activities that are to be wholly financed from future income would not form part of such designation.

10.8.2 Disclosure example

This example includes a note which discloses commitments to pay grants which have not been accrued as well as commitments relating to leases and capital expenditure.

Example *SRE Aid Foundation*

24. Commitments

	2010 Group £'000	2009 Group £'000	2010 Charity £'000	2009 Charity £'000
At 30 September 2010, the charity had commitments as follows: Capital expenditure authorised but not contracted for:	79	200	79	200

Balance sheet

	2010 Group £'000	2009 Group £'000	2010 Charity £'000	2009 Charity £'000
Commitments in respect of grants approved for projects which have not been accrued in the financial statements but will form part of grants:				
Within one year	472	319	472	319
Between one and two years	180	165	180	165
Between two and three years	42	38	42	38
	694	**522**	**694**	**522**
Annual commitments under non-cancellable operating leases for land and buildings which expire:				
Within one year	185	138	137	101
In two to five years	416	281	416	281
Over five years	393	574	372	553
	994	**993**	**925**	**935**
Annual commitments under non-cancellable operating leases for motor vehicles which expire:				
Within one year	1	–	–	–
In two to five years	45	46	28	28
	46	**46**	**28**	**28**

10.9 Defined benefit pension scheme asset or liability

Any asset or liability derived from a surplus or deficit in a defined benefit pension scheme (calculated in accordance with FRS 17: Retirement Benefits) should be included within this category and disclosed on the face of the balance sheet.

A surplus or deficit in a defined benefit scheme will normally give rise to an asset or liability within the unrestricted funds of the reporting charity. The circumstances in which the pension asset or liability may accrue to a restricted fund are set out in paras 433–442.

Recommendations on the application of FRS 17 to charities and the required accounting methods and disclosures are set out in a separate section on accounting for retirement benefits in paragraphs 430–448.

10.10 Share capital

A number of charities (such as industrial and provident societies) are constituted with a share capital. A small number of charities incorporated as companies under the CO Act 2006 may also have share capital. Usually this is a nominal amount (such as £10) and although this is legally 'owners' equity', the prohibition on owners benefiting from this share ownership effectively means that money contributed for share capital forms part of the unrestricted funds of the charity. Nevertheless, company law requires share capital to be shown separately in the balance sheet.

10.11 Revaluation reserve

Charities that are companies are required to report, in respect of their unrestricted funds, the difference between the historic cost of fixed assets (including investment assets) and their revalued amount as a revaluation reserve.

10.12 Pension reserve

When there is a surplus or a deficit on a defined benefit pension scheme that results in an asset or a liability being recognised by the charity, the recognition of the pension asset or liability will result in the creation of a pension reserve. This reserve will be negative in the case of a liability. If the pension asset or liability relates only to unrestricted funds then this reserve will be part of unrestricted funds. If, however, the criteria set out in paras 438–442, are met and the pension asset/liability is allocated to a restricted fund, then the pension reserve will be part of that restricted fund.

10.13 Guarantees

All material guarantees given by the charity, and the conditions under which liabilities might arise as a result of such guarantees, should be disclosed in a note to the accounts.

10.14 Contingent assets and liabilities

A charity may have contingent assets and liabilities as defined in FRS 12 Provisions, contingent liabilities and contingent assets.

A charity should not recognise incoming or outgoing resources or gains and losses arising respectively from contingent assets or contingent liabilities in the SOFA or the balance sheet.

Contingent assets are not recognised because it could result in the recognition of incoming resources that may never be realised. However, when the realisation of the incoming resources is virtually certain, then the asset is not a contingent asset

Balance sheet

and the resource or gain arising should be included in the SOFA as an incoming resource and in the balance sheet as a debtor.

Where it becomes probable that there will be a future outflow of resources to settle an item previously regarded as a contingent liability it should cease to be contingent and should be accrued in the accounts. The amount of the liability should (except in extremely rare circumstances where no reliable estimate can be made) be capable of being estimated with reasonable accuracy at the date on which the accounts are approved.

The probability of a contingent asset or liability resulting in a future transfer of resources (to or from the charity) should be continually assessed and the recognition of the asset or liability should be reviewed as appropriate.

10.14.1 Disclosure

Material contingent assets and liabilities should be disclosed in the notes to the accounts, unless the probability of a future transfer of resources (to or from the charity) is extremely remote – in which case no disclosure is necessary.

The accounts should disclose the nature of each contingency, the uncertainties that are expected to affect the outcome, and a prudent estimate of the financial effect where an amount has not been accrued. If such an estimate cannot be made, the accounts should explain why it is not practicable to make such an estimate.

Where there is more than one contingent asset or liability, they may be sufficiently similar in nature for them to be grouped together as one class and be disclosed in a single statement.

Where a liability has been accrued but there is still a contingent liability arising from the same set of circumstances, the notes to the accounts should link the provision and the contingent liability.

10.15 Loan liabilities

If any specific assets (whether land or other property) of the charity are subject to a mortgage or charge given as security for a loan or other liability, a note to the accounts should disclose:

(a) particulars of the assets which are subject to the mortgage or charge, and
(b) the amount of the loan or liability and its proportion to the value of the assets mortgaged or charged.

Loan liabilities

The amounts and interest and repayment terms of all inter-fund loans (summarised, if necessary) should be disclosed in the notes to the accounts. Loans made to trading subsidiaries, the security provided, the interest payable and the repayment terms should be disclosed as a separate item in the notes to the accounts.

Chapter 11 – Accounting for separate funds

11.1 Introduction

The main purpose of a charity's accounts is to give an overall view of the total resources available to a charity during the period and how those resources have been expended, with the balance sheet showing the position at the year end.

But there are additional requirements for charities. Many receive monies which, either by the donor or by the terms of the appeal, are earmarked for special purposes. Similarly, income generated from assets held in a particular fund may be subject to donor-imposed restrictions as to its use or to the fund to which it belongs. In order to achieve these distinctions between the various funds, the accounting records need to be somewhat sophisticated, tailored to meet the circumstances so that it is known which assets and liabilities are held in which funds.

11.2 What is a 'fund'?

The glossary presented in Appendix 1 to SORP 2005 defines a 'fund' (GL27) as:

'a pool of resources, held and maintained separately from other pools because of the circumstances in which the resources were originally received or the way in which they have subsequently been treated. At the broadest level a fund will be one of two kinds: a restricted fund or an unrestricted fund.'

The accounts should provide a summary of the main funds, differentiating in particular between the unrestricted income funds, restricted income funds and endowment funds. The columnar format of the Statement of Financial Activities (SOFA) (and of the balance sheet, where the option is taken to use a columnar presentation of funds) is designed to achieve this. Depending on the materiality of each, the notes to the accounts should group the restricted funds under one or more heads.

Unrestricted income funds may be either 'general' or 'designated'.

Restricted funds may be 'income' or 'endowment'. Endowment funds may be either 'expendable' or 'permanent'.

11.2.1 Unrestricted income funds

Nearly all charities have a fund which is available to the trustees to apply for the general purposes of the charity as set out in its governing document. This is the charity's 'unrestricted' fund (sometimes called a 'general' fund) because the trustees are free to use it for any of the charity's purposes. Income generated from assets held in an unrestricted fund will be unrestricted income.

11.2.2 Designated funds

A designated fund is a particular form of unrestricted fund, consisting of amounts of unrestricted funds which have been allocated or designated for specific purposes by the charity itself. The use of designated funds for their designated purpose is at the discretion of the trustees. Designated funds are not to be confused with restricted funds. While the former are established as a result of a decision of the trustees, which may be later altered, or rescinded, the latter arise either from donor-imposed restrictions or by the terms of the specific appeal or the governing document in some cases. Designated funds are often employed as buffers to temper the effect on the balance sheet (funds analysis) of, for example, future maintenance costs of buildings. Paragraph 75 to the SORP recommends that the precise purpose of such funds is given in the notes.

11.2.3 Restricted funds

Paragraph 2 of Appendix 3 to the SORP states that restricted funds are 'funds subject to specific trusts, which may be declared by the donor(s), or with their authority (for example, in a public appeal), but still within the wider objects of the charity'. Restricted funds may be restricted income funds, expendable at the discretion of the trustees in furtherance of the charity's pursuits in accordance with the conditions imposed. Or, they may be capital funds, where the assets are required to be invested, or retained for actual use (for example, an historic building).

If the trustees use restricted income in a way which is inconsistent with the restrictions imposed, they may be in breach of trust. Accordingly, it is essential that due care is taken to spend from a particular restricted fund only where the trusts so permit. Nonetheless, expenditure may be charged to a restricted fund which is not, at the time, in credit (or in sufficient credit), provided that there is a genuine anticipation of income which can properly be credited to that fund to meet the expenditure. In order to allow for the income not materialising, the trusts of the fund used to finance the expenditure should be sufficiently widely drawn to permit that expenditure. Expenditure charged to an unrestricted fund should not, subsequently, be recharged to a restricted fund, simply in order to increase the amount of that fund.

Where restricted income has been temporarily invested, prior to being used for a suitable charitable purpose, any income derived from the investment should be added to, and will form part of, the restricted income fund in question – unless specified otherwise by the donor or the terms of the appeal. Conversely, unless a specific purpose has been declared by the donor, or the terms of the appeal, for the application of the income (in which case, such income will be restricted income), that income may be applied for the general purposes of the charity.

The power may be conferred upon the trustees to convert capital funds into expendable income. Were such a power to be exercised, the relevant funds would become restricted or unrestricted income, depending on whether the trusts permit expenditure only for specific purposes or for any of the purposes of the charity.

11.2.4 Endowment funds

Paragraph 3 of Appendix 3 to the SORP states that 'a capital fund where there is no power to convert the capital into income is known as a permanent endowment fund, which must generally be held indefinitely'.

The concept of 'permanence' does not, however, necessarily mean that the assets held in the endowment fund cannot be exchanged, although, in some cases, the trusts will require the retention of a specific asset (for example, an historic building) for actual use. What it does mean is that the fund cannot be used as if it were income – that is, to make payments or grants to others. Where assets held in a permanent endowment fund are exchanged, their place in the fund must be taken by the assets received in exchange. Paragraph 3 of Appendix 3 states that 'exchange' may simply mean 'a change of investment', but it may also mean, for example, 'the application of the proceeds of sale of freehold land and buildings in the purchase or improvement of freehold property'.

All incoming resources and resources expended relating to endowment funds should be included in the SOFA. Paragraph 75 of the SORP recommends that the notes disclose how the funds have arisen. As well as identifying any major individual funds, the notes should also analyse the funds between permanent endowment and expendable endowment.

11.3 Fund structure

Paragraph 75 of the SORP recommends that the accounts should provide information on the structure of the charity's funds so as to disclose the individual fund balances and the reasons for them. Although details of individual funds may be given in the notes, para. 247 of the SORP recommends, and the Regulations require that, as a minimum, the balance sheet provides a summary of the main funds, differentiating between restricted, including capital (endowment), funds and unrestricted, including designated, funds. The decision as to the most appropriate form of presentation is conferred on the trustees, who should have regard both to the complexity of the fund structure and to the need to avoid confusion between the movements on the various funds.

11.4 Reconciliation and analysis of funds

11.4.1 Reconciliation of opening and closing funds

Paragraph 74 of the SORP recommends that the SOFA should provide a reconciliation of the opening and closing balances on all of the funds of the charity. The reconciliation should be analysed between unrestricted and restricted and, in the latter case, between income and capital (that is, endowment) funds. Further analysis of individual funds (that is. in the case of endowment funds, between permanent endowment and expendable endowment) can be relegated to the notes. Any restricted funds in deficit should be separately disclosed and an explanation provided in the trustees' report. These analyses will show that the charity trustees have accounted for the proper administration of individual funds, in accordance with their terms.

11.4.2 Analysis of the total amount of assets and liabilities

Paragraph 75(a) of the SORP recommends that the assets and liabilities should be analysed between the various funds. It is important to be able to distinguish between the assets and liabilities held in the different funds in order to maintain the integrity of those funds.

11.4.3 Are the resources held in an appropriate form?

It is important to provide an indication as to whether or not sufficient resources are held in an appropriate form to enable the funds concerned to be applied in accordance with restrictions imposed. Thus, funds which are to be spent in the short term need to be matched with assets and investments of a short-term nature. If a fund that has to be applied in the short term is represented by assets which cannot reasonably be expected to be realised in the short term, the charity may not be able to apply its funds as directed.

Paragraph 75(b) of the SORP recommends that the notes indicate whether or not sufficient resources are so held, but not what action is being taken by the charity trustees, or what the consequences (if any) might be, if assets are not held in that form. For example, if a charity has a fund which is to be spent in the near future, it should be made clear in the notes whether or not the assets held (or expected to be received) in the fund are liquid assets.

11.4.4 Realised and unrealised elements

Realised and unrealised gains and losses, provisions for depreciation and diminutions in value on assets held in a particular fund form part of that fund. Similarly, provisions for depreciation, or for a permanent fall in value, form part of the fund in which the asset is held.

There is no recommendation to analyse the total amount of each fund between its realised and unrealised elements.

11.4.5 The nature and purpose of each fund

Paragraph 75 of the SORP recommends the disclosure of how each of the funds has arisen and the purpose of each major fund.

Separate sets of statements may be produced for each major fund and linked to a total summary. The trustees should decide on the most suitable form of presentation, bearing in mind the complexity of the fund structure and the need to avoid confusion between the movements on the various funds.

11.5 Transfers between funds

Paragraph 75(d) of the SORP recommends that material transfers out of restricted funds should be shown separately from allocations to designated funds and should be accompanied by an explanation of their nature and purpose.

The Regulations also require the notes to give an itemised analysis of any material movement between any of the restricted funds of the charity, or between a restricted and unrestricted fund, together with an explanation of the nature and purpose of each of those funds.

11.6 Overhead costs

Unless specifically forbidden by the donor or the terms of the trust a reasonable allocation of overhead expenses (for example, governance and costs of generating funds) can be set against restricted funds.

11.7 Disclosures – particulars of individual funds and notes to the accounts

The notes to the accounts should provide information on the structure of the charity's funds so as to disclose the fund balances and the reasons for them differentiating between unrestricted income funds (both general and designated),

Accounting for separate funds

restricted income funds, permanent endowment and expendable endowment as well as identifying any material individual funds among them in particular:

(a) the assets and liabilities representing each type of fund of the charity should be clearly summarised and analysed (for example, investments, fixed assets, net current assets) between those funds
(b) disclosure of how each of the funds has arisen (including designated funds), the restrictions imposed and the purpose of each fund. An indication should be given as to whether or not sufficient resources are held in an appropriate form to enable each fund to be applied in accordance with any restrictions. For example, if a charity has a fund which is to be spent in the near future, it should be made clear in the notes whether or not the assets held (or expected to be received) in the fund are liquid assets
(c) any funds in deficit should always be separately disclosed. An explanation should be given in the Trustees' Annual Report (see para. 55(b)). Designated funds should never be in deficit
(d) explanations should be provided for material movements in the funds. In disclosing details of movements on funds, material transfers between different funds and allocations to designated funds should be separately disclosed, without netting off, and should be accompanied by an explanation of the nature of the transfers or allocations and the reasons for them; and
(e) where, in relation to permanent endowment, a total return approach to investments has been adopted, the notes to the accounts should give particulars of the movements in the value of the unapplied total return for the financial year. The note should reconcile the balance held as unapplied total return at the beginning with that at the end of the financial year.

11.7.1 Disclosure examples

Example AEE Support Centre

12. Analysis of net assets between funds

	General Funds £	Designated Funds £	Restricted Funds £	Total Funds £
Tangible fixed assets	7,500	–	3,750	**11,250**
Investments	9,825	1,829	–	**11,654**
Current assets	5,170	10,000	19,138	**34,308**
Current liabilities	(5,928)	–	(2,456)	**(8,384)**
Net assets at 31 March 2010	**16,567**	**11,829**	**20,432**	**48,828**

In the example below, the movements on all the funds are presented in one note. As the charity has a small number of designated and restricted funds, the presentation of one note brings together the movements on all funds into one clear disclosure.

Disclosures – particulars of individual funds and notes to the accounts

13. Movements in funds

	At 1 April 2009 £	Incoming Resources £	Outgoing Resources £	Transfers £	At 31 March 2010 £
Restricted funds:					
Computer equipment	–	5,000	(1,250)	–	**3,750**
Advice and information	1,316	70,000	(67,008)	–	**4,308**
Outreach	–	80,765	(68,391)	–	**12,374**
Total restricted funds	1,316	155,765	(136,649)	–	**20,432**
Unrestricted funds:					
Designated training project equipment fund	–	–	–	10,000	**10,000**
Designated revaluation fund	1,067	762	–	–	**1,829**
General funds	19,182	115,900	(108,515)	(10,000)	**16,567**
Total unrestricted funds	20,249	116,662	(108,515)	–	**28,396**
Total funds	21,565	272,427	(245,164)	–	**48,828**

Purposes of restricted funds

Computer equipment	The balance will fund future depreciation of computers which were originally purchased using restricted funds and which the donor specified must be retained.
Advice and information	The fund is for the advice and information activity as explained in the trustees' report.
Outreach	This is a fund for outreach work with young people who are vulnerable or falling into drug misuse. The balance arose from a delay in using grants which were given for the purpose of appointing new staff. Staff were appointed late in the year and all the fund will be utilised in forthcoming months.

Purposes of designated funds

Training project equipment	The management committee has designated funds for purchase of new equipment in the training project.
Revaluation fund	The revaluation fund is required by the Companies Act 2006 and represents the amount by which investments exceed their historical cost.

Where a charity has several designated or restricted funds, then separate notes may give more effective presentation and clearer information to the reader. The example below takes this approach. Note 16, the unrestricted funds note, contains an explanation that funds have been designated for possible repairs that may be required under a property lease. A provision for this item cannot be created because the possibility of repairs would not constitute a provision under FRS 12.

Accounting for separate funds

Example – N & J Support Ltd

16. Unrestricted funds of the charity

	General Fund £'000	Designated Funds £'000	Total £'000
Balance at 1 April 2009	1,263	31	1,294
Movement in funds for the year	83	–	83
Transfer of amount designated for future repairs	(136)	136	–
Balance at 31 March 2010	**1,210**	**167**	**1,377**

The trustees have designated funds for repairs which may be required under the lease for property.

17. Restricted funds

	At 1 April 2009 £'000	Incoming Resources £'000	Outgoing Resources £'000	At 31 March 2010 £'000
Piano fund	10	3	5	8
Ceramics residency	3	–	3	–
Jazz course	–	1	1	–
Clay at the park	2	–	–	2
Kennel Ride	2	–	–	2
The ugly show	–	1	1	–
AFC Park capital project	–	73	73	–
	17	**78**	**83**	**12**

The piano fund is for the purchase of a baby grand piano, which was acquired in June 2010.

The ceramics residency fund is to support the appointment of a resident ceramist. The appointment was made at the beginning of September 2009.

The jazz course fund is specifically to underwrite the costs of the jazz weekend held in March 2010 as an attempt to bring professional and amateur musicians together.

The clay at the park fund is to publish documents and create an archive relating to the development of clay craft in the borough.

The Kennel Ride fund is to assist with the charity's project with the young people of Kennel Ride.

The ugly show fund was to underwrite the costs of an exhibition from five artists held in September and October 2009 which explored notions of beauty.

The AFC Park capital project was funded by the Arts Council, which gave the charity a grant of £73,000. This grant was towards the cost of a further feasibility study for alterations, refurbishment and a new extension to the theatre, which is a Grade 2 listed building. It included the appointment of consultants and the payment of professional fees.

A final comprehensive example includes the disclosure of movements in endowed funds.

Example – James Trust

14. Net assets of the group's funds

The group's net assets belong to the various funds (including Advance fees) as follows.

	Fixed assets £'000	Investments £'000	Net current assets £'000	Long-term liabilities £'000	Fund balances £'000
Endowment funds	–	4,033	–	–	4,033
Restricted funds	–	811	275	–	1,086
Unrestricted funds:					
Designated funds					
Advance fees	–	1,939	185	(1,831)	293
Tangible fixed assets fund	9,562	–	(2,000)	–	7,562
Heritage fund	–	250	2	–	252
Non-charitable trading funds	8	–	–	–	8
General Reserve	–	–	1,190	(44)	1,146
	9,570	7,033	(348)	(1,875)	14,380

14A. Endowed funds: movements in the year

	Balance at 1 September 2009 £'000	Incoming endowments £'000	Amounts expended £'000	Transfers and investment gains/(losses) £'000	Balance at 31 August 2010 £'000
Permanent endowments:					
Foundation capital	563	–	–	15	578
Other special trusts:					
Grants and allowances	1,772	8	–	66	1,846
Scholarships and bursaries	1,460	–	–	(17)	1,443
Prize and other funds	168	–	–	(2)	166
	3,963	8	–	62	4,033

Foundation capital represents the original endowment to provide free education. The income of this fund contributes to the free education of pupils whose parents live in Newshire.

Accounting for separate funds

Other special trusts consist of a number of individual trusts and prize funds set up by individual donors.

Each fund is allocated its proportion of investment income and gains and losses and bears its own expenses.

14B. Restricted funds: movements in the year

	Balance at 1 September 2009 £'000	Income £'000	Expended £'000	Transfers and investment gains/(losses) £'000	Balance at 31 August 2010 £'000
New building fund	–	320	(90)	–	230
Grants and allowances	157	112	(112)	(8)	149
Scholarships and bursaries	504	113	(86)	20	551
Prize and other funds	99	28	(21)	4	110
Foundation	44	39	(36)	(1)	46
	804	**612**	**(345)**	**15**	**1,086**

Included above is a transfer of £3,700 from a bursary fund to the grants and allowances fund.

14C. Unrestricted funds: movements in the year

	Balance at 1 September 2009 £'000	Income £'000	Expended £'000	Transfers and investment gains/(losses) £'000	Balance at 31 August 2010 £'000
Designated funds:					
Advance fee income	250	248	(165)	(40)	293
Tangible fixed assets fund	7,374	–	–	188	7,562
Heritage fund	219	20	–	13	252
General reserve	890	8,716	(8,511)	51	1,146
Charity	**8,733**	**8,984**	**(8,676)**	**212**	**9,253**
Non-charitable trading funds	5	1,694	(1,466)	(225)	8
Group	**8,738**	**10,678**	**(10,142)**	**(13)**	**9,261**

Advance fee income represents the amount set aside to cover any future shortfall on the accrued liability for advance fees.

The tangible fixed assets fund represents the net book value of tangible fixed assets less the bank facilities secured on those assets.

The Governors are setting aside, in the Heritage Fund, monies towards the costs of extensions and refurbishment of the school buildings in preparation for the school's centenary celebrations in 2015.

The general reserve fund represents those funds which are unrestricted and not designated for other purposes.

11.8 Total return

The Charity Commission has developed an approach as to how trustees can be given power to allocate investment returns in a flexible way. The power can only be given on an individual charity basis, where charities have asked us for it.

The Charity Commission permits the trustees of endowed charities a power to allocate the return received from investments between present and future beneficiaries in the way they consider best allows them to fulfil their duty to be fair to all beneficiaries, rather than in a way dictated by the standard rules. The standard rules dictate whether a return should be treated as income or added to the capital of the charity.

The power enables trustees to invest funds in a way they judge will produce the best returns, regardless of the way in which they are received (either capital or income).

Trustees' obligations to treat all beneficiaries – present and future – fairly will not change as a result of the introduction of this power. To make sure this obligation is honoured, the power given to trustees will be subject to a number of directions, including a duty to be even-handed in the treatment of beneficiaries.

Trustees will be under a duty to publicly make known that they have used the power. Declaring that the power has been used will be an important feature in guarding against its misuse. Clearly, disclosure in the notes to the financial statements will be needed.

Trustees will also be under a duty to obtain professional investment advice before making use of the power.

The power does not challenge either the principle of permanent endowment or the right of founders to create a permanently endowed charity. Rather, it underlines the importance of considering the needs of both present and future beneficiaries in an even-handed way which is consistent with the objects of the charity – and which recognises that the charity is intended to be permanent.

Chapter 12 – Cash flow statements

12.1 Introduction

Wherever prepared, para. 352 of the charity SORP requires the cash flow statement to comply with FRS 1 (Revised). The object is to show the cash received and used by the charity in the accounting period. As the cash flow statement is considered to be a 'primary statement', it should be accorded the same prominence as the SOFA and, where prepared, the summary income and expenditure account.

12.2 Exemption

Whether or not incorporated under the Companies Acts, charities are exempt from FRS 1 if they satisfy the 'small company' limits for the purposes of, *inter alia*, filing abbreviated accounts with the Registrar. From 6 April 2008, the effective thresholds, to qualify as a small company, are any two of the following three conditions:

- annual turnover or gross income not exceeding £6.5million;
- balance sheet total not exceeding £3.26million, and
- average number of employees not exceeding 50

12.3 Format of cash flow statements

The analysis of the cash movements should accord with the charity's operations as reported in its Statement of Financial Activities (SOFA), and be given in appropriate detail. The starting point will normally be 'net incoming/outgoing resources before revaluations and investment asset disposals'.

Paragraph 7 of FRS 1 requires the cash flow statement to list the inflows and outflows of cash for the period under the following *standard headings*:

- operating activities;
- dividends from joint ventures and associates;
- returns on investments and servicing of finance;
- taxation;
- capital expenditure and financial investment;
- acquisitions and disposals;

Cash flow statements

- equity dividends paid;
- management of liquid resources, and
- financing.

The first seven headings should be in the sequence set out above. Except in those rare circumstances where the presentation would not be a fair representation of the activities of the charity, the cash flow statement should disclose separately, where material, the individual categories of cash flows under those standard headings. In those circumstances, informed judgement should be used to devise an appropriate alternative treatment. The cash flow classifications may be further divided to give a fuller description of the activities of the charity, or to provide segmental information.

Unlike the recommendations for the structure of the SOFA and reconciliation of funds, the SORP contains no recommendation for the cash flow statement to be presented in columnar format if the charity operates more than one fund. This creates an asymmetric presentation.

12.3.1 Operating activities

Cash flows from operating activities are, in general, the cash effects of transactions and other events relating to operating, or trading, activities. FRS 1 states that the cash flow from such activities represents the net increase, or decrease, in cash resulting from the operations shown in the income and expenditure account in arriving at operating profit.

Paragraph 7 of FRS 1 permits operating cash flows to be reported in one of two ways: either by the 'direct method' or by the 'indirect method'. The direct method reports gross operating receipts and payments, including, in the case of charities, cash receipts from fundraising, donations etc., and cash payments in respect of beneficiaries and on behalf of employees to arrive at net cash flows from operating activities. Conversely, the indirect method adjusts, in the form of a reconciliation, the operating result for, for example, depreciation, accruals and prepayments and other items that do not affect cash to arrive at the same net cash flows.

FRS 1 requires the information provided by the indirect method to be given in *all* circumstances. Where only the indirect method information is given, the FRS shows the reconciliation in a note to the cash flow statement, with the statement itself starting with 'Net cash inflow from operating activities'.

A charity may choose to add the information given by the direct method and, where the benefits to users outweigh the costs of obtaining the information, an appendix to the FRS encourages this. Most charities using the indirect method do not offer, voluntarily, the direct method information.

Where information is given in accordance with the direct method, the examples in the FRS position this on the face of the cash flow statement with the indirect method reconciliation given by way of note.

12.3.2 Returns on investments and servicing of finance

These are receipts resulting from the ownership of investments and payments to providers of finance and include interest and dividends. Also included is the interest element of finance lease rentals and interest paid, whether or not capitalised. Excluded are those items required to be classified under other headings.

12.3.3 Capital expenditure and financial investment

The cash flows included in 'capital expenditure and financial investment' are those related to the acquisition or disposal of any fixed asset other than one required to be classified under 'acquisitions and disposals' and any current asset investment not included in liquid resources.

If no cash flows relating to financial investment fall to be included under this heading the caption may be reduced to 'capital expenditure'.

Cash inflows from 'capital expenditure and financial investment' include:

(a) receipts from sales or disposals of property, plant or equipment, and
(b) receipts from the repayment of the reporting entity's loans to other entities or sales of debt instruments of other entities other than receipts forming part of an acquisition or disposal or a movement in liquid resources, as specified respectively in paras 22–24 and 26–28 of the FRS.

Cash outflows from 'capital expenditure and financial investment' include:

(a) payments to acquire property, plant or equipment, and
(b) loans made by the reporting entity and payments to acquire debt instruments of other entities other than payments forming part of an acquisition or disposal or a movement in liquid resources, as specified respectively in paras 22–24 and 26–28 of the FRS.

FRS 1 is silent as regards the positioning of grants received for the purchase of fixed assets. While some charities classify them as investing cash flows, others classify them as part of financing.

12.3.4 Acquisitions and disposals

The cash flows included in 'acquisitions and disposals' are those related to the acquisition or disposal of any trade or business, or of an investment in an entity that is or, as a result of the transaction, becomes or ceases to be either an associate, a joint venture, or a subsidiary undertaking.

Cash inflows from 'acquisitions and disposals' include:

(a) receipts from sales of investments in subsidiary undertakings, showing separately any balances of cash and overdrafts transferred as part of the sale;
(b) receipts from sales of investments in associates or joint ventures, and
(c) receipts from sales of trades or businesses.

Cash outflows from 'acquisitions and disposals' include:

(a) payments to acquire investments in subsidiary undertakings, showing separately any balances of cash and overdrafts acquired;
(b) payments to acquire investments in associates and joint ventures, and
(c) payments to acquire trades or businesses.

12.3.5 Management of liquid resources

The 'management of liquid resources' section should include cash flows in respect of liquid resources.

'Liquid resources' are current asset investments held as readily disposable stores of value. A readily disposable investment is one that is disposable by the reporting entity without curtailing or disrupting its business; and is either:

1. readily convertible into known amounts of cash at or close to its carrying amount, or
2. traded in an active market.

Each entity should explain what it includes as liquid resources and any changes in its policy. The cash flows in this section can be shown in a single section with those under 'financing' provided that separate subtotals for each are given.

Cash inflows in management of liquid resources include:

(a) withdrawals from short-term deposits not qualifying as cash insofar as not netted under para. 9(b) of FRS1; and
(b) inflows from disposal or redemption of any other investments held as liquid resources.

Cash outflows in management of liquid resources include:

(a) payments into short-term deposits not qualifying as cash insofar as not netted under para 9(b) of FRS1; and
(b) outflows to acquire any other investments held as liquid resources

12.3.6 Financing

Financing cash flows comprise receipts or repayments of principal from or to external providers of finance. The cash flows in this section can be shown in a single section with those under 'management of liquid resources' provided that separate subtotals for each are given.

Financing cash inflows include:

(a) receipts from issuing shares or other equity instruments, and
(b) receipts from issuing debentures, loans, notes, and bonds and from other long-term and short-term borrowings (other than overdrafts).

Financing cash outflows include:

(a) repayments of amounts borrowed (other than overdrafts);
(b) the capital element of finance lease rental payments;
(c) payments to re-acquire or redeem the entity's shares (unlikely for a charity), and
(d) payments of expenses or commissions on any issue of equity shares.

Reconciliation to net cash/debt

A note reconciling the movement of cash in the period with the movement in net cash/debt should be given either adjoining the cash flow statement or in a note. The reconciliation is not part of the cash flow statement: if adjoining the cash flow statement, it should be clearly labelled and kept separate. The changes in net cash/debt should be analysed from the opening to the closing component amounts showing separately, where material, changes resulting from:

(a) the cash flows of the entity;
(b) the acquisition or disposal of subsidiary undertakings;
(c) other non-cash changes, and
(d0 the recognition of changes in market value and exchange rate movements.

Where several balance sheet amounts or parts thereof have to be combined to form the components of opening and closing net cash/debt, sufficient detail should be shown to enable the cash and other components of net cash/debt to be respectively traced back to the amounts shown under the equivalent captions in the balance sheet.

Movements in endowments

Movements in endowments should not be included in cash flows from 'operating activities' but should be treated as increases or decreases in the financing section. This is achieved as follows:

Cash flow statements

(a) cash donations to endowment should be treated as additions to endowment in the 'financing' section;

(b) the receipts and payments from the acquisition and disposal of investments should be shown gross in the 'capital expenditure and financial investment' section of the cash flow statement. A single line should then be included in this section showing the net movement in cash flows attributable to endowment investments. A corresponding line should be included in the 'financing' section for the same amount. The line in the 'financing' section should reflect the cash into/(cash out of) the endowment fund whereas it will be the opposite direction in the 'capital expenditure and financial investment' section;

(c) on the rare occasions when payments are made out of permanent endowment this should be shown as a decrease in the 'financing' section, and

(d) transactions which do not result in cash flows should not be reported in the cash flow statement (for example, depreciation, revaluations, accruals) but may need to be disclosed (see para. 276).

12.4 Major non-cash transactions

Paragraph 355(a) of the SORP and para. 46 of FRS 1 require all material transactions not resulting in movements of cash or cash equivalents of the charity to be disclosed in the notes to the cash flow statement, if such disclosure is necessary for an understanding of the underlying transactions. This would include the inception of a finance lease. Fixed assets donated to a charity would, also, be classified as a non-cash transaction and, if material, disclosed.

12.5 Reconciliation with balance sheet figures

Paragraph 355(b) of the SORP requires that movements in cash (and any financing movements) should be reconciled to the appropriate opening and closing balance sheet amounts.

12.6 Comparatives

Paragraph 48 of FRS 1 requires comparatives to be provided for all items in the cash flow statement and such notes thereto as are required. This requirement should extend to the notes reconciling the balance sheet figures – that is, the analyses of changes in cash and cash equivalents and in financing.

12.7 Disclosure examples

The format of the statement is virtually identical to that which is used for commercial companies. In this example cash flows arising from investment income are not considered to be part of the 'operational activities' and hence have been shown within 'returns on investments and servicing of finance'.

Example – *Beth Aid Helpers*

Consolidated Statement of Cash Flow for the year ended 30 September 2010

	Notes	2010 £'000	2010 £'000	2009 £'000	2009 £'000
Net cash inflow from operating activities	26(a)		1,659		827
Returns on investments and servicing of finance					
Deposit interest received		221		195	
Investment income		8		7	
			229		202
Capital expenditure and financial investment					
Payments to acquire tangible fixed assets		(488)		(266)	
Receipts from sales of tangible fixed assets		46		–	
Disposal of fixed asset investments		8		–	
			(434)		(266)
Net cash inflow before management of liquid resources and financing			1,454		763
Management of liquid resources					
Cash added to short term deposits			(1,391)		(1,170)
Increase /(decrease) in cash in the year			63		(407)
Net cash resources at 1 October 2009			1,394		1,801
Net cash resources at 30 September 2010	26(b)		1,457		1,394

26. Notes to consolidated cash flow statement

(a) Reconciliation of surplus of income to net cash inflow from operating activities

	2010 £'000	2009 £'000
Net movement in funds for the year	2,152	498
Investment income	(229)	(202)
Depreciation charges	297	291
Decrease in stocks	185	56
Increase in debtors	(869)	(21)
Increase in creditors	569	102

Cash flow statements

(a) **Reconciliation of surplus of income to net cash inflow from operating activities**

	2009
(Decrease)/increase in grants payable	(**446**) 103
Net cash inflow from operating activities	**1,659** 827

(b) **Analysis of net cash resources**

	2009 £'000	Cash flow £'000	2010 £'000
Cash in hand (note 18)	929	**212**	1,141
Deposits on one day notice (note 18)	567	**243**	810
Overdrafts	(102)	(**392**)	(494)
	1,394	**63**	1,457

Short-term deposits on more than one day's notice are considered to be liquid resources.

In the example below, cash flows from investment income are considered to be part of 'operational activities' as the charity considers investment activities to be an integral part of its operations.

Example   *The PQR Charity*

Consolidated Cash Flow Statement for the year ended 31 March 2010

	Notes	2010 £'000	2009 £'000
Net cash inflow from operating activities	20	**2,090**	595
Capital expenditure and financial investment			
Payments to acquire tangible fixed assets		(**1,990**)	(1,000)
Proceeds from sale of tangible fixed assets		**130**	170
Purchase of investments		(**1,200**)	(865)
Proceeds from sales of investments		**2,300**	915
		760	780
		£'000	£'000
Cash inflow/(outflow) before increase in liquid resources and financing	20	**1,330**	(185)
Financing			
Finance lease payments		(**40**)	(40)
Management of liquid resources			
Increase in short-term deposits		(**400**)	(200)
Increase/(decrease) in cash in the year	20	**890**	(425)

20. Cash flow information for the group

(a) **Reconciliation of changes in resources to net inflow from operating activities**

	2010 £'000	2009 £'000
Net incoming resources before revaluations	**2,155**	150
Gain on sale of tangible fixed assets	(**20**)	(30)

Disclosure examples

(a) Reconciliation of changes in resources to net inflow from operating activities

Depreciation	**380**	270
Decrease in stocks	**100**	450
Increase in debtors	**(765)**	(225)
Increase/(decrease) in creditors	**240**	(20)
Net cash inflow from operating activities	**2,090**	595

(b) Reconciliation of net cash flow to movement in net funds/debt

Increase/(decrease) in cash in the period	**890**	(425)
Cash outflow from decrease in lease financing	**40**	40
Cash outflow from increase in liquid resources	**400**	200
Movement in net funds and debt in the year	**1,330**	(185)
Net funds and debt at 1 April 2009	**3,020**	3,205
Net funds and debt at 31 March 2010	**4,350**	3,020

(c) Analysis of net funds/debt

	1 April 2009 £'000	Cash flow £'000	31 March 2010 £'000
Cash at bank and in hand	200	**890**	1,090
Liquid resources	3,000	**400**	3,400
Finance leases	(180)	**40**	(140)
	3,020	**1,330**	4,350

Chapter 13 – Accounting policies

13.1 Introduction

By recommending that the accounts should include an explanation of the accounting policies used to prepare them, the provisions of the charity SORP mirror the requirements both of the Companies Act 2006 and of FRS 18 Accounting policies.

13.2 FRS 18 Accounting policies

The purpose of FRS 18 is to assist users in the understanding and interpretation of accounts by setting out the principles to be followed in selecting accounting policies and the disclosures needed to help users to understand the accounting policies adopted and how they have been applied.

The FRS promotes the adoption and review of accounting policies most appropriate to the particular circumstances of each entity for the purpose of giving a true and fair view and of sufficient disclosure for users to understand the policies adopted and how they have been applied. The FRS distinguishes between accounting policies which are the principles on which the accounts are prepared and estimation techniques which are the particular methods that an entity may choose to use in order to provide a monetary value for an asset, liability, gain or loss in accordance with the adopted principles in the chosen accounting policies.

The following two notions are emphasised as having a pervasive role in financial statements and hence in the selection of accounting policies:

1. The **'going concern' assumption**: the enterprise will continue in operational existence for the foreseeable future.
2. The **'accruals' concept**: the substance of transactions should be reflected in the accounts in the accounting period in which they occur rather than when any money or other form of consideration is received or paid in respect of the transactions.

The appropriateness of accounting policies and estimation techniques to each entity's particular circumstances should be judged against the four objectives below, balancing these against each other and against the cost of providing information with the likely benefit to the users of the accounts.

Accounting policies

1. **Relevance**: information is provided in a timely manner and has the ability to influence economic decisions of users of the accounts. It will have predictive or confirmatory value or both.
2. **Reliability**: the information faithfully represents transactions being materially complete, free from bias and material error and has been prudently estimated when conditions are uncertain.
3. **Comparability**: information can be compared from one period to another and against other entities. This can usually be achieved through a combination of consistency and disclosure. Industry practices in SORPs developed with public consultation will be particularly persuasive.
4. **Understandability**: the information is capable of being understood by users with a reasonable knowledge of business and economic activities and accounting and a willingness to study the information with reasonable diligence.

13.3 Disclosure of accounting policies

The notes regarding the basis of preparation of the accounts should state that the accounts have been prepared in accordance with:

(a) the SORP and accounting standards or with the SORP and the FRSSE;
(b) the Charities Act 1993 or the CO Act 2006 or other legislative requirement, and
(c) the historic cost basis of accounting except for investments (and if applicable, fixed assets) which have been included at revalued amounts.

If the accounts depart from accounting standards in any material respect, this should be stated in the accounting policies and Annual Report giving the reason and justification for the departure and the financial impact. Similarly the following details should be given for any material departure from the SORP:

(a) a brief description of how the treatment adopted departs from the SORP
(b) the reasons why the trustees judge that the treatment adopted is more appropriate to the charity's particular circumstances; and
(c) an estimate of the financial effect on the accounts where this is needed for the accounts to give a true and fair view

A departure is not justified simply because it gives the reader a more appealing picture of the financial position or results of the charity.

If any branches have been omitted from the accounts the reason for omission must be given although the individual branches do not need to be named. Reference should also be made to any potentially linked organisations (such as supporters associations or subsidiaries not consolidated) explaining the accounting treatment adopted.

13.3.1 Examples

Two examples are presented to illustrate how charities explain the basis of the accounting policies that they have adopted. Slight variations between the examples arise because Example 1 (Boys City Trust) is a company, while Example 2 (Help for Overseas) is unincorporated. Both charities have a subsidiary, and the note explaining the basis of group accounting also shows slight variations.

Example 1   Boys City Trust

Notes forming part of the financial statements for the year ended 31 March 2010

Accounting policies

The financial statements have been prepared under the historical cost convention and in accordance with the Statement of Recommended Practice, *Accounting and Reporting by Charities* (SORP 2005), applicable accounting standards and the Companies Act 2006. The principal accounting policies adopted in the preparation of the financial statements are as follows:

Group financial statements

These financial statements consolidate the results of the charity and its wholly-owned subsidiary HTC Limited on a line-by-line basis. A separate Statement of Financial Activities, or income and expenditure account, for the charity itself is not presented because the charity has taken advantage of the exemptions afforded by s. 408 of the Companies Act 2006 (previously (s. 230 of the Companies Act 1985) and para. 397 of SORP 2005.

Example 2   Help for Overseas

Notes forming part of the financial statements for the year ended 30 September 2010

1.   Principal accounting policies

(a)   **Accounting convention**

The financial statements are prepared under the historical cost convention as modified by the inclusion of investments at market value and in accordance with applicable accounting standards. In preparing the financial statements the charity follows best practice as set out in the Statement of Recommended Practice Accounting and Reporting by Charities (SORP 2005).

(b)   **Group financial statements**

These financial statements consolidate the results of the charity and its wholly-owned trading subsidiary, Aid Overseas Trading Limited, on a

Accounting policies

line-by-line basis. It also includes the results of all the charity's branches, including those overseas. A separate statement of financial activities (SOFA) is not presented because the charity has taken advantage of the provisions of para. 397 of SORP 2005.

13.4 Specific policies

Trustees should explain in the notes to the accounts the accounting policies they have adopted to deal with material items. Explanations need only be brief but they must be clear, fair and accurate. Significant changes to any of the policies from the preceding year must be disclosed in detail. The following are some examples of matters on which the accounting policies should be explained where the amounts involved are material. Trustees should only include those notes which are relevant to their charity.

13.5 Incoming resources policy notes

The policy for including each type of material incoming resource should be given. This will normally be on a receivable basis but may need further details in some cases, for instance:

(a) a description of when a legacy is regarded as receivable;
(b) the basis of recognition of gifts and intangible income, specifically covering when such items are not included in the SOFA and the methods of valuation;
(c) the basis of recognition of all grants receivable, including those for fixed assets, and how the grants are split between the different types of incoming resources;
(d) whether any incoming resources are deferred and the basis for any deferrals (this will normally only apply to contractual incoming resources received or invoiced in advance);
(e) the basis for including subscriptions for life membership;
(f) whether the incoming resources from endowment funds are unrestricted or restricted, and
(g) whether any incoming resources have been included in the SOFA net of expenditure and the reason for this.

13.5.1 Example

The charity below has several sources of income, including both charitable and commercial trading activities, and donations, grants and intangible sources of income.

Example

Accounting policies (extract)

Incoming resources

Charitable trading activities

Income from theatre admission fees is included in incoming resources in the period in which the relevant show takes place.

Commercial trading activities

Income from commercial activities is included in the period in which the group is entitled to receipt.

Donations and grants

Income from donations and grants, including capital grants, is included in incoming resources when these are receivable, except as follows:

- when donors specify that donations and grants given to the charity must be used in future accounting periods, the income is deferred until those periods, and
- when donors impose conditions which have to be fulfilled before the charity becomes entitled to use such income, the income is deferred and not included in incoming resources until the preconditions for use have been met.

When donors specify that donations and grants, including capital grants, are for particular restricted purposes, which do not amount to preconditions regarding entitlement, this income is included in incoming resources of restricted funds when receivable.

Donated services and facilities

Income from donated services and facilities is included in incoming resources at a valuation which is an estimate of the financial cost borne by the donor where such a cost is quantifiable and measurable. No income is recognised when there is no financial cost borne by a third party.

Interest receivable

Interest is included when receivable by the charity.

Accounting policies

13.6 Resources expended policy notes

Policy notes should be presented which explain how the material items of resources expended are treated in the financial statements.

(a) The policy for the recognition of liabilities including constructive obligations should be given. Where the liabilities are included as provisions, the point at which the provision is considered to become binding and the basis of any discount factors used in current value calculations for long-term commitments should be given. This is particularly applicable to grants, the policy for which must be separately identified.

(b) The policy for including items within types of resources expended should be given. In particular the policy for including items within:
  (i) costs of generating funds
  (ii) charitable activities; and
  (iii) governance costs

(c) The methods and principles for the allocation and apportionment of all costs between the different categories of expenditure in (b). This disclosure should include the underlying principle – that is, whether based on staff time, staff salaries, space occupied or some other principle. Where the costs apportioned are significant, then further clarification on the method of apportionment used is necessary, including the proportions used to undertake the calculations.

13.6.1 Example

A thorough example of an accounting policy for resources expended is presented below. The note explains the treatment of the material components of resources expended and how different costs are allocated. Separate notes are presented explaining the components of fundraising costs, support costs and management and administration costs.

Example

Accounting policies (extract)

(d) **Resources expended and basis of allocation of costs**

Expenditure is included when incurred.

Grants payable to partner organisations for relief and development projects are included in the SOFA when approved by the trustees. The value of such grants unpaid at the year end is accrued. Grants where the beneficiary has to meet certain conditions before the grant is released are not accrued but are noted as financial commitments.

Expenditure on operational programmes is recognised in the period in which it has incurred. A designated fund is established for expenditure which has been committed to projects, but remains unspent at the year end.

The majority of costs are directly attributable to specific activities. Certain shared costs are apportioned to activities in furtherance of the objects of the charity. Office costs and property related costs are apportioned on the proportion of floor area occupied by the activity. Staff costs and office costs are allocated in the same proportion as directly attributed staff costs.

(e) **Costs of generating funds**

These include the salaries, direct expenditure and overhead costs of the staff in offices in the UK who promote fundraising, including events.

13.7 Assets policy notes

13.7.1 Fixed assets

The policy for capitalisation of fixed assets for charity use should be stated including:

(a) whether each class of asset is included at cost, valuation or revaluation and the method of valuation where applicable;
(b) the value below which fixed assets are not capitalised;
(c) whether or not heritage assets are capitalised and if not, the reason why (for example, lack of reliable information, cost or benefit reason, etc.), specifying the acquisition and disposal policies for such assets;
(d) the rates of depreciation applying to each class of fixed asset, and
(e) the policy with respect to impairment reviews of fixed assets.

13.7.2 Example

This charity operates two independent schools and presents a detailed accounting policy explaining the treatment of the school buildings and equipment. The note includes details of the most recent revaluation of the buildings and details of the charity's capitalisation policy.

Example

Accounting policies (extract)

(h) **School buildings and equipment**

Capitalisation and replacement

The college land, together with the original college buildings (which are all Grade 1 listed properties), was a gift to the charity in 1903. These assets were

Accounting policies

professionally revalued by Granville & Co, Chartered Surveyors, on 31 August 2009 at £7,500,000, with the college grounds being valued at £6,000,000 and the original buildings at £1,500,000. This valuation has been adopted as the historical cost under the transitional provisions of the Financial Reporting Standard 15. The charity is responsible for keeping the original buildings in fit and useful condition, and these costs are written off as incurred.

Building improvements and extensions subsequent to the original gift costing more than £5,000, together with furniture and equipment costing more than £1,500, are capitalised and carried in the balance sheet at historical cost.

Depreciation

Land is not depreciated. Depreciation of other assets is provided at rates calculated to write off the excess of cost over estimated residual amount evenly over the estimated useful economic lives of each class of asset, subject to annual review.

These rates are currently as follows:

Original cost of freehold buildings	20–50 years
Buildings improvements and extensions	10–20 years
Furniture and equipment	3–10 years
Motor vehicles	4 years

As explained in note 9, heritage assets have not been capitalised or depreciated as no reliable value can be attributed.

13.7.3 Investments

The policy for including investments in the accounts should be given. This should be at market value but may need to be modified for the valuation of:

(a) investments not listed on a recognised stock exchange;
(b) investment properties, and
(c) investments in subsidiary undertakings.

The basis of inclusion in the SOFA of unrealised and realised gains and losses on investments should be stated.

13.7.4 Example

Normally the investments policy note is short and straightforward, as illustrated below.

Example

Accounting policies (extract)

(e) **Fixed asset investments**

Investments are included at closing mid-market value at the balance sheet date. Any gain or loss on revaluation is taken to the SOFA.

13.7.5 Stocks and work in progress

The basis for inclusion of material stocks and work in progress should be given.

13.8 Funds structure policy notes

A brief description should be given of the different types of fund held by the charity, including the policy for any transfers between funds and allocations to or from designated funds. Transfers may arise for example where there is a release of restricted or endowed funds to unrestricted funds or charges are made from the unrestricted to other funds.

The policy for determining each designated fund should be stated.

13.8.1 Examples

Several of the examples present an accounting policy on fund accounting which simply states 'The nature and purpose of each fund are explained in note X'.

Fund accounting

Funds held by the charity are either:

(a) unrestricted general funds – these are funds which can be used in accordance with the charitable objects at the discretion of the trustees
(b) designated funds – these are funds set aside by the trustees out of unrestricted general funds for specific future purposes or projects
(c) restricted funds – these are funds that can only be used for particular restricted purposes within the objects of the charity. Restrictions arise when specified by the donor or when funds are raised for particular restricted purposes.

Further explanation of the nature and purpose of each fund is included in the notes to the financial statements.

Accounting policies

13.9 Other policy notes

These could include policies for the recognition of the following:

(a) pension contributions;
(b) foreign exchange gains and losses;
(c) treatment of exceptional items;
(d) treatment of finance and operating leases, and
(e) treatment of irrecoverable VAT.

The accounting policies in respect of these items would be determined by the SORP and accounting standards. Several of these policies are illustrated in the examples below.

13.10 Full example

This charity is incorporated and has a subsidiary. The charity engages in a variety of activities, and therefore this illustrative example contains a broad range of policies.

Example   *The Complete Charity*

Notes forming part of the financial statements for the year ended 31 March 2010

1. Accounting policies

(a) **Basis of preparation**

The financial statements have been prepared under the historical cost convention, with the exception of investments which are included at market value. The financial statements have been prepared in accordance with the Statement of Recommended Practice (SORP 2005), *Accounting and Reporting by Charities* and applicable accounting standards.

The SOFA and balance sheet consolidate the financial statements of the charity and its subsidiary undertaking. The results of the subsidiary are consolidated on a line-by-line basis.

The charity has adapted the Companies Act formats to reflect the special nature of the charity's activities. No separate SOFA has been presented for the charity alone as permitted by section 408 of the Companies Act 2006 and para. 397 of SORP 2005.

Full example

(b) **Company status**

The charity is a company limited by guarantee. The members of the company are trustees named on page 1. In the event of the charity being wound up, the liability in respect of the guarantee is limited to £1 per member of the charity.

(c) **Fund accounting**

General funds are unrestricted funds which are available for use at the discretion of the trustees in furtherance of the general objectives of the charity and which have not been designated for other purposes.

Designated funds comprise unrestricted funds that have been set aside by the trustees for particular purposes. The aim and use of each designated fund is set out in the notes to the financial statements. Restricted funds are funds which are to be used in accordance with specific restrictions imposed by donors or which have been raised by the charity for particular purposes. The cost of raising and administering such funds are charged against the specific fund. The aim and use of each restricted fund is set out in the notes to the financial statements.

Investment income and gains are allocated to the appropriate fund.

(d) **Incoming resources**

All incoming resources are included in the SOFA when the charity is legally entitled to the income and the amount can be quantified with reasonable accuracy. For legacies, entitlement is the earlier of the charity being notified of an impending distribution or the legacy being received.

Gifts in kind donated for distribution are included at valuation and recognised as income when they are distributed to the projects. Gifts donated for resale are included as income when they are sold. Donated facilities are included at the value to the charity where this can be quantified and a third party is bearing the cost. No amounts are included in the financial statements for services donated by volunteers.

(e) **Resources expended**

All expenditure is accounted for on an accruals basis and has been classified under headings that aggregate all costs related to the category. Where costs cannot be directly attributed to particular headings they have been allocated to activities on a basis consistent with use of the resources. Premises overheads have been allocated on a floor area basis and other overheads have been allocated on the basis of the head count.

Costs of generating funds are those incurred in seeking voluntary contributions and do not include the costs of disseminating information in support of the

Accounting policies

charitable activities. Management and governance costs are those incurred in connection with administration of the charity and compliance with constitutional and statutory requirements.

(f) **Tangible fixed assets and depreciation**

Tangible fixed assets costing more than £1,000 are capitalised and included at cost including any incidental expenses of acquisition.

Depreciation is provided on all tangible fixed assets at rates calculated to write off the cost on a straight line basis over their expected useful economic lives as follows:

Freehold land	nil
Freehold buildings	over 50 years
Project and office equipment	over five years
Computer equipment	over three years
Motor vehicles	over four years
Equipment held under finance leases	over the life of the lease

(g) **Investments**

Investments are stated at market value at the balance sheet date. The SOFA includes the net gains and losses arising on revaluations and disposals throughout the year.

(h) **Stock**

Stock consists of purchased goods for resale. Stocks are valued at the lower of cost and net realisable value. Items donated for resale or distribution are not included in the financial statements until they are sold or distributed.

(i) **Pension costs**

Payments to the charity's defined contribution scheme are charged as an expense as they fall due.

The cost of providing benefits relating to the charity's defined benefit scheme are determined using the projected unit credit method, with actuarial valuations being carried out at each balance sheet date. Actuarial gains and losses are recognised in the Statement of Financial Activities in full in the period in which they occur.

Past service cost is recognised immediately to the extent that the benefits are already vested, and otherwise is amortised on a straight line basis over the average period until the benefits become vested.

The retirement benefit recognised in the balance sheet represents the present value of the defined benefit obligation as adjusted for unrecognised past service cost, and as reduced by the fair value of scheme assets.

(j) **Finance and operating leases**

Rentals applicable to operating leases are charged to the SOFA over the period in which the cost is incurred. Assets purchased under finance lease are capitalised as fixed assets. Obligations under such agreements are included in creditors. The difference between the capitalised cost and the total obligation under the lease represents the finance charges. Finance charges are written off to the SOFA over the period of the lease so as to produce a constant periodic rate of charge.

(k) **Foreign currencies**

Transactions in foreign currencies are recorded at the rate ruling at the date of the transaction. Monetary assets and liabilities are retranslated at the rate of exchange ruling at the balance sheet date. All differences are taken to the SOFA.

13.11 Small charity example

The basis of allocating costs in item (f) is a particular feature to note.

Example   Little Support Ltd

Notes forming part of the financial statements for the year ended 31 March 2010

1. **Accounting policies**

(a) The financial statements have been prepared under the historical cost convention, as modified by the inclusion of fixed asset investments at market value, and in accordance with the Financial Reporting Standard for Smaller Entities (effective April 2008), the Companies Act 2006 and follow the recommendations in the Statement of Recommended Practice Accounting and Reporting by Charities (SORP 2005).

(b) Voluntary income is received by way of donations and gifts and is included in full in the Statement of Financial Activities when receivable. The value of services provided by volunteers has not been included.

(c) Grants, including grants for the purchase of fixed assets, are recognised in full in the SOFA in the year in which they are receivable.

(d) Incoming resources from the charity shop and from investments is included when receivable.

(e) Resources expended are recognised in the period in which they are incurred. Resources expended include attributable VAT which cannot be recovered.

Accounting policies

(f) Resources expended are allocated to the particular activity where the cost relates directly to that activity. However, the cost of overall direction and administration on each activity, comprising the salary and overhead costs of the central function, is apportioned on the following basis, which is an estimate, based on staff time, of the amount attributable to each activity:

Charity shop	0%
Fundraising and publicity	15%
Advice and information	20%
Outreach work	20%
Training project	30%
Governance of the charity	15%

(g) Depreciation is provided at rates calculated to write off the cost of each asset over its expected useful life, which in all cases is estimated at four years. Items of equipment are capitalised where the purchase price exceeds £500.

(h) Investments held as fixed assets are revalued at mid-market value at the balance sheet date and the gain or loss taken to the SOFA.

(i) Unrestricted funds are donations and other incoming resources receivable or generated for the objects of the charity without further specified purpose and are available as general funds.

(j) Designated funds are unrestricted funds earmarked by the management committee for particular purposes.

(k) Restricted funds are to be used for specific purposes as laid down by the donor. Expenditure which meets these criteria is charged to the fund, together with a fair allocation of management and support costs.

Chapter 14 – Other matters to be covered in the notes to the accounts

14.1 Introduction

This chapter considers the following:

- related party transactions;
- trustees' remuneration and benefits;
- trustees' expenses;
- staff costs and emoluments;
- cost of audit, independent examination or reporting accountant services and other financial services;
- *ex gratia* payments, and
- analysis of the net movements in funds.

14.2 Related party transactions

This section of the SORP, primarily dealing with transactions with trustees and connected persons, reflects FRS 8 Related party disclosures. Although the definitions and disclosures can be complex, disclosable transactions will arise 'where the charity has a relationship with another party or parties (the related party) which might inhibit it from pursuing its own separate interests'.

Disclosure in a note to the accounts is required where the reporting charity enters into a related party transaction. Related parties include:

(a) a charity trustee or someone else who is related to the charity (Appendix 1: Glossary), and
(b) someone who is either connected with a charity trustee or to a person who is related to the charity.

A charity can be a related party of another charity – for example:

- if one is the trustee of the other; or
- if one has the power to appoint or remove a significant proportion of the charity trustees of the other, or
- if the two charities are subject to common control (for instance, a majority of trustees in common).

Other matters to be covered in the notes to the accounts

However, they are not necessarily related simply because a particular person happens to be a trustee of both (though if one charity subordinates its interests to the other charity in any transaction because of this relationship then the charities will be related).

Any decision by a charity to enter into a transaction ought to be influenced only by the consideration of the charity's own interests. This requirement is reinforced by legal rules which, in certain circumstances, can invalidate transactions where the charity trustees have a conflict of interest. This does not necessarily mean that all transactions with related persons are influenced by the consideration of interests other than those of the charity, nor that they are liable to invalidation.

However, transparency is particularly important where the relationship between the charity and the other party or parties to a transaction suggests that the transaction could possibly have been influenced by interests other than those of the charity. It is possible that the reported financial position and results may have been affected by such transactions and information about these transactions is therefore necessary for the users of the charity's accounts.

Related party transactions potentially include:

(a) purchases, sales, leases and donations (including donations which are made in furtherance of the charity's objects) of goods, property, money and other assets such as intellectual property rights to or from the related party;
(b) the supply of services by the related party to the charity, and the supply of services by the charity to the related party. Supplying services includes providing the use of goods, property and other assets and finance arrangements such as making loans and giving guarantees and indemnities, and
(c) any other payments and other benefits which are made to trustees under express provisions of the governing document of a charity or in fulfilment of its charitable objectives.

Only material transactions need to be disclosed in the notes to the accounts. Transactions should be disclosed whether or not they are at arm's length.

The following disclosures must be given in respect of each related party transaction:

(a) the name(s) of the transacting related party or parties;
(b) a description of the relationship between the parties (including the interest of the related party or parties in the transaction);
(c) a description of the transaction;
(d) the amounts involved;
(e) outstanding balances with related parties at the balance sheet date and any provisions for doubtful debts from such persons;

Related party transactions

(f) any amounts written off from such balances during the accounting year, and
(g) any other elements of the transactions which are necessary for the understanding of the financial statements.

The disclosure can be given in aggregate for similar transactions and types of related party, unless disclosure of an individual transaction or connected transactions is necessary for an understanding of the impact of the transactions on the accounts of the charity or is a legal requirement.

Some related party transactions are such that they are unlikely to influence the pursuance of the separate independent interests of the charity. These need not be disclosed unless there is evidence to the contrary. Examples are:

(a) donations received by the reporting charity from a related party, so long as the donor has not attached conditions which would, or might, require the charity to alter materially the nature of its existing activities if it were to accept the donation (but any material grant by the reporting charity to a charity which is a related party should be disclosed);
(b) minor or routine unremunerated services provided to a charity by people related to it;
(c) contracts of employment between a charity and its employees (except where the employees are the charity trustees or people connected with them);
(d) contributions by a charity to a pension fund for the benefit of employees;
(e) the purchase from a charity by a related party of minor articles which are offered for sale to the general public on the same terms as are offered to the general public;
(f) the provision of services to a related party (including a charity trustee or person connected with a charity trustee), where the related party receives the services as part of a wider beneficiary class of which he is a member, and on the same terms as other members of the class (for example, the use of a village hall by members of its committee of management, as inhabitants of the area of benefit), and
(g) the payment or reimbursement of out-of-pocket expenses to a related party (including a charity trustee or person connected with a charity trustee – however, see below for disclosures of these).

14.2.1 Examples

This example contains a detailed note explaining the charity's relationship and transactions with several external organisations including local authorities and another charity.

Other matters to be covered in the notes to the accounts

20. Related parties

The charity has a very close relationship with Y Arts Trust, which is a charity, ZF borough council and Q town council, all of which nominate the majority of the trustees and provide funding to enable the charity to carry out its charitable objectives. The following table is a summary of transactions with those entities.

	2010 £'000	2009 £'000
Revenue funding		
ZF borough council	405	501
Q town council	104	100
Y Arts Trust	154	150
	663	751

All the above funding was received under contracts with the charity to provide services – for example, training in drama production, and has been included in the financial statements under the heading *Incoming resources from charitable activities.*

The charity also received a donation in kind, from ZF borough council, for the rent of premises, the value of which could not be quantified and therefore has not been included in these financial statements.

There were no outstanding balances with related parties at 31 March 2010 (2009 – £Nil).

14.3 Trustees' remuneration and benefits

Unlike in the case of the directors of commercial companies, it is not the normal practice for charity trustees, or people connected with them, to receive remuneration or other benefits from the charities for which they are responsible, or from institutions connected with those charities. Detailed disclosures are required, therefore, where the related party is a charity trustee, or a person connected with a charity trustee. The following points should be borne in mind when reporting on related party transactions, where the related party is a charity trustee or a person connected with a charity.

1. The transaction should always be regarded as material, and should, therefore, be disclosed regardless of its size, unless one of the exceptions in para. 229 of the SORP applies.
2. Each type of related party transaction must be separately disclosed. This means, for example, that particulars of remuneration paid to each charity trustee or person connected with a charity trustee, should be given individually in the notes. Where the charity has made any pension arrangements for charity trustees or persons connected with them, the amount of contributions paid and the benefits accruing must be disclosed in the notes for each related party.

3. Where remuneration has been paid to a charity trustee or a person connected with a charity trustee, the legal authority under which the payment was made (for example, provision in the governing document of the charity, order of the Court or Charity Commission) should also be given, as should the reason for such remuneration.
4. Where neither the trustees nor any persons connected with them have received any such remuneration, this fact should be stated.

14.4 Trustees' expenses

Where a charity has met individual expenses incurred by trustees for services provided to the charity, either by reimbursement of the trustee or by providing the trustee with an allowance or by direct payment to a third party, the aggregate amount of those expenses should be disclosed in a note to the accounts. The note should also indicate the nature of the expenses (for example, travel, subsistence, entertainment, etc.) and the number of trustees involved.

Sometimes trustees act as agents for the charity and make purchases on its behalf and are reimbursed for this expenditure – for example, payment for stationery or office equipment. Such expenditure is not related to the services provided by a trustee and there is no need to disclose it. Likewise there is no need to disclose routine expenditure which is attributable collectively to the services provided by the trustees, such as the hire of a room for meetings or providing reasonable refreshment at the meeting.

Where the trustees have received no such expenses, this fact should be stated.

14.4.1 Examples

This example contains a note disclosing details of expenses paid to trustees and details of transactions between the charity and trustees.

7. Trustees' remuneration

The trustees neither received nor waived any emoluments during the year (2009 – £Nil).

Out-of-pocket expenses were reimbursed to trustees as follows.

	2010 Number	2009 Number	2010 £'000	2009 £'000
Travel	2	2	640	530
Visit to Ghana Project	1	–	1,200	65
Other	1	1	40	65
	4	3	1,880	660

Other matters to be covered in the notes to the accounts

During the year, payments of £7,500 were made to the PPS Company for the printing of the Annual Report. Ms S Williams, a trustee of this charity, is a director of that company. Mr H. Sharif, a trustee, is also a trustee of the Hogwarts Foundation, which provided free accommodation to the charity during the year valued at £14,000.

The example below also contains a note disclosing expense payments to trustees. As there are no other transactions with trustees, the resulting note is straightforward.

13. Trustees' remuneration

Trustees are not remunerated. £2,842 was reimbursed for directly incurred travel expenses to 10 trustees (2009 – £1,796 to five trustees).

14.5 Staff costs and emoluments

It is important that the accounts disclose the costs of employing staff who work for the charity, whether or not the charity itself has incurred those costs. This includes seconded and agency staff and staff employed by connected or independent companies. For instance, staff working for a charity may have contracts with and be paid by a connected company. Payments may also be made to independent third parties for the provision of staff. Where such arrangements are in place and the costs involved are material (in relation to the charity's own expenditure), there should be disclosure by way of note which outlines the arrangements in place, the reasons for them and the amounts involved.

The total staff costs should be shown in the notes to the accounts, giving the split between gross wages and salaries, employer's National Insurance costs and pension contributions for the year. An estimate of the average number of full-time equivalent employees for the year should be disclosed in the notes to the accounts, providing sub-categories according to the manner in which the charity's activities are organised.

14.5.1 Higher-paid staff

Where a charity is subject to statutory audit, the notes should also show the number of employees whose emoluments for the year (including taxable benefits in kind but not employer pension contributions) fell within each band of £10,000 from £60,000 upwards. Bands in which no employee's emoluments fell should not be listed.

In addition pension details must be disclosed in total for higher-paid staff as follows:

a) contributions in the year for the provision of money purchase benefits (normally money purchase schemes), and
b) the number of staff to whom retirement benefits are accruing under money purchase and defined benefit schemes respectively.

If there are no employees with emoluments above £60,000 this fact should be stated.

14.5.2 Examples

The following example presents a combined employees and staff costs note which discloses details of a higher-paid employee and acknowledges the support of the charity's volunteers.

12. Employees and staff costs

	2010 No	2009 No
The average number of UK-contracted employees throughout the year, calculated on a full-time equivalent basis, was:		
Trading operation	**98**	96
Marketing operation	**47**	45
Corporate functions	**18**	17
Programmes in the UK	**38**	38
Programmes overseas	**11**	13
	212	209
Staff based overseas on local contracts	**192**	194
	404	403

	2010 £'000	2009 £'000
The costs of employing those staff were:		
Salaries and wages	**3,395**	3,286
National Insurance	**325**	315
Pension scheme	**160**	154
	3,880	3,755

In addition, a great amount of time, the value of which it is impossible to reflect in these financial statements, is donated by thousands of volunteers throughout the UK.

The emoluments of two members of staff, including benefits in kind, are within the range of £60,000 to £69,999 (2009 – one in the range £60,000 to £69,999), not including retirement benefits which are accruing under a defined benefit scheme.

Other matters to be covered in the notes to the accounts

The following example presents a combined staff costs and trustees' remuneration note. The disclosures include details of an *ex gratia* payment.

7. Staff costs and trustees' remuneration

	2010 £'000	2009 £'000
Wages and salaries	**620**	603
Social security costs	**41**	39
Pension costs	**19**	11
Ex gratia payments	**16**	–
	696	653

The *ex gratia* payment was made to a former chief executive for whom no pension provision had been made. The Charity Commission approved payment on 16 December 2009.

No employee earned more than £60,000 per annum (2009 – nil).

The trustees were not paid or reimbursed for expenses during the year.

8. Staff numbers

The average number of full-time equivalent employees (including casual and part-time staff) during the year was made up as follows:

	2010 No	2009 No
Arts department	**11**	11
Administration, marketing and commercial	**14**	13
Technical	**11**	10
Bars and coffee shop	**21**	17
Front of house, box office, cleaning	**20**	21
Course tutors, models	**31**	30
	108	102

14.6 Cost of audit, independent examination and other financial services

The notes to the accounts should disclose separately the amounts payable to the auditor, independent examiner or reporting accountant in respect of:

(a) the costs of their respective external scrutiny, and

(b) other financial services such as taxation advice, consultancy, financial advice and accountancy.

14.7 *Ex gratia* payments

The total amount or value of any:

(a) payment;
(b) non-monetary benefit;
(c) other expenditure of any kind, or
(d) waiver of rights to property to which a charity is entitled,
that is made not as an application of funds or property for charitable purposes but in fulfilment of a compelling moral obligation should be disclosed in the notes to the accounts.

Where trustees require and obtain the authority of the Court, the Attorney General or the Charity Commission, the nature and date of the authority for each such payment should also be disclosed.

Payments which the trustees reasonably consider to be in the interests of the charity (more than a moral obligation) should not be treated as *ex gratia*, even though there is no legal obligation to make them. For example, the trustees may think that it will motivate retained staff and hence benefit the charity if they make redundancy payments over and above the minimum legally required.

14.8 Analysis of the net movement in funds

The net movement of funds represents the increase or decrease in resources available to a charity to deploy in undertaking future activities. Unlike profit or loss in a commercial entity, it should not necessarily be regarded as an indicator of a charity's performance. Charities also further their objectives by investing in tangible fixed assets to provide services or by making investments of a programme-related or socially related nature. Such applications are charitable but do not decrease the funds of a charity.

Charities may also receive gifts of an endowed nature, which are identified separately in the primary accounting statements. Whilst endowments provide a source of income or service generation in future periods they are not available to finance expenditure.

Information on such charitable applications and sources can be ascertained from a charity's cash flow statement (when prepared). A note summarising these effects, when material, can provide valuable information to readers of accounts in interpreting net movements in funds and help the reader understand the

Other matters to be covered in the notes to the accounts

impact of such transactions on the liquid funds of the charity. Where relevant, a charity may choose to provide in the notes to the accounts the following information:

(a) total net movement in funds for the year;
(b) net endowment receipts for the year (value of endowment receipts less any release of expendable endowment to income funds);
(c) net expenditure on additions to functional fixed assets (cost of additions less proceeds of any disposals) for the year, and
(d) net investment in programme-related investments (cost of additions less proceeds of any disposals) for the year.

14.8.1 Example

Statement of changes in resources applied for fixed assets for charity use for the year ended 31 March 2010

	Unrestricted Funds £'000	Restricted Funds £'000	Totals 2010 £'000	Totals 2009 £'000
Net movement in funds for the year	3,065	(810)	2,255	400
Resources used for net acquisitions of tangible fixed assets	(1,100)	(400)	**(1,500)**	(590)
Net movement in funds available for future activities	1,965	(1,210)	**755**	(190)

Chapter 15 – Accounting for retirement benefits

15.1 Introduction

There are two main types of retirement benefit scheme: defined contribution schemes and defined benefit schemes. Definitions for both appear in the glossary (GL 16 and GL 17) of the SORP. Details of how to account for each are included in this section.

A charity participating in a multi-employer defined benefit scheme, where the contributions are set in relation to the current service period only, or where the charity is unable to identify its share of the underlying assets and liabilities on a consistent or reasonable basis, should account for its contributions to the scheme as if it were a defined contribution scheme. Where a charity is unable to identify its share of the underlying assets and liabilities of the scheme, the disclosures set out in para. 446 should be provided.

15.2 Defined contribution schemes

The cost of a defined contribution scheme recognised in the accounts is equal to the contributions payable to the scheme in the accounting period. These pension costs should be allocated across the relevant resources expended categories of the SOFA set out in para. 177. The note disclosures in relation to such schemes are set out in para. 444.

15.3 Defined benefit schemes

There must be a balance sheet recognition of pension assets or liabilities for charities that operate defined benefit pension schemes.

FRS 17 Retirement Benefits substantially affects charities that operate defined benefit schemes (see Appendix 2: FRS 17). The surplus (or deficit) in a defined benefit scheme is the excess (or shortfall) of the value of the assets in the scheme over (or below) the present value of the scheme's liabilities. In accordance with FRS 17 principles:

Accounting for retirement benefits

(a) an asset should be recognised to the extent that the employer charity is able to recover a surplus, either through reduced contributions in the future or through refunds from the scheme; and
(b) a liability should be recognised to the extent that it reflects its legal or constructive obligation of the employer charity.

Similar principles should also be adopted in relation to the provision of death-in-service and incapacity benefits that are not wholly insured, and provided through a defined benefit pension scheme.

Full actuarial valuations of a defined benefit scheme should be undertaken by an independent, qualified actuary at intervals not exceeding three years and updated annually at the charity's balance sheet date to reflect current conditions.

A surplus or deficit in a defined benefit scheme normally gives rise to an asset or liability within unrestricted funds of the reporting charity. The reporting charity will normally be the employer and have control over the future use of a surplus recovered either in the form of reduced contributions or a refund from the scheme. Similarly, where a liability arises through a legal or constructive obligation to make good a deficit, this liability will normally rest with the main charity's unrestricted funds.

15.4 Allocation of retirement benefit costs and gains

The change in the defined benefit asset or liability (other than that arising from contributions payable to the scheme which affect the surplus or deficit in the scheme), should be analysed into the components identified in FRS 17. However, these will only be recognised through the SOFA on full implementation of FRS 17 (see Appendix 2 for FRS 17 implementation date and transitional arrangements).

Pension costs may be allocated between the resources expended categories of the SOFA on the basis of the charity's own computations. The basis of the allocation should be reasonable and consistent. Allocations of pension costs based on the staff costs of employees within the scheme is one approach, although other approaches (for example, allocation based on pension contributions payable), may also produce an equitable allocation. Allocation of the components should be based on the following:

(a) changes relating to current or past service costs and gains, and losses on settlements and curtailments should be allocated to the appropriate resources expended categories set out in para. 432;
(b) pension finance costs arising from changes in the net of interest costs and expected return on assets should be allocated to the appropriate resources

expended categories set out in para. 432 – income arising from these changes should be recognised as an incoming resource and separately disclosed where material;

(c) where past service costs, or gains or losses on settlements or curtailment, are material in the context of the particular expenditure (or income) category in which they are recognised, the amounts should be disclosed as exceptional in accordance with FRS 3 Reporting Financial Performance (see Appendix 2), and

(d) actuarial gains and losses arising should be recognised within the 'gains and losses' categories of the SOFA under the heading 'actuarial gains and losses on defined benefit pension scheme'.

15.5 Restricted funds

A pension asset should be recognised as accruing to a restricted fund only where it can be demonstrated that the economic benefit of the asset will accrue to a particular fund through reduced contributions or refunds. Similarly, a pension liability should be allocated to a particular fund only where it is demonstrable that a constructive liability arises to fund the deficit and could properly be met from the particular fund. Such a situation may arise where staff are specifically engaged on a long-term project funded from restricted income. This allocation may be undertaken on the basis of the charity's own computations. Liaison with the provider of a particular restricted fund may be necessary in order to establish the basis on which any pension asset or liability is allocated to that fund and therefore the pension costs that may be properly charged through it.

Any allocation of a pension asset or liability to a restricted fund should be reviewed on an annual basis. Where staff changes or cessation of a particular project indicate that the economic benefits or obligations will no longer accrue to that particular fund, then the asset or liability should be allocated to the unrestricted funds by means of a transfer of funds through the SOFA.

Where the criteria for the recognition of a pension asset or liability within restricted funds are met, the related pension costs should be recognised within the 'restricted funds' column of the SOFA. The components of the pension cost should be recognised within the same SOFA categories and on the same basis as set out in the preceding paragraphs.

A restricted fund may, however, incur staff costs without the criteria for the recognition of a pension asset or liability within the restricted fund's balance sheet being met. For example, a restricted fund may be of a short-term nature or staff may frequently be transferred between activities, creating uncertainty over which fund will ultimately recover any surplus or meet future contributions resulting from any deficit. In such circumstances, the 'restricted funds' column of the SOFA may still be recharged with an appropriate portion of the current service cost component of the pension cost relating to the staff engaged in activities within restricted funds. Such a recharge within the SOFA would, as with any recharge, also necessitate a balance sheet adjustment between fund balances. The balance sheet of the unrestricted funds should, however, continue to recognise the overall pension asset or liability.

When past service costs and gains and losses on curtailments and settlements arise, such costs may be recharged to restricted funds only when a charity can demonstrate the costs relate to present staff engaged in the activities of the restricted funds.

15.6 Consideration of going concern

The Audit and Assurance Faculty of the Institute of Chartered Accountants in England and Wales (ICAEW) has provided, in 'Technical Release Audit 1/02', guidance for auditors on how they should approach the question of pension liabilities when assessing the going concern of an entity. Although this guidance is directed at auditors, it does have relevance to charities wishing to understand how pension liabilities may affect solvency.

In the view of the Pensions Regulator, and consistent with that of the Audit and Assurance Faculty, an FRS 17 deficit does not of itself automatically raise an issue over the going concern of the charity.

When considering the appropriateness of the going concern concept, trustee directors of charitable companies need to consider the cash flow effects of the agreed pension contributions arising under the scheme, irrespective of whether any FRS 17 deficit is disclosed on or off the balance sheet.

15.7 Reserves policy

SORP 2005 recommends that trustees provide a statement of their reserves policy in their Trustees' Annual Report. Trustees will need to consider explaining to the charity's stakeholders the effects of the inclusion of any pension asset or liability on the charity, notably any impact on its reserves policy; with particular attention being paid to explaining clearly and simply how the accounting disclosures should be interpreted in the context of the charity's finances. Trustees will also need to consider direct communication with major funders, explaining the impact on cash flows.

Where material, the reserves policy statement is likely to differentiate the pension assets or liability from other reserves of the charity. It might explain the actuarial valuation resulting in the pension reserve or deficit and that the corresponding asset or liability does not result in an immediate cash flow impact on the charity that is to say that it is not an asset that can be immediately drawn down nor a liability that must be settled immediately. A brief indication of the cash flow effect (that is, increase or decrease in contributions to the scheme) would put this situation into context.

Although an FRS 17 calculated pension deficit does not result in an immediate equivalent cash commitment, it would not generally be appropriate for trustees to regard an equivalent amount as a designation of charitable funds. To do so would indicate an intention to apply the amount designated to make good the full amount of any reported pension liability and indicate that such funds were unavailable to expend on the charity's general purposes.

A good starting point is for a charity to exclude the FRS 17 calculated asset or liability when calculating free reserves, but then to give careful consideration to the cash flow implications that may arise from the accounting disclosure in terms of increased or reduced contributions.

Where a charity is confident that it can meet contributions from projected future income without significant impact on its planned levels of charitable activity, then it is unlikely that trustees will need to designate any of their existing funds to meet future pension commitments.

Where contribution increases create uncertainty as to the charity's ability to meet them from projected future income, or where such increases would result in a significant curtailment of charitable activities, then urgent consideration by the trustees is required. In such circumstances, immediate actuarial and legal advice is likely to be appropriate; it would be prudent to create a designation insofar as it is anticipated that the ability to make future contributions is dependent upon the assets currently held by the charity.

The Charity Commission has prepared guidance in partnership with the Charity Finance Directors' Group, which looks at issues including the cash flow impacts of pension arrangements on reserves policy. This guidance has been reproduced in **Appendix 6** of this book.

15.8 Disclosures

The disclosure requirements for pension scheme contributions are given in FRS 17. This section summarises the key points.

Where a defined contribution scheme is operated by a charity, the notes to the accounts should disclose:

(a) the nature of the scheme;
(b) the costs for the accounting period, and

(c) the amount of any outstanding or prepaid contributions at the year end.

FRS 17 disclosure requirements for defined benefit pension schemes are detailed, and charities should refer to the text of the standard in completing their disclosure notes. The notes to the accounts should include the following information:

(a) the nature of the scheme;
(b) the date of the most recent full actuarial valuation;
(c) the contributions made in the accounting period and any agreed contribution rates for future years;
(d) the main financial assumptions used at the beginning of the period and at the balance sheet date;
(e) the fair value of scheme assets analysed between equities, bonds and other assets and their expected rates of return;
(f) the actual return achieved on scheme assets;
(g) the present value of the scheme liabilities and the resulting surplus or deficit compared with the fair value of the scheme assets, and
(h) an analysis of the amounts for each of the component parts of the defined benefit costs charged or credited through the SOFA.

Where a charity operating a defined benefit scheme has established that the employer's share of underlying assets and liabilities cannot be identified on a consistent and reasonable basis (for example, by confirmation from the scheme administrators or actuaries), this fact should be disclosed. Any available information about the existence of surplus or deficit in the scheme, and the implications of that surplus or deficit for the employing charity, should be disclosed, together with a brief explanation of the general circumstances giving rise to this position.

When a charity operating a defined benefit scheme discloses a material pension liability, the notes to the accounts or Trustees' Annual Report, in the explanation of the policy on reserves, should explain the impact, if any, on resources available for general application. If a pension liability exceeds the balance on unrestricted funds, the note should also explain any limitations placed on any restricted fund of the charity to contribute to any resource requirements arising from the disclosed liability.

If a material pension asset is disclosed, the notes to the accounts or the Trustees' Annual Report should explain the nature of the economic benefit derived from the asset and give an indication of the period over which any benefit in terms of reduced contributions will accrue to the charity.

Chapter 16 – Application of accounting standards

In preparing accounts which show a true and fair view charities must apply the accounting standards issued by the Accounting Standards Board and the abstracts issued by the Urgent Issues Task Force. The SORP applies the principles from these standards which are relevant to charities. In respect of specific matters it is, however, important that the original accounting standards should be consulted.

This chapter contains a commentary, which has been adapted from Appendix 2 of SORP 2005, of the accounting standards extant at the date of issue of the SORP and their applicability to charities.

16.1 Statements of Standard Accounting Practice (SSAPs)

16.1.1 SSAP 4 *Accounting for government grants*

SSAP 4 deals with the accounting treatment and disclosure of government grants and other forms of government assistance, including equity finance, subsidised loans and advisory assistance. It is also indicative of best practice for accounting for grants and assistance from other sources.

A gift of a tangible fixed asset (or grant to purchase) is recognised in full with the recipient charity's entitlement to the asset. Any restriction on the asset's future use is recognised by allocating the asset to a restricted fund rather than deferring the recognition of the asset. Any residual liability to the donor arising from, for example, the asset's future sale, is disclosed as a contingent liability unless the event that would trigger repayment of the grant becomes probable – in which case, a liability for repayment is recognised.

The SORP provides the most appropriate interpretation of SSAP 4 for charities. In particular, grants for fixed assets should not be deferred, though normally they will have to be accounted for in a separate fund (see paragraph 111).

16.1.2 SSAP 5 *Accounting for value added tax*

SSAP 5 follows the general principle that the treatment of VAT in the accounts should reflect an entity's role as a collector of the tax and VAT should not be included in income or in expenditure, whether of a capital or revenue nature.

Application of accounting standards

However, where the VAT is irrecoverable, it should be included in the cost of the items reported in the financial statements.

Many, if not all, charities will suffer irrecoverable VAT either because they are not registered or have a mixture of activities that are zero-rated and standard-rated, exempt and outside the scope of VAT. The irrecoverable tax should be included in the relevant cost headings on the face of the Statement of Financial Activities and not shown as a separate item, although separate disclosure of the amount may be made in the notes to the accounts.

16.1.3 SSAP 9 *Stocks and long-term contracts*

SSAP 9 gives guidance on the values of stocks and long-term contracts to be included in the balance sheet and on the criteria for recognition of income and expenditure on such items within the profit and loss account (Statement of Financial Activities for charities).

The standard is equally applicable to charities as to other entities.

16.1.4 SSAP 13 *Accounting for research and development*

SSAP 13 provides guidance on three broad categories of activity – namely, pure research, applied research and development. The standard defines these categories and specifies the accounting policies that may be followed for each.

The standard is equally applicable to charities as to other entities.

16.1.5 SSAP 19 *Accounting for investment properties*

SSAP 19 requires investment properties to be included in the balance sheet at their open market value, but without charging depreciation.

The standard is equally applicable to charities as to other entities.

16.1.6 SSAP 21 *Accounting for leases and hire purchase contracts*

SSAP 21 describes how to identify and account for finance leases, operating leases and hire purchase contracts both for the lessee and the lessor.

The standard is equally applicable to charities as to other entities.

16.1.7 SSAP 25 *Segmental reporting*

SSAP 25 requires the disclosure by class of business and by geographical segment of turnover, segment result and segment net assets. The turnover

Financial Reporting Standards (FRSs)

disclosure is required by all companies, otherwise the disclosure is mandatory only for PLCs, banking and insurance companies and those over 10 times the threshold for medium-sized companies.

This will only be applicable to the largest charities. The disclosure requirements in the SORP for details of activities by function meets the spirit of SSAP 25 for turnover by class of activity. The disclosure by geographical region and segment net assets would be additional.

16.2 Financial Reporting Standards (FRSs)

16.2.1 FRS 1 *Cash Flow Statements* (Revised 1996)

FRS 1 (Revised 1996) requires reporting entities within its scope to prepare a cash flow statement in the manner set out in the FRS. Its scope includes, for accounting periods beginning on or after 6 April 2008, two of the following:

1. gross turnover of £6.5million (previously £5.6million);
2. gross assets of £3.26million (previously £2.8million); and
3. employees of 50 or more.

Paragraphs 351–355 *explain the applicability of FRS 1 to charities.*

16.2.2 FRS 2 *Accounting for Subsidiary Undertakings*

FRS 2 sets out the conditions under which an entity qualifies as a parent undertaking that should prepare consolidated financial statements for its group, the parent and its subsidiaries. It also sets out the manner in which consolidated financial statements are to be prepared.

Paragraphs 381–397 *explain consolidation and the applicability of FRS 2 to charities.*

16.2.3 FRS 3 *Reporting Financial Performance*

FRS 3 requires a layered format for the profit and loss (income and expenditure) account, split between continuing, newly acquired and discontinued operations. It has effectively outlawed extraordinary items. The standard also requires a statement of total recognised gains and losses to be shown as a primary statement. A note of historical profits, which is a memorandum item, is also required, as is the disclosure of earnings per share.

The Statement of Financial Activities combines both the income and expenditure account and the statement of total recognised gains and losses and meets charity law. Exceptional items should be disclosed on a separate line within the activity to which they relate. The additional requirements for charitable companies are explained in paras 423–426. Earnings per share is not relevant to charities.

Application of accounting standards

16.2.4 FRS 4 *Capital Instruments*

FRS 4 requires capital instruments to be presented in financial statements in a way that reflects the obligations of the issuer and the impact on shareholders' equity.

Most parts of this standard are superseded by FRS 25.

This standard is not generally applicable to charities following the SORP.

16.2.5 FRS 5 *Reporting the Substance of Transactions*

FRS 5 requires that the substance of an entity's transactions is reported in its financial statements. This means that the commercial effect of a transaction and any resulting assets, liabilities, gains and losses must be shown and that the accounts do not merely report the legal form of a transaction.

This standard is equally applicable to charities as to other entities.

16.2.6 FRS 6 *Acquisitions and Mergers*

FRS 6 sets out the circumstances in which the two methods of accounting for a business combination (acquisition accounting and merger accounting) are to be used. The FRS sets out five criteria that must be met for merger accounting to be used. If they are not met, then acquisition accounting should be used.

The principles of merger accounting are applicable to charities where two or more charities merge. However, where funds are merely transferred from one charity to another, this may constitute a gift or, in the case of a restricted fund, simply the administrative transfer of the restricted fund from one set of trustees to another. Two of the five criteria apply to shareholder's funds and so will not be applicable to charities. Charities cannot merge with non-charitable companies, and so acquisition accounting will have to be used where such companies are acquired.

16.2.7 FRS 7 *Fair Values in Acquisition Accounting*

FRS 7 sets out the principles of accounting for a business combination under the acquisition method of accounting. It gives the meaning of 'identifiable assets and liabilities' and how to determine their fair values. The difference between the sum of these fair values and the cost of acquisition is recognised as goodwill or negative goodwill.

This standard is equally applicable to charities as to other entities where acquisition accounting is used.

16.2.8 FRS 8 *Related Party Disclosures*

FRS 8 determines who and what 'related parties' are, and the disclosures necessary to draw attention to the possibility that the reported financial position and results may have been affected by the existence of related parties and by material transactions with them.

Paragraphs 221–233 *explain the application of FRS 8 with respect to charities.*

16.2.9 FRS 9 *Associates and Joint Ventures*

FRS 9 sets out the definitions and accounting treatments for associates and joint ventures, two types of interests that a reporting entity may have in other entities. The FRS also deals with joint arrangements that are not entities.

Paragraphs 407–418 *explain the applicability of FRS 9 to charities.*

16.2.10 FRS 10 *Goodwill and Intangible Assets*

FRS 10 requires purchased goodwill and intangible fixed assets (where marketable) to be capitalised on the balance sheet and amortised over their life, normally regarded as 20 years, subject to impairment reviews.

FRS 10 covers common occurrences of goodwill and intangible assets. Where a charity has an intangible asset that does not meet the criteria under the standard, it should not be included in the primary statements but details of the asset and its financial effect must be disclosed in the notes to the accounts.

16.2.11 FRS 11 *Impairment of Fixed Assets and Goodwill*

FRS 11 sets out the principles and methodology for accounting for impairments of fixed assets and goodwill. The carrying amount of an asset is compared with its recoverable amount and, if the carrying amount is higher, the asset is written down. Recoverable amount is defined as the higher of the amount that could be obtained by selling the asset (net realisable value) and the amount that could be obtained through using the asset (value in use). Impairment tests are only required when there has been some indication that an impairment has occurred.

Paragraphs 267–272 *explain the applicability of FRS 11 to charities.*

Application of accounting standards

16.2.12 FRS 12 *Provisions, Contingent Liabilities and Contingent Assets*

FRS 12 describes the circumstances in which a provision (a liability that is of uncertain timing or amount) may arise and how it should be measured and recognised in the financial statements. It also describes how to account for contingent assets and liabilities.

FRS 12 is generally applicable to charities. Paragraphs 148–163 *and* 321–329 *describe some particular application points to charities.*

16.2.13 FRS 13 *Derivatives and other Financial Instruments: Disclosures*

The Financial Reporting Standard on derivatives (FRS13) must be followed by a reporting entity that has any of its capital instruments listed or publicly traded on a stock exchange or market. A capital instrument is an instrument issued by a reporting entity as a means of raising finance and includes shares, debentures, loans and debt instruments.

The FRS is therefore neither applicable to nor designed for charities.

Although FRS 13 is not applicable to charities, much of what would need to be disclosed is required in the SORP. *In particular:*

1. *Amongst the requirements of the FRS are those to disclose details of financial assets and liabilities, which can include most current assets and current liabilities, investments and derivatives. Disclosure of all these items is required by the SORP.*
2. *FRS 13 requires disclosure of the financial risk profile of the entity. Disclosure of risks, including financial risk, is required in the Trustees' Annual Report as part of the general disclosure on risk.*
3. *The FRS also requires an explanation of derivatives in particular and this is also required in the SORP.*
4. *The SORP also indicates that the notes to the accounts should disclose what derivative products are in use by the charity and the role that financial instruments play in creating or changing the risks that the entity faces in its activities (see* paras 337–339).

16.2.14 FRS 14 *Earnings per Share*

This is superseded by FRS 21 for accounting periods beginning on or after 1 January 2005.

It is not applicable to charities.

16.2.15 FRS 15 *Tangible Fixed Assets*

FRS 15 sets out the principles of accounting for tangible fixed assets, with the exception of investment properties. In principle, all fixed assets must be capitalised at cost or at a revalued amount. However, where an enterprise chooses to adopt a policy of revaluing some assets, all assets of the same class must be revalued and the valuations kept up to date.

The principles of FRS 15 are generally applicable to charities and are embodied in the balance sheet section of the SORP. *However, there are relaxed criteria for the valuations of charity assets and certain heritage assets need not be capitalised in certain circumstances, as explained in* paras 279–294.

As noted in paras 265 and 266, *where a charity adopts a policy of revaluation of tangible fixed assets, the SORP allows – in the case of land and building s– such valuations to be undertaken by a suitably qualified trustee or employee.*

16.2.16 FRS 16 *Current Tax*

FRS 16 *is generally not applicable to charities. However, the Government is making compensation payments to charities for five years from April 1999 for the removal of ACT credits on the payment of UK dividends. These payments should be included as part of the charity's investment income.*

16.2.17 FRS 17 *Retirement Benefits*

FRS 17 sets out the accounting treatment for retirement benefits such as pensions and medical care during retirement (see Chapter 15). On the full implementation of the standard, the main requirements are:

(a) pension assets are measured using fair values;
(b) pension scheme liabilities are measured using the projected unit method and discounted using the current rate of return on a high quality corporate bond of equivalent term and currency to the liabilities;
(c) the pension scheme surplus (to the extent it can be recovered) or deficit is recognised on the balance sheet (note that a five year history of assets, liabilities and experience gains/losses is also now required, and
(d) the movement in the scheme surplus/deficit is analysed by:
   (i) the current service cost and any past service cost, recognised in operating profit
   (ii) the interest cost and expected return on assets, recognised as other finance costs; and
   (iii) actuarial gains and losses recognised in the statement of total recognised gains and losses

This standard is *equally applicable to charities.*

Application of accounting standards

Specific guidance on the application of the standard is given in the special section beginning at para. 430.

16.2.18 FRS 18 *Accounting Policies*

FRS 18 sets out the principles to be followed in selecting accounting policies and the disclosures needed to help users to understand the accounting policies adopted and how they have been applied.

Its objective is to ensure that:

(a) an entity adopts the accounting policies most appropriate to its particular circumstances for the purposes of giving a true and fair view;
(b) the accounting policies adopted are reviewed regularly to ensure that they remain appropriate, and are changed when a new policy becomes more appropriate to the entity's particular circumstances, and
(c) sufficient information is disclosed in the financial statements to enable users to understand the accounting policies adopted and how they have been implemented.

It requires disclosure of the extent to which financial statements comply with any relevant SORP. Where an entity's financial statements fall within the scope of a SORP, the entity should state the title of the SORP and whether its financial statements have been prepared in accordance with the SORP's current provisions. In the event of a departure, the entity should give a brief description of the departure from recommended practice, the reasons why the treatment adopted is judged more appropriate, details of any disclosures recommended by the SORP that have not been provided and the reasons why they have not been provided.

The appropriateness of accounting policies adopted is judged against the objectives of:

(a) relevance;
(b) reliability;
(c) comparability, and
(d) understandability.

This standard is equally applicable to charities as to other entities. The disclosure of compliance with any relevant SORP has particular relevance in the context of the charity sector where adherence to SORP *2005 is expected.*

The implementation of this SORP may involve the analysis and presentation of incoming resources and resources expended across different SOFA categories and the allocation of support costs to activity categories within the SOFA. The SOFA for the preceding period should be restated to ensure consistent presentation.

Financial Reporting Standards (FRSs)

Although this SORP does not change the basis of asset and liability recognition, it does provide more detailed guidance on the recognition of performance-related grants, which may result in some charities amending their accounting policies and where the effect of such a policy change is material, a restatement of comparative amounts will be necessary.

16.2.19 FRS 19 *Deferred Tax*

FRS 19 requires full provision to be made for deferred tax assets and liabilities arising from timing differences between the recognition of gains and losses in the financial statements and their recognition in a tax computation.

The general principle underlying the requirements is that deferred tax should be recognised as a liability or asset if the transactions or events that give the entity an obligation to pay more tax or less tax in the future have occurred at the balance sheet date.

This standard is not generally applicable to charities, due to tax exemptions available.

However, the standard will be of relevance in consolidated accounts that include non-charitable subsidiaries, particularly those that adopt a policy of full or partial profit retention rather than full distribution of taxable profits through Gift Aid.

Where it is a subsidiary's practice to make a Gift Aid payment of all of its taxable profits to its parent charity, subsequent to its reporting year end, which qualifies for tax relief in that earlier period, a provision for deferred tax is unlikely to be necessary.

16.2.20 FRS 20 *Share-based Payment*

This standard is not applicable to charities.

16.2.21 FRS 21 (IAS 10) *Events after the Balance Sheet Date*

FRS 21 has replaced SSAP 17 *Accounting for post balance sheet events*. It sets out the recognition and measurement requirements for the following two types of event after the balance sheet date;

1. Those that provide evidence of conditions that existed at the balance sheet date for which the entity shall adjust the amounts recognised in its financial statements or recognise items that were not previously recognised (adjusting events) – for example, the settlement of a court case that confirms the entity had a present obligation at the balance sheet date.
2. Those that are indicative of conditions that arose after the balance sheet date for which the entity does not adjust the amounts recognised in its financial statements (non-adjusting events) – for example, a decline in

Application of accounting standards

market value of investments between the balance sheet date and the date when the financial statements are authorised for issue.

FRS 21 applies for accounting periods beginning on or after 1 January 2005.

It is equally applicable to charities as to other entities.

The determination after the balance sheet date of the amount of a Gift Aid payment to a parent charity by a subsidiary undertaking is an adjusting event, if the subsidiary had a present legal (for example, a deed) or a constructive obligation at the balance sheet date. Where a present obligation is demonstrable at the year end, an adjustment is made where post-balance sheet calculations provide greater accuracy in the measurement of the existing liability —for example, to equate the Gift Aid liability more closely to taxable profits.

Designations reflect intentions as to the future application of funds held at a particular balance sheet date and do not reflect an external transaction or present obligation to a third party. As such, they fall outside the scope of FRS 21. However, the spirit and reasoning behind the standard would suggest that charities should designate for future projects or plans envisaged at the balance sheet date and adjust such estimates to accord with any more accurate information that becomes available after the year end.

16.2.22 FRS 22 (IAS 33) *Earnings per share*

This standard only applies to entities whose ordinary shares are traded or that are in the process of issuing such shares.

This standard supersedes FRS14 for accounting periods beginning on or after 1 January 2005.

It is not applicable to charities.

16.2.23 FRS 23 (IAS 21) *The Effects of Changes of Foreign Exchange Rates*

An entity may carry on foreign activities in two ways. It may have transactions in foreign currencies or it may have foreign operations. In addition, an entity may present its financial statements in a foreign currency. FRS 23 prescribes how entities should include foreign currency transactions and foreign operations in their financial statements and how they should translate financial statements into a presentation currency.

The standard applies to entities applying FRS 26. In effect, this means listed entities are required to apply the standard for accounting periods beginning on or after 1 January 2005, and unlisted entities preparing their accounts in

Financial Reporting Standards (FRSs)

accordance with the fair value accounting rules set out in the Companies Acts will be required to adopt it for accounting periods beginning on or after 1 January 2006.

This standard replaces the requirements set out in SSAP 20 from when the new standard is applied.

This standard is applicable to charities that are applying FRS 26.

16.2.24 FRS 24 (IAS 29) *Financial Reporting in Hyperinflationary Economies*

FRS 24 prescribes how an entity whose functional currency is the currency of a hyperinflationary economy, should report its operating results and financial position. It also provides guidance on determining whether an economy is hyperinflationary.

The standard applies to entities applying FRS 26. In effect, this means listed entities are required to apply the standard for accounting periods beginning on or after 1 January 2005. Unlisted entities preparing their accounts in accordance with the fair value accounting rules set out in the Companies Acts will be required to adopt it for accounting periods beginning on or after 1 January 2006.

Where this standard is applied, it replaces UITF 9.

This standard will not apply to charities unless the functional currency in which they report is subject to hyperinflation and FRS 26 has been adopted.

16.2.25 FRS 25 (IAS 32) *Financial Instruments: Disclosure and Presentation*

The objective of FRS 25 is to enhance the understanding by users of accounts of the significance of financial instruments to an entity's financial position, performance and cash flow.

The presentation requirements of this standard deal with the classification of capital instruments issued between debt and equity and the implications of that classification for dividends and interest expense. The presentational disclosures required by the standard apply to accounting periods beginning on or after 1 January 2005 with earlier adoption not being permitted.

The disclosure requirements apply to entities applying FRS 26 only. In effect this means listed entities are required to apply the standard for accounting periods beginning on or after 1 January 2005 and unlisted entities preparing their

Application of accounting standards

accounts in accordance with the fair value accounting rules set out in the Companies Acts will be required to adopt it for accounting periods beginning on or after 1 January 2006.

Presentational requirements apply to charities for accounting periods beginning on or after 1 January 2005.

Disclosure requirements apply to charities that are applying FRS 26.

16.2.26 FRS 26 (IAS 39) *Financial Instruments: Recognition and Measurement*

FRS 26 introduces for the first time requirements for the measurement of financial instruments. It implements in full the measurement and hedge accounting provisions of IAS 39 as published by the International Accounting Standards Board.

This standard applies to listed entities for accounting periods beginning on or after 1 January 2005.

Unlisted entities preparing accounts in accordance with fair value accounting rules set out in the Companies Acts are required to apply the standard for accounting periods beginning on or after 1 January 2006, and may voluntarily apply it for accounting periods beginning on or after 1 January 2005.

This standard is applicable to charities that are companies and which adopt an accounting policy that measures financial instruments at fair value for accounting periods beginning on or after 1 January 2006.

16.2.27 FRS 27 *Life Assurance*

FRS 27 applies to all entities with a life assurance business (including a life reinsurance business), and is effective for accounting periods ending on or after 23 December 2005, except that some smaller friendly societies are exempt until 2006 or 2007.

This standard will only apply to charities in the event of them undertaking life insurance business.

16.2.28 FRSSE *Financial Reporting Standard for Smaller Entities*

The FRSSE brings together the relevant accounting requirements and disclosures from the other accounting standards and UITF abstracts, simplified and modified as appropriate for smaller entities. The FRSSE is an optional standard but entities adopting it are exempt from applying all the other accounting standards and UITF abstracts. Financial reporting is continually evolving and therefore the FRSSE needs to be updated, roughly on an annual basis, to reflect new or revised accounting standards and UITF abstracts.

Paragraphs 5.2.1–5.2.2 in Appendix 5 explain the applicability of the FRSSE to smaller charities. Whilst it can be followed there are certain principles and notes within the SORP which apply to all charities and must be included in the financial statements.

16.3 Urgent Issues Task Force (UITF) Abstracts

16.3.1 UITF Abstract 4 *Presentation of long-term debtors in current assets*

Such items should be separately disclosed on the face of the balance sheet or in the notes to the accounts.

This is equally applicable to charities as to other entities.

16.3.2 UITF Abstract 5 *Transfers from current assets to fixed assets*

This is applicable in principle to charities, but unlikely to arise in practice.

16.3.3 UITF Abstract 9 *Accounting for operations in hyper-inflationary economies*

See also FRS 24.

This is only applicable to charities that operate in countries where such conditions exist.

16.3.4 UITF Abstract 11 *Capital instruments: issuer call options*

See also FRS 25 and FRS 26.

This is not generally applicable to charities.

16.3.5 UITF Abstract 15 *Disclosure of substantial acquisitions*

This is not generally applicable to charities.

Application of accounting standards

16.3.6 UITF Abstract 17 *Employee share schemes*

This is not applicable to charities.

16.3.7 UITF Abstract 18 *Pensions costs following the 1997 tax changes in respect of dividend income*

Note: This is to be to be replaced by FRED 20.

The probable reduction in actuarial value as a result of pension schemes no longer being able to claim tax credits on dividends should be spread over the remaining service lives of current employees, in line with SSAP 24.

This is equally applicable to charities as to other entities.

16.3.8 UITF Abstract 19 *Tax on gains and losses on foreign currency borrowings that hedge an Investment in a foreign enterprise*

This is not generally applicable to charities.

16.3.9 UITF Abstract 21 *Accounting issues arising from the proposed introduction of the euro*

This is generally applicable to charities, although it will have limited impact unless the UK adopts the euro.

16.3.10 UITF Abstract 22 *The acquisition of a Lloyd's business*

This is not applicable to charities.

16.3.11 UITF Abstract 23 *Application of the transitional rules in FRS 15*

This provides transitional rules on the use of previous period adjustments where tangible fixed assets that were previously treated as a single asset are identified as having two or more major components with substantially different useful economic lives.

This is equally applicable to charities as to other entities.

16.3.12 UITF Abstract 24 *Accounting for start-up costs*

This abstract addresses whether or not start-up costs that cannot be included within the cost of a fixed asset may nevertheless be carried forward. Start-up costs that do not meet the recognition criteria under relevant accounting standards should not be carried forward, but recognised as an expense when incurred.

This is equally applicable to charities as to other entities.

16.3.13 UITF Abstract 25 *National Insurance contributions on share option gains*

This is not applicable to charities.

16.3.14 UITF Abstract 26 *Barter transactions for advertising*

An entity involved in publishing or broadcasting may agree to provide advertising in exchange for advertising services provided by its customers, rather than for cash consideration. Income from advertising undertaken on such a barter basis is only recognised where persuasive evidence exists that the advertising opportunity could have been sold for an equivalent sum of cash.

This is equally applicable to charities as to other entities.

16.3.15 UITF Abstract 27 *Revisions to estimates of useful economic life of goodwill and intangible assets*

This abstract states that a change from non-amortisation of goodwill or intangible assets, on the grounds that the life of the asset is indefinite, to amortisation over a period of 20 years or less, should not be reported as a change in accounting policy. In such a circumstance, the carrying amount of the goodwill or intangible asset should be amortised over the revised remaining useful life.

Goodwill rarely arises in the context of charity accounts; the treatment of intangible assets applies equally to charities as to other entities.

16.3.16 UITF Abstract 28 *Operating lease incentives*

A lessor may provide an incentive for the lessee to enter into a new or renewed operating lease. It requires that the relevant income or expense be recognised over the life of the asset, or until a market rent will be payable, on a straight-line basis unless another systematic basis is more representative of benefit flows.

Application of accounting standards

This is equally applicable to charities as to other entities.

16.3.17 UITF Abstract 29 *Website development costs*

Websites are used for a variety of activities, including promotion of services and goods, taking orders and provision of information. Many entities incur significant costs in developing such websites. Certain website development costs may be capitalised only where they lead to the creation of an enduring asset delivering benefits at least as great as the amount capitalised.

This is generally applicable to charities.

However, charities' websites may also provide economic benefit without being related to cash flow – for example, the provision of educational information to beneficiaries of the charity. To the extent that the relationship to such benefits is sufficiently certain, such costs may be capitalised.

16.3.18 UITF Abstract 30 *Date of award to employees of shares or rights to shares*

This is not applicable to charities.

16.3.19 UITF Abstract 31 *Exchanges of businesses or other non-monetary assets for an interest in a subsidiary, joint venture or associate*

Entities may transfer businesses or other non-monetary assets in exchange for equity in a subsidiary, joint venture or associate. This abstract deals with accounting for such transactions in consolidated accounts – dealing in particular with the issues surrounding reporting the transaction at fair values or book values.

This is equally applicable to charities as to other entities.

16.3.20 UITF Abstract 32 *Employee benefit trusts and other intermediate payment arrangements*

This abstract applies when an entity sets up and transfers funds to an employee benefit trust (or other intermediary) and the trust's accumulated assets are used to remunerate the entity's employees (or other service providers). The abstract clarifies how the principles for FRS 5 *Reporting the Substance of Transactions* should be applied.

This is not generally applicable to charities.

16.3.21 UITF Abstract 33 *Obligations in capital instruments*

This abstract deals with the classification of capital instruments. A capital instrument, other than a share, which involves an obligation to transfer economic benefits will be treated as a liability in the single entity financial statements of the issuer – unless that obligation would not be considered in accordance with the going concern concept.

See also FRS 25 and FRS 26.

This is equally applicable to charities as to other entities.

16.3.22 UITF Abstract 34 *Pre-contract costs*

This abstract is intended to bring consistency to the treatment of costs incurred in bidding for and securing contracts to supply products or services.

It requires costs incurred before it is virtually certain that a contract will be obtained to be charged immediately as expenses. Directly attributable costs incurred after that point should be recognised as an asset and charged as expenses during the period of the contract.

This is equally applicable to charities as to other entities.

16.3.23 UITF Abstract 35 *Death-in-service and incapacity benefits*

This abstract clarifies the accounting required by FRS 17 *Retirement Benefits* for the cost of death-in-service and incapacity benefits, where such benefits are provided through a defined benefit pension scheme. The abstract requires that, where the benefits are not wholly insured, the uninsured scheme liability and the cost for the accounting period should be measured, in line with other retirement benefits, using the projected unit method. The effect is that the valuation of uninsured benefits reflects the current period's portion of the full benefits ultimately payable in respect of current members of the scheme; the cost of insured benefits is determined by the relevant insurance premiums.

This is equally applicable to charities as to other entities.

16.3.24 UITF Abstract 36 *Contracts for sales of capacity*

Entities in some industries (such as telecommunications and electricity) sell rights to use capacity on their networks, sometimes entering into exchange or reciprocal

Application of accounting standards

transactions ('capacity swaps'). This abstract sets out the limited circumstances under which transactions in capacity should be reported as sales, and the proceeds reported as turnover.

This is not generally applicable to charities.

16.3.25 UITF Abstract 37 *Purchases and sales of own shares*

See also FRS 25 and FRS 26.

This is not applicable to charities.

16.3.26 UITF Abstract 38 *Accounting for ESOP trusts*

This is not applicable to charities.

Chapter 17 – Consolidated accounts

17.1 Introduction

The 1993 Act and the previous Regulations did not contain provisions relating to consolidation. This matter was left entirely to the SORP which recommends that consolidated accounts are prepared for a charity and the subsidiary (usually non-charitable) undertakings it controls. The purpose is to show a true and fair view of the state of affairs and activities of the charity and its subsidiary undertakings as a whole. The Charities Act 2006 now puts non-company charities in the same legal position as company charities (see section **4.10.4** in Chapter 4).

17.2 Changes made by SORP 2000

SORP 2000 introduced the requirement for consolidation to be performed on a line-by-line basis, bringing the SORP completely into line with FRS 2. It also brought in exemption criteria where, if the gross income of the charitable group is less than (the threshold for a statutory audit), then it is necessary to consolidate.

The SORP introduced disclosure requirements and accounting principles for associates, joint ventures and joint arrangements, which are consistent with FRS 9.

17.3 How are parent and subsidiary undertakings defined?

17.3.1 The Companies Act 2006 and FRS 2

In summary, an undertaking is a parent undertaking to a subsidiary undertaking if:

(a) it holds a majority of the voting rights in the subsidiary undertaking;
(b) it is a member of the subsidiary undertaking and has the right to appoint or remove a majority of its board of directors;
(c) it has the right to exercise a dominant influence over the subsidiary undertaking by virtue of:
(d) provisions contained in the subsidiary undertaking's Memorandum or Articles; or
(e) a control contract

Consolidated accounts

(**Note**: It is not necessary for the parent undertaking to be a member of the subsidiary undertaking in this case), and

it is a member of the subsidiary undertaking and controls, alone, pursuant to an agreement with other shareholders or members, a majority of the voting rights in the undertaking

Subsidiaries also include sub-subsidiaries.

17.3.2 SORP 2005

'Parent undertaking' and 'subsidiary undertaking' are defined in the glossary appended to the SORP as follows:

> 'In relation to a charity, an undertaking is the parent undertaking of another undertaking, called a subsidiary undertaking, where the charity controls the subsidiary. Control requires that the parent can both direct and derive benefit from the subsidiary.
>
> (a) Direction is achieved if the charity or its trustees:
>
> > (i) hold or control the majority of the voting rights, or
> >
> > (ii) have the right to appoint or remove a majority of the board of directors or trustees of the subsidiary undertaking, or
> >
> > (iii) have the power to exercise, or actually exercise, a dominant influence over the subsidiary undertaking or
> >
> > (iv) manage the charity and the subsidiary on a unified basis
>
> (b) Benefit derived can either be economic benefit that results in a net cash inflow to the charity or can arise through the provision of goods or services to the benefit of the charity or its beneficiaries.

The SORP's definition is therefore based on the Companies Act, to which reference should be made, if necessary.

Paragraphs 388–392 set out some guidance on applying the definition of 'subsidiary undertaking'. A charity, however constituted, should be regarded as a subsidiary undertaking where the parent charity has the power to exercise, or actually exercises, dominant influence or control over the subsidiary or the parent and subsidiary are managed on a unified basis. This can arise in any of the following situations:

(a) the charity trustees and/or members and/or employees of the parent charity are, or have the right to appoint or remove, a majority of the trustees of the subsidiary charity;

(b) the governing document of the subsidiary charity reserves to the parent charity's trustees and/or members the right to direct, or to give consent to, the exercise of significant discretions by the trustees of the subsidiary charity, and
(c) the objects of the subsidiary charity are substantially or exclusively confined to the benefit of the parent charity.

The basis for treating a non-company charity as a subsidiary is that the connection between it and some other charity is such that the operating and financial policies of the former are likely to be set in accordance with the wishes of the latter. This is likely to be the case where one of the relationships described in the previous paragraph exists, but trustees may, in a particular case, be able to produce evidence to the contrary.

A further instance where the relationship is similar to that of a parent and subsidiary undertaking may arise where the parent charity transacts with another undertaking in such a way that all the risks and rewards of the transactions remain with the parent undertaking – for instance, through transfers of assets to another entity whilst retaining exclusive use of those assets and the costs of maintaining them. Such undertakings are regarded as quasi-subsidiaries and should be accounted for in accordance with Financial Reporting Standard 5 (FRS 5).

Where the objects of a charity are substantially or exclusively confined to the benefit of another charity, the issue of control requires particular consideration. For example, friends' groups, on occasion, form separate charities to give support to an established charity whilst retaining legal discretion as to the nature and timing of their support. In such cases, the formal powers identified above may not exist, but dominant influence may arise less formally. Alternatively, the benefiting charity may set out in outline the nature or timing of the support it wants to achieve. Again, the parent charity may intervene on a critical matter. Where evidence exists of such dominant influence being exercised, the criteria for consolidation should be regarded as being met.

17.4 What are the requirements governing the preparation of consolidated accounts?

17.4.1 The Companies Act 2006 and FRS 2

Both the Companies Act 2006 and FRS 2 (para 21) exempt a parent undertaking from preparing consolidated accounts if:

(a) the parent undertaking is a wholly owned subsidiary undertaking and its immediate parent undertaking is established under the law of a Member State of the European Union. Exemption is conditional on compliance with

certain further conditions set out in section 400 Companies Act 2006 (previously, s. 228(2) of the Companies Act 1985);
(b) the parent undertaking is a majority-owned subsidiary and meets all the conditions for exemption as a wholly owned subsidiary undertaking set out in (a) above as well as some additional conditions;
(c) all of the parent undertaking's subsidiary undertakings are permitted or required to be excluded from consolidation by section 402 of the Companies Act 2006 (previously, s. 229 of the 1985 Act), or
(d) the group is small and is not an ineligible group, as defined in s. 398 of the Companies Act 2006 (previously, s. 248 of the 1985 Act). A group is ineligible if any of its members is a public company, a banking institution or an insurance company.

17.4.2 SORP 2005

Paragraphs 383–385 discuss the requirement to prepare consolidated accounts. The general rule is that a parent charity should prepare consolidated accounts, including all its subsidiary undertakings, except where:

(a) FRS 2 provides for the exclusion of certain subsidiary undertakings from consolidation; or
(b) the gross income, after consolidation adjustments, of the group in the accounting period is no more than the threshold for a statutory charity audit; or
(c) the results of the subsidiary undertaking(s) are not material to the group; or
(d) the subsidiary is not a company and, by virtue of being a special trust or a charity subject to a uniting direction under s. 96(5) or (6) of the Charities Act 1993, has had its accounts aggregated with that of the parent charity.

In respect of item (b), the present level of gross income for audit exemption is £500,000. This applies in place of the more generous exemptions on the grounds of size which are permitted by the Companies Act 2006 and FRS 2.

FRS 2 allows subsidiaries to be excluded from consolidation in certain limited circumstances (severe long-term restrictions which substantially hinder the exercise of the parent undertaking's rights over the subsidiary undertaking's assets or management or subsidiary held only for sale). It is unlikely that these exclusions will generally apply to a charitable group.

Charities utilise subsidiary undertakings for a variety of purposes including undertaking non-charitable trading, for investment purposes and carrying out charitable activities. The difference between profit and not-for-profit undertakings is not sufficient of itself to justify non-consolidation. However, where a subsidiary undertaking is a registered company that is insolvent and is being wound up, the subsidiary undertaking can be excluded from consolidation.

Charitable subsidiaries

Most non-company charitable subsidiaries will be included in the aggregated accounts of the controlling charity, as they will either be restricted funds or endowment funds of the charity. However, on occasion, a charity may control another charitable entity that does not meet the definition of a special trust – for example, because the objects of the subsidiary are wider than those of the parent charity. Where the tests for control (the parent's ability to direct and benefit) are met, the charitable subsidiary should be consolidated. Benefit to a parent charity may arise where the services and benefits provided by the charitable subsidiary to its own beneficiaries also contribute to the objectives of the parent charity or to the cash flow of the parent charity. Where (unusually) a subsidiary charity's objects are substantially different from the parent charity, the benefit test of control will not be met, and so no consolidation should take place.

A subsidiary that is a charity with objects narrower than its parent will need to be accounted for by the use of one or more restricted fund columns in the consolidated accounts.

17.5 Method of consolidation

SORP 2005 specifies that the 'line-by-line' method of consolidation, used in FRS 2, should be applied to the consolidation of charitable groups.

All items of incoming resources and resources expended should be shown gross after the removal of intra-group transactions. Clearly, it is desirable that similar items are treated in the same way. For instance, operating activities for generating funds in the charity should be combined with similar activities in the subsidiary, and charitable activities within the charity should be combined with charitable activities in the subsidiary. Similarly, costs of generating funds and/or administration costs in the subsidiary should be aggregated with those of the charity.

Each charity should choose appropriate line headings within the permissible format of the Statement of Financial Activities and suitable amalgamations of activities. The headings should be expanded and changed to reflect the underlying activities of the group. In practice, it may not be possible to find exactly matching items between the subsidiary undertaking and the parent charity; in which case, segmental information should be provided so that the results of the parent charity and each subsidiary undertaking are transparent.

Thus, the sales of a trading subsidiary would be consolidated as an 'activity for generating funds' under 'incoming resource from generated funds' whilst the cost of sales would be consolidated within 'costs of generating funds'. However, the

Consolidated accounts

presentation of a separate summary profit and loss account for the trading subsidiary within the notes to the financial statements would aid understanding.

17.6 Disclosures

17.6.1 All charities with subsidiary undertakings

There should be a separate comment in the Trustees' Annual Report concerning the performance of the charity's subsidiary undertakings (see Chapter 7).

The notes to the accounts should state the aggregate amount of the total investment of the charity in its subsidiary undertakings and, unless the subsidiary is not material, it should state in relation to each one:

(a) its name;
(b) particulars of the charity's shareholding or other means of control;
(c) how its activities relate to those of the charity;
(d) the aggregate amount of its assets, liabilities and funds, and
(e) a summary of its turnover and expenditure and its profit or loss for the year (or equivalent categories for charitable subsidiary undertakings)

Similar details should be provided relating to any minority interest external to the charity held in the subsidiary undertakings, including any restrictions that may be placed on the group's activities.

If a charity has a large number of subsidiary undertakings such that this disclosure would result in information of excessive length being given, the information need only be given in respect of those undertakings whose results or financial position materially affected the figures shown in the charity's annual accounts. The full disclosure must be made available (in the same way as the accounts) to any member of the public upon request.

There is a requirement that – at the end of the financial year – the following be disclosed for each undertaking that is a subsidiary of the parent:

(a) its name, and:
    (i) if it is a company outside Great Britain, its country of incorporation, or
    (ii) if a non-company, the address of its principal place of business;
(b) under which of the conditions the undertaking is a subsidiary, and
(c) the identity of each class of share held by the parent (and the group) and the proportion of the nominal value held.

In addition to these disclosures, paragraph 33 of FRS 2 requires disclosure of:

(a) the proportion of voting rights held by the parent and its subsidiary undertakings, and
(b) an indication of the nature of its business.

17.6.2 Where consolidated accounts are prepared

SORP 2005 specifies that where consolidated accounts are prepared, the method of consolidation should be stated in the policy notes, along with notification of which subsidiaries are included and which are excluded from the consolidation.

Segmental information may need to be provided where the aggregation and adjustments required to consolidate financial information may obscure information about the different undertakings and the activities included in the consolidated accounts. It is important that the presentation adopted and disclosure in the notes are sufficiently detailed to distinguish the key results of the charity from those of its subsidiary undertakings. Examples of those items that should be separately disclosed include the costs of generating funds, governance costs and the costs of charitable activities.

In consolidated accounts, funds or reserves retained by subsidiary undertakings, other than funds used in carrying out the charity's objects, should be included under an appropriate 'separate fund' heading in the balance sheet (for example, 'non-charitable trading funds').

17.6.3 In the entity accounts of the parent where consolidated accounts are not (required to be) prepared

If consolidated accounts are not prepared, then the trustees should give the reasons in a note to the charity's accounts, with reference to each excluded subsidiary undertaking.

There is a requirement that the following be disclosed:

(a) the name of each subsidiary undertaking, and:
  (i) if it is a company outside Great Britain, its country of incorporation, or
  (ii) if a non-company, the address of its principal place of business;
(b) the identity of each class of share held by the parent and the proportion of the nominal value held;
(c) unless the subsidiary undertaking is included in the accounts using the equity method of accounting, the aggregate amount of its capital and reserves as at the end of its financial year and of its profit or loss for that year, and

(d) where the disclosures in (c) are provided and the subsidiary undertaking's year end is not co-terminous with that of the parent, its year end (that is, the last before that of the parent's).

Paragraph 22 of FRS 2 requires a parent undertaking not preparing consolidated accounts to state that its accounts present information about it as an individual undertaking and not about its group.

17.6.4 For subsidiaries excluded from consolidation

The Companies Act 2006 and paragraph 26 of FRS 2 both require the names of subsidiary undertakings excluded from consolidation to be stated, together with the reasons for their exclusion.

Unless included in the accounts by way of the equity method of accounting, there is a requirement that the aggregate amount of each subsidiary undertaking's share capital and reserves as at the end of its financial year and of its profit or loss for that year be stated.

In addition, para. 31 of FRS 2 requires disclosure of:

(a) particulars of the balances between the excluded subsidiary undertakings and the rest of the group;
(b) the nature and extent of transactions of the excluded subsidiary undertakings with the rest of the group;
(c) unless the excluded subsidiary undertaking is equity-accounted, any amounts included in the consolidated accounts in respect of:
  (i) dividends received and receivable from that undertaking; and
  (ii) any reduction in the period in respect of the investment in that undertaking or amounts due from that undertaking; and
(d) for subsidiary undertakings excluded from consolidation because of different activities, their separate accounts. Summarised financial information may be provided unless the excluded subsidiaries account for more than 20 per cent of any of the group's operating profits, turnover or net assets. The group amounts should be measured by including all excluded subsidiary undertakings.

17.7 Approval and filing of consolidated accounts

Accounts for each member of the group (that is, parent and subsidiary undertakings) should be prepared for approval by the respective boards of trustees and/or directors. The consolidated group accounts should then be prepared by the parent charity.

Paragraphs 396 and 397 of SORP contains guidance on how charities in England and Wales that have prepared consolidated accounts can meet the requirements of the Charities Act 1993 to file the individual charity's accounts with the Charity Commission. Where the group and parent charity's accounts are included in the same set of consolidated accounts, as well as two balance sheets, there should be two SOFAs (one for the group and one for the parent). However, consolidated accounts that omit the SOFA for the parent charity are often filed with the Charity Commission. The Charity Commission is prepared to accept these accounts as long as the assets and liabilities of the charity can be distinguished from those of its subsidiary (or subsidiaries) and that the turnover and results of the subsidiary (or subsidiaries) are clearly stated. However, the Charity Commission retains the power to require the production and filing of any individual charity SOFA and, similarly, members of the public have a legal right to request this statement.

17.8 Accounting for associates, joint ventures and joint arrangements

SORP 2005 contains extensive guidance on the accounting for and disclosure of associates, joint ventures and joint arrangements. This guidance applies the requirements of FRS 9 to charities.

Where associates, joint ventures and joint arrangements exist, consolidated accounts should be prepared, subject to the exemptions in para. 383 of the SORP.

17.8.1 Identification

Associate

Where a charity has a long-term participating interest in another undertaking and exercises significant influence over its operating and financial policy, then this is likely to be an associate undertaking. Where a charity beneficially holds 20 per cent or more of the voting rights in any undertaking, it will be presumed to have a participating interest and significant influence over its operating and financial policy, unless the contrary is shown.

Charities providing grants or making programme-related investments may, on occasion, combine funding with the provision of advice or expertise and may be invited by the recipient charity to provide or nominate a charity trustee with particular skills or expertise. Where the recipient charity operates with a small trustee body, this might be construed as creating an associate. An associate will be created if the nomination or appointment is used in conjunction with a formal or informal agreement to exercise significant influence through direct involvement

Consolidated accounts

in setting the recipient charity's operating and financial polices. Where the charity trustee appointment is simply used to provide advice or expertise to the recipient charity, whilst allowing the charity to adopt its own policies and strategies, then an associate relationship is unlikely to be created.

Joint venture

In a joint venture, a separate entity is jointly controlled by two or more undertakings, each of which has a say in the operations of the joint venture, so that no *one* investing undertaking controls the joint venture but all of them together can do so. It is possible for a charity to beneficially hold 20 per cent or more of the voting rights in an undertaking, but for the management arrangements to be such that control is clearly shared with the other partners, and hence the undertaking is a joint venture as opposed to an associate.

Joint arrangements

Often charities also undertake joint arrangements where they may carry out activities in partnership with other bodies but without establishing a separate legal entity.

17.8.2 Methods of accounting for associates, joint ventures and joint arrangements

Associates

Associates should be included in the accounts based on the net equity method. The consolidated Statement of Financial Activities should show the net interest in the results for the year in the associates as a separate line after the 'net incoming resources before transfers' line. On the balance sheet, the net interest in associates should be shown as a separate line within fixed asset investments.

Where there are gains and losses on investments and unrealised gains on other fixed assets, the net share relating to associates should be shown on a separate line of the SOFA.

Joint ventures

Joint ventures should be accounted for on a gross equity method. This requires the reporting entity to present its share of the gross incoming resources of joint ventures on the face of the consolidated profit and loss account. However, this does not form part of the group incoming resources and must be clearly distinguished. For charities, this can be achieved by including gross incoming resources from joint ventures in the Statement of Financial Activities on a line-by-line basis with an additional line showing the total share of gross

Accounting for associates, joint ventures and joint arrangements

incoming resources from joint ventures as a reduction in total incoming resources. In addition, a line showing the net interest in the results for the year in the joint ventures as a separate line after the 'net incoming resources before transfers' line must be included (this may be combined with that of the associates). On the balance sheet the share of the gross assets and the gross liabilities should be shown in a linked presentation within fixed assets investments.

Where there are gains and losses on investments and unrealised gains on other fixed assets, the gross share relating to joint ventures should be shown either on a separate line or combined with the appropriate lines on the statement of financial activities.

Joint arrangements

Where there is a joint arrangement, the charity's gross share of the incoming resources and resources expended and the assets and liabilities should be included in the accounts in the same way as for a branch, as per paras 51–55. If under the arrangement the charity is jointly and severally liable for an obligation, it should accrue the part of the obligation for which it is responsible and treat the part of the obligation that is expected to be met by the other parties as a contingent liability.

17.8.3 Disclosure

The following disclosures should be given in respect of each associate and joint venture and this will normally comply with FRS 9:

(a) its name;
(b) the charity's shareholding and other interests in it;
(c) the nature of the activities of the associate or joint venture, and
(d) the charity's interest in the results, showing separately its share in:
  (i) gross incoming resources, by type;
  (ii) the costs of generating funds;
  (iii) expenditure on charitable activities;
  (iv) expenditure on management and administration;
  (v) net results (where tax is payable, the share of the results pre-tax and post-tax and the share in the tax should be shown);
  (vi) gains or losses on investments, and the share in unrealised gains on other fixed assets;
  (vii) fixed assets;
  (viii) current assets;
  (ix) liabilities under one year;
  (x) liabilities over one year;
  (xi) the different funds of the charity;
  (xii) contingent liabilities and other commitments, and

(xiii) particulars of any qualifications contained in any audit or other statutory report on its accounts, and any note or reservation in those accounts to call attention to a matter which, apart from the note or reservation, would properly have been referred to in such a qualification.

For joint arrangements the notes to the accounts should provide appropriate details of the charity's commitments in the arrangement.

17.8.4 Disclosure examples

The following example is a company charity which has a trading subsidiary. The charity prepares consolidated accounts and the SOFA and balance sheets are presented below. In addition, the note explaining the activities and summarising the results of the subsidiary is also presented.

Table 17.1 *Consolidated Statement of Financial Activities (including Income and Expenditure Account) for the year ended 31 March 2010*

	Notes	Unrestricted Funds £'000	Restricted Funds £'000	Total Funds 2010 £'000	Total Funds 2009 £'000
Incoming resources					
Operation of theatre and arts centre	3	1,200	–	**1,200**	1,259
Activities for generating funds:					
Commercial trading operations	4	549	–	**549**	296
Donations		12	79	**91**	79
Interest receivable		18	1	**19**	16
Total incoming resources		1,779	80	**1,859**	1,650
Less cost of generating funds:					
Commercial trading operations	4	337	2	**339**	280
Net incoming resources available					
for charitable application		1,442	78	**1,520**	1,370
Charitable activities					
Cost of operation of theatre and arts centre	5	1,209	81	**1,290**	1,230
Governance costs	6	150	2	**152**	113
Total charitable expenditure		1,359	83	**1,442**	1,343
Total resources expended		1,696	85	**1,781**	1,623
Movement in total funds for the year					
Net income/(expenditure) for the year		83	(5)	**78**	27
Total funds brought forward		1,294	17	**1,311**	1,284
Total funds carried forward	16,17	1,377	12	**1,389**	1,311

The statement of financial activities includes all gains and losses recognised in the year.

All incoming resources and resources expended derive from continuing activities.

Table 17.2 *Consolidated and Charity Balance Sheets as at 31 March 2010*

	Notes	Group 2010 £'000	Group 2009 £'000	Charity 2010 £'000	Charity 2009 £'000
Fixed assets					
Tangible assets	10	830	824	830	824
Investments	4	–	–	1	1
		830	824	831	825
Current assets					
Stock	11	217	213	203	212
Debtors	12	207	206	272	206
Cash at bank and in hand		423	319	314	319
		847	738	789	737
Creditors: amounts falling due within one year	13	242	195	185	195
Net current assets		605	543	604	542
Total assets less current liabilities		1,435	1,367	1,435	1,367
Creditors: amounts falling due after more than one year	15	46	56	46	56
		1,389	1,311	1,389	1,311
Unrestricted funds					
General	16	1,210	1,263	1,210	1,263
Designated	16	167	31	167	31
		1,377	1,294	1,377	1,294
Restricted funds	17	12	17	12	17
		1,389	1,311	1,389	1,311

Approved by the trustees on 19 August 2010 and signed on their behalf by

A Met

Trustee

Chapter 18 – Company charities

18.1 Introduction

There is a problem with charity reporting concerning company charities that are subject to the requirements of both the Companies Act 2006 and the Charities Act 2006, and which, in England and Wales, must file accounts with both Companies House and the Charity Commission. The 1995 SORP contained limited guidance on the particular problems of company charities. This is addressed in SORP 2005, as in SORP 2000, by a separate section of guidance which addresses the main problems arising from applying the requirements of both the Companies Act and the Charities Act (both now 2006) and the SORP.

18.2 Accounts and reports

Company charities must comply with the Companies Act 2006 with respect to the form and content of their accounts. The Act also stipulates the contents of the annual (directors') report. Strictly, the directors of company charities, in England and Wales, have to prepare both that report and the Trustees' Annual Report under Part VI of the Charities Act 1993, but the Charity Commission is prepared to accept the directors' report for filing under Part VI if it also contains the necessary information. Company charities (unlike non-company charities) do not have the exemption to omit the names of the directors from the annual report.

The Companies Act 2006 requires a company to prepare annual financial statements that give a true and fair view of its state of affairs at the end of the year and of its profit and loss for that year. In addition, the directors are required to adapt the headings and subheadings of the balance sheet and profit and loss account in any case where the special nature of the company's business requires such adaptation.

The requirements to show a true and fair view and to adapt the accounts for the special nature of charity mean that there is a strong presumption that company charities will, in all but exceptional circumstances, have to comply with this SORP in order to meet the requirements of company law. Particulars of any material departures from this SORP are required to be disclosed. A departure is not justified simply because it gives the reader a more appealing picture of the financial position or results of the charity.

18.3 The Statement of Financial Activities and the summary income and expenditure account

A long-standing confusion which arose from the 1995 SORP was whether company charities had to prepare both a SOFA and an income and expenditure account. The regulatory position is as follows:

- all company charities registered under the Companies Act 2006 must include an income and expenditure account in their financial statements, and
- the SOFA, a requirement of the SORP, is designed to include all the gains and losses of a charity which would be found in the income and expenditure account and the statement of total recognised gains and losses as required by FRS 3.

A separate income and expenditure account is may not therefore be required for company charities.

A separate income and expenditure account probably will be required where the income and expenditure account cannot be separately identified within the SOFA and there are items that may be open to challenge if they are included in an income and expenditure account. This might arise when there are:

(a) movements on endowment (capital) funds during the year, and
(b) unrealised gains and losses arising during the year.

Whilst unrealised gains and losses are not allowed in the income and expenditure account, most of these are included in the SOFA below the point at which a conventional income and expenditure account would end.

In practice, material considerations mean that in many cases a separate income and expenditure account will not be presented. This arises because the degree of the presentational difference between the surplus or deficit as reported in the SOFA and the net surplus or deficit as reported under the Companies Act is not deemed to be significant. Where a separate income and expenditure is not presented, a note on the face of the SOFA should disclose the amount of net income under Companies Act reporting requirements.

18.4 Presentation of the summary income and expenditure account

Where the SOFA of a company charity does not include any of the items mentioned above, there may be no need to produce a separate summary income and expenditure account. However, the headings in the SOFA must be changed so that:

(a) the title clearly indicates that it includes an income and expenditure account and statement of total recognised gains and losses (if required), and
(b) there is a prominent subtotal entitled 'net income/(expenditure) for the year' which replaces or is in addition to the heading of 'net incoming/(outgoing) resources for the year'.

Care must also be taken to ensure that all realised gains and losses are included in the SOFA in such a way that they fall within the bounds of the headings for (a) and (b) above within the income and expenditure account. Particular attention may need to be given to impairment losses and reversals which, in accordance with the guidance in FRS 11, are realised in some circumstances and unrealised in others.

Where a summary income and expenditure account is required, it should be derived from and cross-referenced to the corresponding figures in the SOFA. It need not distinguish between unrestricted and restricted income funds, but the accounting basis on which items are included must be the same as in the SOFA. It should show each of the following elements separately in respect of continuing operations, acquisitions and discontinued operations:

(a) gross income from all sources;
(b) net gains or losses from disposals of all fixed assets belonging to the charity's income funds;
(c) transfers from endowment funds of amounts previously received as capital resources and now converted into income funds for expending;
(d) total income (this will be the total of all incoming resources – other than revaluation gains – of all the income funds but not for any endowment funds);
(e) total expenditure out of the charity's income funds, and
(f) net income or expenditure for the year.

In practice, the format may need to be modified to comply with specific statutory requirements or with those of the charity's own governing document.

Where consolidated accounts are prepared, a summary income and expenditure account should be included for the group (when it is required).

18.5 The balance sheet format

If a columnar format is chosen, then company charities will still have to show the funds of the charity as a single line, or as split between the various different types of fund, in order to comply with the Companies Act requirements.

18.6 Revaluation reserve

Where fixed assets are revalued upwards, a revaluation reserve will arise – being the difference between the original depreciated cost or valuation of the asset and the revalued amount. Separate reporting of the reserve is not significant for charities as they do not distribute profits, but a revaluation reserve will, nevertheless, arise. This will form part of the funds in which the revalued assets are held. In certain circumstances (as described in FRS 11 and 15), impairment losses or other downward revaluations can be offset against the revaluation reserve.

To comply with the Companies Act 2006, company charities must separately disclose the revaluation reserve within the funds section on the face of the balance sheet, but may change the heading as appropriate. This may best be effected by use of a prominent inset.

18.7 Summary financial information

Company charities should follow the recommendations in paras 371–379, but their summary financial information must also include a statement indicating whether or not the statutory accounts for the relevant year (or years) have been delivered to the Registrar of Companies.

Any summary financial information prepared by a company charity will almost all be non-statutory (the statutory option for the publication of summary financial statements only applies to listed companies), and the auditor's report cannot be published with it without the statutory accounts to which it relates. This means that, in effect, companies can produce summarised accounts without the backing of an audit report.

18.8 Disclosure examples

In the following example, taken from a company charity, technically a separate income and expenditure account is required because the 'net movement in funds' includes both realised and unrealised gains. As the difference between any surplus under Companies Acts requirements is not materially different from that presented, the difference is noted at the bottom of the SOFA.

As the SOFA incorporates an income and expenditure account, the heading of the statement refers to this fact.

Disclosure examples

Table 18.1 *Consolidated Statement of Financial Activities (incorporating an Income and Expenditure Account) for the year ended 31 March 2010*

	Notes	Unrestricted Funds £'000	Restricted Funds £'000	Totals 2010 £'000	Totals 2009 £'000
Incoming resources					
Incoming resources from generated funds					
Donations and gifts	2	4,130	3,200	**7,330**	6,000
Legacies	3	2,150	–	**2,150**	1,330
Building appeal	17	–	400	**400**	900
Activities for generating funds:					
Merchandising income	4	1,140	–	**1,140**	900
Incoming resources from charitable activities					
Government grants for residential care	17	–	700	**700**	400
Fees for residential care		1,200	–	**1,200**	1,000
Investment income	5	350	50	**400**	475
Net gain on disposal of fixed assets		20	–	**20**	30
Total incoming resources		8,990	4,350	**13,340**	11,035
Resources expended					
Cost of generating funds:					
Fundraising costs		480	210	**690**	550
Building appeal costs	17	–	45	**45**	110
Merchandising costs	4	870	–	**870**	710
Investment management fees		80	10	**90**	110
		1,430	265	**1,695**	1,480
Charitable activities:					
Residential care costs		1,400	1,030	**2,430**	2,545
Childcare		1,000	2,400	**3,400**	3,350
Emergency services		1,800	1,300	**3,100**	2,800
Information and education		90	10	**100**	300
Governance costs		320	140	**460**	410
		4,610	4,880	**9,490**	9,405
Total resources expended	6	6,040	5,145	**11,185**	10,885
Net incoming/(outgoing) resources before transfers		2,950	(795)	**2,155**	150
Transfers between funds	17	15	(15)	**–**	–
Net incoming/(outgoing) **resources**		2,965	(810)	**2,155**	150

Company charities

	Notes	Unrestricted Funds £'000	Restricted Funds £'000	Totals 2010 £'000	Totals 2009 £'000
Net gains on investment assets	11	100	–	100	250
Net movement in funds		3,065	(810)	**2,255**	400
Fund balances brought forward at 1 April	17	6,300	3,900	**10,200**	9,800
Fund balances carried forward at 31 March	17	9,365	3,090	**12,455**	10,200

All of the above results are derived from continuing activities. All gains and losses recognised in the year are included above. The surplus for the year for Companies Act purposes comprises the net incoming resources for the year plus realised gains on investments, and was £2,225,000 (2009 – £230,000). Page 10 gives details of changes in resources applied for fixed assets for charity use.

The following example is from a Scottish charity, which is required by Scottish charity accounts regulations and law to present a separate income and expenditure account. A statement of total recognised gains and losses is also presented in order to report unrealised investment gains.

Table 18.2 *Statement of Financial Activities for the year ended 31 March 2010*

	Notes	Unrestricted Funds £'000	Restricted Funds £'000	Endowment Funds £'000	Totals 2010 £'000	Totals 2009 £'000
Incoming resources						
Incoming resources from generated funds						
Activities for generating funds						
rental income		11,761	–	–	**11,761**	15,576
Donations and legacies	2	123,328	–	–	**123,328**	28,565
Millennium appeal income	2	–	1,490,367	–	**1,490,367**	372,525
Incoming resources from charitable activities						
Grants and fees for care and education of children	3	1,381,047	–	–	**1,381,047**	1,491,997
Investment income	4	258,266	–	–	**258,266**	205,181
Total incoming resources		1,774,402	1,490,367	–	**3,264,769**	2,113,844
Cost of generating funds	5	–	(82,975)	–	**(82,975)**	(242,282)

Disclosure examples

	Notes	Unrestricted Funds £'000	Restricted Funds £'000	Endowment Funds £'000	Totals 2010 £'000	Totals 2009 £'000
Net incoming resources available for charitable application		1,774,402	1,407,392	–	**3,181,794**	1,871,562
Charitable activities						
Teaching and care of children	6(a)	794,227	–	–	**794,227**	733,870
Running costs and maintenance of school	6(b)	793,340	–	149,621	**942,961**	706,524
Governance costs	7	69,950	14,321	–	**84,271**	62,242
Total charitable expenditure		1,657,517	14,321	149,621	**1,821,459**	1,502,636
Total resources expended		1,657,517	97,296	149,621	**1,904,434**	1,744,918
Net incoming/(outgoing) resources before transfers		116,885	1,393,071	(149,621)	**1,360,335**	368,926
Transfers in respect of fixed assets additions	14	–(1,401,229)	1,401,229		–	–
Gains on investments		–	–	209,329	**209,329**	2,550,912
Net movement in funds for the year		116,885	(8,158)	1,460,937	**1,569,664**	2,919,838
Total funds at 1 April 2009	14	194,224	(135,085)	8,185,985	**8,245,124**	5,325,286
Total funds at 31 March 2010	14	311,109	(143,243)	9,646,922	**9,814,788**	8,245,124

Table 18.3 Income and expenditure account for the year ended 31 March 2010

	Notes	2010 £'000	2009 £'000
Income			
Donations, legacies and Millennium Appeal income	2	1,613,695	401,090
Grant from Scottish Executive	3	902,978	923,854
Local authority fees	3	478,069	568,143
Investment income	4	258,266	205,181
Rental income		11,761	15,576
		3,264,769	2,113,844

Company charities

	Notes	2010 £'000	2009 £'000
Charitable expenditure			
Costs of generating funds	5	82,975	242,282
Teaching and care of children	6	794,227	733,870
Running costs and maintenance of school	6	942,961	706,524
Governance costs	7	84,271	62,242
		1,904,434	1,744,918
Operating surplus for the year		1,360,335	368,926
Realised (loss)/gain on sale of investments		(29,843)	109,434
Surplus for the year		1,330,492	478,360
Statement of total recognised gains and losses			
Surplus for the year		1,330,492	478,360
Unrealised gain on investment	10	239,172	2,441,478
Total gains and losses recognised since 31 March 2010		1,569,664	2,919,838

All activities relate to continuing operations.

There is no difference between the surplus on ordinary activities for the year stated above and its historical cost equivalent.

Chapter 19 – Accounting for branches

19.1 Introduction

The 1995 SORP formally required non-company charities, for the first time, to incorporate the transactions of their branches into their accounts. In many cases, this meant not only a dramatic change in the format and size of the figures in charity accounts, but also formalising branch accounting procedures and, often, the preparation of branch returns. SORP 2000 introduced clearer guidelines in terms of what constituted a branch.

Apart from a diversity of purpose, charities have a diversity of structure. Some charities have local branches which form part of the registered charity, with one charity number. If the charity is an incorporated company, section 386 of the Companies Act 2006 (previously s. 221 of the Companies Act 1985) requires the charity to obtain returns from its branches and incorporate these in the national accounts. For such branches, the charity will need to comply with s.5 of the 1993 Act and state the fact that it is a registered charity on, *inter alia*, all branch notices, advertisements, cheques, invoices and receipts.

Other charities may have local groups that are autonomous and, therefore, registered as main charities. They are subject to compulsory registration with the Commission, under s. 3 of the 1993 Act if, broadly, they either use or occupy land, have permanent endowment or have gross income of more than £1,000 p.a. from any source. They will have their own accounts and their own body of trustees.

Some charities may have a mix of local branches and autonomous groups.

Who accounts for what? It is extremely important that charity trustees recognise and account for all subsidiary charitable funds, special trusts and branches it controls, because the relevant income and expenditure thresholds identified in the 1993 Act relate to those of the charity as a whole, including its special trusts and controlled branches. Because many charities do not fall neatly into one category or another, this is a complex area requiring legal advice in cases of doubt. It is understood that, in any particular case, the Charity Commission will provide further guidance to charity trustees on request.

19.2 What is a branch?

Before considering the accounting requirements, it is essential to understand what constitutes a branch for these purposes. Branches are defined in the SORP (in Appendix 1, the glossary) as follows:

Accounting for branches

' "Branches" (which may also be known as supporters' groups, friends' groups, members' groups, communities or parishes which are part of a common trust etc) are entities or administrative bodies set up, for example, to conduct a particular aspect of the business of the reporting charity, or to conduct the business of the reporting charity in a particular geographical area. They may or may not be legal entities which are separate from the reporting charity.

For the purpose of this SORP a "branch" is either:

(a) simply part of the administrative machinery of the reporting charity; or
(b) a fund shown in the accounts as a restricted or endowment fund. Two types of entity are covered by this category, each of which should be treated as linked to the reporting charity for accounting purposes:

   (i) a separate legal entity which is administered by or on behalf of the reporting charity and whose funds are held for specific purposes which are within the general purposes of the reporting charity. "Legal entity" means a trust or unincorporated association or other body formed for a charitable purpose. The words "on behalf of" should be taken to mean that, under the constitution of the separate entity, a substantial degree of influence can be exerted by the reporting charity over the administration of its affairs; or,

   (ii) in England and Wales, a separate legal entity not falling within (b) which the Charity Commission has united by a direction under s96(5) or 96(6), Charities Act 1993 should be treated as linked to the reporting charity for accounting purposes.

This definition has been adopted to reflect the provisions of the Charities Act 1993 allocating responsibility for accounting in the case of multicellular charities. FRS 2 expressly disapplies its requirements where they are not consistent with a particular statutory accounting framework. Consequently, charitable bodies which are controlled by other charitable bodies will not normally be subject to the requirements of that standard as they will be treated as "special trusts" under the Charities Act 1993 or will be the subject of a direction as mentioned above [in paragraph (b)(ii)].

Some of the characteristics of a branch are:

(a) it uses the name of the reporting charity within its title;
(b) it exclusively raises funds for the reporting charity and/or for its own local activities;
(c) it uses the reporting charity's registration number to receive tax relief on its activities;

(d) it is perceived by the public to be the reporting charity's local representative or its representative for a particular purpose;
(e) it receives support from the reporting charity through advice, publicity materials, etc.

If the branch exists to carry out the primary objects of the charity, typically it will receive funds from the reporting charity for its work and may be staffed by employees of the reporting charity.

If the branch is not a separate legal entity, all funds held by a branch will be the legal property of the reporting charity, whether or not the branch has a separate bank account.

Organisations which are not Branches

Some charities may be known as "branches" within a particular organisational or network structure, but if their level of administrative autonomy from the reporting charity – as determined by their constitutions – is such that legislation requires them to be treated as separate accounting entities, then they should not be regarded as "branches" for accounting purposes but should prepare separate accounts for submission to the appropriate regulatory authority.

Other examples of organisations which are not "branches" for the purpose of these recommendations include:

(a) groups of people who occasionally gather together to raise funds for one or a number of different charities; and
(b) special interest groups who are affiliated to a particular charity, but do not themselves undertake charitable activities (including fundraising for the charity).'

19.3 Accounting requirements

Paragraphs 77–81 of the SORP cover the accounting requirements in respect of branches as follows:

77. Before preparing accounts, trustees must be quite clear as to the legal structure of the charity. A charity may operate through branches to raise funds and/or carry out its charitable purposes. Branches as defined in the glossary will be accounted for as part of the whole charity. But if both reporting charity and the branches are companies, company law requires each entity to prepare its own accounts. In such a case, one annual report should normally be prepared to cover both the reporting charity and its branch(es) and consolidated accounts should be prepared in accordance with paragraphs 381 to 406.
78. Separate legal entities which may be known as branches but do not fall within the definition of a branch in the Glossary should prepare their own

Annual Report and Accounts and, if they are connected charities the relationship should be explained in the trustees report (see paragraph 44 (f)).
79. All branch transactions should be accounted for gross in the reporting charity's own accounts excluding those transactions which net off eg. branch to branch transactions o[r] those between the branches and the head office. Similarly all assets and liabilities of the branch including, for example, funds raised but not remitted to the reporting charity at the year end should be incorporated into the reporting charity's own balance sheet. This provision need not apply where the transactions and balances of the branches in aggregate are not material to the charity's accounts.
80. Funds raised by a branch for the general purpose of the reporting charity will be accounted for as unrestricted funds in the accounts of the main charity. (Comment: Such funds are sometimes treated as designated funds if they are retained by the branch.) Funds raised by a branch for specific purposes of the reporting charity will need to be accounted for as restricted funds in the accounts of the main charity. Funds held for the general purposes of a branch which is a separate charity should usually be accounted for as restricted funds in the accounts of the reporting charity.
81. Where a branch is not a separate legal entity, its accounts must form part of the accounts of the reporting charity but it may be in the interests of local supporters and beneficiaries for additional accounts to be prepared covering only the branch.

19.4 Further considerations

19.4.1 Fund accounting

In addition to the requirements of para. 80 of SORP (above), there may be instances where a donor gives funds for use by, or is led to believe that funds collected will be used only for, a specific branch. In these cases, the funds should normally be treated as restricted funds in the accounts of the charity (that is, they can only be used by that specific branch).

19.4.2 Branch returns

In order to properly reflect the transactions and funds of its branches, a charity may need to consider what information it requires from the branches – either on a regular basis, or simply at the end of each financial year. Whilst this information will need to be accurate and supported by reliable records (which may be subject to audit, either locally or by the auditors of the main charity), careful consideration will have to be given to the effect that any formal requirements may have on those who run the branches and who will frequently be volunteers who do not have a detailed accounting knowledge. Trustees' responsibilities extend to branches and they must, therefore, satisfy themselves as to the general management and conduct of all branches, including the proper recording of transactions and details of any branch assets and liabilities at any time.

If the time taken between the year end and the preparation of the accounts is short, it might be appropriate to consider preparing branch returns for a slightly earlier date, provided the treatment is consistent each year and that there are no material transactions in the intervening period. If this policy is adopted, it should be made clear in the notes to the accounts.

19.4.3 Omission of branches from accounts

Paragraph 360 of the SORP requires the omission of any branches from the accounts to be given, although individual branches do not need to be named. Reference should also be made to any potentially linked organisations (such as supporters' associations or subsidiaries not consolidated), explaining the accounting treatment adopted.

19.4.4 External scrutiny of branches

Trustees may need to consider either regular or periodic external scrutiny of branch accounts (alternatively, they may be covered by internal audit procedures). The cost of any such scrutinies should be identified and disclosed separately in the accounts of the main charity.

19.4.5 Local branches constituted as separate autonomous bodies

Where local branches are separately registered charities and autonomous, separate accounts should be prepared and separate annual returns submitted. Whether or not this represents conclusive evidence, such branches should not be included in the accounts of the main charity, unless it seems that their public accountability might be open to question. In such a case, their registration with the Charity Commission should be re-examined. In determining the level of autonomy, there may be circumstances in which consideration should be given to the principles of FRS 5 and whether the branch might be deemed to be a 'quasi-subsidiary'. Some of the questions which might be asked in the absence of the 'special trust' situation include the following.

1. Does the main charity have legal control over the branches' constitution and administration, including the power of intervention?
2. Are the branches financially dependent on the main charity, other than for grant funding?
3. Does the main charity have the right to control the use of the branches' resources for its own purposes to the detriment of the branch?

4. What would happen if a branch were in financial difficulties? Would creditors have access only to the branch funds and branch trustees?
5. What would happen to surplus funds if a branch were dissolved?

The litmus test of whether or not there is sufficient autonomy may be obscured in circumstances where there is a mix of independence and control. In some situations the main charity may have limited controls over the local branches, although their management and administration may, in all other respects, be independent. In others, local groups may, for example, use the national charity number for fundraising purposes, but be autonomous in most other respects.

19.5 Connected charities

'Connected charities' are generally covered under the heading of 'related parties'. They are defined in the glossary to the SORP as those which have common, parallel or related objects and activities; and either:
   a) common control; or
   b) unity of administration (for example,. shared management).

Within this category may be charities that come together under one umbrella organisation or which are part of a federal structure.

Chapter 20 – Summary financial information and statements

20.1 Introduction

The presentation of summary financial information and statements has become a regular feature of UK financial reporting. Some charities publish financial information or summaries in a format different from the statutory accounts. Such information or summaries are often included in a non-statutory annual review or in fundraising literature. There are two basic types of such summaries:

a) summarised financial statements which should be based on the full financial statements and communicate key financial information without providing the greater detail required in the full accounts (for example, as contained in the notes to the accounts), and
b) summary financial information which presents information on a particular aspect of a charity's finances – for example, an analysis of incoming resources or expenditure on particular activities of a charity. Such information does not purport to summarise the full statutory accounts.

20.1.1 Distinction between summarised financial statements and summary information

The characteristics distinguishing between summarised financial statements and summary information are set out in the table below.

Table 20.1 The key characteristics of summarised financial statements and summary financial information

Summarised financial statements	Summary financial information
Include a summary of the SOFA and the balance sheet.	Draws information only from specific parts of the accounts.
The summary is derived from statutory accounts.	May be based on interim accounts or other financial information, as well as statutory accounts.

Summarised financial statements	Summary financial information
A financial statement that purports to be a Statement of Activities or a balance sheet or summary thereof.	Makes no reference to either of these primary statements.
Represents the entire finances of a charity or a charity group, for example,.	Represents analysis of a particular activity or region.

20.2 What are the requirements relating to summary financial information and statements?

There are no accounting provisions in the 1993 Act relating to the content of, or reporting on, summarised financial statements and information published by non-company charities. However, for company charities, the provisions of sections 434 and 435 of the Companies Act 2006 (previously, s. 240 of the Companies Act 1985) relating to the publication of non-statutory financial statements do apply. The recommendations set out in the SORP in relation to summarised financial statements are consistent with these statutory provisions applying to companies.

As the form of summarised financial statements and information may vary, depending on the purpose for which they are prepared, the SORP acknowledges that it is impractical to provide detailed guidance on their content. However, the general principles that should be followed are set out in the SORP, in paras 34 and 371–379.

Regardless of the intended circulation of any summary financial information or summarised financial statements, the full Annual Report and accounts must always be produced.

Any summarised financial statements should:
a) contain information on both the SOFA and the balance sheet;
b) be consistent with the statutory accounts, and
c) not be misleading – either by omission or through inappropriate amalgamation of information.

Summary financial information will not necessarily contain information on both the SOFA and balance sheet, but should nevertheless present information consistent with the statutory accounts, and should not be misleading either by omission or through inappropriate amalgamation of information.

What are the requirements relating to summary financial information and statements?

Summarised financial statements

Summarised accounts should be accompanied by a statement signed on behalf of the trustees, giving the following details (para. 377):

a) that they are not the statutory accounts but a summary of information relating to both the SOFA and the balance sheet;
b) whether or not the full accounts from which the summarised financial statements are derived have, at that point, been externally scrutinised (whether by audit, independent examination, or reporting accountant's report);
c) where they have been externally scrutinised, whether the report contained any concerns (such as a qualified opinion, limitation of scope, etc.);.
d) where the report contains any concerns (for example, is qualified, contains an explanatory paragraph or emphasis of matter), sufficient details should be provided in the summarised financial statements to enable the reader to appreciate the significance of the report;
e) where accounts are produced only for a branch of the charity, it must be clearly stated that the summarised financial statements are for that branch only and have been extracted from the full accounts of the reporting charity (giving its name);
f) details of how the full annual accounts, the external scrutiny report (as applicable) and the trustees' annual report may be obtained;
g) the date on which the annual accounts were approved, and
h) for charities registered in England and Wales, say whether or not the Trustees' Annual Report and accounts have been submitted to the Charity Commission.

If the full accounts have been externally scrutinised (whether audited, independently examined or subject to a reporting accountant's report) the external scrutineer should attach a statement giving an opinion as to whether or not the summarised financial statements are consistent with the full annual accounts.

Summary financial information

Any other summary financial information, in whatever form, which does not include information on the SOFA and the balance sheet must be accompanied by a statement signed on behalf of the trustees as to:

a) the purpose of the information;
b) whether or not it is from the full annual accounts;
c) whether or not these accounts have been audited, independently examined or subject to a reporting accountants report, and
d) (details of how the full annual accounts, trustees report and external examiners report (as appropriate) can be obtained.

Summary financial information and statements

Company charities

Company charities are required to comply with the provisions in the Companies Act 2006 relating to non-statutory accounts. Non-statutory accounts are any balance sheet or profit and loss account that a company publishes that relates to, or purports to deal with, any financial year, but which does not qualify as full individual accounts or full group accounts in respect of that financial year (see sections 434 and 435 Companies Act 2006 (previously, s. 240 (5) of the Companies Act 1985). For this purpose, a company publishes a balance sheet or a profit and loss account whenever it publishes, issues or circulates it (or makes it available in any other way for public inspection) with a view to its being read by the public generally or by any class of members of the public.

If a company charity publishes non-statutory accounts, sections 434 and 435 of the Companies Act 2006 (previously, s. 240 (3) of the Companies Act 1985) requires a statement to be appended, indicating:

a) that they are not the company's statutory accounts;
b) whether the statutory accounts have been delivered to the Registrar;
c) whether the auditors or reporting accountant have made a report on the statutory accounts, and
d) whether the auditor's report was qualified or contained a statement under s. 498 of the Companies Act 2006 (previously, s. 237 of the Companies Act 1985) (accounting records or returns inadequate, accounts not agreeing with records and returns or failure to obtain necessary information and explanations), or whether any report by the reporting accountant was qualified.

A company charity must not publish either the auditor's or reporting accountant's report with the non-statutory accounts.

Chapter 21 – Small charities

21.1 Introduction

What is a 'small charity'?

This chapter summarises the regulatory framework as it applies to smaller charities. For the purposes of this chapter, a small charity is one which due to its size does not have to adopt all the requirements of the SORP. However, this encompasses charities of various sizes. The regulatory framework applicable to charities allows various reporting options and regulatory requirements of charities, which are determined by levels of income and expenditure.

By December 2008 there were nearly 170,000 main registered charities on the Charity Commission register with total income of over £48 billion. Forty-seven per cent of these registered charities have income of £10,000 or less, and they represent less than one per cent of total income recorded. Charities with income over £500,000 (approximately five per cent of those on the Register) received nearly 90 per cent of the total income recorded. The very diverse nature of the charity sector is further shown by the fact that the largest 722 charities (those with income over £10 million) received over £23 billion, which represents forty-eight per cent of the total income received.

Table 21.1 *Distribution of charity income (as at 31 December 2008)*

Annual income	Number of main charities	%	Annual income (£bn)	%
£0 to 10,000	79,813	47.4	0.262	0.5
£10,001 to £100,000	48,834	29.0	1.697	3.5
£100,001 to £500,000	16,069	9.6	3.626	7.5
£500,001 to £5,000,000	7,518	4.5	11.204	23.2
£5,000,000 plus	1,586	0.9	31.611	65.3
Sub-total	**153,820**	**91.4**	**48.400**	**100.0**
Not yet known	14,534	8.6	0.000	0.0
TOTAL	**168,354**	**100.0**	**48.400**	**100.0**

The table indicates that small charities (that is, those with an annual income under £500,000) numbered 144,716 (or nearly 86 per cent) of the 168,354 charities on the Register, but that accumulated between them only 11.5 per cent of total charity income in 2008.

Many of the smaller charities are managed, and have services provided, entirely by lay volunteers. More often than not, there are no professional resources, nor, if there were, would there be any, or enough, financial resources to pay for them. Some of those who work with these charities took the view that the proposals of the exposure draft to the 1995 SORP were onerous and likened them to the use of a sledgehammer to crack a nut. One of the major concerns was the threshold then prevailing of £25,000 for the preparation of accounts to a true and fair view standard and the burden that compliance with that duty would have imposed on those charities. It is clearly important to strike a proper balance between the requirements for supervision and the need to minimise burdens. Developments in charity reporting after the issue of the 1995 SORP continued to consider the requirements of smaller charities and, where appropriate, allow disclosure concessions.

21.2 The Charities Act 2006

The present application of the regulatory requirements of the Charities Act 2006 is set out in SI No.629 The Charities (Accounts and Reports) Regulations 2008.

21.2.1 Charities whose gross income does not exceed £5,000

The Charities Act 2006 requires charities to register only if their annual income is over £5,000, regardless of whether or not they have a permanent endowment or the use or occupation of land. If they do register, they will be subject to the same requirements as those set out in section **21.2.2** below.

Charities, whose gross income does not exceed £5,000, must maintain proper accounting records, can prepare their accounts on the receipts and payments basis and must make those accounts available to the public on request.

There is no statutory requirement for any form of external scrutiny, although one may be required by, for example, the governing document. There is also no duty to prepare a Trustees' Annual Report or to submit the accounts to the Charity Commission.

21.2.2 Charities whose gross income does not exceed £10,000

The 1993 Act introduced a new regulatory band – a 'light touch' band which had not previously been in existence. It is for those charities which have gross income and total expenditure that do not exceed £10,000 in a financial year.

Charity trustees must keep proper accounting records and, except in the case of a company charity, can elect to prepare their accounts on the receipts and payments basis. As with the above band, this will allow many small charities (for example, local lay-volunteer charities) which use treasurers who may have had little or no training and experience in accounting, but have diligently trained themselves in bookkeeping, to continue to act for them.

If such charities elect to prepare the accounts on the accruals basis, however, those accounts must be prepared in accordance with the Regulations, although these allow some concessions from disclosure. There is no requirement to:

(a) provide a statement that the accounts have been prepared in accordance with applicable accounting standards (FRSs/SSAPs or the FRSSE) and the SORP, nor to provide particulars of, and reasons for, any material departure;
(b) provide particulars of the cost to the charity of providing trustees' indemnity insurance, and
(c) adhere to the standard expenditure headings in the SOFA.

There is no statutory requirement for an independent examination although, again, an examination or audit may be required – for example, by the governing document or by the Charity Commission.

The trustees must prepare an annual report, but it may be simplified. The Regulations require the following legal and administrative details to be provided in that report:

(a) the name of the charity as it appears in the register and any other name by which it makes itself known;
(b) the charity registration number;
(c) its principal address, and
(d) (the names of the charity trustees, or – where a charity has more than 50 – the names of 50 of those trustees, including any charity trustee who is also an officer (for example, chair or treasurer) of the charity and the name of any other person who has at any time during the financial year been a charity trustee.

In the case of a particular charity or class of charities, or of a particular financial year of a charity or class of charities, the regulations allow the Charity Commission to dispense with the requirement(s), in (c) and/or (d) above, to give the principal address and/or name of a trustee, where it is satisfied that such a disclosure could lead to that person (for example, the trustee of a women's refuge) being placed in any personal danger.

The report on the activities in the Trustees' Annual Report must specify the financial year to which the report relates and be a brief summary of the charity's main activities and achievements during the year in relation to its objects. The Trustees' Annual Report must be dated and signed by one, or more, of the charity trustees, each of whom must be authorised to do so. .

Small charities

A description of the charity's trusts must be provided.

As there is no requirement for them to submit their annual report to the Charity Commission, such charities do not routinely engage in the surveillance regime. However, if the Charity Commission requests the report,, the charity trustees must submit it within the prescribed time limit: where that request is made before the end of seven months after a financial year to which that report relates, within ten months of the end of that financial year; in any other case, within three months of the date of the request. In either case, the Charity Commission may, for any special reason, allow a longer period.

The trustees are required to keep, for at least six years from the end of the financial year to which a report relates, any annual report that they have not been required routinely to submit to the Charity Commission.

If registered, these charities are asked – but not as a statutory requirement – to provide the Charity Commission with factual information to enable it to keep the public register up to date.

21.2.3 Charities whose gross income does not exceed £100,000

The trustees must maintain proper accounting records and (except in the case of a company) can elect to prepare their accounts on the receipts and payments basis.

To whatever standard the accounts are prepared, they must be independently examined or audited. A charity's governing document may demand a level of scrutiny higher than that required by the Charities Act 2006. Where an audit is required to be carried out by a registered auditor, the option to have an independent examination is removed. In certain circumstances, the intention of the document may be unclear, having been constructed to comply with a regulatory framework in place at that time. In these circumstances, the trustees may seek an amendment to the document.

The accounts must be submitted to the Charity Commission, together with the Annual Report containing the same information as required by charities in the above band, within 10 months of the end of the financial year (or such longer period as the Charity Commission may allow). These charities will also have to submit an annual return.

21.2.4 Charities whose gross income exceeds £100,000 (but whose gross income does not exceed £500,000 and whose total assets are less than £2.8 million)

The accounts must be prepared on the accruals basis in accordance with the Regulations.

The accounts must be submitted to the Charity Commission, together with the annual report. The Regulations allow the report to be simplified, as outlined above.

An annual return will also need to be submitted.

21.3 The Charities 1993 Act versus the Companies 2006 Act

As regards the standard to which accounts are prepared, trustees of all company charities must prepare accounts that show a true and fair view of the company charity's results for the year and its state of affairs at the year end. Accordingly, however small they are, they cannot take advantage of the provisions allowing the preparation of accounts on the receipts and payments basis. The 1993 Act is, however, less demanding. The trustees of non-company charities, whose gross income in a financial year does not exceed £100,000, may elect to prepare a simplified set of accounts on the receipts and payments basis. This set of accounts is not required to give a true and fair view, either of the financial activities of the year or of the state of affairs at the date of the year end. Where a non-company charity's gross income exceeds that figure in a financial year, a statement of accounts must be prepared to give a true and fair view, thus complying with all applicable FRSs, SSAPs and the revised SORP.

For accounting periods beginning on or after 27 February 2007 (that is, 31 March 2008 year ends), a company charity whose gross income is greater than £90,000 but not greater than £500,000 (and where its balance sheet total is not greater than £2.8million) will normally require an audit exemption report (Reporting Accountants report) to be prepared in accordance with the specified requirements.

For accounting periods beginning on or 1 April 2008 (that is, 31 March 2009 year ends), a company charity whose gross income is greater than £90,000 but not greater than £500,000 (and where its balance sheet total is not greater than £2.8million) will require an independent examination to be prepared in accordance with the specified requirements. This measure harmonises the provisions for both non-company and company charities. The 1993 Act used to be more demanding than the Companies Act. While a non-company charity with gross income between £10,000 and £90,000 was required, as a minimum, to submit its accounts for examination by an independent examiner, a company charity meeting the relevant criteria is exempt from the provisions relating both to audit and to audit exemption reports. Thus, it may be possible for trustees to set up a company charity, hide behind the veil of incorporation and not have the accounts subjected to any form of independent scrutiny, other than any additional monitoring that the Charity Commission may choose to undertake.

Small charities

This inconsistency was resolved by Charities Act 2006 by placing unincorporated and incorporated charities under the very same degree of scrutiny (see **section 4.10.3** of Chapter 4)

21.4 Preparing accounts on the receipts and payments basis

21.4.1 The Charity Commission's guidance

The following legal considerations apply in respect of the eligibility to prepare accounts on the receipts and payments basis.

1. In England and Wales, charities whose accounts' 'form and content' are governed by the Charities Act 1993 may choose between preparing accruals accounts and receipts and payments accounts, provided that their gross income is not over £100,000. (See section **4.14** of Chapter 4)
2. Scottish charities whose accounts are prepared under regulations made under the Charities and Trustee Investment (Scotland) Act 2005 may prepare receipts and payments accounts, provided that their gross receipts are not over £100,000.
3. Small company charities must always prepare accruals accounts and are not covered by these concessions.

There are no statutory requirements governing the structure, presentation and content of accounts prepared on the receipts and payments basis. However, the Charity Commission has developed guidance, which is detailed below.

There are many relatively small charities with very simple structures and no control of other organisations. The vast majority of them will have cash and deposit accounts but few other assets. Apart from company charities (which must always prepare accruals accounts), these charities will often find that receipts and payments accounts meet both their needs and those of others who read their accounts. This form of accounts contains a summary of money received and money spent during the year and a list of assets.

Receipts and payments accounts have the following general features.

1. The accounting statements showing what happened during the financial year summarise only cash movements (compared with resource movements in accruals accounts).
2. A statement listing assets and liabilities is required (in place of a balance sheet required by accruals accounts).
3. No asset valuations are required, unless an evaluation is essential to a meaningful description of the asset (they may be provided if trustees so wish).

Preparing accounts on the receipts and payments basis

4. (Notes to the accounts are not often necessary, although it is recommended that these are prepared where doing so would increase the user's understanding of the accounts. The regulations made under the Law Reform (Miscellaneous Provisions) (Scotland) Act 1990 require notes on certain matters to be provided, where applicable. It is recommended that notes on related party transactions and trustee remuneration should always be given, as well as information on significant non-monetary resources.
5. They do not claim to show a true and fair view of the charity's financial activities and state of affairs. Accounting standards, which are primarily concerned with the presentation of a true and fair view, will therefore not generally apply to such accounts.
6. The only accounting convention always applicable to receipts and payments accounts is comparability through consistency – that is, they are prepared in a consistent way from year to year. Where valuations are provided the estimates should also be relevant, reliable and understandable and normally the going concern concept will also apply.

Receipts and payments accounts and statements of assets and liabilities may be organised in any way that the trustees feel appropriate. There is also flexibility in extending the titles as long as they include 'Receipts and Payments' and 'Statement of Assets and Liabilities' ('Statement of Balances' in Scotland). However, there are some general principles that trustees should be aware of, detailed below.

1. In this context 'cash' includes near cash (bank and building society current and deposit accounts) where the amount deposited (the 'capital' sum) is not at risk and is not subject to withdrawal term conditions.
2. Bank balances must be reconciled for unpaid cheques and deposits before the receipts and payments accounts are drawn up. Cheques paid out but not cleared through the bank must not be counted as creditors. Cash received but not yet banked is still cash in the hands of the charity and must be accounted for.
3. Trust law requires that trustees should be able to account separately for each trust fund they manage. It will therefore be important for trustees to account separately for cash belonging to unrestricted funds, restricted funds and endowment funds. This may be achieved by using a columnar receipts and payments account (similar to the SOFA) or by having three (or more) separate accounts. As with accruals accounts, it is acceptable to add together all restricted funds in one statement and all endowment funds in another, though the bookkeeping records must enable accounts to be drawn up for each separate trust fund.
4. Receipts and payments accounts will normally summarise the cash movements in that all payments for similar purposes (for example, wages) and receipts for similar purposes (such as donations) should be grouped together and not shown separately. Two forms of grouping of expenditure

Small charities

      are normally used: by nature (wages, rent, electricity, etc.) or by function (charitable expenditure, fundraising costs, etc.).
5. When summarising, any form of grouping of receipts and payments is acceptable.
6. The statement of assets and liabilities should be adequate to show the readers of the accounts what assets are controlled by the trustees. There is no need to list all the individual assets but the list should be comprehensive in covering all classes of asset held by the charity trustees. No valuation of assets held is required, unless an evaluation is essential to a meaningful description of the asset – for example, in the case of cash and other monetary assets, the cash value would be given. Trustees may add values if they wish and the valuation rules given earlier in relation to accruals accounts should be followed in this case.

Where receipts and payments accounts are subjected to external examination, this will normally be done by an independent examiner. However, the Practice Note 11 'The Audit of Charities in the United Kingdom' (Revised) December 2008 does allow for the audit of receipts and payments accounts by a registered auditor (though a 'true and fair' opinion cannot be given) and so an audit provision does not demand the production of accruals accounts. Occasionally, there is a requirement (for example, by the governing document or by a donor) for both an audit by a registered auditor and for accruals accounts to be prepared.

The recommendations given by the SORP are minimum ones, and charities should feel free to include more information if they think this will help readers understand the accounts.

Accounting for the smaller charity

The Charity Commission has prepared a guide, *Guidance for small charities about the SORP* ('the Guide'), for those charities preparing their accounts on the receipts and payments basis.

21.4.2 General principles

The only accounting policy that applies to accounts prepared on the receipts and payments basis is that of consistency.

The principle of materiality applies. Trustees should regard an item as material unless they 'can justify its omission …on the grounds that it is too trivial to influence the reader. In cases of doubt, the item should be regarded as material and should be included in the accounts or report'.

A note to the accounts should state that they have been prepared under the receipts and payments basis. That note should also state that the accounts comply with the appropriate legal requirements – that is, that the gross recorded income from all sources did not exceed £100,000 and that the charity is not a company incorporated under the Companies Acts.

Where a charity has branches, or local groups, which raise funds in the charity's name, funds raised, and any expended, and any assets and liabilities should be included in the charity's receipts and payments account and statement of assets and liabilities. This will mean obtaining accounting returns from branches, or groups, to add to the figures for head office. To avoid double-counting, intra-charity transactions should be eliminated.

Where both restricted and unrestricted funds are held, the receipts and payments account should distinguish cash received and paid between the funds. This can be done in several ways – for example, by preparing separate receipts and payments accounts for each fund, or by preparing one receipts and payments account which is appropriately sectionalised.

Comparatives should be provided for all headings.

21.4.3 Classification of receipts and payments

The Guide lists headings under which receipts and payments may be classified. Given that all charities are different, these headings are not obligatory, and trustees are free to use headings that are more appropriate to their charity.

21.4.4 The receipts and payments account

All cash receipts, including receipts in respect of grants, should be included in the receipts and payments account when the cash is actually received. Non-monetary benefits can present accounting problems. Donations in the form of assets should be included only when the assets are sold. If the assets have not been sold at the year end, and are still in the trustees' possession, they should be included in the statement of assets and liabilities with a note of the fund of which they form part. Donations for onward distribution (for example, clothing) are not cash and should not appear in the receipts and payments account, but described in the annual report. Other benefits received (for example, in the form of intangible income) should be described in the annual report in a way which properly illustrates their value and importance to the charity.

Legacies that the charity has been informed of, but not received at the year end, should be included in the statement of assets and liabilities only if the trustees have a legally enforceable right to receive them. They should be described, not as the assets themselves, but as the right to the assets. The description should also explain the circumstances under which the rights have arisen

All trading receipts, whether or not directly connected with the charity's purposes, should be shown gross, as should proceeds from fundraising events. Profits covenanted by non-charitable companies carrying out activities that the charity itself may not carry out should be shown separately from other receipts.

Tax recovered on interest or other income received should be shown separately from the income to which it relates. Refunds claimed but not received at the year end should be included in the statement of assets and liabilities with a suitable explanation.

21.4.5 The statement of assets and liabilities

Cash and bank deposits should be shown as the first heading. (**Note**: Deposits held for fixed periods should be classified as investments, as the trustees do not have immediate access to the funds).

Debts and other monies owed to the charity (for example, loans or tax refund claims) should be classified as other monetary assets.

Assets or property held by the charity for investment purposes should be classified as investment assets. These will include stocks and shares, cash deposits held for a fixed term, interests in land, and shares in a charity's own non-charitable trading company. Their value to the charity should be given in the notes. If an asset is difficult or expensive to value, the note should include the estimated market, or insured, value at the year end. In the case of land (with or without buildings), the note should provide the address and a brief description of the property. The Guide believes it will be helpful to disclose the original cost to the charity of the land and to describe briefly the age and condition of any buildings. Where the charity is subject to the Trustee Investments Act 1961, a note should analyse investments between each of the ranges.

Assets held by the charity for its own use should be separately categorised. These will include land and buildings, motor vehicles, office and any specialised equipment, and shares in a charity's non-charitable company providing charitable services. All assets should be included, including those being purchased under a hire purchase agreement or finance lease and those which cannot be sold because the governing document prohibits disposal. A note should provide information to allow a user to gain a clear picture of their value to the charity. The age, condition and estimated market (or insured) value of each major asset should be given. If an asset has no market value, either because the law or the governing document prohibits its sale, or because the asset is not saleable (for instance, a statue or monument), this fact should be disclosed.

Liabilities should be analysed between current and non-current liabilities. For 'major' liabilities, the actual date on which the liability falls due should be given, if known.

Where a liability (for example, a hire purchase liability) relates directly to an asset, the relationship should be explained. The number and frequency of instalments, together with the amount of each instalment should be provided.

If a charity has undertaken to make a charitable payment on some future date, it should be shown as a liability only if the charity is legally bound to make the payment, or the payment is unavoidable in the interests of the charity. A commitment is not to be treated as a liability where it becomes legally binding if, and only if, a condition is fulfilled in the future. Conditional charitable liabilities should be described separately from current and non-current liabilities.

Guarantees given by the charity should be disclosed, as should their nature and likely expiry date.

Any other liability that the trustees think likely to become payable at some future time should also be disclosed, together with an explanation of how and why it arises.

It should be stated to which fund each asset and liability relates.

21.4.6 Trustees' annual report

For charities preparing their accounts on the receipts and payments basis, the trustees' annual report is likely to be their main publicity document. To be effective, every effort should be made to get the best use from the report by conveying useful information in a clear and convincing manner.

The Guide recommends that the report should 'identify the charity, how it is constituted, its aims and officers, and provide a brief but comprehensive review of the year's activities and achievements, including the main features of the accounts'.

Legal and administrative details

Paragraph 20 recommends the following details are provided:

(a) the charity's full name;
(b) the charity's registered number;
(c) its principal address (**Note**: The Guide states that, if the charity does not have use of its own office, this will be the address of the person acting as the charity's correspondent);
(d) the nature of its governing document;
(e) the names of the charity trustees, which should include officeholders (for example, chair, treasurer), together with the names of those persons who can appoint trustees

Small charities

> (Notes: (1) If there are more than 50 charity trustees, the Guide and the Regulations allow only 50 to be given.
> (2) The Guide recommends disclosure of the following: if the charity trustees are incorporated, a statement to that effect; the names of its directors (or other persons managing it) or any corporate trustee acting as a sole trustee; the names of any custodian trustees; and the principal officers or employees of the charity);

(f) the names and addresses of the charity's main advisers;
(g) a note of any restrictions imposed by the governing document that limit the charity's activities, and
(h) a brief summary of any specific investment powers in the governing document.

The disclosures recommended in (d), (f), (g) and (h) are revised SORP recommendations only.

The Guide states that the Charity Commission may dispense with the recommendation to disclose the principal address of the charity trustees where it is satisfied that its disclosure could lead to that person being placed in any personal danger. The Guide is unclear, however, whether, in similar circumstances, the names of the trustees also need not be disclosed.

Narrative information

The Guide states that the following information 'should enable the reader to gain a proper understanding of the financial information given in the accounts'.

(A) Aims and organisation

In order to explain what the charity is trying to achieve and how it is going about it, para. 21.1 recommends that the following are provided:

(a) a brief summary of the charity's trusts;
(b) an explanation of how the charity is organised, and
(c) details of, and reasons for, any major changes in aims or organisation since the last report.

(B) Review of progress and achievements

A brief summary of the charity's main achievements during the year in relation to its objects should be provided (para. 21.2). This should show how the charity's work has developed towards fulfilling its aims, what progress has been made on any special projects and how the charity has responded to any important events of the year.

Preparing accounts on the receipts and payments basis

(C) Review of financial activities and affairs

Regarding the review of the financial activities and affairs, para. 21.3 recommends that the following information is disclosed insofar as it is applicable:

(a) a review of any major cash or non-cash transactions, showing how the charity's activities have been financed;
(b) any important events which have occurred since the year end;
(c) where available, figures demonstrating the impact the charity is making (**Note:** The Guide suggests numbers of beneficiaries helped, calls on the charity's services, etc., compared with the estimated number of those in need and the charity's existing capacity to help);
(d) in order to pursue its work, the extent of the charity's reliance on the future continuance of any substantial voluntary help, gifts in kind, unquantifiable free facilities or services received by the charity during the year;
(e) a review of the trading performance of any subsidiary company;
(f) if the charity has any substantial liabilities, obligations or commitments, a review of the adequacy and availability of its cash and non-cash resources to meet them;
(g) a list of any assets mortgaged as security for a loan or other liability. The amount of the loan outstanding at the year end should also be given and compared with the current value of the assets mortgaged;
(h) brief particulars, with names of recipients, of any grants of cash or other assets to the value of £1,000 or more made in the year to institutions (including other charities);
(i) if there have been any transactions with connected persons, an explanation of the nature of the relationships and a description of the transactions;
(j) any payments (including repayments of expenses) made to the trustees out of the charity's funds or by connected persons;
(k) any trustee indemnity insurance premiums paid from the charity's funds;
(l) the total of any *ex gratia* payments made by the charity (that is, where the trustees believe that they are under a moral obligation but cannot justify the payment as being within the charity's objects. The trustees should confirm that any necessary authority, such as an Order of the Charity Commission, has been received and provide the date on which it was given, and
(m) where the charity acts as custodian trustee:
  (i) details of any assets for which it is responsible;
  (ii) the name and aims of the charity concerned;
  (iii) particulars of any special arrangements made for segregation and safe custody of the assets, and
  (iv) how this activity furthers its own objects.

Other than (m), these disclosures are additional to those required by statute and allow a reader to better understand the charity's work.

The Guide states that disclosures in (g), (h), (j), (k) and (l) are only to be provided in the Annual Report 'if not disclosed in the accounts or explanatory notes'.

Small charities

Change in accounting basis

For each year in which the charity changes from accruals accounts to receipts and payments accounting, or vice versa, the corresponding amounts for the previous financial year should be restated on the basis of the new accounting policy.

21.5 Accruals accounting for the smaller charity

The Charity Commission also published a further publication, *Accruals accounting for the smaller charity*, for those non-company charities that:

(a)   have gross income not exceeding £100,000 for a financial year, and
(b)   do not have branches or investment assets.

This publication lifts those parts from the 1995 SORP that are likely to be of relevance to these charities when they choose to prepare their accounts on the accruals rather than the receipts and payments basis. Again, this publication continues to be of relevance to the smaller charity which wishes to prepare accruals accounts.

21.6 The application of the Financial Reporting Standard for Smaller Entities (FRSSE)

Any charity (whether or not it is a company) which is beneath the thresholds for small companies as described in the Companies Acts can follow the FRSSE in preparing its financial accounts, except where it conflicts with the SORP – in which case, the SORP should be followed. Where consolidated accounts or receipts and payments accounts are produced, smaller entities cannot follow the FRSSE in preparation of their accounts.

In following the FRSSE, the accounts will meet most of the requirements of the SORP for smaller entities. However, the following points should be noted:

(a)   the accounts should include a SOFA in place of a profit and loss account and statement of total recognised gains and losses;
(b)   the principles of fund accounting should be adopted throughout the accounts. This will include appropriate descriptions of the funds and notes showing the composition of the funds and the differentiation of funds on the balance sheet;
(c)   all investments, including investment properties, must be shown at market value;

(d) those foreign exchange gains and losses which may be allowed to be taken to reserves (as prescribed in the FRSSE) must be shown in the gains and losses section of the SOFA;
(e) those exceptional items which are required to be shown after operating profit must be shown in an appropriate place on the SOFA, and
(f) if a charity applying the FRSSE prepares consolidated accounts, it should apply the relevant accounting practices and disclosures required by accounting standards and the SORP, in relation to consolidated accounts.

21.7 Charities with gross income not exceeding £500,000 (England and Wales)

Accounting statements of smaller charities

The SORP provides a number of concessions for smaller charities that are not subject to a statutory audit. The concessions cover the SOFA and notes to the accounts and are as follows.

(a) In relation to the SOFA, smaller charities do not need to analyse either resources expended or incoming resources by activity categories within the SOFA. They may instead choose resource classifications to suit their circumstances.
(b) Where a small charity adopts an alternative approach to analysis within the SOFA, certain note disclosures may no longer be necessary – for example, where these disclosures relate to the constituent costs of an activity category or where relevant information is provided on the face of the SOFA. The disclosure paragraphs affected by this are given in the table below.

Table 21.2 Disclosure concessions for small charities

Details	Paragraph references
Analysis of activities that have generated funds	122
Analysis of incoming resources from charitable activities	146
Support costs analysis	166–167
Apportionment of costs	175–176
Breakdown of costs of generating voluntary income	183–184
Analysis of fundraising trading costs	186
Analysis of charitable activity costs	191–194
Analysis of grant making or associated support costs by activity	202, 203(b)

Small charities

Details	Paragraph references
Analysis of governance costs	212

(a) Smaller charities are not required to give details of staff emoluments in bands (para. 236).

These concessions are intended to reduce the detail of reporting requirements placed on smaller charities, though any such charity wishing to follow the full recommendations of the SORP is encouraged to do so.

Trustees' Annual Reports of smaller charities in England and Wales

In England and Wales, all registered charities are required to produce a Trustees' Annual Report. Regulations made under the Charities Act 1993 provide for charities that are not subject to a statutory audit to produce an abbreviated Trustees' Annual Report. This concession applies to all charities required to produce the report, and includes charitable companies.

The minimum content of the abbreviated Trustees' Annual Report is summarised in the table below.

Table 21.3 *Minimum content of abbreviated Trustees' Annual Reports*

		SORP paragraph
Reference and Administrative Details of the Charity, its Trustees and Advisers	Name of the charity	41(a)
	Other name by which a charity makes itself known	41(a)
	Charity registration number (or Scottish Charity Number), if any	41(b)
	Company registration number (if applicable)	41(b)
	Address of the principal office of the charity	41(c)

		SORP paragraph
	Names of the charity's trustees or trustee(s) for the charity on the date the report was approved.(where any charity trustee is a body corporate, the names of the directors of that body corporate should also be provided)	41(d)
	Names of any other person who served as a charity trustee in the financial year	41(e)
Structure, Governance and Management	Nature of the governing document and how the charity is (or its trustees are) constituted	44(a)
	Methods adopted for the recruitment and appointment of new trustees	44(b)
Objectives and Activities	Summary of the objects of the charity as set out in its governing document	47(a)
	Summary of the main activities undertaken in relation to those objects	47(e)
Achievements and Performance	Summary of the main achievements of the charity during the year	(54)
Financial Review	Policy on reserves	55(a)
	Details of any fund materially in deficit, the circumstances giving rise to the deficit and the steps being taken to eliminate the deficit	55(b)
Funds Held as Custodian Trustee on Behalf of Others	Description of the assets held in this capacity	59
	Name and objects of the charity (or charities) on whose behalf the assets are held and how this activity falls within their own objects	59
	Details of the arrangements for safe custody and segregation of such assets from the charity's own assets	59

Chapter 22 – Risk management

22.1 Introduction

The requirement for trustees to confirm in the Trustees' Annual Report that they have identified the major risks to which the charity is exposed, and that systems or procedures have been established to manage those risks was introduced in Chapters 6 and 7. This disclosure requirement was possibly the most significant change in SORP 2000; the revised Charities SORP, published in March 2005, recommends that this statement, with further details where appropriate, is included in the 'Structure, Governance and Management' section of the Trustees' Annual Report (para. 45 of the 2005 SORP). If the charity is not subject to statutory audit, then the trustees can omit this disclosure, although the statement, and the underlying action in relation to risk management processes, are encouraged as best practice for all charities.

This chapter explains further the issues that trustees should consider when managing risk and preparing the disclosures. The chapter also explains why risk management is an important issue for charities.

22.2 Why risk management?

Responding to risk is something that all organisations, including charities and other non-profit organisations, are doing on a daily basis, on one level or another. But how do organisations know that these responses, whether through individual or collective efforts, are complete, appropriate and effective?

Risk is the 'chance or possibility of danger, loss, injury or other adverse consequences'. Being 'at risk' means being exposed to danger or loss. These definitions reinforce the widely held perception that risk has primarily negative connotations.

Risk is used increasingly in the context of the business environment to refer to real and potential events which reduce the likelihood of an organisation achieving its business objectives. Business objectives can be threatened through opportunities not being spotted or gains not being maximised, as well as through things going wrong. This introduces an important upside to risk as it includes the potential for reward, opportunities and change.

Risk management

Risk management is about containing and minimising the downside and exploiting the upside and opportunities. It is about taking risks knowingly rather than by mistake and without due care.

Figure 22.1 below highlights the factors that interlink to form a credible starting point for effective risk management. Fundamental to the process is the development of a critical risk register based around the charity's key objectives.

Figure 22.1 *The risk management 'wheel'*

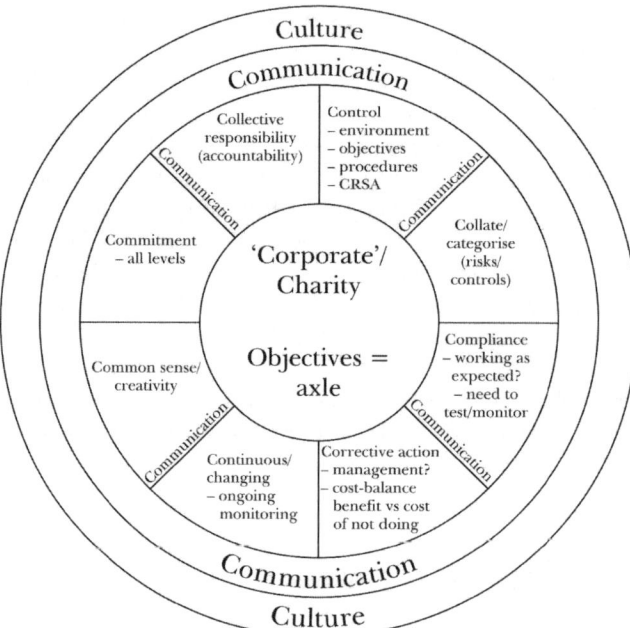

22.3 Charity objectives

Central to the risk management process, and the 'hub' of the wheel, are the charity, or corporate, objectives. In order to identify the risks facing the charity, there is a prerequisite to understand what it is trying to achieve. Connecting the management of the charity and the achievement of its objectives to the management of the risks threatening these objectives is necessary to ensure that the risk management process is relevant, effective and sustainable.

22.4 Critical risk register

Once the charity's objectives have been made explicit, the process of identifying the threats to their achievement, or 'risks', can begin. The trustees should formally identify the significant risks faced by the charity, or at least review and endorse the process by which they have been identified. The trustees should also be able to show that they are aware of such risks and that they have thought about how they may evolve.

One way to do this is to develop a 'critical risk register'. The precise format the register takes will depend on the needs and nature of the organisation concerned. It is more likely to be used on an ongoing basis if it is constructed as a user-friendly, practical and straightforward document.

At this level, it is important that the risks are not defined too narrowly. A thought-provoking, if not uncomfortable, starting point might be to think about what sort of events keep the trustees 'awake at night', or what sort of newspaper headlines would be a disaster for the charity. It may also be helpful to think about the near misses of the past – either in relation to the charity or to others in a similar position. Think about the actual or potential losses made (not necessarily financial), as well as instances when opportunities were not spotted and hence not used to the charity's best advantage.

22.5 Collate, prioritise and categorise

The ability to prioritise and to focus on the important and the likely risks is key to critical risk management. For each risk identified, there should be a balanced assessment of the probability of its occurrence and its impact on the charity should it materialise. Categorising the risks into 'high', 'medium' or 'low' may be enough as long as there is a clear, shared understanding by the trustees of what the definitions mean, and of what is and is not acceptable.

It is important to remain focused on the significant risks and to not get bogged down; therefore, the trustees should primarily be concerned at this stage with those risks that threaten the achievement of the high-level objectives identified in the first stage of the exercise.

There are various ways of classifying risks – for example, by function within the charity (fundraising, personnel, etc.) or by category (strategic, operational, regulatory, financial). The categories chosen must be relevant and clearly defined – classifying by function may be the easiest way initially, but it is important to ensure that cross-functional risks are not overlooked. The trustees may decide that the classification is not as important as being able to show how risks relate to the charity's objectives. Increasingly, charities are finding that threats to their reputation are paramount. For example, perhaps there are 'reputational risks' in terms of the success, or otherwise, of high-profile fundraising campaigns or events; or risks in terms of not delivering the services required by members and other stakeholders of a major membership charity; or risks of the charity being brought into disrepute by the actions of branches or volunteers. The trustees should consider how best to capture and categorise 'reputational risks' of this nature.

At this stage, it should be assumed that there are no controls or only very weak controls in place – effectively, the trustees should be assessing the 'gross risk'.

22.6 Controls

Having identified and assessed the 'gross' risk, it is important to review the control processes the charity has in place to prevent the risks occurring in the first place, and those that mitigate the impact of the risk should it occur. At this level, it is important to identify the strength of the overall control environment, before diving into the lower-level detail of the individual controls and processes themselves.

Assessing the strength of the perceived controls on a high, medium and low basis should be a good starting point – again, as long as these terms are defined and clearly understood. Once the key elements of the internal control system have been identified and evaluated, it is then possible to arrive at a 'net' or 'residual' risk position.

At this point, the trustees should have the basis of an effective critical risk register, which identifies the main threats (risks) to the achievement of the charity's objectives and links these to the main control processes already in place. But this is only the starting point.

22.7 Continuity and change

The trustees will need to know that the risks are being managed on an ongoing basis and that the controls identified continue to operate effectively and as expected.

As the environment in which the charity is operating changes, so do the risks it faces. For example, how will the trustees ensure that risks previously categorised as non-critical remain that way, and that no new risks have emerged? The type and level of risk the trustees are prepared to accept may change over time, depending on external factors as well as the charity's 'appetite' for, and tolerance of, risk. The nature or effectiveness of the controls may also change as staff move on or processes become more streamlined or technological.

A review process needs to be clearly defined – for example, in terms of the scope and frequency of reviews, who should perform them, the nature of reporting and the actions that will be taken to address the findings.

The trustees may find that they need an independent function such as internal audit to assist with these reviews. The need for this, whether in-house or outsourced, should be periodically reviewed.

The use of control risk self assessment (CRSA) techniques that involve staff at all levels in identifying and managing risk in their own areas may also be considered as a way of helping to ensure that the risk management process is effective at an operational level.

22.8 Commitment and responsibility

Effective risk management relies on the commitment of the trustees, management and staff at all levels. Trustees should expect to set the scene and demonstrate commitment to drive the risk management process. The key is to get people involved. Different contributions can be valuable in ensuring that there is awareness of the issues facing others, as well as of the cumulative effect. This is one of the benefits of introducing a CRSA process.

An effective ongoing risk management process also depends on the clear allocation of responsibilities and accountability – of the trustees, management, other employees, and internal audit (if relevant). The key is to ensure that the respective roles and responsibilities are properly aligned and are agreed and understood.

22.9 Communication

Communication throughout the risk management process is paramount. Some of the key areas that will need to be actively defined, communicated and discussed are:

(a) charity objectives;
(b) whether there is adequate information being communicated about the objectives and the risks;
(c) whether the communication is timely, relevant and reliable (Does it consider the future and not just review the past?);
(d) what happens to communication should things go wrong;
(e) authority, roles and responsibility and accountability to ensure that people understand what is expected of them (These need to be clearly defined so that they are not misinterpreted), and
(f) the trustees should make it clear what its risk management expectations are – of the Board of Trustees, of management and other staff and internal audit – in relation to identifying, evaluating, monitoring and reporting risk.

The trustees may also want to ensure that there is communication with the charity's stakeholders and users – whether in the initial stages of risk identification or later, when the charity wants to highlight the positive steps being taken in relation to risk management. However, it is important not to get distracted by specific requests and issues and to keep a balanced perspective.

22.10 Creativity

An example of a risk register page has deliberately not been presented in this chapter, as the key to effective risk management is for each charity to find something that works for them. Factors which are instrumental in making the process work have been highlighted, without being precise about the output itself. It is up to each organisation concerned to adapt these, be creative and come up with something relevant and appropriate for its own circumstances – something that works and which captures the essence of the organisation, its passion, its objectives and its work.

There will be elements of judgment and perception, and probably debates and disagreements – this is all part of the art of risk management. It is important to capture the spirit of risk management and make it more than just another set of procedures.

22.11 Costs

There will be a cost to this process, particularly in terms of people's time. However, this needs to be weighed against the cost of not doing anything – and also the fact that additional opportunities and rewards may not otherwise be identified. The trustees may also find that, when identifying the controls relevant to the critical risks, they uncover processes that are unnecessary. Savings may be made in resources or staff time.

22.12 Culture

However the trustees decide to implement risk management processes, the method needs to fit with the culture of the organisation, and also to become part of that culture. If the process does not take account of this, then the risk management process is likely to stall. The more closely the process is aligned to the culture of the charity, the less bumpy the ride will be.

Ultimately, this means that risk management activities should be incorporated into the charity's normal management and governance processes and should not be seen as exercises divorced from what the charity is trying to achieve. Do not underestimate the cultural change which may be required, or the 'people issues'.

22.13 How can risk be managed?

Having identified the major risks, trustees need to make a decision on the method of managing them. They need to set a policy to help make decisions about the levels of risk that can be accepted on a day-to-day basis and those matters that need to be referred to them.

The following approach describes four basic strategies that can be applied to an identified risk:

1. transferring the financial consequences to third parties or sharing it (for example, insurance, outsourcing);
2. completely avoiding the activity giving rise to the risk (for example, a potential grant or contract not taken up
3. managing or mitigating risk; or
4. accepting the risk (for example, assessed as an inherent risk that cannot be avoided if the activity is to continue).

The process of risk management extends beyond simply setting out systems and procedures. Trustees will need to monitor and assess the systems put in place.

22.14 What types of risk do charities face?

Charities face some level of risk in most of the things that they do. No single list or classification of risk can ever be regarded as complete. Key areas of risk arising from both internal and external factors need to be considered. The charity sector is incredibly diverse. Additionally, there are vast ranges in the nature of activities and external influences that charities experience. The following is a brief outline of one possible classification system, together with examples of risks that may fall into each category:

- **Governance risks** – for example, inappropriate organisational structure, difficulties in recruiting trustees with relevant skills, conflict of interest;
- **Operational risks** – for example, service quality and development, contract pricing, employment issues, health and safety issues, fraud and misappropriation;
- **Financial risks** – for example, accuracy and timeliness of financial information, adequacy of reserves and cash flow, diversity of income sources, investment management;
- **External risks** – for example, public perception and adverse publicity, including reputational issues, demographic changes, government policy, and
- **Compliance with law and regulation** – for example, breach of trust law, employment law, and regulatory requirements of particular activities, such as fundraising or the running of care facilities.

The role of trustees

The responsibility for the management and control of a charity rests with the trustee body. As such, their involvement in the key aspects of the risk management process is essential, particularly in setting the parameters of the process and in the review and consideration of the results. This should not be interpreted as meaning that the trustees must undertake each aspect of the process themselves. In all but the smallest charities, trustees are likely to delegate elements of the risk management process to managers, ensuring at the same time that they themselves, as trustees, review and consider the key aspects of the process and results. The level of involvement should be such that the trustees can make the required statement on risk management with reasonable confidence. This is likely to involve:

- ensuring that the identification, assessment and mitigation of risk is linked to the achievement of the charity's operational objectives;
- ensuring that the process covers all areas of risk;
- ensuring that the process seeks to produce a risk exposure profile that reflects the trustees' views as to levels of acceptable risk;
- reviewing and considering the principal results of risk identification, evaluation and management, and
- ensuring that the risk management is ongoing and embedded in management and operational procedures.

22.15 Identifying and managing risk

There are several models that can be used to identify and manage risk. There is no requirement or obligation on trustees to adopt any particular model or approach, but each of these models has a number of core elements and they are commended as being essential for a proper understanding of risk management. Although these elements can be used as 'steps' or 'stages', it is very likely that trustees will need to revisit each stage as their knowledge of the charity's risk profile increases. The key stages are likely to include:

- establishing risk policy;
- identifying risks and controls;
- assessing risk;
- evaluating which action needs to be taken, and
- periodic monitoring and assessment.

A charity that has identified the major risks it faces, and established systems to mitigate such risks, will be able to make a positive statement on risk in its Trustees' Annual Report. This will help to demonstrate the charity's accountability to its various stakeholders (beneficiaries, donors and other funders, employees, and the general public).

An effective risk management strategy can help ensure that:

- the charity's aims are achieved more effectively;
- significant risks are known and monitored, enabling trustees to make a more effective contribution, and
- forward planning is improved.

22.16 Conclusion

The ideas presented in this chapter should provide a challenging and practical starting point for any organisation to embark on effective risk management.

It is important that there is a response to risk – just because trustees may not want to actively identify the key risks facing the organisation does not mean that the risks are not there. The process is called risk management, not risk elimination – it will not necessarily make the risks go away but, performed properly, the exercise should enable a more informed response to them. Risk identification and management should be viewed positively and real benefits, such as the identification and maximisation of opportunities, should be sought. The process should assist the achievement of the charity's objectives more efficiently or quickly, and should not be a hindrance.

Unfortunately, it will not stop poor human judgement, human error, deliberate circumvention of procedures, management override and unforeseen circumstances, but it should help the charity to anticipate these, detect them quickly and at least mitigate the effects.

Risk management should not be seen purely as a compliance issue or as being solely focused on the prevention of a 'disaster'. The process will enable trustees to focus on the mitigation of risks that would prevent the charity achieving its strategic objectives. In so doing, charities will be able to take opportunities and develop them with an understanding of the risks faced, and with confidence that reasonable steps have been taken to mitigate those risks.

Annex – Case study – risk assessment letter

Extract of a letter written to a Goldwins' client who sought advice in this area.

Dear ….

Risk management

The Charity Commission published the revised SORP (Statement of Recommended Practice) 'Accounting and Reporting by Charities' in October

2000 and this SORP is effective for all accounting periods beginning on or after 1 January 2001.

Included in its recommendations is a requirement by trustees to confirm in their annual report that 'the major risks to which the charity is exposed, as identified by the trustees, have been reviewed and systems have been established to mitigate those risks'. The thought process behind risk management is based on the principles outlined in the Turnbull Report, which was written for listed companies in the commercial sector.

Charities can define risk as 'any event or action that may adversely effect the organisation's ability to achieve its charitable objectives and execute its strategies'. Risk is now extended to all areas of the charity's operations and includes not just financial risk but all aspects of business risk, including reputational risk.

Charities need to implement systems of internal control that manage the risks that are significant to the fulfilment of their charitable objectives, with a view to safeguarding the charity's assets and ensuring that the charity is effectively fulfilling its objectives. Risk can now be categorised under the following three headings:

- hazard – the risk of bad things happening
- uncertain outcomes – the risk of not meeting expectations
- missed opportunities – the risk of failing to exploit promising possibilities.

The concept of mitigating risk should be seen as an opportunity for charities. Risk management should not be seen as a defensive activity but rather as a beneficial proactive process. Risk management involves identifying risks and devising strategies to deal with them. The following options can be considered when dealing with a risk:

- accept the risk
- transfer the risk by insuring against it
- reduce the risk
- minimise the impact of the risk (for example, contingency planning)
- monitor the risk and exploit any potential upside.

A necessary prerequisite to risk management is a sound internal control system that is imbedded in the day-to-day processes of the charity. It needs to be capable of reacting to both external and internal changes.

A successful risk management process has to align itself with the organisation's goals and needs to be supported by the trustees, management, staff and volunteers of the charity. It also needs to be communicated effectively throughout the charity and has to be adaptable to environmental and other changes. A simple but structured framework is preferred.

Annex – Case study – risk assessment letter

The following have been identified as key risks to most charities:

- loss of major funder
- regulatory breaches
- adverse public relations – reputational risk
- industrial action
- increased competition for funds
- changing economic conditions (for example, September 11)

There is no hard and fast rule about how a risk management process should be tackled, but the following five areas should be considered:

- identification of potential risks
- prioritising of risks
- mitigation by taking appropriate action
- review to test effectiveness of this action
- report to trustees and management team.

Please do not hesitate to contact me if you require any further clarification in this area.

Yours sincerely

ANTHONY EPTON
Charities partner

Chapter 23 – Audit of charities

23.1 Introduction

In December 2008, the Auditing Practices Board (APB) published Practice Note 11 *The Audit of Charities in the United Kingdom* (Revised). This Practice Note contains guidance on the application of Auditing Standards issued by the APB to the audit of charities in the UK. The preface to Practice Note 11 advises that:

The Practice Note is supplementary to, and should be read in conjunction with, International Standards on Auditing (ISAs) (UK and Ireland), which apply to all audits undertaken in the United Kingdom. It sets out the special considerations relating to the audit of charities which arise from individual ISAs (UK and Ireland). The Practice Note does not provide detailed guidance on the audits of charities. Where no special considerations arise from a particular ISA (UK and Ireland), no material is included.

The Practice Note supersedes the previous guidance included in Practice Note 11 'The audit of charities in the United Kingdom' (Revised) issued by the APB in April 2002, and takes account of significant regulatory and other developments affecting charities since 2002, including:

- the replacement of Statements of Auditing Standards by ISAs (UK and Ireland),
- the implementation of the Companies Act 2006 for accounting periods commencing on or after 6 April 2008,
- changes to the Charities Act 1993 which apply to charities in England and Wales for accounting periods commencing on or after 1 April 2008,
- changes arising from the introduction of the Charities and Trustee Investment (Scotland) Act 2005 which apply to charities in Scotland for accounting periods commencing 1 April 2006 and
- the establishment of the Office of the Scottish Charity Regulator (OSCR).

PN 11 (Revised) December 2008 is based on legislation and regulations that became effective at 1 November 2008. It is anticipated that there will be subsequent changes in the following three areas:

- Charitable Incorporated Organisations (CIOs) (see section **4.9** in Chapter 4);
- reporting thresholds (see section **4.14** in Chapter 4), and

Audit of charities

- changes to the regulation of charities in Northern Ireland (see section **29.3** in Chapter 29).

In conducting an audit of a charity, including that of a non-company charity whose gross income does not exceed £100,000 and whose accounts may be prepared on the receipts and payments basis, auditors should have regard both to the ISAs in general and to Practice Note No. 11 *The Audit of Charities in the United Kingdom* (Revised) December 2008 (will now be referred to as PN 11).

The purpose of all Practice Notes issued by the APB, is to assist auditors in applying Auditing Standards of general application to particular circumstances and industries. While the Practice Notes are persuasive, rather than prescriptive, they are indicative of good practice, even though they may have been developed without due process.

For those audits conducted in the public sector, PN 11 is to be used together with Practice Note 10 'The Audit of Financial Statements of Public Sector Bodies in the United Kingdom (Revised)'.

The main areas of legislation that affect charity audits are:

- all company charities – the Companies Act 2006;
- charities in England and Wales – the Charities Act 1993 as amended by the Charities Act 2006;
- all Scottish registered charities – the Charities and Trustee Investment (Scotland) Act 2005, and
- non-company charities in Northern Ireland – the Charities Act (Northern Ireland) 1964.

23.2 Adoption of International Standards on Auditing (UK and Ireland)

Practice Note 11 (PN 11), issued in April 2002, was revised in December 2008 as a result of the issue of International Standards on Auditing (UK and Ireland) (ISAs) by the APB, and in the light of the Companies Act 2006 and Charities Act 2006. The APB published UK and Ireland versions of the full set of current ISAs, which are effective for audits commencing on or after 15 December 2004.

The new standards apply to all audits, regardless of size, and are therefore just as relevant to the audits of charities as to the audits of companies.

The ISAs usually result in some more work in audit planning, risk assessment, the identification, documentation and testing of controls, considering the possibility that fraud has taken place and obtaining appropriate audit evidence.

23.3 The special audit features of charities

The December 2008 revision of PN 11 acknowledges that there will be a great diversity of charities in respect to constitution, activity and size. In planning and performing the audit of a charity, auditors should have regard to the special features of charities, which may affect any charities however large or small. These features have an impact upon the assessment of risk, upon the consideration of compliance with laws and regulations and upon the detailed collection of audit evidence, as well as the reporting of the results of the audit. The six special features are set out in sections **23.3.1 – 23.3.6** below.

23.3.1 Governance

Overall responsibility for the preparation and presentation of the Trustees' Annual Report and the annual financial statements of an individual charity rests with the trustees. Trustees have responsibility for any losses the charity may incur from mismanagement of its funds, which can include supporting charitable projects that are outside the objects detailed in the charity's constitution, or investing funds in investments not permitted by the constitution. The Charity Commission may take action against individual trustees, which can include disqualification from acting as trustee of any charity. Auditors must ensure that trustees of their charity clients fully understand their duties and responsibilities. Traditionally, many trustees have seen their appointment as a mark of their support for the charity and therefore do not appreciate the full magnitude of their responsibilities. An effective audit service must include, where necessary, a process of trustee education to ensure that responsible controls and leadership are given.

23.3.2 Operating structures and branches

Where a charity undertakes activities through branches or other affiliated groups, rather than through a central structure, the accounting treatment is determined by the legal relationship between the various entities. If the branches come under the control of the trustees of the main charity, the SORP requires the branches to be accounted for in the financial statements of the main charity. Many charities have excluded branches from their accounts in the past and, therefore, are now including them in the full financial statements for the first time.

The inclusion of branches in the financial statements gives rise to a series of audit problems. The aggregation may prove to be complex, including many small entities whose local treasurers may be difficult to contact and slow to complete and return the 'consolidation packs'. In total, these branches may be material, and a process of review by rotation may be needed. This may affect the assessment of audit risk and, because of the implications for the level of audit work, the fee quotation.

Audit of charities

If the charity has subsidiaries, then they must be consolidated. Similar considerations to the audit of branches apply. Company and non-company charities are not permitted to take advantage of the statutory exemption from preparing group accounts which apply to small and medium-sized companies (see section **4.10.4** of Chapter 4). If the subsidiary undertakes trading or fundraising activities, then difficulties in auditing the completeness of its income may affect the audit opinion given for the 'group' as a whole.

23.3.3 Sources of income

Many charities derive a significant proportion of their income from voluntary sources, such as donations in the form of cash or cheques or in kind. There is unlikely to be any supporting documentation for these sources of income and the pattern of income may be difficult to predict with any degree of accuracy.

Audit procedures which can be applied to test income for completeness and accuracy include tests to enable reliance to be placed upon the control procedures implemented by the charity. Relevant controls may include post-opening procedures to ensure that all cheques received are recorded or the strict controls that should be operated when a charity conducts a public collection. Some analytical procedures may be appropriate, such as reviewing actual collections against expectations, budgets and prior years. If a charity tends to expend the funds it raises and, historically, maintains a low level of reserves, then matching expenditure to income may be an appropriate audit test.

Income generated by branches and other supporting groups may also be difficult to test for completeness and accuracy, because of the lack of control of the main charity over the supporting group and variations in the fundraising activities of individual groups. In such cases, it is particularly important to review the charity's procedures for ensuring that funds are remitted by its supporters and that the charity's income recognition policy has been complied with.

23.3.4 Restricted funds

Charities may not use restricted funds for general purposes, and must separately disclose their funds in the financial statements. Misuse of restricted funds constitutes a breach of duty by the trustees. Consequently, auditors must give close attention to the presentation of restricted funds and the reporting of movements in these funds. Therefore, the normal principles of materiality do not apply when reviewing and testing restricted funds.

23.3.5 Trading activities

The existence of trading activities needs to be taken into account when planning the audit, and the implications of any breaches in the taxation status of the charity must be considered. Charities may engage in trading as a primary purpose or trade for the purposes of raising funds. However, if the charity is deemed to be trading for profit or engages in any trade that is contrary either to charity law or to its constitutional objects, then its exemption from taxation may be questioned.

23.3.6 Public interest

The charity sector has a high public profile, and an individual charity will typically receive greater public interest in its activities than would a trading activity of similar size. Charities handle large sums of money given by the general public and receive generous taxation exemptions. Charities often receive grants and other allowances and must be seen to account properly for these. The auditors may receive unwelcome attention as a result of deficiencies identified in the accounts of a charity client, or because of general comments or concerns regarding the activities of the charity that arise. The audit of a charity has high risks attached to it in terms of public exposure, and the importance of its proper conduct must be communicated to all members of the engagement team. Equally, of course, the importance of the auditors' duty of confidentiality, and the confidential nature of the procedures for 'whistle blowing' to the Charity Commission must be emphasised (see section **23.8.2** of Chapter 23).

23.4 Reporting requirements

The audit opinion of a non-company charity must explicitly state whether the accounts:

- are properly prepared in accordance with the requirements of the Charities Act 1993, and
- give a true and fair view of the state of affairs at the year end and the incoming resources and application of the resources in the year.

Under the Companies Act 2006, in the case of company charities, the audit opinion must explicitly state whether the accounts:

(a) are properly prepared in accordance with the Companies Act 2006;
(b) give a true and fair view of the state of affairs at the year end and the incoming resources and application of the resources, including its income and expenditure, in the year, and
(c) the auditors of a charity, whether company or non-company, must also report by exception if:
 (i) proper accounting records have not been kept;
 (ii) accounts do not agree to the accounting records, or
 (iii) they have not received all the information or explanations that they require.

Audit of charities

The reporting requirement is modified for a non-company charity that prepares receipts and payments accounts. In this case, the auditor must explicitly report that:

- the receipts and payments account and the statement of assets and liabilities are properly prepared in accordance with the Charities Act 1993, and
- the account and the statement adequately distinguish any material special trust or other restricted fund of the charity.

When addressing ISA 200 (Overall Objectives of the Independent Auditor and the Conduct of an Audit in Accordance with International Standards on Auditing), PN 11 states that auditors should not accept or perform work that they are not competent to undertake. Once satisfied, the auditor should perform his or her work with 'an attitude of professional scepticism'.

PN 11 outlines the following differences between audits undertaken in accordance with the Companies Act 2006 and those in accordance with charity legislation.

1. The prescribed statement must be included on a company's balance sheet, if the directors are taking exemption from the Companies Act 2006 requirements.
2. The consistency of the annual report and the financial statements must be reported under the Companies Act 2006. This is not the case under charity law.
3. The senior statutory auditor must sign a Companies Act 2006 audit report. Under charity law, audit reports are still signed in the name of the firm.
4. The auditor is able to limit his or her liability under the Companies Act 2006. This is not available under charity law.

23.5 Terms of audit engagement

ISA 210 (Agreeing the Terms of Audit Engagement) states that the auditors and the client should agree on the terms of engagement, which should be recorded in writing. Therefore, written terms of engagement should be in existence for all charity audit clients, regardless of the charity's legal form.

The engagement letter should clearly summarise the responsibilities of the trustees and of the auditors, the scope of the engagement and the form of the reports to be given.

The particular characteristics of charities give rise to several considerations when setting out the terms of engagement.

Addressee

The engagement letter should be addressed to the authority within the charity who had the responsibility to appoint the auditor. Usually, for a non-company charity, this will be the trustees, although the auditors should review the constitution of the charity to confirm the appointing authority. The trustees should be asked to return to the auditors a signed copy of the letter, which acknowledges their confirmation of the terms of engagement. If the trustees are not involved in the day-to-day management of the charity, a copy of the letter should be sent to the persons who have this responsibility.

Scope of the audit

The engagement letter should state which legislation or regulations govern the requirement for the charity to have an audit and should state which subsidiary or branches and funds of the charity fall within the scope of the audit.

Form of reports

An outline of the form of report to be given should be specified in the letter, together with the details of any other special report that the auditors are required to give. The need for such a report might arise when the charity is in receipt of special income, such as government or local authority grants.

23.5.1 Example engagement letters for charity audits in England and Wales

The following letter has been reproduced from Appendix 3 of PN 11 (Revised).

Non-company charity (accruals basis)

The following paragraphs should be inserted into the auditor's standard letter of engagement for non-company charities in England & Wales which are preparing financial statements on an accruals basis:

As trustees of the charity, you are responsible for maintaining proper accounting records and an appropriate system of internal control for the charity. You are also responsible for preparing the annual report and financial statements which give a true and fair view and have been prepared in accordance with applicable accounting standards and the Charities Act 1993 ('the Act') and regulations thereunder.

As trustees of a charity, you are under a duty to prepare an annual report for each financial year complying in its form and content with regulations made under the Charities Act 1993. You should also have regard to the SORP, issued

Audit of charities

by the Charity Commission for England & Wales, and any subsequent amendments or variations to this statement.

Under the Charities Act 1993 we have a statutory responsibility to report to you as trustees whether in our opinion the financial statements comply with the requirements of regulations made under that Act and whether they give a true and fair view of the state of affairs of the charity at the end of the financial year and of the incoming resources and application of the resources of the charity in that year. In arriving at our opinion, we are required to consider the following matters, and report on any in respect of which we are not satisfied:

- whether proper accounting records have been kept by the charity and proper returns adequate for our audit have been received from branches not visited by us in accordance with Section 41 of the Charities Act 1993;
- whether the charity's balance sheet and income and expenditure account are in agreement with the accounting records and returns;
- whether we have obtained all the information and explanations which we consider necessary for the purpose of our audit; and
- whether the information given in the Trustees' Annual Report is consistent with the financial statements.

Under the Charities (Accounts and Reports) Regulations 2008 and the SORP you are required to report as to whether you have given consideration to the major risks to which the charity is exposed, and to the systems designed to manage those risks. We are not required to audit this statement, or to form an opinion on the effectiveness of the risk management and control procedures.

We have a statutory duty to report to the Charity Commission such matters (concerning the activities or affairs of the charity or any connected institution or body corporate) of which we become aware during the course of our audit which are (or are likely to be) of material significance to the Commission in the exercise of their powers of inquiry into, or acting for the protection of, charities (The Charities (Accounts and Reports) Regulations 2008).

From time to time we may have to rely on oral representations by management which are uncorroborated by other audit evidence. Where they relate to matters which are material to the financial statements, we will request that you provide written confirmation of them. In particular, where misstatements in the financial statements that we bring to your attention are not adjusted, we are required to obtain your reasons in writing.

Charitable company

Alternative paragraphs for a charity in England and Wales which is incorporated under the Companies Act 2006 and does not exceed the small company thresholds (as defined by the Companies Act 2006):

For all paragraphs in non-company (accruals basis) heading, the term charity can be replaced with charitable company.

1. Reference in the first paragraph above to the "Charities Act 1993" should be replaced with "Companies Act 2006".
2. The second paragraph above should be replaced with "As trustees of a charity, you have a duty under the Companies Act 2006 to prepare a directors' report for each financial year and also an annual report complying in its form and content with regulations made under the Charities Act 1993. You should also have regard to the Statement of Recommended Practice 'Accounting and Reporting by Charities (revised 2005)' ('SORP'), issued by the Charity Commission for England & Wales, and any subsequent amendments or variations to this statement".
3. In the first section of the third paragraph above replace "you as trustees" with "the members". In the first section, also replace "comply with the requirements of regulations made under that Act" with "have been properly prepared in accordance with the Companies Act 2006". In the first bullet point delete "in accordance with Section 41 of the Charities Act 1993".

23.6 Audit planning

23.6.1 Features of charity audits

When planning the audit of a charity, auditors should consider the following special features of their client and how these features may affect their audit approach:

(a) existence of special regulations governing the conduct of charities;
(b) sources of income which may include grants from public authorities or funds held on trust. Breaches of the conditions relating to the use of such income can have serious implications for the charity;
(c) tax relief dependent upon the charity complying with the governing document submitted to HM Revenue & Customs;
(d) activities of the charity which bring it within the scope of other regulations as well as those relating to charities;
(e) the level of involvement in the administration of the charity which can be expected of (typically unpaid) trustees, and
(f) the way in which the charity is managed on a day-to-day basis (for example, systems within the organisation for controlling income, expenditure and staff resources).

PN 11 suggests that auditors consider the following areas at the planning stage:

- applicable accounting framework;
- governance arrangements;
- operating structures;
- activities in relation to objects;
- related or connected parties;
- statutory duty to report to regulators, and
- need for any special audit reports.

23.6.2 The regulatory framework

At the planning stage of the audit, the auditors must ascertain under which law and regulations the client operates, and both understand them and be aware of any changes in these since the last audit. The form of law and regulations under which the charity operates will influence both the charity's reporting responsibilities and the duties of the auditor.

23.6.3 The operations of the charity

The auditors must then undertake and review the details of the charity's activities and organisation, as this is essential for assessing the risk of misstatement arising from potential fraud, error or non-compliance with the relevant law and regulations. Information can be built up from sources within the charity – such as minutes, budgets and plans, and procedures manuals – and from external sources ,such as specialist publications and information providers.

23.6.4 The structures of the charity

The reporting structures of the charity and the resulting audit approach will be determined by the legal form that the charity has adopted for its operations. The main structures which could be adopted are:

(a) groups, in which activities are conducted by separate legal entities that are controlled by the charity;
(b) associated undertakings, where the charity has a participating interest in the other undertaking and exercises a significant degree of influence over its operations;
(c) operations conducted by a separate administrative entity such as a subcommittee of the charity which does not have a separate legal identity from the charity itself;
(d) 'subcontracting' by the charity of its activities to non-controlled organisations, and
(e) branches.

23.6.5 Groups

When planning the audit of a charity that has a group structure, the auditors must ascertain if audits of the members of the charity's group are to be performed and whether they or another firm has been engaged to perform the audits that are required. If the results or financial position of the other members of the group are material in relation to the principal charity, the auditors must determine the level of evidence they require to support their opinion on the group accounts from the auditors of the members of the group, and issue written instructions to those auditors, setting out the information and reports that are required.

23.6.6 Branches

A branch of a charity may or may not be a separate legal entity. It may be either;

- a part, either geographical or functional, of the overall operation of the charity, or

- a separate legal entity which, for accounting purposes, is required to be grouped with the main charity.

The SORP requires the main charity to prepare accounts that aggregate (that is, consolidate) its results, assets and liabilities with those of its branches. The auditors must plan their procedures to ensure that they are able to conclude that proper returns have been received from the branches they have not visited. Usually, the auditors will visit, in rotation, a number of the branches of the charity to review branch transactions and procedures.

If the branch is a separate legal entity, then although aggregation is required, it must also prepare separate accounts and receive an audit or an independent examination if its income or expenditure falls within the relevant qualification bands.

23.6.7 Overseas operations

If the charity has an overseas operation, the auditors must, as part of their planning, ensure that they have a clear understanding of the relationship between the overseas operation and the main charity. If the overseas operation constitutes a separate legal entity that is controlled by the main charity, consolidated accounts should be prepared which incorporate the charity and its overseas operation. If the overseas operation constitutes a branch, its results and financial position should be aggregated together with those of the main charity. If grants or donations are paid to a local entity, then it is unlikely that a branch or subsidiary relationship arises.

23.7 Materiality

There is a distinction between the auditors' consideration of materiality in planning the audit, and that prevailing at the time of evaluating the results of audit procedures. The assessment of materiality at the planning stage determines the nature, timing and extent of audit tests. The materiality of matters found in the course of audit work is considered both in relation to their possible impact on the financial statements, and in relation to applicable regulations and other factors governing the conduct of individual charities. If the auditors are engaged to make additional reports – for example, in respect of restricted grants – it will be appropriate for them to make a separate assessment of materiality specifically for the purposes of such additional engagements.

Where a charity operates through branches or subsidiaries, their contribution to the result and financial position of the charity may not be known at the time of planning the audit. In this case, the auditors consider how to decide the likely results of branches or subsidiaries by reference to such procedures as:

- discussion with management;
- consideration of problems or particular issues encountered in previous years, to see whether there is an identifiable pattern suggestive of weak management or fraud, for example;
- consideration of previous year figures, and
- any budgeted or preliminary results.

On such evidence, the auditors then incorporate the resulting best estimate into the materiality calculation for the audit as a whole.

Often, a split materiality figure is appropriate for the audit of a charity – because of the different magnitude of current income and expenditure reported in the SOFA and fixed assets and investments presented on the balance sheet.

Restricted funds

Many charities may receive funds that are subject to specific trusts, which must be accounted for separately (unless grouped together if, individually, they are comparatively small) in accordance with the Charities SORP. It is not necessary in every case to set a different monetary materiality level for such funds. However, materiality may be influenced by considerations such as legal and regulatory requirements, which may result in different materiality considerations being applied to particular aspects of the financial statements. Auditors should therefore consider whether this is appropriate when planning the nature and extent of their work in relation to restricted funds. Any breaches of the terms of trusts relating to restricted funds that come to the auditors' attention in the course of their work, regardless of materiality to the financial statements as a whole, need to be considered in terms of their significance to the auditors' report on the financial statements and brought to the attention of trustees, as a failure on the part of the trustees to comply with the terms of trusts may place them in breach of their responsibilities.

23.8 Consideration of laws and regulations

23.8.1 Introduction

Auditors are required to be alert for instances of possible or actual non-compliance with the law or regulations. In the case of charities, relevant laws and regulations include trust law, and hence specific requirements regarding the use of restricted funds and preservation of any permanent endowments (capital funds).

The regulatory framework relevant to the operations of a charity can be divided into the following categories:

- those relating directly to the preparation of the charity's financial statements, or the inclusion or disclosure of specific items in the financial statements;
- those that relate to the independent audit or review of the charity's financial statements, and
- those that provide a legal framework within which the charity conducts its activities and which are central to the charity's ability to conduct its activities.

- Auditors need to be aware of the regulatory framework applicable to each charity that they act for. Details of the framework should be recorded on the permanent file and the implications of regulatory changes must be considered. With regard to any regulatory breach of which they become aware, the auditors must consider the implications for the financial statements and for the audit opinion and whether a whistle-blowing duty arises. The regulatory structure of a charity is determined by its own constitution and by conditions imposed upon it by statute, regulators, the courts and other third parties.

23.8.2 Whistle blowing

Auditors have a duty to report to the Charity Commission on any matters that they believe are of 'material significance' to the Charity Commission. Usually, a matter is 'materially significant' if the actions of the trustees have put, or are likely to put, the funds of the charity at risk. Such matters would include, for example:

- the discovery of expenditure not in accordance with the trust deed;
- material weaknesses in the trustees' control over the charity's affairs, and

- where insufficient explanations or records were available to enable the audit or examination to be completed satisfactorily.

This arrangement is similar to those for other regulated bodies such as pension schemes and registered financial services entities.

No additional audit procedures need be performed to seek to identify such matters. However, all staff involved in the audit need to be aware of this reporting responsibility, and the firm of auditors needs to have in place procedures for reporting and assessing matters that give rise to concern and a possible need to 'blow the whistle'.

23.8.3 Charity governing documents

In addition to the external regulations that govern the activities of a charity, the charity's own governing documents will define the objects of the charity and the powers and responsibilities of its trustees. The documents may contain special provisions regarding the disclosure of information in the financial statements or may extend the reporting requirements of the auditors. The charity's governing documents are extended by any subsequent will, trust or other instruction which imposes a restriction upon any present or future funds of the charity.

23.8.4 Laws relating directly to the preparation of the financial statements

As part of their audit, auditors must ensure that the charity is presenting its financial statements in accordance with the reporting regulations and the SORP, as well as any special reporting requirements imposed by the charity's own governing documents. Normally, this is evidenced by the use of a disclosure checklist, together with a file note explaining how compliance with any special requirements has been checked.

Auditors should also check whether the charity's governing documents contain any special provisions regarding the disclosure of information in the financial statements or reporting requirements for the auditors. Users of the financial statements of a charity reasonably expect that the transactions recorded within them are authorised by the governing document of the charity and are in furtherance of the charity's objects. In order to give a true and fair view, due regard needs to be given to disclosure of any non-compliance with the governing document.

Auditors therefore familiarise themselves with the charity's governing documents and, in planning and conducting their audit, will:

- ensure that their audit procedures cover compliance with the governing document

- consider any changes in the charity's activities proposed by the trustees to ensure that these comply with the governing document, and
- be alert to new or unusual transactions which may not be in accordance with the governing document.

23.8.5 Laws and regulations central to the charity's conduct of its business

Auditors are required to carry out specified steps to help identify possible or actual instances of non-compliance with those laws and regulations that are central to the entity's ability to conduct its business.

Laws and regulations that are central to the charity's ability to conduct its activities are those where:

- compliance is a prerequisite of obtaining a licence to operate, or
- non-compliance may reasonably be expected to result in the charity ceasing operation, or would call into question its status as a going concern.

If these laws and regulations are breached, the following consequences may arise:

- appointment by the Charity Commission of a receiver and manager (due to primary breaches of laws and regulations applying to charities generally);
- loss of those licences that are necessary to continue a major element of the charity's work, and
- financial liabilities which are likely to exceed the available resources of the charity.

Examples of laws that apply to the activities of charities include:

(a) laws on raising funds through lotteries, including betting, gambling, lotteries and amusements legislation;
(b) laws relating to the generation of income by commercial and professional fundraisers;
(c) laws relating to the generation of income through house-to-house or street collections, and
(d) the Trustee Act 2000.

Specific regulations which apply to the operations of individual charities would include:

(a) the Children Act 1989 requirements in respect of day care or respite care
(b) the requirements of the Registered Homes Act 1984 (as amended) in respect of nursing homes
(c) clinical waste requirements under the Environmental Protection Act and their implications for hospitals and hospices, and

(d) food safety and hygiene regulations and their implications for residential care homes, village halls and community buildings.

Breaches of laws and regulations that apply to a particular type of activity may also result in fines, the financial consequences of which may, in particular instances, be significant. Severe financial consequences may also arise from failure to comply with grant conditions or taxation law.

Compliance with grant conditions

Charities receiving grants of public funds (including lottery funds) are normally required to meet certain specific conditions. Expenditure outside grant conditions can lead to disallowance and repayment. Such conditions might include, for example, the requirement to produce audited accounts regardless of the size of the charity.

Compliance with taxation law

Charities are exempt from tax on most (but not all) types of income and on capital gains, provided that the income and capital gains are applicable, and are applied to, qualifying charitable purposes. There is, however, no general exemption from VAT for charities.

23.9 Audit risk

The purpose of ISA 315 (*Obtaining an understanding of the entity and its environment and assessing the risks of material misstatement*) is to establish standards and to provide guidance on obtaining an understanding of the entity and its environment, including its internal control, and on assessing the risks of material misstatement in a financial statement audit.

The principles of obtaining and using knowledge of the charity to be audited are the same as those applying to the audit of any entity. The auditor's responsibilities in this respect are not related to the level of fee charged for the audit: for example, the same knowledge and understanding of the client charity are required in respect of audits carried out on an honorary basis as for audits carried out for a commercial fee.

23.9.1 Understanding the entity and its environment, including its internal control

ISA 315 specifies that 'the auditor should obtain an understanding of relevant industry, regulatory, and other external factors including the applicable financial reporting framework'.

Each charity is different and the forms of constitution can vary widely through the sector. Understanding the client is therefore vital and a full permanent file is essential. ISA 315 refers to the importance of proper understanding of the activities, organisation and constitution of individual clients. In respect of charities, auditors should be particularly aware of:

- the constitution – which will come in many forms depending upon the origins of the charity and charity's structure;
- the constitutionally defined objectives and investment powers;
- the accounting system and controls established by the charity;
- the operational structure of the charity and the nature of its relationship with branches, affiliated groups and other supporters, and
- the principal sources of income of the charity, which may include fundraising activities which can be difficult to audit for completeness and trading activities which can give rise to threats to the taxation status of the charity.

23.9.2 The regulatory framework

Provision for the oversight of charities differs across the United Kingdom, with separate regimes in England and Wales, in Scotland and in Northern Ireland.

The auditor needs to ascertain which laws and regulations apply to the jurisdiction within which the charity operates, and understand them. This involves keeping up to date with those laws and regulations that relate to charities generally and to the client charity in particular.

A key element in understanding the entity is a knowledge and understanding of the charity's governing document. There are many different types of governing instrument or constitution which will determine the objects of the charity and the powers of its trustees, and the audit approach needs to be adapted accordingly. Particular issues include any limitations in objectives placed on the charity by its governing document, or terms and restrictions placed on material gifts or donations received.

23.9.3 Special features of charities

Knowledge of the charity's activities and organisation is essential for ascertaining the risk of material misstatement arising from fraud, error, or non-compliance with applicable law and regulations. The auditor considers special features of charities (that is, the nature and sources of income, restricted funds, trading and charitable status, taxation and operating structures and branches) in order to plan and carry out audit work effectively and efficiently, and to provide a yardstick against which to evaluate the evidence gained from audit procedures.

Audit of charities

Sources of income often include grants – for example, from public authorities or other charities. Such grants are often made for specific purposes and are subject to conditions, breach of which can have serious implications for the charity. Developments in the public sector mean that auditors of a public authority donor may have, or may seek, the right of access to the charity's records to follow through and verify the use made of the grant. In addition, grants from public bodies are increasingly subject to clawback provisions requiring repayment if a charity breaches specified conditions.

Where charities receive funding to undertake operational activities, the auditor ascertains whether such income is received under contract (which is generally unrestricted income) or by way of grant for provision of a specific service (which normally gives rise to restricted income). As well as distinguishing whether the income is restricted or not, the nature of the terms and conditions may affect taxation considerations (for example, the VAT treatment).

The trustees of smaller charities may not have formal documentation of their activities, which could be used to chart the charities' progress through the year, although auditors may be able to encourage trustees to keep such records. The most useful source of information in these circumstances is likely to be discussion with the trustees.

23.9.4 Branches

The auditor needs a clear understanding of the legal structure of a charity. A charity may operate through branches to raise funds or carry out particular aspects of its charitable activities. The auditor needs to understand whether the structure adopted by a charity falls within the definition of a branch in the SORP. The principles set out in the SORP apply whether operations are carried out in the UK or overseas.

Branches that fall within the SORP definition will be accounted for as part of the whole charity. Therefore, the omission of branches, where material, will affect the audit opinion. The auditor also needs to be aware that some charities will use the term 'branches' outside of its SORP meaning to describe a network of charities that are administratively autonomous and, as such, are separate accounting entities. The constitutional provisions in such cases may require careful consideration.

23.9.5 Overseas activities

The considerations noted above apply equally where activities are carried out overseas. The auditor takes into account the fact that significant aspects of a charity's business may be conducted in conditions or locations that impede access. In these circumstances, auditors will need to ensure that they are able to assess the full extent of the activities, and have the necessary understanding of the regulatory environment in which significant activities are carried out – for example, in relation to taxation and employment law. The auditor also needs to be aware of the Charity Commission's guidance on charities working internationally.

23.9.6 Connected entities

The structure and management of any connected entities should be considered – in particular, the degree to which connected entities are managed and controlled by the trustees and management of the charity. Where the charity is not a company and/or where the connected entity is not a subsidiary, the auditor of the connected entity normally owes duties of confidentiality to that entity. In these cases, the charity's auditor will ordinarily wish to put arrangements in place through the trustees of the charity and directors of the connected entity to allow the connected entity, and its auditor, to give the auditor of the charity such information and explanations as may reasonably be required for the purposes of the auditor's duties. The charity's auditor also considers discussing his or her particular responsibilities under the Charities Acts and the Regulations with the auditor of the connected entity, so that these are fully understood.

23.9.7 Accounting policies

ISA 315 specifies that 'the auditor should obtain an understanding of the entity's selection and application of accounting policies and consider whether they are appropriate for its business and consistent with the applicable financial reporting framework and accounting policies used in the relevant industry'.

FRS 18 (*Accounting Policies*) requires a statement that the financial statements have been prepared in accordance with the relevant SORP and provides details of any departures from recommended practice and disclosures. This means that it is normally necessary to follow the SORP in order to give a true and fair view.

23.9.8 Incoming resources

The SORP states that incoming resources should be recognised, when prudent and practical. Recognition is dependent on legal entitlement, reasonable certainty of receipt and the monetary value being measurable with reasonable certainty. The use of autonomous branches, agents or loosely affiliated volunteer groups for fundraising needs to be considered when determining the appropriate method of income recognition. The auditor of a charity needs to understand clearly the basis and terms on which such fundraising services are provided to it.

23.9.9 Estimates

The SORP provides detailed guidance on appropriate accounting policies and measurement bases. In applying these policies and bases, the use of estimates and estimation techniques will often be necessary to determine the monetary value of assets and liabilities, and to determine the allocation of costs within the SOFA. The auditor seeks to ensure that techniques selected by trustees enable the financial statements to give a true and fair view. The auditor ensures that the financial statements disclose a description of those estimation techniques adopted, including the underlying principles, that are significant in order to comply with FRS 18 and the SORP.

23.9.10 Objectives and strategies

ISA 315 specifies that 'the auditor should obtain an understanding of the entity's objectives and strategies, and the related business risks that may result in material misstatement of the financial statements'.

The auditor considers the possibility of non-compliance by the charity with its governing document which may cause the financial statements to not give a true and fair view. Each charity is bound to comply with the terms of its governing document, which may, for example, take the form of a trust deed, a will, a constitution or the Memorandum and Articles of Association of a company. The governing document sets out the objects of the charity and determines the powers of its trustees, and may also set out more detailed rules for conducting its work. Failure to comply with the governing document's terms may constitute a breach of trust and, in particular, in England and Wales may form grounds for intervention by the Charity Commission.

In order to understand the charity's business risks and strategies fully, the auditor also considers the ways in which the charity organises its affairs, including, for example, the use of volunteer staff and branch offices, and the carrying out of overseas activities and/or trading activities.

23.9.11 Measurement of financial performance

ISA 315 specifies that 'the auditor should obtain an understanding of the measurement and review of the entity's financial performance'.

The auditor obtains an understanding of the performance indicators used by the differing levels of management – for example, trustees, audit committee (if in existence), chief executive, finance director, and department heads. The auditor also considers what steps have been taken by trustees and senior management in respect of cost allocations and setting a reserves policy.

23.9.12 Internal controls

ISA 315 specifies that 'the auditor should obtain an understanding of internal control relevant to the audit'.

The maintenance of an effective system of internal control is at least as important for charities as it is for other entities (if not more so), since it is a fundamental duty of charity trustees to protect the property of their charity and to secure its application for the objects of the charity. Failure to do so can render the trustees personally liable for any loss occasioned by the charity. Guidance leaflets entitled CC8 *Internal Financial Controls for Charities* and CC10 *The Hallmarks of an Effective Charity* have been published by the Charity Commission, and these provide a useful point of reference for auditors.

23.9.13 The regulatory framework

Certain charities (for example, those that are also registered friendly societies), are subject to specific reporting requirements in respect of internal controls. In such cases, the auditors should plan their audit to enable them to give an opinion that there is a satisfactory system of control over transactions.

23.9.14 The operations of charities

There is a very wide variation between different charities in terms of size, activity and organisation, so that there can be no 'standard' approach to internal control systems and audit risk assessments. Charities undertake a variety of activities, through varying structures that may include both UK and overseas branches, which will present widely different risks. Internal control systems will be developed in relation to the specific risks associated with income sources, the activities undertaken, and location and staffing arrangements.

23.9.15 Control environment

PN 11 requires charity auditors to consider the control environment in which a charity operates. The role, attitude and actions of the trustees are fundamental in shaping the control environment of a charity. Factors to consider include:

- the amount of time committed by trustees to the charity's affairs;
- the skills and qualifications of individual trustees;
- the frequency and regularity of trustee meetings and the level of attendance at these meetings;
- the form and content of trustee meetings;
- the independence of trustees from each other;
- the division of duties between trustees;

Audit of charities

- the supervision by the trustees of relatively informal working arrangements, which are common when employing volunteers;
- the degree of involvement in, or supervision of, the charity's transactions on the part of individual trustees;
- the level of delegation by trustees to senior management and the formality of this delegation, and
- the committee structure of the organisation.

Other features of the control environment will depend on the size, activities, organisation and corporate governance structures of the charity but might include:

(a) a recognised plan of the charity's structure, showing clearly the areas of responsibility and lines of authority and reporting – where the charity does not have staff, and is administered entirely by the trustees, there can still be an agreed division of duties, provided that there is adequate monitoring by the body of trustees as a whole;

(b) segregation of duties where charities have more than one member of staff (whether paid or not) – in larger charities, such segregation could include involvement of staff from outside the finance department in certain transactions: for example, in providing a first signatory for cheques;

(c) supervision by trustees of activities of staff where segregation of duties is not practicable;

(d) competence, training and qualification of paid staff and any volunteers appropriate to the tasks they have to perform;

(e) involvement of the trustees in the recruitment, appointment and supervision of senior executives;

(f) access of trustees to independent professional advice where necessary;

(g) budgetary controls in the form of estimates of income and expenditure for each financial year and comparison of actual results with the estimates on a regular basis, and

(h) communication of results of such reviews to the trustees on a regular basis so as to facilitate their review of performance and enable them to initiate action where necessary.

23.9.16 Risk assessment

ISA 315 specifies that 'the auditor should obtain an understanding of the entity's process for identifying business risks relevant to financial reporting objectives and deciding about actions to address those risks, and the results thereof'.

The SORP requires charities with annual income in excess of £500,000 to include a statement in the Trustees' Annual Report confirming that the major risks to which the charity is exposed, as identified by the trustees, have been reviewed and systems have been established to mitigate those risks. As a result of this, charities will often maintain a risk register. Where this is the case, the auditor reviews this register. In smaller charities this may not be the case, and so the auditor refers to paragraph 79 of ISA 315.

23.9.17 Restrictions on income

For charities it is important that the systems in place are able to capture accurately any restrictions placed on income – whether imposed by the donor or as a result of the charity's fundraising initiatives. The systems should also ensure the documentation supporting the restrictions on the income is retained and easily accessible. The auditor assesses these systems as part of the process of obtaining an understanding of the information systems.

23.9.18 Control activities

Aspects of the control activities that specifically apply to charities are described below. Control activities that are not specific to charities – such as segregation of duties or physical security of tangible assets – are not included in the examples, but are also relevant to the auditors' assessment of the components of audit risk.

A particular difficulty for charity trustees in establishing control activities can stem from the use of volunteers (often recruited on a part-time basis) who are not formally accountable to them, unlike employees. Nevertheless, it is important for charities raising a significant proportion of income through volunteers, such as street collectors, to ensure that those volunteers are adequately supervised and controlled. The examples below are not intended to be comprehensive: there may be other control activities that will be relevant to a particular charity, and control activities that are of general application (such as segregation of duties or physical security of tangible assets) which are not included in the examples given below. The nature and extent of the activities will clearly depend on the size of the charity.

Cash donations

Donations – collecting boxes and tins

- numerical control over collecting boxes and tins;
- satisfactory sealing of boxes and tins so that any opening prior to recording is apparent;
- regular collection and recording of proceeds from collecting boxes, and
- dual control over counting and recording of proceeds.

Other cash receipts

- clear directions to staff on how to handle cash donations, and
- advice to donors on where to make donations securely

Postal receipts

- unopened mail kept securely;
- dual control over the opening of mail;
- immediate recording of donations on the opening of mail or receipt of cash, and
- agreement of bank paying-in slips to record receipts by an independent person.

Receipts over the internet

- sending a confirmation of receipt to the donor, and
- controls over the writing up of daybooks,

Text giving:

- IT controls to ensure texts received are processed correctly with adequate audit trail.

Other donations

Gift aid

- establish procedures to ensure donations are initially recorded correctly with tax compliance issues being met;
- regular checks and follow-up procedures to ensure due amounts are received;
- regular checks to ensure all tax repayments have been obtained, and
- structured archive system in place to ensure documentation is retained for seven years.

Legacies

- comprehensive correspondence files maintained in respect of each legacy, and numerically controlled searches of agency reports of legacies receivable;
- regular reports and follow-up procedures undertaken in respect of outstanding legacies, and
- security of chattels received as legacies and procedures to establish their value and proper realisation.

Donations in kind and intangible income

- all types of activity: immediate recording of donated assets;
- in the case of charity shops, separation of recording, storage and sale of stock, and
- procedures for recording donated services.

Other income

Fundraising activities

- records maintained for each fundraising event;
- comparable controls maintained over receipts as for normal donations, and
- comparable controls maintained over expenses as for administrative expenses.

Central and local government grants and loans

- regular checks that all sources of income or funds are fully exploited and appropriate claims made;
- ensuring income or funds are correctly applied in accordance with the terms of the grant or loan, and
- comprehensive records of applications made and follow-up procedures for those not discharged.

Fixed assets

Existence of assets

- a register of fixed assets, including donated assets.

Valuation

- donated assets recorded at approximate market value and, where appropriate, depreciation calculated and recorded in accordance with proper assessment of future benefits deriving from assets' use.

Use of funds

Restricted funds – records maintained of the following:

- separate revenue and assets;
- terms controlling application of fund monies, and
- application of fund monies.

Grants to beneficiaries

- records maintained of all requests for material grants received and their treatment;
- checks made of the *bona fides* of applicants for substantial grants, and that amounts paid are *intra vires;*
- minutes maintained of all grants committee meetings with records of decisions made including the recording of conflicts of interest, and

Audit of charities

- adequate documentation given to the committee for it to base its decision on the facts.

Related party transactions

- annual declaration of interests provided by all trustees.

Branch operations

Many charities carry out their operations through branches based either in the UK or overseas. Set out below are the control activities that the charity may implement:

(a) regular reports or returns to the charity's head office by any branch, office or individual representative of the charity, checks to ensure that all these are received, and a mechanism for monitoring branch activities – for example, by comparison of expenditure to budget;
(b) prompt investigation of any report of the misuse of the charity's name;
(c) internal controls of equivalent standard to those of the main charity in any branch where the trustees of the charity have direct control;
(d) existence of an accounts manual and the standardisation of procedures at all branches;
(e) proper acknowledgements of remittances to and from abroad;
(f) clarity of instructions and guidelines regarding receipt and transfer of income, to identify the point at which it belongs to the main charity;
(g) controls over recruitment and appointment of staff to run branch operations;
(h) defined authorisation limits and responsibilities for local staff in ordering and paying for goods and services;
(i) if the amounts involved are material, periodic checks by internal audit or head office personnel;
(j) retention of documents for local inspection (for example, at overseas locations if local law requires this) or for periodic transmission to the head office, and
(k) in the case of overseas branches, controls over treasury operations – for example, to ensure that unspent cash balances are held in hard currencies and in secure holdings where the overseas economy is inflationary and conditions are unstable.

23.9.19 Assessing the risks of material misstatement

ISA 315 specifies that 'the auditor should identify and assess the risks of material misstatement at the financial statement level, and at the assertion level for classes of transactions, account balances, and disclosures'.

Audit risk

PN 11 identifies certain features of charities that may affect the risk of material misstatement. These include:

(a) the complexity and extent of regulation;
(b) the significance of donations and cash receipts;
(c) the extent of donations over the internet or by credit card;
(d) difficulties of the charity in establishing ownership and timing of voluntary income where funds are raised by non-controlled bodies;
(e) lack of predictable income or a precisely identifiable relationship between expenditure and income, which makes it difficult for the charity to ensure that the income to which it is entitled is actually received;
(f) uncertainty of future income, which can make consideration of future operations and viability of the charity difficult;
(g) the scope of the objects and powers given by charity's governing documents, which is often narrower than that given in the equivalent documents for commercial entities. Failure to act in accordance with those objects and powers is more likely to have consequences for the financial statements, and therefore the auditors' report, than would a transaction by a commercial company that is not permitted by its Memorandum or Articles of Association;
(h) restricted funds held by many charities which require special considerations as to use and accounting;
(i) the extent and nature of trading activities must be compatible with the entity's charitable status;
(j) the complexity of tax rules (whether income tax, capital gains tax, Value Added Tax or business rates) relating to charities;
(k) the sensitivity of certain key statistics, such as the proportion of resources used in administration and fundraising, and
(l) the need to maintain adequate resources for future expenditure whilst avoiding the build-up of reserves which could appear excessive to potential donors or be incompatible with the entity's charitable status.

A common feature of most charities is the receipt of voluntary income, which may be received by way of cash donations or donations in kind. Unlike the income of commercial entities, voluntary income will not always be supported by invoices or equivalent documentation. Therefore, it can be difficult to obtain assurance on the completeness and accuracy of recorded donations.

The level of income from donations cannot be predicted with any great accuracy, as people's pattern of giving may change – due, for example, to economic hardship or competing demands on limited resources. It is also difficult to establish a relationship between donations and other figures in the financial statements, as expenditure levels may not have any direct relationship with such income. Where voluntary cash donations are received, the trustees need to make arrangements to institute appropriate controls, to the extent practicable, to ensure that all income is properly accounted for, and the charity's auditors are likely to rely on evidence concerning those controls in order to form a view on the completeness of the income shown in its financial statements.

The completeness of incoming resources, overseas operations and restricted funds are likely to be significant risks affecting charity audits.

23.9.20 Fraud

The purpose of this ISA is to establish basic principles and essential procedures, to provide guidance on the auditor's responsibility to consider fraud in an audit of financial statements and to expand on how the standards and guidance in ISA 315 and ISA 330 (*The auditor's procedures in response to assessed risk*) are to be applied in relation to the risks of material misstatement due to fraud.

The trustees of a charity are responsible for the prevention and detection of fraud in relation to the charity, even if they have delegated some of their executive functions to senior staff.

They are expected to safeguard charity assets and reserves through the implementation of appropriate systems of control. The auditor of a charity is responsible for forming an opinion on whether or not financial statements show a true and fair view; and to this end the auditor plans, performs and evaluates audit work in order to have a reasonable expectation of detecting material misstatements in the financial statements arising from error or fraud.

Many charities receive funds that have restrictions placed upon them. These funds are held on trust and must be applied to the purpose for which they were given. The misappropriation of funds constitutes a breach of trust, whether it was intentional or accidental. In planning, performing and evaluating the audit work, the auditor considers the risk of material misstatement arising from such breaches of trust.

The auditor considers the possibility that the charity's records of incoming resources to which it is legally entitled may be incomplete as a result of fraud. A common type of fraud against charities is the diversion of donations to bank or building society accounts that they do not control. Sources of audit evidence as to whether incoming resources from appeals and other 'non-routine' sources have been fully recorded can involve the assessment and testing of internal controls, and comparison of donations actually received by the charity with past results for similar appeals, to budgets and to statistics for response rates for charities in general.

PN 11 identifies certain features of charities which may increase the risk of fraud. These include:

(a) widespread branches or operations, such as those established in response to emergency appeals in countries where there is no effective system of law and order;
(b) the use of volunteers and/or inexperienced staff;
(c) transactions (income and expenditure) often undertaken in cash;
(d) unpredictable patterns of giving (in cash, by cheque, and through donations in kind) by members of the public, in terms of both timing and point of donation;
(e) the limited involvement of trustees in key decision making or monitoring;
(f) inconsistent regulation across international borders, and
(g) international transfer of funds.

Reviewing the minutes of meetings of the board of trustees, finance committee and audit committee helps the auditor evaluate whether any fraud risk factors are present.

A particular difficulty in applying analytical procedures to the audit of charities is that certain items in the financial statements can be very difficult to predict. The usefulness of individual procedures depends on the scale and nature of activities undertaken, but examples of measures that can be adopted include:

- comparison of actual income and expenditure to previous years' figures and trends;
- comparison of actual to budgeted results;
- comparison of actual expenditure to the auditor's own estimate of the expenditure that would be reasonable for the particular transaction under review;
- comparison of results of an individual branch to those of similar branches of the main charity;
- checking charity shops' sales revenue between different periods (for example, monthly), and against other shops operating in similar locations;
- analysis of efficiency ratios, such as staff or administration costs as a percentage of benefits delivered or grants made, or the ratio of operating costs to income (in this respect, care needs to be taken to compare the results of charities of similar sizes, since larger charities tend to benefit from economies of scale), and
- comparison of actual cash donations received as a result of fundraising activities with the amount that could be expected on the basis of charity statistics, if any are available.

It is likely to be helpful to analyse voluntary income into its different sources and then design analytical techniques appropriate to each source. For example, funds can be raised through television or radio appeals, street collections, trading activities, special events, telephone canvassing and postal appeals. The income raised through special events may be predicted and controlled through

Audit of charities

budgeting, whereas industry statistics and the charity's own past experience may provide a useful indication of the amount likely to be raised from a postal appeal.

In situations where there is suspicion of money laundering, the Serious Organised Crime Agency (SOCA) will need to be informed. Auditors have reporting obligations under the Proceeds of Crime Act 2002 and the Money Laundering Regulations 2007 to report knowledge or suspicion of money laundering offences.

23.10 Audit evidence

Auditors must collect sufficient appropriate audit evidence to enable them to form conclusions on which to draw their audit opinion. In this section, emphasis is placed upon the forms of audit evidence which should be collected in order to address the risk characteristics and planning considerations that have been discussed earlier.

23.10.1 Sources and completeness of income

The income of charities depends upon a number of different sources, ranging from grants by government departments to occasional cash donations by members of the public in response to street collections. Whilst it is the trustees' responsibility to safeguard the assets and income of the charity, the voluntary nature of some elements of its income raises considerations concerning the methods available to the trustees for the purposes of ensuring that all income to which the charity is entitled is correctly accounted for. These considerations differ from those in commercial concerns: the amount of voluntary donations cannot be determined in advance, nor can a charity be regarded as necessarily entitled to funds, even when the amounts can be predicted, before they are donated to it. Trustees of a charity cannot be held responsible for the security of money or other assets that are intended for its use until that money or assets are within the control of the charity.

The most effective source of audit evidence regarding the completeness of income is from the operation of the charity's system of internal control. The auditors should document the income recording systems, identify the controls within the system, and perform tests on these controls to ascertain if the controls are effective. Controls on which the auditors could seek to place reliance would include the following:

1 Controls over postal receipts
    (a) unopened mail to be kept securely;
    (b) incoming post to be opened in the presence of at least two people;
    (c) maintenance of a post log;
    (d) recording of cheques and cash received;
    (e) checking to agree paying-in slips with the record of receipts, and

(f) regular bank reconciliations to ensure that recorded receipts are in fact paid into the bank account.
2. Controls over street and similar cash collections
   (a) collecting boxes to be individually numbered, sealed and controlled, and
   (b) collections to be counted in the presence of the collector and receipted.
3. Controls over fundraising events
   (a) separate records to be kept for each event;
   (b) procedures for controlling cash and cheque receipts similar to those for cash collections, and
   (c) use of pre-numbered tickets for events when tickets are sold, and reconciliation of those to recorded income.

Audit evidence for the completeness of income may also be drawn from using internal historical data as a guide to the level of income that may be expected from the charity's various fundraising activities. Assurance may also be drawn from assessing and placing reliance upon the budgeting and internal management reporting procedures of the charity.

Receipts from legacies

The auditors must ensure that the charity's accounting policy has been consistently applied. Usually, legacies are recognised on a receipts basis, which is a departure from the strict principles of accruals accounting. However, such an approach can be justified on the grounds of uncertainty as to the timing and amount of the receipts, as well as of prudence.

Evidence as to the completeness of legacies can be obtained from review of minutes and from placing reliance on the charity's controls over cash receipts.

Receipts from fundraisers

If the charity makes use of external fundraisers, the auditors should check the fundraising agreement (which is required by the Charities Act 1992) and any other relevant documentation, to ascertain the basis on which the receipts due to the charity are to be computed and when these funds were transferred to the charity.

Receipts from branches, associates and supporters' associations

The auditors should ascertain the nature of the relationship between the charity and its branches and other associated organisations to determine the basis on which funds are raised for the charity and how the funds are to be remitted.

If control over fundraising events is imposed by the main charity, the auditors should identify the relevant controls and seek to place reliance upon them. If funds are raised by an associated body that is not controlled by the main charity, the same control conditions apply as for other donations. Audit reliance can be obtained from the past history of volume and timing of receipts from associated bodies. The auditors may also seek to request associate bodies to confirm directly to them details of the amounts remitted.

Income from grants

In the case of grant-funded charities, an examination of the grant applications and correspondence is a useful way of verifying completeness of income. It may also be possible to obtain direct confirmation of the amounts receivable from the grant provider.

Non-cash donations

Satisfactory operation of internal controls may enable the auditors to obtain sufficient appropriate audit evidence as to the recognition and measurement of donations made by way of goods, other assets or services. The trustees of a charity should develop procedures for recording donations in kind and ensure that the policy for valuing the assets or services received is consistent with the SORP. The basis of any valuation of non-cash donations should be clearly stated in the notes to the financial statements and consistently applied. The auditors consider whether the policy is reasonable in the circumstances and has been properly applied.

Loss of income through fraud

Auditors consider the possibility that the charity's records of income to which it is legally entitled may be incomplete as a result of fraud. A common type of fraud against charities is the diversion of donations to bank or building society accounts that they do not control. Sources of audit evidence as to whether income from appeals and other 'non-routine' sources has been fully recorded can involve the assessment and testing of internal controls, and a comparison of donations actually received by the charity with past results for similar appeals and statistics for response rates for charities in general.

23.10.2 Expenditure

Verification of the accuracy and validity of the charity's expenditure should include consideration that the charity's expenditure is properly applied in accordance with the terms of the governing document. If funds are expended on non-charitable activities, tax reliefs may be forfeited and legal actions may be brought against the trustees.

If the charity has made donations of goods, services or other funds, the auditors must obtain evidence that these were for charitable purposes that fall within the charity's objectives. Audit evidence can be obtained from the assessment of the charity's controls for making and awarding donations, and for monitoring the use of the donation by the recipients.

In some cases, expenditure may be difficult to test. For example, the charity may operate in a war or disaster zone or it may undertake a significant amount of cash expenditure and hold few supporting records for this expenditure.

23.10.3 Branches, subsidiaries and overseas operations

If the charity does not fully control a branch or an associated operation, the auditors must consider the nature of the controls that have been instituted to ensure that the assets and income arising from these operations are recognised and safeguarded, and that the information received is reliable. Returns made by the branch to the charity should be reviewed by the auditors to ensure that all returns have been received and reviewed by the charity, and any matters arising have been addressed.

Where a branch, subsidiary or associated operation which is to be included in the main accounts of the charity is audited or examined by another auditor or examiner, the principal auditor should seek to obtain sufficient appropriate audit evidence by:

- issuing instructions to the secondary auditors or examiners, detailing the scope of the work to be performed and the form of the report to be issued;
- issuing a standard questionnaire for completion by the secondary auditors or examiners, and
- requesting, direct from the secondary auditors or examiners, a report of the principal matters arising and conclusions.

If the reports from the other auditor or examiner indicate potential problems and in particular qualified opinions, which in aggregate could cover a substantial part of the charity's transactions, the principal auditors should assess whether it is possible for additional audit procedures to be performed, in order to obtain further evidence so that an unqualified opinion can be given.

23.10.4 Fixed assets (including investments)

Evidence must be obtained that the fixed assets of the charity exist and that none are omitted from the financial statements. In particular, auditors must ensure that all donated fixed assets have been recognised in the financial statements, both as an asset and as income, and that the value given to the asset is appropriate. Evidence needs to be obtained that the charity has title to its fixed assets, by inspection of deeds, invoices or from review of the terms under which gifts were

Audit of charities

received. If an asset has not been capitalised, because it is deemed to be inalienable or historic or because neither a cost nor a market value can be attached to it, the auditors should assess whether the treatment is appropriate and whether the disclosures regarding the treatment in the financial statements are sufficient.

Audit evidence as regards investments will include ensuring that:

(a) the trustees have title to all investments;
(b) all investment transactions are properly authorised;
(c) the charity is complying with any constitutional restrictions on its investment powers;
(d) investment income is complete, and
(e) all investment gains or losses (realised and unrealised) and income are allocated to the correct fund.

23.10.5 Bank reports for audit purposes

In December 2007, the APB issued Practice Note 16 (Revised), which recommends that bank audit letters include the names of all the legal entities covered by the request, together with the main account sort code and account number for each of the entities. The Practice Note provides examples of the new standard request forms that should be adopted (see Annex 1). This Practice Note applies to accounting periods beginning on or after 26 December 2007.

23.10.6 Charitable loans

If the charity has made loans of a charitable nature, then doubt may arise as to their recoverability. In particular, provision would be expected if the loan is unsecured, has 'soft' terms or there are doubts as to the whereabouts of the recipient.

23.10.7 Application of funds

Evidence must be obtained that the charity has properly accounted for its individual funds in accordance with the terms of its constitution and the terms of trust for the individual funds. The auditors should ensure that all funds are correctly classified and that they have a correct record of the terms of each fund. Checks should be performed to ensure that the movements on each fund are authorised and properly recorded. If a fund has ceased during the year, evidence must be obtained that any remaining balances have been properly expended or transferred. Auditors should ensure that all income and expenditure, and assets and liabilities have been correctly allocated between relevant funds.

23.10.8 Analytical review

Analytical procedures may prove to be an efficient and effective source of audit evidence because certain of the transactions of a charity, and particularly many of a charity's sources of income, lack detailed documentary support. There may also be a high degree of predictability over the income and expenditure of a charity, with both the major income-raising programmes and expenditure projects placed well in advance. The administrative expenditure of the charity may be relatively fixed and therefore straightforward to predict.

PN 11 suggests that the following analytical procedures could be used to generate relevant audit evidence:

(a) comparison of actual income and expenditure to previous years' figures and trends;
(b) comparison of actual to budgeted results;
(c) comparison of actual expenditure to the auditors' own estimate of expenditure that would be reasonable for the particular transaction under review;
(d) comparison of results between branches;
(e) checking the sales revenue of shops and trading activities between different periods;
(f) comparison of actual cash donations received as a result of fundraising activities with the amount that could have been expected on the basis of available charity statistics, and
(g) analysis of efficiency ratios (for example, staff cost as a percentage of benefits received.

23.11 Audit completion

23.11.1 Representation letters

As with any audit, the auditors should obtain a representation letter. In the case of a charity, the usual source is the trustees. In many charities executive management is separate from the trustees – in these situations, the letter of representation must still be received from the trustees as they have the responsibility for preparing and presenting the financial statements. An example letter, shown below, has been drafted from ISA 580 (*Management representations*). The example letter needs to be adapted to the charity's specific circumstances, which means that some points will need to be deleted and others added.

Example letter

Goldwins
Chartered Accountants
75 Maygrove Road
West Hampstead
London NW6 2EG

Audit of charities

Dear Sirs

Representation Letter

This representation letter is provided in connection with your audit of the financial statements for the year ended 31 December 2008 for the purpose of expressing an opinion as to whether the financial statements give a true and fair view of the financial position and of the results of the operations for the year then ended in accordance with the financial reporting framework. We acknowledge our responsibility for the fair presentation of the financial statements in accordance with the financial reporting framework.

We confirm, to the best of our knowledge and belief, the following representations:

- There have been no irregularities involving management or employees who have a significant role in internal control or that could have a material effect on the financial statements.
- All books of account and supporting documentation and all minutes of meetings of shareholders and the board of directors have been made available to you.
- The financial statements are free of material misstatement, including omissions.
- The entity has complied with all aspects of contractual agreements that could have a material effect on the financial statements in the event of non-compliance. There has been no non-compliance with requirements of regulatory authorities that could have a material effect on the financial statements in the event of non-compliance.
- We have no plans or intentions that may materially alter the carrying value or classification of assets and liabilities reflected in the financial statements.
- We have no plans to abandon lines of product/services or other plans or intentions that will result in any excess or obsolete inventory, and no inventory is stated at an amount in excess of net realisable value.
- The entity has satisfactory title to all assets and there are no liens or encumbrances on the entity's assets, except for those disclosed in the financial statements.
- We have recorded or disclosed, as appropriate, all liabilities, both actual and contingent.
- There have been no events subsequent to period end which require adjustment of or disclosure in the financial statements or notes.
- We acknowledge our responsibility for the design and implementation of internal control to prevent and detect fraud.
- We have disclosed the results of our assessment of the risk that the financial statements may be materially misstated as a result of fraud.

Audit completion

- We have disclosed our knowledge of fraud or suspected fraud affecting the entity involving management, employees who have significant roles in internal control or others where the fraud could have a material effect on the financial statements.
- We have disclosed our knowledge of any allegations of fraud, or suspected fraud, affecting the entity's financial statements communicated by employees, former employees, analysts, regulators or others.
- We have disclosed all known actual or possible non-compliance with laws and regulations whose effects should be considered when preparing financial statements, including the actual or contingent consequences which may arise from the non-compliance.
- We have corrected all misstatements brought to our attention by the auditor.
- We have disclosed all relevant information regarding the identification of related parties and the adequacy of related party disclosures in the financial statements.
- Our plans for the future justify our belief the entity is a going concern.
- All income has been recorded, all restricted funds have been properly applied, all constructive obligations for grants have been recognised and all correspondence with regulators has been made available to the auditor, including any serious incident reports.

Yours faithfully

....

DIRECTOR

Date

The final bullet point follows PN 11 recommendation that charity auditors may need to additionally confirm.

Examples of other matters where confirmation of representations may be necessary:

- material accounting estimates – confirming basis of estimation;
- lack of evidence – material representations where no other evidence available;
- trustees' or directors' opinions – confirmations of opinions
- provisions for doubtful debts;
- contentious legal matters;
- accounting policies – confirming appropriately adopted and disclosed; and
- bank or loan facilities – confirming no breaches of covenant or terms.

23.11.2 Review of financial statements

The objective of the review of the financial statements is to consider the overall view presented, together with the conclusions formed on the audit evidence collected, to ensure that there is a reasonable basis for the audit opinion.

Audit of charities

The view conveyed by the financial statements should be consistent with and reflect the operations of the charity during the year and the auditor's knowledge of the charity. There should be consistency between the financial statements and non-financial information issued by the charity and with the impression of the charity's activities conveyed by internal documents such as the minutes of meetings of its trustees and committees.

Other points which should be considered when reviewing the financial statements include:

- disclosure of income from fundraising activities;
- the capitalising of expenditure on fixed assets;
- apportionment of administrative expenses;
- recognition of income from donations and legacies;
- treatment of exceptional items, and
- presentation of special or irregular income or expenditure.

23.11.3 Going concern

Auditors need to consider the going concern of the charity on which they are reporting and the appropriateness of any disclosures that the trustees have made with regard to going concern. As with any entity, the auditors may need to refer to these disclosures in their report or qualify their opinion.

Basis for preparation of financial statements

In considering factors relating to a charity's status as a going concern, it is necessary to take account of the particular circumstances of that charity which may affect its ability to continue its activities. Auditors consider the availability of future funding and whether uncertainties exist which require disclosure in the financial statements. The charity's purpose may also require consideration: some charitable activities are focused on a specific purpose and, once this is achieved, the charity may cease to operate.

Circumstances where a charity may cease to be a going concern

The following list gives examples of conditions that can give grounds for concern that a charity may not be a going concern:

- inability to finance its operations from its own resources;
- a decision by the trustees to curtail or cease activities;
- transfer to, or takeover by, another entity of the charity's activities;
- loss of essential resources or key staff;
- existence of tax liabilities that cannot be met from existing resources;

- loss of clients (for example, where a public authority ends a practice or contract to refer (and pay for) clients to the charity);
- loss of operating licence (for example, for a residential care home);
- significant changes in strategy of major funders, and
- significant decline in donations by the public.

There are many indicators of potential going concern problems, such as an excess of liabilities over assets. Although the most significant factor ensuring the future viability of many charities is public goodwill, this is difficult, if not impossible, to value and cannot be included in the balance sheet, nor can auditors rely solely on the existence of goodwill as evidence to support the going concern assumption.

The 'credit crunch' and the resulting recessionary times (see **Chapter 32**) have placed great strains on charities' income streams. Auditors need to be particularly alert to this issue, and it is quite likely that going concern issues will feature in current audit reports. In December 2008 the APB issued Bulletin 2008/10 on going concern issues during the current economic conditions This recognises that the economic environment leads to uncertainty over:

- bank lending intentions and the availability of finance more generally;
- the impact of the recession on a company's own business, and
- the impact of the recession on customers and suppliers.

One consequence is expected to be an increase in the disclosures in annual reports and accounts about going concern and liquidity risk. Auditors will need to ensure that they fully consider going concern assessments and only refer to going concern in their auditor's reports when appropriate.

The operations of charities

The timing of cash flows may present special considerations in the audit of charities. This is particularly true of charities receiving grants of money from central government, as monies are only voted on an annual basis even though there may be a working presumption that funding will continue for future years. Some charities may be unable to finance long-term commitments other than through short-term fundraising. There may be difficulties or delays in converting current assets into cash – for example, where a grant is obtained for reimbursement of expenses already incurred but is not paid for a number of months.

It may also be difficult for charities to cut back on a project or grant funding in the event of a liquidity problem, because it may not have the discretion to do so under the terms of its own funding. It is possible for a charity to have an apparently large bank balance and yet to be unable to meet general liabilities as they fall due, because the balance in question belongs to one or more restricted funds.

It is particularly important to consider whether the balance sheet of the charity includes restricted funds or similar assets that cannot be applied to meet the general liabilities of the charity. Auditors should also check whether short-term liabilities are matched by short-term, unrestricted assets, and whether any commitments for future expenditure are reasonable.

Assessment of a charity's financial strength or weakness is complicated by the uncertainty of future income to which most charities are subject. Regular or predictable income, from sources such as deeds of covenant, endowments and investments, forms a comparatively small part of most charities' revenues, and it would be impossible to obtain confirmation of future giving from donors. Charities generally see themselves as competing for scarce resources, and the impact of competition, such as another charity operating in the same sector or area, can be profound. Other factors outside the control of charities are constraints on spending by members of the public, either through loss of personal income, or through a change in spending patterns.

Obtaining evidence

The Trustees' Annual Report may contain an indication of future expected income based on past donations or patterns of giving. In addition to this information, the auditors consider the level of skills available to the charity in its trustees and staff, and their track record and commitment. The auditors' opinion on the financial statements is only qualified if they consider that:

- the scope of their work is limited by an inadequate or inappropriate consideration of going concern by the trustees; or
- there is insufficient disclosure of relevant circumstances to enable the financial statements to give a true and fair view, or
- the basis used in the preparation of the financial statements was inappropriate.

Where there is fundamental uncertainty about the future viability of the charity, but the auditors consider that both the measures taken by the trustees in relation to assessment of going concern and disclosure of any matters needed for a proper understanding of the circumstances were adequate, their opinion would not be qualified in respect of going concern. In these circumstances, the auditors include an explanatory paragraph in the basis of opinion section of their report.

In considering going concern, it may be helpful for the auditors to include the following points in discussions with trustees:

(a) the nature of management information systems covering future income and expenditure;
(b) the level of forecast future expenditure, divided between that which is committed and that which is discretionary;
(c) the level of 'known' future income (deriving from sources such as endowments, investments, and deeds of covenant – assessment of the latter making allowances for deeds terminated due to unforeseen circumstances);
(d) where the charity relies for a significant part of its funding on one or more major institutional donors or granting authorities such as local authorities, whether it would be practicable to obtain a degree of comfort from such funders as to their future support for the charity;
(e) shortfall of identifiable future income on forecast expenditure needing to be made up by voluntary donations of cash or other resources;
(f) past patterns of income and expenditure;
(g) lists of projects supported, or awards made, in the year and planned for the following year;
(h) the level of uncommitted reserves remaining available to the charity;
(i) comparison of previous budgets to actual performance;
(j) the reasonableness of the assumptions underlying the current budgets;
(k) any reliance on support by the charity's bankers, major donors, or public authorities;
(l) concentration on provision of services to a particular category of beneficiaries or objects for which future funding or demand may be limited, and
(m) any special operating licences or similar conditions.

23.11.4 Related parties

The principles of FRS 8: *Related Party Disclosures* apply to charities, together with a series of disclosures given in the SORP in respect of transactions with trustees and connected persons. The auditors consider the steps taken by the trustees to identify and record related party transactions and remain alert, in carrying out their audit, for evidence of such transactions that are not included in the information provided by the trustees.

It is a fundamental principle of trust law that a trustee should not benefit directly or indirectly from his or her trust. This means that neither charity trustees nor persons connected with them should transact business with the charity (or with any company owned by the charity), except where the transaction, and any benefit (including remuneration) derived from it, is either expressly permitted by the charity's governing document, or permission has been obtained from an appropriate authority (for example, in the case of charities based in England or Wales, the Charity Commission).

23.11.5 Other information presented with the financial statements

Other information may be issued by the charity in a combined publication with the audited financial statements. Auditors should check such information to ensure that there are no inconsistencies which could either confuse readers of the accounts, or cast doubt on the reliability of the audited information. Examples include:

(a) statements by the patron, president, chairman of the trustees and/or chief executive of the charity;
(b) an operating and financial review;
(c) a statement concerning arrangements for corporate governance, based on the Combined Code of Best Practice for listed companies;
(d) a treasurer's report;
(e) financial summaries, and
(f) projections of future expenditure based on planned activity.

Additional care will be needed where, for example, the annual report and the financial statements are prepared at the same time but by different personnel, so that their content is largely independent.

The SORP requires charity trustees to state in their report that the major identified risks to which the charity is exposed have been reviewed and that systems have been established to mitigate such risks. If the auditor becomes aware of any apparent misstatements or inconsistencies in other information published together with the audited financial statements, he or she should seek to resolve them. Whilst auditors are not expected to verify any risk management statement made by trustees, they are likely to become aware of the steps taken by the trustees to identify and mitigate identified financial risks through their work in assessing audit risk. They may also become aware of non-financial risks during the course of their audit. If, after discussion with the trustees, any significant misstatement or apparent inconsistency identified by the auditors in relation to a corporate governance or risk management statement remains in the Trustees' Annual Report, the auditors should consider reporting this in the opinion section of their report. It should be noted that, as this does not give rise to a qualified audit opinion on the financial statements, the auditors' comments may be included under the heading 'other matters'. Where trustees include information concerning corporate governance in a charity's annual report, they may request the auditors to review and report on that information.

23.11.6 Communication of audit matter with those charged with governance

ISA 260 requires the auditor to always issue written communications to those charged with governance – that is, the trustees – even if the content of the communication is limited to merely explaining there is nothing the auditor wishes to draw attention to. For the communication to be effective, it must be two-way and not exclusively in writing.

Examples of what would be included in such a communication include any material weaknesses in the system of internal control and any breaches in the administration of the charity.

23.12 Audit reports

Bulletin 2009/2 was issued in April 2009 and supersedes Bulletin 2006/6. It is effective for accounting periods ending on or after 5 April 2009. It deals with a number of changes to the auditor's report as a result of s. 495 of the Companies Act 2006. There is now a so-called 'three-part-opinion'. The auditor will have to give an opinion as to whether the annual accounts:

- give a true and fair view of the state of affairs and profit or loss for the year;
- have been properly prepared in accordance with the relevant financial reporting framework, and
- have been prepared in accordance with the requirements of the Companies Act 2006.

The responsibilities section of the auditor's report has been changed to reflect reference to the directors' responsibility to not approve the accounts unless they are satisfied that they show a true and fair view (s. 393 of the Companies Act 2006).

Auditors will also have to report, by exception, on (amongst other matters):

- whether reference to adequate (previously 'proper') accounting records (s. 498 of the Companies Act 2006), have been kept, and
- reference to disclosure of directors' remuneration to include benefits, pensions and compensation for loss of office (ss. 412 and 498 of the Companies Act 2006).

The form and content of the auditors' report on the financial statements of a charity should follow the general principles of ISA 700 (*The Auditors' report on financial statements*), whether the charity is a company or not. A review of the detailed requirements of the reports is given below, followed by examples of unqualified reports in respect of:

(a) company charities, and
(b) non-company charities.

23.12.1 Review of contents of audit reports

Addressee

The audit report of a charity that is a company should be addressed to the members, as this is a requirement of the Companies Act. In respect of non-company charities, the Regulations specify that the report should be addressed to the trustees, unless the auditors have been appointed by the Charity Commission – in which case, the report should be addressed to the Commission.

Statement of trustees' responsibilities

Although the general duties of charity trustees are identical regardless of the constitution, the specific responsibilities will vary according to the constitution and legal status of the charity.

In respect of company charities, the duties of the trustees are specified in the Companies Act, and the form of responsibility statement recommended in ISA 700 should normally be used.

Where a charity is not subject to regulation, apart from that applicable to charities, the form of words set out below should either be included in the text of the auditors' report or the report should contain a reference to the page in the package of report and accounts where it is situated. (See section **2.5** of Chapter 2.)

Responsibilities of the auditors

The responsibilities of the auditors will be defined by the reporting regime to which the charity is subject and the form of opinion that the auditors are required to give.

In respect of a company charity, the auditors are reporting under the Companies Act to the members and the responsibility statement set out in ISA 700 should be given.

If the charity is non-company, the responsibility statement should state what the auditor is required to report upon, and specify that the auditors have been appointed under and are reporting in accordance with the requirements of the Charities Act 1993.

Basis of opinion

Whether the auditors have been appointed under and are reporting in accordance with the Companies Act or the Charities Act 1993, the basis of forming the opinion is essentially the same. The auditors are required to apply International Auditing Standards to form the opinion and they have similar rights under both Acts to receive all required information and explanations.

Opinion

The wording of the opinion paragraph must reflect the regulations to which the charity is subject.

Company charities

The auditors must give an opinion on the truth and fairness of the view given of the state of affairs (balance sheet) of the charity at the reporting date and of its incoming resources and application of resources (SOFA) for the period to that date. An opinion must also be given on the truth and fairness of the view given by the income and expenditure account for the period to the reporting date. The financial statements must be properly prepared in accordance with the primary legislation – that is, the Companies Act.

Non-company charities

The auditors' opinion differs from that for a company charity because the Regulations specify that an opinion is required on the truth and fairness of the view given by the balance sheet and the SOFA. No mention of income and expenditure is required. The financial statements must be properly prepared in accordance with the primary legislation – the Charities Act 1993.

Signature and date

The normal requirements regarding the signature and the date of the auditors' report apply to charities. Whether the charity is constituted as a company or is non-company, the designation 'Registered Auditors' must be used. For accounting periods beginning on or after 6 April 2008, the auditor must sign as Senior Statutory Auditor for company charities only (see section **30.5** of Chapter 30).

23.12.2 Example audit reports

In March 2009, the APB published Bulletin 2009/1 (*Auditor's Reports – Supplementary Guidance for Auditors of Charities with 31 March 2009 Year Ends*). This much-awaited guidance made it very clear, however, that it referred only to accounting periods beginning on or after 1 April 2008 but beginning before 6 April 2008 – that is, 31 March 2009 year ends.

The Companies Act 2006 applies to company charities whose accounting periods begin on or after 6 April 2008, and the APB have stated that separate guidance will be published later in 2009 for these charities. It is hoped that this subsequent guidance will also refer to group accounts and FRSSE adoption. The two examples below are taken from Bulletin 2009/1, but it must be emphasised that these example reports are only applicable for 31 March 2009 year ends.

Audit of charities

For accounting periods beginning on or after 1 April 2008, company charities that are 'small' for the purposes of the Companies Act and do not exceed the Companies Act 1985 audit threshold (see section **30.8.2** of Chapter 30) may take advantage of audit exemption from the Companies Act audit, but will nevertheless require an audit under the Charities Act if they are above the Charities Act audit threshold. Any election to take audit exemption under the Companies Act 1985 will require a statement to this effect on the charity's balance sheet.

If a company charity is not 'small, its audit will remain under the Companies Act, as was previously the case.

Example 1 – *'Small' company charity registered only in England and Wales, audited under the Charities Act 1993*

INDEPENDENT AUDITORS' REPORT TO THE MEMBERS OF XYZ CHARITY LIMITED

We have audited the financial statements of (name of charity) for the year ended 31 March 2009 which comprise the [state primary financial statements such as the Statement of Financial Activities, the Summary Income and Expenditure Account, the Balance Sheet, the Cash Flow Statement] and the related notes. The financial statements have been prepared under the accounting policies set out therein.

Respective responsibilities of trustees and auditors

The responsibilities of the trustees (who are also the directors of the company for the purposes of company law) for preparing the Trustees' Annual Report and the financial statements in accordance with applicable law and United Kingdom Accounting Standards (United Kingdom Generally Accepted Accounting Practice) are set out in the Statement of Trustees' Responsibilities.

The trustees have elected for financial statements not to be audited in accordance with the Companies Act 1985. Accordingly, we have been appointed as auditors under section 43 of the Charities Act 1993 and report in accordance with regulations made under section 44 of that Act.

Our responsibility is to audit the financial statements in accordance with relevant legal and regulatory requirements and International Standards on Auditing (UK and Ireland).

We report to you our opinion as to whether the financial statements give a true and fair view and are properly prepared in accordance with the Charities Act 1993. We also report to you if, in our opinion, the information given in the Trustees' Annual Report is not consistent with those financial statements, if the charity has not kept sufficient accounting records, if the charity's financial statements are not in agreement with these accounting records or if we have not received all the information and explanations we require for our audit.

We read the Trustees' Annual Report and consider the implications for our report if we become aware of any apparent misstatements within in.

Basis of audit opinion

We conducted our audit in accordance with International Standards on Auditing (UK and Ireland) issued by the Auditing Practices Board. An audit includes examination, on a test basis, of evidence relevant to the amounts and disclosures in the financial statements. It also includes an assessment of the significant estimates and judgements made by the trustees in the preparation of the financial statements, and of whether the accounting policies are appropriate to the charity's circumstances, consistently applied and adequately disclosed.

We planned and performed our audit so as to obtain all the information and explanations which we considered necessary in order to provide us with sufficient evidence to give reasonable assurance that the financial statements are free from material misstatement, whether caused by fraud or other irregularity or error. In forming our opinion we also evaluated the overall adequacy of the presentation of information in the financial statements.

Opinion

In our opinion;

- the financial statements give a true and fair view, in accordance with United Kingdom Generally Accepted Accounting Practice, of the state of affairs of the charity as at 31 March 2009, and of its incoming resources and application of resources, for the year then ended; and
- the financial statements have been properly prepared in accordance with the Charities Act 1993.

[Name of firm]

Registered Auditors

[Town/City]

Date:

Where the financial statements are published with surround information in addition to the Trustees' Annual Report, the paragraph below replaces the paragraph 'We read the Trustees' Annual Report and consider the implications for our report if we become aware of any apparent misstatements within it.'

[We read other information contained in the Annual Report, and consider whether it is consistent with the audited financial statements. The other

Audit of charities

information comprises only [list all documents published with the financial statements such as the Chairman's Statement and the Trustees' Annual Report]. We consider that implications for our report if we become aware of any apparent misstatements or material inconsistencies with the financial statements. Our responsibilities do not extend to other information].

Example 2 – *Non-company charity registered in England and Wales*

INDEPENDENT AUDITOR'S REPORT TO THE TRUSTEES OF XYZ CHARITY

We have audited the financial statements of (name of charity) for the year ended 31 March 2009 which comprise [state primary financial statements such as the Statement of Financial Activities, the Balance Sheet, the Cash Flow Statement] and the related notes. The financial statements have been prepared under the accounting policies set out therein.

Respective responsibilities of trustees and auditors

The trustees' responsibilities for preparing the Trustees' Annual Report and the financial statements in accordance with applicable law and United Kingdom Accounting Standards (United Kingdom Generally Accepted Accounting Practice) are set out in the Statement of Trustees' Responsibilities.

We have been appointed as auditors under section 43 of the Charities Act 1993 and report in accordance with regulations made under that Act. Our responsibility is to audit the financial statements in accordance with relevant legal and regulatory requirements and International Standards on Auditing (UK and Ireland).

We report to you our opinion as to whether the financial statements give a true and fair view and are properly prepared in accordance with the Charities Act 1993. We also report to you if, in our opinion, the information given in the Trustees' Annual Report is not consistent with those financial statements, if the charity has not kept sufficient accounting records, if the charity's financial statements are not in agreement with these accounting records or if we have not received all the information and explanations we require for our audit.

We read the Trustees' Annual Report and consider the implications for our report if we become aware of any apparent misstatements within it.

Basis of audit opinion

We conducted our audit in accordance with International Standards on Auditing (UK and Ireland) issued by the Auditing Practices Board. An audit includes examination, on a test basis, of evidence relevant to the amounts and disclosures in the financial statements. It also includes an assessment of the significant estimates and judgements made by the trustees in the preparation of the financial statements, and of whether the accounting policies are appropriate to the charity's circumstances, consistently applied and adequately disclosed.

We planned and performed our audit so as to obtain all the information and explanations which we considered necessary in order to provide us with sufficient evidence to give reasonable assurance that the financial statements are free from material misstatement, whether caused by fraud or other irregularity or error. In forming our opinion we also evaluated the overall adequacy of the presentation of information in the financial statements.

Opinion

In our opinion;

- the financial statements give a true and fair view, in accordance with United Kingdom Generally Accepted Accounting Practice, of the state of affairs of the charity as at 31 March 2009, and of its incoming resources and application of resources, for the year then ended; and
- the financial statements have been properly prepared in accordance with the Charities Act 1993.

[Name of firm]

Registered Auditors

[Town/City]

Date:

Where the financial statements are published with surround information in addition to the Trustees' Annual Report, the paragraph below replaces the paragraph 'We read the Trustees' Annual Report and consider the implications for our report if we become aware of any apparent misstatements within it.'

[We read the other information contained in the Annual Report, and consider whether it is consistent with the audited financial statements. The other information comprises only [list all documents published with the financial statements such as the Chairman's Statement and the Trustees' Annual Report]. We consider the implications for our report if we become aware of any apparent misstatements or material inconsistencies with the financial statements. Our responsibilities do not extend to other information].

23.12.3 Receipts and payments accounts

A non-company charity whose gross income is not more than £100,000 per annum may prepare receipts and payments accounts rather than full accruals accounts. If such a charity elects to receive an audit of its accounts the audit report reflects, with the statement of trustees' responsibilities, that the accounts have been prepared in accordance with the Charity Commission's guidance for smaller charities. The auditors are required, in this situation, to report on the presentation of the assets and liabilities, at the reporting date, and the receipts and payments for the period to that date, as well as on the proper preparation of the accounts. There is no requirement to report on the accounts in terms of their truth and fairness.

23.12.4 Fundamental uncertainties and qualified opinions

The reporting of a matter arising from the audit of a charity which gives rise to a fundamental uncertainty or of circumstances which require the auditors to present a qualified opinion should follow the principles of ISA 700.

23.12.5 Reports on summarised accounts

Where a charity prepares summarised accounts, the SORP requires that there should be a statement from the auditor stating whether or not the summarised accounts are consistent with the full accounts. Practice Note 11 (Revised) December 2008 recommends that the report is made to the Trustees in the following form:

Independent Auditor's statement to the Trustees of XYZ Charity

We have examined the summarised financial statements for the year ended ... set out on pages ...

Respective responsibilities of trustees and auditor

The trustees are responsible for preparing the summarised financial statements in accordance with applicable United Kingdom law and the recommendations of the Charities SORP.

Our responsibility is to report to you our opinion on the consistency of the summarised financial statements (within the summarised annual report) with the full annual financial statements and the Trustees' Annual Report.

(We also read the other information contained in the summarised annual report and consider the implications for our report if we become aware of any apparent misstatements or material inconsistencies with the summarised financial statements.)

We conducted our work in accordance with Bulletin 2008/3 issued by the Auditing Practices Board.

Opinion

In our opinion the summarised financial statements are consistent [are not consistent] with the full annual financial statements and Trustees' Annual Report of XYZ Charity for the year ended. (in the following respects ...)

Statutory auditor   *Address*

Date

23.13 Reporting to the Charity Commission

The new Regulations require the auditors of both company and non-company charities to communicate to the Charity Commission certain matters of which they become aware in their capacity as auditors of the charity.

The Regulations specify that auditors are required to communicate matters which are of 'material significance' in the context of the Charity Commission's powers to institute enquiries or act for the protection of charities. Matters which are of 'material significance' will primarily arise from the identification of a significant loss or misapplication of a charity's property or funds, or from the identification of a significant risk to the charity's property or funds resulting from maladministration or misuse of assets.

The Charity Commission does not expect to receive reports on minor matters which have been resolved and where the charity has suffered no loss.

Appendix 5 of PN 11 (Revised) December 2008 lists eight examples (which are the same for Independent Examiners) of 'material significance' as set out below.

1. Matters suggesting dishonesty or fraud involving a significant loss of, or a major risk to, charitable funds or assets. Examples include:
   (a) evidence of false accounting, theft or misappropriation of assets by any charity trustee or senior employee
   (b) evidence of a material application of charitable funds for a non-charitable purpose
   (c) evidence that gives reasonable cause to doubt the honesty or integrity of a charity trustee or the trustee body
   (d) evidence that any charity trustee is a person disqualified from acting as a charity trustee under s. 72 of the Charities Act 1993 and not having obtained a waiver from disqualification (disqualification may arise from a conviction involving dishonesty or deception, undischarged bankruptcy, sequestration, a composition or arrangement with creditors, a disqualification or removal order); and

(e) evidence of a charity trustee, employee or agent knowingly or recklessly providing the Charity Commission with information which is false or misleading in a material respect (s. 11 of the Charities Act 1993).

2. Failure(s) of internal controls, including failure(s) in charity governance, that resulted in a significant loss or misappropriation of charitable funds, or which leads to significant charitable funds being put at major risk. Examples include:
   (a) evidence that the trustee body as a whole has failed to exercise proper control over the administration and management of the charity's affairs and activities, having due regard to the nature of its trusts and activities;
   (b) evidence of recklessness on the part of the trustee body as a whole giving rise to a significant risk of a material loss or misapplication of charitable funds;
   (c) absence of adequate arrangements by the charity trustees to monitor functions delegated to third parties;
   (d) uncertainty as to who are the trustees;
   (e) a lack of adequate security or control over the assets of the charity; and
   (f) the auditors being prevented from continuing with or completing the audit as a result of insufficient records being available or insufficient explanations being given in answer to questions raised.

3. Matters leading to the knowledge or suspicion that the charity or charitable funds have been used for money laundering or such funds are the proceeds of serious organised crime or that the charity is a conduit for criminal activity.

4. Matters leading to belief or suspicion that the charity, its trustees, employees or assets, have been involved in or used to support terrorism or proscribed organisations in the UK or outside of the UK.

5. Evidence suggesting that in the way the charity carries out its work relating to the care and welfare of beneficiaries, the charity's beneficiaries have been or were put at significant risk of abuse or mistreatment.

6. Significant or recurring breach(es) of either a legislative requirement or the charity's trusts. Examples include:
   (a) a significant breach of the law relating to fundraising undertaken by professional fundraisers or commercial participators. In particular a failure to make the required statement as to the method of remuneration, the failure to pay all cash and cheques so raised to the charity gross, and a failure to enter into a proper agreement with the charity (part II of the Charities Act 1992 (ss. 58–64 as amended) and the Charitable Institutions (Fund-Raising) Regulations 1994);
   (b) a material inaccuracy in the completion of an annual return made under s48 1993 Act which is not immediately corrected on identification;

(c) receipt by any charity trustee (or person connected with a trustee) of remuneration or other benefits from the assets of the charity without proper powers or consent;

(d) a charity entering into a significant transaction with a charity trustee (or person connected with a charity trustee) without proper authority which gives rise to a conflict of interest or may be to the benefit of the trustee or connected person;

(e) a significant *ex gratia* payment or waiver of entitlement given to any person connected with the charity without proper authority under s. 27 of the Charities Act 1993.

(f) a significant breach of law or regulation, not specific to a charity, that could prevent the charity from undertaking a significant part of its activities – for example, loss of registration in a residential care charity; and

(g) a reckless investment made contrary to the proper advice and investment criteria requirements of the Trustee Act 2000.

7. A deliberate or significant breach of an Order or Direction made by a charity regulator under statutory powers including suspending a charity trustee, prohibiting a particular transaction or activity or granting consent on particular terms involving significant charitable assets or liabilities.

8. The notification on ceasing to hold office or resigning from office, of those matters reported to the trustees.

23.13.1 Ceasing to hold office

In addition to the duty to report matters of material significance, the Regulations (para 35) provides that, where an auditor appointed by trustees ceases for any reason to hold office, he or she shall send

(a) to the trustees a statement of any circumstances connected with his or her ceasing to hold office which he or she considers should be brought to their attention; or, if he or she considers that there are no such circumstances, a statement that there are none, and

(b) a copy of any statement sent to the trustees under this paragraph (except a statement that there are no such circumstances) to the Charity Commission.

Matters that may require consideration in relation to this duty include:

(a) disagreement over opinions expressed or to be expressed in an auditors' report;

(b) disagreement over any disclosure made or to be made to the Charity Commission in respect of a matter of material significance;

(c) disagreement over any accounting policy, assumption, financial judgment or disclosure made in the accounts or in the preparation of the accounts;

(d) concerns over any matter which is believed to give rise to a material risk of a loss of charitable funds; and

(e) lack of co-operation or obstruction in the context of an audit.
(See section **23.16.6** below.)

23.13.2 Discussing matters of material significance with trustees

The trustees are the persons principally responsible for the management of the charity. Auditors will therefore normally bring a matter of 'material significance' to the attention of the trustees and seek their agreement on the facts and circumstances. However, where the auditors conclude that a duty to report arises they should bring the matter to the attention of the regulator without undue delay. The trustees may wish to report the matters identified to the Charity Commission themselves and detail the actions taken or to be taken. Whilst such a report from the trustees may provide valuable information, it does not relieve the auditors of the statutory duty to report directly to the Charity Commission.

The Charity Commission has indicated that where a matter that is potentially of material significance is identified by the auditors, but has already been rectified by the trustees, then a reporting duty will not arise unless there has been significant pecuniary loss to the charity or the matter casts doubt on the honesty and integrity of the trustees. If the auditors are uncertain as to whether a matter has been rectified, it would be advisable to report to the Charity Commission.

23.13.3 Auditors' right to report to the Charity Commission

In the case of charities in England and Wales, the circumstances giving rise to a duty to report are equivalent to those applicable to regulated entities in the financial sector. In the financial sector a separate statutory right (as opposed to a duty) to report to the appropriate regulator also exists and may be used by auditors. Similarly, auditors of charities may become aware of circumstances which in their opinion do not give rise to a duty to report to the Charity Commission but which should be brought to its attention. Such matters should be considered in conjunction with the ISAs and, where any report is made, auditors may rely on the protection afforded by general law.

23.13.4 Contents of a report to the Charity Commission

The Charity Commission has indicated that a report concerning a matter of material significance should be sent to the 'reporting officer' at the relevant office of the Charity Commission. The Charity Commission has indicated that a report should follow the format provided by the standard, that is to:

- state the name of the charity and its registration number;
- state that the report is made under the Regulations;

- state that the report is prepared in accordance with the ISAs;
- describe the context in which the report is given;
- describe the matter giving rise to the report;
- request that the Charity Commission confirms that the report has been received, and
- state the name of the auditors, the date of the report, the date of any oral report made to the Charity Commission and the name of the officer to whom the report was made.

Auditors are not relieved of their duty to make a written report where an oral report has been previously made to the Charity Commission or by any informal discussions of the issue with Charity Commission staff. Similarly, auditors are not relieved of their duty to report on the basis that any other party has provided relevant information, whether written or oral, to the Charity Commission.

The report sets out such information as is relevant to a proper understanding of the matter reported. It explains how the matter was identified, and the extent to which it has been investigated and discussed with the charity's trustees. The report also describes any steps taken by the trustees to rectify the reportable matter.

Where trustees wish to make a submission to the Charity Commission as to the circumstances and steps being taken to address a reportable matter, the auditors may attach such a memorandum or report prepared by the trustees to their report. Where such additional information is provided auditors refer to the additional information in their report, and indicate whether or not they have undertaken additional procedures to determine whether any remedial actions described have been taken.

23.14 Adding value

How can the charity audit actually add value to the charity?

It has been suggested that 'the auditor is the person who comes into the battlefield and bayonets the wounded'. This does not have to be the case. The charity audit can indeed be a beneficial, useful and purposeful exercise.

It is important to set out some initial ground rules. The first of these is that the auditor should act with, and not oppose, the finance team. The auditor should be perceived as acting on the side of his or her client rather than as a potential adversary or, worse still, finger-waving law enforcer. The notion of an understanding auditor is derived from the fact that the word 'audit' comes from the Latin word *audire* meaning 'to hear'. The audit process should therefore be a listening and receptive one.

Secondly, although an audit is likely to be merely an annual event, a good auditor should maintain contact with his or her client all year round and not just react to nasty surprises. To this end, reviewing minutes of finance meetings throughout the year and not just at the year end will enable the auditor to anticipate rather than react to important client issues. A proactive auditor is a necessary ally of the charity's finance team.

Specific areas in which the audit process can be beneficial to a charity are as follows.

Accounting

Minimally, the auditor should be able to provide comfort that the accounts comply with all statutory and legislative requirements. In addition, the SORP needs to be adhered to. Few in the charity world need reminding just how highly regulated it already is. This is not by chance, as the public place great confidence in charities being able to perform effectively and the price charities have to pay for this is greater public accountability. A recent survey put the amount of income generated from the sector at over £46 billion per annum.

There is no hiding from the fact that charity is big business. There may well be no financial 'bottom line' in a charity's accounts but nonetheless charities do need to be fully accountable. A good auditor will ensure that his or her charity client is fully up to date with all statutory and financial legislation. If the accounts are well audited, then the disclosures will be fully implemented to show greater transparency of the figures and the charity will be able to tell its story better and more effectively. This may result in greater funding opportunities and, if the charity really produces a good set of accounts and annual report, it could be short-listed for the Charity Online Accounts Awards which are co-sponsored by the ICAEW.

Taxation

The previous remit of measures introduced by Gordon Brown as Chancellor of the Exchequer entitled 'Getting Britain Giving' transformed the UK into arguably the most liberal tax-efficient giving regime in the world. There are now a whole host of taxation and fundraising opportunities to be taken advantage of. A good auditor will be able to communicate these and tailor them as appropriate.

For example, certain wealthy donors can now benefit from share gift relief which, where used optimally, can attract up to 80% tax relief for the individual donor. The new payroll giving measures allow an individual to donate 40p but for a charity to receive £1. Thirdly, the opportunities under gift aid are amazing. It really has never been so easy to give. It is now possible, with the correct mechanisms, for charity collection boxes to be treated as gift aid and tax reclaims made on them.

Sections 43 and 47 of the Local Government Finance Act 1988 provide a mandatory 80% relief from non-domestic rates. Careful negotiations can, however, yield a further 20% discretionary relief (see section **25.11** in Chapter 25).

Fundraising

Charities need to consider how to divert their fundraising resources between donor recruitment and donor development. Recruiting donors into a charity for the first time is particularly difficult. This should be considered as a long-term strategy. The Pareto principle teaches us that 80% of a charity's income can come from 20% of its donors. Donor development is inherently more profitable. However, charities also need to balance this with ensuring a constant flow of new donors. It is in the charity's interest that the fundraisers of the charity are able to find these 20% and do not waste their time and resources elsewhere. Auditors can help identify lifetime values, which are defined as the 'total net contributions that a customer generates during his lifetime'. Understanding the fundraising cycle is also important. This consists of:

- *Need and case* (mission statement – case for support);
- *Research* – market, qualitative, prospective;
- *Strategy* – implementation of campaign, and
- *Consolidation* – database management.

Fundraising now operates in an environment where the goalposts have moved, caused principally by the changes in gift aid. In terms of segmenting constituencies of support, prioritising approaches and developing appeals, fundraisers will need to be more subtle in their dealings. A heavy-handed approach is not what is required. As there is potentially a larger donor 'cake' than before, fundraisers need to use more guile and adapt their plans if they wish to obtain as large a share as possible. Minimally, fundraisers should endeavour to ensure that all current donors now donate under the gift aid rules. For corporate donors, fundraisers need to make the message clear that because these donations are now treated gross, companies need to 'gross up' the amount they previously donated, in order for the charity to benefit by the equivalent amount.

Governance and law

This is a very wide-ranging area and a good auditor will be able to advise on the following topics:

- **The most suitable mode of forming the charity.**

    The more contracts a charity enters into, the more likely a company limited by guarantee will be the most beneficial structure. However, if it is envisaged that the charity is to be run by just a handful of members, then forming a charitable trust may be a more simple and convenient mechanism. Later in 2010, CIOs should become available (see section **4.9** in Chapter 4).

- **Payment of trustees is a particularly topical subject**.

  The Charities Act 2006 has provided further opportunities to pay trustees for services provided. Auditors should be well placed to advise in this area.

- **Public benefit**

  The review of the Register of Charities currently being undertaken, in light of the public benefit requirements, places an emphasis on charities being required to justify how they achieve 'public benefit'. Many potential charities will need to consider if there is a need that they believe their new organisation meets and therefore merits registration. The concept of social value equalling a public benefit would need to be considered here by any charity adviser.

- **Advice on meetings, procedures and administration**

  This can be provided by a charity auditor. Similarly, the relationship between trustees, paid staff and volunteers can be codified by an impartial outside party. To this extent, the auditor can help ensure that trustees communicate better and more effectively with each other by providing external guidance to their report-writing procedures and policy implementation.

- **Apportionment of responsibilities**

  The auditor can also help establish better lines of demarcation between trustees and management. In reality, the buck stops with the trustees but they are entitled to delegate to their management team. The most common scenario for policy formation is where policies are jointly decided between trustees and staff, but there are many variations on this theme.

- **Risk management**

  Strategic planning can help direct the charity's efforts and energies to optimise all the resources that are made available to it. The charity auditor can help formulate a balanced risk management policy backed up with sound internal financial controls. It is the SOFA that aims to report on just how effectively the charity achieved this use of resources.

The day may soon be with us where it will be the client ringing up and pestering the auditors, asking them when they can book in their audit, rather than the other way round as is often currently the case.

23.15 Ethical Standards

23.15.1 Introduction

In April 2008 the APB published revised Ethical Standards for Auditors (ESs), which become effective for audits of financial statements for periods commencing on or after 6 April 2008. This followed a review of the ESs by the APB which concluded that there was no need to make major changes to the standards, except for amendments which:

- are needed to comply with UK and Irish legislation that implements the EU Statutory Audit Directive;
- are required in order that the ESs continue to adhere to the principles of international ethical standards, or
- add clarity to the existing standards and assist their implementation in practice.

Although the standards remain principle-based, they include many bold paragraphs which draw some very rigid lines. The original ESs became effective at the same time as ISAs.

The revised ESs are:

- ES1 (Revised) – *Integrity, objectivity and independence*;
- ES2 (Revised) – *Financial, business, employment and personal relationships*;
- ES3 (Revised) – *Long association with the audit engagement*;
- ES4 (Revised) – *Fees, remuneration and evaluation policies, litigation, gifts and hospitality*;
- ES5 (Revised) – *Non-audit services provided to audit clients*, and
- ES *Provisions Available for Smaller Entities* (PASE) (Revised).

ES5 (Revised) and 'PASE' cause the most confusion and are now considered in more detail below.

23.15.2 ES 5 – Non-audit services provided to audit clients

The standard requires:

(a) any person proposing to provide a non-audit service (for example, accounts preparation work) to inform the engagement partner, and
(b) the engagement partner, before accepting engagement for a non-audit service, to:

(i) consider if an informed third party would consider it inconsistent with the audit objectives;
(ii) assess the related threats, and
(iii) identify and assess available safeguards.

Then, if the engagement partner assesses that an informed third party would regard it as inconsistent, the standard says that the firm should either not provide the service or resign as auditor.

Where safeguards cannot reduce the threats to an acceptable level, the firm should either not provide the service or resign as auditor: or alternatively the engagement partner should, if uncertain, consult with the ethics partner.

The engagement partner should:

(a) inform the client of all ethical matters involving the proposed provisions of the non-audit service including safeguards, and
(b) document the reasoning and the safeguards taken.

Whilst all the ethical threats are identified and described, particular attention is paid to the management threat. This is a threat to objectivity and independence. The notes to the standard review each type of threat individually and how providing other services can be the cause of such a threat. The standard then looks at each specific non-audit service and identifies the individual threats and safeguards relating to each and sets out specific requirements. For charity assignments, a common problem will arise as a result of the provision of accounting services.

Informed management

When considering the management threat, the standard concludes that in the absence of 'informed management' it is unlikely that any safeguards can eliminate or reduce this threat to an acceptable level.

Informed management is defined as a 'member of the management who is capable of making independent decisions or judgements on the basis of information provided'.

To avoid the management threat:

- the non-audit services result in recommendations based on transparent analyses or providing the client a choice between reasonable alternatives, and
- a capable member of the management team has been designated to receive the results of the non-audit service and make any judgements or decisions required.

Ethical Standards

If there is informed management, an assessment can be made of the safeguards necessary to reduce any threats to an acceptable level.

Accounting services

These are defined as services involving:

(a) maintenance of accounting records, and
(b) preparation of financial statements.

They do not include advice on implementation of accounting standards or the SORP.

These services create self-review and management threats. The significance of the threat will depend on the nature of the service.

The standard states that, unless there is 'informed management' and there are appropriate safeguards, there is a risk of the auditor taking a management role. Accountancy advice as a by-product of the audit process and not the result of a separate engagement does not give rise to any threat.

The standard suggests as examples of safeguards, that the following steps are taken:

(a) accounting services provided by the audit firm are performed by partners and staff who have no involvement in the external audit of the financial statements;
(b) accounting services are reviewed by partner or a staff member not part of the audit team, and
(c) the audit of the financial statements is reviewed by an audit partner who is not involved in the audit engagement, to ensure that the accounting services performed have been properly and effectively assessed in the context of the audit of the financial statements.

23.15.3 ES Provisions available for Smaller Entities (PASE)

The definition of a charity that qualifies as small, and can therefore take advantage of PASE, is 'any charity with income of no more than £6.5 million for accounting periods beginning on or after 6 April 2008'. The previous threshold was £5.6 million. As a result, many audits of charities will be able to utilise these provisions.

Option 1 – Alternative provision

For charities that qualify to apply PASE, auditors are not required to apply safeguards to address the self-review threat, provided that:

- the client has 'informed management', and
- the audit firm extends the cyclical inspection of completed engagements that is performed for quality control purposes (that is, carries out 'cold' file reviews).

Option 1 is the preferred option.

Option 2 – Exemption

For charities that qualify to apply PASE, the prohibitions in ES5 relating to providing non-audit services (IT, internal audit, tax, corporate finance and transaction-related accounting) do not have to be adhered, to provided that:

- the auditor discusses objectivity and independence issues with the client, and
- makes the necessary disclosures detailed below.

Disclosure requirements

Where advantage has been taken of an exemption that partner should ensure that:

- the audit report discloses this fact in a separate paragraph having no effect on the opinion paragraph, and
- either the financial statements or the auditor's report discloses the type of non-audit services provided or the fact that a former audit engagement partner has joined the client.

The sample wording offered for inclusion in the audit report is:

'We have undertaken the audit in accordance with the requirements of APB Ethical Standards including APB Ethical Standard – Provisions Available for Small Entities, in the circumstances set out in note [x] to the financial statements'.

23.16 Recent auditing issues

The following section addresses a series of recent developments in charity auditing, and these are

1. Entity and environment;
2. Internal control;
3. Auditing income;
4. Communication with the client;
5. Whistle blowing responsibilities;
6. Auditor appointment and resignation, and
7. Clarity ISAs.

23.16.1 Entity and environment

The standards dealing with risk (ISA 315 and ISA 330) require more documentation of risk assessments and are more prescriptive on the audit approach to be adopted. There is much more emphasis on auditors gaining an understanding of the entity's objective and strategies and management's procedures for identifying and addressing business risks, and on the evaluation of the design and implementation of internal controls.

There is already a requirement for the trustees of most charities to confirm in their report each year that they have identified the major risks to which the charity is exposed and established systems to mitigate these. Auditors need to understand the review the process that the trustees have adopted and also to understand the performance indicators used by the various levels of management.

In undertaking their risk assessment, ISA 315 also envisages auditors obtaining evidence from a wider range of sources, including discussions with management outside the finance function, analytical procedures, observation and inspection.

The auditors need to have a clear understanding of the legal structure of the charity, particularly where it operates through branches or joint ventures, either within the UK or overseas. An understanding of the legal structure may also be important in establishing the point at which expenditure is actually incurred.

23.16.2 Internal control

The auditor needs to identify the control procedures in place over these risks. They must then design tests of controls to ensure the controls have been applied effectively throughout the period. In addition, these significant areas will need to be tested substantively (either analytical procedures or tests of detail) in order for the auditor to gain sufficient assurance.

There is a need for auditors to understand the charity's selection and application of accounting policies and consider whether they are appropriate. In particular, this will include policies relating to income recognition and those involving the use of estimates and estimation techniques. Auditors should also understand how trustees and senior management allocate costs between the relevant headings within the SOFA and how the reserves policy is developed and monitored.

An effective system of internal control is as important for charities as for any other entity, possibly more so given the stewardship role of the trustees.

23.16.3 Auditing income

There are 3 areas which will typically present significant risks in the context of a charity audit. These are:

- completeness of income;
- overseas activities, and
- restricted funds.

Completeness of income

There is considerable discussion on the difficulty of predicting levels of voluntary income with any degree of certainty and of establishing relationships between donations and other figures in the accounts, and the limitations on the use of analytical procedures in these circumstances. It is difficult to audit what is not there. The emphasis is very much on:

- the need for trustees to develop appropriate systems and procedures to record and safeguard voluntary income as soon as it comes within their control; and
- the need for the auditors to understand these arrangements and confirm that they work effectively in practice.

In practice, it will be necessary to summarise all the income levels in a 'lead schedule', listing the statutory accounts headings. From there it will be possible to use this lead schedule as a summary of overall evidence obtained on incoming resources. Some income streams will only require limited evidence that can be annotated on the schedule; others will need to be cross-referenced to where the auditor has obtained assurance from internal controls, analytical procedures or other substantive tests.

Overseas operations

Where access may be difficult, the auditors need to ensure that they have sufficient information to assess the full extent of the charity's activities – for instance, the terms of tax or employment law.

Restricted funds

Restricted funds can give rise to a significant risk of misstatement, bearing in mind that their misappropriation constitutes a breach of trust, regardless of whether it is intentional or accidental. Auditors will need to consider the internal control procedures established by the charity to identify restricted funds at the time of receipt and to ensure that they are used only for the purpose specified.

23.16.4 Communication with the client

Another aspect of the UK and Ireland versions of the ISAs is that a distinction is drawn between 'management' and 'those charged with governance'. This is of particular importance as there is now a requirement to discuss certain matters with both groups. For many audits, they are one and the same people. However, on some audits there is a clear distinction between the management of a charity and the overall board of trustees.

Under ISAs, as a minimum, the auditor will need to discuss:

- the management's/trustees' arrangements for assessing, identifying and responding to fraud risk;
- how, if at all, management/trustees communicate this to each other and to other staff and volunteers, and
- any knowledge of actual, suspected or alleged fraud affecting the charity.

23.16.5 Whistle blowing responsibilities

Section 44 of the Charities Act 1993, as amended by the Charities Act 2006, places a duty on the auditors of both a non-company charity and a company charity (previously only non-company charity) to report matters of 'material significance' to the Charity Commission.

The duty to report arises where the auditors, in the course of their audit, identify a matter, which relates to the activities or affairs of the charity or of any connected institution or body, and which the auditors have reasonable cause to believe is likely to be of material significance for the purposes of the exercise by the Charity Commission of its functions under sections 8 or 18 of the Charities Act 1993.

Subject to compliance with money laundering legislation on 'tipping off', in the circumstances leading to a right or duty to report, the auditors are entitled to communicate to charity regulators in good faith any information or opinions relating to the business or affairs of the entity or any associated body without contravening the duty of confidence owed to the entity. In addition, in England and Wales, the Charities Act 1993 provides additional statutory protection for the auditors as no duty, for example confidentiality, is regarded as contravened merely because of any information or opinion contained in the report.

The reporting of a matter of material significance is a separate report from the auditors' report on the accounts. The Charities Act 1993 requires the report to be made immediately the matter comes to the auditors' attention; in England and Wales the Charities Act 1993 requires that this is done in writing.

Audit of charities

It is not part of the reporting duty of auditors to perform any additional work as a result of this statutory duty nor are they specifically required to find reportable matters. Auditors should, however, have sufficient procedures within their planning to ensure that they have sufficient understanding to enable them to identify situations which may give them reasonable cause to believe that matter should be reported.

23.16.6 Auditor appointment and resignation

For private companies, the appointment of auditors will generally be made by the members by ordinary resolution. This should be done within 28 days of the circulation of the accounts for the previous year. The auditors' term of office will run from the end of the 28-day period following circulation of the accounts until the end of the corresponding period the following year. Auditors are now deemed to be re-appointed unless the company decides otherwise.

The revised rules about statements that auditors have to make when leaving a company in ss. 519 to 525 of the Companies Act 2006 apply to resignations on or after 6 April 2008.

For company charities, the Companies Act 2006 also requires the following actions for the departing auditor:

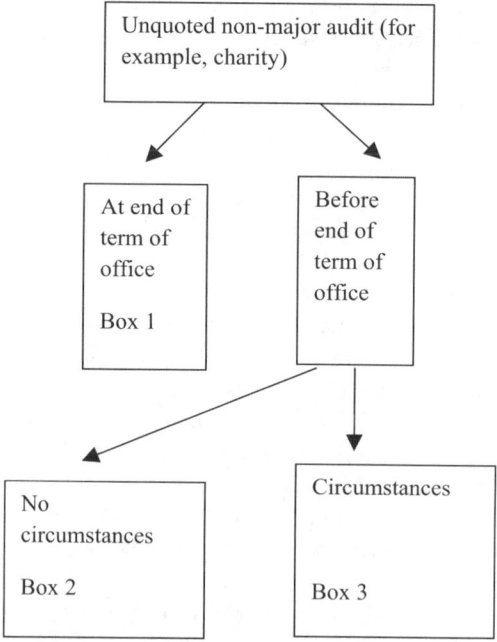

Box 1

1. A statement of any circumstances connected with the auditor ceasing to hold office must be filed at the company's Registered Office by the auditor within 14 days. If there are no circumstances connected with leaving office, then a statement must be made (s. 519 of the Companies Act 2006).

Box 2

1. A statement that there are no circumstances connected with the auditor ceasing to hold office must be filed at the company's Registered Office by the auditor within 14 days (s. 519 of the Companies Act 2006).
2. A note must be sent to the audit authority by the auditor informing it that he has ceased to hold office. This must be accompanied by a copy of the statement of circumstances. As this states that there are no circumstances, there must be an additional statement of the reasons for ceasing to hold office. The auditor should be careful here: he could be at risk if he refers to something that should have been reported to the members or creditors in the statement of circumstances.
3. The company must also notify the audit authority that the auditor has ceased to hold office and give a statement of the reasons for the auditor ceasing to hold office.

Box 3

1. A statement of the circumstances connected with the auditor ceasing to hold office must be filed at the company's Registered Office by the auditor within 14 days (s. 519 of the Companies Act 2006).
2. A notice must be sent to the audit authority by the auditor informing it that he has ceased to hold office. This must be accompanied by a copy of the statement of circumstances.
3. The company must also notify the audit authority that the auditor has ceased to hold office. The notice must be accompanied by a statement of the reasons for the auditor ceasing to hold office or a copy of the auditor's statement of circumstances.

23.16.7 Clarity ISAs

In October 2008 the APB published a consultation paper on whether UK and Irish Auditing Standards should be updated for the new International Auditing Standards generated by the International Auditing and Assurance Standards Board ('IAASB'). During 2008, the ICAEW and APB were active in alerting the UK profession and relevant service providers to the profession to the need to prepare for Clarity ISAs.

Audit of charities

Clarity ISAs should be applicable to all audits. However for audits of smaller entities, there may need to be some differences. For instance, on audits of smaller entities, it may be appropriate to vary the extent of required communications to those charged with governance or the level of audit documentation required without in any way affecting the level of evidence gathering and therefore assurance provided by the audit.

The APB has been recommended to avoid the introduction or retention of any discretionary requirements through the current mechanism of 'ISA pluses'. Although it is accepted that UK law and regulation introduces certain requirements for the auditor that are not to be found in the Clarity ISAs, there is no consensus that it would be appropriate for these to be drawn to the attention of auditors. It is therefore recommended that the requirements of UK Auditing Standards go no further than the requirements of the IAASB's standards unless separate UK law or regulation dictates otherwise.

There is general support for the IAASB's project to revise and redraft ISAs. The Clarity project has combined both the re-drafting of all and the revision of 16 current ISAs. The re-drafting of auditing standards to make them clearer is a welcome move towards simplicity.

The revisions made to certain ISAs have been prompted by developments in financial reporting and the observations and recommendations of international regulators. In light of developments such as the credit crunch and poor public reporting, it is appropriate for requirements to have been increased in certain areas.

The APB has announced its intention to update its auditing standards for the new, clarified, International Standards on Auditing (ISAs) issued by the International Auditing and Assurance Standards Board (IAASB). The new UK and Irish auditing standards will be effective for audits of financial statements for periods ending on or after 15 December 2010. There are strong indications that certain other territories will seek to introduce Clarity ISAs as national Generally Accepted Auditing Standards ('GAAS') in 2010.

It will be practicable for some firms to apply these ISAs to 2010 audits, provided that the APB's approach to UK and Ireland pluses are exposed and finalised swiftly during 2009 and that, going forwards, UK and Ireland pluses are restricted to requirements imposed by UK law or regulation.

A single set of principles-based auditing standards that are scalable to all entities is being considered. This is also consistent with the concepts that audits, no matter the size of the entity are intended to provide a similar level of assurance to users of the audited financial statements.

Recent auditing issues

Annex 1 Bank report requests
(to be typed on auditor's own note paper)

REQUEST FOR BANK REPORT FOR AUDIT PURPOSES – STANDARD

In accordance with the agreed practice for provision of information to auditors, please forward information on our mutual client(s) as detailed below on behalf of the bank, its branches and subsidiaries. This request and your response will not create any contractual or other duty with us.

1. **BANK NAME & ADDRESS**

2. **AUDITOR CONTACT DETAILS**

   Name and address of auditor

   Contact number

   Contact name

   Period end date (DD/MM/YYYY)

   Date of request (DD/MM/YYYY)

3. Companies or other business entities

Company	Main account sort code	Main account number

4. Authority to disclose information

   Authority already held and dated (DD/MM/YYYY)   OR   Authority Attached

Annex 1 Bank report requests (to be typed on auditor's own note paper)

5. Acknowledgement

Please complete this section if an acknowledgement is required.

Acknowledgement required	☐ by email	Reference number to be quoted	[_____]
OR	☐ by post	(template attached)	

6. Additional information required

Trade Finance	☐ One of the facility account numbers	[_____]
Derivative & Commodity Trading	☐ One of the facility account numbers	[_____]

Chapter 24 – Independent examination

24.1 Introduction

Current charity law embodies the concept that, for most charities, some form of independent external scrutiny of accounts is required.

For accounting periods beginning on or after 1 April 2008, the trustees of both company and non-company charities

- whose gross income is less than £500,000;
- whose gross income exceeds £100,000 and whose gross assets are not more than £2.8 million

may elect to have an independent examination, subject to any other formal regulatory or constitutional requirement.

For charities whose gross income is less than £10,000 in a particular year, there is no statutory requirement for any form of independent scrutiny. Trustees may, of course, seek the assurance of an examination where they consider it appropriate.

24.2 What is an 'independent examination'?

Independent examination was introduced by the Charities Act 1993 and inserted a new layer into the scrutiny process. Independent examination provides a higher level of assurance than an audit exemption report, but is a less onerous form of scrutiny than an audit. As there is a fine dividing line between a full audit and no meaningful scrutiny, the aim of an independent examination is to find some middle ground. The more onerous requirements imposed on the independent examiner are a recognition of greater public expectation, as regards the level of assurance provided on the proper administration of the charity and its funds by the charity trustees.

The examiner is not required to form an opinion as to whether the accounts show a true and fair view. Rather, the objective of the examination is to enable the examiner to state whether, on the basis of procedures carried out, anything has come to his or her attention that causes him or her to believe that the account and statement (or statement of accounts) is not prepared, in all material respects, in accordance with the financial reporting framework. In other words, it is a form of negative assurance. For the purposes of expressing negative assurance, the examiner should be able to obtain sufficient appropriate evidence – primarily through enquiries and analytical procedures – to be able to draw conclusions.

Other matters which may cause concern are reported on an exception basis, if they arise during the course of the examination.

Section 43(7)(b) of the Charities Act 1993 (the Act) enables the Charity Commission to give directions, as it considers appropriate, with respect to the carrying out of such an examination. These are contained in its booklet CC32 Independent Examination of Charity Accounts Examiners' Guide. The Charity Commission has also published a booklet CC31 Independent Examination of Charity Accounts Trustees' Guide. Both booklets were updated in October 2008.

There are 10 specific directions which the examiner must address, seven of which apply to all accounts and a further three of which (7, 8 and 9) only apply when accruals accounts are prepared. Each direction is accompanied by explanatory guidance. The Charity Commission stresses that, as with any guidance, the procedures suggested and the examples given cannot meet all circumstances that may arise in the course of an examination, and judgement will need to be exercised by examiners in the context of their work. The directions and guidance in CC32 are reproduced below (see section **24.8**), together with commentary.

24.3 Who is an independent examiner?

An independent examiner is defined in s. 43(3)(a) of the Act as 'an independent person who is reasonably believed by the trustees to have the requisite ability and practical experience to carry out a competent examination of the accounts'.

It seems somewhat ironic that, while the level of assurance provided by an independent examination is higher than that provided by an audit exemption report, the qualifications required of an independent examiner are less demanding.

In accordance with s. 43(7)(a) of the Act, the Charity Commission has given guidance to charity trustees in connection with the selection of an independent examiner. For ease of reference, that guidance is given as **Annex 1** to this chapter. Charity trustees should take all necessary steps to satisfy themselves that the examiner is independent and has the requisite ability and practical experience to discharge the responsibilities. If trustees follow this guidance, it states that they can be satisfied that they will have taken all reasonable steps to obtain a competent independent examination of their accounts.

24.4 Who is an 'independent person'?

For an examiner to be independent, the guidance states that the individual should have no connection with the charity's trustees which might inhibit the impartial conduct of the examination. Whether or not such a connection exists will depend on the particular circumstances, but the guidance lists those persons who, as a minimum, would normally be considered to have such a connection.

Examiners should have regard to appropriate ethical considerations: these include integrity, objectivity, independence, professional competence and due care and confidentiality.

24.5 Which persons would have the 'requisite ability'?

The suitability of an independent examiner, as well as the quality both of the examiner's credentials and of the evidence for these credentials, will depend on the particular circumstances and the size and nature of the charity's transactions. As regards the quality and evidence of credentials, trustees should consider obtaining references.

The standard of scrutiny that an examiner can be expected to exercise is likely to vary, depending on qualifications and experience, and this should be reflected in the trustees' decision on the appointment of a suitable person. A higher standard of care would be required of a qualified accountant.

For charities seeking an independent examiner who is not necessarily a qualified accountant, the Association of Charity Independent Examiners (ACIE) can provide assistance and the names of suitably qualified examiners, who are required to act within a code of ethics.

24.6 What is 'practical experience'?

Prospective independent examiners should have practical experience that is relevant to the charity. This could be achieved by:

(a) having had an involvement in the financial administration of a charity of a similar nature;
(b) having acted successfully as an independent examiner on previous occasions for such charities, or
(c) having relevant practical experience in accountancy or commerce.

Independent examination

24.7 Selection procedures

Charity trustees should:

(a) discuss fully with the prospective examiner the work of the charity and their expectations;
(b) ensure that the prospective examiner is familiar with:
 (i) the Charity Commission's directions to independent examiners and the nature of the report required;
 (ii) where a statement of accounts is prepared in accordance with **s. 42(1) of the Act**, the form and content of the **Regulations**, the methods and principles with which that statement must be prepared and the SORP, and
(c) ensure that the letter of engagement recognises and does not limit the examiner's statutory duties.

24.8 The Charity Commission's Directions

The Directions (which must be followed) are reproduced in bold print.

24.8.1 Examination and accounting thresholds

Direction 1

The examiner shall carry out specific procedures as are considered necessary to provide a reasonable basis on which to conclude:

(a) that an examination is required under section 43(3) of the Charities Act 1993 and that section 43(2) (audit) does not apply to the charity, and
(b) where the charity is a small company charity, that it is exempt from audit in accordance with section 477 of the Companies Act 2006, and
(c) where accounts are prepared under section 42(3) of the Charities Act 1993, that the charity trustees may properly elect to prepare accounts under this subsection.

Guidance

1.1 Trustees may elect for independent examination (under section 43(3)) and, for non-company charities only, if their charity is eligible, elect for the preparation of Receipts and Payments accounts (under section 42(3)). For either election to be valid, the charity must be within the relevant income bands specified by legislation.

The examiner should take reasonable steps to confirm:

The Charity Commission's Directions

- the charity's gross income for the financial year or aggregate value of assets does not exceed the threshold for independent examination. If gross income exceeds £500,000 or gross income exceeds £100,000 and the aggregate value of assets (before deduction of liabilities) exceeds £2.8million then an audit is required;
- where the charity is a parent charity with one or more subsidiaries (for example, a trading company), that the aggregate gross income of the parent charity and its subsidiaries after consolidation adjustments does not exceed £500,000 (as above this threshold group accounts must be prepared which will require an audit);
- where the charity operates branches and these branches are part of the charity (and are not separately registered charities), that any income received by the branches has been included in the gross income of the charity;
- if receipts and payments are being prepared, that the charity is not a company incorporated under company law and that the gross income received in the period is £100,000 or less;
- whether the gross income exceeds £10,000 (because below this threshold no examination is required by law);
- whether the charity's governing document requires any form of professional audit, and
- whether any grant condition demands an audit of the accounts.

1.2 Carrying out these procedures at an early stage should prevent the work of the examiner being duplicated by professional audit, which would add to the expense for the charity. Where the charity is not eligible for independent examination, the accounts should be referred back to the trustees to appoint an auditor where the threshold is exceeded or to consider a voluntary examination where the charity's gross income is below £10,000.

1.3 Gross income for threshold purposes should be calculated in accordance with the methods set out in Appendix 1. If accounts are prepared on the accruals basis, then the level of income should be considered on the accruals basis. Where accounts are prepared on the receipts and payments basis then the level of income should be considered on the basis of money actually received.

1.4 The examiner should consider at an early stage of the examination the level of income disclosed by the accounting records and by the trial balance. The examiner does, however, need to remain alert to any additional information which may come to attention during the course of the examination which indicates that an income threshold has been crossed.

1.5 The reasonable steps taken to confirm the income of the charity and the outcome of that research should be documented in accordance with Direction 2.

1.6 Where the trustees have requested and obtained in advance from the Commission approval for an independent examination instead of an audit, the examiner should obtain a copy of the approval letter from the Commission and make reference to it in the examiner's report.

1.7 The thresholds for audit, independent examination and for Receipts and Payments accounts are kept under review. The Government has provided for a review of these thresholds following the Charities Act 2006 and consequently it is important to confirm the thresholds that apply. It is therefore recommended that, prior to the independent examination taking place, the thresholds are confirmed. Details of all current thresholds can be found by viewing the accounting or publication pages on the Commission's website – http://www.charitycommission.gov.uk.

1.8 The thresholds for independent examination and the assets threshold for audit are likely to be raised with effect for financial years beginning from a date in mid-2009 (see section 4.14 in Chapter 4) and the guidance will be updated once these planned changes take effect.

Comment

The examiner must always maintain an awareness that an audit may be a requirement

(a) of the charity's governing document; or
(b) under another parallel statutory regime; or
(c) placed on the charity by a donor as a condition of accepting a grant, or other finance.

Many charities have related charitable funds or branches with varying degrees of independence and differing constitutions. Given that the relevant income and expenditure thresholds identified by the 1993 Act relate to those of the charity as a whole, including its special trusts and controlled branches, the examiner needs to ensure that these entities are properly constituted and accounted for.

The examiner should be aware that, under section 96(5) of the Charities Act 1993, the Charity Commission is able to direct that, for all or any of the purposes of that Act, an institution established for any special purposes of, or in connection with, a charity shall be treated as forming part of that charity, or as forming a distinct charity. Further, the Charities (Amendment) Act 1995 has inserted subsection 95(6) into the 1993 Act, enabling the Charity Commission to direct that, for all or any purposes of the Act, two or more charities having the same charity trustees shall be treated as a single charity.

The specific procedures appear more demanding than those in respect of an audit exemption report, where the reporting accountant is required to perform such procedures as are necessary to provide a reasonable basis on which to form an opinion on whether – having regard only to, and on the basis of, the information in the accounting records – the company is entitled to exemption from audit.

In order to verify the level to which the accounts should be prepared and subject to scrutiny, the examiner must remain alert to any information that comes to light which indicates that income or expenditure may have been unrecorded and that, consequently, a threshold has been exceeded. For example, income may have been deferred to a future financial year to circumvent the preparation of a statement of accounts or an audit being carried out.

Where it becomes apparent that the gross income or total expenditure has exceeded the limits above which an audit is required, the examiner will need to notify the trustees. Provided that he or she is a registered auditor, a fresh engagement can be agreed with the charity.

24.8.2 Documentation

Direction 2

The examiner shall record the examination procedures carried out and any matters which are important to support conclusions reached or statement provided in the examiner's report.

Guidance

2.1 The examiner's working papers should provide details of the work undertaken and support any conclusions reached, and record any matters of judgment (where accruals accounts are prepared see Direction 8) which may arise. Working papers should normally be retained by the examiner for six years from the end of the financial year to which they relate, and would include:
- a communication with the trustees which confirms their appointment as the independent examiner. Independent examiners charging a fee or receiving any form of payment should prepare a letter of engagement;
- a letter of engagement, where appropriate, from the independent examiner to the trustees, together with evidence that this has been accepted by the trustees (for example, a copy of the engagement letter signed by a representative of the trustees);
- relevant information extracted or obtained from the governing document, trustees' meeting minutes and a record of discussions with the charity's trustees and the charity's staff;
- notes as to how any areas of concern identified have been resolved, including meetings with trustees and charity staff, together with details of any verification procedures used;
- where verification procedures have been used, details of checks or vouching carried out during the examination, the conclusions reached and any areas of concern identified;

Independent examination

- where items are added together as a single entry in the accounts, schedules showing the breakdown of accounting items that have been aggregated for accounts disclosure purposes;
- copies of any trial balance and the accounts;
- the Trustees' Annual Report where accruals accounts are prepared (sight of the Trustees' Annual Report is required under Direction 9 where accruals accounts are prepared; it is recommended but not required where Receipts and Payments accounts are prepared); and
- in exceptional circumstances, copies of any written assurances that the examiner required of the trustees confirming amounts included within the accounts.

2.2 Where the examiner has cause to resign or is unable to complete his independent examination, he should consider the circumstances carefully and decide if there is a duty to report to the Commission – for example, if he has been prevented from completing the examination or has been obstructed by trustees or charity staff in carrying out his examination. Even if there is no duty to report, the examiner may decide that he has identified matters which he wishes to report because he considers them to be relevant to the work of the Commission.

Comment

The examiner should document all matters that are important in providing the evidence to support his report.

In addition to the above, the documentation should include:

(a) a description of the accounting records and systems and a conclusion as to whether proper accounting records have been maintained;
(b) evidence of the planning process;
(c) any disclosure checklist which has been used, and
(d) a letter of representation.

A separately documented work programme is not considered to be necessary, provided that the work planned and performed and the conclusions reached are fully recorded.

24.8.3 Understanding the charity

Direction 3

The examiner shall obtain an understanding of the charity's constitution, organisation, accounting systems, activities and nature of its assets, liabilities, incoming resources and application of resources in order to plan the specific examination procedures appropriate to the circumstances of the charity.

Guidance

3.1 For a proper examination to be carried out, it is important for the examiner to have an understanding of what the charity is aiming to do and how it goes about doing it. The examiner will need to know about the operations, structure and objectives of the charity. This understanding will help the examiner to plan his independent examination by identifying major projects and important activities of the charity, possible problems or concerns and to provide background to his analytical review. The steps taken by an examiner would normally include:

- consideration of the governing document of the charity, paying particular attention to the charity's objects, powers and obligations;
- consideration of any matters which would give rise to a statutory duty to make a report to the Commission;
- discussions with trustees and, where appropriate, the charity's staff, to understand the activities, structure, aims and objectives by which the charity seeks to achieve its objects for the public benefit;
- discussions with the trustees and, where appropriate, the charity's staff, about the activities of the charity in order to gain an insight into any special circumstances and problems affecting the charity;
- reviewing the minutes of trustees' meetings to find out about details of major events, plans, decisions and any changes to the trustee body, and
- obtaining details of the accounting records maintained and methods of recording financial transactions.

3.2 Normally a discussion with one of the trustees and the person who prepared the accounts should provide all the information or explanations required. However, if during the independent examination the examiner identifies a lack of formal trustee meetings, or of an absence of minute-keeping or appropriate record-keeping, or over reliance on a key individual, he may then the examiner may need to confirm or discuss significant matters with two or more of the trustees and/or members of the charity's staff to gain the necessary background information for the examination.

Comment

The examiner should properly plan his or her work. Knowledge of the charity, its constitution, organisation, activities and accounting systems and the nature of its assets, liabilities, incoming resources and their application is necessary so that he or she can design appropriate procedures and make relevant enquiries of the charity trustees.

Although the independent examiner is required to make a positive statement in his or her report if there have been any material expenditure or actions which do

Independent examination

not appear to be in accordance with the charity's trusts, a separate direction is not provided. Nonetheless, while not required to carry out specific procedures to identify such breaches, the examiner needs to have an understanding of the objectives and activities of the charity to be able to identify such breaches when carrying out the work he or she is required to do.

The examiner should use the same materiality as would be applied were an audit carried out. This is because the judgement of what is or is not material is made by reference to the information on which the examiner is reporting and the needs of those relying on that information, and not on the level of assurance provided.

Many charities publish summarised accounts in addition to the full accounts required by law. In planning the examination of the full accounts, the examiner should ascertain whether summarised accounts are to be prepared.

It will usually be more efficient for the examiner to carry out work on the summarised accounts at the same time as carrying out the examination of the full accounts. In the past, some charities have published their annual reviews, containing summarised accounts, after publication of the full accounts. The examiner should encourage the trustees to have this in mind when they are planning the timetable for the preparation of the full accounts.

24.8.4 Accounting Records

Direction 4

The examiner shall review the accounting records maintained in accordance with section 41 of the Charities Act 1993, or, in the case of a charity that is a company, the accounting records maintained in accordance with section 386 of the Companies Act 2006, in order to provide a reasonable basis for the identification of any material failure to maintain such records.

Guidance

4.1 The charity trustees are responsible for maintaining the accounting records. This is an important responsibility and an absence of well organised and complete accounting records gives rise to a significant risk of misstatement and loss from fraud, theft, or the misappropriation of charitable funds.

4.2 The examiner is required to review the accounting records with a view to identifying any material failure to maintain such records in accordance with the trustees' legal duty. A simple review should indicate whether records or vouchers (invoices, receipts, claims and similar paperwork) have been kept to support the accounts and whether they appear reasonably complete. Further evidence of the completeness of those records may come from any vouching undertaken following the analytical review. For trustees of non-company charities their duty is under section 41(1) of the 1993 Act. For trustees (normally the directors) of charitable companies their legal duty is under section 386 of the Companies Act 2006.

4.3 The review procedures are not aimed at identifying the occasional omission or insignificant error, but at identifying any significant failure to maintain records in a manner consistent with the statutory requirements.

4.4 Accounting records should be well organised and capable of ready retrieval and analysis. The records may take a number of forms, for example book form, loose-leaf binder or computer records.

4.5 The accounting records should:
- be up to date;
- be readily available, and
- provide the basic information from which the financial position can be ascertained, not only at the year end, but also on any selected date.

4.6 The accounting records should contain:
- details of all money received and expended, the date, and the nature of the receipt or expenditure; and
- details of assets and liabilities.

4.7 Smaller charities may not have maintained nominal ledgers to record assets and liabilities, and in such instances the requirements can generally be met by maintaining a simple record of transactions and files for unpaid invoices and amounts receivable. A record of stocks and fixed assets is also generally necessary to meet the accounting requirements.

4.8 Charitable companies are required by s386 of the Companies Act 2006 to maintain accounting records that contain:
entries from day to day of all sums of money received and expended by the company and the matters in respect of which the receipt and expenditure takes place; and
a record of the assets and liabilities of the company.

4.9 Charitable companies dealing in goods must also maintain stock records, the particular requirements for which are set out in s386(4) of the Companies Act 2006.

Comment

The examiner is required to state whether any matter has come to his or her attention, in connection with the examination, which gives him or her reasonable cause to believe either that the accounts are not in agreement with the accounting records or that proper accounting records have not been kept. The requirement to keep and maintain proper accounting records is fundamental to the administration, protection and use of funds for the purposes for which they have been given.

It is worth noting that the Charity Commission expects that a record of fixed assets is generally necessary to meet the accounting requirements. Thus, for those charities that have not yet done so, a fixed asset register will need to be compiled.

Independent examination

24.8.5 Comparison with accounting records

Direction 5

The examiner shall compare the accounts of the charity with the charity's accounting records in sufficient detail to provide a reasonable basis on which to decide whether the accounts are in accordance with such accounting records.

Guidance

5.1   It is necessary to compare the accounts with the underlying accounting records to be satisfied that the accounts properly show what income the charity has received, how it has spent its charitable funds; and, where transactions relate to restricted or endowment funds, that these have been properly recorded and identified in the accounts.

5.2   Where accounts are prepared on the accruals basis, all balances in the accounts will need to be compared with the trial balance or any nominal ledger maintained.

5.3   Where accounts are prepared on the receipts and payments basis, a direct comparison with the cash records of the charity should be carried out if no nominal ledger is kept. Records for receipts and payments accounts may amount to bank statements, a file of receipts and invoices, and a simple listing of transactions in a book, or on paper, or entries in a spreadsheet of amounts paid and received with an explanation by each amount.

5.4   Where entries for transactions are not made directly into the nominal ledger, test checks will also be necessary on the posting of entries from books of prime entry (e.g. cash book, any sales or purchase ledgers or other day books recording transactions) to the trial balance itself. Similar checks are necessary even where accounting records are maintained by using computer accounting packages.

5.5   A review of bank reconciliations, payroll summaries and control accounts prepared will provide a useful check as to the completeness of posting from the primary accounting records where the transaction is first recorded (the books of prime entry).

5.6   There is no requirement for accounting entries to be checked against source documents (eg invoices, supplier statements, purchase orders, gift aid records etc) unless concerns arise during the course of the examination or following the analytical review (Direction 6) which cannot be resolved by seeking explanations from the trustees (or, where appropriate, the charity's staff) or the explanations given are insufficient.

5.7   Whilst the charity trustees are responsible for the preparation of accounts, on occasion the examiner may also prepare the statutory accounts on behalf of the trustees. The preparation of accounts will not generally impinge on

independence provided that the examiner ensures that the requirements of the Directions are met and provided that:
- the accounting records (the books of prime entry) have been maintained by another person, and
- the examiner has had no direct involvement in the day-to-day management or administration of the charity.

Comment

Postings from the books of prime entry to the general ledger should be checked in each direction. There is no initial requirement for accounting entries to be checked against source documents (for example, invoices). Unlike an audit exemption report, however, source documents may need to be checked if concerns arising during the course of the examination cannot be resolved by explanation.

24.8.6 Analytical procedures

Direction 6

The examiner shall carry out analytical procedures to identify unusual items or disclosures in the accounts. Where concerns arise from these procedures, the examiner must seek an explanation from the charity trustees. If, after following such procedures, the examiner has reason to believe that in any respect the accounts may be materially misstated then additional procedures, including verification of the asset, liability, incoming resource or application, must be carried out.

Guidance

6.1 The analytical review is an important part of the independent examination. For receipts and payments accounts the analytical review involves comparing the analysis of the cash received and the cash spent in the current year with the previous year to identify any significant changes from year to year. For accruals accounts the analytical review involves both the SOFA and the Balance Sheet, with the analysis comparing both the income and the expenditure and the movement in Balance Sheet values in the current year with the previous year. The examiner of accruals accounts will be looking for material values which require review.

6.2 It is important that the examiner looks carefully at the accounts to see if they reveal any significant or unusual items, unexpected fluctuations, or inconsistencies with other financial information. It is important that the analytical review is documented carefully in the examiner's working papers. In carrying out the analytical review, steps taken would normally include:
- comparing the accounts with those for comparable prior periods;
- comparing the accounts with any budgets or forecasts that have been produced;

Independent examination

- considering whether incoming resources are consistent with known fundraising sources, for example the history of cash collections or fundraising events, grants received, income from trading, or income from the sale of donated goods;
- considering whether the spending of charitable resources is consistent with the payroll details, and the activities and the objects of the charity – it is important to have obtained a proper understanding of the nature of the charity's activities and affairs for this aspect of the review to be successful;
- considering whether the liabilities and current assets disclosed are consistent with the scale and type of activities undertaken, or in the case of receipts and payments accounts whether all significant assets and liabilities are listed;
- considering whether fixed asset investments are producing income consistent with the nature of assets held;
- considering whether any tangible fixed assets held are consistent with the scale and type of activities undertaken by the charity, and
- where accruals accounts are prepared, confirming with the trustees that they are satisfied that the charity is a going concern and that there are no post balance sheet events requiring adjustments to be made to the accounts or disclosure in the notes to the accounts.

6.3 Where analytical review procedures identify any unusual items, unexpected fluctuation or inconsistency, then explanations should be sought from the charity trustees or, where appropriate, the charity's staff.

6.4 Only if the explanations provided by the charity trustees or, where appropriate, the charity's staff, do not satisfy the examiner, will additional procedures be necessary. It is important to document in the working papers what items the examiner has found which required further explanation or review and any additional procedures undertaken to confirm those items or matters. Such procedures may include:
- physical inspection of a tangible fixed asset;
- verification of title to an asset;
- inspection of third party documentary evidence (e.g. invoice, contract or agreement) to verify an expense or liability or to confirm an amount of income received or receivable;
- third party certification of a bank balance, or other asset held including the custody of investment certificates; and
- checking of a post year end receipt or payment to confirm recoverability of a debt or the amount of a liability.

6.5 A comprehensive list of analytical procedures, and of additional procedures where concerns arise, is beyond the scope of this publication, and will to an extent be an area in which t he examiner will need to exercise judgement and to draw on experience as to what is reasonable given the size and nature of the charity's activities.

Comment

The examiner is required to carry out analysis and review procedures of the accounts to identify any unusual items, disclosures or omissions.

Where concerns arise, the examiner must seek and obtain satisfactory information and explanations from the charity trustees. If, after making these enquiries, the examiner still has reason to believe that the accounts may be materially misstated, he or she must carry out additional procedures as necessary to give that negative assurance. These additional procedures take the form of audit procedures and include the verification of an asset or liability, or the vouching of an incoming resource or application of that resource.

Analytical procedures may include:

(a) comparing the accounts with those of previous periods and, if available, with budgets and forecasts;
(b) obtaining explanations from the trustees for any unusual fluctuations or inconsistencies;
(c) considering the effect of any unadjusted errors – individually and in aggregate, bringing those to the attention of the trustees and determining how they will influence the report on the examination;
(d) reading the accounts to consider, on the basis of the information which has come to the examiner's attention, whether the accounts appear to conform with the basis of accounting indicated;
(e) considering the adequacy of the disclosures and their suitability as to classification and presentation;
(f) enquiring of the trustees concerning, for example:
  (i) whether all transactions have been recorded;
  (ii) whether the accounting policies comply with applicable accounting standards and SORPs, whether they have been applied appropriately and consistently and, if not, that disclosures have been made of any changes, and
  (iii) changes in the charity's activities and accounting principles and practices;
(g) reading the minutes of trustees' and any executive committees' meetings in order to identify matters which could be important to the examination;
(h) enquiring about the existence of transactions with related parties, how such transactions have been accounted for and whether related parties have been properly disclosed;
(i) enquiring about commitments and contingencies, and
(j) obtaining a letter of representation.

A full understanding of the objectives and activities of the charity will be necessary in order for the analytical review work to be properly performed.

Independent examination

24.8.7 Form and content of accounts

Direction 7

The examiner shall carry out such procedures as the examiner considers necessary to provide a reasonable basis on which to decide whether or not the accounts prepared under section 42(1) of the Charities Act 1993 comply with the form and content requirements of the 2008 Regulations including their preparation in accordance with the methods and principles set out in the Statement of Recommended Practice: Accounting and Reporting by Charities (the SORP); or in the case of a charity that is a company, whether or not the accounts are prepared in accordance with sections 396 of the Companies Act 2006, and are prepared in accordance with the methods and principles of the SORP.

Guidance

7.1 By far the majority of non-company charities have a gross income of £100,000 or less and are eligible to prepare receipts and payments accounts. A minority of charities – those with a gross income in excess of £100,000 and all charitable companies irrespective of their income – should prepare accruals accounts in accordance with the SORP. On occasion the examiner may encounter receipts and payments accounts which are accompanied by a balance sheet instead of a Statement of Assets and Liabilities. Provided that no non-cash items have been put through the receipts and payments accounts the examiner should treat those accounts as receipts and payments accounts, otherwise the accounts should be regarded as accruals accounts and should be examined accordingly.

7.2 The 2008 Regulations draw heavily on the recommendations of the SORP. Where accruals accounts are prepared, the examiner will require access to the SORP and an understanding of its principles to ensure compliance with the 2008 Regulations.

7.3 Where accounts are prepared under section 42(1) (the accruals basis), the 2008 Regulations require the accounts to be prepared in accordance with the method and principles of the SORP. The SORP requires all charities preparing accruals accounts to prepare a Statement of Financial Activities, balance sheet, and accompanying notes to the accounts. Charities eligible for independent examination enjoy greater flexibility and Appendix 5 of the SORP details all the concessions that are available for smaller charities preparing accruals accounts.

7.4 The 2008 Regulations concerning the content of accounts do not apply to the accounts of charitable companies. The accounts of charitable companies must be prepared in accordance with section 396 of the Companies Act 2006. The trustees of a charitable company must prepare accounts to give a 'true and fair' view, and this will generally involve compliance with accounting standards and the SORP. Financial Reporting Standard 18, Accounting Policies, requires particular disclosures to be made and explanations to be provided where a SORP has not been followed.

7.5 The examiner should review accruals accounts in sufficient detail to be able to identify any significant non-compliance with the 2008 Regulations or with the methods and principles of the SORP. This will involve a review of the format of the Statement of Financial Activities and Balance Sheet and the inclusion of necessary notes to the accounts. These review procedures should be sufficiently detailed to enable the examiner to decide whether or not any non-compliance with the 2008 Regulations or the SORP should be identified in the examiner's report.

7.6 A set of compliant accounts in the SORP format is available for non-company charities in the Charity Commission's *Accruals Accounts Pack* (CC17).

Form and content of accounts

7.7 For charitable companies, section 396 of the Companies Act 2006 requires the preparation of individual accounts. In the case of not-for-profit undertakings, including charities, the Companies Act 2006 section 474(2) substitutes an income and expenditure account for the profit and loss account. In addition a balance sheet is required and additional information is to be provided in the notes. The SORP requires all charities preparing accruals accounts to prepare a Statement of Financial Activities, Balance Sheet, and accompanying notes to the accounts. A charitable company will therefore usually submit a Statement of Financial Activities that incorporates an income and expenditure account; it may, however, opt to submit both an income and expenditure account and a Statement of Financial Activities. In such cases the examiner will review the two statements for consistency.

7.8 The 2008 Regulations do not specify the form and content of accounts prepared on a receipts and payments basis. The Commission does provide a pro forma layout for such accounts in its *Receipts and Payments Accounts Pack* (CC16).

7.9 The threshold for the preparation of receipts and payments accounts has been raised to £250,000 gross income (previously £100,0000) with effect for financial years ending on or after 1 April 2009 and the guidance will be updated once this planned change takes effect.

Comment

This procedure differs from that specified for an audit exemption report. An independent examiner is required to state whether or not any matter has come to his or her attention that causes him or her to believe that the statement of

Independent examination

accounts does not comply with any of the requirements (except the requirement to show a true and fair view) of the Regulations which prescribe the form and content of the statement of accounts. A reporting accountant is, however, only required to state whether the accounts have been drawn up in a manner consistent with the specified accounting requirements. The use of the words 'comply with' implies that the focus is on whether the statement of accounts complies with the substance of the legal requirements and not merely on whether it is in the required legal form.

For the majority of charities, a disclosure checklist should be completed.

As regards fixed assets, for example, detailed procedures may include the following:

(a) obtaining, or preparing, a lead schedule;
(b) considering whether fixed assets are included in the balance sheet under the appropriate caption in the format prescribed by the Regulations and recommended by the revised SORP;
(c) considering whether they are included on a basis permitted by the revised SORP;
(d) discussing with the trustees the capitalisation policy, additions to, and disposals from, fixed assets and enquiring whether all movements and profits and losses have been properly accounted for;
(e) *if necessary, vouching additions and disposals to supporting documentation;
(f) *if necessary, verifying fixed assets by establishing title or physical verification;
(g) discussing with the trustees the policy for depreciation and whether it is consistent with previous years;
(h) considering whether fixed assets are being written off systematically over their useful economic lives;
(i) comparing depreciation rates with prior periods;
(j) considering whether fixed assets have suffered a permanent diminution in value;
(k) enquiring of the trustees that all information, e.g. regarding fixed assets not capitalised, is disclosed in the accounts;
(l) enquiring of the trustees whether any of the fixed assets are subject to any form of security and, if so, that the details are fully disclosed in the statement of accounts;
(m) discussing with the trustees whether all lease agreements are properly reflected in the statement of accounts, and
(n) enquiring of the trustees whether all capital commitments are identified and properly disclosed

* Only if the explanations received are not satisfactory.

24.8.8 Accounting policies, estimates and judgements

Direction 8

When accounts are prepared under section 42(1) of the Charities Act 1993, or in the case of a charity which is a company, prepared under section 396 of the Companies Act 2006, the examiner shall review the accounting policies adopted and consider their consistency with the Statement of Recommended Practice: Accounting and Reporting by Charities (the SORP) and their appropriateness to the activities of the charity. The examiner must also consider and review any significant estimate or judgment that has been made in preparing the accounts.

Guidance

8.1 Receipts and payments accounts report cash book transactions in the period and so are not affected by this Direction. If accounts are prepared on the receipts and payments basis under section 42(3), the only fundamental accounting concept which applies is that of consistency of presentation within the accounts. Accounting policies and judgmental issues have less relevance since the receipts and payments account is simply a factual record of money actually received and spent. The statement of assets and liabilities is a simple schedule of information.

8.2 Further guidance as to the form and content of receipts and payments accounts can be found in the notes included in Charity Commission's *Receipts and Payments Accounts Pack* (CC16).

8.3 Accounts prepared on an accruals basis involve the use of accounting policies that determine how transactions and events are reflected in accounts and estimates. Judgement may be necessary to arrive at monetary values to be included in accounts, for example the length of time over which an asset is to be depreciated.

8.4 Where accounts are prepared under section 42(1) (the accruals basis) or where the trustees prepare accounts to give a 'true and fair' view under the Companies Act 2006 section 396, the accounting policies adopted, and also any estimates or judgments made in preparing the accounts, may have a material effect on both the financial activities and state of affairs disclosed by the accounts. Such matters therefore require careful consideration by the examiner although the examiner does not have to form an opinion on whether the accounts give a 'true and fair' view.

8.5 The examiner should be satisfied that accounts are prepared on a basis consistent with the going concern assumption and accruals concept, and evaluate the accounting policies adopted and applied for appropriateness to the activities of the charity and consistency with the SORP. The accounting

Independent examination

policies adopted should ensure a relevant, reliable, comparable and understandable accounts presentation.

8.6 Where the accounts are not prepared on a going concern basis, the examiner should consider the alternative basis upon which they are prepared and ensure that the basis of preparation is adequately disclosed in the accounting policies section of the notes to the accounts.

8.7 The examiner should evaluate whether the accounting policies adopted are consistent with the methods and principles set out in SORP. Where the accounting policies are not consistent with the SORP, this should be drawn to the attention of the charity trustees and, if the effect on the accounts is material, the matter should be reported in the examiner's report unless corrected.

8.8 Where accounts are produced under the Companies Act the trustees must prepare the accounts to give a 'true and fair' view. However, the examiner is not required to provide an opinion as to whether the accounts give a 'true and fair' view. Where accounting policies are not consistent with the SORP, this should be drawn to the attention of the charity trustees by the examiner, and the item(s) in question, if the inconsistency is material, should be reported in the examiner's report unless corrected.

8.9 The SORP requires any departure from its recommendations to be explained in the notes to the accounts of both company and non-company charities. A departure is only justifiable if it is necessary in order to give a 'true and fair' view and such circumstances will be rare. In the case of a departure, the examiner will need to check that the explanation required by the SORP has been provided. Where a material departure has not been adequately justified or explained, the examiner should make a comment in their report.

8.10 The examiner must evaluate the reasonableness of any estimates or judgments made in preparing the accounts where these are material to the accounts. Matters that may require consideration include:
- transfers to or from restricted fund accounts;
- valuation of gifts in kind;
- valuation of fixed asset investments where no market prices exist;
- estimates resulting from transactions not being fully recorded in the accounting records, and
- where an activity based approach has been adopted, the allocation of costs between the various expenditure categories of the Statement of Financial Activities.

Comment

The policies adopted by the charity trustees should comply with the fundamental accounting concepts and be appropriate to the activities of the charity. Unlike a reporting accountant, the examiner would need to consider, for example, the going concern concept.

Unlike a reporting accountant, the examiner must consider the reasonableness of any estimates or judgements which are material to the statement of accounts and whether that statement complies with applicable accounting standards and SORPs.

24.8.9 Trustees' Annual Report

Direction 9

When accounts are prepared under section 42(1) of the Charities Act 1993, or in the case of a charity which is a company, prepared under section 396 of the Companies Act 2006, the examiner shall compare the accounts to any financial references in the Trustees' Annual Report (if any), identifying any major inconsistencies, and consider the significance such matters will have on a proper and accurate understanding of the charity's accounts.

Guidance

9.1 If accounts are prepared on the receipts and payments basis under section 42(3) there is no requirement placed on the examiner to consider the Trustees' Annual Report. The examiner may, nevertheless, find the Annual Report a useful guide to the activities of the charity.

9.2 The Trustees' Annual Report (or for a company charity the combined trustees' and directors' report) provides a report of the charity's activities during the financial year. The Charity Commission publication *Charity Reporting and Accounts: The Essentials April 2008* (CC15a) sets out the information that should be contained in the Trustees' Annual Report. The legal requirements concerning the Trustees' Annual Report that apply to both company and non-company charities are set out in the 2008 Regulations.

9.3 Procedures should be directed at identifying inconsistencies between the Trustees' Annual Report and the accounts which are misleading or which contradict the financial information contained in the accounts. For example, a review should identify where amounts stated in the Annual Report are not consistent with those in the accounts or the nature or scale of activities described are inconsistent with the level of activity disclosed in the accounts. The level of reserves stated in the Annual Report should be consistent with amounts disclosed in the charity's balance sheet.

9.4 Where inconsistencies are identified which are significant, this should be drawn to the attention of the charity trustees. If no appropriate amendment is made to the Annual Report, then details of the matter should be provided in the examiner's report.

Comment

Any material inconsistency between the accounts is expressed with reference to the accounts, as this relates to the relevant power in the Charities Act 1993. Conversely, the equivalent provision in the Companies Act 2006 is with reference to the directors' report.

24.8.10 Examiner's report

Direction 10

The examiner shall review and assess all conclusions drawn from the evidence obtained from the examination and consider the implications on the report to be made under Regulation 31 of the 2008 Regulations. If the examiner has cause to make a positive statement on any matter arising from the provisions of Regulation 31(h) or 31(i), or to make a statement on any matter arising from the provisions of Regulation 31(j), then the examiner must ensure so far as practicable that the report gives a clear explanation of the matter and of its financial effects on the accounts presented.

Guidance

10.1 The examiner's report is the outcome of an independent examination and is addressed to the trustees. It either confirms that all the matters the examiner is required to review as set out by the 2008 Regulations have been met, or identifies which requirements have not been met, together with any matters that need reporting for the benefit of the reader's understanding of the charity's accounts. The examiner needs to consider carefully the conclusions drawn from his examination, and the impact of these conclusions on their report.

10.2 The 2008 Regulations set out the legal requirements for an independent examiner's report. An independent examination is not an audit and the examiner is required to consider a limited number of specified matters in his report and to confirm that nothing has come to his attention in the course of his examination which leads him to conclude that certain requirement have not been met. The report provides 'negative' assurance requiring the examiner to give an opinion only on a matter where he has found that a requirement has not been met. The matters to be reported on are listed in paragraph 10.4.

10.3 The first part of the examiner's report is a factual statement. The report must state:
- the examiner's name and address and the name of the charity concerned;

- the financial year in respect of which the accounts to which the report relates have been prepared, and where the charity is a charitable company, that the accounts do not require an audit in accordance with Part 16 of the Companies Act 2006;
- if the gross income exceeds £250,000, the qualification which enables the examiner to act as an independent examiner;
- any relevant professional qualification the examiner holds;
- in the event of the independent examination being allowed by dispensation in place of an audit, the date when the Commission dispensed with the requirement for an audit;
- that the report provided relates to an independent examination carried out under section 43 of the 1993 Act and that the examination has been conducted in accordance with the Directions given by the Commission.

10.4 After making these statements, the examiner must then state whether or not any matter has come to their attention, in connection with the examination, which gives reasonable cause to believe that in any material respect:
- where the charity is not a company, accounting have not been kept in accordance with section 41 of the Charities Act 1993; or
- where the charity is a charitable company, the accounting records have not been kept in accordance with section 386 of the Companies Act 2006; or
- the accounts do not accord with the accounting records; or
- where the accounts are prepared on an accruals basis for a non-company charity under section 42(1) of the Act 1993, they do not comply with the requirements of the 2008 Regulations setting out the form and content of charity accounts; (a charity's accounts consist of a Statement of Financial Activities and balance sheet and notes and are prepared in accordance with the methods and principles set out in the Statement of Recommended Practice), or
- where the accounts are prepared for a charitable company, the accounts do not comply with section 396 of the Companies Act and the methods and principles of the SORP.

10.5 Where any of the above matters have been identified, and the failure is considered material, there should be a clear explanation of the nature of the failure and, where it can be estimated, its financial effects on the accounts.

10.6 Where the concern relates to non-compliance in respect of the form and content of the accounts or material inconsistency with the SORP, the matter should be raised first with the charity trustees to seek the necessary amendment to the accounts.

10.7 The examiner in the second part of the report is also required to state whether or not any matter has come to their attention in connection with the examination to which, in the examiner's opinion, attention should be drawn in the report to enable a proper understanding of the accounts to be reached. It is expected that only significant matters will be reported.

Independent examination

Where accruals accounts are prepared, attention is drawn to matters which are material to the accounts. These matters should be brought to the attention of the charity trustees first with a view to seeking an amendment or adjustment to the accounts; but, if concerns remain, the matter should be addressed in the examiner's report. Where reported, the matter concerned should be fully explained together with the financial effects on the accounts.

10.8 There is also a requirement to provide a statement if the following specific matters have become apparent to the examiner during the course of the examination:
- any material expenditure or action which appears not to be in accordance with the trusts of the charity;
- any failure to be provided with information and explanation by any past or present trustee, officer or employee that is considered necessary for the examination, and
- in the case of accruals accounts any material inconsistency between the accounts and the Trustees' Annual Report, and in the case of a charitable company with the director's report.

10.9 In order to identify any material expenditure or activities undertaken outside the objects of the charity, an understanding of the stated objects of the charity, as set out in its governing document, is necessary. Small or immaterial levels of expenditure on purposes outside of the objects of the charity will not generally be included in the examiner's report. Material expenditure, or significant actions, contrary to the trusts of the charity would be a significant concern, and details should be included on the examiner's report. The examiner need not carry out specific checks or procedures to identify such breaches, but such matters when identified must be included in the examiner's report. The examiner will also need to consider whether a separate report of the matter needs to be sent to the Commission.

10.10 Any failure to be provided with information and explanations may seriously hamper an examination. If information and explanations requested are not provided to the examiner's satisfaction, this fact must be included in the examiner's report. A refusal to provide information or explanations is a serious matter and a separate report to the Commission may again be necessary

10.11 In the case of accounts prepared on an accruals basis, any major inconsistency between the accounts and the Trustees' Annual Report may give rise to misunderstanding. This should be brought to the attention of the charity trustees with a view to the amendment of the discrepancy. If the trustees decline to agree to change their Annual Report, or where concerns still exist this must be stated in the examiner's report.

10.12 For NHS charities independently examined by an examiner appointed by the Audit Commission or the Auditor General for Wales, the examiner has equivalent reporting duties that are set out in Regulation 32 of the 2008 Regulations.

Comment

The report should contain a clear expression of negative assurance. The examiner should review and assess all conclusions drawn from the evidence obtained as the basis for that expression.

Matters may come to the examiner's attention which cause him or her to express a qualification, in the relevant parts) of the examiner's report, of the negative assurance provided. For example, the Regulations require the examiner to state whether, during the examination, a matter has come to his or her attention which causes him or her to believe that the statement of accounts does not comply with the requirements of the Regulations. This might be the case where a current asset is stated at cost, rather than at its net realisable value, in which case an 'except for' report may be appropriate. Alternatively, there may be circumstances – for example, the non-consolidation of a subsidiary – where the matter is so material to the statement of accounts that an 'adverse' statement should be given.

The examiner is required to state whether or not any matter has come to his or her attention, in connection with the examination, to which, in his or her opinion, attention should be drawn in the report to enable a proper understanding of the accounts to be reached.

There may have been a limitation on the scope of the examiner's procedures. For example, a limitation of scope may be imposed by circumstances (where parts of the accounting records have been lost or destroyed, for instance). Alternatively, a limitation of scope may have been imposed by the directors (for example, where they refuse to provide information or explanations requested by the examiner).

Verification of the completeness of voluntary donations can often be a problem for the auditors of charities. Given the scope of the examination, however, that problem should not arise for the examiner. The procedures he or she will need to adopt will be restricted to:

(a) comparing the results with previous years and those expected for the current year and discussing significant variations with the trustees:
(b) discussing with the trustees whether the recognition of income has taken place in the correct accounting period, and
(c) ensuring that, where accruals accounts are prepared, the accounting policy is clearly stated and that the accounting records have been maintained in accordance with that policy.

Examples of examiners' reports are reproduced as **Annex 2** to this chapter.

24.8.11 Reports to the Charity Commission

As well as the 10 directions, there is also a statutory duty to report to the Charity Commission.

Independent examination

Direction

Sections 44A and 68A of the Charities Act 1993 place a duty upon the independent examiners of both non-company and company charities to make a report to the Charity Commission where, in the course of their examination, they identify a matter, which relates to the activities or affairs of the charity or of any connected institution or body and which the examiner has reasonable cause to believe is likely to be of material significance for the purposes of the exercise by the Commission of its functions under section 8 or 18 of the Charities Act 1993.

Guidance

11.1 In addition to making an examination report on the accounts, the examiner has a separate legal responsibility to report to the Charity Commission if a matter of material significance to the regulatory functions of the Commission is identified. This duty applies to both company and non-company charities which are registered with the Commission and to charities which are currently excepted from registration with the Commission.

11.2 It is important to emphasise that there is neither a legal duty nor an expectation that the examiner will actively go looking for matters of material significance that need to be reported. However, where the examiner comes across such matters as part of his work, he must make a report to the Commission. Normally the matter will relate to the year upon which the examiner is reporting and the examiner is not required to review the previous year's accounts and records. However, where a matter comes to light relating to a previous financial year which would give rise to a duty to report, then the examiner should still make a report.

11.3 The Commission and The Office of the Scottish Charity Regulator (OSCR) have agreed a shared list of 8 matters of material significance that should always be reported by an independent examiner. These are set out below:

- Matters suggesting dishonesty or fraud involving a significant loss of, or a major risk to, charitable funds or assets.
- Failure(s) of internal controls, including failure(s) in charity governance, that resulted in a significant loss or misappropriation of charitable funds, or which leads to significant charitable funds being put at major risk.
- Matters leading to the knowledge or suspicion that the charity or charitable funds have been used for money laundering or such funds are the proceeds of serious organised crime or that the charity is a conduit for criminal activity.

- Matters leading to belief or suspicion that the charity, its trustees, employees or assets have been involved in, or used to support, terrorism or proscribed organisations in the UK or outside of the UK.
- Evidence suggesting that in the way the charity carries out its work relating to the care and welfare of beneficiaries, the charity's beneficiaries have been or were put at significant risk of abuse or mistreatment.
- Significant or recurring breach(es) of either a legislative requirement or the charity's trusts.
- A deliberate or significant breach of an Order or Direction made by a charity regulator under statutory powers including suspending a charity trustee, prohibiting a particular transaction or activity or granting consent on particular terms involving significant charitable assets or liabilities.
- Any notification or matter reported to the trustees on resigning as independent examiner or matter that the examiner is aware of on resignation or ceasing to act that falls within the categories of reportable matters set out above.

11.4 Volunteer independent examiners may not encounter these situations very often when reviewing the accounts of charities; and so to help them, and to help all examiners, some illustrative examples are provided in Appendix 5 of CC32 of matters of material significance and where they may be identified in the course of the examiner's work.

11.5 The examiner must make a report to the Commission only if in the course of his independent examination he identifies a matter which he has reasonable cause to believe is likely to be of material significance for the purposes of the exercise by the Commission of its formal inquiry powers under section 8 or 18 of the Charities Act 1993.

11.6 The duty to report relates to information or evidence obtained from the examiner's work undertaken in following the Commission's Directions or whilst acting in the capacity of the examiner of a charity. A reporting requirement would not arise from minor breaches of trustees' obligations, or isolated administrative errors that are unlikely to jeopardise the charity's assets or amount to misconduct or mismanagement.

11.7 The duty to report applies to the examiner who must make a report, whether or not the matter has already been notified to other regulators or agencies and whether or not the trustees have already advised the Commission, for example, by making a serious incident report. In any event the examiner must keep the particular matters of material significance in mind as he carries out their examination.

11.8 Where the matter to be reported concerns terrorism, then the matter must be immediately reported to the Police before the examiner makes his report to the Commission.

Independent examination

11.9 Where the matter to be reported concerns money laundering, those examiners who are charging a fee are providing an accountancy service and so are governed by the Money Laundering Regulations and should advise the Serious Organised Crime Agency in the first instance. However, it is not expected that notifying the Commission, itself a regulator, will give rise to a 'tipping off' offence.

11.10 In preparing to make a report to the Commission on a matter of material significance, the examiner should gather together the relevant information or evidence about the matter and make a note of the significant concern(s) identified. The examiner may find it helpful to discuss the matter first with the trustees unless the matter concerns the honesty or integrity of the trustees. In particular, matters that involve terrorism or money laundering must always be immediately reported to the Police or Serious Organised Crime Agency and care exercised to ensure risks of 'tipping off' do not arise.

11.11 There should not be a delay in sending a report to the Commission as the duty to report is immediate. However, the Commission recognises that the examiner will need some time to consider the information or evidence identified and where appropriate to seek clarification or further explanation from the trustees. Where the trustees wish to explain the actions they have taken or propose to take, this may be appended to the examiner's report.

11.12 Where a reporting duty arises, the examiner should report the matter either by e-mail to Whistleblowing@charitycommission.gsi.gov.uk or in writing to Charity Commission Direct, PO Box 1227, Liverpool, L69 3UG. The e-mail or letter should be headed 'Independent Examiner reporting a matter of material significance' and should provide the following information:
- the examiner's name and contact address, telephone number and/or e-mail address;
- the charity's name and registration number (if applicable);
- a statement that the report is made in accordance with section 44A of the Act 1993;
- under which of the eight headings of reportable matters (see paragraph 11.3) the report is being made;
- a description of the matter giving rise to concern and the information available on the matter reported; and, where possible, an estimate of the financial implications;
- where the trustees are attempting to deal with the situation, a brief description of any steps being taken by trustees of which the examiner has been made aware;
- if the report concerns terrorist, money laundering or other criminal activity, whether the examiner has notified the Serious Organised Crime Agency and/or Police as appropriate; and
- if the report concerns the abuse of vulnerable beneficiaries, whether the examiner has informed the Police and/or Social Services.

11.13 Section 44A of the 1993 Act also provides a discretionary power or right for the examiner to make a report to the Commission where the examiner becomes aware of a matter, where there is reasonable cause to believe the matter is likely to be relevant to the exercise of any of the Commission's functions. This is a very broad right and enables the examiner to advise the Commission of any matters that may be relevant to the Commission's functions but where the matter does not fall clearly within the category of being of material significance. This right might be used by an examiner, for example, where a matter has been identified that the examiner believes the Commission's input is necessary for its resolution.

11.14 It is not appropriate to give a list of issues where this discretionary power might be used because it is widely drawn and there is no obligation on the examiner to make a report. Examiners are encouraged not to report small or insignificant matters, particularly where such matters have been satisfactorily resolved internally or the matter can be resolved by the examiner through discussion with the trustees in the first instance.

11.15 Where the examiner is exercising his discretion to report a matter, the examiner should report either by e-mail to Whistleblowing@charitycommission.gsi.gov.uk or in writing to: Charity Commission Direct, PO Box 1227, Liverpool, L69 3UG. The examiner should:
- state the charity's name and registration number (if applicable);
- state the examiner's name and contact address, telephone number and/ or e-mail address;
- state that the report is made using the examiner's power of discretion to report a matter relevant to the work of the Commission in accordance with section 44A of the Act 1993;
- describe the matter and the examiner's view of its relevance to the work of the Commission, and, where possible, provide an estimate of the financial implications, and
- where the trustees are attempting to deal with the situation, give a brief description of any steps being taken by the trustees of which the examiner is aware.

11.16 Appendix 5 of CC32 provides further advice, particularly for volunteer examiners, on matters of material significance that may be reportable to the Commission. It also provides examples of how a letter to the Commission might be set out where a reportable matter is identified or where the examiner chooses to exercise his discretionary power or right to report a matter. Where a report is made to the Commission under these provisions, the examiner cannot be held to be in breach of any duty to the trustees or the charity, for example breach of confidence. The examiner enjoys legal protection in relation to the information or opinions contained in the report made to the Commission.

Independent examination

Comment

Examples are reproduced as **Annex 3** to this chapter.

In order to avoid deluging the Charity Commission, matters that do not lead to a material loss or misapplication of funds, and which belong in a report to the trustees, should not be reported.

24.9 Reporting on summarised accounts

There is no statutory requirement for an independent examiner of a company charity to report on summarised accounts. The terms of engagement may, however, include the provision of a separate report to enable the trustees to follow the SORP's principles. Where summarised accounts are issued, the procedures that the independent examiner will adopt should be similar to those that auditors will adopt. These are discussed in **Chapter 20**.

Reporting on summarised accounts

Annex 1 – Guidance on the selection of an examiner Charity Commission guidance under section 43(7)(a) of the Charities Act 1993

Guidance from the Charity Commission to charity trustees on the selection of a person for appointment as an independent examiner. References to sections are references to the 1993 Act.

1. The requirement for an independent examination

1.1 The following criteria determine eligibility for independent examination:
- Charities with a gross income in the current year exceeding £10,000 must have their accounts independently examined, or may choose to have the accounts audited.
- All charities whose gross income is more than £500,000 must have a professional audit. Trustees cannot opt for an independent examination if this threshold is exceeded.
- All charities whose governing document requires them to have an audit must do so (although if this means a higher level of scrutiny is necessary than otherwise required by the 1993 Act we are prepared to consider an amendment to the governing document to accord with the 1993 Act provisions).

1.2 The charity trustees should take steps to ensure that a competent examination takes place and they will therefore wish to consider most carefully the suitability of a prospective independent examiner.

1.3 Charity trustees are entitled to pay reasonable remuneration to an independent examiner for services rendered and if they are unable to obtain the services of a competent examiner on a voluntary basis, should be prepared to pay such remuneration and regard it as a proper charge on the assets of the charity.

2. The independent examiner

2.1 An independent examiner as described in section 43(3)(a) is 'an independent person who is reasonably believed by the charity trustees to have the requisite ability and practical experience to carry out a competent examination of the accounts'. Once a charity's gross income exceeds £250,000, the examiner must be a person who is a member of one of the

Annex 1 – Guidance on the selection of an examiner – guidance s. 43(7)(a)

following bodies listed in the 1993 Act and should be allowed by the rules of that body to undertake the roles of independent examiner:
- Institute of Chartered Accountants in England and Wales
- Institute of Chartered Accountants in Scotland
- Institute of Chartered Accountants in Ireland
- Association of Chartered Certified Accountants
- Association of Authorised Public Accountants
- Association of Accounting Technicians
- Association of International Accountants
- Chartered Institute of Management Accountants
- Institute of Chartered Secretaries and Administrators
- Chartered Institute of Public Finance and Accountancy; or
- Association of Charity Independent Examiners

If the charity's annual income is below £250,000, the independent examiner does not need to have an appropriate qualification but will need to be independent and appropriately experienced.

3. An independent person

3.1 For an examiner to be independent, that individual should have no connection with the charity trustees which might inhibit the impartial conduct of the examination.

3.2 Whether this connection exists will depend upon the circumstances of a particular charity but the following persons at least will normally be considered to have such a connection:
 (a) the charity trustees or anyone else who is closely involved in the administration of the charity;
 (b) a major donor to, or major beneficiary of, the charity; or
 (c) a close relative, spouse, partner, business partner or employee of any person who falls within sub-paragraph (a) or (b) above.

4. Requisite ability

4.1 In the House of Lords' debate on the Charities Bill, it was stated that 'an independent examiner must obviously be competent for the task that he is to do and he must be familiar with accounting methods, but he need not be a practising accountant. We have in mind ... people such as bank or building society managers, local authority treasurers or retired accountants. They would all be suitable as independent examiners'.

4.2 The quality of evidence of ability which is required will depend upon the size and nature of the charity's transactions. Charity trustees should consider taking independent references on the capability of the prospective independent examiner to carry out this function.

5. Practical experience

5.1 Charity trustees should satisfy themselves that prospective examiners have practical experience relevant to the charity in question which might be by virtue of that person having:

Annex 1 Guidance on the selection of an examiner – guidance s. 43(7)(a)

- had an involvement in the financial administration of a charity of a similar nature; or
- acted successfully as an independent examiner on previous occasions for such charities, or
- relevant practical experience in accountancy or commerce.

6. Selection procedures

6.1 Charity trustees should discuss fully with the prospective examiner the work of the charity and their expectations. They should ensure that the prospective independent examiner is conversant with the Charity Commission Directions to independent examiners and the nature of the independent examiners' report prescribed by relevant Regulations made under section 44(1)(c). Where the accounts are prepared under section 42(1), the examiner should also be conversant with the Regulations made under section 42(1) as to the form and content of those accounts and the relevant SORP.

6.2 Charity trustees should take all necessary steps to satisfy themselves as to the matters referred to in paragraphs 3 to 5 above.

6.3 Charity trustees should ensure that any written terms of engagement recognise and do not limit the examiner's statutory duties.

6.4 Charity trustees who follow these guidelines and gain suitable assurances from prospective examiners and from any references can be satisfied that they have taken all reasonable steps to obtain a competent independent examination of their accounts for the period in question.

Annex 2 – Examples of Independent examiner's reports

Example 1: Independent Examiner's unqualified report (for non-company charity – gross income less than £250,000)

Independent Examiner's Report to the Trustees of ABC Trust

I report on the accounts of the Trust for the year ended 30 April 2009, which are set out on pages — to —.

Respective responsibilities of trustees and examiner

The charity's trustees are responsible for the preparation of the accounts. The charity's trustees consider that an audit is not required for this year under section 43(2) of the Charities Act 1993 (the 1993 Act) and that an independent examination is needed.

It is my responsibility to:

- examine the accounts under section 43 of the 1993 Act;
- to follow the procedures laid down in the general Directions given by the Charity Commission under section 43(7)(b) of the 1993 Act; and
- to state whether particular matters have come to my attention.

Basis of independent examiner's report

My examination was carried out in accordance with the Charity Commission's Directions. An examination includes a review of the accounting records kept by the charity and a comparison of the accounts presented with those records. It also includes consideration of any unusual items or disclosures in the accounts, and seeking explanations from you as trustees concerning any such matters. The procedures undertaken do not provide all the evidence that would be required in an audit, and consequently no opinion is given as to whether the accounts present a 'true and fair view' and the report is limited to those matters set out in the statement below.

Independent examiner's statement

In connection with my examination, no matter has come to my attention:

(1) which gives me reasonable cause to believe that in any material respect the requirements:

Example 2: Independent Examiner's unqualified report (for company charity)

- to keep accounting records in accordance with section 41 of the 1993 Act; and
- to prepare accounts which accord with the accounting records and comply with the accounting requirements of the 1993 Act,

have not been met; or

2) to which, in my opinion, attention should be drawn in order to enable a proper understanding of the accounts to be reached.

Name:

Relevant professional qualification or body:

Address:

Date:

Example 2: Independent Examiner's unqualified report (for company charity – gross income more than £250,000)

Independent examiner's report to the trustees of WXY Charitable Company

I report on the accounts of the company charity for the year ended 30 April 2009, which are set out on pages — to —.

Respective responsibilities of trustees and examiner

The trustees, who are also the directors of the company for the purposes of company law, are responsible for the preparation of the accounts. The trustees consider that an audit is not required for this year under section 43(2) of the Charities Act 1993 (the 1993 Act) and that an independent examination is needed. The charity's gross income exceeded £250,000 and I am qualified to undertake the examination by being a qualified member of ICAEW.

Having satisfied myself that the company charity is not subject to audit under company law and is eligible for independent examination, it is my responsibility to:

- examine the accounts under section 43 of the 1993 Act;
- follow the procedures laid down in the Directions given by the Charity Commission under section 43(7)(b) of the 1993 Act; and
- to state whether particular matters have come to my attention.

Basis of independent examiner's report

My examination was carried out in accordance with the Directions given by the Charity Commission. An examination includes a review of the accounting

Annex 2 – Examples of Independent examiner's reports

records kept by the company charity and a comparison of the accounts presented with those records. It also includes consideration of any unusual items or disclosures in the accounts, and explanations sought from you as trustees concerning any such matters. The procedures undertaken do not provide all the evidence that would be required in an audit and consequently no opinion is given as to whether the accounts present a 'true and fair view' and the report is limited to those matters set out in the statement below.

Independent examiner's statement

In connection with my examination, no matter has come to my attention:

(1) which gives me reasonable cause to believe that in any material respect the requirements:
- to keep accounting records in accordance with section 386 of the Companies Act 2006; and
- to prepare accounts which accord with the accounting records, comply with the accounting requirements of section 396 of the Companies Act 2006 and with the methods and principles of the Statement of Recommended Practice: Accounting and Reporting by Charities

have not been met; or

(2) to which, in my opinion, attention should be drawn in order to enable a proper understanding of the accounts to be reached.

Name:

Relevant professional qualification or body:

Address:

Date:

Example 3: Independent Examiner's qualified report – failure to identify a restricted fund Receipts and Payments accounts (non–company charity)

Independent examiner's report to the trustees of EFG Trust

I report on the accounts of the Trust for the year ended 30 April 2009, which are set out on pages — to —.

Example 3: Independent Examiner's qualified report

Respective responsibilities of trustees and examiner

The charity's trustees are responsible for the preparation of the accounts. The charity's trustees consider that an audit is not required for this year (under section 43(2) of the Charities Act 1993 (the 1993 Act)) and that an independent examination is needed.

It is my responsibility to:

- examine the accounts under section 43 of the 1993 Act;
- to follow the procedures laid down in the general Directions given by the Charity Commission under section 43(7)(b) of the 1993 Act, and
- to state whether particular matters have come to my attention.

Basis of examiner's statement

My examination was carried out in accordance with the Charity Commission's Directions. An examination includes a review of the accounting records kept by the charity and a comparison of the accounts presented with those records. It also includes consideration of any unusual items or disclosures in the accounts, and explanations sought from you as trustees concerning any such matters. The procedures undertaken do not provide all the evidence that would be required in an audit and consequently no opinion is given as to whether the accounts present a 'true and fair view' and the report is limited to those matters set out in the statement below.

Independent examiner's qualified statement

The trustees have prepared receipts and payments accounts but have not separately identified restricted funds within those accounts. At the end of one church service a special appeal was held for a mission to Samarkand, but the money was banked together with the routine collection and no separate record kept of the amount received. The accounts show the expenditure on the mission to Samarkand was separately identified and amounted to £2,837. The trustees pointed out that the banking for that service was £1,978 against an average weekly banking of £1,275, but they have now put in place a protocol to ensure that any appeals are now counted and banked separately.

In connection with my examination, no other matter except that referred to in the above paragraph has come to my attention:

(1) which gives me reasonable cause to believe that in any material respect the requirements:
   - to keep accounting records in accordance with section 41 of the 1993 Act; and
   - to prepare accounts which accord with the accounting records and comply with the accounting requirements of the 1993 Act

Annex 2 – Examples of Independent examiner's reports

           have not been met; or
(2) to which, in my opinion, attention should be drawn in order to enable a proper understanding of the accounts to be reached.

Name:

Relevant professional qualification or body:

Address:
Date:

Annex 3 – Examples of deliberate or reckless misconduct

Deliberate or reckless misconduct in the administration of a charity

Matters that give rise to a reporting duty primarily concern the improper use of charity assets which has resulted, or could result from the deliberate or reckless misconduct of one or more of the charity trustees in the administration of the charity. The following are examples of such misconduct.

1. Where a deliberate abuse of charity assets by one or more of the charity trustees has come to the examiner's attention, a reporting duty will arise. Matters that require consideration will include:
evidence of false accounting by any charity trustee;
evidence of theft or misappropriation by any charity trustee, and
evidence giving rise to doubts as to the honesty or integrity of any charity trustee.

2. A breach of legislative requirement or an action contrary to the trusts of the charity may also need to be reported. However, a reporting duty will only arise if information or evidence exists which indicates that such an action was taken or sanctioned deliberately or recklessly by a charity trustee. Moreover, a reporting duty would only arise if, as a result of such action, the charity suffered or was likely to suffer a material loss or misapplication of its assets. Matters that may require consideration include:
   - a material application of funds clearly outside the objects of the charity;
   - a breach of law or regulation that could jeopardise future activities or result in a material pecuniary loss (for example, an attempt to evade any direct or indirect tax properly payable), and
   - an attempt by any charity trustee to obtain an improper pecuniary benefit for himself or another and/or to the detriment of the charity.

3. The charity trustees are responsible for the control and management of a charity's affairs. Where there has been a gross neglect of these duties which has resulted, or could result, in a material loss of charity assets, consideration will need to be given as to whether this has arisen from deliberate or reckless misconduct by the charity trustees in the administration of the charity. Factors that will require consideration include:
   - a failure of the trustee body to meet or consider issues affecting the charity;

Annex 3 – Examples of deliberate or reckless misconduct

- a gross failure on the part of the trustee body to keep accounting records, and
- evidence of indifference or recklessness on the part of a charity trustee or the trustee body – for example, evidence that professional advice has been disregarded without due consideration or a failure to take action in the case of fraud within or affecting the charity.

Chapter 25 – Trading income

25.1 Main statutory exemption

The main statutory exemptions from tax for the income of a charity are contained in section 505 of the Income and Corporation Taxes Act 1988 (ICTA 1988). These exemptions relate to:

(a) income from land;
(b) income assessable under Case III of Schedule D, such as bank interest, gift aid payments, and annual payments, and
(c) trading income.

In this chapter the various trading income exemptions are considered.

The restrictions, which apply to trading income received by charities, are more restrictive than for all other types of income except that received under Schedule D Case VI. A charity is exempt from tax on the profits of any trade carried on in the UK or elsewhere, which is:

(a) exercised in the course of the actual carrying out of a primary purpose of the charity; or
(b) mainly carried out by beneficiaries of the charity, or
(c) the turnover of a non-primary purpose trade falls below certain limits

provided that it is applied solely for charitable purposes.

In light of the above, the aim of this chapter is to explain how HMRC treats trading profits of charities for tax purposes. It will also look at the exemptions from tax available for trading profits both under statute (mentioned above) and by concession. It will then look at some common trading activities and also give some guidance on calculating the amount of the profits of a trade carried on by a charity. Towards the end of the chapter there is a section describing ways in which non-exempt trading profits can be passed to a charity in such a way that no tax will be payable. Finally, the factors to take into account when a charity invests in a trading company are examined.

25.2 What is a trade?

Many charities carry on trades, either as part of their charitable activities or to raise funds. Many charities often fail to take account of the possibility of trading because they are of the opinion that 'we are not trading because we are not a commercial body'. However, what matters from a tax point of view is not the type of body but the type of activity being carrying on. The key question to consider, therefore, is whether the activity of the charity amounts to the carrying on of a trade for income tax purposes. The definition of a trade is very wide. Section 832 of ICTA 1988 states that 'trade includes every trade, manufacture, venture or concern in the nature of trade'. This is a very wide definition and, over the years, the courts have established a number of so-called 'badges of trade'. These are:

- profit-seeking motives
- existing trade connections
- repetition
- method of finance
- interval between purchase and sale
- selling organisation
- inheritance or donation – method of acquisition
- operations pending sale; and
- nature of asset.

Normally, a trade involves the sale of goods or services to customers as part of a commercial enterprise. A one-off or occasional venture may be treated as a trade for tax purposes if it involves the sale of goods or the provision of services for profit.

In most cases it will be clear whether an activity is, or is not, a trade. However, sometimes it will not be easy to decide whether there is a trade – for example, when a one-off transaction has taken place. There will be a need to look at all of the circumstances surrounding the activity.

At this stage, when deciding whether activity amounts to a trade, it is irrelevant that the profits are intended to be used for charitable purposes.

'The profit cannot be taxable because we are using it for a charity' is a very common misunderstanding, which can be very expensive. It is necessary to distinguish clearly between expenditure that is incurred in the earning of the income and expenditure that effectively amounts to the disposal of the income. The former will be an allowable expense in calculating the profit (or loss) from the venture whilst the latter has no immediate bearing on the tax position at all.

Trading by charities can take a number of forms. However, general trades carried on by charities fall into one of two broad categories:

(a) trades that are exercised in the course of the actual carrying-out of a primary purpose of a charity (for example, a religious charity selling religious books) or where the trade is carried on mainly by its beneficiaries (the manufacture and sale of poppies by ex-servicemen); or

(b) trades that are not themselves part of the primary purpose of the charity but which are designed to raise funds to be applied for charitable purposes (for example, sales of promotional items).

25.3 Statutory exemption from tax

The legislation provides very limited exemption from tax for the profits of a trade carried on by charities. To qualify for exemption the profits must be used solely for the purposes of the charity. In addition the trade must satisfy one of the three following conditions:

(a) the trade must be exercised in the course of the actual carrying out of the primary purpose of the charity (a 'primary purpose trade') or be ancillary to this primary purpose trade, or
(b) the work in connection with the trade must be mainly carried out by beneficiaries of the charity, or
(c) the turnover of a non-primary purpose trade must fall below certain limits

If a trade does not satisfy one of the above conditions, the profits of the trade will not be exempt from tax regardless of whether or not they are used for the purposes of the charity. However some fundraising events may qualify for a concessionary relief under an extra-statutory concession which will be described in more detail below.

25.4 Trading activities of charities

It will be helpful before we look at the above exemptions to consider some of the various types of activities of charities, which could be regarded as trading.

Sponsorship

Sponsorship is often an important source of funds for many charities. If it is a simple donation, with nothing required in return, then there will be no question of trading. It should, however, be borne in mind that sponsors could not expect to get any tax relief against profits for their payment. For this reason, sponsors usually look for some tangible return for their generosity – for example, a prominent display of their name, the opportunity to advertise in the event programme or perhaps complimentary tickets to a function. Once this happens, the charity moves into a much greyer area, where trading becomes a possibility.

The activity will move into a trade where a charity incorporates large and prominent displays of the sponsor's logo or corporate colours, or mentions specific products or services in publicity for events. Where the charity, in return for sponsorship, allows the sponsor access to its membership mailing list, once again it will become a trading situation. Similarly, where a charity takes steps to actively endorse a product of the sponsor, that too will be regarded as trading.

Once it has been determined that sponsorship payments are trading income in the charity's hand, the next step is to consider whether the sponsorship arrangement is a trade in its own right or part of the income of a wider trade.

Where the sponsorship is intended to fund an activity of the charity which is in itself a trade, the payment will be regarded as part of the income of that trade, so that the tax treatment will follow the tax treatment of the profits of that trade. For example, where a business angel sponsors a stage production at a theatre, the sponsorship payments will be regarded as part of the income of a trade of putting on the stage production. Whether or not the sponsorship income in such a case would be exempt from tax would depend on whether or not the trade was exercised in the course of the actual carrying out of a primary purpose of the charity.

Lotteries

Charities may run lotteries in order to raise funds for their charitable purposes as defined in sections 3 and 5 of the Lotteries and Amusements Act 1976. Lotteries are undertaken on a clear profit motive.

The profits of such a lottery – whether promoted by charities or by subsidiary companies on their behalf – are exempt from tax, provided that the lottery is conducted within the requirements of this Act and the lottery profits are applied solely to the purpose of the charity.

Where a subsidiary company, rather than the charity, is registered as the society under section 5 of the Lotteries and Amusements Act 1976, for tax purposes, the lottery profits will belong to the company and not to the charity. The exemption will not apply and the company will need to pass the profits to the charity under gift aid (see below) to obtain relief from tax.

Charity shops

Charity shops are a common feature of many high streets. To the extent that the shops sell only donated goods, such as clothes or bric-a-brac, there will be no problem because HMRC accepts that the charity is merely turning donations in kind into cash donations. The sale of goods that have been donated to a charity is not trading. This is so even where the donated goods are sorted, cleaned and given minor repairs. However, if the goods are subjected to significant refurbishment or to any process that brings them into a different condition for sale than that in which they were donated, the sale proceeds may regarded as trading income.

Many charity shops also buy in a variety of goods, in which case the sale proceeds of those goods will be seen as a trading activity. Where a charity shop sells both donated goods and bought-in stock, the trading activities will need to be separately identified from the non-trading activities.

This situation might arise in a shop run by a charity whose aim is to enhance the skills of disabled people. The shop might sell, for example:

- books, CDs and videos donated for sale – not trading
- wooden toys made by disabled people ('primary purpose trading'), and
- bought-in soft toys ('non-primary purpose trading'), the only purpose of which is to raise funds.

In this case, the only trading being conducted is that in wooden toys and soft toys. The trade is separated into its primary purpose and non-primary purpose elements.

Christmas cards

Christmas cards are a common means of fundraising. The activity is clearly a commercial one and is in competition with commercial card manufacturers and is therefore seen as a trading activity.

Affinity card schemes

Affinity card schemes are an ever-increasing way in which charities raise money. They operate in a way under which the charity allows its name to be used by credit card companies who produce specifically designed cards. The key advantage for the credit card company is access to the charity members, who will be encouraged to use the card because the charity will benefit both from the original take-up of the card and from the usage of it. In such cases, there are usually two transactions involved – the licence of the charity name and logo, which will not be regarded as a trading activity (see below) and the sale by the charity of its mailing list of members. That list is a commercial asset and its exploitation will be regarded as a trading activity.

Payments for use of a charity's logo

Where a charity allows its logo to be used, in return for payment, by a business as an endorsement for one or more of the business's products or services, and the charity likewise promotes the endorsement in its own literature, the payments are likely to be trading income of the charity.

Payments **solely** for the use of a charity's logo may be annual payments rather than trading income. Whether payments for use of the logo are considered to be annual payments will depend on the precise terms of the agreement for the use of the logo. The payment must be made under a legal obligation, recur each year and be a pure donation in the hands of the charity. The charity can reclaim the tax that the payer deducts when making annual payments, provided that the income is applied solely for charitable purposes.

Profits from lettings

Rental income from land and buildings received by a charity is exempt from tax under section 505 of ICTA 1988, provided that it is applied for charitable purposes. This may arise from either land or buildings that are held as investment property by the charity or from property that is not being used by the charity. For example, a college may let its buildings as conference facilities outside term time.

However, if services are provided in addition to the use of land and buildings, such as the provision of food or the use of office facilities, these activities may become trading activities. Each case needs to be considered on its own facts.

25.5 Primary purpose trades

As mentioned above, trading activities that are exercised in the course of the actual carrying out of a primary purpose of the charity are exempt from tax. This exemption from tax is only available if the profits are applied solely for the purposes of the charity. Primary purpose trades will be identified from the charity's trust deed, constitution or other governing document.

Typical examples of primary purpose trading include:

(a) the charging of fees by a school fulfilling the primary object of advancement of education;
(b) the holding of an exhibition by an art gallery or museum in return for admission fees;
(c) the sale of tickets for a theatrical production staged by a theatre that has charitable status;
(d) the provision of healthcare services by hospitals in return for payment;
(e) the provision of residential accommodation by a residential care charity in return for payment, and
(f) the sale of certain educational goods by an art gallery or museum.

In each of the above examples it is assumed that the organisation carrying on the activity is a charity and that it is part of the organisation's charitable objects to undertake the activity described.

25.5.1 Ancillary trading

Ancillary trading contributes indirectly to the successful furtherance of the purposes of the charity. This is treated as part of 'primary purpose trading' for both charity law and tax purposes. The level of annual turnover in trading which is said to be ancillary may have a bearing on the question of whether or not the trading really is ancillary, but there is no specific level of annual turnover beyond which trading will definitely not be regarded as ancillary. Trading is not regarded as ancillary to the carrying out of a primary purpose of the charity simply because its purpose is to raise funds for the charity.

The exemption from tax also extends to other trades that are not primary purpose activities in themselves but which are ancillary to the carrying-out of a primary purpose so that they can still be said to be exercised in the course of the actual carrying-out of a primary purpose. Examples would be:

(a) the sale of relevant books for the benefit of students by a school or college;
(b) the provision of a crèche for the children of students by a school or college in return for payment;
(c) the sale of food and drink in a cafeteria to visitors to exhibits by an art gallery;
(d) the sale of food and drink in a restaurant or bar to members of an audience by a theatre, and
(e) the sale of confectionery, toiletries and flowers to patients and their visitors by a hospital or by a 'league of friends' group.

25.5.2 Non-primary purpose trading

Non-primary purpose trading is trading intended to raise funds for the charity, as distinct from trading which in itself furthers the charity's objects. Charities may engage in such trading only where no significant risk is involved. Charity law permits charities to carry on non-primary purpose trading in order to raise funds, provided that the trading involves no significant risk to the assets of the charity. The 'significant risk' to be avoided here is that the turnover is insufficient to meet the costs of carrying on the trade, and the difference has to be financed out of the assets of the charity.

Whether or not the risk of non-primary purpose trading is 'significant' depends on a number of factors, including:

- the size of the charity;
- the nature of the business;
- the expected outgoings;
- the projected turnover, and
- the sensitivity of business profitability to the ups and downs of the market.

There is no general exemption from corporation tax (or income tax in the case of charitable trusts) on the profits of non-primary purpose trading carried on by a charity, even where the profits are all applied for the charity's purposes. However, the small-scale exemption and the fundraising exemption may still apply.

25.5.3 Mixed trades

An example of 'mixed trades' is a shop that is run by a charity providing a public art gallery, and which may sell a range of goods, some connected with furthering the charity's primary purpose (for example, books relating to an exhibition, copies of the charity's paintings) and some not so connected (for example, promotional pens, mugs and tea towels).

Although in general terms a charity will actually only have one trade, for tax purposes, this type of mixed primary and non-primary purpose trading activity must be treated as two separate trades. In these circumstances, section 505 (1B) of ICTA 1988 (introduced by section 56 of the Finance Act 2006) deems the primary purpose and non-primary purpose parts of the trade to be two separate trades. The trade deemed to be primary purpose is exempt, as long as its profits are used for charitable purposes. The trade deemed as non-primary purpose is taxable, although the exemption for small trading can apply to this trade. Any receipts or expenses relating to the overall trade should be apportioned to the separate trades on a reasonable basis.

There are situations where trades are not wholly primary purpose trades. In such cases, a trade might amount in part to a primary purpose trade but may not be wholly a primary purpose trade. One example of this is the letting by a school or college of accommodation for students in term time, and for tourists outside term time. Another is the sale of food and drink in a theatre restaurant both to members of the audience and to the general public. In such circumstances, the trade might not qualify as a primary purpose trade because part of the trade is not related to a primary purpose. In practice, HMRC will accept that all of the profits of the trade will be within the exemption of tax if:

(a) the part of the trade that is not within the primary purpose is not large (that is, less than £50,000 per annum) in absolute terms, and
(b) the turnover of that part of the trade is less than 10 per cent of the turnover of the whole trade.

Where the profits of the trade cannot be exempted because part of the trade is not related to a primary purpose and it represents 10 per cent or more of the whole trade, the whole of the profits may be liable to tax, including that part of them that is related to a primary purpose.

If a charity incurs a loss from its non-primary purpose trading, the loss in connection with the trading will be regarded as 'non-charitable expenditure', within the meaning of s. 506(1) of the 1988 Act. This could result in a restriction of the charity's tax exemptions on other income and/or gains.

The Charity Commission's view is that incurring such a loss would only amount to a breach of trust if the loss had been incurred irresponsibly. There would, in the Charity Commission's view, be no breach of trust, if:

- there was a rational expectation that the trading would be successful;
- subsidiary, and
- the expenditure which gave rise to the loss was within the powers available to the trustees.

This treatment applies for accounting periods commencing on or after 22 March 2006. Previously, this type of trading was treated as wholly primary purpose or wholly non-primary purpose, depending on the size of the non-primary purpose element. Trustees of charities carrying on this type of trading will need to consider whether any restructuring is desirable.

Example 1

Charity A carries on a trade with an annual turnover of £60,000. Of this, £55,000 is primary purpose and £5,000 is not. Because the non-primary purpose turnover is less than 10 per cent of the total and less than £50,000, the whole trade is treated as primary purpose.

Example 2

Charity B carries on a trade with an annual turnover of £100,000. Of this, £85,000 is primary purpose and £15,000 is not. Because the non-primary purpose turnover exceeds 10% per cent of the total, the whole trade is treated as non-primary purpose.

25.5.4 Trades where the work is carried out by the beneficiaries of the charity

If the trade does not fall within the definition of primary purpose trades, the profits may be exempt because the beneficiaries of the charity mainly carry out the trade. This exemption was introduced in 1921 to provide exemption for the sale of works provided by disabled people. That type of activity would clearly still be relevant today, as would the sale of goods produced in developing countries and sold through aid shops or through mail order.

Where work carried out by beneficiaries has a therapeutic, remedial or educational value, the profits from the trade will often also qualify for exemption from tax as a primary purpose trade. But the exemption of tax is not restricted to such trades. It covers all trades where the work is mainly carried out by beneficiaries. Examples include:

(a) a farm operated by students of an agricultural college;
(b) a restaurant operated by students as part of a catering course run by a further education college, and
(c) the sale of goods manufactured by disabled people who are beneficiaries of a disability charity.

Often, as is the case in the above examples, employees, contractors or volunteer workers who will not rank as beneficiaries of the charity may carry out part of the work of the trade. In these circumstances, exemption will still be available, provided that it can be shown that beneficiaries of the charity carry out the greater part of the work in connection with the trade.

Also, a charity may wish to pay salaries to beneficiaries who work in a trade carried out by the charity. This will mean that the beneficiaries will become employees of the charity. Provided that they can still properly be regarded as beneficiaries of the charity, the exemption of the trading profits will not be affected. PAYE must operate on the earnings of beneficiaries who are employed by a charity in the same way as for other employees.

Some of the work of a trade may be carried out by employees, contractors or volunteer workers who will not rank as beneficiaries of the charity. In these circumstances exemption under s. 505 (1)(e)(ii) of ICTA 1988 will still be available, provided that it can be shown that the greater part of the work in connection with the trade is carried out by beneficiaries of the charity.

For chargeable periods beginning on or after 22 March 2006, s. 505 (1B)(b) of ICTA 1988 extends the exemption where the work is carried out partly but not mainly by beneficiaries. The part carried out by beneficiaries is deemed to be part of the charity's exempt beneficiary trade. Receipts or expenses relating to the overall trade should be apportioned to the separate parts on a reasonable basis

25.5.5 Small-scale exemption

In addition to the above exemptions, there is also a statutory exemption for profits of small trading carried on by charities that would not otherwise be already exempt. The small-scale exemption is an exemption from corporation tax (or income tax in the case of charitable trusts) on the profits from small-scale non-primary purpose trading and the income from some other business activities carried on by charities. It applies only where all the relevant profits or income are applied for the charity's purposes. It does not apply where the trading profits or other income are exempt from tax on some other basis.

Before a charity considers whether this particular statutory exemption applies, it should first consider whether the statutory concession for fundraising activities is of relevance (see below).

The new exemption applies to the profits of all trading activities that are not already exempt from tax, provided that:

- the total turnover from all of the activities does not exceed the annual turnover limit; or

Primary purpose trades

- if the total turnover exceeds the annual turnover limit, the charity had a reasonable expectation that it would not do so, and
- the profits are used solely for the purposes of the charity.

The annual turnover limit is:

(a) £5,000, or
(b) if the turnover is greater than £5,000, 25 per cent of the charity's gross income, subject to an overall limit of £50,000.

These limits are reduced proportionally if the chargeable period is less than a year.

The following table represents the application of these rules.

Table 25.1 Exemption limits on profits from trading activities

Total gross income of the charity	Maximum permitted sales turnover
Under £20,000	£5,000
£20,000–£200,000	25% of charity's total gross income
Over £200,000	£50,000

The definition of sales turnover is income that would be taxable under Schedule D Case 1 as a trade, or under Case VI, and which is not exempt under any other section. Gross income means the total receipts of the charity for the year from all sources (grants, donations, investment income, trading receipts, etc).

Small trading exemption examples

A charity sells Christmas cards to raise funds. This trading is not primary purpose, nor does it fall to be considered under ESC C4 because it is not raising income from a fund-raising event.

Example 1

- Assume this is the only taxable trading activity.
- The turnover from the Christmas cards amount to £4,500 in the year.
- Any profits will be exempt from tax, because the turnover does not exceed £5,000.

Example 2

- A charity has a turnover from non-primary purpose trading of £40,000 for the year.

Trading income

- Its total incoming resources for the year are £160,000 (including the £40,000 turnover).
- Profits will be exempt from tax because the turnover from the non-exempt trading does not exceed either:
  (i) 25 per cent of the total incoming resources (£160,000 @ 25% = £40,000), or
  (ii) the overall upper limit of £50,000.

Example 3

- A charity has turnover from non-primary purpose trading of £40,000 for the year.
- Its total incoming resources amounted to £150,000.
- The £40,000 turnover exceeds the annual turnover limit (£150,000 @ 25% = £37,500).
- However, the profits on sales may still be exempt from tax for this year if the charity had a reasonable expectation at the start of the year that the turnover would not exceed the limit.

Example 4

- A charity has turnover of £60,000 for the year.
- Its total incoming resources only amounted to £150,000.
- The turnover exceeds the overall upper limit of £50,000.
- The profits on sales may still be exempt from tax for this year if the charity had a reasonable expectation at the start of the year that the turnover would not exceed that limit.

This could happen either because the turnover was underestimated or because the gross income of the charity was overestimated. It will be necessary in such cases to convince HMRC that the 'reasonable expectation' existed. HMRC will consider any evidence the charity may have to satisfy the reasonable expectation test.

HMRC has indicated that the type of evidence needed to demonstrate the levels of turnover and income which were expected might include minutes of meetings at which that matter was discussed, copies of cash flow forecasts, business plan and the previous year's accounts.

It may be the case that the charity has carried on the trading activity for a number of years and might be able to show that the turnover increased unexpectedly compared with early years. Alternatively, the charity might have started carrying out the trading activity in the year in question and might be able to show that the turnover was higher than it forecasted when it decided to start the activity. Similarly, the charity's gross income might be lower than it forecast –

for example, because the charity did not receive a grant for which it had budgeted or it was received in a subsequent accounting period.

25.6 Chargeable periods beginning on or after 22 March 2006

Typically, a charity will have only one trade. This follows from case law. In order to safeguard the exemptions from tax, which it is intended that charities should enjoy, it has been necessary to divide the charity's trade into a number of different statutory forms, which, for chargeable periods beginning on or after 22 March 2006, include 'deemed trades'.

For chargeable periods beginning on or after 22 March 2006, the position is as follows:

a) Primary purpose common

All trading exercised in the course of carrying out a primary purpose of the charity (for example, a religious charity selling religious texts, a charitable school charging fees to pupils, or a charitable clinic charging fees to patients or selling medicines). This, together with (d) below, is referred to for convenience as 'primary purpose trading' (see s. 505 (1)(e)(i) of ICTA 1988). Not taxable.

b) Beneficiary (main) unusual

Trading that is not primary purpose ('non-primary purpose') but carried out mainly by beneficiaries (for example, the manufacture and sale of items by disabled people). Together with (f) below, it is referred to for convenience as beneficiary trading (see s. 505 (1)(e)(ii) of ICTA 1988). Not taxable. This is an unusual scenario as much trading that appears to be beneficiary trading will be covered by the primary purpose exemption.

c) Non-primary purpose unusual

Trading that is not part of the primary purpose of the charity, but which typically is undertaken to raise funds to be applied for charitable purposes (for example, sales of promotional items). This, together with (e) and (g) below, is referred to for convenience as 'non-primary purpose trading'. It is unusual for all the trading of a charity to be non-primary purpose. Unless this is carried out mainly or partly by beneficiaries (see (b) and (f)), non-primary purpose trading is taxable as it enjoys no exemptions – apart from the small trading exemption.

d) Deemed primary purpose trade common

Where a charity's trade is carried out partly in the course of carrying out a primary purpose of the charity, and partly for non-primary purposes, s.505 (1B) of ICTA 1988 deems each part as a separate trade for tax purposes. The trade deemed primary purpose is not taxable (see s. 505 (1B)(a) of ICTA 1988).

e) Deemed non-primary purpose trade common

Where a charity's trade is carried out partly in the course of carrying out a primary purpose of the charity, and partly for non-primary purposes, s.505 (1B) of ICTA 1988 deems each part as a separate trade for tax purposes. The charity's trade deemed non-primary purpose is not exempt from tax, unless the work is carried out mainly or partly by beneficiaries (see s. 505 (1)(d)(ii) of ICTA 1988) – or the small trading exemption applies.

f) Part beneficiary (exempt) unusual

Where the work in connection with a charity's trade is carried out partly by beneficiaries, that part is deemed to be a separate trade, which enjoys exemption from tax (see s. 505(1)(B) of ICTA 1988). Both these deemed trades and the trades where work is mainly carried on by beneficiaries are referred to for convenience as 'beneficiary trades'.

g) Part beneficiary (taxable) unusual

Where the work in connection with a charity's trade is carried out partly by beneficiaries, the part not carried out by beneficiaries is deemed to be a separate trade, which, assuming it is non-primary purpose, will be taxable unless the small trading exemption applies (see s. 505 (1B)(b) of ICTA 1988).

For chargeable periods beginning before 22 March 2006, only (a), (b) and (c) above applied. The profits of non-primary purpose trading carried on by charities that fall outside the statutory and concessional exemptions ((c), (e) and (g) above) will be taxable. In general, where charities have taxable trading, those constituted as trusts are subject to income tax, while other charities are subject to corporation tax. Profits from primary purpose and beneficiary trading are exempt, so long as they are applied for charitable purposes.

25.7 Extra-statutory concession relief for fundraising activities

As indicated above, before a charity considers whether an exemption for small trading applies, it should first determine whether the extra-statutory concession for fundraising activities is of relevance.

This extra-statutory concession applies specifically to fundraising events. If an event falls within the concession, HMRC will not seek to tax the profits arising from it. The full text of the concession is set out below and you will see that it mirrors the VAT exemption for similar activities.

25.7.1 The concession

'Certain events arranged by voluntary organisations or charities for the purpose of raising funds for charity may fall within the definition of 'trade' in s832 ICTA 1988, with the result that any profits will be liable to income tax or corporation tax. Tax will not be charged on such profits provided:

(a) the event is of a kind which falls within the exemption of VAT under Group 12 of Sch. 9 of the VAT Act 1994; and
(b) the profits are transferred to charities or otherwise applied for charitable purposes.

In addition, the following conditions must apply:

1. the event must be organised by a charity, or a trading subsidiary or another qualifying body, for the charity's own benefit;
2. trading is not being undertaken through a series of events (multiple events – such as, say, a regular weekly dinner dance);
3. accommodation for the event is not provided for more than 2 nights' duration; and
4. there may be no more than 15 events of the same kind in a charity's financial year at any one location by a charity (including its trading subsidiary) or qualifying body.

Following the merger of the Inland Revenue and Customs and Excise into HM Revenue & Customs (HMRC) on 18 April 2005, there is a joint Charities Unit within the new structure. This joint unit will decide whether the extra-statutory concession applies in individual cases.

HMRC regards the following as different kinds of events, which may be held for fundraising purposes:

- dinner dances, discos or barn dances;
- live performances, for example concerts, theatrical productions, ballets, gymnastic performances, puppet shows and similar events with a paying audience;
- film, video or DVD showings;
- fetes, fairs and festivals;
- horticultural shows;
- exhibitions, for example of objects of artistic, historical, cultural, educational, religious, scientific, mechanical, sporting, ecological or environmental interest;
- bazaars, jumble sales, car boot sales and good-as-new sales;
- games of skill, knowledge or ability, including contests and quizzes;
- firework displays;
- meals, such as dinners, lunches, teas and barbecues;
- auctions of donated goods; (donated goods are zero-rated for VAT, as opposed to exempt, and this enables VAT to be recovered on

costs associated with the sale; donated goods sold at an event can still qualify for zero rating, as opposed to exemption), and
- auctions of bought in-goods (which may attract VAT).

Although the above list is quite extensive, there are other factors, such as frequency and turnover, which are considered by HMRC.

Eligible events are restricted to 15 events of the same kind in any one location by a charity (including its trading subsidiary) or qualifying body in the charity's financial year. The restriction prevents distortion of competition with other suppliers of similar events, which do not benefit from tax exemption. If the charity holds 16 or more events of the same kind at the same location during its financial year, none of the events will qualify for exemption.

Similar kinds of events held in different locations would qualify for exemption provided that all other conditions were met. For example, 20 balls held by a national charity, each in different towns in the same financial year, would all qualify for relief.

All fundraising events where the gross takings are no more than £1,000 per week, such as coffee mornings, are VAT exempt and are excluded from the 15 event limit. The £1,000 limit relates to the income of the event prior to any costs being deducted.

To ensure that commercial businesses are not put at a disadvantage, if a commercial organisation alleges disadvantage, HMRC would look carefully into the matter and any subsequent action would depend upon the particular circumstances. A charity would have the right to appeal against the decision.

If an event falls outside the terms of the concession, and is not covered by the statutory exemptions, the profits may be taxable.

If the charity believes that a particular event or series of events will not fall within the concession, it may be possible to organise the events so as to minimise the amount of tax payable. For instance, the charity might set a basic minimum charge (which will be taxable) and invite those attending the event to supplement this with a voluntary donation. The additional contribution will not be taxable if all of the following conditions are met:

(a) it is clearly stated on all publicity material, including tickets, that anybody paying only the minimum charge will be admitted without further payment
(b) the additional payment does not give you any particular benefit (for example, admission to a better seat in an auditorium); the extent of further contributions is ultimately left for the ticket holder to decide (even if the organiser indicates a desired level of donation). These

further contributions may be made under the gift aid scheme, subject to their meeting the requirements of the scheme

(c) for film, or theatre performances, concerts, sporting fixtures and similar events the minimum charge is not less than the usual price for the particular seat of a normal commercial event of the same type; and

(d) for dances, dinners and similar functions, the sum of the basic minimum charge is not less than the total cost incurred in arranging the event.'

25.8 Calculating the profits of the trade

The profits of trades carried on by charities which fall outside the statutory and concessional exemptions described will be taxable. The whole of the profits will be taxable despite the possibility that part of the activities of a trade might be said to fall within one of the exemptions. The profits –including capital allowances, if applicable – should be calculated in the same way as for any other trader. However, there are some factors that may be particularly relevant when calculating the profits of a trade carried on by a charity.

As well as deducting direct expenditure of the trade when calculating the profits, the charity should deduct indirect expenditure that it has incurred and which is attributable to the trade. For example, it would be right and proper to allocate to the trade some part of the cost of premises, employee costs and other related expenditure.

The proper basis of apportionment of indirect costs will depend on the facts.

It should be noted that where a charity receives goods or services in its trade at no cost or at less than their full market value, HMRC will only charge those profits calculated on a commercial basis. Thus, where a charity has received goods or services free, or at less than their full market price, the charity may deduct a notional market price when computing the profits of the trade.

25.9 Using a trading company

Charities carrying a trade outside the statutory and concessional exemptions usually arrange for the trade to be carried on by a wholly owned trading company. Using this approach, it is possible for the trading profits to be applied for charitable purposes tax free. This is done by donating all the trading company's profits to the charity either by way of a 'profit-shedding' deed of covenant or by gift aid.

There is nothing to prevent a trading company continuing to base the amount of profits to be transferred on a legally binding agreement such as a deed of covenant. However, all charitable payments made by a company to a charity will attract tax relief under the gift aid scheme (see Chapter 28).

25.10 Financing the trading company

Before commencing a trade, the trustees of a charity need to be certain that the business is viable and that it will generate sufficient additional resources for the charity after taking into account the costs in terms of both money and time that it will expend. Without a robust business plan, the trustees will be unable to quantify the risk of a loss arising rather than a profit. The other thing to be considered at all times is the reputation of the charity. This is often one of the most valuable assets that the charity has; and if anything is done that could cause loss of this reputation, it would be very difficult to regain.

Financing the trading company is an important area, particularly when the trading company is about to start and considerable funds are required. One way is by putting in funds in the form of shares, but it must be remembered that the greater the shareholding by the charity, the greater is the risk to the funds of the charity. There are two other options: loans from the charity and outside funding.

The Charity Commission does not like to see large amounts of unsecured lending by a charity to its trading subsidiary. It regards such an arrangement as putting the assets of the charity at too great a risk.

The preferred option of the Charity Commission is for there to be some outside funding of the trading company. This would come from a financial institution such as a bank. Any such borrowing would involve a commercial rate of interest, which would usually increase with the level of risk that the bank manager perceives to be involved.

Whilst it is important to get the initial funding of a company right, the problems often come after trading has begun and can often arise directly as a result of the tax planning that triggered the creation of the company. The basic arrangement of a profit-shedding deed of covenant is that all taxable profits are transferred back to the charity. The result is that the company will never be in a position to build up reserves of profits to fund its own development and the charity will be required to keep putting in funds.

In reality the same money could go round in a circular route of company profit > payment to charity > loan from charity to company. Unless some money actually comes to rest in the charity, the whole venture would be somewhat pointless. The potentially circular system is one that concerns both the Charity Commission and HMRC.

25.11 Business rates

Sections 43 and 47 of the Local Government Finance Act 1988 provide a mandatory 80 per cent relief from non-domestic (business) rates. Charities benefit from a mandatory 80 per cent rate relief for the premises that they occupy. This relief extends to charity shops. The remaining 20 per cent is discretionary and will be awarded by the local authority to whom the rates are payable. The following principles are relevant when applying for discretionary relief from national non-domestic rates:

1. The purposes of the organisation making the application should be charitable or non-profit making and should be concerned with education, recreation, social welfare, science, literature or the fine arts or be otherwise philanthropic, and the property that is the subject of an application should be used for such purposes.
2. Membership should be open to all sections of the community.
3. Organisations should be encouraged to promote their facilities to particular groups in the community – for example, young people, women, older age groups, use by schools and casual public.
4. Organisations should provide training, education or assistance with the development of skills.
5. The organisation should provide facilities that indirectly relieve the local authority of the need to do so or which enhance or supplement those which are provided.
6. The club should be affiliated to local or national organisations – for example, local arts or sports councils.
7. Membership should be drawn mainly from local residents.

25.12 Stamp duty land tax (SDLT)

SDLT came into effect on 1 December 2003, replacing stamp duty, which had been in place since the 17th century. Stamp duty was a voluntary tax and involved stamping the legal documents with the amount of tax paid. The introduction of SDLT helped close the tax gap by making the tax enforceable for the first time. SDLT is a modern self-assessed tax on land transactions involving any estate, interest, right or power in or over land in the United Kingdom.

The exemption for charities is given in the following ways for the purposes of stamp taxes:

1. Section 129 of the Finance Act 1982 (stamp duty exemption) – the exemption is given for a 'body of persons established for charitable purposes only or to the trustees of a trust so established'.

2. Schedule 8 of the Finance Act 2003 (SDLT exemption) – relief is given to a 'charity'. 'Charity' is defined as 'a body or trust established for charitable purposes only'.

Details of all land transactions involving a charity must still be submitted to HMRC and the relief applicable to charities claimed.

Relief from SDLT is available to charities on the purchase of an interest in land (a chargeable interest) if two conditions are met. There are:

(a) the purchasing charity must intend to hold the chargeable interest for qualifying charitable purposes. This means:
  (i) for use in furtherance of the charitable purposes of the purchaser or another charity, or
  (ii) as an investment, the profits of which are applied to the charitable purposes of the purchaser, and
(b) the transaction must not have been entered into for the purposes of avoiding SDLT by either the purchaser or any other person.

Loss of Charity Relief

Charity relief will be withdrawn if the charity ceases to be a charity within three years of the transfer or (where it still owns property) ceases to use the property for charitable purposes in the three-year period.

Where the relief is lost because the charity ceases to be a charity or the property ceases to be used for charitable purposes, this is a 'disqualifying event' and a further land transaction return (LTR) must be filed within 30 days of the disqualifying event.

In these circumstances, provision is made for the relief previously granted on a transaction to be clawed back. The amount chargeable is the SDLT that would have been chargeable in respect of the relevant land transaction as if charities relief had not applied, or an appropriate proportion of that SDLT if a derived interest is held. An appropriate proportion is calculated having regard to what was acquired in the relevant transaction and what is being used for non-charitable purposes.

25.13 Stamp duty reserve tax (SDRT)

Fund or investment managers will assume responsibility for retaining evidence to support claims for SDRT charity exemption. From 1 April 2009, fund or investment managers are allowed to forward a prior application seeking an approved arrangement with HMRC Stamp Taxes and be allocated a unique HMRC reference number.

Where a charity buys chargeable securities, exemption from SDRT can be claimed. In practice, the exemption is secured by the exchange member or qualified dealer (as the 'accountable person' for SDRT purposes) who is purchasing the shares either directly on behalf of the charity, or on instructions from a fund or investment manager with an underlying client (or clients) who is a charity, and who would otherwise be accountable for the tax. When reporting the transaction to CREST, the exchange member or qualified dealer inputs the CREST Transaction Stamp Status (TSS) value 'S' and enters the HMRC Charities (formerly Inland Revenue FICO) or Charity Commission's reference number in the Charity ID field.

HMRC needs to be able to verify that the exemption claimed in this way is properly due and will want to be satisfied on the following two matters. An accountable person must be able to demonstrate that:

(a) instructions to purchase shares have been received from a client that is a bona fide charity, or from a client acting for and on behalf of an underlying client that is a bona fide charity, and
(b) checks have been undertaken to verify that the charity is, and continues to be, a registered charity and eligible for exemption from SDRT.

Trading income

Annex Trading by charity – flow chart

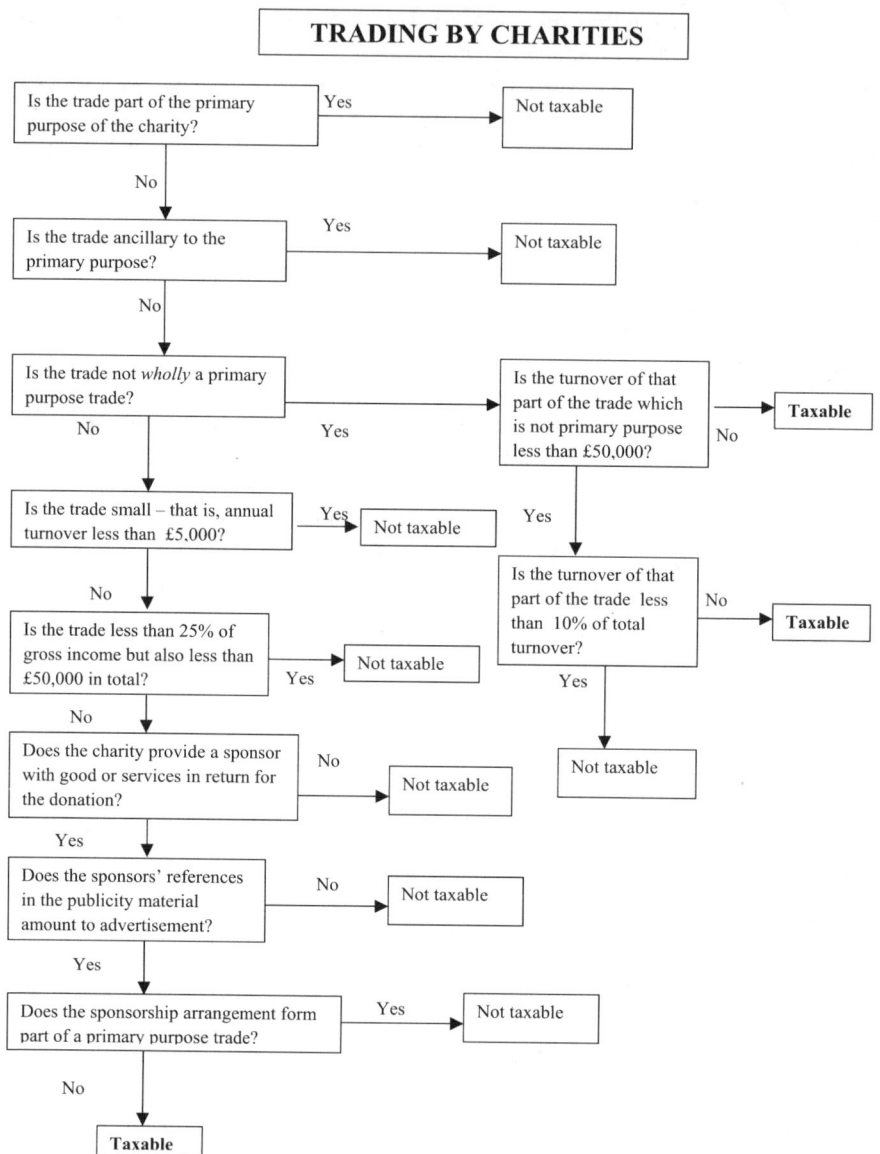

Chapter 26 – Employment taxes

26.1 Introduction

There is a popular, but erroneous, belief that because charities are exempt from tax on their own income, they are also outside the scope of other requirements of the Taxes Acts. Unfortunately, this approach seems to colour the view that many charities take toward their responsibilities as employers, but this is extremely dangerous. It is perhaps not surprising that in light of the above far too many charities appear before employment tribunals.

Charities, which are employers, are treated like any other employer for the PAYE requirements. From the perspective of HM Revenue & Customs (HMRC), recovery of unpaid PAYE and National Insurance contributions (NICs) from the charitable sector is highly profitable. It seems to be the Revenue's view that almost any person who receives regular sums from a charity for services is likely to be an employee.

Notwithstanding the fact that the taxation of employees is a complex area and is fraught with many difficulties, it is an area where charities, like other employers, need to have a sound understanding of both statute law and case law.

26.2 Casual, temporary and volunteer workers

An employment protection case, *Carmichael and another v National Power plc* (House of Lords) ([1999] 1 WLR 2042) upheld that individuals engaged on a casual 'as required basis' are not employees. This ruling will be of significance to the many charities that use casual, temporary and/or volunteer workers. In such cases, there is usually a need to avoid an employment relationship because of the fact that employees qualify for an increased number of statutory rights, including minimum notice periods, redundancy payments, maternity pay and the right not to be unfairly dismissed.

In the case in question, the individuals had agreed to work for National Power plc as guides showing visitors around as and when work arose. While they did not have to accept work, neither did the company guarantee to provide it. Since National Power was not obliged to offer work and the worker was not obliged to accept work when requested, there was no employment relationship. There was no 'mutuality of obligation,' which is an essential feature of any contract of employment.

Employment taxes

Many charities often enter into similar relationships with workers, the essence of the relationship being that work will be irregular and that the individual is only paid for work that he or she does and that the charity has no obligation to provide work. The relationship must not include the understanding that the worker is obliged to accept the work offered, despite the fact that it might be irregular.

The more difficult area to monitor is to ensure that the pattern of work has not led to an expectation on the part of the worker that he or she will be offered work when he or she is available and in preference to others. If this were the case, it could be argued that the worker has become a part-time employee. Unfair dismissal in such cases could result in substantial financial awards.

The benefits of the *Carmichael* case in providing clarification of employment law as it currently stands could, however, be short-lived. There are indications that the Government is about to abandon the concept of an 'employee' status and replace it with a definition of 'worker' in extending statutory employment protection. This term is already used in various pieces of employment legislation. Where used, a 'worker' is defined as including any individual who contracts to do or perform any work or services personally, but excludes those in business on their own account. Casual and temporary charity workers would appear to come within that broader definition.

The Government has also stated that it is committed to examining what it considers to be the abuse of 'zero hour' contracts. By including the term 'worker' rather than 'employee' in more recent employment legislation, this would tackle many of these perceived abuses. One would hope that there would still be a place for casual arrangements that are based on the genuine wishes of both parties, without giving rise to statutory rights.

We are in the process of changing both the status of casual, temporary and volunteer workers and also the rights to which they are entitled. It is therefore important that all charities that use such workers understand the changes as soon as they are implemented and appreciate how they will affect the working relationship with what is often an invaluable part of their total workforce.

26.3 Is somebody an employee or self-employed?

The question of identifying whether an individual is an employee or self-employed is one which affects both income tax and National Insurance. A person who is self-employed cannot be in receipt of income assessable under Schedule E, and so the PAYE regulations cannot be applied.

The problem with the question of whether or not a charity worker is an employee is that it is often a hard one to resolve. The very nature of charity work, which often implies a strong sense of vocation, is an additional complicating factor. It is therefore important to look at all the circumstances surrounding the relationship between the two parties and to come to some conclusion about the nature of that relationship.

HMRC has updated its guidance in this area. It now has an Employment Status Indicator (ESI), which is an online toolkit. HMRC also provides a list of the questions that should be asked in determining workers' status.

Determining your worker's employment status

In many situations, it will be straightforward to know your workers' employment status. In general terms, they are:

- employed – if they work for you and do not have the risks of running a business, or
- self-employed – if they are in business on their own account and are responsible for the success or failure of that business.

Listed below is a series of questions that will help determine your workers' employment status. The same questions also apply for a casual or part-time worker.

An individual worker is likely to be **employed** if the answer is 'yes' to most of the following questions:

1. Does the worker have to do the work himself or herself?
2. Can you tell the worker where to work, when to work, how to work or what to do?
3. Can you move the worker from task to task?
4. Does the worker have to work a set number of hours?
5. Is the worker paid a regular wage or salary?
6. Can the worker get overtime pay or bonus payments?
7. Is the worker responsible for managing anyone else engaged by you?

Your worker is likely to be **self-employed** if the answer is 'yes' to one or more of these questions:

1. Can the worker hire someone to do the work, or take on helpers at his or her own expense?
2. Can the worker decide where to provide the services of the job, when to work, how to work and what to do?
3. Can the worker make a loss as well as a profit?
4. Does the worker agree to do a job for a fixed price, regardless of how long the job may take?

If you cannot answer 'yes' to any of the above questions, your worker is still likely to be **self-employed** if you can answer 'yes' to most of the following questions:

- Does the worker risk his or her own money?
- Does the worker provide the main items of equipment (not the tools that many employees provide for themselves) needed to do the job?
- Does the worker have to correct unsatisfactory work in his or her own time and at his or her own expense?

The first point to note in looking at any employment or self-employment position is that there is no statutory definition of 'employment': rather it is a term that has evolved, and continues to evolve, over many years in the courts.

Certain key factors need to be considered and it is these that help determine whether or not a particular contract is one of employment. Key factors are as follows.

Control

A worker will not be an employee unless there is a right to exercise 'control' over the worker. The *right* of control is important, rather than the *actual* control. Where 'the charity' has the right to determine how the work is done, this is a strong pointer towards employment; but it is not an essential feature. Equally, a right to determine what work is carried out is also a strong pointer toward employment. A working relationship that involves no control is unlikely to be one of employment.

Control would include being told what work is to be carried out at any particular time by a team leader. It would also include the right to say how the work should be carried out, even if in practice such control is not normally necessary. However, if the contractor has a free hand over how his or her work is carried out and when, even though there may be an overall deadline for completion, control will be limited. This would be the case even if the worker is required to keep the charity fully informed about progress, and the charity has the right to require the worker to modify proposals if any of them seem unsatisfactory.

The right to get a substitute or helper to do the job

Personal service is an essential element of a contract for employment. If a worker has the freedom to choose whether to do the job personally or hire somebody else to do it for him or her, that person is probably self-employed. Similarly, if that person can hire someone else to provide substantial help, he or is probably self-employed.

A right of substitution must relate to the key components of the contract and not just some ancillary part of the contract.

It will probably not be sufficient merely to include a right of substitution in a contract. Rather, there will be a need for the worker to be able to satisfy HMRC that either substitution actually took place or there was a real possibility that substitution could have taken place. In other words, the charity was in reality willing to accept a suitably qualified substitute.

Provision of equipment

A self-employed worker generally provides whatever equipment is needed to do the job. The provision of significant equipment that is fundamental to the engagement is of particular importance. For example, if an IT consultant is engaged to undertake a specific piece of work and works exclusively at home, using his or her own computer equipment, this will be a strong pointer towards self-employment. If on the other hand, the consultant is provided with office space and computer equipment, this would point towards employment.

Financial risk

Financial risk supports a case for self-employment, and this can take many forms – for example, quoting a fixed price for a job with the consequent risk of bearing the additional cost if the job overruns or having to correct any bad workmanship in one's own time. This could apply where there is a ceiling on the number of days or hours that the charity is willing to pay for in relation to a specific project, unless unforeseen difficulties arise. Financial risk would also occur where the worker purchases materials and assets needed for the task in hand.

Basis of payment

Employment usually results in a fixed wage or salary paid weekly or monthly and may include payments of overtime and/or a bonus scheme. Self-employment tends to result in a fixed sum for a particular job. Where a worker gets paid an hourly rate, this would point towards employment. The basis of the payment is closely linked to whether or not there is an opportunity to profit from sound management. People who are paid by the job will often be in this position.

Rights of employment

Employees are often entitled to sick pay, holiday pay, pensions, expenses, etc. However, not all employees receive such entitlements – for example, those on short-term engagements. Self-employed individuals working for a charity would not expect to receive such entitlements. Similarly, a right to terminate an engagement by giving notice of a specified length is a common feature of employment. It is less common in a self-employment situation, where termination normally ends on the completion of the task unless the terms of the contract are breached.

Employment taxes

Length of engagement

Long periods working for one charity may be typical of employment, but are not conclusive. It is still necessary to consider all the terms and conditions of each contract.

The above are some of the factors that would influence a decision on whether or not there is an employment situation. The final decision is not taken, however, by merely adding up the number of factors pointing towards employment and comparing that result with the number of factors pointing towards self-employment. The correct approach is to stand back and look at the picture as a whole to see if the overall effect is that of a person in business on his or her own account or of a person working as an employee in somebody else's business. Mummery J made this point in *Hall v Lorimer (1994)* BTC 473 when he remarked:

> 'It is a matter of evaluation of the overall effect of the detail, which is not necessarily the same as the sum total of the individual details. Not all details are of equal weight or importance in any given situation. The details may also vary in importance from one situation to another'.

It follows from this that there are no hard and fast rules that can be applied. In general terms, each case must be considered on its own facts, with key factors isolated. For this reason, if a charity is in doubt as to whether or not a particular worker is an employee or not they should seek appropriate professional advice.

The problem with just accepting HMRC's booklet is that it gives a rather simplistic view of the question of determining employment or self-employment. As mentioned above, there is no statutory definition of these terms. Rather, our understanding of what constitutes employment or self-employment has come from many court cases. The problem is that case law sometimes gives a somewhat mixed message.

This can be seen by considering two recent cases on the issue of 'substitution'. It is considered that much of the argument in future with the HM Revenue & Customs will revolve around the 'substitution' clause when determining the question of employment vs. self-employment.

The case of *Express and Echo Publications v Tanton* [1999] **IRLR** 367 is illustrative. There were many factors in this case that pointed toward Mr Tanton (a delivery driver employed by Express and Echo) being under a contract of employment. However, included within the contact was the following clause:

> 'In the event that the contractor is unable or unwilling to perform the services personally he shall arrange at his own expense entirely another suitable person to perform the services'.

In addition, the contract stated:

> 'In the event that the contractor provides a relief driver, the contractor must satisfy the company that such a relief driver is trained and is suitable to undertake the services'.

Gibson LJ held:

> '... that, where a person who works for another was not required to perform his services personally, as a matter of law the relationship was not one of employee or employer; and accordingly, Clause 3.3 of the contract (not to perform any services personally) was a provision wholly inconsistent with the contract being one of service'.

The case should be compared with the case of *MacFarlane and Skivington v Glasgow CC* [2000] EAT/1277 heard by the Employment Appeals Tribunal. The appeal raised the issue of whether the two appellants, qualified gymnastic instructors, were employees of the city council or self-employed. The appellants lodged a claim for unfair dismissal and constructive dismissal. The council required them to sign a new contract, but the appellants contended that the new contract would effectively make them self-employed. The council contended that they had been self-employed all along.

The tribunal went through the facts of the situation and came to the following provision:

> 'If for any reason one of the applicants was unable to take a class she would contact a replacement from the register of coaches maintained by the respondent, and arrange for her class to be covered by a member of the register'.

It was the applicant who was enabled to select the replacement coach rather than the council, but the substitute had to come from the council's list. The arrangement for the replacement was to be made by the applicant, not the council. A provision for substitution would only be available when an applicant was 'unable' to take a class, although the inability could be for any reason.

The tribunal was of the opinion that the applicants were employees except for one fact that a substitute could be provided. This was in light of the *Tanton* case.

The tribunal found the following differences between the two cases:

1. The appellants in this case could not simply choose not to attend or not to work in person. Only if the appellant was unable to attend, could she arrange for another to take her class.
2. The appellants could not provide just anyone who was suitable as a replacement for her but only someone from the council's own registers. To that extent, the council could veto a replacement and also could ensure that

such persons that were named on the register were persons in whom the council could have trust and confidence.
3. The council itself sometimes organised the replacement.
4. The council would not pay the appellant for the time served by the substitute but instead paid the substitute direct. There is no finding as to what the substitutes were paid, nor that they were paid the same as the appellants, nor that the appellants had any say in what the substitutes were paid.

The Employment Appeal Tribunal allowed the appeal.

What we can learn from these two cases is that the more restricted the limitations are on acceptance of substitution, the less likely it is that substitution will support an argument for self-employment.

Despite the above difficulties in deciding whether or not somebody is employed or self-employed, the question of status is one that the charity employer should not duck. It is vital for any situations where categorisation could be an issue that this should be highlighted at an early stage and a decision taken with professional help. Whilst there is a strong incentive for a charity to argue that workers are self-employed as a way to avoid the need to pay the cost of secondary (employer's) NICs, such an incentive needs to be tempered by reality.

It is often argued that a letter from a worker's accountant that he or she is self-employed is sufficient evidence of employment status. This is not the case, as it is possible that the circumstances of the engagement with the charity may be very different from the worker's normal activities.

As explained above, if a charity is in any doubt, it should seek professional advice. Failure to deal with the matter properly could mean that the charity is required to meet not only the tax that should have been deducted from payments, but also the associated employee and employer's NICs. Of course, this could happen after the employee has left the charity, with little chance of obtaining any recompense from the employee in question.

26.4 Tax advantages for charities

Employees of charities enjoy a number of small tax advantages.

Benefits in kind

The usual rule is that a director of a company is within the scope of the benefit in kind legislation even though he or she earns less than £8,500 per annum. This rule does not apply to the director of a company charity. Such a person is only chargeable to tax on benefits in kind if his or her total emoluments for the year, including benefits in kind, exceed £8,500.

Living accommodation

The usual rule is that a company director who works part-time cannot escape the living accommodation charge even though the accommodation may be necessary for the employee's duties, or it is customarily provided for the better performance of his or her duties. This does not apply to a director of a company charity.

Ministers of Religion

Ministers of Religion enjoy reliefs relating to living accommodation and the deductibility of certain expenses.

Non-resident employees of missionary societies

Non-residential employees enjoy personal allowances that are normally available only to UK residents.

26.5 Schedule E liability of beneficiaries of charities

When providing grants from a charity to a beneficiary, one needs to consider if this constitutes an emolument of the beneficiary's employment and is therefore liable to tax under PAYE. An example would be a payment to augment a person's income, say a clergyman, by his church.

26.6 National Insurance Contributions (NICs)

It has been announced that, from April 2011, there will be a 0.5 per cent increase in NICs for employees, employers and the self-employed. The charity sector is very staff intensive and this will no doubt place a further strain on already stretched finances.

Chapter 27 – VAT

27.1 Introduction

There is no universal VAT relief for charities. Unlike the situation with the direct tax system, a charity is generally treated like any other person or business within the VAT system.

There are some reliefs in the VAT system designed for charities. Most of these will apply to all charities, regardless of whether they are VAT-registered. Others are designed to relieve VAT-registered charities of VAT in certain circumstances.

Before looking at the special reliefs that are available to all charities, first we shall consider how the normal rules of the VAT system apply to charities generally.

27.2 How VAT applies to charities

The application of VAT to charities is complex, initially, and it is necessary to explain concepts and terms.

VAT is a tax on consumption. It works by VAT-registered businesses charging *output VAT* on their taxable supplies and in return being able to recover *input VAT* incurred on purchases. The concept of *business* is crucial to the operation of the tax. It determines if an activity is within the scope of VAT or not. A *non-business* activity is *outside* the scope of VAT.

Also crucial to charities is the concept of *supply*. An activity will only be within the scope of VAT if it involves something being provided in return for a payment (which can be non-monetary). If the 'something' would have been provided irrespective of whether the payment was made, then there is no supply. The payment is not consideration and is outside the scope of VAT. In the charity sector the most common example of outside-the-scope receipts are donations.

A supply will have a VAT liability. This liability will determine whether output VAT needs to be accounted for on sales and whether input VAT incurred on purchases can be recovered. The liabilities are as follows:

Taxable Supplies	— Standard rated	17.5 per cent*
(allow input VAT recovery)	— Zero rated	0 per cent
	— Reduced rate	5 per cent

Taxable Supplies	— Standard rated	17.5 per cent*
Exempt Supply	— Exempt	
(restrict input VAT recovery)		

(*Note: For the period from 1 December 2008 to 31 December 2009, a reduced rate of 15 per cent applies)

It is estimated this temporary 2.5 per cent VAT reduction will save charities around £70 million. This includes VAT savings of £800,000 for Cancer Research UK, £200,000 for RNLI and £100,000 for Action for Blind People.

For periods after 1 May 2009, charities whose taxable supplies exceed the VAT registration threshold (currently £68,000 per annum) are obliged to notify HMRC and register for VAT. It is also possible to register for VAT voluntarily if the turnover of taxable supplies is below the registration limit. This will only be worthwhile if you expect VAT repayments to exceed payments.

27.3 The meaning of business

Whether an activity is regarded as 'business' is a question that forms the foundation of the VAT system.

The concept of business governs both someone's obligation to charge output VAT and also their ability to recover input VAT. It is important to note that 'business' for VAT purposes has a different meaning from 'trading' as used by the Charity Commission and/or HMRC in the context of direct tax.

An entity is generally seen as being in 'business' in VAT terms if it does something for consideration – that is, in money or payment in kind. This something could be providing goods or services. Historically, it has not mattered why the entity undertakes the activity (for example, it could be inspired by altruism), whether it could ever be a profitable activity, or indeed who pays for the goods and services provided. What matters is that the entity makes a compulsory charge to someone for providing something in return.

The question is one that often causes charities problems. The question is relevant, not only in determining the treatment of a charity's income, but also in determining whether it qualifies for certain reliefs – for example, in respect of property used 'or a relevant charitable purpose'.

It is not always the case that 'non-business' is 'good'. This is because VAT cannot be recovered in respect of non-business activities, and often a charity will want to argue that its income is business income to improve VAT recovery.

The standard tests for whether an activity constitutes a business were laid down in the Lord Fisher and Morrison's Academy cases, namely:

1. The activity should be a 'serious undertaking earnestly pursued' or 'a serious occupation not necessarily confined to commercial or profit-making undertakings'.
2. The activity should be an occupational function actively pursued with recognisable or reasonable continuity.
3. The activity should have a measure of substance to the extent that such measure could be shown in VAT returns.
4. The activity should be conducted in a regular manner and on sound and recognised business principle.
5. The activity should be predominantly concerned with making supplies for a consideration.
6. The taxable supplies made should be of a kind which, subject to differences of detail, are commonly made by those who seek to profit by them.

Profit motive

HMRC has long held that a profit motive is not necessary in determining a business purpose. This view has been supported by a number of UK and EU court cases. In fact the EC Sixth Directive uses the broader term 'economic activity' rather than 'business'. However, two recent High Court decisions (*Yarburgh and St. Paul's Community Project Limited*) have called into question HMRC's long-standing policy.

The cases both concerned zero rating property construction, on the grounds that the buildings would be used for a 'relevant charitable purpose'. HM Customs & Excise (as it was known then) lost the Yarburgh case in 2003, but issued a *Business Brief* (04/2003) effectively saying that it would disregard the decision.

In the St. Paul's case, the charity constructed a building and leased it for a nominal rent to another charity. The Court followed the Yarburgh decision in holding that the rents received did not constitute business income because they were so far below market value (in the St Paul's case, 60 to 70 per cent of the market value) and the activity was in accordance with the objects of the charity. Here, a charity that provided subsidised nursery places attempted to obtain its new building zero-rated (see section **27.13.1** below). HMRC ruled that the charity was engaged in making an exempt supply of nursery services and, as it made a charge to parents, was engaged in a business activity. This meant that zero rating could not apply. The charity argued that it was providing subsidised places and that it was carrying out its charitable activities, which were inherently non-business. The matter went before the High Court and the charity was successful.

HMRC has accepted that the judgment sets a precedent for nursery charities, but it is resisting arguments that the judgment has a more general application. It seems likely that the matter will eventually be resolved before the Courts when another test case is heard. This fairly wide definition given to the term 'business' means that charities that have separate trading companies may still find that the charity itself undertakes business activities for VAT purposes. If the value of these business supplies exceeds the annual registration threshold (currently £68,000 per year), the charity will be potentially automatically registrable for VAT if it is not already registered.

Again, HMRC has sought to minimise the impact of the decision by saying it does not agree that the activities were non-business. However, it will accept that the provision of nursery and crèche facilities by charities (along the same lines as Yarburgh and St Paul's) is not a business. This statement appears to be overly restrictive, and charities making supplies below cost should consider whether they could benefit from these decisions, bearing in mind that non-business treatment will not always give the best result.

27.4 VAT recovery for VAT-registered charities

VAT recovery for charities is a two-stage process. The first stage is to determine if the goods or services in question have been purchased for a business rather than a non-business purpose. VAT incurred for business purposes is potentially recoverable; VAT on non-business expenses is not. Charities are likely to undertake both business and non-business activities, meaning that a significant amount of the VAT they incur will be irrecoverable. VAT that is used to undertake both business and non-business activities is usually apportioned. This calculation is made using a business/non-business method.

As an alternative to an apportionment, charities are able to take advantage of the *Lennartz* principle. This allows them to recover all the VAT they incur at the time of purchase and then account for output VAT on the non-business use in future periods. *Lennartz* gives charities a cash flow advantage, albeit at the cost of increased administration (see section **27.15.3** below). Prior to August 2005, HMRC sought to restrict the application of the principle to land transactions. Following a European Court case, HMRC now accepts that it can apply to all transactions.

Following the business/non-business apportionment stage of VAT recovery, the charity must confront partial exemption. This is potentially one of the more complex areas of VAT, partly because of the existence of an assortment of anti-avoidance provisions and overrides. Partial exemption works by allowing VAT that is used to make *taxable supplies* to be recovered and restricting recovery of VAT used to make *exempt supplies*. VAT used to make both taxable and exempt supplies is apportioned using a *partial exemption method*. Unless HMRC has agreed an alternative, the default or *standard method* uses an income calculation to determine recovery.

There is also a standard method override provision which may automatically apply if certain conditions are met. It will effectively force the charity to agree a special VAT recovery method with HMRC,

If the amount of irrecoverable VAT resulting from the partial exemption stage is relatively low, special *de minimis* rules allow full recovery. These rules do not apply to VAT restricted under the first business/non-business apportionment.

When undertaking a partial exemption calculation, it is obviously important to ensure that supplies are correctly categorised as taxable or exempt.

There are two types of supply that allow a charity to recover VAT:

1. taxable supplies   — standard rate   – 17.5 per cent*
— reduced rate   – 5 per cent
— zero rate   – 0 per cent
2. supplies outside the scope

(***Note**: For the period from 1 December 2008 to 31 December 2009, a reduced rate of 15 per cent applies)

The VAT legislation assumes that everything undertaken or sold for a payment will be a standard-rated supply unless it is listed as being reduced rate, zero rated or exempt.

Following the VAT case involving The Church Of England Children's Society, HMRC accepts that where a charity engages the services of professional fundraisers to collect donations from the public, this can be considered a general overhead and is therefore a cost component of the charity's economic activity. As such, VAT charged by the professional fundraiser on his or her fees can be recovered according to the charity's overhead recovery rate

27.5 The treatment of grants

When someone provides a grant, the VAT system does not generally recognise that the grantor is buying a service or a good. This is because in most cases, the grantor is not personally consuming what is being paid for. The reason for the grantor making the payment is to enable the grant recipient to undertake its activities and not to provide a benefit to the grantor. The VAT system therefore generally treats grants as being outside the scope of VAT, and VAT is not chargeable. An activity, that is entirely funded by grants will automatically be non-business for VAT purposes.

In practice, there is often a grey area between what constitutes a grant and what is a genuine payment for goods or a service, which falls within the VAT system. Increasingly, grant-making organisations are setting stricter criteria on how their money is spent and on whom it is spent. Consequently, in many cases, it is now possible to make the argument that grants are in fact payments for a supply to the grant provider. The question becomes particularly problematic when charities enter into contracts with government departments. Regardless of the terms of the agreement, government bodies often try to argue that they are giving an outside-the-scope grant to prevent themselves being charged VAT.

In some cases, treating the payment as taxable may be beneficial. If the person providing the grant is able to recover any VAT charged to him or her, then treating the payments as being within the VAT system will be beneficial for the charity. This is because the charity will be able to recover any VAT that it incurs when undertaking the activity. It must be pointed out that this is a very technical and contentious area of the tax and one where it usually pays to take professional advice.

27.6 Donations

Donations are treated as outside the scope of VAT when the person paying the money has no right to receive something in return other than a token.

If a charity gives a donor benefits in return for the payment, the situation is less clear-cut. In many cases, the money is treated as consideration for a taxable supply. A common example occurs with sponsorship. Charities that grant publicity rights or logo use in return for a payment will generally be making taxable supplies.

Providing that the sponsor is able to recover VAT, this will not be a problem. In fact, if corporate donors are able to fully recover VAT, it will often be beneficial to structure the consideration so that the payment becomes subject to VAT. This is because it is generally the case that the greater the taxable supplies made by a charity, the higher will be its VAT recovery proportion.

27.7 Examples of business and non-business activities

Table 27.1 Classification of charitable activities as business or non-business

Type of activity	Classification
Admission charges	Business
Advertising	Business
Affinity/promotion cards	Business (may also have non-business donational elements if organised correctly)

Type of activity	Classification
Catering	Business
Export of goods	Business
Free services	Non-business
Free admissions	Non-business
Fundraising events	Generally business
Organising leagues	Non-business
Share deal-up	Non-business
Sponsorship	Business/non-business depending on what is provided
Subscriptions	Business

27.8 Business membership and supporters' subscriptions

If someone has to pay a fee in order to receive a particular benefit, then this is a business activity. Organisations that provide membership benefits which mainly take the form of zero-rated publications may find that they are able to obtain ongoing refunds of VAT on their associated costs. If this is the case, a voluntary VAT registration is worth considering.

27.9 VAT reliefs that apply to all charities

Some VAT reliefs apply to all charities, regardless of whether or not they are VAT-registered.

27.9.1 Advertising zero rate

No VAT will be charged to charities on advertising that they purchase.

This relief includes all charity advertisements purchased for whatever purpose. The relief is not available to trading companies (which could be subsidiaries of the charity) Therefore, it includes adverts for recruitment, as well as fundraising and making known a charity's objects.

The relief applies to all forms of advertising media that the charity may purchase, including:

- badges;
- balloons;
- banners;

VAT

- carrier bags;
- cinema ads;
- flags;
- internet ads;
- posters;
- radio ads;
- television ads;
- teletext, and
- skywriting by light aircraft.

To obtain the relief, the charity may need to demonstrate to their supplier that it qualifies.

The relief applies to purchases of space or time in advertising media that are owned and controlled by third parties. It is not designed to allow charities to buy VAT-free goods. Therefore, although the owner of a light aircraft will be able to zero rate any supply of any skywriting he or she might undertake for a charity, he or she could not sell the actual plane at a zero rate if the charity wanted to buy it. A different concession allows charities to obtain some fundraising goods VAT-free (this is covered later).

It is also important to note that the relief only applies to advertisements provided to the charity. It does not apply to advertisements provided by the charity. If the charity gets advertising income – for example, through its website or magazine – this is not zero-rated.

27.9.2 Advertising zero-rate exceptions

It should be noted that there are some important exceptions.

The relief applies only to charities, and not to their associated trading companies or other persons. It does not apply to selective advertising such as direct mail, e-mail or telesales.

In practice, this exclusion can be problematic. If a charity obtains direct advertising through a supplier who produces and prints general leaflets for a selected audience, then, in theory, there are two liabilities. The production of the written material would normally be zero-rated. However, the supply of the mailing service (for example, the data processing, labelling, etc.) will be standard-rated.

As HMRC policy is now to see single supplies as much as possible, the old option of apportioning is not always available – although some suppliers will still apply this policy and even have permission to do so. If there is a single supply and the direct mail element is the most prominent (and in practice direct mail lists are often the largest expense), then it will be a single standard-rated supply.

If charities do obtain direct marketing services involving printed matter, it may pay them to take advice as planning here can obtain sizeable savings.

27.9.3 In-house costs

Supplies of goods or services that are purchased by charities to enable them to produce or design their own advertisements are excluded from the relief.

27.10 Donated goods

The donation of goods *to* a charity which will then be sold, let or exported is zero rated.

This relief means that donors who supply equipment to charities do not have to account for output VAT. This is a useful relief for charity shops.

The relief applies for charities and also persons (organisations and private individuals) who have agreed in writing to donate any profits from the sale or leasing of the goods to the charity. Therefore, private individuals or companies can obtain zero rating on goods provided to them which they are bound to use to raise money (through sale or lease).

27.10.1 Sales of donated goods by charities

The sale or letting of donated goods *by* a charity is zero rated. This relief also applies to persons who have agreed in writing to donate any profits they make from the sale to a charity.

This means that not only are sales of these goods by charities zero rated, but also sales by their trading subsidiaries and indeed any other person or organisation that agrees to raise money on their behalf.

For the zero rating to apply, the sale or letting must be to the general public rather than a selected few. The exception to this concerns goods that charities sell specifically to people who are disabled or in receipt of some forms of state benefit. This rule means that, for example, a corporate donor cannot buy a new mainframe computer and donate it to a charity on the understanding that it will then be leased back to the donor VAT free.

27.11 Goods used by charities to collect donations

A charity may obtain certain goods which it intends to use for collecting donations VAT free.

This relief applies to the following:

(a) lapel stickers, ribbons or attachments that are intended to be given away in return for an anticipated donation of £1 or less;
(b) collecting receptacles designed specifically for collecting donated money, such as moulded plastic collecting boxes or other receptacles that bear the name of the charity. The relief does not cover receptacles which incorporate an element of amusement – for example, helter skelter boxes;
(c) bucket lids designed to provide a secure seal for collecting money;
(d) pre-printed letters appealing solely for money for the charity;
(e) envelopes that are overprinted with an appeal request, and
(f) pre-printed collecting envelopes used for door-to-door collection.

It should be noted that these reliefs are provided by extra-statutory concession rather than by legislation. Unfortunately, this means that they are effectively in HMRC's gift and thus liable to be interpreted as strictly or loosely as an HMRC officer may decide.

27.12 Reliefs for medical goods

The legislation provides for a number of quite complex reliefs for charities that buy goods to provide care, or carry out medical or surgical treatment for people or animals, or that are engaged in medical research. As these charities are quite specialised, they are outside the scope of this book.

Charities that engage in this type of work should take advice either from professional advisors or from HMRC as to whether any reliefs will apply.

27.13 Charity buildings

27.13.1 New buildings

Normally, anyone purchasing construction services will be charged VAT by the builder or architect, etc. For normal businesses that are VAT-registered and able to recover any VAT charged to them, this is not a problem. Unfortunately, for charities that are likely to engage in a sizeable amount of non-business activity, it can cause difficulty. In order to assist charities, the legislation allows them to obtain zero-rated construction services, provided that certain conditions are met.

The principal condition is that the charity may obtain zero-rated construction for a building that it intends to use for a non-business purposes. (For guidance on what is a non-business purpose see section **27.3** above.)

HMRC is prepared to accept that a building can be treated as being used for a non-business activity if:

(a) the building is used solely for non-business activity for 90 per cent or more of the time it is available for use;
(b) 90 per cent or more of the floor space of the building is used for non-business activity, or
(c) 90 per cent or more of the people using the building are engaged solely in non-business activity..

It should be noted that concessions (a) and (b) can only be applied to the *whole* of a building. In practice, many charities will be in a position where the relief will not apply because they have commercial or trading activities that mean that the business use of the building will exceed ten per cent. This is an area where it is possible to obtain VAT savings by careful planning, and on which it pays to take professional advice.

It is very important that if a charity is purchasing the freehold or obtaining a leasehold of an interest in a new building that it will use for 'relevant charitable purposes', it needs to issue the vendor a special zero-rating certificate before the relevant date. The absence of this certificate could jeopardise the zero-rating treatment even if all the other conditions for zero rating are met.

If a charity constructs a building for non-business use and subsequently the use of the building changes, there are provisions within the legislation which may require the charity to pay back the VAT it has saved. The main focus on when the clawback applies will be whether the charity knew from the beginning that the rule concerning the 10 per cent business use would be breached.

27.13.2 Listed buildings

One of the most peculiar features of the VAT system is the way it treats listed buildings. Normal repairs to such buildings will always attract VAT. However, alterations that require listed building approval can in certain circumstances be zero rated.

If a charity owns a listed building and makes alterations to it, with the intention of using the building for a non-business charitable purpose (or residential purposes,) then it can obtain the work zero rated.

27.14 VAT reliefs that apply to VAT registered charities only

27.14 1 Fundraising

Fundraising events can be treated as VAT exempt (see section **25.7** of Chapter 25).

VAT

The VAT legislation incorporates an exemption for fundraising events held by charities. An exempt supply is one where, although no VAT needs to be accounted for on sales, no VAT is recoverable on related expenses. It follows that, although VAT exemption applies to all charities, in practice it will only be of benefit to charities that would otherwise need to account for VAT on the activity – that is, charities either registered for VAT, or charities which, but for the exemption, would be liable for VAT registration.

The VAT legislation allows a charity to treat a supply of goods or services in connection with an event as exempt if its primary purpose is the raising of money (and it is promoted as such) – for example, it is advertised as a fundraiser.

The exemption will apply to all income raised as part of an event, unless there is an aspect of it that would otherwise be zero rated. Fundraising events include:

- auctions of goods that have been purchased;
- car boot sales and jumble sales;
- concerts and stage performances
- dinners, discos and balls;
- endurance events;
- exhibitions;
- fairs and fetes;
- films;
- firework displays
- games of skill, such as a quiz;
- garden shows;
- sponsored walks, and
- sports events.

The relief is only designed to apply to fundraising events rather than to a charity's normal trading activities. In order to make this distinction, the legislation incorporates rules which state that if more than 15 similar events are held in the same place within the year, then the exemption cannot apply. All fundraising events where the gross takings are no more than £1,000 per week are VAT exempt. Theses events are excluded from the 15-event limit. In practice, this means that nearly all fundraising events can be covered by the exemption. The exemption will not apply if the event includes the provision of accommodation.

The downside of a VAT exemption as opposed to zero rating is that VAT on associated purchases cannot be recovered. This means that in some cases treating an event as exempt may not be a sensible option. If, for example, the people attending the event would be able to recover any VAT charged to them on admission, there is no point in treating the event as exempt. If, however, the attendees are members of the public and the charity is charged little VAT in putting on the event, then the exemption is a benefit. Fortunately, because of the way the legislation is drafted, it is normally possible for a charity to change what would otherwise have been an exempt event into a taxable one if it will benefit by doing so.

27.15 Recent developments

27.15.1 Land and property

HMRC has announced that the long-awaited changed to the option to tax (OTT) legislation will take effect from 1 June 2008. These changes include the following:

1. The insertion of legislation regarding the revocation of an OTT which has been in place for 20 years or more. The earliest date for a revocation will be 1 August 2009 (that is, 20 years after the implementation of the OTT legislation on 1 August 1989)
2. Options will lapse if a business has not had an interest in a property on which it opted to tax in the previous six years.
3. The time after which an OTT can be revoked, once made, will be increased from three months to six months. In addition, the condition regarding not having recovered VAT will be removed. Of course, any VAT recovered in respect of an opted property will be repayable on revocation.
4. The rules regarding the OTT affecting all members of a VAT group, even after they have left the group, will be relaxed. A key change is that, if a company leaves a VAT group, it will no longer have an OTT on VAT group properties unless it has an interest in the properties.
5. Redefinition of what is covered by the OTT. Broadly, in future it will cover land and buildings on the land. However, it will be possible to write to HMRC to remove the option from a new building where a previous property had been opted.
6. Where permission to opt to tax is required, the option will be effective from the date on which the application for permission is received by HMRC, or a later date as agreed. Currently, the option is only effective from a date it is notified, after permission has been received.
7. New procedures for disapplying the OTT on a building that will be used as a dwelling or for a relevant residential purpose.
8. The introduction of an OTT which automatically covers all properties to be acquired, with effect from the date of acquisition.

27.15.2 Challenge events

If the charity insists that participants make a payment before being able to participate, HMRC believes that a supply has been made to the participant. The supply is the deposit, booking fee or payment of percentage of the fundraising target. If, on the other hand, the charity does not insist on such a payment, the event is outside the scope.

If the event does not qualify for the fundraising exemption, the charity needs to determine whether it is acting as the principal or agent. If it is as principal, then the charity must account for VAT under the Tour Operator Margin Scheme (TOMS). Alternatively, if the charity is the agent, then it must account for VAT on the commission received from the principal.

The charity will be acting as agent, if it meets the following three conditions:

(a) both the charity and principal agree that the charity is the agent;
(b) the charity discloses the names of the principal to the participants in the terms and conditions, and
(c) the charity is not taking any significant commercial risk in running the event.

27.15.3 Lennartz regulations

Lennartz accounting applies to land, buildings, vehicles, computers, etc. but not to intangible assets. Assets may be bought and be used for both business and non business purposes. It may be possible to treat the asset as a business asset and recover all the input VAT, subject to the capital goods scheme. All output VAT can be paid out on the non-business use.

Since 1 November 2007, regulations have governed how this self-supply charge is calculated. The VAT-bearing cost is spread over 10 years for land and buildings and over five years for other assets. The portion of non-business use is multiplied by the depreciation on the asset, and VAT is charged on this amount. For example, if a building cost £500,000 plus £75,000 VAT (at the current rate of 15 per cent), depreciation over 10 years is £50,000 output VAT a year (£12,500 per VAT quarter). Assuming non-business use of 40 per cent, the output VAT would be £750 (that is, £12,500 × 40% × 15% = £750). If the assets are also in the capital goods scheme, then both schemes must operate together.

27.15.4 Independent living units

HMRC believes that the construction of houses or flats in the grounds of care homes cannot usually be zero rated. This will be the case if there is a planning condition to the effect that the dwelling cannot be used independently from the care home, or if separate disposal is prohibited. Such residential units will also not be zero rated where there is a relevant residential purpose for which the units do not qualify in themselves. If the letting of the units is non-business, then there may be a relevant charitable purpose. In the JRF Sharples Tribunal case, sheltered house were built in the grounds of a care home and separate use was not prohibited. The disposal of the freehold was prohibited but not the disposal of the long lease. The Tribunal found that the sale of the lease was a 'disposal', so the construction could be zero rated.

27.15.5 Staff hire concession

Employment agencies only charge VAT on their commission – that is, the margin. For seconded staff, there is no VAT on the reimbursed salary costs. Similarly, disabled workers have no VAT charged on the reimbursed salary costs for sheltered placement schemes.

From 1 April 2009, this agency staff concession has been removed. However, the secondment and disabled worker concessions will stay in place. This will have an effect on those charities using agency staff for non-business or exempt activities. The withdrawal of the concession will affect temps, care staff and agency teachers. Renegotiating commission with agencies and staff sharing arrangements should be considered to mitigate the impact of this.

27.15.6 Voluntary disclosures

Since 1 July 2008, a charity has only needed to make a voluntary disclosure if the error is greater than:

- £10,000, and
- one per cent of business turnover, up to limit of £50,000

From 1 September 2008, interest will be charged on all voluntary disclosure underpayments, even if the amount is below the disclosure threshold.

Chapter 28 – Giving to charities

28.1 Introduction

There are numerous ways in which an individual can give to charity in a tax-efficient manner. These include:

- gift aid and deeds of covenant;
- give-as-you-earn schemes;
- through tax returns;
- legacies;
- gifting shares and securities;
- gifting property, and
- giving by businesses.

This section deals with the characteristics of each, together with some associated pitfalls.

28.2 Gift aid

28.2.1 Gift aid for individuals

The original gift aid scheme, which was introduced in 1990, was designed to encourage charitable giving within the United Kingdom. It was significantly revised and improved in 2000. In particular, the scheme was simplified for donations made by individuals on or after 6 April 2000.

The main changes were:

- to abolish the £250 minimum limit for gift aid donations, so that the scheme now applies to any donation, whether large or small, regular or one-off;
- to withdraw the separate tax relief for payments made under a deed of covenant and to give relief for all such payments under the gift aid scheme;
- to create a simpler and more flexible gift aid declaration in place of the previous requirement for donors to give a gift aid certificate with each gift aid donation to a particular charity;
- to allow donors to give a written gift aid declaration by post, fax or internet, or give an oral declaration either over the phone or face to face;
- to extend the class of individuals that can use the new gift aid scheme, and

- to apply the new gift aid measures to covenanted payments falling due on or after 6 April 2000 and to all other donations made on or after that date.

As explained above, from 6 April 2000 the £250 minimum limit for gift aid donations was abolished. From that date, charities have been able to reclaim tax on any donation made by individuals – whether large or small, regular or one-off – provided that the other conditions are satisfied. From an administrative point of view, each charity will need to decide, after considering its own circumstances, whether or not it wishes to reclaim tax on small gift aid donations. For some charities, it may not be cost-effective to claim on donations below a certain threshold; for others, it may be cost-effective to claim on all gift aid donations.

Whether or not the charity decides to make a claim on a gift aid donation, it will still be possible for a donor to claim higher-rate tax relief on the gross amount of the donation, provided that he or she has completed a gift aid declaration, and has met the other conditions of the scheme.

From 6 April 2000 the following individuals have been able to make valid gift aid payments:

- individuals who are resident in the UK;
- individuals who are Crown Servants or members of the UK Armed Forces serving overseas, and
- other non-resident individuals, provided that they have income or capital gains charged to UK tax at least equal to the gross amount of the donation.

Donations must be a payment of a sum of money and cannot be made in kind.

From 6 April 2000, donors have to pay an amount of income tax and/or capital gains tax, whether at the basic rate or some other rate, equal to the tax deducted from the donations. Prior to that date, they needed to have paid income tax at the basic rate equal to the tax reclaimed by the charity on their donations.

The change means that donors who previously may have paid tax at a marginal rate between the lower and basic rate of tax (and therefore had not paid enough tax at the basic rate to cover the tax reclaimed by the charity) will no longer have additional tax to pay.

Prior to 6 April 2000, donors could only claim higher-rate tax relief on donations against income tax they paid. From 6 April 2000, donors have been able to claim higher-rate tax relief for their donations against both income tax and/or capital gains tax.

It should be noted that the position of taxpayers making gift aid donations could change from one tax year to the next. Charities are therefore recommended to remind donors on a regular basis of the need for them to have paid sufficient income and/or capital gains tax on their donations. This could be done, for example, by way of a newsletter and does not have to be a separate letter to each donor.

28.2.2 Gift aid declarations

As mentioned above, gift aid certificates for each donation to a charity have been replaced by a simpler and more flexible gift aid declaration.

Before a charity can reclaim tax on a donation by an individual, it must have received a gift aid declaration from the donor containing certain information and confirming that the donation is to be treated as a gift aid donation. Without this declaration, a donation from an individual will not qualify under the gift aid scheme.

Donors will be able to give the charity a declaration:

- in advance of their donation, at the time of their donation, or at any time after their donation (subject to the normal time limit within which tax can be reclaimed – normally within six years);
- to cover a single donation or any number of donations, or
- in writing (for example, by post, by fax or electronically through the internet) or orally (for example, over the phone or face to face).

Oral declarations must be confirmed by written notification from the charity, showing the information set out below, plus a note explaining that the oral declaration can be cancelled retrospectively within 30 days. The notification should also include the date on which the donor gave the charity the declaration and the date on which the charity sent the written record to the donor.

The amount of information required by law on a gift aid declaration has been kept to the minimum. All gift aid declarations must contain:

- the donor's name;
- the donor's address;
- the charity's name;
- a description of the donation to which the declaration relates;
- a declaration that the donations are to be treated as gift aid donations, and
- a note explaining the requirement that the donor must pay an amount of income tax and/or capital gains tax equal to the tax deducted from his or her donations.

There is no statutory requirement for a declaration to be signed and dated. However, a date is needed on the declaration where it serves to identify that a particular donation or donations are to come within the scheme. For example, if the declaration states that 'all donations I make from today are to be gift aid donations', clearly a date would be required. A date would not be required, however, where the declaration stated, for example, 'all donations I make to the charity from 6 April 2010'.

Other than the information required by law, charities may wish to add further information and notes of their own on their declaration forms. It may also be necessary to add further information to satisfy other legal requirements. For example:

- if the charity plans to use the information provided by the donor for any use other than reclaiming tax, the Data Protection Act 1998, it is required to explain this, and
- if a charity registered in England and Wales incorporates a gift aid declaration in appeals literature, it is required by the Charities Act 1993 to include a statement that it is a registered charity. Under Scottish law, Scottish charities are required to include a statement that they are recognised charities.

Gift aid declarations can be incorporated into other documents, such as standing order mandates for deeds of covenant.

HM Revenue & Customs (HMRC) does not produce an official gift aid declaration, and charities are required to design their own gift aid declarations. HMRC does, however, provide in its *Guidance Notes to Charities* a model declaration form that charities can use or adapt if they wish.

It should be noted that donors are entitled to cancel the declarations at any time. They may do so by notifying the charity via any form of communication. The charity should keep a record of the cancellation of a declaration, including the date of the donor's notification.

Subject to oral declarations, the cancellation of a declaration only has effect in relation to donations received by the charity on or after the date on which the donor notifies the charity of the cancellation, or such later date as the donor may specify in the cancellation.

28.2.3 Oral declarations

As mentioned above , oral declarations can be cancelled within the period of 30 days after the donor has been being sent his or her written record. The cancellation will have retrospective effect, so that it will be as if the declaration had never been made.

For some time now, the charity sector has been looking for a simpler regime for securing gift aid when donations are made over the telephone. Before relief could be claimed, the charity had either to obtain written or internet confirmation from the donor or to write to each telephone donor to confirm that gift aid could be claimed following a telephone donation. Where a charity was involved in a large public appeal, this could easily cost hundreds of thousands of pounds each time.

The person taking the declaration on behalf of the charity might recite information already held by the charity to the donor and ask him or her to confirm it, rather than asking the donor to recite the information.

If a charity receives an oral declaration, and it does not keep an audible (and auditable) recording of the donor's oral declaration, it must send the donor a written record of the declaration, which must include:

- all the details provided by the donor in his oral declaration;
- an explanation that the donor must pay an amount of income tax and/or capital gains tax equal to the tax deducted from his or her donations;
- an explanation of the donor's entitlement to cancel the declaration retrospectively within 30 days;
- the date on which the donor gave the charity the oral declaration, and
- the date on which the charity sent the written record to the donor.

An oral declaration will not be effective unless and until the charity, or its representative, sends the donor the written record of the declaration.

The charity cannot reclaim tax in respect of a donation covered by an oral declaration until it has sent the written record. Once the written record has been sent, the charity can reclaim tax in respect of any donations covered by the declaration, even if they were received before the written record was sent. If the oral declaration is cancelled within the 30-day period, however, any reclaimed tax will have to be repaid to HMRC.

The written record of the declaration does not have to be recorded on paper. For example, the charity's representative might record the details on a computer, with an electronic copy being emailed to the donor, or a hard copy sent by post. If the charity uses an electronic means of recording the donor's information, it will need to demonstrate to HMRC at an audit that the electronic recording of the information generates a written record sent to the donor.

In the case of a donor who has given the charity an oral declaration and then cancels it within 30 days of being sent the written record, it will be as if the declaration had never been made.

Charities need to maintain a store of digitally recorded telephone calls, emails and text messages for six years. Supporting equipment to enable this could potentially prove very expensive.

There is a further problem with using this kind of technology in that statistical evidence suggests that individuals are far more likely to give a telephone donation if they are connected with a human being rather than to an automated recorded message. Speaking to a person is apparently an important part of the decision-making process when people make telephone donations. The organisers of large public appeals are aware that, when potential donors are connected to a back-up automated service when operators are busy, there is a significant fall-off in the number of callers who actually make a donation.

Fundraising professionals believe that the inclusion of such a warning in a recorded message will of itself deter a proportion of callers from making a donation.

It is naïve to assume that all potential donors will have a good enough understanding of their own tax status to be certain that they are not going to be leaving themselves with a tax bill as a result of making a charitable donation.

28.2.4 Declarations linked to sponsored events

The person being sponsored may ask the sponsors to make a separate declaration to the charity for which he or she is raising the money. This is likely to be a one-off donation type of declaration supplied to the participant by the charity.

Rather than one-off donation types of declaration, it is possible for charities to design a sponsorship form that can also be used as a joint declaration form. HMRC suggests that the declaration is placed at the head of each sheet, with each sponsor being able to opt to have his or her sponsorship money paid to the charity as a gift aid donation – for example, by ticking a box. The recommended method is to have the following boxes below the declaration for each sponsor to complete:

(a) sponsor's full name;
(b) address (including postcode);
(c) amount pledged;
(d) amount collected;
(e) date collected; and
(f) tick-box to have amount treated as a gift aid donation.

The details outlined in the first points (a) to (c) above will be collected from the sponsors by the participant prior to the event, with the other details being entered on the form when the money is collected.

28.2.5 Gifts of goods to charity

HMRC has provided revised guidelines on 'gifting goods to charities'.

Charities have often asked whether they can reclaim repayments of income tax under gift aid when donors provide them with goods rather than cash. The answer is 'no' because one of the requirements of gift aid is that it is a gift of money to the charity.

However, there may be a practical solution to this problem. If the charity and/or its trading subsidiary agree with the donor to sell the item on the donor's behalf, the donor can then give the proceeds to the charity, and can in turn claim gift aid. The charity or its subsidiary is acting as agent for the donor in respect of the sale.

When the item is sold, the charity must inform the donor of the sale price, and the donor must be given the opportunity to change his or her mind about giving all or part of the proceeds to the charity. This is to ensure that the gift is purely voluntary, which is a specific requirement of gift aid. It also protects the donor from giving more than he or she wished to give if the asset is sold for a greater sum than expected. As a by-product, it stops the charity from running the risk of any allegations of inappropriate practice. HMRC would normally expect the donor to be given at least 21 days in which to change his or her mind. This allows time for postal delays, illness and holidays.

In practice, it is likely that the charity will have a written agreement with the donor, which:

(a) establishes the charity or its subsidiary as an agent to sell the item(s) on behalf of the donor;
(b) itemises the goods to be sold;
(c) obtains a gift aid declaration from the donor, and
(d) informs the donor of the nature of the scheme and that the donor has the option of claiming the cash when notified of the sale price.

In order to simplify the matter, one would normally expect the gift aid declaration to be obtained at the time that the goods are accepted, rather than after they are sold.

The staff of the charity and/or its subsidiary would need to have systems in place to ensure that this process is secure. Systems will also need to be introduced in order to determine which goods are covered by this scheme from both identification and accounting points of view.

Gift aid claims can be made in the normal way. Claims can be submitted as soon as the donor either confirms his or her wish to donate the sales proceeds or after the 21-day period has elapsed. In addition to the gift aid declaration, the charity would need to be able to produce any agreement that confirms that the charity or subsidiary is acting as the donor's agent. Documentation confirming the sale proceeds, and that the donor has had the opportunity to receive all or part of the proceeds rather than donating them, should also be retained.

Because this system is more likely to be used for high value items, the donor may need to know the sale price to calculate his or her capital gains tax, although the chattel exemption and annual allowances may help. For gift aid purposes, individuals will need to know how much they are giving, as they will be able to claim any higher rate tax relief that may be due.

28.2.6 Gift aid for companies

Gift aid donations made by companies to charities must be paid without deduction of income tax. Since no income tax is deducted, no declarations are required. Consequently, charities cannot reclaim tax on donations they receive from a company.

Charities often set up 100 per cent wholly owned subsidiaries to carry out trading activities that fall outside the tax exemptions offered to charities. Such companies often enter into a 'profit–shedding' deed of covenant with the parent charity, or gift aid arrangements, under which they pay to the charity a sum equivalent to the profits assessable to corporation tax.

Unlike other types of companies, charity-owned companies have nine months from the end of the accounting period in which to determine the amount they wish to give or are obliged to pay to the charity under a profit-shedding deed or gift aid payment. They are then able to claim the deduction against the corporation tax profits of the accounting period to which the payment relates.

28.3 Deeds of covenant

Deeds of covenant have been a popular form of giving to charity for some time. In many cases, they remain popular despite the relaxation of the various gift aid regulations. To satisfy the requirements of HMRC, there are several criteria that must be fulfilled. The way in which the covenant is worded is of paramount importance, and the following points should be noted:

(a) a covenant form must state that it is a deed;
(b) the covenant form must be signed and delivered by the covenantor in the presence of a witness;
(c) a covenant must provide for annual payments to be made year by year and must cover a minimum period;
(d) a covenant cannot be backdated, and
(e) a covenant must be capable of lasting more than three years (in practice, covenants are usually drawn up for a four-year period).

As for gift aid, regular payments made by individuals and companies before April 2000 to a charity under a deed of covenant were paid after the deduction of basic rate tax. The charity could claim back from HMRC the basic rate tax deducted from the payment.

The individual must have paid at least as much income tax at the basic rate as the amount of tax reclaimed by the charity on the payment. If the amount reclaimed by the charity exceeded the amount paid by the covenantor, HMRC might require the individual to pay the tax difference. Companies were required to deduct basic rate tax from the covenanted payment and pay it over separately to HMRC.

If the individual paid tax at the higher rate, he or she could get tax relief on the payment on the difference between the basic and higher rates of tax on the grossed-up amount. A company deducts the gross amounts of the payments it charges in its corporation tax computation.

There is no longer a separate tax relief for payments made by an individual (or a company) under a deed of covenant – all tax relief for such payments is under the gift aid scheme. The deed of covenant will stand in place of the gift aid declaration. However, any donation made outside the terms of the deed, or after expiry of the deed, must be covered by a separate gift aid declaration.

Payments made under a deed of covenant must be covered by a gift aid declaration. Where a charity wishes to continue with the use of deeds of covenant for donors, these can also be used as declarations, provided that all the information required in the declaration is given in the deed.

The abolition of a separate tax relief for payments made under a deed of covenant to a charity does not mean that such deeds will cease to exist, but it does mean that they are no longer required.

Some charities have decided to maintain deeds of covenant from their supporters in order to secure a regular flow of income. If they do so, they will need to make sure they also obtain a gift aid declaration from the donor, or ensure that the deed contains the necessary elements required in such a declaration.

28.4 Benefits received by donors

Charities may wish to give a token of appreciation by way of a 'thank you' to donors for their donations. Modest benefits received in consequence of making a donation will not stop the donation from qualifying as a gift aid donation, provided that its value does not exceed certain limits.

The donor benefit rules contain two limits for the value of the benefit that a donor, or a person connected with the donor, may receive in consequence of

Giving to charities

making a donation. If the value of the benefits received exceeds either of these limits, the donation will not qualify as a gift aid donation. A donation will not qualify if:

- the value of the benefit exceeds the limits in the table set out below, or
- the value of the benefit, plus the value of any benefits received in consequence of any gift aid donation made by the same donor to the same charity earlier in the same tax year, exceeds £500 (the so-called 'aggregate value test' – see below).

The limits for the relevant value tests are set out below.

Table 28.1 *Limits set on value of benefits for a donation to qualify as gift aid*

Amount of donation	Value of benefits
£100	25 per cent of the donation
£101–£1,000	£25
In excess of £1,000	5 per cent of the donation

These limits apply separately to each donation.

In addition to satisfying the relevant value test, the value of the benefits received in consequence of the donation must also satisfy the 'aggregate value test' if the donation is to qualify as a gift aid donation. In other words, the value of the benefits received in consequence of making the donation, plus the value of any benefits received in consequences of any gift aid donations by any donor to the same charity earlier in the same tax year, must not exceed £500.

The valuation of donor benefits can be difficult. The starting point should be to look at the value of the benefits made available. Where the item or service, or a comparable item or service, is sold to the public (whether by the charity or someone else) on arm's length terms (for example, a ticket to attend a sporting event), the value of the benefit will generally be the sale price to the public. Where the value of the benefit is less immediately obvious, the charity will need to determine how much someone dealing with it at arm's length would be prepared to pay for the benefit. Evidence might be obtained from similar transactions in the commercial sector.

The value to be arrived at is the value to the recipient. Consideration in the form of third-party discount could cost the charity nothing to provide but will still be of value to the recipient.

Working out the value of benefits

The value of a benefit is always the value to the recipient, not the cost to the charity of providing the benefit. Even if a charity gets a discount on the cost of any benefits given to donors, the benefit must still be given its full value when working out whether a donation qualifies for gift aid.

Valuing goods and services

For many benefits, the value is simply the retail value of the item or service. If a donor receives a free theatre ticket, the value of the benefit is the face value of the ticket.

Where a retail value cannot be found, the charity must work out how much someone would be prepared to pay for the item or services by looking at similar commercial transactions.

Valuing attendance at a non-ticketed event

Where a benefit is attendance at an event that is not open to the public (so that there is no ticket price), the benefit should be valued by dividing the cost to the charity of staging the event by the number of people attending the event.

Valuing benefits in return for life membership subscriptions

Where a benefit is given in return for a life membership subscription, to arrive at the benefit value an estimate of the value of all the benefits that will be received over the first 10 years of the membership should be calculated.

Valuing benefits that are discounts

Where the benefit is a discount on goods or services (which an individual donor may or may not take advantage of), the valuation can be based on the average take-up of the benefit by all the charity's donors.

28.4.1 Fundraising dinners

Problems have arisen where HMRC believed that donations made were not in fact voluntary donations, but more of an amount to cover the ticket price. Additionally, where HMRC accepted the voluntary nature of the donation, benefit rules were breached. In both cases, HMRC would not allow gift aid to be applied.

For gift aid to be applicable, it must be clear that the donations made are voluntary in nature. This can best be achieved in the following ways:

1. Using the phrase 'suggested voluntary donation' on invitations. No set ticket price is charged and the voluntary donation can be made before the event or on the night through an appeal or pledge cards. Gift aid can now apply as normal.

Giving to charities

2. Charging a *de-minimis* amount for the ticket price to cover the approximate cost per head. Any subsequent donations would therefore not be in breach of any benefit rules and gift aid can apply.

28.4.2 Challenge events

There has been a widespread increase in charities offering participants ever more challenging ways of raising money. Sponsored walks still exist, but now there are increased fundraising activities, such as trekking, running, triathlons, climbing and car rallies, to name but a few.

Participants may be asked to pay a non-refundable deposit or registration fee of, say, £250 but will then be required to raise an additional minimum amount through sponsorship of, say, £3,000 in return for being allowed to participate. The charity will, however, have to pay a third party, say, £600 per participant – a sum which represents the actual cost of the event (travel, insurance, provision of specialist equipment, food, accommodation, etc.). The value of the benefit to the participant is his or her cost of participating in the event, less the registration fee (that is, in this example, £600 – £250 = £350). Where the value of the benefit exceeds the permitted levels, gift aid will not be available. If the participant pays the full cost of the trip (that is, £600 in this example), then all sponsorship paid, whether by connected persons or otherwise, qualify for gift aid as there is no benefit to the participant from the sponsors' donations. A person is 'connected to the donor' if he or she is:

- the donor's husband, wife, civil partner or linear relative – for example, son, daughter, parent, grandparent, or grandchild;
- any linear relative of the donor's wife, husband or civil partner , or
- a company under the control of the donor, or under the control of any of the above.

Otherwise it may well be difficult, as a result of the benefit rules, for donations made by the participant himself or herself or by a connected person, to qualify for gift aid.

Sponsorship payments made by people who are not connected to the participant can be made under gift aid. So, if all the sponsorship raised by a participant is donated by persons not connected to the participant, then all of those individual payments qualify for gift aid.

The value of benefits must be equal to or below the following limits:

(a) for a donation – up to £100, the value of the benefits must not exceed 25 per cent of the donation;
(b) for a donation of £101 to £1,000, the value of the benefits must not exceed £25;

(c) for a donation of £1,000 to £10,000, the benefits must not exceed 5 per cent of the donation. So a donor can make a £1,000 donation but only receive benefits up to £50, and

(d) for a donation above £10,000, the benefits must not exceed £500.

In our example, donations from the donor plus connected persons must be at least £7,000 (that is, 5% × £7,000 = £350) in order for gift aid to be applied to them.

The benefit limits listed above are for gift aid purposes only. For VAT purposes, a donation is a voluntary payment for which no benefit is given in return. If a charity gives a donor a benefit in return for a payment, the normal VAT rules apply, and the full amount paid is consideration for a supply of goods or services.

28.4.3 Admissions to view charity property

Special rules apply in the case of admissions to view charity property. This includes land and buildings, artefacts, works of art, plants, animals and scientific property.

Charities that charge an admission fee to visit and view their property will not be able to claim gift aid on the fee, as it is not a gift. For example, if a charity charges a £25 admission fee to view a property, none of the money raised from the admission sales qualifies for gift aid. The money made counts towards its trading profit and is not a donation. In certain circumstances, however, HMRC will allow the payment to qualify for gift aid where the visitors view the property in return for a voluntary donation.

Only voluntary donations qualify for gift aid. A charity can ask its visitors to make a voluntary donation that meets either of the following two conditions:

1. the donation is 10 per cent greater than the normal admission fee, or
2. the donation allows admission for a period of at least 12 months.

Where the donation is 10 per cent more than the normal admission fee

This applies where a visitor has the option of paying the normal admission fee, but instead chooses to make a gift in the form of a donation that is at least 10 per cent more than the normal admission fee. In return for the donation, the charity must allow the visitor the same right of admission as a normal paying visitor would receive.

In this case the whole amount received from the visitor qualifies for gift aid, not just the additional 10 per cent. It is important that all visitors are clearly made aware that the option to donate the 10 per cent extra is entirely voluntary.

Giving to charities

Charities could use this option for daily admissions, but any admission period of less than 12 months can be included, provided that members of the public could still purchase the same right of admission.

Where the donation allows admission for at least a 12 month period

This applies where charities accept a donation that gives the donor the right of admission to view charity property for a period of at least one year, at all times that the property is open to members of the public. It includes annual membership subscriptions that meet the conditions to be regarded as donations.

Charities can either:

(a) accept a donation that allows free admission for all visits during the period covered. They can still specify up to five days when the right of free admission does not apply. A visitor who chooses to make a donation but does not complete a gift aid declaration must also be given free admission for the same period on the same terms, or
(b) accept a donation and grant a right of admission on payment of a reduced fee, which must apply for the first and all subsequent visits during the period covered. In this case, only the initial donation qualifies for gift aid. The first and subsequent admission fees are not donations, but are payments of a charge for admission to view the property. A visitor who chooses to make a donation but does not complete a gift aid declaration must also be able to gain the same reduced rate admission on the same terms for his or her first and all subsequent visits. Charities are free to decide what minimum level of donation they will accept before granting a right of admission for a year or more.

In either of the above cases, donations only qualify for gift aid when:

- the donations are supported by an appropriate gift aid declaration;
- visitors are offered a clear choice about whether they make a donation or pay the normal admission price for entry to view a property;
- the donor's right of entry to view a property is exactly the same as for visitors paying the normal admission price to view the same property; and
- all the other conditions of the gift aid scheme are met, including the benefit rules.

28.4.4 Membership subscriptions

To be treated as a gift and qualify for gift aid, any subscription payments to a charity must be for membership only and not allow the personal use of facilities.

Members will still be able to:

- receive periodic newsletters produced by the charity to explain its work Where a charity sends literature to its donors, HMRC accepts that the value of the literature will be nil, provided that it is produced for the purpose of describing the work of the charity. The material must be relevant to the furtherance of the objects of the charity. The fact that the literature has a cover price and is also on sale to members of the public is not relevant;
- visit and view the work of the charity – for example, a wildlife conservation charity allowing members admission to view its conservation work, and
- take part in activities that form part of the charity's objectives – for example, a youth organisation providing group craft workshops as part of its educational objectives.

Any additional benefits provided to members must be within a certain value, based on the amount of the donation.

If a charity offers family membership, HMRC will regard the membership subscription as a gift to the charity by an individual donor and it will qualify for gift aid, provided that the individual donor is included in the family membership and has given a gift aid declaration to the charity and all the conditions of the gift aid are met.

Membership subscriptions that do not qualify for gift aid

Any membership subscription that gives the member rights to personal use of the charity's services or facilities would not be treated as a gift and so would not qualify for gift aid. This might include:

- using the equipment of a charitable sports centre;
- providing coaching or tuition to individuals, whether alone or in a group, and
- allowing members the free or discounted use of facilities that were not available on similar terms to non-members – for example, the use of a swimming pool or golf course.

28.4.5 Charity auctions

Where an individual successfully bids for goods or services at a charity auction, his or her payment for the item is not a donation and therefore is not strictly a gift to charity. However, HMRC recognises that sometimes payments made for goods and services auctioned for charity will intentionally be more than their retail value. In these circumstances, HMRC will treat payments as donations which will qualify for gift aid provided that the other rules of the scheme are met and the benefits do not exceed certain limits.

For donations to qualify for gift aid, any benefits provided – including the value of the items auctioned – must be below the limits as set out in sections **28.4** and **28.4.2** above.

Giving to charities

If the auction lot is commercially available, then that commercial value can be used as the value of the benefit. For example, if a football shirt from the local team, which is widely available in local shops for a retail price of £60, is auctioned for £100, then the value of the benefit to the bidder is £60 even though the bidder pays £100.

If the goods or services are not commercially available, the value of the item auctioned is the price paid by the successful bidder. A bidder is likely to be prepared to pay more for such an item because it is unique. For example, if a football shirt that is signed by players in the local team, which cannot be purchased in the local shops, is auctioned for £200, the value of the benefit to the bidder is £200.

When a benefit given to a donor would exceed the benefit limits, it is still possible for the donor's payment to be split between an amount to 'buy' the benefit and an amount that is treated as a gift. To do this the value or cost of the item auctioned is taken away from the amount paid, and the remainder is treated as the qualifying gift aid donation. Gift aid can only be applied to the remainder if:

- the benefit (the item purchased in the auction) can be purchased separately, and
- the donor is aware of the value of the benefit at the time the donation is made.

For auction items, the option to buy only applies where:

- the item is commercially available, and
- the donor is aware, at the time of making a successful bid, that the item could be purchased separately and its price.

For example, David bids for tennis lessons given by a professional tennis coach at an auction. He is told at the start of the auction that the tennis lessons can be bought commercially for £60. David successfully bids £200 for the lessons. In this case, the benefit limit is exceeded because the value of the benefit (£60) is more than the benefit limit (£25), so the payment will not qualify for gift aid. So, instead, David decides to buy the benefit, by taking the cost of the benefit away from the total amount bid. The £140 difference (£200 paid, less the benefit of £60) now qualifies for gift aid.

Why do so many charity auction donations fail to qualify for gift aid?

If the goods or services are not commercially available, the value of the item auctioned is the price paid by the successful bidder. Often, charity auction lots are unique and as the successful bid represents the value of that lot to the bidder, the amount paid is the value placed on the benefit. As the value of the benefit is 100 per cent of the amount paid, the donation will not qualify for gift aid.

HMRC examples of whether gift aid applies to auction items

Item type	Is item commercially available?	Market value	Price at auction	Benefit value	Does payment qualify for gift aid?
Book	Yes	£10	£100	£10	Yes – the benefit value is less than 25 per cent of the donation.
Book signed by a celebrity	Yes, but enhanced	£10 +	£100	£100	No – the benefit value is the value of the donation.
Handbag donated by a celebrity	Yes	Not applicable	£100	£100	No – the benefit value is the value of the donation.
Professional tennis lessons	Yes	£50	£100	£50	No – the benefit value is more than 25 per cent of the donation.
Dinner with a celebrity	No	Not applicable	£100	£100	No – the benefit value is the value of the donation.

28.4.6 Lotteries and raffles

Outright payments to a charity in return for services, rights or goods are not gifts to charity and so are not eligible for gift aid. This includes payments for raffle or lottery tickets: the purchase of any right to participate in a tombola or similar event (for instance, an offer such as 'If you give us a donation of £50, we will give you five tickets.') also cannot be a charitable payment. A payment to purchase a raffle ticket from a charity is not a gift to that charity but a payment for the right to enter the raffle. It is immaterial that the chance or expectation of winning a prize is small or that the value of the prize may be negligible.

28.4.7 Charity vouchers

Charity vouchers cannot themselves be used to purchase services, rights or goods. They cannot be used for:

- specific school fees and/or private education;
- purchase of goods such as books or food;
- admission to events, such as concerts, dinners and jumble sales, or
- purchase of raffle or lottery tickets.

Charity vouchers can only be used in respect of purely voluntary donations.

28.5 Payroll giving (GAYE – give as you earn)

Payroll giving provides tax relief at source for individuals who give to charity by direct deduction from their pay. Once an employee has signed up to the scheme, the employer simply deducts the relevant amounts from the employee's pay before deducting tax under PAYE and sending the payment to the charity.

A number of improvements have been made to payroll giving, including the fact that there are now no limits on the amount that can be given. The mechanism of the scheme is that the employer deducts amounts specified by the employee from gross pay, and this amount is not taxable to the employee. In most cases, the employee will receive a book of vouchers (similar to a chequebook) from the Charities Aid Foundation (CAF), which he or she can then use to make gifts to charities of his choice. The charity is not entitled to reclaim any further tax on these payments.

The CAF acts as a type of clearing house and pays funds into the charity concerned at the request of the employee. It performs a similar service for individuals who can set up an account for using covenanted donations. The donor issues instructions to the CAF to pay amounts to specified charities from the accounts.

28.6 Giving through the tax return

28.6.1 Carry back

In addition to payments during the tax year, any individual taxpayer may make gift aid payments for the period from the beginning of the tax year to the date on which his tax return is submitted to HMRC, provided that the return is submitted by the normal deadline of 31 January. Such payments are treated as though made in the previous tax year. This is a valuable relief to individuals, as such giving can be used to reduce a tax liability and/or receive higher-rate tax relief.

28.6.2 Charitable giving through self assessment

Taxpayers can nominate a charity to receive a tax repayment due to them as a result of making the tax return. The donation can only be made to one charity. Each charity on the HMRC list has been given a unique code, which should be used on the tax return to identify the charity to receive the donation. The taxpayer can donate the whole repayment or specify an amount. Donors can make a gift aid declaration on the tax return itself. Higher-rate taxpayers will be able to claim the relief due to them in the tax return for year in which the donation was made

28.7 Legacies

Transfers to charities are exempt from inheritance tax and thus reduce the tax burden on an estate. There are several ways in which wills can be drafted to maximise the effect of this relief, particularly where the estate is substantial and the testator wishes to split the disposition between a charity or charities and individuals. A certain amount of planning can ensure that even a small pecuniary legacy to a charity can be structured so as to take advantage of maximum tax reliefs available.

28.8 Gifting shares and securities

Individuals can get income tax relief on gifts of certain shares, securities and other investments to charities. This is in addition to the existing capital gains tax relief on gifts of assets to charities.

Companies can get corporation tax relief on gifts to charities for the same type of investments. This is in addition to relief from corporation tax on capital gains arising from gifts to charities of shares, securities and other assets.

As far as the charity is concerned, the item received can be sold immediately (or later) and the proceeds used for charitable purposes or it can be retained as an investment.

The types of investment that qualify for the tax relief are:

- shares and securities listed or dealt on the UK Stock Exchange, including the Alternative Investment Market;
- shares and securities listed or dealt on any overseas recognised stock exchange;
- shares in a UK-authorised unit trust;
- shares in a UK open-ended investment company, and
- holdings in certain foreign collective investment schemes (broadly, these are schemes established outside the UK that are equivalent to unit trust and open-ended investment companies).

Individuals normally claim their relief in their self-assessment tax returns. Companies should claim the relief in their corporation tax self-assessment returns.

The amount of relief that can be claimed is the market value of the investment on the day that it is given to the charity. The date on which the gift is made is the day on which the whole of the beneficial ownership of the investments is transferred to the charity. This is usually the date on which the donor signs the stock transfer form. There might be additional costs of making the gift – for example, a broker's fee can also be claimed. Any amount of consideration or the value of any benefits received by the donor or persons 'connected' with them, in connection with the gift, must be deducted from the amount of the relief.

The following examples illustrate how the amount of relief is calculated.

Example 1

Philippe owns 5,000 shares in ABC Ltd, a company quoted on the London Stock Exchange. The shares are given to a charity when they are worth £5 each. A broker's fee of £50 is charged for handling the transaction. As a token of gratitude, the charity gives the donor tickets to an event worth £250.

The deduction that the donor can make is:

	£
The value of the shares	25,000
Add: the broker's fees	50
	25,050
Less: the value of the benefit received	(250)
	24,800

Charities are able to ask donors to sell shares on their behalf. In such instances, the donor can still obtain these tax reliefs. The donors will, however, require evidence from the charity, such as an exchange of letters, showing that they have made the gift of the investment to the charity and that the charity asked them to dispose of the investments on their behalf. Otherwise, they will be treated as having made a disposal on their own account and the cash gift to the charity may be treated as a gift aid donation. No capital gains tax relief (as detailed below) would be available in that case.

In addition to income tax and corporation tax relief, there is already relief from capital gains tax or corporation tax on chargeable gains for gifts of assets to charities. Conversely, a donor cannot take advantage of a loss for capital gains tax purposes. This relief relates to all chargeable assets gifted to charities and not just the assets that qualify for the income tax and corporation tax relief.

Where assets are given to a charity, or sold to a charity for no more than their cost, the donor is treated as having disposed of them for such an amount as gives rise to neither a gain nor a loss.

On any subsequent disposal by a charity, the calculation of any gain is based on the date and cost of the donor's original acquisition.

A question that is often asked is whether it is better to sell the investment and give the proceeds to the charity using gift aid. For companies, it will usually be better to give the shares to the charity. If no chargeable gain will arise on the sale, then there is no difference between the two methods. For individuals, it depends on their circumstances and whether they wish the charity or themselves to gain the greater benefit from the tax relief. The following example demonstrates the difference.

Example 2

Rebecca is a higher-rate taxpayer with shares worth £100,000. If she sells them, she would make a net gain of £25,000 after all reliefs and allowances, and be liable to capital gains tax. The first option is for Rebecca to sell the shares and give the proceeds to the charity under gift aid.

	£
Gross proceeds of sale of shares	100,000
Less capital gains tax (£25,000 @ 18%)	(4,500)
Net proceeds after capital gains tax	95,500

Under **gift aid**, the charity can recover from HMRC the amount of the gift multiplied by the basic rate income tax that Rebecca has suffered. If Rebecca gives £95,500 to a charity under gift aid, the charity can reclaim:

	£
£95,500 × 22/78 (the effective rate in three-year transitional period 6 April 2008 – 5 April 2011), which equals	26,935
When this is added to the gift the charity receives in total, £95,500 + £26,935 =	122,435
Rebecca claims tax relief on the difference between the basic rate (20%) and the higher rate (40%) on £122,435 (20% × £122,435) = £24,487	
So the gift has cost her £100,000 – £24,487	75,513
The second option is for Rebecca to give her shares (**shares aid**) to the charity.	£
The charity receives shares to sell or retain as investments	100,000
Rebecca gets tax relief on £100,000 at the higher rate of tax (40%)	(40,000)
So the gift has cost Rebecca £100,000 – £40,000 =	60,000

Under the first option, the charity received £122,435 as opposed to £100,000 received under the second option. However, the gift has cost Rebecca £75,513 under the first option, but only £60,000 under the second option.

Example 3

Shares aid	Gift aid
Charity receives £50,000	Sell shares £50,000
Tax relief for donor = £50,000 @ 40% income tax relief = £20,000	Capital gains tax £10,000 @ 18% = £1,800
	Net proceeds gifted £48,200
	Charity receives £61,795 (£48,200 + £13,595 gift aid (22/78 × £48,200)
Cost to donor	**Cost to donor**
£50,000	£50,000
(20,000)	Higher rate of tax on gross gift (61,795 @ 20%) = (£12,359)
£30,000	**£37,641**

28.9 Gifting land and buildings

The relief mentioned above for the gifting of shares and securities to charities was extended in April 2002 to include land and buildings. The relief is identical to that for the gifting of shares and securities, and therefore all the same opportunities exist.

28.10 Giving to charity by businesses

Businesses can give to charities in a number of ways other than pure gifts of money. These include:

- gifts of land, buildings, shares and securities;
- gifts of equipment or trading stock, and
- secondment of employees.

As regards tax relief for the donor, there are different rules for each type of gift. These need to be understood by both the business community and the charitable sector as the availability of the reliefs may encourage business donations.

Gifts of land, buildings, shares and securities

The tax relief for such gifts is explained in sections **28.8** and **28.9** above.

Gifts of equipment or trading stock

Relief can be obtained if a business gives either an item manufactured or sold in the course of its trade, or machinery or plant used in the course of the trade.

When a business gives away an article manufactured or sold in the course of its trade, nothing is included as a trading receipt in the profit and loss account for the item. In this way, the business gets relief for the cost of the item in calculating the profit of the trade.

Similarly, if a business gives away a fixed asset, it will have no disposal proceeds for capital allowance purposes. The total capital allowances given to the business for the fixed asset will be equal to its cost.

Secondment of employees to charity

Relief is given to companies, sole traders or partnerships that provide assistance to charities by seconding employees to them on a temporary basis, by treating the employment costs of the individual as a business expense.

28.11 Recent changes

The 2008 Budget announcements are particularly helpful to charities as they cover a number of issues, including gift aid, and represent a great achievement for the sector in the concessions and measures that have been announced.

28.11.1 Gift aid

Following the announcement in Budget 2007 that the basic rate of income tax would be cut from 22 per cent to 20 per cent from 2008/09 (that is, from 6 April 2008), the Government launched a consultation on the gift aid scheme in June 2007. The consultation closed on 30 September 2007 and the Government's response was published on Budget Day, 12 March 2008.

As a result of that consultation, a range of amendments to the scheme have been announced. These are aimed at increasing the take-up of gift aid over the long term. They include major reform to the auditing process, a comprehensive programme for bringing smaller charities into gift aid, a redesign of the guidance, outreach to 5,000 new charities through the launch of targeted marketing tools, and a number of other administrative changes.

Transitional relief – charities

Most importantly, a transitional relief will be available for three years (2008/09 to 2010/11 inclusive) to counteract the loss of income which charities would

Giving to charities

have suffered as a result of the reduction in the basic rate of income tax from 22 per cent to 20 per cent with effect from 6 April 2008.

The Government estimates that this will be worth around £300 million to the charity sector as a whole. Charities will submit claims at the new basic rate, and HMRC will adjust the repayment made to include the transitional relief. Claims for the transitional relief will have to be made within two years of the year in which the donation was received.

Transitional relief – donors who are higher-rate taxpayers

The transitional relief that is available to charities does not affect the additional tax relief that may be claimed by higher-rate taxpayers who make donations under gift aid. They are still able to claim tax relief for their donations in the amount of the difference between the basic and the higher rates of income tax.

The net cost to the donor of a donation with a gross value to the charity of £100 will vary as shown in the table below, assuming the basic rate of income tax continues to be 20 per cent.

Table 28.2 *The varying net cost to the donor for making a donation of £100 (for incomes up to £100,000)*

	Up to 5 April 2008	6 April 2008 to 5 April 2011	After 5 April 2011
Charity			
Cash donation	£78.00	£78.00	£80.00
Charity recovers	£22.00	£22.00	£20.00
Charity receives	£100.00	£100.00	£100.00
Donor			
Cash donation	£78.00	£78.00	£80.00
Higher-rate relief	£18.00	£19.50	£20.00
Net cost to donor	**£60.00**	**£58.50**	**£60.00**

Thus, in consequence of the reduction in basic rate tax and the transitional relief, during the three years to 5 April 2011, the net cost to higher-rate taxpayers of making a donation to charity goes down; so, arguably, they can afford to give more. If they continued to give an amount with a net cost to donor of £60 during these three years, it would be worth £102.56 per annum to the charity.

Increase in income tax for high earners

From April 2010, people with taxable income over £150,000 will pay tax on the excess at 50 per cent. There will also be a staged reduction to nil in personal allowances for people with 'adjusted net incomes' above £100,000. Donors will therefore see their tax reliefs increase correspondingly.

Table 28.3 *Higher rate income tax increases to 50 per cent for incomes over £150,000*

		2009/10		2010/11
		£		£
Donation		1,000		1,000
Gross donation to the charity – £1,250				
(ignoring transitional supplement)				
Higher rate tax relief				
(40% – 20% basic rate × £1,250)		250		
(50% – 20% basic rate × £1,250)				375
Net cost to donor		**750**		**625**

This table demonstrates that the increase in the top tax rate to 50 per cent will reduce the 'cost' of Gift Aid Donations.

Additionally, the £1 reduction in personal allowances for each £2 of net adjusted income over £100,000 creates a marginal tax rate of 60 per cent on incomes between £100,000 and £112,950. Since income for this purpose is after Gift Aid contributions, a gross donation of £1,250 will actually "only" cost the donor £500 in this income range.

28.11.2 HMRC auditing of gift aid

One of the major areas highlighted by the sector during the 2007 consultation was that of HMRC audits. Although some respondents commented that HMRC auditors provided practical and helpful advice, there is a widespread view that preparation for an audit and the audit itself impose a considerable administrative burden, as well as the 'fear factor'. As a result of these concerns, the Government has announced a number of new measures and reforms.

From 12 March 2008, charities and community amateur sports clubs will be allowed to repair errors identified within an audit sample, before the error rate is extrapolated across the gift aid claim. 'Repaired' means that the charity finds the missing declaration, or obtains a new (or fully completed) declaration from the donor.

Also, from 12 March 2008, there will be a *de-minimis* error level of four per cent, below which charities claiming under £2,500 per year will not be penalised for errors in their gift aid claims. HMRC says that this means that two-thirds of Gift aid claimants will not be penalised for errors in record-keeping. The four per cent limit will be applied to the level of errors after repair rather than before.

HMRC will introduce a 'yellow card' warning system which will apply to earlier years, rather than make recoveries for those years where either the amount or the level of errors is small (see table below). When a 'yellow card' is issued, the scheme will include the provision of advice on remedial action regarding how the charity should prevent errors in its record-keeping in the future, to give support to the charities and assist them in understanding gift aid and in rectifying errors for future claims. If the necessary action has not been taken by the next time HMRC examines the claims by the charity, it will then go back and recover the amount calculated to be the excess tax reclaimed for any earlier years.

The *de-minimis* limited and 'yellow card' system will apply as shown below.

Table 28.4 *How the de-minimis limited and 'yellow card' system will apply*

Repaired error level	Amount at stake	Action at audit 1
Less than 4%	Less than £100	No recovery in year of audit or earlier years – no card issued.
Less than 4%	Less than £500	Recovery in year but not earlier years – no card issued.
Less than 4%	More than £500	Recovery in year but not earlier years – 'yellow card' issued.
More than 4%	Less than £500	Recovery in year but not earlier years – 'yellow card' issued.
More than 4%	More than £500	Recovery in year and earlier years.

Claims process and record-keeping

This is another related area, which charities have found a real burden. To afford some relief, the following relaxations have been announced:

1. From 12 March 2008, the process for making claims is adjusted so that charities can aggregate donations under £10 in claims up to a total of

£500. This will mean that charities that have collected donations of money for which they have also received a gift aid declaration, will have the option of making a claim without having to list all the donors on the repayment claim form.

2. **From 1 April 2010, the time limit for making gift aid claims (and indeed other tax claims) will be reduced to four years from the end of the tax year to which the claim relates.** The current time limit is five years 10 months for charitable trusts and six years for charitable companies. (The current limits are determined by the regimes for self-assessment for personal tax and corporation tax respectively, and are being changed as part of an overhaul of the regime relating to time limits and penalties).

Guidance and awareness

On Budget Day 2008, HMRC launched a gift aid web-based information service at *www.direct.gov.uk/giftaid*, together with a detailed programme of upgrades to HMRC guidance. These will both be developed in partnership with the sector and will result in a comprehensive online source of guidance.

A gift aid toolkit has been developed. This contains all the tools and guidance needed to run a successful gift aid scheme, and will be available to over 5,000 newly-registering and 20,000 existing registered charities.

Small charities

In order to address the particular needs of small charities identified in the 2007 consultation, the Government has announced an extension of the Tax-effective Giving Initiative. This will be delivered via the Institute of Fundraising, which will give charities access to training, resources and advice on operating tax-efficient giving schemes, including gift aid. A Small Charities Training Programme will target charities with an annual turnover of less than £1million, so that small local charities can access guidance and training on gift aid. In order to help charitable community and voluntary groups access the benefits of gift aid, the use of local 'umbrella charities' will be promoted. A new online gift aid mentoring forum for charities will also be developed.

28.11.3 Substantial donor legislation

The substantial donor rules are anti-avoidance rules that were brought in by s. 54 of the Finance Act 2006. The aim of the rules is to prevent tax avoidance whereby a taxpayer (an individual or a company) gets tax relief on a donation to a charity, but the charity in return provides benefits to the donor (for example, by entering into transactions with them on non-arm's length terms). The effect of the rules is to actually penalise the charity for entering into particular transactions with a substantial donor. The charity becomes liable to tax on the value of the transaction. A 'substantial donor' is a donor who makes a donation of £25,000 or more in any one tax year, or £150,000 in any period of six years.

The transactions penalised are:

(a) the provision of services by the charity or the donor;
(b) buying, selling, exchanging or letting property by either party to the other;
(c) the provision of financial assistance by either party;
(d) payment of remuneration by the charity to the donor, and
(e) investment by the charity in the business of a substantial donor.

In all cases, the transactions that are penalised include transactions with individuals or companies connected with the donor.

There are many problems with the application of these rules. After numerous representations by the charity sector, HMRC and the Treasury undertook a joint consultation in 2008 and made a number of proposed changes. The general response from the sector was that, while these changes did improve the application of the rules in certain areas, they did not substantively address the significant structural problems inherent in the legislation. The following further recommendations were made by the charity sector:

1. The rules should be abolished and (if necessary) replaced by rules that would be easier to understand and operate, and did not penalise innocent transactions.
2. If the existing rules were retained, there should be a provision to exempt all transactions on arm's length terms where there was no tax-avoidance motive, and the charity should only be taxed on the value of any benefit it provided to the donor.
3. There should be a clearance procedure so that charities could obtain certainty about whether a transaction would be penalised or not.

The Pre-Budget Report in November 2008 promised 'a detailed response early next year' (that is, in 2009). However, the 2009 Budget produced only one change to the regime – an increase in the size of donations which, over a six-year period, qualify the donor as a substantial donor and bring transactions with them into the regime.

However, the 2009 Budget Report states that 'The Government has considered its response to the consultation on the anti-avoidance rules around substantial donors to charity. Further informal consultation with the sector to develop new rules based around an effective anti-avoidance purpose test. The Government aims to bring forward proposals at the 2009 Pre-Budget Report, with a view to legislating in 2010.'

28.11.4 Tax administration

The changes to the administration of the tax system announced following the Carter review will affect charities' statutory tax returns.

Tax returns for trusts

For charities constituted as trusts, the changes apply to returns for the 2007/08 tax year onwards. The deadline for paper returns has been brought forward to 31 October, so that the deadline for paper returns for the year ended 5 April 2008 is 31 October 2008. However, for returns filed online, the deadline remains at 31 January, with the result that the deadline for 2007/08 returns filed online will be 31 January 2009. The payment date for any tax due remains at 31 January, however the return is filed. Charities only have to submit a tax return when they receive a notice requiring them to do so or have income that is not exempt; they do not have to submit returns routinely on an annual basis.

28.12 List of statutory references

1. Gift aid (individual) – Sections 414–428 of the Income Tax Act 2007
2. Gift aid declaration regulations – SI No. 2074 2000
3. Gift aid (company) – Section 339 of the Income and Corporation Taxes Act 1988 (as amended by Section 40 of the Finance Act 2000)
4. Transactions with substantial donors – Section 54 of the Finance Act 2006
5. Non-charitable expenditure – Section 55 of the Finance Act 2006
6. Trade profits – Section 56 of the Finance Act 2006
7. Gift aid relief for companies wholly owned by one or more charities – Section 57 of the Finance Act 2006
8. Extension of restriction on gift aid payments by close companies – Section 58 of the Finance Act 2006
9. Gift of shares, securities and real property – Sections 587B and 587BA of the Income and Corporation Taxes Act 1988
10. Gifts of land and buildings – Section 587C of the Income and Corporation Taxes Act 1988
11. Payroll giving – Sections 713–715 of the Income Tax (Earnings & Pensions) Act 2003
12. Payroll giving regulations – SI No. 2211 1986 (as amended by SI.00/759 and SI.00/2083)
13. Loans to Charities Section 620 (1) and (5) Income Tax (Trading Other Income) Act
14. Charitable tax exemptions – Section 505 of the Income and Corporation Taxes Act 1988
15. Small trading exemption – Section 46 of the Finance Act 2000
16. Capital Gains Tax exemption for charities – Section 256 of the Taxation of Chargeable Gains Act 1992
17. Capital Gains Tax exemption for Gifts to Charities – Section 257 of the Taxation of Chargeable Gains Act 1992
18. Qualifying Investments and Loans – Schedule 20 of the Income and Corporation Taxes Act 1988

Giving to charities

19. Definition of a Charity for Tax and Overseas Donations – Section 506 of the Income and Corporation Taxes Act 1988
20. Gifts in kind to charities – Section 83A of the Income and Corporation Taxes Act 1988.
21. Community Amateur Sports Clubs (CASCs) – Schedule 18 of the Finance Act 2002.

Chapter 29 – Charities in Scotland, Northern Ireland and the Republic of Ireland

29.1 Scope of SORP 2005

The accounting recommendations of this SORP apply to all charities in the United Kingdom that prepare accounts on the accruals basis to give a true and fair view of a charity's financial activities and financial position, regardless of their size, constitution or complexity.

Whilst charities in the Republic of Ireland do not fall within the scope of this SORP, they may choose to comply with its recommendations. If a charity based in the Republic of Ireland chooses to adopt this SORP's recommendations, it is encouraged to disclose that fact.

Charity accounts are accompanied and complemented by information that does not form part of the financial statements. Within the UK such accompanying information is primarily provided by charities through a Trustees' Annual Report. However, the legal requirements for an annual report and its contents differ according to the charity reporting frameworks that apply within the separate legal jurisdictions of the UK. The SORP recognises that such accompanying information is very important for users of charity accounts in understanding the activities and achievements of a charity as a whole, and it therefore provides best practice recommendations for the content of such reports.

In England and Wales these best practice recommendations are underpinned by law, and in Scotland and Northern Ireland – whilst the recommendations are considered to be consistent with the law – they should be regarded as voluntary best practice recommendations supplementing legal requirements.

29.2 Scotland

The Office of the Scottish Charity Regulator (OSCR) has been established as a monitoring and regulatory body for the charity sector in Scotland. Scottish charity law was changed by the Charities and Trustee Investment (Scotland) Act 2005, which received Royal Assent on 14 July 2005. The Scottish Parliament has approved new accounting regulations, and the Charities Accounts (Scotland)

Regulations 2006 apply to accounting periods beginning on or after 1 April 2006. The following principal secondary legislation is also applicable:

- The Charities Accounts (Scotland) Amendment Regulations 2007;
- The Charities References in Documents (Scotland) Regulations 2007, and
- The Charities Reorganisation (Scotland) Regulations 2007.

The Charities and Trustee Investment (Scotland) Act 2005 also determines the format and level of scrutiny of Scottish charity accounts. It should be noted that the vast majority of Scottish charities have annualéé income of less than £100,000. In fact, approximately two thirds of the 24,000 charities on the Scottish register have annual income below £25,000. Charities must prepare their accounts in accordance with section 44 of the 2005 Act. Accounts prepared on the accruals basis must follow SORP 2005. Under the Regulations, charities with income less than £100,000 can prepare a simpler form of receipts and payments accounts, unless:

- the charity is a company, or
- the charity's constitution prevents it.

29.2.1 Annual monitoring

One of OSCR's key objectives is to plan and introduce a proportionate regime of monitoring and supervision of Scottish charities. Sections 22, 28 and 29 of the 2005 Act give OSCR power to make enquires and obtain the necessary information from charities. Every year, all charities are issued with an annual return. Charities with income over £25,000 for the preceding year will also receive a supplementary monitoring return which seeks some additional information, such as transactions with trustees and connected trading companies. Unlike in England and Wales, accounts, annual returns and monitoring returns are required to be submitted to OSCR within nine months of the year end.

29.2.2 Charity Register

All charities either managed or controlled from Scotland or with significant operations in Scotland will have to provide the following basic information to OSCR:

(a) the name of the charity;
(b) its principal office;
(c) its charitable purposes, and
(d) whether it is part of a designated religious body.

29.3 Northern Ireland

29.3.1 Charities Act (Northern Ireland) 2008

The relevant legislation is the Charities Act (Northern Ireland) 2008, which establishes a Northern Ireland Charity Commission as the main regulator. The Act creates new charitable purposes and introduces a public benefit requirement. There will be a new requirement for charities in Northern Ireland to register with this new commission.

The long-awaited new charities legislation for Northern Ireland received Royal Assent on 9 September 2008. Many of the provisions of the Charities Act require secondary legislation and, as such, will be introduced in stages. The Department for Social Development anticipates that all parts of the Act should become fully operational by early 2011. A separate Charity Commission has been appointed.

The first main business of the new Commission is to consult on public benefit guidance. It is envisaged that charities will not be required to register with the Charity Commission until the spring of 2010, with the first reporting requirements happening the following year. The new rules for fundraising and public collections are not likely to take effect until 2011.

The Charities Act (Northern Ireland) 2008 is very similar to the reforms that have been introduced in the rest of the UK, but is not identical. It represents the first major reform of charity law in Northern Ireland for some considerable time. The main objectives of the Act are:

- to modernise and update the law;
- to introduce a new advisor and regulator in the form of the Charity Commission for Northern Ireland , and
- to allow openness and transparency on the operations of the sector

This Act is the largest piece of legislation particular to Northern Ireland that has come before the Assembly. It will put the charity sector on a firm foothold for the future and should also help to increase public confidence and therefore strengthen the sector.

Table 29.1 Implementation timetable

September 2008	Royal Assent granted
March 2009	Appointment of Charity Commissioners
March 2009	First Commencement Order introduced
March 2009	NI Charity Commission established

April 2009	Consultation on public benefit
May 2009	Second Commencement Order on meaning of charitable purpose and public benefit test
September 2009	Third Commencement Order to introduce charities register
April 2010	First charity registrations
April 2011	First financial returns and reports

The legislation also provides statutory definitions of *charity* and *charitable purpose*, sets out new rules with regard to fundraising and collections, and introduces a new form of charitable body. All charities, regardless of size, will be required to report annually to the new regulator with their annual accounts either audited or independently examined.

The Charities Implementation Team in the Department has set up a Charity Regulation Stakeholder Forum to consider the implications of the new Charities Act. The Charities Act 2006 (which applies in England and Wales) and The Charities and Trustees Investment (Scotland) Act (which applies in Scotland) do not apply in Northern Ireland.

The Act also sets up a new organisation, the Charity Commission for Northern Ireland (CCNI), and a process for anyone to make an appeal against the decision made by the CCNI, the Charity Tribunal for Northern Ireland. Sections 6 to 11 (and Schedule 1) of the Act list the Charity Commission's objectives, purpose, general duties and powers. The Commission will be a non-departmental public body (NDPB) supported by the Department for Social Development (DSD).

Charity Commission personnel

The Commission will have a Board comprising a Chief Commissioner, a Deputy Chief Commissioner and up to five Charity Commissioners, all on a part-time basis. The public appointment process will be overseen by the Office of the Commissioner for Public Appointments in Northern Ireland.

The Commission will be responsible for up to 16 staff, including:

- a Chief Executive;
- a Head of Registration & Compliance;
- a Head of Investigation & Enforcement, and
- a Head of Finance & Administration.

It will take some time for the CCNI to become fully operational, so initially some staff may be seconded from DSD to provide support. Later, the CCNI will make its own appointments.

Charity Commission structure

The Commission will make a Management Statement and Financial Memorandum which gives details about how the Commission will work. This document will include:

1. How the Commission will meet its objectives and how this will support the aims of the Department for Social Development (DSD).
2. Guidelines and rules regarding how the Commission will carry out all its tasks.
3. Details of how and when public funds are paid to the Commission and of how the Commission will be answerable for its work.

The Accounting Officer for DSD will make the Chief Executive of the Commission its Accounting Officer. The Commission will set up and look after its own internal reviews following Treasury and Department for Finance and Personnel guidance. An independent audit committee will be set up within the Charity Commission Board.

Charity Commission budget

The CCNI has an annual operating budget of £800,000. This will largely go towards the cost of salaries and to meet the overheads of running the organisation. It will also support the important work of providing information on the changes and requirements to be met by charities. The budget is secured by DSD on behalf of CCNI.

Charitable Purposes and Public Benefit

The definition of charitable purposes will be significantly widened to 12, including those long-established charitable purposes such as the relief of poverty, the advancement of religion and the advancement of education, but there are also additional specific purposes, including:

(a) the advancement of health or the saving of lives;
(b) the advancement of citizenship or community development;
(c) the advancement of the arts, culture, heritage or science;
(d) the advancement of amateur sport;
(e) the advancement of human rights, conflict resolution or reconciliation, or the promotion of religious or racial harmony or equality and diversity;
(f) the advancement of environmental protection or improvement;
(g) the relief of those in need by reason of youth, age, ill-health, disability, financial hardship or other disadvantage;
(h) the advancement of animal welfare, and
(i) and other purposes analogous to or within the spirit of any of the above.

However, there will no longer be any presumption that what is being done is for the public benefit and each charity will have to be established for one of the 12 charitable purposes **and** prove that what it is doing is for the public benefit.

To demonstrate public benefit, a charity will need to identify what the benefit is, how it relates to the aims of the charity and how any benefit is gained or is likely to be gained by a section of the public. This will be measured against the 'disbenefit' incurred by the public – for example, whether there is any harm or detriment that arises from what is proposed. The new Charity Commission is required to produce detailed guidance on how the public benefit test will be applied.

Charity Commission for Northern Ireland

This will be a body corporate which is to be independent with its members appointed by the DSD. The Commission has a number of objectives and general functions. It will determine whether an institution is or is not a charity, encourage and facilitate the better administration of charities, identify and investigate apparent misconduct or mismanagement of charities and take remedial or protective action, issue public collection certificates for fundraising and disseminate information. It will be responsible for keeping the register of charities.

It is important to note that all Northern Ireland charities will be required to register with the Commission and it is the responsibility of the charity's trustees to do so.

Charities will still have to apply to HMRC, in Bootle, for tax exemptions as this is a totally separate matter and automatic tax exemption status does not follow from charity registration.

Non-Northern Ireland charities and dual registration

New to the Act is Section 167, which deals with 'Section 167 Institutions'. These are institutions that are not charities under Northern Ireland law but which operate for charitable purposes in or from Northern Ireland. It is likely that this part of the Bill will be amended slightly, and that there will be a mandatory requirement for such bodies to register in Northern Ireland even if they are registered elsewhere. They will have to produce a financial statement and statement of activities relating to their operations for charitable purposes in or from Northern Ireland. This is of interest to national or international clients who also have a presence or branch or carry out operations in Northern Ireland.

The detail of how registration of a charity in other parts of the UK or in the Republic of Ireland will be recognised in Northern Ireland is a matter of ongoing discussion and the Regulators Forum (made up of representatives from each UK jurisdiction and Ireland) is looking at this issue.

Powers of the Charity Commission

The Charity Commission will oversee the reporting requirements of Northern Ireland charities and it will have significant powers, such as:

(a) to institute enquiries into a charity and to require it to produce accounts and documents and to attend and give evidence;
(b) to make a published public report of the results of such enquiry;
(c) to call for documents and search records;
(d) to disclose information to any other public body throughout the United Kingdom or outside the United Kingdom:
(e) to remove trustees from the membership of a charity;
(f) to appoint an interim manager;
(g) to give specific directions for the protection of the charity, and
(h) to direct the application of charity property.

Charity Tribunal

The Bill also provides the establishment of a new Charity Tribunal, which will hear appeals from decisions taken by the Charity Commission and also carry out some of the functions previously carried out by the Attorney General.

Cy-près

The Act simplifies the cy-près procedure so that the Charity Commission can undertake this function and this should make it less expensive and simpler for a charity where the purposes for which property has been given to the charity need to be altered.

Regulation and reporting

The Act introduces a new duty on all charity trustees to keep accounting records and to prepare and submit a statement of accounts. There are also set requirements for annual audit or independent examination of charity accounts. The level of scrutiny and 'audit' required depends on the gross income. Company charities continue to be governed by the provision of the companies' legislation (currently being amended by the Companies Act 2006). Auditors should note their duty to report matters to the Charity Commission, which extends the reporting requirements of auditors of charities beyond those of a company auditor.

Trustees are required to prepare an Annual Report, reporting on the activities of the charity during the year and to file an Annual Return. All of these measures will address the lack of information currently available on the charity sector and provide specific information to enable year-by-year comparisons and transparency.

Trustees

Trustees will also be under more scrutiny. There will be powers to disqualify trustees and rights for the Commission to remove them from office. On the other hand, the Charity Commission will be able to relieve a trustee (together with auditors and independent examiners) of liability for a breach of trust or duty where the person acted honestly and reasonably and ought fairly to be excused.

For the first time trustee indemnity insurance is to be put into statutory form, subject to an overriding requirement for charity trustees to be satisfied that this is in the best interests of the charity for such insurance to be purchased, and subject to any express prohibition on the purchase of such insurance set out in the charity's trust instrument.

Company charities

There are new rights for the Charity Commission in relation to windings-up and restorations of companies that have been struck off the register, and consent of the Charity Commission will be required for an alteration – for example, to a charitable company's Memorandum of Association.

Charitable incorporated institutions

The Act introduces a new concept of a charitable incorporated organisation (CIO), which is a body corporate with a constitution and which can be a company limited by shares or guarantee. It will be possible to convert an existing charitable company or industrial and provident society to a charitable incorporated organisation. This should avoid dual regulation in that the CIO is accountable only to the Charity Commission and not the Companies Register.

Public collections and fundraising

There will be major changes to public charitable collections, where a certificate and a permit must be obtained by the Charity Commission. The fundraising provisions also cover television and multimedia appeals, and new provisions deal with the control of fundraising by the professional fundraisers – where an express agreement will be required, with the institution engaging a person that satisfies the prescribed requirements.

Mergers

There are also new and helpful provisions to simplify charity mergers and to deal with gifts made to a charity that has subsequently merged with another body.

Religious charities

There are specific provisions allowing certain religious charities that meet the criteria to apply for designated religious status, which means that they would not be subject to the same level of scrutiny by the Commission as the other charities, at least not in the first instance. However, all religious charities will still need to register and file accounts and reports.

Summary

The Act makes major changes to existing law, as follows.

1. It repeals the existing charities legislation – the 1964 Act and the 1987 Order.
2. It makes changes to the law on fundraising.
3. It creates new charitable purposes.
4. It establishes a Charity Commission for Northern Ireland with powers of investigation and sanction.
5. It creates reporting obligations for charities in the form of accounts, annual reports and annual returns.
6. It sets up the Charity Tribunal, and it provides for a new type of charity – a charitable incorporated organisation.

29.3.2 Charity accounts

Until the Charities Act (Northern Ireland) 2008 is fully implemented, the Charities Act (NI) 1964 Northern Ireland and Charities (NI) Order 1987 remain in force.

Under section 27 of the Charities Act (NI) 1964 Northern Ireland, charities are required to:-

(a) keep proper books of account;;
(b) prepare consecutive statements of account consisting of:
  (i) a receipts and payments account or an income and expenditure account; and
  (ii) if the charity's property exceeds £500, and the Department so directs, a balance sheet, and
(c) preserve the accounts for at least seven years.

These requirements are less stringent than those that apply in the rest of the UK, and trustees of at least the larger and more active charities may wish to go a bit further than the Act requires, since trustees have a general duty to act in the best interests of their charity and, in some cases, this might imply preparing more thorough accounts than are strictly required.

The DSD is not in a position to offer detailed advice on charity accounts. However, the Charity Commission produces a series of leaflets on charity accounts which will be of use to any trustee taking a detailed interest in this subject.

The accounting regime described in the Charity Commission leaflets is based on the Statement of Recommended Practice (SORP) on Accounting by Charities. This is a fairly technical guide covering all aspects of accounting by charities, which is probably of most interest to people with accountancy qualifications, and is intended to set the standard for such accounts. This means that accounts prepared in accordance with it (or the Charity Commission leaflets that are based on it) can be assumed to be in line with current best practice and are unlikely to be challenged.

29.3.3 Charity administration

It is often assumed that the system of charity administration is the same throughout the United Kingdom. This is not the case. One system covers England and Wales and is operated by the Charity Commissioners. The second is operated in Scotland by the Office of the Scottish Charities Regulator, while a different one is operated in Northern Ireland by the DSD. All three systems are based on different legislation and differ widely in their details, though the basic principles are the same, and the system of tax relief is the same throughout the UK.

The most obvious difference between the system in England, Wales and Scotland and that in Northern Ireland is that the former includes a system of compulsory registration for most types of charity: this does not currently exist in Northern Ireland.

Where a charity is being established in Northern Ireland, it is normally advisable for application to be made to the HMRC for charitable status for tax purposes, as explained earlier. There may be cases where it is unnecessary to do this; but where an organisation is able to enjoy fiscal advantages from doing so, a failure to apply may raise doubts in the minds of the public as to whether it is a bona fide charity or is being properly administered.

29.3.4 The Department for Social Development

The DSD is the charity authority for Northern Ireland: Charities Branch of its Voluntary & Community Unit handles the normal day-to-day work. Most of its functions are carried out under the Charities Act (Northern Ireland) 1964 and the Charities (Northern Ireland) Order 1987, but it has no statutory role in connection with setting up new charities. Its main functions concern giving consent to the disposal of land or buildings by charity trustees, who usually cannot sell or otherwise dispose of property without specific consent, and making Schemes to change the objects of charities whose original functions can no longer be carried out effectively.

Apart from its specific functions under the legislation, a major part of the Branch's work consists of giving informal advice to trustees and their solicitors. Charities Branch is always prepared to discuss any problem that a charity or would-be charity faces, and even if the matter is outside its area of responsibility, it can often suggest approaches that have proved successful for other charities, or refer trustees to other sources of advice or assistance.

29.3.5 Charity legislation in Northern Ireland

The following Acts are those which affect most charities. There are others which only affect a few charities, who should already be aware of them.

Legislation under which the Department for Social Development has functions

1. House-to-House Charitable Collections Act (NI) 1952.
   Orders made under:
   (a) House-to-House Charitable Collections Regulations (NI) 1952, and
   (b) House-to-House Charitable Collections Regulations (NI) 1953.
2. Charities Act (NI) 1964
   Orders made thereunder:
   (a) Charities Central Investment Fund Scheme (NI) 1965, and
   (b) Charities Central Investment Fund Order 1988.
3. Charities (NI) Order 1987.

Other legislation relating to charities

While the Department for Social Development does not have any formal functions under the following provisions, they affect charities in relation to the subjects shown:

House-to-house and street collections

1. Police, Factories etc. (Miscellaneous Provisions) Act 1916.
   Orders made thereunder:
   (a) Collections in Streets or Public Places Regulations 1927.
   (b) Collections in Streets or Public Places Regulations 1963.

General powers and duties of trustees

2. Trustee Act (NI) 2001.

Fundraising by means of lotteries

3. Betting, Gaming, Lotteries and Amusements (NI) Order 1985 (Part IV) as amended by Betting and Lotteries (NI) Order 1994.
   Regulations made thereunder:

(a) Gaming and Lotteries (Variation of Monetary Limits) Order (NI) 1990.
(b) Lotteries Regulations (NI) 1994.

29.3.6 The Charities Act (Northern Ireland) 1964: a summary

The bulk of the work of the Department in relation to charities is done under this Act. Sections concerning technical matters which do not affect the rights, power and duties of charity trustees have been omitted from the list below.

Section comments

1 Applications for opinion etc. of Ministry

The Department may give a formal written opinion which, in certain circumstances, protects trustees if they act in accordance with it in a doubtful case. It is not every question that arises in the administration of a charity upon which the opinion of the Department under this section would be appropriate, although trustees are often given informal advice.

2 Certification of cases to Attorney-General

The Department may certify cases to the Attorney-General.

3 Power to call for documents and search records

The Department may examine charity records in certain circumstances.

4 Publication of charitable gifts in wills

The Department receives copies of all wills containing charitable bequests from the Probate Registry, and has powers to ensure that bequests are properly applied.

5 Compromises of claims by or against charities

The Department may sanction the compromise of a claim by or against a charity.

6 Transfer of certain administrative actions to Ministry

The Department may intervene in a court case involving a charity in certain circumstances.

7 Receipts given by Ministry

Where a gift or bequest cannot be paid because there are no trustees to give a valid receipt, the Department may accept the sum and give a receipt.

8 Funds in court

The Department may apply for the trusteeship of unused charitable funds held in Court.

9 Taxation of solicitor's bill

The Department may in certain circumstances order that a charity's solicitor's bill of costs be taxed – that is, checked by an officer of the court to see that items are properly charged.

10 & 11 Incorporation schemes for charity trustees & Further provisions as to schemes under s.10

The Department may make a scheme incorporating the trustees of a charity. This gives them perpetual succession, avoids the need for repeated deeds appointing new trustees, and formalises the administration of the charity.

12 Appointment of new charity trustees

If all the trustees of a charity are dead or otherwise unable to act, and if new trustees cannot conveniently be appointed otherwise than by the Court or the Department under this section, the Department may with the consent of the Attorney-General make an order appointing new trustees.

13 Cy-près powers of Ministry

Where a charity can no longer function properly because its original objects cannot be carried out effectively and its assets do not exceed £50,000, the Department may in certain circumstances make a cy-près scheme to alter its objectives. The new objectives must be as near as possible to the original.

14 Misdescribed charitable beneficiaries in wills

This section provides for the application, in certain circumstances, of gifts in wills not exceeding £2,500 where the gift is made to misdescribed charitable beneficiaries. It allows the Department, with the consent of the Attorney-General, to provide for the alternative application of the gift. If it were not for the existence of this section, an application to the Court might be required.

15 Acceptance of charity property by Ministry

The trustees of any charity, with the Department's consent, may transfer the trusteeship to the Department under this section. The Department then becomes the sole trustee and is responsible for the proper running of the charity, although local administrators are usually appointed.

16 Proceedings to recover charity property

The Department may in certain circumstances institute court proceedings to recover charity property.

17 & 18 Leases of and improvements to charity lands & Sale, exchange or mortgage of charity lands

Where a charity does not have power to lease, sell, exchange, mortgage, or surrender the lease of its property, the Department may give it such power if it considers that it is for the benefit of the charity to do so.

19 & 20 Redemption of rent-charges etc. payable to charity & Redemption of rent-charges etc., charged on charity's land

The Department may give trustees power to redeem a rent charge payable by or to the charity if it is satisfied that to do so would be for the benefit of the charity.

21 Effect of transactions under ss. 17 to 20

This section sets out further provisions in relation to sections 17, 18, 19 and 20.

22 & 23 Occasions for applying property cy-près & Application cy-près of gifts of donors unknown or disclaiming

These sections define the circumstances in which a cy-près scheme can be made. See section 13 above.

24 Gifts for mixed purposes

This section gives the Department power to deal with certain cases where property is given for mixed charitable and non-charitable purposes.

25 Common investment schemes

This section empowers the Department to set up common investment schemes.

26 Power of two-thirds of trustees to act for certain purposes

Where a charity has at least four trustees, two-thirds of them (fractions counting up) can legally carry out certain functions. In general, the Department prefers applications to it to be made by all the trustees.

27 Duty to keep accounts

This section imposes a duty on trustees to keep proper accounts.

28 Deposit of deeds etc., with Ministry for safe keeping

This section provides that trustees may deposit documents with the Department for safekeeping.

29 Applications to Court

Where there is or is alleged to be a breach of any charitable trust, or the advice or order of the Court is required in connection with the administration of any charitable trust, any interested party, including the Department, may apply to the Court for whatever action may in the circumstances be necessary.

30 Enforcement of requirements made by the Ministry

This section provides for the enforcement of certain of the Department's orders and schemes.

31 Value of land, etc., for purposes of Act

This section sets out how the value of land or a periodical payment is to be determined for the purposes of the Act.

32 Costs and expenses of Ministry

This section provides for the Department to recover expenses. The costs of publishing statutory notices in newspapers in connection with sections 12 and 13 above are the only expenses that normally arise.

33 Annual report by Ministry

This section requires the Department to produce an annual report

34 Interpretation

This section defines certain terms used in the Act.

29.3.7 The Charities (Northern Ireland) Order 1987: a summary

This Order is largely concerned with giving the trustees of small charities the power to wind up their charities. The following list of Articles omits those whose purpose is to amend the Charities Act (Northern Ireland) 1964 since they have already been taken account of in the previous section on that Act.

Article comments

Resolution by trustees of old charity to alter objects

3. The trustees of a local charity for the relief of poverty may, in some circumstances, alter its objects, subject to the Department's concurrence.

Power for trustees of small charities to transfer whole property to another charity

4. The trustees of a charity with an income of less than £200 per annum may, in some circumstances, transfer all its assets to another similar charity, subject to the Department's concurrence.

Power for very small charities to spend capital

The trustees of a charity with an endowment of £25 or less (not consisting of land) and an annual income of £5 or less, may in some circumstances expend the charity's capital.

Effect of alteration of instruments establishing charity as a body corporate

9(1) If a charitable company alters its Memorandum and Articles of Association so that it ceases to be charitable, all its property must continue to be used for its original objects..

9(2) Where a charity is a company, any alteration of the objects clause in its Memorandum and Articles of Association is ineffective without the prior written consent of the Department.

9A Limits the application of certain Articles of the Companies (NI) Order 1986 to charitable companies.

9B Where a company is a charity and its name does not include the words 'charity' or 'charitable' the fact that it is a charity must be stated on all its letters, notices, bills, cheques, conveyances, invoices, receipts, etc.

29.4 Republic of Ireland

Charities in the Republic of Ireland have adopted the previous SORPs as a matter of 'best practice', even though the SORP has no legal status in the Republic.

29.4.1 The Charities Bill 2007

The Department of Community, Rural and Gaeltacht Affairs published the Charities Bill 2007 in April 2007. The publication of the Bill brings the modernisation of charity legislation one step closer to enactment in the Republic. It provides for the following:

(a) the establishment of a statutory body for the regulation of charities, to be called the Charities Regulatory Authority;
(b) a Register of Charities;
(c) a definition of charitable purpose;
(d) the creation of a Charity Appeals Tribunal, and
(e) an update of fundraising legislation.

The Bill entitled an Act to provide for the better regulation of charitable organisations, and, for that purpose, to provide for the establishment of a body to be known as An tÚdarás Rialála Carthanas (or, in the English, the Charities Regulatory Authority), to provide for the dissolution of the Commissioners of Charitable Donations and Bequests for Ireland; to make provision in relation to the regulation and protection of charitable organisations and charitable trusts; to provide for the registration of charitable organisations; to provide for the establishment of a body to be known as the Charities Appeals Tribunal to hear appeals from decisions of the Charities Regulatory Authority; to make provision in relation to fundraising by or on behalf of registered charitable organisations; to provide for the repeal of certain provisions of the Charities Act 1961; and to provide for matters connected therewith.

29.4.2 Irish move towards common charity legislation

Northern Ireland and the Republic of Ireland have agreed to coordinate their charity legislation to ensure that the sector is regulated consistently across the island.

There needs to be public confidence in charitable work, and the establishment of charity regulators in the North and the South will provide the structure for governance, accountability and transparency. This will be achieved through unified legislation. New legislation in the Republic of Ireland is to match that across the border as closely as is practicable.

Chapter 30 – The Companies Act 2006

30.1 Introduction

The Department of Trade and Industry (DTI) started the process of updating company law back in March 1998. This Act finally received Royal Assent on 8 November 2006, the same day as the Charities Act 2006. It is now known as the Companies Act 2006. It has 1,300 sections and 10 schedules. The Act represents the largest single piece of legislation ever passed by Parliament.

Following the lengthy review period, the Act brings company law into the 21st century. It is a consolidating Act and when it has been fully implemented, which is due to happen by 1 October 2009, the Companies Act 1985 will be repealed. Although the Act is largely deregulatory in nature for private companies, there is now stronger emphasis on appropriate levels of corporate governance being applied. All charities that are set up as companies limited by guarantee (CLGs) are affected by this legislation.

A welcome amendment made at a late stage means that the new Act incorporates and replaces the provisions of the 1985 and 1989 Companies Acts and the 2004 Companies (Audit, Investigations and Community Enterprise) Act, except for the self-standing provisions on community interest companies and provisions on investigations (which go wider than companies). It is hoped that the Act will make life much easier for all who are involved in company law.

Responsibility for the implementation of this Act is that of the Department for Business Enterprise & Regulatory Reform (BERR), which has replaced the DTI.

30.2 Objectives

The Government had four key objectives in its reform of company law. The overriding purpose has been to 'think small first' – that is, to treat smaller companies as the norm, with additional provision for public companies, as opposed to the other way round, which has been the tendency of much of the existing law.

The four objectives were:

1. Enhancing shareholder engagement and a long-term investment culture

(a) codification of directors' duties;
(b) specific responsibility of directors to ensure that accounts give a true and fair view;
(c) authority in statute for derivative actions;
(d) simplification of the law regarding directors' loans and property transactions;
(e) enhancement of the rights of indirect investors, and
(f) electronic communication of company documents and information to members.

It is likely that the codification of directors' duties will result in more court cases where interpretation of the legislation will be sought. It is doubtful whether the nature and outcome of the above actions will change greatly as a result of this legislation.

2. Ensuring better regulation and a 'think small first' approach

(a) private companies not being required to hold an AGM;
(b) extended use of written resolutions;
(c) abolition of the restrictions on private companies' providing financial assistance for the purchase of their own shares, and
(d) reduction of capital without the need for Court sanction.

These provisions are useful as far as they go, but may not make very much difference to the directors of private companies, many of whom have already taken advantage of the elective regime first allowed by Companies Act 1989.

3. Making it easier to set up and run a company

(a) simplification of a private company's model Articles, and incorporation into the Articles of clauses previously in the Memorandum:
(b) ability of a company to have unlimited objects as the 'norm', and
(c) confidentiality of directors' home addresses.

A simpler set of Articles will be an advantage for private companies' management, as will the relaxation of restrictions on the objects clause, which will benefit in particular owner-managed companies, which do not normally need to restrict their objects. Directors should bear in mind that external investors may not be so enthusiastic about unrestricted objects, which can be seen as permission to directors to do what they like.

4. Providing flexibility for the future.

The Government's intention is for future legislation to be enacted largely by means of statutory instrument. This may save time, although there will be a risk of parts of the new Act being overtaken by statutory instruments and of the law becoming ever more inaccessible.

30.3 Directors' duties

30.3.1 Companies in general

For the first time, directors' duties are enshrined in statute, having up until now been governed by case law. The Government accepted the recommendations of the Company Law Review that the codification should reflect the current state of the law without making fundamental changes to the fiduciary nature of directors' duties. The DTI had set up the Company Law Review as an independent group of experts, practitioners and business people in 1998. Their aim was to review the law and advise on how company law could be brought up to date.

The legislation aims to codify the modern interpretation of 'the best interests of the company as a whole' as the fulfilment of the company's stated objects. This may not necessarily coincide with the interests of the major shareholders.

The Act states that the general duties of directors, including shadow directors, are owed to the company and are based on common law rules and equitable principles. As with the common law duties, the duties set out in the Act are complementary and may overlap. They do not prevent a director from complying with other laws relevant to running a company.

30.3.2 Statutory duties

Seven statutory duties have been set out, four of which came into force on 1 October 2007 and the remaining three on 1 October 2008.

The first four duties

All these duties implement previous common law rulings.

1. The duty to act within powers conferred by the company's constitution

That is, the company's Memorandum and Articles. The Articles may impose stricter conditions on directors than the law requires but they may not themselves breach the law. Directors must exercise their powers only for the purposes for which they are conferred.

2. The duty to promote the success of the company for the benefit of its members as a whole.

For company charities this can be interpreted to mean furthering the charity's purposes and objectives. This is because company charities exist to help their beneficiaries, not their members.

In carrying out this duty, directors should have regard to (but can then disregard) the following points:

(a) the likely consequences of any decision in the long run;
(b) the interests of the company's employees;
(c) the need to foster business relationships with suppliers, customers and others;
(d) the impact of the company's operations on the community and the environment;
(e) the desirability of maintaining a reputation for high standards of business conduct;
(f) the need to act fairly as between members of the company.

This duty enshrines in statute what is commonly referred to as 'enlightened shareholder value'. The success of the company means the benefit of the members as a whole.

It is possible for the objects of the company to conflict with the direct benefit to the members. The Act makes it clear that the objects should have priority.

3. The duty to exercise independent judgement.

This means that directors must be free to use their own discretion – unless they are acting in accordance with an agreement restricting that discretion, or in accordance with the company's constitution. Directors are usually permitted in a company's Articles to delegate their functions in accordance with the Articles.

4. The duty to exercise reasonable care, skill and diligence.

This includes an objective task to act as a reasonable person would but, additionally, any particular skills a director possesses have to be used in a subjective manner by that director.

This section takes up the common law standard expected of directors, which is itself based on the standard set in section 214 of the Insolvency Act 1986 (wrongful trading), where 'reasonable skill, care and diligence' means:

- the knowledge, skill and experience that may reasonably be expected of (a director), and
- the general knowledge, skill and experience that the director has.

The remaining three duties

5. The duty to avoid conflicts of interest.

There is some relaxation of the very strict principles which have been applied by the Courts.

A director now has positive obligations to avoid situations in which he or she has, or can have, a direct or indirect interest or duty that conflicts or possibly may conflict with the interests of, or his duty to, the company, unless the matter cannot reasonably be regarded as likely to give rise to a conflict. This is now a wider definition of what constitutes 'conflict'.

However, if the matter is properly authorised by the other independent directors, then this will suffice. Companies will therefore be well advised to adopt thorough internal 'conflict procedures' to help identify existing or potential conflicts, provide disclosure to the Board, clarify authorisation procedures and review their Articles of Association.

This new power for the directors relaxes the usual conflicts of interest provisions, thus allowing a conflicted director to participate in voting and be counted in the quorum. For charitable companies, the power must be included in the Articles. Many charities wishing to take advantage of this will need to amend their articles, as this is not a provision commonly found in charity constitutions.

There are two main reasons for all company boards to check the provisions in the company's articles dealing with conflicts of interest, as follows:

(a) having the right wording in the Articles can protect a director from liability for breach of the duty owed to the company to avoid a conflict of interest. Historically, the risk of such an action has been very small; nevertheless, building in suitable protection is sensible, and

(b) as a matter of good governance, all boards should have clear procedures for dealing with conflicts. The more workable the procedures, the more likely they will be remembered and followed in practice.

Other areas to review include draft agendas (which should include a default item to note any interests declared) and minutes, which should record any interests disclosed and any authorisations of conflicts. Although having a register of directors' interests is no longer a statutory requirement, it is often worth having one to track all disclosures of interests and all authorisations made.

Directors of a charity's trading subsidiary have to be particularly aware of these new rules and consider where an actual or potential conflict of interest arises. It may require the trading subsidiary to amend its Memorandum and Articles, or seek specific authority from the charity to enable directors to properly address these duties where conflict of interest situations arise.

The Companies Act 2006

In addition to obtaining authority, it will be vital to put in place formal procedures and policies to ensure effective disclosure of interests to enable transparency and appropriate conflict management, all of which will need to be properly documented.

Essentially the new rules split conflicts into:

- 'transactional conflicts' – that is, conflicts arising from transactions between the director and the company, and
- a broad range of other conflicts arising from any 'situation' – most commonly, a conflict of duties.

Typical areas where a conflict of duties will arise are where the director of the trading company is also an employee or trustee of the charity. The definition of a conflict covers actual and potential conflicts and direct and indirect interests. The scope of this duty is therefore extremely broad and in considering whether an interest exists and a conflict might arise, a director's family or other connected people must also be considered.

If appropriate authorities are not obtained and the new procedures not followed, directors of trading subsidiaries risk breaching duties imposed by the Companies Act 2006.

The Charity Commission considers that directors of company charities are already under a duty to avoid conflicts of interest. Conflicts of interest include those arising from:

- any personal financial interest in a transaction with the charity – for example, where a director receives payment from the charity for services or goods, and
- conflicts of duty which do not involve any material benefit to a director – for example, where a director is also a trustee of another charity which might be in competition with the charity ('conflicts of loyalty').

From 1 October 2008, directors are under a specific statutory duty to avoid a situation in which they have, or can have, a direct or indirect interest that conflicts, or possibly may conflict, with the interests of the company (see s. 175(1) of the Companies Act 2006).

In the case of company charities, this duty does not apply to a conflict of interest arising in relation to a transaction or arrangement with the company if this is permitted by the company's Articles of Association (see s. 175(3) of the Companies Act 2006 as modified for company charities by s. 181).

Where a benefit or a transaction which may give rise to a conflict of interest is authorised by an order of the Charity Commission, the duty to avoid a conflict of interest does not apply (see s. 26(5)A of the Charities Act 1993).

In addition, authorisation may be given by the unconflicted directors to a conflict of interests where the company's constitution includes provision that enables them to provide such authorisation (see s. 175(5) as modified by s. 181). Such authorisation is not necessary where the conflict arises from a transaction or arrangement with the company that is authorised by the Memorandum or Articles of the company.

6. The duty not to accept benefits from third parties

This is where the benefit has been conferred by virtue of the directorship. All corporate hospitality situations should be notified to the Board to ascertain whether or not any such benefits arise.

This is an example of a duty that overlaps with others (for example, the duty to exercise independent judgement and avoid of conflicts of interest). 'Benefits' are not specified, but would clearly include bribes. 'Third parties' exclude the company itself or other companies in a group. The duty is not infringed if acceptance of the benefit could not give rise to a conflict of interest.

7. The duty to declare interest in proposed transaction or arrangement.

This refers specifically to transactions between a director and the company. Shareholder approval is no longer required, unless the Articles stipulate it. The disclosure is merely to the other directors, either at a board meeting or by notice. No disclosure is required if the transaction could not give rise to a conflict of interest – for example, a director of a retailer buying goods from one of its shops.

30.4 Community interest companies

30.4.1 Introduction

The legal structure known as a Community Interest Company (CIC) has been available since July 2006. Since then, around 1,500 CICs have been formed. CICs are limited companies with special additional features, created for the use of people who want to conduct a business or other activity for community benefit and not purely for private advantage. CICs cover a range of activities, including theatre, recycling, sport, health services and childcare. Many social entrepreneurs did not want to operate under the auspices of a charity. Company law was therefore adapted to allow for a new type of company.

CICs must prepare and deliver to Companies House a 'community interest company report', made up to the same date as the accounts, regardless of the size of the company or the exemptions taken advantage of. This report gives details of the way in which the CICs activities have benefited the community, together with some other relevant information. The report, form CIC34, is available online from www.cicregulator.gov.uk.

There are increasing opportunities for CICs to step in to provide state services. One of the merits of the CIC as against the charity model is that a CIC can have a full executive board – that is, the employees can serve on the board. Equally, a CIC can have a mixture of executive and non-executive directors who can be paid. Running a service business (using the charity model) with a board of volunteer trustees who only meet, say, quarterly is not normally an appropriate governance structure where a business needs constantly to adapt to the demands of a challenging environment.

30.4.2 The unique features of CICs

A CIC can be either a company limited by guarantee (CLG) or a company limited by shares (CLS). CIC status is effectively grafted on top of existing company law, making use of the fact that company law is kept up to date on a regular basis and that most of the difficult areas of company law have been resolved through court decisions down the years.

A CIC has to include the words 'Community Interest Company', 'CIC' or 'Community Interest Public Limited Company' (or the Welsh equivalent) in its title.

Before it can register, a CIC has to pass the community interest test ('Might a reasonable person consider that its activities are being carried on for the benefit of the community?') There are certain activities, however, that cannot pass the test, such as being a political party or an organisation established to promote political purposes.

A fundamental feature of the CIC is the 'asset lock'. Until the CIC existed, there was no easy way of ensuring that a non-charitable public body could not be converted for private benefit. As with a charity, 'once a CIC, always a CIC', although a CIC can convert into a charity.

In the case of a CIC that is a CLS, there is a cap on distributions imposed by the regulations (the dividend cap). The current dividend cap is five per cent above the Bank of England base rate and 35% per cent of the company's distributable profits in any one year. If the full amount (subject to the cap) is not distributed in one year, the unused amount may be carried forward and used in the next.

If a CLS redeems or buys back its shares, it may only pay par. In the event of the winding-up of a company, the shareholders only receive par value on their shares. They get no uplift – not even for inflation.

This effectively means that the capital growth in the company belongs to the CIC rather than to the shareholders. The shareholders get a return more akin to an interest payment or return on a bond. Hence, in many ways there is no need to use a CLS unless the particular share mechanisms are useful for governance purposes. Moreover, financing a CIC by bonds rather than shares is effective in tax terms, since interest is payable pre-tax whereas dividends are payable post-tax. On the other hand, of course, bonds appear as a liability on a balance sheet whereas share capital appears as an asset.

New companies that wish to become CICs have to apply to the Registrar of Companies in the normal way, but they also have to be approved by the CIC Regulator. Existing companies can convert into CICs, but the CIC Regulator still has to approve the conversion papers. This means that electronic incorporations are not possible for CICs.

30.4.3 Tax reliefs

The big problem for CICs, however, is that as yet no tax reliefs have been given to them by the Government. This contrasts with the position of charities, which receive very attractive tax reliefs. It is also different from the position of investors in for-profit companies. CIC investors are not at present given a complete tax write-off against their investments, and any interest they receive is taxable. Changes to this tax treatment would provide further incentives to encourage investment in social enterprise.

CICs offer social entrepreneurs a ready-made legal vehicle for operating their socially minded businesses. To make them work better still, the Government should now consider affording CICs the appropriate tax reliefs.

30.5 Senior Statutory Auditor (SSA)

The APB has issued Bulletin 2008/6 *The "Senior Statutory Auditor" under the United Kingdom Companies Act 2006* as guidance on Section 503(3) of the Companies Act 2006, which requires, where the auditor is a firm, that the auditor's report must be signed by the SSA in his or her own name, for and on behalf of the auditor. This requirement applies to auditor's reports for financial years beginning on or after 6 April 2008. The only restriction in the Companies Act 2006 is that the person identified as an SSA of the company must be eligible for appointment as auditor of the company in question.

Subject to meeting this requirement, the APB has decided that the term SSA has the same meaning as the term 'engagement partner', which is defined in ISA (UK and Ireland) 220 as follows: 'The partner or other person in the firm who is responsible for the audit engagement and its performance, and for the auditor's report that is issued on behalf of the firm, and who, where required, has the appropriate authority from a professional, legal or regulatory body'.

The Companies Act 2006

This appears very straightforward but there are a number of problems that can arise as a result of the requirement for the SSA to sign personally – nobody else can sign on his or her behalf. Problem areas are dealt with in the bulletin and summarised in the questions and answers below.

Question 1: What are the requirements if the audit firm changes the SSA during the engagement?

Answer: The new SSA must review the audit work performed to the date of the change. The review procedures must be sufficient to satisfy the new SSA that the audit work performed to the date of the review has been planned and performed in accordance with professional standards and regulatory and legal requirements.

Question 2: What will be the implications if the SSA is unable to be present to sign the auditor's report?

Answer: Under section 503(3) of the Companies 2006, the SSA must sign the auditor's report. Another partner, or responsible individual, is not able to sign for and on behalf of the SSA. If the SSA is unable to continue to take responsibility for the direction, supervision and performance of the audit, the audit firm must appoint a replacement SSA. If the SSA is absent but is still able to, and does, take responsibility for the direction, supervision and performance of the audit, the SSA may sign the auditor's report using electronic means (for example, email or fax).

Question 3: What will be the implications if the auditor's report needs to be signed on a particular date and the SSA is unable to be present to sign the auditor's report on that date?

Answer: The APB suggests that it would be pragmatic for the auditor firm to have a contingency plan as to who would succeed as SSA in the event that the audit is at an advanced stage but the SSA is unable to sign the auditor's report. If another audit partner is actively involved in the audit engagement, a suitable contingency plan may be for that other partner to work in parallel with the SSA and be able to take over as SSA if the need arises. If no other partner has worked in parallel with the SSA, then the APB is of the view that in such exceptional circumstances it is permissible for the engagement quality control reviewer to be appointed as the replacement senior statutory auditor where:

(a) the engagement quality control reviewer has completed his or her review, and
(b) the audit is at an 'advanced stage', as defined by Bulletin 2008/2, which deals with the auditor's association with preliminary announcements

This is subject to the condition that the engagement quality control reviewer is eligible to be appointed as the SSA. Once an engagement quality reviewer has been appointed as a replacement SSA, he or she can no longer act as the engagement quality control reviewer because his or her objectivity may have been impaired through assuming the role of SSA.

30.6 Filing dates

For accounting reference periods which begin on or after 6 April 2008, private companies will now have nine months (previously, 10 months) to submit their accounts to Companies House after the end of each accounting reference period.

In practice the interpretation of 'month' is as follows. If the accounting reference date is the last day of the month, the period allowed for filing accounts would end with the last day of the appropriate month. For example, a private company with an accounting reference date of 30 April 2010 has until midnight on 31 January 2011 to deliver its accounts, *not 30 January 2011*.

For a company's first set of accounts, where those accounts cover a period of more than 12 months, the new filing date is 21 months from the date of incorporation (previously 22 months from end of month of incorporation) for private companies or three months from the accounting reference date, whichever is longer.

For example, a private company incorporated on 1 January 2009 with an accounting reference date of 31 January has until midnight on 1 October 2010 (**21 months from the date of incorporation**) to deliver its accounts, not until *31 October* 2010.

30.7 Late filing penalties

The table of penalties is set out below.

Table 30.1 *Late filing penalties*

Accounts delivered	Private company penalty
Not more than one month late	£150 (previously £100)
More than one month but not more than three months late	£375 (previously £100)
More than three months but not more than six months late	£750 (previously £250)
More than six months late	£1,500 (previously £500 up to 12 months late, then £1,000)

The Companies Act 2006

The new penalties came into force from 1 February 2009. Previously, once a set of accounts was late, the directors had three months before the penalty increased. This has changed, so now there is an incentive to file within the first month of being late, before the penalty increases.

In addition, where there is a failure to comply with filing requirements in relation to the previous financial year (and that the previous financial year had begun on or after 6 April 2008), the penalty will be double that shown in the table above.

30.8 Small companies

30.8.1 Introduction

A small company can prepare and submit accounts according to special provisions in the Companies Act 2006 and the relevant regulations. This means that it can choose to disclose less information than would otherwise be the case.

30.8.2. Qualifying as small

Conditions to qualify as a small company

The provisions outline the conditions for a company or a group to qualify as small. There are separate conditions for a small company to be exempt from audit.

Under the Companies Act 2006, the criteria for a company or a group to qualify as small or to claim audit exemption are not materially different from those contained in Companies Act 1985, except for the fact that under the new Act, the size thresholds have been increased by 20 per cent.

Non-group companies qualifying as small and exemption from audit

Section 381 of the Companies Act 2006 states that the small companies' regime applies to a company for a financial year in relation to which it qualifies as small and it is not excluded from the regime. In respect of companies that are not part of a group, the qualifying conditions are outlined in s. 382 of the Act.

For accounting periods beginning on or after 6 April 2008, to qualify as small a company in its first financial year, a company needs to meet at least two of the following three conditions:

(a) have annual turnover not exceeding £6.5million (or £5.6million for accounting periods beginning before 6 April 2008);
(b) have a balance sheet total not exceeding £3.26million (or £2.8million for accounting periods beginning before 6 April 2008), and
(c) have no more than 50 employees.

In respect of subsequent years, the company will only incur a change in its status – for example, from medium to small or from small to medium – if it respectively meets or fails two of the three conditions above for both the current and the preceding financial year. The above is commonly referred to as the **two-year rule** and its tenet has remained unchanged from the provisions of the 1985 Act.

It is important to realise that the increased Companies Act 2006 thresholds also apply retrospectively to any financial years beginning before 6 April 2008 in determining whether a company qualified as small in the earlier period. It needs to be stressed that the 2006 thresholds will only be applicable retrospectively in the context of determining the status of a company for years beginning after 6 April 2008 – that is, to ascertain the small entity status of a company for years beginning before that date, the 1985 Act thresholds will still apply.

Section 384 of the Companies Act 2006 lists the companies that are excluded from the small companies' regime. The exclusions mirror those contained in the 1985 Act and affect other public companies and members of ineligible groups.

Audit exemptions

The conditions for exemption from audit for a company that is not part of a group are included in s. 477 of the 2006 Act. To be exempted from audit in respect a financial year beginning on or after 6 April 2008, a company needs to meet all of the following conditions:

(a) that the company qualifies as a small in relation to that year;
(b) that its turnover in that year is not more than £6.5 million, and
(c) that its balance sheet total for that year is not more than £3.26 million.

A company will therefore need to qualify as a small company in accordance with the criteria stated in the paragraph above before it can test its turnover and balance sheet conditions to obtain audit exemption. It is important to state that if the company fails just one of the conditions, it will not be able to be exempted from audit.

There is also no equivalent of the two-year rule as far as audit exemption is concerned, and the relevant conditions need to be fulfilled in the specific year for which exemption is to be claimed. The fact that the conditions had or had not been met in earlier years is not relevant.

Section 478 of the Companies Act 2006 lists those companies that are excluded from the possibility of obtaining audit exemption. The exclusions mirror those contained in the 1985 Act and includes public companies.

Qualification as small and audit exemption for group companies

Companies can be part of a group by virtue of being a parent, a subsidiary, or both at the same time. A company that is part of a group only by virtue of being a subsidiary will qualify as small by meeting the same conditions that apply to a non-group company, as contained in section 382 of the Companies Act 2006, that have been discussed above. The exclusions from the small companies' regime outlined in section 384 of the Act will apply equally to such a company, and particular care should be taken to verify whether the company is a member of an ineligible group.

A company that is the parent of a group or a parent and subsidiary in a group needs to meet the qualifying conditions set in section 383 of the Act to qualify as small, in addition to meeting the general conditions prescribed by s. 382 and explained above.

Section 383 requires that a parent company qualifies as small in respect of a financial year only if the group headed by it qualifies as a small group. A group would qualify as small in its first financial year if it meets at least two of the following three conditions:

(a) aggregate turnover not more than £6.5 million net or £7.8 million gross;
(b) aggregate balance sheet total not more than £3.26 million net or £3.9 million gross, and
(c) aggregate number of employees not more than 50.

In respect of subsequent years, the group will only incur a change in its status – for example, from medium to small or from small to medium, if it respectively meets or does not meet two of the three conditions above for both the current and the preceding financial year. The two-year rule is therefore applicable to groups as well as companies in determining the qualification as small or medium.

In relation to the aggregate turnover and balance sheet total, *net* means figures after any set-offs and other adjustments made to eliminate group transactions, while *gross* means without such set-offs and adjustments. It is important to notice that a group could satisfy any relevant requirement on the basis of either the net or the gross figure; therefore, a mix of gross and net figures – that is, net group turnover and gross balance sheet total – could be used to meet the qualifying conditions.

In a manner similar to that for companies, the Companies Act 2006 thresholds can be applied retrospectively to establish the size of the group for any previous years, when that is instrumental in determining the size of the group for financial years beginning on or after 6 April 2008. The exclusions of s. 384 also apply to a parent company, and such a company and all of its subsidiaries could be excluded from the small companies' regime if the group was an ineligible group.

The availability of audit exemption to a company that is part of a group – that is, either a parent or a subsidiary – is regulated by s. 479 of the Companies

Act 2006. A company that was, at any time during the financial year, a group company would not be entitled to audit exemption in respect of that year, unless all the following conditions are met:

- that the group qualifies as a small group in relation to that year and it was not at any time in that year an ineligible group;
- that the group's aggregate turnover in that year is not more than £6.5 million net or £7.8 million gross, and
- that the group's aggregate balance sheet total for that year is not more than £3.26 million net or £3.9 million gross.

Any group company would therefore need to ascertain if the group of which it is part qualifies as a small before it can claim audit exemption. Both the group's aggregate turnover and balance sheet total would then need to be tested and must meet the size conditions to qualify for the exemption. It has to be noted that any relevant requirements can be met on the basis of either the gross or the net figure and therefore a mix of gross and net figures can be used to satisfy the criteria.

A group company can also be exempted from audit if, throughout the whole of the period in which it was part of a group, it was both a subsidiary and dormant.

30.8.3 Exemptions available for small companies

Small companies can prepare and file simpler, less detailed accounts than those required by large and medium companies. The requirements for companies subject to the small companies' regime are set out in Parts 15 and 16 of the Companies Act 2006. The Companies Act 2006 and Regulations also set out what the directors' report of a small company must contain. Such a report does not have to contain a business review or a statement as to the amount that the directors recommend be paid by way of dividend. If the company has taken advantage of the small companies' exemption in preparing the directors' report, it must contain a statement to that effect above the directors' signature.

A company can file a copy of the accounts that it prepared for its members under the small companies' regime, or it can deliver an abbreviated version of these accounts. The content of abbreviated Companies Act accounts can be found in the Companies Act 2006 and in Schedule 4 to the Small Companies and Groups (Accounts and Directors' Report) Regulations 2008.

If the accounts are abbreviated, a special auditor's report is required. This must state that, in the auditor's opinion, the company is entitled to deliver abbreviated accounts in accordance with s. 444 (3) of the Companies Act 2006 and that they have been properly prepared in accordance with the regulations made by the

Secretary of State. This report is not needed if the company is exempt from audit. Small companies preparing Companies Act accounts can deliver an abbreviated balance sheet.

If accounts (whether abbreviated or not) are prepared in accordance with the provisions applicable to small companies, a statement must be included in a prominent position on the balance sheet that the accounts have been prepared in accordance with the special provisions applicable to companies subject to the small companies' regime.

For accounting periods beginning on or after 6 April 2008, the balance sheet must contain the following statements above the director's signature:

'For the year ending .... (dd/mm/yyyy) the company was entitled to exemption from audit under section 477 of the Companies Act 2006 relating to small companies.

Directors' responsibilities:

- The members have not required the company to obtain an audit of its accounts for the year in question in accordance with section 476.
- The directors acknowledge their responsibilities for complying with the requirements of the Act with respect to accounting records and the preparation of accounts.

These accounts have been prepared in accordance with the provisions applicable to companies subject to the small companies' regime'.

30.9 Auditors limiting their liability

Section 536 of the Companies Act 2006 requires any liability limitation agreement to be authorised by the members, unless the members themselves have waived the need for such approval. The agreement will need to be fair and reasonable. It can only last for one financial year at a time.

30.10 Auditors' rights to information

This was enacted under The Companies (Audit, Investigations and Community Enterprise) Act 2004. Its aim was to restore confidence in company reporting in various ways. For company charities, the measures enhancing the rights of auditors are as follows.

Auditors of all companies now have the right to require information and explanations not only from officers of a company (always a rather vague term which included 'managers') but from any employee who holds relevant information. The full list is (s. 8):

(a) any officer or employee of the company;
(b) any person holding a company's books, accounts or vouchers;
(c) any subsidiary of the company;
(d) any officer, employee or auditor of the subsidiary, and
(e) any person who fell within (a) to (d) at a time to which the required explanations relate (that is, the current auditor has the right to question past officers)

It is now a criminal offence for such a person not only to give false information but also to fail to give information when required.

Statement in directors' report

Section 9 requires the directors' report to state (for each director) that:

(a) so far as the director is aware, there is no relevant audit information of which the company's auditors are unaware, and
(b) he or she has taken all the steps that he or she ought to have taken as a director in order to make himself or herself aware of any relevant audit information and to establish that the company's auditors are aware of that information.

This raises particular issues for directors of company charities who may be part-time and/or non-executive. The Act says that in determining the extent of a director's duty, 'the following considerations are relevant:

(a) the knowledge, skill and experience that may reasonably be expected of a person carrying out the same functions as are carried out by the director in relation to the company, and
(b) (so far as they exceed what may reasonably be so expected) the knowledge, skill and experience that the director in fact has.'

Company charities should ensure that all their directors who are also trustees are aware of this new requirement and that systems are in place to enable all the directors to make this declaration. It may be helpful to remember that 'non-executive director' is not a concept enshrined either in common law or in current company legislation. Directors, whatever their actual role within their company, have similar responsibilities in the eyes of the law. The overriding requirement is for directors to act in the best interests of the company as a whole. This duty is reflected in s. 418 of the Companies Act 2006.

30.11 Other measures (affecting company charities)

30.11.1 Disclosure on emails and websites

From 1 January 2007, all emails and websites must contain the following information:

The Companies Act 2006

- the company's name;
- the company's place of registration and registration number;
- the address of the company's registered office, and
- if the company is exempt from using the word 'limited' in is name, the fact that it is limited.

Formal correspondence between a company and its members can be conducted by email or other forms of ecommunication defined by the Act, subject to certain conditions (ss 1143 – 1148 and Schedules 4 and 5).

30.11.2 Company Meetings

Annual general meetings (AGMs)

From October 2007, private companies will no longer need to hold AGMs (see s. 336 of the Companies Act 2006). Should they choose to do so, 14 days' notice (previously, 21 days' notice) will be required. Members still have a right to receive accounts.

Extraordinary general meetings

The category of 'extraordinary' general meetings has been discontinued. Meetings of the company are now simply 'general meetings'. Although only 14 days' notice is required for a general meeting, the Articles can make provision for longer notice, and directors may wish to do so for certain types of general meeting, such as AGMs or general meetings at which special resolutions are being considered.

Short notice meetings

Where members wish to call a company general meeting at short notice, s. 307 of the Companies 2006 requires a minimum of 90 per cent of the members to support this proposal.

Members' right to appoint proxies

Members of company charities have the right to appoint proxies, and notices of general meetings must refer to this right (see ss 324 and 325).

Written resolutions

Members may agree in writing to resolutions – there is no longer a requirement for unanimity. Instead, a simple majority is needed for ordinary written resolutions and a 75 per cent majority for special written resolutions (see ss 282 and 283 and ss 288 to 300).

Casting vote

A chairperson under Articles adopted after 1 October 2007 cannot have a casting vote (except where that was previously permitted by the Articles).

30.11.3 Company secretary

From April 2008, private companies will not have to appoint a company secretary. Should they choose to do so, the company secretary will have the same powers and responsibilities as before (see s. 270).

30.11.4 Company formation

From 1 October 2009, the Memorandum of Association will become an historical document which, with various accompanying documents, will simply record the facts at the time of incorporation. It will be the Articles, rather than the Memorandum, that will set out the principles under which the company conducts its business. The new Articles will comprise a single document.

Companies set up before 1 October 2009 with a Memorandum and Articles of Association will not need to make any changes – all operative clauses in the Memorandum, including the objects, will be deemed to be part of the Articles when this provision comes into force (see s.18 and s. 28). The Charity Commission does not believe that it will be necessary for company charities to amend their Memorandum and Articles in order to comply with the new duties.

New companies will be able to take advantage of the new default model Articles of Association, which will be set out in clear language. There is no requirement for companies to set out their objects in any documentation.

New company charities will be automatically exempt from using the word 'limited' (see s.60 (1a)).

30.11.5 Directors' age

Since 1 October 2008, the minimum age for a director has been 16 (see s. 157).

30.11.6 Natural person

Private companies can have a sole director and no company secretary, but the director has to be a 'natural person' – that is, an individual not corporate body (see s. 155).

30.11.7 Directors' service addresses

From 1 October 2009, every director must provide Companies House with both his or her usual residential address and, for each directorship held, a service address. The service address, which can be the registered office address, will be on the public record and will be public information, but the residential address will be protected information. If the director chooses to use his or her residential address as the service address, the fact that the two addresses are the same would not be apparent from the public record.

The residential address will only be available to prescribed regulatory authorities, such as the police and HMRC, and it may also be made available to credit reference agencies

Chapter 31 – Recent developments in SORP 2005

31.1 Scope of the SORP

The SORP Committee published the most recently revised SORP on 4 March 2005. The purpose of the revised SORP was to update the previous SORP published in October 2000. A second edition of SORP 2005 was published in May 2008. The second edition updated SORP 2005 for the Charities Act 2006 and the Companies Act 2006 references, and it also provides specific guidance for small charities in its introduction.

Since the advent of FRS 18, the SORP is effectively compulsory for all charities (except where a more specific SORP applies) as to divert from the SORP would require true and fair override disclosures. In the case of non-company charities, the full version of the SORP will be applicable for those above the audit threshold, and a 'mini' SORP (see Appendices 5.3 and 5.4 of SORP 2005) for those below it but whose income is above £100,000. Below £100,000 income, a non-company charity can prepare receipts and payments accounts, which are not covered by the SORP. The 'mini' SORP reduces the level of detail needed for various reporting requirements – for example, there is no requirement in the SOFA to analyse resources by activity.

In the case of company charities, the full version of the SORP applies for those charities above the audit threshold and a 'mini' SORP applies for those below it.

SORP 2005 now limits its recommendations to accruals accounts. The Charity Commission will continue to provide and develop separate guidance, including pro-forma accounts and report packs, for charities that prepare cash-based receipts and payments accounts. Where receipts and payments accounts are prepared, trustees in England and Wales will be able to rely on these packs to provide comprehensive guidance and will no longer need to refer to the SORP in preparing their accounts and reports.

In order to assist charities adopting SORP 2005, the Charity Commission has produced several examples of Trustees' Annual Reports and Accounts. These can be accessed on the Charity Commission website.

31.2 SORP 2005 – Information Sheet 1

The Charity Commission and the Office of the Scottish Charity Regulator (OSCR) are the joint SORP-making body. They are required by the ASB's code of practice to undertake annual reviews of the SORP. These reviews are conducted by the SORP Committee, which considers:

- any implications for the SORP of new or proposed accounting standards;
- any evidence of widespread failure to follow any part of the guidance, and
- any developments within the sector that suggest that further guidance on accounting matters is desirable.

In 2007, the SORP Committee issued *Information Sheet 1* to assist practitioners in their preparation of financial statements. *Information Sheet 1* does not form part of the SORP, nor has it been reviewed by the ASB. Instead, it attempts to explain and illustrate what is already recommended by the SORP, although it does not carry the authority of the SORP. The topics covered are:

- accounting treatment for grants;
- disclosures for grant-making charities;
- investment management costs;
- bank interest and other finance costs;
- the business review and company charities, and
- the operating financial review and reporting charities.

31.2.1 Accounting for grants receivable

The implementation of SORP 2005's treatment for grants receivable has caused some difficulties in interpretation. To address this point, the Charity Commission has published further guidance in Charities SORP 2005 *Information Sheet 1*.

The problem revolves around the fact that a charity now has two main areas to allocate its income:

(a) incoming resources from generated funds (including voluntary income), and
(b) incoming resources from charitable activities.

Strictly speaking, if a charity receives a grant to deliver its services, then this could be classified under heading (a) as the grant may be of a purely voluntary nature.

However, it is more accurate to describe this type of income under heading (b). This will enable the matching of income for a particular charitable activity with the expenditure for the same charitable activity. This was one of the main goals underlying the rewriting of SORP 2005.

The fact that a grant may be for a restricted purpose makes it more likely, but not necessarily conclusively, to be akin to a performance-related grant. SORP 2005 requires this type of grant to be shown under heading (b). This will certainly be true where a charity receives contractual income by providing goods or service to beneficiaries.

The Charities SORP 2005 *Information Sheet 1* states that if the grant creates a 'service requirement', then it should be included under heading (b). If, however, service requirement criteria are lacking, then heading (a) will be more appropriate. In practice, this is likely to be very rare as normally, even where the conditions attached to grants do not create specific performance-related conditions, the funding is still for particular services and should therefore be shown under heading (b).

Only those grants received for general purposes and/or core funding, with no particular service requirement, should be shown under heading (a).

31.2.2 Disclosures for grant-making charities

The Charities Act 2006 provides that 'there shall be no provision in the Regulations made under section 42 of the Charities Act 1993 that requires the trustees of a charity that is a charitable trust created by any person (the settlor), to disclose in the statement of the accounts, either the identities of recipients of grants made out of the funds of the charity, or the amounts of any individual grants so made, if the disclosure would fall to be made at a time when the settlor or any spouse or civil partner of his was still alive' Further grant disclosure exemptions in addition to those already set out in SORP para. 200 are now available.

The disclosures of the names of institutions supported by grants, and the amount of funding they received, will be discretionary in law during the lifetime of the settlor (or of his or her spouse or civil partner) of a charitable trust that has funded the grant. This discretion does not extend to charities registered or operating in Scotland.

31.2.3 Investment management costs

A key principle of the SORP is that all incoming resources should be reported gross. For unit trusts or common investment funds, investment management costs may be included within the bid-offer spread, or recovered by transaction and portfolio charges rather than by a fee charged directly to the charity.

Where it is not practicable to ascertain the actual or a notional apportionment of costs charged to the individual participants of such schemes with reasonable accuracy, then it is permitted for investment income received to be reported without any adjustment.

31.2.4 Bank interest and other finance costs

Interest and other finance costs may arise from short-term borrowing to fund working capital, or from longer-term borrowing to fund the operating assets of a charity. Preparers of accounts have questioned whether such interest costs should be allocated to activities funded by the loan rather than being regarded as a cost of generating funds.

The SOFA provides an activity classification of costs. Where interest has arisen in order to finance a particular activity, then it would generally be allocated to that activity. Interest costs that cannot be directly allocated to a particular activity will generally be apportioned on a reasonable basis, as with other support costs.

31.2.5 Business review and company charities

Section 417 of the Companies Act 2006 requires the Directors' Report to include a 'business review' but small companies are exempt from this reporting requirement by virtue of s. 417(1). Approximately the top 500 company charities will have to include in their report:

- a fair review of the business, and
- a description of principal risks and uncertainties facing the company

In practice, charities subject to statutory audit (through their compliance with the SORP's recommendations) are likely to be compliant with the requirements of the business review, provided that they include an explanation of the risks and uncertainties that they face.

31.2.6 The operating and financial review (OFR)

The SORP does not create any requirement for charities to prepare an OFR. However, the SORP's recommendations for a Trustees' Annual Report already cover a number of the key disclosures recommended by the ASB in a statement of best practice, *Reporting Statement: Operating and Financial Review*, issued in January 2006.

The *Reporting Statement* was developed as best practice and is not mandatory, even for quoted companies. Where the trustees, particularly of larger charities, choose to expand their reporting to encompass a full OFR, they are encouraged to make reference to the *Reporting Standard*. Indeed, the principles put forward by the statement may also be helpful to trustees more generally in the preparation of their annual report.

The *Information Sheet* includes a table (shown below) which the SORP Committee believes may be helpful to charities that are considering expanding their annual report into a full OFR. The particular areas that the SORP Committee considers are not currently addressed by the SORP are highlighted in bold in the table.

Table 31.1 Key elements of an operating and financial review

Contents of best practice OFR	SORP 2005
A balanced and comprehensive analysis consistent with the size and complexity of the business of: (a) development and performance in the financial year (b) position at the end of the year (c) main trends and factors underlying the development, performance and position during the year (d) main trends and factors which are likely to affect future development, performance and position so as to assist 'members' to assess the strategies adopted and potential for success	Paras 36, 47, 53 & 57
In supplementing the accounts, provide additional explanations of amounts and explain the conditions and events that shaped the information in the financial statements.	Paras 10, 21, 35 & 36
Key elements of disclosure: (a) nature of the business including a description of the market, competitive and regulatory environment and entity's objectives and strategies (b) development and performance, both in the financial year and in the future (c) resources, principal risks and uncertainties and relationships that may affect long-term value (d) position of the business, including **liquidity** performance both in the financial year and in the future	Paras 47, 53, 55 & 57
Details of particular matters, where appropriate, to provide a balanced and comprehensive analysis: (a) **environmental matters** and related policies (b) **employees** and related policies (c) **social and community issues** and related policies (d) persons with whom entity has contractual or other arrangements essential to the business (e) other matters	Paras 44 & 51
Director's strategies for achieving the objectives of the business	Para 47
Include key performance indicators (KPI) – both financial, and where appropriate, non-financial – used by directors to assess progress against their stated objectives	Para 53
For each KPI disclosed, disclose key matters including definition and calculation	

31.3 Charities accounts survey

31.3.1 Introduction

A recent survey of charity accounts carried out by the ICAEW's Quality Assurance Department (QAD) revealed concerns about quality at the smaller end of the charities sector.

It was evident from QAD's results that many of the quality deficiencies identified in the survey were attributable to a lack of knowledge and awareness of the technical requirements or responsibilities in examining small charity accounts or were probably due to process or quality check issues. While many good practices were also seen, overall the majority of accounts judged to be deficient indicated a lack of familiarity with the necessary form and content of charity accounts and with the appropriate reports.

31.3.2 Why survey charity accounts?

QAD, in discharging its public interest role and its objective of helping members and firms to maintain quality standards, undertook a survey of accounts of charities with income between £10,000 and £250,000. This range was pegged just above the level at which charities are required to file accounts and just below the previous audit requirement threshold in force at that time. QAD's overall intention was to assess the quality of professional accounting services in an area of public interest. Its particular aim was to assess compliance with the relevant SORP and other applicable regulations.

31.3.3 Survey results and conclusions

The accounts surveyed were rated according to the quality of presentation and compliance. The ratings ranged from 'good' to 'very poor' in line with defined criteria. While 26 per cent of the sample were rated as 'good', 36 per cent were rated as either 'poor' or 'very poor', which cannot be viewed as an acceptable outcome.

The major areas of concern based on the survey findings are summarised as follows:

- **The Independent Examiner's Report** – This was the most common area of concern. Firstly, there was frequently a failure to use the required report wording. A number of reports suggested that the accounts were audited, when in fact they were not. Secondly, independent examiners did not always realise that the appointment is on an individual basis and that, while a firm might be referenced in the report, it should be only as a business address.

- **Trustees' Annual Report** – These are mandatory under both the 2000 and the 2005 SORP for all charities sampled, yet a number of the smaller charities did not provide them. Also, several of the Trustees' Annual Reports that were provided lacked the required disclosures, such as trustee details, information on structure and governance and a statement about major risks. Also, a number of reports were not signed or dated.
- **Accounts formats** – In the main, QAD found that the SORP formats were complied with, but there were errors – for example, an endowment fund might not be shown separately in the SOFA.

31.4 Updated Financial Reporting Standard for Smaller Entities (FRSSE)

The ASB has issued a revision of the FRSSE (effective April 2008) to bring it into line with the Companies Act 2006. This FRSSE is applicable for accounting periods beginning on or after 6 April 2008. Early adoption is not permitted; hence, smaller companies should continue to use the previous FRSSE (effective January 2007) for earlier accounting periods.

This has largely been an updating exercise with little of substance changing. The main impact of the Companies Act 2006 is to set out the accounting and reporting requirements for small companies in a separate regulation.

The most significant changes include:

- a 20 per cent increase in the thresholds for qualifying as a smaller company;
- a requirement to report separately political donations and charitable donations;
- an increase in the threshold for reporting these donations (now £2,000), and
- removal of the requirement to disclose authorised share capital.

31.5 Small charity disclosures

31.5.1 Exemptions

Significant exemptions are given to charities with income below the audit threshold, allowing them flexibility in the analysis provided in their SOFA and considerably reducing the level of disclosures in both their Trustees' Annual Report and notes to the accounts. By referring to statutory audit requirements in the SORP, the revised accounting disclosure exemptions will automatically apply. These are now set at gross income levels of £500,000.

Concessions available to smaller charities are now summarised in a new Appendix 5. Particularly useful is Table 11, which summarises the minimum disclosure requirements for the Trustees' Annual Report. Appendix 5 also contains guidance on the use of the FRSSE and details regarding which charities may use cash-based receipts and payments accounts.

Non-company charities with annual income below £100,000 are allowed to prepare receipts and payments accounts. All charities (preparing accruals accounts) with annual income below the statutory audit threshold are allowed to take advantage of some important presentational and disclosure exemptions and do not need to base their accounts on 'activities', but can instead use natural classifications, an option that provides greater flexibility.

31.5.2 Abbreviated accounts

There is no provision for non-company charities to file abbreviated accounts (although there are some small disclosure concessions). In theory, company charities can file abbreviated accounts at Companies House. However, as they also have to file full accounts at the Charity Commission, many do not bother with two sets of accounts.

31.6 SORP 2005 – Information Sheet 2

Information Sheet 2 is the SORP Committee's response to the ASB's *Interpretation for Public Benefit Entities of the Statement of Principles for Financial Reporting*, which was published in June 2007. The purpose of the *Interpretation* was to provide a coherent framework for the development of SORPs and to assist with new or emerging issues. The SORP Committee concluded that there was no need to amend anything in SORP 2005 in the light of the ASB publication, but *Information Sheet 2* has been issued to give further clarity on current good practice. Published in June 2008, *Information Sheet 2* addresses the following issues:

- objective of financial statements;
- multi-period liabilities;
- residual interest and designations;
- donated services;
- grants for financing capital projects, and
- accounting for business combinations.

These issues are covered in greater detail in sections **31.6.1** to **31.6.6** below.

31.6.1 Objective of financial statements

SORP 2005 stresses the importance of financial reporting for a wide range of users of financial information. Unlike profit-oriented entities, which prepare their accounts for investors, public entities (such as charities) have no primary interest group and there is therefore no one defining class of users for charity accounts.

31.6.2 Multi-period liabilities

SORP 2005 recognises constructive obligation in addition to those liabilities created by specific conditions in relation to delivering a specific service. A general or policy statement of behalf of the charity of its intention to provide goods or services to a beneficiary will, of itself, be insufficient ground to create a liability. The exact accounting treatment depends on whether:

- the charity cannot realistically withdraw from the obligation;
- the commitment has been communicated to the recipient; and
- the commitment is performance-related.

31.6.3 Residual interest and designations

In charity accounting, residual interests are known as 'funds'. As distinct from the SORP, the Interpretation requires that in the rare situations where the ultimate interest in a winding-up would be required to be distributed in a special way, this fact needs to be disclosed. The *Interpretation* largely views designated funds in the same light as the SORP.

31.6.4 Donated services

Examples of donated services or facilities might include circumstances where:

- staff on secondment from a commercial organisation still have their salary paid by that organisation, or
- the costs of long-term rent-free accommodation are borne by the landlord.

SORP 2005 requires the inclusion of such income (measured as the value to the charity) whenever this can reasonably be quantified and measured – that is, there is an economic contribution. SORP 2005 does not extend this analysis to volunteering.

The SORP states that where charities receive substantial amounts of voluntary help, such help should not be accounted for in the SOFA, but should be dealt with in the notes to the accounts or in the Trustees' Annual Report. This area has proved to be quite controversial as there are many who believe that a suitable valuation and financial quantification of volunteers' time should go into the SOFA itself. To date, no suitable valuation of the intangible asset has been agreed upon.

The *Interpretation* states that in situations where volunteering has an economic impact on an entity, this fact requires recording in the financial statements. However, it goes on to recognise that measuring this with a sufficient degree of reliability will not be possible in practice. If the charity:

- can provide reliable measurement of the economic benefit; and
- would otherwise have purchased the service

then a financial recognition should be recorded in the accounts.

31.6.5 Grants for financing capital projects

The *Interpretation* follows SORP 2005 in that capital grants should be recognised in the SOFA. There would have to be very stringent conditions placed on the capital grant to justify its deferral. Such rare situations would mean the capital grant is more akin to a capital contribution resulting in a financial interest for the 'donor'.

31.6.6 Accounting for business combinations

The accounting options provided by SORP 2005 are consistent with the *Interpretation*. Any negative goodwill arising under FRS 10 *Goodwill and Intangible Assets* should be treated as a gift in the SOFA.

31.7 Financial Reporting Exposure Draft (FRED) 42 – Heritage Assets

FRED 40 *Accounting for Heritage Assets* was published in December 2006. The ASB's aim was to improve the quality of financial reporting for heritage assets by entities such as museums holding collections of art, antiques and books and also entities that own and manage landscape or buildings for their environmental or historical qualities.

The proposals required entities, wherever practicable, to report collections of heritage assets at valuation in their annual accounts. If it was not practicable to obtain a valuation, the collection should not be reported in the balance sheet. Enhanced disclosures were required, regardless of whether or not collections were reported in the balance sheet, and illustrative disclosures (including details of the nature and scale of heritage assets held and policies for their acquisition, preservation, management and disposal) were included in the FRED.

Criticisms of FRED 40 included the opinion that it overlooked or understated the significance of the following issues:

- the cost and subjectivity of annual valuations;

- the difficulties of auditing these valuations, and
- the reluctance of entities to reveal the proper value of their assets.

In consequence, there was a significant reduction in the recognition of heritage assets.

As a result, in June 2008 the ASB published a revised and retitled FRED – FRED 42 *Heritage Assets* – which is largely based on the current FRS 15 approach but with enhanced disclosures.

The main features of FRED 42 are:

1. Enhanced disclosures should apply to all entities that hold heritage assets, regardless of whether these assets are reported in the balance sheet. The disclosures will provide more information about the entity's total holding of heritage assets and its stewardship of these assets.
2. The enhanced disclosures will include the accounting policies adopted for heritage assets and the extent to which they are recognised in the accounts. The disclosures should provide readers with an understanding of the asset values being reported as well as the entity's policy for holding such assets.
3. Accounting for heritage assets should follow the requirements of FRS 15.
4. Because the ASB favours valuations rather than leaving assets at historical cost, it allows entities to use internal valuations without the need for a full valuation every five years.

31.8 Trustees' Annual Report

31.8.1 Introduction

SORP 2005 clarifies the reasons why the Trustees' Annual Report is such a key document. An important theme is that the Trustees' Annual Report should report matters that cannot be adequately covered in the financial statements. It is an opportunity for trustees to 'tell their story'. The word 'reporting' was added to the title of the previous SORP, SORP 2000, to emphasise this added aspect. Whilst most of the detailed content of the report was required by the previous two SORPs, SORP 2005 builds on these past recommendations by adding a number of disclosures to the report, including:

- the name of the chief executive (or senior staff);
- the induction and training provided for new trustees;
- details of any social or programme-related investments;
- principal funding sources, and
- details of any social, environmental and ethical concerns taken account of in the investment policy.

Perhaps more significant, however, is that SORP 2005 presents the recommendations for the report in a more structured way using the following seven sections:

(a) reference and administrative details;
(b) structure, governance and management;
(c) objectives and activities;
(d) achievements and performance;
(e) financial review;
(f) plans for future periods, and
(g) funds held as custodian trustee

SORP 2005 does give some important exemptions to smaller charities – that is, charities whose income is less than that required for a statutory audit.

31.8.2 Trustee induction and training

Included within the guidance on 'Structure, Governance and Management' (para. 44c of SORP 2005) section of the Trustees' Annual Report is a requirement to disclose 'the policies and procedures adopted for the induction and training of trustees'. While trustee induction is important, the ongoing training of trustees must not be neglected. Once undertaken, trustee training arrangements need to be recorded in the report.

31.8.3 Achievements and performance

A new section in the Trustees' Annual Report provides greater clarity as to the disclosure expected about the achievements and performance of the charity and of any subsidiary undertakings in the year. A summary of any measures or indicators used by the charity to assess its achievements should be included in the report (see para. 53 of SORP 2005).

This requirement extends similar disclosure now required for large charities in the Summary Information Returns (see **section 31.9** below). A good report may address achievements and performance under the following three headings:

- **Outputs** – These represent 'countable' units and are the direct product of programmes or activities of the charity. They could be children immunised, animals relocated, classes taught, training courses delivered or people attending workshops. In themselves they are not the objectives of the organisation. They should be quantifiable and may be explained using tables and charts.
- **Outcomes** – These are the benefits or changes for intended beneficiaries. They tend to be less tangible and therefore less countable than outputs. Outcomes are usually planned and are therefore set out in charity's

objectives. It may well be difficult in practice to define outcomes and to be able to claim them as a result of a charity's activities.

- **Impact** – This covers all the changes resulting from an activity, project or organisation. It includes intended as well as unintended, both negative and positive, and long-term and short-term effects. Impact reporting should not be confused with reporting on outcomes. Some of the best Trustees' Annual Reports will tackle impact reporting in an intelligent manner.

In understanding the above definitions, it is also helpful to define the following two categories:

- **Inputs** – These are the resources that contribute to a programme or activity, including income, staff, volunteers and equipment. Most of them are reflected in the accounts but certain inputs (such as volunteering) are not. An out-of-date chart of accounts can lead to some charities experiencing difficulty in correctly linking inputs to activities.
- **Activities** – These are what an organisation does with its inputs in order to achieve its mission. In many cases, they can inform the expenditure headings in the SOFA and the reporting of outputs and outcomes.

In addition to providing details of fundraising performance, any material expenditure for future income generation should be explained, together with the effect on both current and future income generation.

SORP 2005 also recognises that factors outside the control of the charity may impact on its ability to achieve the objectives set. Where relevant, details of such factors should be included within the report.

31.9 Standard information return (SIR)

In 2003 the Charity Commission was asked by the Home Office to implement the recommendation in the Strategy Unit report *Private Action, Public Benefit* to introduce an annual SIR which highlights key qualitative and quantitative information about charities that have an income of £1million and above.

The Charity Commission then set up an external reference group of charity representatives, the NCVO, and others with expertise in the sector, in order to develop the SIR and draft supporting guidance notes. Following a consultation period, the SIR was introduced and implemented as a new Part C of the Annual Return 2005.

The SIR is intended to comprise a summary of the key information already reported in the Trustees' Annual Report and Accounts.

There are eight questions in the SIR. Questions 2, 6 and 8 are governance related, with question 6 ('What is the charity's financial health at the year end?')

being an appeal opportunity for the charity. Questions 1, 3, 4 and 7 are all performance related and consider the area of public benefit. Question 5, on income, expenditure, activities and fundraising, lends itself to the inevitable drawing-up of league tables, as displayed within the sector.

31.10 SORP for the future

31.10.1 Introduction

In February 2008, the ASB's Committee on Accounting for Public Benefit Entities (CAPE) asked the SORP Committee to consider six areas for further research, including:

1. the structure of primary statements – for example, SOFA terminology, FRS2 consistency, columnar approach, approaches of other public entity bodies (start with resources expended at top of page);
2. the use of designated funds – window-dressing;
3. the treatment of capital grants – consistency with SSAP 4;
4. multi-period funding – consistency with FRS12, interpretation of constructive obligations', performance-related grants;
5. narrative reporting – difficulty in narrating achievements 'annually' as often a charity is at a point on a route map as part of an overall strategy, and
6. combinations – no merger accounting under IFRS.

These six areas formed the basis for the Charity Commission's six months of research to gauge stakeholders' views on how well the current SORP is performing.

31.10.2 Stakeholder roundtable events

The SORP Committee conducted a series of 24 stakeholder roundtable events to gauge the views and concerns of a variety of users. This research phase was completed in April 2009. The feedback will determine how the next SORP is developed. The particular stakeholder groups were:

(a) preparers of small accounts;
(b) preparers of large accounts;
(c) audit firms;
(d) Government funders;
(e) donors and financial supporters;
(f) media and analysts, and
(g) academics.

The Committee realised that timely and high-quality reporting was essential for maintaining public trust. This requires accounts and reports to be transparent in order to provide stakeholders with unbiased, comparable and understandable information.

Preliminary recommendations from these events include:

1. reduction in governance-related disclosures in Trustees' Annual Report;
2. clarification of SOFA terminology;
3. performance reporting and stewardship to remain important;
4. clarification as to when full SORP (as opposed to 'mini' SORP) disclosures are and are not required (and what they are);
5. inclusion of social and environmental (including ethical) reporting;
6. consideration of long-term outcomes;
7. the need to reflect both the letter and the spirit of the legislation – a charity can achieve full SORP compliance, yet at the same time produce unintelligible accounts, and
8. removal of duplication by combining Trustees' Annual Report (currently required for compliance purposes) and Annual Review (currently required for marketing purposes).

31.10.3 SORP for small charities

There is a genuine desire in the sector to reduce unnecessary complexity and aim for greater clarity. The concerns of smaller charities need to come to the fore. The Committee is particularly conscious that nearly 90 per cent of all charities have income under £500,000 (figure as at December 2008 – see **section 21.1** of Chapter 21). Small charities face situations where accountancy skills are often in short supply, where there is strong reliance on trustees and volunteers, and where funding and achievements are likely to be local. The Committee therefore needs to be receptive to small charities' needs. This means that reports should concentrate on outcomes and impacts, allowing charities more flexibility to tell their story.

It is hoped that a more user-friendly, less technical SORP will emerge. This does not mean that small charities can take donors for granted, as reports and accounts are still required under charity law. Transparency will, however, mean that small charities are still able to demonstrate effectiveness and provide the necessary level of confidence in the sector. So one of the aims of the next SORP will include maintaining donor confidence with the minimal amount of burden. Reporting needs to be simple, direct and, above all, proportionate.

31.10.4 International issues

The actual timing of the next SORP will be determined by the ASB's own timetable for converging UK Generally Accepted Accounting Practice (UK

GAAP) with International Financial Reporting Standards (IFRSs). As it is unlikely that this will occur in 2009, the next SORP is unlikely to be published before 2010. IFRSs place the emphasis on decision-making for the future as opposed to stewardship. In fact, private companies have little reporting to their owners, so the role of stewardship also needs to be carefully analysed by the Committee. The ASB is considering a three-tier approach to IFRS convergence:

1. Full IFRSs for listed entities;
2. International Accounting Standards Board (IASB) Small and Medium-sized Entities (SME) standard based on IFRS – Private Entity Standards, and
3. IFRS compliant FRSSE – for smaller entities

The ASB is also considering issuing its own not-for-profit standard. Ideally, a single framework and standard (that is IFRS compliant) needs to be devised for charities. If a satisfactory not-for-profit conceptual framework is not reached in time, the initial IFRS-compliant Charities SORP may well be an adaptation of a commercial standard relying heavily on the ASB's existing conceptual approach *Statement of Principles for Financial Reporting: Interpretation of Public Benefit Entities*.

The International Public Sector Accounting Standards Board (IPSASB) focuses on the accounting and financial reporting needs of national, regional and local governments, related governmental agencies, and the constituencies they serve. It addresses these needs by issuing and promoting benchmark guidance and facilitating the exchange of information among accountants and those who work in the public sector or rely on its work.

A key part of the IPSASB's strategy is to converge the International Public Sector Accounting Standards (IPSASs) with the IFRSs issued by the IASB. To facilitate this strategy, the IPSASB has developed guidelines or 'rules of the road' for modifying IFRSs for application by public sector entities. The Committee may well need to consider the role of the IPSASB in the implementation process as the standards the IPSASB have already produced may be of assistance to the Committee in the convergence process.

Chapter 32 – Managing in a downturn

32.1 Recent survey

A survey jointly published in December 2008 by the Charity Finance Directors' Group (CFDG), PwC and the Institute of Fundraising showed that charities were already taking proactive measures to protect themselves from future financial instability. Prudent initiatives carried out so far include:

- 32 per cent of charities putting capital projects on hold, and
- 34 per cent of charities planning to restrict IT projects

In further evidence of good management and monitoring:

- 74 per cent of charities reported that they felt they had adequate budget setting and regular monitoring systems in place;
- 47 per cent of charities expected to take pre-emptive actions ahead of potential increases in costs or reductions in income, and
- 50 per cent of the charities had even identified positive advantages of the downturn, with 62 per cent of charities expecting to increase their fundraising activities in the coming months, in order to fundraise out of the downturn.

Overall, charities are not expecting a growth in income, but they are wary of predicting what the next few years may hold for them. It is as difficult for them as for other organisations to guess what will happen in the near future. The report showed that with the right tools, knowledge and support, charities can weather the 'credit crunch', and in some cases it may even provide opportunities for further fundraising. Charity finance directors will need to show real leadership and work proactively to guide charities through the uncertain times ahead. Action must be taken now in order to make the most efficient use of available resources and thus maximise the support for the beneficiaries that charities exist to help.

32.2 Key points

The following key points emerged from the survey:

1. While there are obvious anxieties in the sector, a significant number of charities actually see opportunities arising.

Managing in a downturn

2. The message from the previous recession is that there is a significant lead time from recession to the full impact on consumer spending, and then again until spending returns to pre-recession levels.
3. There are factors at play today which suggest that the lead time might be shorter, while the impact will be no less prolonged.
4. All experience shows that recessions can be viewed as similar to 'pit stops' in a grand prix, with those organisations that use the time to reassess their position emerging stronger, and those that do not being at risk of falling behind.

32.2.1 Fundraising

Each area of fundraising is subject to different pressures, and those charities that have a mixed and diverse fundraising strategy will be better placed than those that have underinvested in the past. Fundraisers need to be effective at making the point to their boards and chief executives that cutting back on their investments in income generation now will guarantee that the downturn has a knock-on effect well into the inevitable recovery period that will follow. Those that use this period to build a solid and diverse fundraising strategy will accelerate away from the pack once recovery begins. Relationships are equally vital with corporates, trusts, major donors, potential legacy prospects and individual givers.

There is some evidence that smaller charities are more optimistic about the future than their larger equivalents. This optimism may be well placed as smaller charities have close relationships and can carry out a more detailed interpretation of the impact. However, as the larger charities have greater resources to analyse the impact, it is possible that their greater pessimism may be based on detail that smaller charities do not possess.

32.2.2 Effective financial management

Charities now, more than ever, require strong strategic panning to battle against these difficult times. It is most likely to be weak financial management that will result in charities failing. At the heart of all this lies strong governance within the charity structure. Strong governance will facilitate strategic planning and this in turn will be achieved through risk assessment. Trustees will then be able to set realistic and revised reserves policies that will constantly be reviewed. Such charities will be able to deliver timely and meaningful management information that will further enhance the effective financial management process.

Throughout this process, trustees need to be aware that they have an obligation to safeguard the charity's assets, and this may well require them to ask difficult questions. Conducting several 'what if' scenarios may be required. In implementing their decision making, trustees need to be aware of the time taken to reach the necessary decisions and contingency plans. There is no time like the present.

32.2.3 Strategic planning

Charities should have in place a long-term strategy to meet their charitable objects. This strategy should cover finance, operations and governance. During the downturn, it is imperative that charities remain strategic in their focus. Consideration of all options should be made and trustees should not avoid difficult questions. Activities may need to be prioritised and even basic questions, such as 'Should we survive as a stand-alone charity?' or 'Are we able to generate funds more cost-effectively?', should be addressed.

32.2.4 Risk assessment

Budgets – including income and expenditure, cash flow and balance sheet forecasts – should be drawn up at a level of detail to allow trustees to understand the impact of the downturn and other risks. Such detailed scenario planning should take place for all realistic contingencies – such as, 'What if our fundraised income declined by 30 per cent?' This should enable the charity to understand what it would do in the event of those contingencies materialising.

Only then will trustees know how to react. This process of planning should not be underestimated. Seeking agreement amongst the trustees on what may be very difficult decisions will, of itself, take time, as not every trustee will necessarily have the same view.

32.2.5 Reserves policy

The charity's reserves policy will need to be reviewed in the light of the scenario planning above. If a charity has a risk-based policy already, then this should make life easier; if there is not a risk-based policy, then now is the time to put one in place. The extent to which reserves are utilised in order to 'smooth' the effect of the downturn will be a key decision, as will the extent to which activities should be reduced yet further if reserves are insufficient in order to build up a reserve.

32.2.6 Investment policy

The charity's investment policy will need to be reviewed in light of the current economic environment. Firstly, policies must address the risks associated with investments, whether the risks are accepted by the charity or whether action is taken to mitigate these risks. Policies and procedures should be sufficient to ensure that the will of the trustees is communicated, documented and adhered to.

Secondly, charities should consider the return of investments and their relative liquidity; how changes in the actual return will impact the fulfilment of the charity's objectives, and, if necessary, how such risks can be addressed.

Finally, the value of many charities' investments has dropped dramatically in recent times. Additionally, the fact that interest rates are at an all time low, means that investment income streams have also dwindled.

32.2.7 Management information

Detailed and appropriate management information will be vital to a charity's understanding of the extent to which the downturn is affecting its performance. The better the information, the earlier the charity will be aware of any issues and the longer it will have to implement a response. This is about optimising the charity's chances of surviving and prospering in this downturn.

32.3 Conclusion

There will be winners and losers during this downturn, as with any other. Winners will have considered their environment, implemented good management, have strong cash resources and used reserves appropriately. Recessions tend to result in polarisation: the strong get stronger and the weak either fail or lose their identity through enforced merger. Medium-sized charities could be particularly hard hit as they may be too small to absorb large losses but too large to be flexible enough to adapt.

1. Take a closer look

The goalposts are moving, so charities need to understand the true picture and not what they would like to believe is the case. What is their driver? What do they do best and why? This will enable them to understand better how they are being impacted by the downturn.

2. Act decisively

With increased uncertainty and volatility it is important to take tough decisions early. Focus on the key drivers of value and the key risks across the charity. Do not sit back and wait. The winners will be those who position themselves to take advantage of the upturn.

3. Cash is king

There is a well-known management mantra: 'Sales is vanity, profit is sanity and cash is reality'.

Charities need to ensure that their finances and working capital are in good order, protect their liquidity and re-examine their treasury, financing, funding and pension exposures. They also need to monitor their performance against financial and non-financial key performance indicators (KPIs). This can be achieved through adopting a 'hands-on' and proactive approach to cash management.

4. Focus on what really matters

Evaluate which activities, projects and channels create or destroy value. Revisit the existing programmes. Which initiatives could be stopped or deferred? It is important to focus on core activities. New projects can account for excessive management time and resources.

5. Manage your cost base

Focus on enhancing operational performance. Charities need to go for targeted rather than 'across–the-board' cuts, extract better value, reduce unnecessary complexity and look at whether their business model needs to change.

6. Reliable management information

Charities need the right management information. Clearly defined KPIs are therefore essential. Decision-making needs to be based on facts to facilitate reaching decisions faster. Watch out for negative free reserves, which are indicative of going concern problems.

7. Plan for different scenarios

Winners demonstrate agility and flexibility and they model a range of financial, operational and workforce scenarios that reflect the impact of the downturn on their charity. Again, this allows them to adapt quickly to explore strategic options.

8. Recognise the value of your people

Regular and clear communication with employees is key to their performance. Identify key talent and develop appropriate incentives for them. Retaining and motivating the best people is critical for the future.

9. Take your stakeholders with you

Evaluate the likely impact of the downturn on your funders and other stakeholders. Charities need to make sure that they understand their agendas.

Managing in a downturn

Perception is often reality, so maintaining regular and open dialogue is essential. A clear communication strategy is important. Trustees need to be both robust and transparent in their decision-making, whilst not glossing over the truth

10. Take advantage of the opportunities

Do not stop innovating or investing in those areas of growth that are needed for the future and do not forget the charity brand. Have an eye for the future, so think beyond the next quarter.

Annex

Performance management

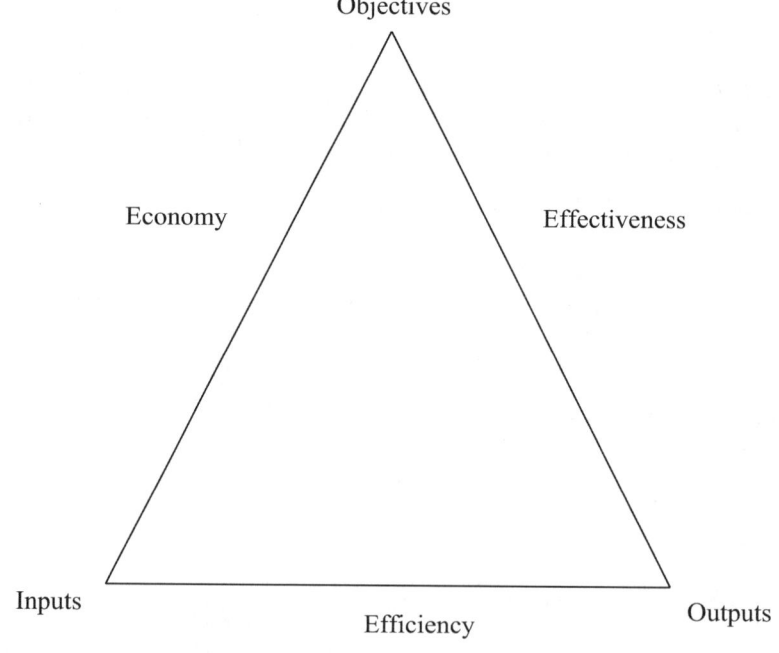

In coping with difficult times, charities need to be particularly conscious of their performance management. The above figure lists the 3Es which demonstrate how a charity can best achieve value for money in performing its activities. *Economy* requires minimal expenditure consistent with the objectives, *efficiency* considers the relationship between outputs to inputs, and *effectiveness* considers the relationship between outputs and objectives.

In the commercial world, efficiency is particularly important as it measures the relationship between cost inputs and revenue outputs. In the not-for-profit sector, non- financial data is especially important. Effectiveness may well be considered more important than efficiency. In the commercial world, the profit figure, or 'bottom line' is paramount but in the not-for profit sector, there is no 'bottom line'.

Appendix 1 – The Charities (Accounts and Reports) Regulations 2008

STATUTORY INSTRUMENTS

2008 No. 629

CHARITIES

The Charities (Accounts and Reports) Regulations 2008

Made - - - - -	*6th March 2008*
Laid before Parliament	*10th March 2008*
Coming into force	*1st April 2008*

£7.50

Appendix 1 – The Charities (Accounts and Reports) Regulations 2008

STATUTORY INSTRUMENTS

2008 No. 629

CHARITIES

The Charities (Accounts and Reports) Regulations 2008

Made - - - -	6th March 2008
Laid before Parliament	10th March 2008
Coming into force - -	1st April 2008

The Minister for the Cabinet Office makes the following Regulations in exercise of the powers conferred by sections 42, 44, 45 and 86(3) of and paragraphs 3, 4, 6, 10 and 15 of Schedule 5A to the Charities Act 1993(**a**).

In accordance with section 86(4) of that Act he has consulted such persons and bodies of persons as he considers appropriate.

PART 1
GENERAL

Citation and commencement

1. These Regulations may be cited as the Charities (Accounts and Reports) Regulations 2008 and come into force on 1st April 2008.

Interpretation

2.—(1) In these Regulations—

"the 1960 Act" means the Charities Act 1960(**b**);

(**a**) 1993 c.10. Section 42 was amended by the Charities Act 1993 (Substitution of Sums) Order 1995 (S.I. 1995/2696) and by the Charities Act 2006 (c. 50), Schedule 8, paragraph 133. Section 44 was amended by the Charities Act 2006, Schedule 8, paragraphs 96 and 137. Section 45 was amended by the Deregulation and Contracting Out Act 1994, section 29, the Companies Act 1985 (Audit Exemption) Regulations 1994 (S.I. 1994/1935), the Regulatory Reform (National Health Service Charitable and Non-charitable Trust Accounts and Audit) Order 2005 and the Charities Act 2006, Schedule 7 and Schedule 8, paragraphs 96 and 138. The amendments made to section 45 by Schedule 7 to the Charities Act 2006 are not yet in force. Sections 43 to 47 of and Schedule 5A to the 1993 Act were also amended by the Charities Act 2006 (Charitable Companies Audit and Group Accounts) Order 2008 (S.I. 2008/527). The amendments made by that Order have effect in relation to financial years of charities beginning on or after 1st April 2008. Section 86 was amended by the Trustee Act 2000 (c. 29), Schedule 2, paragraph 2 and Schedule 4, the Charities and Trustee Investment (Scotland) Act 2005 (asp. 10), Schedule 3, paragraph 9, and the Charities Act 2006 (c. 50), Schedule 7, paragraph 6 and Schedule 8, paragraph 165. The amendments made by Schedule 7 of the 2006 Act are not yet in force. The functions exercisable by the Secretary of State under sections 43 to 45 of the Charities Act 1993 were transferred to the Minister for the Cabinet Office by the Transfer of Functions (Third Sector, Communities and Equality) Order 2006 (S.I. 2006/2951).

(**b**) 1960 c. 58. The 1960 Act was repealed in part by the Charities Act 1993 (c. 10). The provisions remaining in force are repealed by the Charities Act 2006, Schedule 9. The relevant entry in Schedule 9 to the 2006 Act has not yet been commenced.

Appendix 1 – The Charities (Accounts and Reports) Regulations 2008

"the 1985 Act" means the Companies Act 1985(**a**);

"the 1993 Act" means the Charities Act 1993;

"the 2006 Act" means the Charities Act 2006(**b**);

"the 2005 Regulations" means the Charities (Accounts and Reports) Regulations 2005(**c**);

"auditable charity" means a charity the accounts of which for the financial year in question are required to be audited in pursuance of any statutory requirement;

"authorised person" has the meaning given by section 31 of the Financial Services and Markets Act 2000(**d**);

"charitable subsidiary undertaking" means a subsidiary undertaking that is a charity;

"common deposit fund" means a common deposit fund established by a scheme under section 22A of the Charities Act 1960(**e**) or section 25 of the 1993 Act;

"common investment fund" has the meaning given by paragraph (2);

"director"—

(a) in relation to a body corporate whose affairs are managed by its members, means a member of the body corporate;

(b) in any other case, includes any person occupying the position of a director by whatever name called;

"English National Health Service Charity" has the meaning given by section 43A(7) of the 1993 Act;

"ex gratia payment" means any such application of the property of a charity, or any such waiver by a charity of any entitlement to receive any property, as is capable of being authorised under section 27(1) of the 1993 Act;

"fixed assets" means the assets of a charity which are intended for use or investment on a continuing basis;

"fund" means particular assets of a charity held on trusts which, as respect the purposes for which those assets are held or the powers of the charity trustees to use or apply those assets, are not identical to the trusts on which other assets of the charity are held;

"investment fund" means a common deposit fund or a common investment fund;

"non-charitable subsidiary undertaking" means a subsidiary undertaking that is not a charity;

"parent charity" has the meaning given by paragraph 1 of Schedule 5A to the 1993 Act;

"relevant financial year" means the financial year in respect of which—

(a) the statement of accounts is prepared;

(b) the receipt and payments account and statement of assets and liabilities are prepared; or

(c) group accounts are prepared;

"reserves" means—

(a) in relation to a charity, those assets in the unrestricted fund of a charity which the charity trustees have, or can make, available to apply for all of any its purposes, once they have provided for—

   (i) the liabilities of the unrestricted fund; and

   (ii) any commitments of the charity or other planned expenditure intended to be met from the assets of the unrestricted fund;

(**a**) 1985 c. 6.
(**b**) 2006 c.50.
(**c**) S.I. 2005/572.
(**d**) 2000 c. 8. There have been amendments to the Financial Services and Markets Act 2000 which are not relevant for the purposes of these Regulations.
(**e**) section 22A of the Charities Act 1960 was inserted by section 16 of the Charities Act 1992 (c. 41).

Appendix 1 – The Charities (Accounts and Reports) Regulations 2008

    (b) in relation to any body that is not a charity, the net assets or liabilities of the body that are disclosed in the body's balance sheet for the financial year in question;

"restricted fund" means any fund of a charity other than an unrestricted fund;

"the SORP" means the Statement of Recommended Practice for Accounting and Reporting by Charities, issued by the Commission on 4th March 2005(**a**);

"special case charity" means—

    (a) a charity which is a registered social landlord within the meaning of the Housing Act 1996(**b**) and whose registration has been the subject of a notice under section 3(3)(a) of that Act;

    (b) a charity which has during the financial year in question—

        (i) conducted an institution in relation to which a designation made, or having effect as if made, under section 129 of the Education Reform Act 1988(**c**) has effect;

        (ii) received financial support from funds administered by a higher education funding council within the meaning of the Further and Higher Education Act 1992(**d**) in respect of expenditure incurred or to be incurred by the charity in connection with that institution; and

        (iii) incurred no expenditure for charitable purposes other than the purposes of that institution or any other such institution; and

"subsidiary undertaking" has the meaning given by paragraph 1 of Schedule 5A to the 1993 Act;

"trustee for a charity" means a person other than the charity itself ("A") or a charity trustee of A who holds title to property belonging to A and includes a custodian trustee and a nominee;

"unrestricted fund" means a fund which is to be used, or applied, in any way determined by the charity trustees of a charity for the furtherance of the objects of the charity;

"Welsh National Health Service Charity" has the meaning given by section 43B(4) of the 1993 Act.

(2) Subject to paragraph (3), in these Regulations, "common investment fund" means a common investment fund established by a scheme under section 22 of the 1960 Act or section 24 of the 1993 Act.

(3) A fund is not a "common investment fund" for the purposes of these Regulations if its trusts provide for property to be transferred to that fund only by or on behalf of a participating charity of which the charity trustees are the trustees appointed to manage the fund.

(4) Where the scheme or schemes regulating an investment fund allocates responsibility for the exercise of a function of a charity trustee to a particular person, "charity trustees", in relation to that investment fund, includes the person to whom the relevant function has been allocated.

Financial year of a charity which is not a company

3.—(1) The financial year of a charity which is not a company ("relevant charity") is, for the purposes of the 1993 Act and regulations made under that Act, to be determined in accordance with this regulation.

(2) The first financial year of a relevant charity is the period beginning with the day on which the charity is established and ending with—

(a) Copies of the SORP can be obtained from the Charity Commission's website: http://www.charitycommission.gov.uk/investigations/sorp/sorp05docs.asp. Printed copies can be obtained from CCH on 0870 777 2906 or customerservices@cch.co.uk (quoting product code CCSORP) or via the CCH website: http://www.cch.co.uk . There may be a charge for obtaining printed copies of the SORP.
(b) 1996 c. 52. Eligibility for registration as a social landlord is determined in accordance with section 2 of that Act. Section 3(3)(a) of the 1996 Act was amended by the Charities Act 2006 (c.50), Schedule 8, paragraph 184. There are other amendments to the 1996 Act not relevant for the purposes of these Regulations.
(c) 1988 c. 40. Section 129 of the 1988 Act was amended by section 72(1) of the Further and Higher Education Act 1992 (c. 13).
(d) 1992 c. 13.

Appendix 1 – The Charities (Accounts and Reports) Regulations 2008

    (a) its accounting reference date; or

    (b) such other date, not more than seven days before or after the accounting reference date, as the charity trustees may determine.

(3) Subsequent financial years of a relevant charity—

    (a) begin with the day immediately following the last day of the charity's previous financial year; and

    (b) end with—

        (i) its accounting reference date; or

        (ii) such other date, not more than seven days before or after the accounting reference date, as the charity trustees may determine.

(4) For the purposes of this regulation, the "accounting reference date" of a relevant charity is—

    (a) in relation to the first financial year of the charity, such date, not less than 6 months and not more than 18 months after the date on which the charity was established as the charity trustees may determine;

    (b) in relation to a subsequent financial year of the charity—

        (i) the date 12 months after the previous accounting reference date of the charity; or

        (ii) subject to paragraphs (5) and (7), such other date, not less than 6 months and not more than 18 months after the previous accounting reference date of the charity as the charity trustees may determine.

(5) The charity trustees may only exercise the power in paragraph (4)(b)(ii) in respect of a restricted financial year with the consent of the Commission.

(6) In paragraph (5), "restricted financial year" means a financial year beginning immediately after—

    (a) a financial year in respect of which the charity trustees had exercised the power in paragraph (4)(b)(ii) above or in regulation 6(4)(b) of the 2005 Regulations;

    (b) a financial year ("A") where A began immediately after a financial year in respect of which the charity trustees had exercised the power in paragraph (4)(b)(ii) above or in regulation 6(4)(b) of the 2005 Regulations.

(7) The charity trustees may exercise their power under paragraph (4)(b)(ii) so as to determine an accounting reference date less, or more, than 12 months from the beginning of the financial year only where they satisfied that there are exceptional reasons to do so.

Application, revocation, savings and transitional provisions

4.—(1) The 2005 Regulations are revoked.

(2) Despite paragraph (1) and subject to paragraphs (3) and (4), the 2005 Regulations continue to apply in respect of a financial year of a charity which began before 1st April 2008.

(3) The duty in regulation 7(5) of the 2005 Regulations continues to apply only in respect of matters of which an auditor became aware of—

    (a) before 1st April 2008; and

    (b) during a financial year ending on or before 31st March 2008.

(4) These Regulations apply in respect of a financial year of a charity which—

    (a) begins on or after 1st April 2008; or

    (b) is a transferred year.

(5) Despite paragraph (4)—

    (a) nothing in these Regulations applies to a charity which is an exempt charity;

    (b) the group accounts provisions do not apply in respect of a transferred year.

(6) In this regulation—

Appendix 1 – The Charities (Accounts and Reports) Regulations 2008

    (a) "accounts determination" means—

        (i) in relation to an investment fund, a determination that regulation 6 of these Regulations rather than regulation 4 of the 2005 Regulations is to apply to the statement of accounts prepared in respect of the financial year in question;

        (ii) in relation to any other charity, a determination that regulation 8 of these Regulations rather than regulation 3 of the 2005 Regulations is to apply to the statement of accounts prepared in respect of the financial year in question;

    (b) "group accounts provisions" means—

        (i) Part 3;

        (ii) Chapter 3 of Part 4;

        (iii) in so far as it applies to audits carried out under paragraph 6 of Schedule 5A to the 1993 Act, Chapter 3 of Part 4,

    of these Regulations

    (c) "report determination" means—

        (i) in relation to an investment fund, a determination that regulation 38 of these Regulations rather than regulation 12 of the 2005 Regulations is to apply to the annual report prepared in respect of the financial year in question;

        (ii) in relation to any other charity, a determination that regulation 40 of these Regulations rather than regulation 11 of the 2005 Regulations is to apply to the annual report prepared in respect of the financial year in question;

    (d) "transferred year" means a financial year of a charity—

        (i) which began before 1st April 2008; and

        (ii) in respect of which the charity trustees may make and make an accounts determination and a report determination.

(7) The charity trustees of a charity may not make an accounts determination or a report determination in respect of financial year beginning before 1st April 2008 if—

    (a) the charity is a special case charity; or

    (b) before that date they have—

        (i) approved the accounts of the charity prepared in respect of that financial year; or

        (ii) authorised the signature of an annual report prepared in respect of that financial year in accordance with the 2005 Regulations.

PART 2

FORM AND CONTENT OF STATEMENTS OF ACCOUNT

General

5. The requirements as to the form and content of a statement of accounts of a charity to be prepared under section 42(1) of the 1993 Act are prescribed—

    (a) in the case of an investment fund, in regulation 6;

    (b) in the case of special case charity, in regulation 7;

    (c) in the case of any other charity, in regulation 8.

Form and content of statement of accounts: investment funds

6.—(1) This regulation applies to a statement of accounts prepared by the charity trustees of an investment fund in accordance with section 42(1) of the 1993 Act.

Appendix 1 – The Charities (Accounts and Reports) Regulations 2008

(2) The requirements as to form and content of a statement of accounts to which this regulation applies are prescribed in paragraphs (3) to (8).

(3) Subject to paragraph (4), the statement of accounts must consist of—

   (a) a statement of total return which satisfies the requirements prescribed in Part 1 of Schedule 1;

   (b) a statement of changes in net assets which satisfies the requirements prescribed in Part 2 of Schedule 1; and

   (c) a balance sheet which satisfies the requirements prescribed in Part 3 of Schedule 1.

(4) In the case of any financial year of a common deposit fund in which there are no gains or losses on disposal or revaluation of assets, paragraph (3) has effect as if sub-paragraph (b) were omitted.

(5) The statement of accounts must be prepared in accordance with the methods and principles specified or referred to in Part 4 of Schedule 1.

(6) There must be provided by way of notes to the accounts the information specified in Part 5 of Schedule 1.

(7) The balance sheet must—

   (a) if the scheme or schemes regulating the investment fund allocates responsibility for preparing the accounts to a particular person, be signed and dated by that person;

   (b) in any other case, be signed by at least one of the charity trustees of the investment fund, each of whom has been authorised to do so.

(8) Where the balance sheet of an investment fund is signed by one or more of the charity trustees in accordance with paragraph (7)(b), the balance sheet must specify the date on which the statement of accounts of which the balance sheet forms part was approved by the charity trustees.

Form and content of statement of accounts: special case charities

7.—(1) This regulation applies to a statement of accounts prepared by the charity trustees of a special case charity in accordance with section 42(1) of the 1993 Act.

(2) The requirements as to form and content of a statement of accounts to which this regulation applies are prescribed in paragraphs (3) to (5).

(3) The statement of accounts must consist of—

   (a) an income and expenditure account; and

   (b) a balance sheet showing the state of affairs of the charity as at the end of the relevant financial year.

(4) The statement must be prepared in accordance with the following principles—

   (a) the income and expenditure account must give a true and fair view of the income and expenditure of the charity for the relevant financial year; and

   (b) the balance sheet must give a true and fair view of the state of affairs of the charity at the end of that year.

(5) The balance sheet must—

   (a) be signed by at least one of the charity trustees of the charity, each of whom has been authorised to do so; and

   (b) specify the date on which the statement of accounts of which the balance sheet forms part was approved by the charity trustees.

Appendix 1 – The Charities (Accounts and Reports) Regulations 2008

Form and content of statement of accounts: charities other than investment funds or special case charities

8.—(1) This regulation applies to a statement of accounts prepared by the charity trustees of a charity which is not an investment fund or a special case charity in accordance with section 42(1) of the 1993 Act.

(2) The requirements as to form and content of a statement of accounts to which this regulation applies are prescribed in paragraphs (3) to (11).

(3) The statement of accounts must consist of—

(a) a statement of financial activities showing the total incoming resources and application of the resources, together with any other movements in the total resources, of the charity during the relevant financial year; and

(b) a balance sheet showing the state of affairs of the charity as at the end of the relevant financial year.

(4) The statement of accounts must be prepared in accordance with the following principles—

(a) the statement of financial activities must give a true and fair view of the incoming resources and application of the resources of the charity in the relevant financial year;

(b) the balance sheet must give a true and fair view of the state of affairs of the charity at the end of the relevant financial year;

(c) where compliance with paragraphs (5) to (10) would not be sufficient to give a true and fair view as required under sub-paragraph (a) or (b), the additional information necessary to give a true and fair view must be given in the statement of accounts or in notes to the accounts;

(d) if in special circumstances compliance with any of the requirements of paragraphs (5) to (10) would be inconsistent with giving a true and fair view, the charity trustees must depart from the relevant requirement to the extent necessary to give a true and fair view.

(5) The statement of accounts must be prepared in accordance with the methods and principles set out in the SORP.

(6) Subject to paragraphs (7) to (9), the statement of accounts must, in relation to any amount required to be shown in the statement of financial activities or in the balance sheet for the relevant financial year, show the corresponding amount for the financial year immediately preceding the relevant financial year.

(7) Where a charity has more than one fund, only amounts corresponding to the entries in the statement of financial activities relating to the totals of both or all of the funds of the charity need be shown.

(8) Where the corresponding amount referred to in paragraph (6) is not comparable with the amount to be shown for the item in question in respect of the relevant financial year, the corresponding amount is to be adjusted.

(9) Where—

(a) the effect of paragraphs (4) and (5) is that there is nothing to be shown in respect of a particular item for the relevant financial year; but

(b) an amount was required to be shown in respect of that item in the statement of accounts for the financial year immediately preceding the relevant financial year,

paragraphs (4) and (5) have effect as if an amount were required to be shown in the statement of accounts for the relevant financial year, and that amount were nil.

(10) There must be provided by way of notes to the accounts the information specified in Schedule 2.

(11) The balance sheet must—

(a) be signed by at least one of the charity trustees of the charity, each of whom has been authorised to do so; and

Appendix 1 – The Charities (Accounts and Reports) Regulations 2008

   (b) specify the date on which the statement of accounts of which the balance sheet forms part was approved by the charity trustees.

PART 3
PREPARATION OF GROUP ACCOUNTS
CHAPTER 1
GENERAL

Meaning of "aggregate gross income"

9.—(1) For the purposes of Schedule 5A to the 1993 Act the aggregate gross income for a financial year of a group consisting of a parent charity and its subsidiary undertaking or undertakings is to be determined by eliminating all group transactions for that year from the group income for that year.

(2) For the purposes of this regulation—
- (a) "corresponding financial year" has the meaning given by paragraph (3);
- (b) "gross income" means, in relation to a non-charitable subsidiary undertaking, the amount of income of that undertaking that would be construed as its gross income were it a charity;
- (c) "group income" means the aggregate of—
    - (i) the gross income of the parent charity for the financial year;
    - (ii) the gross income of each charitable subsidiary undertaking of that parent charity for the corresponding financial year; and
    - (iii) the gross income of each non-charitable subsidiary undertaking of that parent charity for the corresponding financial year.
- (d) "group transactions" means—
    - (i) all income and expenditure relating to transactions between members of the group;
    - (ii) all gains and losses relating to transactions between members of the group;
- (e) "member of a group" is to be construed in accordance with paragraph 1 of Schedule 5A to the 1993 Act;

(3) Subject to paragraph (4), "corresponding financial year" in relation to a subsidiary undertaking means—
- (a) in the case of a subsidiary undertaking whose financial year ends with that of the parent charity, that year;
- (b) in any other case, the financial year of the subsidiary undertaking ending immediately before the end of the financial year of the parent charity.

(4) If the figures for the corresponding financial year of a subsidiary undertaking cannot be obtained without disproportionate expense or undue delay, the latest available figures are to be taken.

Financial years of subsidiary undertakings

10.—(1) For the purposes of Schedule 5A to the 1993 Act the financial years of subsidiary undertakings are to be determined in accordance with this regulation.

(2) The financial year of a charitable subsidiary undertaking is to be determined in accordance with section 97 of the 1993 Act.

(3) The financial year of a non-charitable subsidiary undertaking is a period in respect of which a profit and loss account of the undertaking is required to be made up (by its constitution or by the law under which it is established), whether that period is a year or not.

Appendix 1 – The Charities (Accounts and Reports) Regulations 2008

Requirement for financial years of a parent charity and its subsidiary undertakings to coincide

11. The charity trustees of a parent charity must secure that, except where in their opinion there are good reasons against it, the financial year of each of its subsidiary undertakings coincides with its own financial year.

CHAPTER 2

FORM AND CONTENT OF GROUP ACCOUNTS

Form and content of group accounts: general

12. The requirements as to the form and content of group accounts to be prepared under paragraph 3(2) of Schedule 5A to the 1993 Regulations are prescribed—

    (a) in the case of a parent charity that is an investment fund, in regulation 13;

    (b) in the case of a parent charity that is a special case charity, in regulation 14;

    (c) in the case of any other parent charity, in regulation 15.

Form and content of group accounts: parent charities that are investment funds

13.—(1) This regulation applies to the group accounts prepared by the charity trustees of a parent charity that is an investment fund under paragraph 3(2) of Schedule 5A to the 1993 Act.

(2) The requirements as to the form and content of the group accounts to which this regulation applies are prescribed in paragraphs (3) and (4) and regulation 16.

(3) The group accounts must consist of—

    (a) a consolidated statement of total return dealing with the total return of the parent charity and its subsidiary undertakings in the relevant financial year;

    (b) a consolidated statement of changes in net assets dealing with the changes in the net assets of the parent and its subsidiary undertakings in the relevant financial year;

    (c) a consolidated balance sheet dealing with the state of affairs of the parent and its subsidiary undertakings as at the end of the relevant financial year.

(4) The group accounts must be prepared in accordance with the following principles—

    (a) the consolidated statement of total return must give a true and fair view of the total return of the parent charity and its subsidiary undertakings in the relevant financial year;

    (b) the consolidated statement of changes in net assets must give a true and fair view of the changes in the net assets of the parent charity and its subsidiary undertakings between their position at the beginning of the relevant financial year and their position at the end of that year;

    (c) the consolidated balance sheet must give a true and fair view of the state of affairs of the parent charity and its subsidiary undertakings at the end of the relevant financial year.

(5) The group accounts must comply so far as practicable with—

    (a) paragraphs (3) and (4) of;

    (b) in so far as it relates to paragraphs 14 and 15 of Schedule 1, paragraph (5); and

    (c) paragraph (6) of,

regulation 6 as if the parent charity and its subsidiary undertakings required to be included in the group accounts were a single charity.

Form and content of group accounts: parent charities that are special case charities

14.—(1) This Regulation applies to the group accounts prepared by the charity trustees of a parent charity that is a special case charity under paragraph 3(2) of Schedule 5A to the 1993 Act.

Appendix 1 – The Charities (Accounts and Reports) Regulations 2008

(2) The requirements as to the form and content of the group accounts to which this regulation applies are prescribed in paragraphs (3) and (4) and regulation 16.

(3) The group accounts must consist of—

- (a) a consolidated income and expenditure account dealing with the income and expenditure of the parent charity and its subsidiary undertakings for the relevant financial year;
- (b) a consolidated balance sheet dealing with the state of affairs of the parent charity and its subsidiary undertakings as at the end of the relevant financial year.

(4) The group accounts must be prepared in accordance with the following principles—

- (a) the consolidated income and expenditure account must give a true and fair view of the income and expenditure of the parent charity and its subsidiary undertakings as a whole in the relevant financial year;
- (b) the consolidated balance sheet must give a true and fair view of the state of affairs of the parent charity and its subsidiary undertakings as at the end of the relevant financial year.

(5) The group accounts must comply with the requirements of paragraph (5) of regulation 7 as if the parent charity and its subsidiary undertakings required to be included in the group accounts were a single charity.

Form and content of group accounts: parent charities that are not investment funds or special case charities

15.—(1) This regulation applies to the group accounts prepared by the charity trustees of a parent charity other than a parent charity to which regulation 13 or 14 applies under paragraph 3(2) of Schedule 5A to the 1993 Act.

(2) The form and content of the group accounts to which this regulation applies are prescribed in paragraphs (3) to (5) and regulation 16.

(3) The group accounts must consist of—

- (a) a consolidated statement of financial activities showing the total incoming resources and application of the resources, together with any other movements in the total resources, of the parent charity and its subsidiary undertakings in the relevant financial year; and
- (b) a consolidated balance sheet showing the state of affairs of the parent charity and its subsidiary undertakings as at the end of the relevant financial year.

(4) The group accounts must be prepared in accordance with the following principles—

- (a) the consolidated statement of financial activities must give a true and fair view of the total incoming resources of the parent charity and its subsidiary undertakings and the movements in the total resources of the group during the relevant financial year;
- (b) the consolidated balance sheet gives a true and fair view of the state of affairs of the parent charity and its undertakings as at the end of the relevant financial year.

(5) The group accounts prepared under this regulation must—

- (a) so far as practicable comply with the requirements of paragraphs (6) to (10) of regulation 8 as if parent charity and its subsidiary undertakings were a single charity; and
- (b) in any case where the parent charity is a company, be prepared as if its charity trustees had been required to prepare a statement of accounts under section 42(1) of the 1993 Act.

(6) Where paragraph (5)(b) applies, there is substituted for paragraph 1(w) of Schedule 2—

> "(w) where the company has exercised its power under section 225 of the 1985 Act to determine an accounting reference date earlier or later than 12 months from the beginning of the financial year, a statement of their reasons for doing so.".

Appendix 1 – The Charities (Accounts and Reports) Regulations 2008

Form and content of group accounts: general requirements

16.—(1) In addition to complying with regulation 13, 14 or 15, as the case may be, the group accounts prepared by the charity trustees of any parent charity under paragraph 3(2) of Schedule 5A to the 1993 Act must comply with the requirements prescribed in this regulation.

(2) The group accounts must be prepared in accordance with applicable accounting principles and in particular must make the adjustments or include the information prescribed in this regulation.

(3) The group accounts must incorporate in full the information contained in the individual accounts of the parent charity and its relevant subsidiary undertakings, subject to such consolidation adjustments, if any, as may be appropriate in accordance with applicable accounting principles.

(4) Where the financial year of a relevant subsidiary undertaking differs from that of the parent charity, the group accounts must be made up from—

- (a) the accounts of the relevant subsidiary undertaking for its most recent financial year ending before the last day of the parent financial year, provided that financial year ended no more than three months before the parent financial year ended; or
- (b) interim accounts prepared by the relevant subsidiary undertaking as at the end of the parent financial year.

(5) Where an undertaking becomes a subsidiary undertaking of a parent charity, that event must be accounted for in the group accounts by the acquisition method or merger method of accounting as appropriate in accordance with applicable accounting principles.

(6) Where the parent charity or a relevant subsidiary undertaking—

- (a) has an interest in an associated undertaking or participates in the management of a joint venture and that associated undertaking or joint venture is not itself a subsidiary undertaking of the parent charity; or
- (b) participates in a joint arrangement,

the interest of the parent charity or subsidiary undertaking in that associated undertaking, joint venture or joint arrangement must appear in the group accounts as appropriate in accordance with applicable accounting principles.

(7) The consolidated balance sheet must identify as a separate item any minority interest in the net assets or liabilities of any relevant subsidiary undertaking as appropriate in accordance with applicable accounting principles.

(8) The consolidated statement of financial activities, consolidated income and expenditure account or consolidated statement of changes in net assets, as relevant, must identify as a separate item any minority interest in the net movement of the funds of a relevant subsidiary undertaking as appropriate in accordance with applicable accounting principles.

(9) In this regulation—

- (a) "applicable accounting principles" means, in relation to a parent charity that is required to prepare group accounts, the methods and principles set out in—
    - (i) the financial reporting standards and statements of standard accounting practice issued by the body known as The Accounting Standards Board(a) ("the Board") that are relevant to the preparation of those accounts by that parent charity;
    - (ii) any abstract issued by the committee of the Board known as the Urgent Issues Task Force which is relevant to the preparation of those accounts by that parent charity; and
    - (iii) any statement of recommended practice (including the SORP) issued by a body recognised by the Board for the purpose of issuing guidance on the standards in paragraph (i) relevant to the preparation of those accounts by that parent charity.

(a) The Accounting Standards Board was established under the articles of association of The Accounting Standards Board Limited.

Appendix 1 – The Charities (Accounts and Reports) Regulations 2008

(b) "parent financial year" means the financial year of the parent charity in respect of which the group accounts are prepared;

(c) "relevant subsidiary undertaking" means a subsidiary undertaking of the parent charity which is not excluded under regulation 19 from the group accounts required to be prepared for the parent financial year.

Group Accounts: departure from the general rules

17.—(1) Where compliance with the group accounts requirements is not sufficient to comply with any requirement to give a true and fair view, the necessary additional information must be given in the group accounts or a note to them.

(2) If in special circumstances compliance with any of the group accounts requirements is inconsistent with a requirement to give a true and fair view, the charity trustees must depart from the relevant provision to the extent necessary to give a true and fair view.

(3) Particulars of any departure under paragraph (2), the reasons for it and its effect must be given in a note to the group accounts.

(4) In this regulation "group accounts requirements" mean the requirements prescribed by regulation 13, 14 or 15, as the case may be, and regulation 16.

CHAPTER 3

EXCEPTIONS TO THE REQUIREMENT TO PREPARE GROUP ACCOUNTS

Exceptions relating to requirement to prepare group accounts

18. The sum specified for the purposes of paragraph 4(2) of Schedule 5A to the 1993 Act is £500,000.

19.—(1) The circumstances in which a subsidiary undertaking may be excluded from group accounts required to be prepared under paragraph 3(2) of Schedule 5A to the 1993 Act are—

(a) subject to paragraph (2), where the inclusion of the subsidiary undertaking is not material for the purposes of giving a true and fair view;

(b) severe long term restrictions substantially hinder the exercise of the rights of the parent charity over the assets or management of the undertaking;

(c) the information which is necessary for the preparation of the group accounts cannot be obtained without disproportionate expense or undue delay;

(d) the interest of the parent charity in the undertaking is held exclusively with a view to subsequent resale.

(2) Two or more subsidiary undertakings may only be excluded from the group accounts under paragraph (1)(a) if they are not material when taken together.

PART 4

SCRUTINY OF ACCOUNTS

CHAPTER 1

GENERAL

Duties of auditors: general

20. The duties of an auditor carrying out an audit of the accounts of a charity are—

(a) in the case of an audit carried out under section 43 of the 1993 Act, specified—

(i) where the auditor is carrying out an audit of a statement of accounts prepared under section 42(1) of the 1993 Act, in regulation 24;

Appendix 1 – The Charities (Accounts and Reports) Regulations 2008

  (ii) where the auditor is carrying out an audit of individual accounts of a company that is a charity prepared under Part 7 of the 1985 Act, in regulation 25;

  (iii) where the auditor is carrying out an audit of a receipts and payments account and a statement of assets and liabilities prepared under section 42(3) of the 1993 Act, in regulation 26;

 (b) in the case of an audit carried out under section 43A of the 1993 Act, specified in regulation 27;

 (c) in the case of an audit carried out under section 43B of the 1993 Act, specified in regulation 28.

21. The duties of an auditor carrying out an audit of the group accounts of a parent charity under paragraph 6 of Schedule 5A to the 1993 Act, specified in regulation 30.

Duties of examiners: general

22. The duties of an independent examiner with respect to the making of a report in respect of an examination carried out by him under section 43 of the 1993 Act are specified in regulation 31.

23. The duties of an examiner with respect to the making of a report in respect of an examination carried out by him under section 43A or 43B are specified in regulation 32.

CHAPTER 2

AUDIT OF INDIVIDUAL CHARITY ACCOUNTS

Duties of auditors: audit of a statement of accounts prepared under section 42(1) of the 1993 Act

24.—(1) Where a statement of accounts has been prepared under section 42(1) of the 1993 Act for the relevant financial year, the auditor carrying out the audit of those accounts under section 43 of that Act must make a report on that statement to the charity trustees which—

 (a) states the name and address of the auditor and the name of the charity concerned;

 (b) is signed by him or, where the office of auditor is held by a body corporate or partnership, in its name by a person authorised to sign on its behalf;

 (c) states that the auditor is a person falling within paragraph (a) or, as the case may be, paragraph (b) of section 43(2) of the 1993 Act;

 (d) is dated and specifies the financial year in respect of which the accounts to which it relates have been prepared;

 (e) specifies that it is a report in respect of an audit carried out—

  (i) under section 43 of the 1993 Act; and

  (ii) in accordance with regulations made under section 44 of that Act;

 (f) states whether in the auditor's opinion the statement of accounts complies with—

  (i) the requirements of regulation 6, 7 or 8, as relevant; and

  (ii) in particular whether—

   (aa) the balance sheet gives a true and fair view of the state of affairs of the charity at the end of the relevant financial year; and

   (bb) the true and fair view requirements specified in paragraph (2) are satisfied.

 (g) where the auditor has formed the opinion that—

  (i) accounting records have not been kept in respect of the charity in accordance with section 41 of the 1993 Act;

  (ii) the statement of accounts does not accord with those records;

Appendix 1 – The Charities (Accounts and Reports) Regulations 2008

- (iii) any information contained in the statement of accounts is inconsistent in any material respect with any report of the charity trustees prepared under section 45 of the 1993 Act in respect of the relevant financial year; or
- (iv) any information or explanation to which he is entitled under regulation 33 has not been afforded to him,

contains a statement of that opinion and of the grounds for forming it.

(2) The true and fair view requirements specified for the purposes of sub-paragraph (f)(ii)(bb) of paragraph (1) are—

- (a) in the case of a charity to which regulation 6 applies—
  - (i) the statement of total return gives a true and fair view of the incoming resources and application of the resources of the investment fund in the relevant financial year;
  - (ii) the statement of changes in net assets gives a true and fair view of the movements in the net assets of the investment fund between their position as at the beginning of the relevant financial year;
- (b) in the case of a charity to which regulation 7 applies, the income and expenditure account gives a true and fair view of the income and expenditure of the charity in the financial year in question;
- (c) in the case of a charity to which regulation 8 applies, the statement of financial activities gives a true and fair view of the incoming resources and application of the resources of the charity in the relevant financial year

(3) The auditor must, in preparing his report carry out such investigations as will enable him to form an opinion as to the matters specified in sub-paragraphs (f) and (g) of paragraph (1).

Duties of auditor: audit of accounts prepared under Part 7 of the Companies Act 1985

25.—(1) Where individual accounts have been prepared by the charity trustees of a charity which is a company under Chapter 1 of Part 7 of the 1985 Act, the auditor carrying out the audit of those accounts under section 43 of the 1993 Act must make a report on those accounts to the charity trustees which—

- (a) states the name and address of the auditor and the name of the charity concerned;
- (b) is signed by him or, where the office of auditor is held by a body corporate or partnership, in its name by a person authorised to sign on its behalf;
- (c) states that the auditor is a person falling within paragraph (a) or, as the case may be, paragraph (b) of section 43(2) of the 1993 Act;
- (d) is dated and specifies the financial year in respect of which the accounts to which it relates have been prepared;
- (e) confirms that the accounts were not required to be audited in accordance with Part 7 of the 1985 Act;
- (f) specifies that it is a report in respect of an audit carried out under section 43 of the 1993 Act and in accordance with regulations made under section 44 of that Act;
- (g) states whether in the auditor's opinion—
  - (i) the company's individual accounts comply with the requirements of section 226A of the 1985 Act, and in particular whether—
    - (aa) the income and expenditure account gives a true and fair view of the income and expenditure of the charity for the relevant financial year; and
    - (bb) the balance sheet gives a true and fair view of the state of affairs of the charity as at the end of that year;
  - (ii) in any case where the charity has prepared a statement of financial activities in addition to complying with the requirements of the 1985 Act, that statement gives a true and fair view of the charity's incoming resources and application of resources in the relevant financial year;

Appendix 1 – The Charities (Accounts and Reports) Regulations 2008

(iii) in any case where the accounts state that they have been prepared in accordance with the methods and principles in the SORP, those methods and principles have been followed;

(h) where the auditor has formed the opinion that—

(i) accounting records have not been kept in respect of the charity in accordance with section 221 of the 1985 Act;

(ii) the charity's individual accounts do not accord with those records;

(iii) any information contained in those accounts is inconsistent in any material respect with—

(aa) any report of the charity trustees prepared under section 45 of the 1993 Act in respect of relevant financial year; or

(bb) the report prepared in respect of the relevant financial year under section 234 of the 1985 Act; or

(iv) that any information or explanation to which he is entitled under regulation 33 has not been afforded to him,

contains a statement of that opinion and of the grounds for forming it.

(2) The auditor must in preparing his report carry out such investigations as will enable him to form an opinion as to the matters specified in sub-paragraphs (g) and (h) of paragraph (1).

Duties of auditors: audit of a receipts and payments account and a statement of assets and liabilities prepared under section 42(3) of the 1993 Act

26.—(1) Where an account and statement have been prepared under section 42(3) of the 1993 Act for the relevant financial year the auditor carrying out the audit of the accounts under section 43 of that Act must make a report on those accounts to the charity trustees which—

(a) states the name and address of the auditor and the name of the charity concerned;

(b) is signed by him or, where the office of auditor is held by a body corporate or partnership, in its name by a person authorised to sign on its behalf;

(c) states that the auditor is a person falling within paragraph (a) or, as the case may be, paragraph (b) of section 43(2) of the 1993 Act;

(d) is dated and specifies the financial year in respect of which the accounts to which it relates have been prepared;

(e) specifies that it is a report in respect of an audit carried out under section 43 of the 1993 Act and in accordance with regulations made under section 44 of that Act;

(f) states whether in the auditor's opinion—

(i) the account and statement properly present—

(aa) the receipts and payments of the charity for the relevant financial year; and

(bb) its assets and liabilities as at the end of that year;

(ii) the account and statement adequately distinguish any material special trust or other restricted fund of the charity;

(g) where the auditor has formed the opinion that—

(i) accounting records have not been kept in respect of the charity in accordance with section 41 of the 1993 Act;

(ii) the account and statement do not accord with those records; or

(iii) any information or explanation to which he is entitled under regulation 33 has not been afforded to him,

contains a statement of that opinion and of the grounds for forming it.

(2) The auditor must in preparing his report carry out such investigations as will enable him to form an opinion as to the matters specified in sub-paragraphs (f) and (g) of paragraph (1).

Appendix 1 – The Charities (Accounts and Reports) Regulations 2008

Duties of auditors of the accounts of English National Health Service Charities

27.—(1) The duties of an auditor carrying out an audit of the accounts of an English National Health Service Charity under section 43A of the 1993 Act are specified in this regulation.

(2) Where—
   (a) the accounts of the charity in respect of the relevant financial year are required to be audited by section 43A(2) of the 1993 Act; or
   (b) an auditor is appointed by the Audit Commission under section 43A(3)(a) of the 1993 Act to audit the accounts of the charity and the charity has prepared a statement of accounts under section 42(1) of that Act for the relevant financial year,

regulation 24 applies to the auditor with the modifications specified in paragraph (3).

(3) The specified modifications to regulation 24 are—
   (a) for paragraph (1)(c) there is substituted—
      "(c) states that the auditor is a person appointed under section 43A(2) or, as the case may be, section 43(3)(a);";
   (b) in paragraph (1)(d) for "section 43" there is substituted "section 43A".

(4) Where—
   (a) the charity has prepared an account and statement have been prepared under section 42(3) in respect of the relevant financial year; and
   (b) an auditor has been appointed by the Audit Commission under section 43A(3)(a) of the 1993 Act to audit those accounts,

regulation 26 applies to the auditor with the modifications specified in paragraph (5).

(5) The specified modifications to regulation 26 are—
   (a) for paragraph (1)(c) there is substituted—
      "(c) states that the auditor is a person appointed under section 43A(3)(a);";

(6) in paragraph (1)(d) for "section 43" there is substituted "section 43A".

Duties of auditors of accounts of Welsh National Health Service Charities

28.—(1) The duties of an auditor carrying out an audit of the accounts of a Welsh National Health Service Charity under section 43B are specified in this regulation.

(2) Where—
   (a) the accounts of the charity in respect of the relevant financial year are required to be audited under section 43B(2) of the 1993 Act; or
   (b) the Auditor General for Wales elects under section 43B(3) of the 1993 Act that the accounts of the charity be audited and the charity has prepared a statement of accounts under section 42(1) of that Act for the relevant financial year,

regulation 24 applies to the Auditor General for Wales with the modifications specified in paragraph (3).

(3) The specified modifications to regulation 24 are—
   (a) the requirement in paragraph (1)(a) to provide the name and address of the auditor is omitted;
   (b) paragraph (1)(c) is omitted;
   (c) in paragraph (1)(e) for "section 43" there is substituted "section 43B".

(4) Where—
   (a) the charity has prepared an account and statement have been prepared under section 42(3) of the 1993 Act in respect of the relevant financial year; and
   (b) the Auditor General for Wales elects under section 43B(3) of the 1993 Act that the accounts of the charity be audited,

Appendix 1 – The Charities (Accounts and Reports) Regulations 2008

regulation 26 applies to the Auditor General for Wales with the modifications specified in paragraph (5).

(5) The specified modifications to regulation 26 are—

(a) the requirement in paragraph (1)(a) to provide the name and address of the auditor is omitted;

(b) paragraph (1)(c) is omitted;

(c) in paragraph (1)(e) for "section 43" there is substituted "section 43B".

CHAPTER 3
AUDIT OF GROUP ACCOUNTS

Audit of accounts of larger groups

29. The sum prescribed as the relevant income threshold for the purpose of paragraph 6(1)(a) of Schedule 5A to the 1993 Act is £500,000.

Duties of auditors carrying out an audit of group accounts under paragraph 6 of Schedule 5A to the Charities Act 1993

30.—(1) Where group accounts prepared under paragraph 3(2) of Schedule 5A to the 1993 Act are required to be audited under paragraph 6 of that Schedule, the auditor must make a report on those accounts to the charity trustees of the parent charity which—

(a) states the name and address of the auditor and the name of the parent charity concerned;

(b) is signed by him or, where the office of auditor is held by a body corporate or partnership, in its name by a person authorised to sign on its behalf;

(c) states that the auditor is—

(i) if section 43A of the 1993 Act applies in relation to the relevant financial year, a person appointed by the Audit Commission;

(ii) if section 43B of that Act applies in relation to the relevant financial year, is the Auditor General for Wales;

(iii) in any other case, is a person falling within paragraph (a) or, as the case may be, paragraph (b) of section 43(2) of that Act;

(d) is dated and specifies the financial year in respect of which the accounts to which it relates have been prepared;

(e) where the parent charity is a company, confirms that the charity trustees were not required by section 227 of the 1985 Act to prepare group accounts for that year;

(f) specifies that it is a report in respect of an audit carried out under paragraph 6 of Schedule 5A to the 1993 Act and in accordance with regulations made under section 44 of that Act (as modified by paragraph 8 of Schedule 5A to that Act);

(g) states whether in the auditor's opinion the group accounts—

(i) in the case of a parent charity to which regulation 13 applies, comply with the requirements of regulation 13 and in particular whether—

(aa) the consolidated statement of total return gives a true and fair view of the total return of the parent charity and its subsidiary undertakings during the relevant financial year;

(bb) the consolidated statement of changes in net assets gives a true and fair view of the changes in the net assets of the parent charity and its subsidiary undertakings during the relevant financial year;

Appendix 1 – The Charities (Accounts and Reports) Regulations 2008

      (cc) the consolidated balance sheet gives a true and fair view of the state of affairs of the parent charity and its subsidiary undertakings at the end of the relevant financial year;

  (ii) in the case of a parent charity to which regulation 14 applies, comply with the requirements of regulation 14 and in particular whether—

      (aa) the consolidated balance sheet gives a true and fair view of the state of affairs of the parent charity and its subsidiary undertakings at the end of the relevant financial year; and

      (bb) the consolidated income and expenditure account gives a true and fair view of the income and expenditure of the parent charity and its subsidiary undertakings as a whole in the relevant financial year;

  (iii) in the case of a parent charity to which regulation 15 applies, comply with the requirements of regulation 15 and in particular whether—

      (aa) the consolidated balance sheet gives a true and fair view of the state of affairs of the parent charity and its subsidiary undertakings as at the end of relevant financial year;

      (bb) the consolidated statement of financial activities gives a true and fair view of the total incoming resources of the parent charity and its subsidiary undertakings and the movements in the total resources of the group in the relevant financial year;

(h) where the auditor has formed the opinion that—

  (i) any information contained in the group accounts is inconsistent in any material respect with any report of the charity trustees prepared—

      (aa) under section 45 of the 1993 Act in respect of the relevant financial year; or

      (bb) where the parent charity is a company, with the report prepared in respect of that financial year under section 234 of the 1985 Act;

  (ii) any information or explanation to which he is entitled under regulation 33 has not been afforded to him;

contains a statement of that opinion and of the grounds for forming it.

(2) The auditor must, in preparing his report carry out such investigations as will enable him to form an opinion as to the matters specified in sub-paragraphs (g) and (h) of paragraph (1).

CHAPTER 4

INDEPENDENT EXAMINATION OF INDIVIDUAL CHARITY ACCOUNTS

Independent examination of individual charity accounts

31. An independent examiner who has carried out an examination of the accounts of a charity under section 43 of the 1993 Act must make a report to the charity trustees which—

(a) states his name and address and the name of the charity concerned;

(b) is signed by him;

(c) is dated and specifies—

  (i) in all cases, the financial year in respect of which the accounts to which it relates have been prepared;

  (ii) where the charity whose accounts are being examined is a company, confirms that the accounts are not required to be audited under Part 7 of the 1985 Act;

(d) if the gross income of the charity in that year exceeds the sum specified in section 43(3A) of the 1993 Act, specifies the basis on which he qualifies to act as independent examiner in accordance with that section;

(e) states any, or any other, relevant professional qualifications or professional body of which he is a member;

Appendix 1 – The Charities (Accounts and Reports) Regulations 2008

(f) where the accounts are being examined in the circumstances specified in regulation 34(3)(b), states the date when the Commission dispensed with the requirements of section 43(2) of the 1993 Act;

(g) specifies that it is a report in respect of an examination carried out under section 43 of the 1993 Act and in accordance with any directions given by the Commission under subsection (7)(b) of that section which are applicable;

(h) states whether or not any matter has come to the examiner's attention in connection with the examination which gives him reasonable cause to believe that in any material respect—

    (i) accounting records have not been kept in respect of the charity in accordance with—

        (aa) where that charity is a company, section 221 of the 1985 Act;

        (bb) in any other case, section 41 of the 1993 Act;

    (ii) the accounts do not accord with those records;

    (iii) in the case of an examination of a statement of accounts which has been prepared under 42(1) of the 1993 Act, the statement of accounts does not comply with any of the requirements of regulations 6, 7 or 8 as relevant other than any requirement to give a true and fair view;

    (iv) in the case of the examination of the accounts prepared under Part 7 of the 1985 Act, the charity's accounts—

        (aa) do not comply with the requirements of section 226A of the 1985 Act other than any requirement to give a true and fair view;

        (bb) in any case where those accounts state they have been prepared in accordance with the SORP, have not in fact been prepared in accordance with the methods and principles set out in the SORP;

(i) states whether or not any matter has come to the examiner's attention in connection with the examination to which, in his opinion, attention should be drawn in the report in order to enable a proper understanding of the accounts to be reached;

(j) contains a statement as to any of the following matters that has become apparent to the examiner during the course of the examination, namely, that—

    (i) there has been any material expenditure or action which appears not to be in accordance with the trusts of the charity;

    (ii) any information or explanation to which he is entitled under regulation 32 has not been afforded to him;

    (iii) in the case of an examination of a statement of accounts which has been prepared under section 42(1) of the 1993 Act, any information contained in the statement of accounts is inconsistent in any material respect with any report of the charity trustees prepared under section 45 of the 1993 Act in respect of the financial year in question;

    (iv) in the case of an examination of accounts prepared under Part 7 of the 1985 Act, any information contained in the accounts is inconsistent in any material respect with any report of the charity trustees prepared under section 45 of the 1993 Act or the report prepared under section 234 of the 1985 Act in respect of the financial year in question.

CHAPTER 5

EXAMINATION OF THE ACCOUNTS OF ENGLISH AND WELSH NATIONAL HEALTH SERVICE CHARITIES

Examination of the accounts of English and Welsh National Health Service Charities

32. Where a person has carried out an examination of the accounts of an English National Health Service charity under section 43A of the 1993 Act, or the Auditor General for Wales has

Appendix 1 – The Charities (Accounts and Reports) Regulations 2008

carried out an examination of the accounts of a Welsh National Health Service charity under section 43B of that Act, that person or, as the case may be, the Auditor General for Wales must make a report to the charity trustees which—

  (a) states the name of the charity concerned, and, in the case of an examination under section 43A, the name and address of the examiner;
  (b) is signed by him;
  (c) is dated and specifies the financial year in respect of which the accounts to which it relates have been prepared;
  (d) in the case of an examination under section 43A, states any relevant professional qualifications or professional body of which he is a member;
  (e) specifies that it is a report in respect of an examination carried out under section 43A, or, as the case may be, section 43B, of the 1993 Act and, in the case of an examination under section 43A, in accordance with any directions given by the Commission under subsection (5) of that section which are applicable;
  (f) states whether or not any matter has come to the examiner's attention in connection with the examination which gives him reasonable cause to believe that in any material respect—
    (i) accounting records have not been kept in respect of the charity in accordance with section 41 of the 1993 Act;
    (ii) the accounts do not accord with those records;
    (iii) in the case of an examination of a statement of accounts which has been prepared under 42(1) of the 1993 Act, the statement of accounts does not comply with any of the requirements of regulation 6, 7 or 8, as relevant, other than any requirement to give a true and fair view;
  (g) states whether or not any matter has come to the examiner's or, as the case may be, the Auditor General for Wales', attention in connection with the examination to which, in his opinion, attention should be drawn in the report in order to enable a proper understanding of the accounts to be reached;
  (h) contains a statement as to any of the following matters that has become apparent to the examiner or, as the case may be, the Auditor General for Wales, during the course of the examination, namely, that—
    (i) there has been any material expenditure or action which appears not to be in accordance with the trusts of the charity, or
    (ii) any information or explanation to which he is entitled under regulation 33 has not been afforded to him, or
    (iii) in the case of an examination of accounts a statement of which has been prepared under section 42(1) of the 1993 Act, any information contained in the statement of accounts is inconsistent in any material respect with any report of the charity trustees prepared under section 45 of the 1993 Act in respect of the financial year in question.

CHAPTER 6
MISCELLANEOUS

Audit and independent examination: supplementary provisions

33.—(1) Any person carrying out an audit or examination of the accounts of a charity under sections 43, 43A or 43B of or paragraph 6 of Schedule 5A to the 1993 Act has a right of access to any books, documents and other records (however kept) which relate to the charity concerned and which the person concerned considers it necessary to inspect for the purpose of carrying out the audit or examination.

Appendix 1 – The Charities (Accounts and Reports) Regulations 2008

(2) Such a person is entitled to require, in the case of the charity concerned, such information and explanations from past or present charity trustees of, or trustees for, the charity, or from past or present officers or employees of the charity, as he considers it necessary to obtain for the purposes of carrying out the audit or examination.

(3) An auditor carrying out an audit of the group accounts of a parent charity under paragraph 6 of Schedule 5A to the 1993 Act also has—

    (a) a right of access to any books, documents and other records (however kept) which relate to any of the subsidiary undertakings included in group accounts and which the auditor considers it necessary to inspect for the purpose of carrying out the audit;

    (b) the right to require, in the case of any such subsidiary undertaking, such information and explanations from—

        (i) in the case of a subsidiary undertaking which is a charity, past or present charity trustees of, or trustees for, that charity;

        (ii) in the case of any subsidiary undertaking which is not a charity from the subsidiary undertaking itself and from past or present officers or employees of that undertaking;

    as he considers it necessary to obtain for the purposes of carrying out the audit;

    (c) the right to require the charity trustees of the parent charity to take all such steps as are reasonably open to them to obtain from any such subsidiary undertaking such information and explanations as he may reasonably require for the purposes of carrying out the audit.

(4) For the purposes of this regulation, "officer" includes any auditor or other person appointed to scrutinise the accounts of any such undertaking.

Dispensations from audit or examination requirements

34.—(1) The Commission may—

    (a) in the circumstances specified in paragraph (2), dispense with the requirements of section 43(2) or (3) of the 1993 Act in the case of a particular charity;

    (b) in the circumstances specified in paragraph (3) dispense with those requirements in respect of a particular financial year of a charity;

    (c) in the circumstances specified in paragraph (4) dispense with the requirements in paragraph 6(4)(a) of Schedule 5A to the 1993 Act in the case of a particular charity;

    (d) in the circumstances specified in paragraph (5) dispense with those requirements in respect of a particular financial year of a charity.

(2) The circumstances specified for the purposes of paragraph (1)(a) are where the Commission is satisfied that the accounts of the charity concerned—

    (a) are required to be audited in accordance with any statutory provision contained in or having effect under an Act of Parliament which imposes requirements which, in the opinion of the Commission, are sufficiently similar to the requirements of section 43(2) for those requirements to be dispensed with;

    (b) have been audited by the Comptroller and Auditor General or the Auditor General for Wales.

(3) The circumstances specified for the purposes of paragraph (1)(b) are where the Commission—

    (a) is satisfied that the accounts of the charity concerned for the financial year in question have been, or will be, audited or examined in accordance with requirements or arrangements which, in the opinion of the Commission, are sufficiently similar to the relevant requirements of section 43 of the 1993 Act applicable to that financial year of that charity for those requirements to be dispensed with;

    (b) considers that, although the financial year in question of the charity concerned is one to which section 43(2) of the 1993 Act applies, there are exceptional circumstances which justify the examination of the accounts by an independent examiner instead of their audit in accordance with that subsection.

(4) The circumstances specified for the purposes of paragraph (1)(c) are where the Commission is satisfied that the group accounts of the parent charity concerned—
  (a) are required to be audited in accordance with any statutory provision contained in or having effect under an Act of Parliament which imposes requirements which, in the opinion of the Commission, are sufficiently similar to the requirements of paragraph 6(4)(a) of Schedule 5A for those requirements to be dispensed with;
  (b) have been audited by the Comptroller and Auditor General or the Auditor General for Wales.

(5) The circumstances specified for the purpose of paragraph (1)(d) are where the Commission is satisfied that the group accounts of the parent charity concerned for the financial year in question have been, or will be, audited in accordance with requirements or arrangements which, in the opinion of the Commission, are sufficiently similar to the requirements of paragraph 6(4)(a) of Schedule 5A for those requirements to be dispensed with.

(6) The Commission must make it a condition of a dispensation granted under this regulation that the charity trustees send to the Commission any report made to the trustees with respect to the accounts of that charity for the relevant financial year of which it requests a copy.

(7) The Commission must make it a condition of a dispensation granted under paragraph (3)(b) that the charity trustees comply with the requirements of section 43(3) of the 1993 Act as if they were able to make and had in fact made an election under that section that the accounts of the charity for the relevant financial year be examined by an independent examiner.

(8) The Commission may revoke a dispensation granted under this regulation if the charity trustees fail to comply with a condition imposed under paragraph (6) or (7).

Ceasing to hold office

35.—(1) Where an auditor appointed by charity trustees or under section 43A(2) or (3)(a) ceases for any reason to hold office he must send—
  (a) to the charity trustees—
    (i) a statement of any circumstances connected with his ceasing to hold office which he considers should be brought to their attention; or
    (ii) if he considers that there are no such circumstances, a statement that there are none;
  (b) a copy of any statement sent to the charity trustees under sub-paragraph (a)(i) to the Commission.

Auditors appointed by the Commission

36.—(1) Subject to paragraph (2), in the case of an auditor appointed by the Commission, any report required by any of the provisions of this Part to be made to the charity trustees must instead be made to the Commission.

(2) This regulation does not apply in the case of an English or Welsh National Health Service Charity.

PART 5
ANNUAL REPORTS

General

37.—(1) The report and information to be contained in the annual report prepared by the charity trustee's of a charity are prescribed—

Appendix 1 – The Charities (Accounts and Reports) Regulations 2008

- (a) in the case of a non-parent investment fund, in regulation 38;
- (b) in the case of a parent investment fund, in regulation 39.
- (c) in the case of a non-parent charity, in regulation 40;
- (d) in the case of a qualifying parent charity, in regulation 41.

(2) In this Part—
- (a) "non-parent charity" means a charity—
    - (i) which is not an investment fund; and
    - (ii) is—
        - (aa) not a parent charity; or
        - (bb) a parent charity but the charity trustees are not required to prepare group accounts in respect of the financial year to which the annual report relates;
- (b) "non-parent investment fund" means an investment fund which—
    - (i) is not a parent charity; or
    - (ii) is a parent charity but the charity trustees are not required to prepare group accounts in respect of the financial year to which the annual report relates;
- (c) "parent investment fund" means an investment fund—
    - (i) which is a parent charity; and
    - (ii) the charity trustees of which are required to prepare group accounts in respect of the financial year to which the annual report relates;
- (d) "qualifying parent charity" means a charity—
    - (i) which is not an investment fund; and
    - (ii) the charity trustees of which are required to prepare group accounts in respect of the financial year to which the annual report relates.

Annual Reports: non-parent investment fund

38.—(1) This regulation applies to the annual report prepared under section 45(1) of the 1993 Act by the charity trustees of a non-parent investment fund.

(2) The report on the activities of the investment fund during the year which is required to be contained in the annual report must—
- (a) specify the financial year to which it relates;
- (b) be a review of the significant activities of the investment fund during that year, including details of—
    - (i) the aims and objectives which have been set for the investment fund during the year,
    - (ii) the policies adopted for achieving those aims and objectives; and
    - (iii) the achievements of the investment fund, measured by reference to the aims and objectives which have been set;
- (c) provide any other significant information which the charity trustees consider would assist charities participating in the investment fund to make an informed judgement on the suitability to the charity of the investment fund as an investment for the charity;
- (d) specify any material events affecting the investment fund which have occurred since the end of the year;
- (e) contain a statement as to the steps (if any) taken to consider whether any person to whom functions in respect of the management of the investment fund has been delegated has complied with the terms of the delegation; and
- (f) be signed—
    - (i) if the scheme or schemes regulating the investment fund allocates responsibility for preparing the report to a particular person, by that person;

Appendix 1 – The Charities (Accounts and Reports) Regulations 2008

(ii) in any other case, by at least one of the charity trustees of the investment fund, each of whom has been authorised to do so.

(3) The information relating to an investment fund and to its trustees and officers which is required to be contained in the annual report is—

(a) the name of the investment fund as it appears in the register of charities and any other name by which it makes itself known;

(b) the number assigned to the investment fund in the register;

(c) the principal address of the investment fund;

(d) particulars, including the date, of any scheme or schemes containing provisions which regulate the purposes and administration of the investment fund;

(e) the name of any person or body of persons entitled under any such scheme or schemes to appoint any charity trustee of the investment fund, and a description of the method provided by any such scheme or schemes for such appointment;

(f) a description of the objects of the investment fund;

(g) a description of the organisational structure of the investment fund;

(h) the name of any charity trustee of the investment fund, on the date of the signature of the report, where paragraph (2)(f)(i) applies, and otherwise on the date when the authority referred to in paragraph (2)(f)(ii) is given, and, where any such person is a body corporate, the name of any person who is a director of the body corporate on that date;

(i) the professional qualifications of any individual person referred to in sub-paragraphs (e) or (h);

(j) the name of any other person who has, at any time during the financial year in question, been a charity trustee of the investment fund;

(k) the name of any person who is, in relation to the investment fund, a trustee for the charity on the date referred to in sub-paragraph (h);

(l) the name of any other person who has, at any time during the financial year in question, been, in relation to the investment fund, a trustee for the charity;

(m) a description of any functions relating to the management of the investment fund which have been delegated (including the maintenance of the register of charities participating in the investment fund), and of the procedures adopted to ensure that those functions are discharged consistently with the scheme or schemes by which the investment fund is regulated, and with the investment policies adopted for the investment fund;

(n) the name and address of any person to whom any such functions in respect of the management of the investment fund have been delegated or who have been instructed to provide advice on investment matters; and

(o) a statement as to which, if any, of the persons whose names are given in accordance with the provisions of sub-paragraphs (h), (j), (k), (l) or (n), are authorised persons.

Annual Reports: parent investment funds

39.—(1) This regulation applies to an annual report prepared in accordance with section 45(1) of the 1993 Act by the charity trustees of a parent investment fund.

(2) The report on the activities of such an investment fund and of its subsidiary undertakings, during the year which is required to be contained in the annual report prepared under section 45 of the 1993 Act in respect of each financial year of the investment fund must—

(a) specify the financial year to which it relates;

(b) be a review of the significant activities of the investment fund and of its subsidiary undertakings during that year, including details of—

(i) the aims and objectives which have been set for the investment fund and its subsidiary undertakings during the year and identifying, in the case of subsidiary

Appendix 1 – The Charities (Accounts and Reports) Regulations 2008

        undertakings, how these aims and objectives support the investment activities of the investment fund;

        (ii) the policies adopted for achieving those aims and objectives; and

        (iii) the achievements of the investment fund and of its subsidiary undertakings, measured by reference to the aims and objectives which have been set;

(c) where the total of capital and reserves in any of the investment fund's subsidiary undertakings was materially in deficit at the beginning of the financial year, contain particulars of the steps taken by the relevant undertaking or undertakings to eliminate that deficit;

(d) provide any other significant information which the charity trustees consider would assist charities participating in the investment fund to make an informed judgement on the suitability to the charity of the investment fund as an investment for the charity;

(e) specify any material events affecting the investment fund which have occurred since the end of the relevant financial year;

(f) contain a statement as to the steps (if any) taken to consider whether any person to whom functions in respect of the management of the investment fund has been delegated has complied with the terms of the delegation; and

(g) be signed—

    (i) if the scheme or schemes regulating the investment fund allocates responsibility for preparing the report to a particular person, by that person;

    (ii) in any other case, by at least one of the charity trustees of the investment fund, each of whom has been authorised to do so.

(3) The information relating to a parent investment fund, to its trustees and officers, and to its subsidiary undertakings, which is required to be contained in the annual report is—

(a) the name of the investment fund as it appears in the register of charities and any other name by which it makes itself known;

(b) the number assigned to the investment fund in the register;

(c) the principal address of the investment fund;

(d) particulars, including the date, of any scheme or schemes containing provisions which regulate the purposes and administration of the investment fund;

(e) the name of any person or body of persons entitled under any such scheme or schemes to appoint any charity trustee of the investment fund, and a description of the method provided by any such scheme or schemes for such appointment;

(f) a description of the objects of the investment fund;

(g) a description of the organisational structure of the investment fund, and of its subsidiary undertakings;

(h) the name of any charity trustee of the investment fund, on the date of the signature of the report, where paragraph (2)(g)(i) applies, and otherwise on the date when the authority referred to in paragraph (2)(g)(ii) is given, and, where any such person is a body corporate, the name of any person who is a director of the body corporate on that date;

(i) the professional qualifications of any individual person referred to in sub-paragraphs (e) or (h);

(j) the name of any other person who has, at any time during the financial year in question, been a charity trustee of the investment fund;

(k) the name of any person who is, in relation to the investment fund, a trustee for the charity on the date referred to in sub-paragraph (h);

(l) the name of any other person who has, at any time during the financial year in question, been, in relation to the investment fund, a trustee for the charity;

(m) a description of any functions relating to the management of the investment fund which have been delegated (including the maintenance of the register of charities participating

Appendix 1 – The Charities (Accounts and Reports) Regulations 2008

in the investment fund), and of the procedures adopted to ensure that those functions are discharged consistently with the scheme or schemes by which the investment fund is regulated, and with the investment policies adopted for the investment fund;

(n) the name and address of any person to whom any such functions in respect of the management of the investment fund have been delegated or who have been instructed to provide advice on investment matters; and

(o) a statement as to which, if any, of the persons whose names are given in accordance with the provisions of sub-paragraphs (h), (j), (k), (l) or (n), are authorised persons.

(4) In this regulation "subsidiary undertaking" does not include a subsidiary undertaking which is excluded from group accounts in accordance with regulation 19.

Annual reports: non-parent charity

40.—(1) This regulation applies to an annual report prepared in accordance with section 45(1) of the 1993 Act by the charity trustees of a non-parent charity.

(2) The report on the activities of a charity during the year which is required to be contained in the annual report prepared under section 45 of the 1993 Act—

(a) must specify the financial year to which it relates;

(b) must—

  (i) in the case of a charity which is not an auditable charity, be a brief summary setting out—

  (aa) the main activities undertaken by the charity to further its charitable purposes for the public benefit; and

  (bb) the main achievements of the charity during the year.

  (ii) in the case of a charity which is an auditable charity, be a review of the significant activities undertaken by the charity during the relevant financial year to further its charitable purposes for the public benefit or to generate resources to be used to further its purposes including—

  (aa) details of the aims and objectives which the charity trustees have set for the charity in that year, details of the strategies adopted and of significant activities undertaken, in order to achieve those aims and objectives;

  (bb) details of the achievements of the charity during the year, measured by reference to the aims and objectives which have been set;

  (cc) details of any significant contribution of volunteers to these activities;

  (dd) details of the principal sources of income of the charity; and

  (ee) a statement as to whether the charity trustees have given consideration to the major risks to which the charity is exposed and satisfied themselves that systems or procedures are established in order to manage those risks;

(c) must—

  (i) where—

  (aa) any fund of the charity was in deficit at the beginning of the relevant financial; and

  (bb) the charity is one in respect of which a statement of accounts has been prepared under section 42(1) of the 1993 Act for that financial year,

  contain particulars of the steps taken by the charity trustees to eliminate that deficit;

  (ii) contain a statement by the charity trustees as to whether they have complied with the duty in section 4 of the 2006 Act to have due regard to guidance published by the Commission; and

  (iii) be dated and be signed by one or more of the charity trustees, each of whom has been authorised to do so.

Appendix 1 – The Charities (Accounts and Reports) Regulations 2008

(3) Subject to paragraphs (4) to (7), the other information relating to a charity and to its trustees and officers which is required to be contained in the annual report is—

    (a) the name of the charity as it appears in the register of charities and any other name by which it makes itself known;

    (b) the number assigned to it in the register and, in the case of a charitable company, the number with which it is registered as a company;

    (c) the principal address of the charity and, in the case of a charitable company, the address of its registered office;

    (d) the name of any person who is a charity trustee of the charity on the date when the authority referred to in paragraph (2)(c)(iii) above is given, and, where any charity trustee on that date is a body corporate, the name of any person who is a director of the body corporate on that date;

    (e) the name of any other person who has, at any time during the relevant financial year been a charity trustee of the charity;

    (f) the name of any person who is a trustee for the charity on the date referred to in sub-paragraph (d);

    (g) the name of any other person who has, at any time during the relevant financial year been a trustee for the charity;

    (h) particulars, including the date if known, of any deed or other document containing provisions which regulate the purposes and administration of the charity;

    (i) the name of any person or body of persons entitled by the trusts of the charity to appoint one or more new charity trustees and a description of the method provided by those trusts for such appointment;

    (j) a description of the policies and procedures (if any) which have been adopted by the charity trustees for the induction and training of charity trustees and where no such policies have been adopted a statement to that effect;

    (k) a description of the organisational structure of the charity;

    (l) a summary description of the purposes of the charity;

    (m) a description of the policies (if any) which have been adopted by the charity trustees for the selection of individuals and institutions who are to receive grants or other forms of financial support out of the assets of the charity;

    (n) a statement regarding the performance during the financial year of the investments belonging to the charity (if any);

    (o) where material investments are owned by a charity, a description of the policies (if any) which have been adopted by the charity trustees for the selection, retention and realisation of investments for the charity including the extent (if any) to which social, environmental or ethical considerations are taken into account;

    (p) a description of the policies (if any) which have been adopted by the charity trustees for the purpose of determining the level of reserves which it is appropriate for the charity to maintain in order to meet effectively the needs designated by its trusts, together with details of the amount and purpose of any material commitments and planned expenditure not provided for in the balance sheet which have been deducted from the assets in the unrestricted fund of the charity in calculating the amount of reserves, and where no such policies have been adopted, a statement to that effect;

    (q) a description of the aims and objectives which the charity trustees have set for the charity in the future and of the activities contemplated in furtherance of those aims and objectives;

    (r) a description of any assets held by the charity or by any charity trustee of, or trustee for, the charity, on behalf of another charity, and particulars of any special arrangements made with respect to the safe custody of such assets and their segregation from assets of the charity not so held and a description of the objects of the charity on whose behalf the assets are held.

(4) The Commission may, where it is satisfied that, in the case of a particular charity or class of charities, or in the case of a particular financial year of a charity or class of charities—

  (a) the disclosure of the name of any person whose name is required by any of sub-paragraphs (d), (e), (f), (g) and (i) of paragraph (3) to be contained in the annual report of a charity could lead to that person being placed in any personal danger, dispense with the requirement in any of those sub-paragraphs so far as it applies to the name of such person;

  (b) the disclosure of the principal address of the charity in accordance with paragraph (3)(c) above could lead to any such person being placed in any personal danger, dispense with that requirement.

(5) In the case of a charity having more than 50 charity trustees on the date referred to in paragraph (3)(d)—

  (a) paragraph (3)(d) has effect as if for "name of any person who is a charity trustee of the charity" there were substituted "names of not less than 50 of the charity trustees of the charity, including any charity trustee who is also an officer of the charity"; and

  (b) paragraph (3)(e) has effect as if, at the end of that paragraph, there were inserted "other than the name of any charity trustee whose name has been excluded from the report in pursuance of sub-paragraph (d)".

(6) In the case of a report prepared under section 46(5) of the 1993 Act (excepted charities which are not registered), paragraph (4) has effect as if—

  (a) in sub-paragraph (a) from "as it appears in the register of charities" to the end; and

  (b) in sub-paragraph (b) "the number assigned to it in the register and,",

were omitted.

(7) Sub-paragraphs (j), (k), (m), (n), (o) and (q) of paragraph (3) do not apply to a charity which is not an auditable charity.

Annual Reports: qualifying parent charities

41.—(1) This regulation applies to an annual report prepared in accordance with section 45(1) of the 1993 Act by the charity trustees of a qualifying parent charity.

(2) The report on the activities of such a parent charity and its subsidiary undertakings, during the year, which is required to be contained in the annual report prepared under section 45 of the 1993 Act in respect of each financial year of the charity must—

  (a) specify the financial year to which it relates;

  (b) be a review of the significant activities undertaken by the charity during the relevant financial year to further its charitable purposes for the public benefit or to generate resources to be used to further its purposes including details of—

    (i) the aims and objectives which the charity trustees have set for the parent charity and its subsidiary undertakings in that year;

    (ii) the strategies adopted and the significant activities undertaken, in order to achieve those aims and objectives;

    (iii) the achievements of the parent charity and its subsidiary undertakings during the year, measured by reference to the aims and objectives which have been set;

    (iv) any significant contribution of volunteers to these activities; and

    (v) the principal sources of income of the parent charity and of its subsidiary undertakings;

  (c) contain a statement as to whether the charity trustees have—

Appendix 1 – The Charities (Accounts and Reports) Regulations 2008

   (i) given consideration to the major risks to which the parent charity and its subsidiary undertakings are exposed; and

   (ii) satisfied themselves that systems or procedures are established in order to manage those risks;

(d) where any fund of the parent charity was in deficit at the beginning of the financial year in question, contain particulars of the steps taken by the charity trustees to eliminate that deficit;

(e) where the total of capital and reserves in any of the parent charity's subsidiary undertakings was materially in deficit at the beginning of the financial year, contain particulars of the steps taken by the relevant undertaking or undertakings to eliminate that deficit,

(f) contain a statement by the charity trustees as to whether they have complied with the duty in section 4 of the 2006 Act to have due regard to guidance published by the Commission; and

(g) be dated and be signed by one or more of the charity trustees, each of whom has been authorised to do so.

(3) Subject to paragraphs (4) to (6), the information relating to a qualifying parent charity, to its trustees and officers, and to its subsidiary undertakings, which is required to be contained in the annual report is—

(a) the name of the parent charity as it appears in the register of charities and any other name by which it makes itself known;

(b) the number assigned to the parent charity in the register and, in the case of a charitable company, the number with which it is registered as a company;

(c) the principal address of the parent charity and, in the case of a charitable company, the address of its registered office;

(d) the name of any person who is a charity trustee of the parent charity on the date when the authority referred to in paragraph (2)(g) is given, and, where any charity trustee on that date is a body corporate, the name of any person who is a director of the body corporate on that date;

(e) the name of any other person who has, at any time during the financial year in question, been a charity trustee of the parent charity;

(f) the name of any person who is a trustee for the parent charity on the date referred to in sub-paragraph (d);

(g) the name of any other person who has, at any time during the financial year in question, been a trustee for the parent charity;

(h) particulars, including the date if known, of any deed or other document containing provisions which regulate the purposes and administration of the parent charity;

(i) the name of any person or body of persons entitled by the trusts of the parent charity to appoint one or more new charity trustees, and a description of the method provided by those trusts for such appointment;

(j) a description of the policies and procedures (if any) which have been adopted by the charity trustees of the parent charity for the induction and training of charity trustees, and where no such policies have been adopted a statement to this effect;

(k) a description of the organisational structure of the parent charity and of its subsidiary undertakings;

(l) a summary description of the purposes of the parent charity;

(m) a description of the policies (if any) which have been adopted by the charity trustees of the parent charity for the selection of individuals and institutions who are to receive grants, or other forms of financial support, out of the assets of the charity;

(n) a statement regarding the performance during the financial year of—

Appendix 1 – The Charities (Accounts and Reports) Regulations 2008

    (i) any investments belonging to the parent charity; and

    (ii) any investments belonging to the parent charity's subsidiary undertakings, where those investments are material to the group accounts;

(o) where—

    (i) investments are owned by a qualifying parent charity or any of its subsidiary undertakings; and

    (ii) those investments are material to the group accounts,

    a description of the policies (if any) which have been adopted by the charity trustees, or as the case may be the subsidiary undertaking, for the selection, retention and realisation of investments, including the extent (if any) to which social, environmental or ethical considerations are taken into account;

(p) where the charity trustees have adopted polices for the purpose of determining the level of reserves which it is appropriate to maintain in order to meet effectively the needs designated by its trusts—

    (i) a description of those policies including in particular whether account has been taken of any reserves held by its subsidiary undertakings in determining the appropriate level of reserves;

    (ii) details of the amount and purpose of any material commitments and planned expenditure not provided for in the balance sheet which have been deducted from the assets in the unrestricted fund of the charity in calculating the amount of reserves;

(q) if the charity trustees have not adopted policies falling within sub-paragraph (p), a statement that no such policies have been adopted;

(r) a description of the aims and objectives which the charity trustees have set for the parent charity in the future, and of the activities contemplated in furtherance of those aims and objectives;

(s) a description of any assets held by the parent charity or by any charity trustee of, or trustee for, the charity, on behalf of another charity, and particulars of any special arrangements made with respect to the safe custody of such assets and their segregation from assets of the charity not so held and a description of the objects of the charity on whose behalf the assets are held.

(4) The Commission may, where it is satisfied that, in the case of a particular charity or class of charities, or in the case of a particular financial year of a charity or class of charities–

(a) the disclosure of the name of any person whose name is required by any of sub-paragraphs (d), (e), (f), (g) and (i) of paragraph (3) above to be contained in the annual report of a charity could lead to that person being placed in any personal danger, dispense with the requirement in any of those sub-paragraphs so far as it applies to the name of that person; or

(b) the disclosure of the principal address of the charity in accordance with paragraph (3)(c) above could lead to any such person being placed in any personal danger, dispense with that requirement.

(5) In the case of a charity having more than 50 charity trustees on the date referred to in paragraph (3)(d)—

(a) that sub-paragraph has effect as if for the words "name of any person who is a charity trustee of the charity" there were substituted the words "names of not less than 50 of the charity trustees of the charity, including any charity trustee who is also an officer of the charity"; and

(b) paragraph (3)(e) has effect as if, at the end of the sub-paragraph, there were inserted the words "other than the name of any charity trustee whose name has been excluded from the report in pursuance of sub-paragraph (d)".

(6) In the case of a report prepared under section 46(5) of the 1993 Act (excepted charities which are not registered), paragraph (3) above shall have effect as if–

Appendix 1 – The Charities (Accounts and Reports) Regulations 2008

(a) in sub-paragraph (a) the words from "as it appears in the register of charities" to the end, and

(b) in sub-paragraph (b) the words "the number assigned to it in the register and,",

were omitted.

(7) In this regulation, "subsidiary undertaking" does not include a subsidiary undertaking which is excluded from the group accounts in accordance with regulation 19.

6th March 2008

Phil Hope
Parliamentary Secretary of State
Cabinet Office

SCHEDULE 1

Regulation 6

STATEMENTS OF ACCOUNTS: INVESTMENT FUNDS

PART 1

STATEMENT OF TOTAL RETURN

1. The statement of total return must show—

(a) the net gain or loss on investments, gross income, total expenditure and total return of the investment fund; and

(b) the total amount distributed or due, including interest paid or payable, to participating charities out of the investment fund,

during the relevant financial year.

2. Subject to paragraph 4, the information required by paragraph 1 must be analysed by reference to—

(a) net gains or losses on investments analysed as arising from—

(i) non-derivative securities;

(ii) derivative contracts;

(iii) forward currency contracts;

(b) gains or losses on other assets;

(c) gross income, divided into—

(i) dividends in respect of shares;

(ii) scrip dividends;

(iii) interest on securities;

(iv) interest on deposits at banks and building societies;

(v) underwriting commission; and

(vi) other income;

(d) expenses incurred in the administration of the investment fund, divided into—

(i) fees payable in respect of investment management services provided to the investment fund;

Appendix 1 – The Charities (Accounts and Reports) Regulations 2008

- (ii) fees payable in respect of the maintenance of the register of charities participating in the investment fund;
- (iii) fees payable in respect of any audit of the accounts of the investment fund;
- (iv) fees payable to the person carrying out such an audit in respect of other services for the investment fund provided by him;
- (v) fees payable in respect of the safe custody of the assets of the investment fund;
- (vi) fees payable in respect of other administrative services provided to the investment fund; and
- (vii) other expenditure divided into such categories as reasonably enable the user to gain an appreciation of the expenditure incurred;
- (e) interest incurred in the administration of the investment fund;
- (f) net income of the investment fund before taxation calculated as follows—

    A-B

    where

    A is the total amount entered under paragraph (c),

    B is the aggregate of the total amounts entered in that statement pursuance of paragraphs (d) and (e);
- (g) tax borne by the investment fund in respect of income, profits or gains during the relevant financial year, divided into—
    - (i) income tax or capital gains tax to which the investment fund is liable in the United Kingdom; and
    - (ii) overseas tax;
- (h) net income of the investment fund after taxation calculated as follows—

    A-B

    where

    A is the amount entered under paragraph (f),

    B is the amount entered under paragraph (g);
- (i) total return of the investment fund before distributions which is calculated by aggregating the amounts entered under paragraphs (a), (b) and (h);
- (j) the amount distributed or due in respect of income and accumulation shares, and interest paid or payable to charities who have deposited sums during the relevant financial year;
- (k) the change in value of the investment fund resulting from its activities calculated as follows—

    A-B

    where

    A is the amount entered under paragraph (i)

    B is the amount entered under paragraph (j).

3. In the case of a common investment fund established by a scheme which, in pursuance of section 22(5) of the 1960 Act or section 24(5) of the 1993 Act, includes provision for enabling sums to be deposited by or on behalf of a charity on the basis that (subject to the provisions of the scheme) the charity shall be entitled to repayment of the sums deposited and to interest thereon at a rate determined by or under the scheme, the analysis required by paragraph 2 must distinguish between—

- (a) the amount of capital and income to be shared between charities participating otherwise than by way of deposit; and

Appendix 1 – The Charities (Accounts and Reports) Regulations 2008

(b) the amount of capital and income that is required in respect of the liabilities of the investment fund for the repayment of deposits and for interest on deposits (including amounts required by way of reserve).

4. Where a sub-paragraph of paragraph 2 requires information to be divided into separate categories, the division of that information into such separate categories may, if the charity trustees so elect, be effected instead by means of a note to the accounts made in pursuance of Part 5 of this Schedule.

PART 2

STATEMENT OF CHANGE IN NET ASSETS

5. The statement of change in net assets must provide a reconciliation between—

   (a) the net assets of the investment fund at the beginning of the relevant financial year; and

   (b) the net assets of the investment fund at the end of that year.

6. The reconciliation referred to in paragraph 5 must show—

   (a) the value of the net assets at the beginning of the relevant financial year;

   (b) the change in value of the investment fund calculated in accordance with paragraph 2(k);

   (c) the value of the net assets at the end of the relevant financial year;

   (d) particulars of any other items necessary to provide the reconciliation required by paragraph 1 above; and

   (e) in the case of a common investment fund—

       (i) the amount or value of any property transferred to or withdrawn from the investment fund during the relevant financial year by participating charities; and

       (ii) the amount of any distribution of income due in respect of accumulation shares.

7. In the case of a common investment fund to which paragraph 3 applies, the analysis required by paragraph 6 must distinguish between—

   (a) the amount of capital and income to be shared between charities participating otherwise than by way of deposit; and

   (b) amount of capital and income that is required in respect of the liabilities of the investment fund for the repayment of deposits and for interest on deposits (including amounts required by way of reserve).

PART 3

BALANCE SHEET

8. The balance sheet must show the state of affairs of the investment fund as at the end of the relevant financial year by reference to the information specified—

   (a) in the case of a common investment fund to which paragraph 3 does not apply, in paragraph 9;

   (b) in the case of a common investment fund to which paragraph 3 applies, in paragraph 10;

   (c) in the case of a common deposit fund, in paragraph 11.

9. In the case of a common investment fund to which paragraph 3 does not apply, the specified information is—

   (a) tangible fixed assets for use by the investment fund;

   (b) investments;

   (c) other assets, divided into—

Appendix 1 – The Charities (Accounts and Reports) Regulations 2008

- (i) debtors;
- (ii) deposits and loans;
- (iii) cash at bank and in hand; and
- (iv) others;
- (d) total assets calculated by aggregating the amounts entered under of paragraphs (a), (b) and (c);
- (e) derivative liabilities;
- (f) other liabilities, divided into—
  - (i) creditors;
  - (ii) bank overdrafts;
  - (iii) other loans; and
  - (iv) distributions payable to participating charities;
- (g) total liabilities calculated by aggregating the amounts entered under paragraphs (e) and (f);
- (h) net assets which is calculated as follows—

  A-B

  where

  A is the amount entered under paragraph (d),

  B is the amount entered under paragraph (g).

10. In the case of a common investment fund to which paragraph 3 applies, the specified information is—

- (a) in relation to the amount of capital and income to be shared between charities participating otherwise than by way of deposit, the information specified in paragraph 9;
- (b) in relation to the amount of capital and income that is required in respect of the liabilities of the investment fund for the repayment of deposits and for interest on deposits (including amounts required by way of reserve), the information specified in paragraph 11.

11. In the case of a common deposit fund, the specified information is—

- (a) cash at bank and in hand;
- (b) debtors;
- (c) deposits and investments, divided into—
  - (i) deposits at the Bank of England;
  - (ii) deposits with a person who has permission under Part 4 of the Financial Services and Markets Act 2000 to accept deposits;
  - (iii) other bank deposits;
  - (iv) other deposits; and
  - (v) other investments;
- (d) current assets not included in paragraphs (a) to (c);
- (e) tangible fixed assets for use by the common deposit fund;
- (f) gross assets which is calculated by aggregating the amounts entered under paragraphs (a) to (e);
- (g) sums deposited by participating charities;
- (h) other liabilities, divided into—
  - (i) creditors;
  - (ii) bank overdrafts;

Appendix 1 – The Charities (Accounts and Reports) Regulations 2008

      (iii) other loans; and

      (iv) interest accrued or payable to participating charities;

  (i) sums held as an income reserve on trust for existing depositors; and

  (j) total liabilities which is calculated by aggregating the amounts entered under paragraphs (g), (h) and (i).

12. Despite the requirement in paragraph 11(c) to divide into separate categories the information to be provided by dividing the information into separate categories, the division of that information into those categories may, if the charity trustees so elect, be effected instead by means of a note to the accounts made in pursuance of Part 5 of this Schedule.

PART 4

METHODS AND PRINCIPLES

13.—(1) The statement of total return must give a true and fair view of the incoming resources and application of the resources of the investment fund in the relevant financial year.

(2) The balance sheet must give a true and fair view of the state of affairs of the investment fund at the end of the relevant financial year.

(3) The statement of changes in net assets must give a true and fair view of the movements in the net assets of the investment fund between their position at the beginning of the relevant financial year and their position at the end of that year.

(4) Where compliance with Part 1, 2, 3 or 5 of this Schedule would not be sufficient to give a true and fair view, the necessary additional information shall be given in the accounts or a note to them.

(5) If in special circumstances compliance with any of the provisions of Parts 1, 2, 3 or 5 of this Schedule is inconsistent with the requirement to give a true and fair view—

  (a) the charity trustees must depart from that provision to the extent necessary to give a true and fair view; and

  (b) particulars of any such departure, the reasons for it and its effect must be given in a note to the accounts.

14.—(1) Subject to paragraphs (2) and (3), in respect of every amount required—

  (a) by paragraph 2 to be shown in the statement of total return,

  (b) by paragraph 6 to be shown in the statement of changes in net assets;

  (c) by paragraph 9, 10 or 11 to be shown in the balance sheet,

the corresponding amount for the financial year immediately preceding the relevant financial year must also be shown.

(2) Where that corresponding amount is not comparable with the amount to be shown for the item in question in respect of the relevant financial year—

  (a) the former amount must be adjusted; and

  (b) particulars of any material adjustment under this sub-paragraph must be disclosed in a note to the accounts.

(3) Where the effect of paragraph 13 is—

  (a) that in the relevant financial year there nothing required to be shown by one or more of the provisions specified in sub-paragraph (1) above in respect of a particular item; but

  (b) an amount was required to be shown by that provision for that item in the statement of accounts prepared for the financial year immediately preceding the relevant financial year,

sub-paragraph (1) has effect as if such an amount were required to be shown in the relevant financial year and that amount were nil.

Appendix 1 – The Charities (Accounts and Reports) Regulations 2008

15. The values at which assets and liabilities of an investment fund are recorded in the balance sheet, and the recognition bases for gains and losses, must be determined in accordance with the methods and principles set out in the IMA SORP.

PART 5

NOTES TO THE ACCOUNTS

16.—(1) The information to be provided by way of notes to the accounts, insofar as not provided in the statement of accounts, is—

    (a) a description of the accounting policies adopted for the investment fund and in particular—

        (i) the basis of valuation of investments;

        (ii) the recognition of dividend income or interest; and

        (iii) the conversion of any amounts expressed in currency other than pounds sterling;

    (b) a description of the accounting assumptions made by the investment fund, including—

        (i) any material change in these assumptions;

        (ii) the reason for such change; and

        (iii) its effect (if material) on the accounts;

    (c) where the charity trustees have during the relevant financial year—

        (i) entered into any transaction, agreement or arrangement made for the purpose of minimising the risk of loss to the investment fund in consequence of fluctuations in interest rates or in the market value of securities or in the rates of foreign exchange; or

        (ii) entered into any other transaction in financial futures or options relating to shares, securities, foreign currency or into any other financial instrument the value of which is dependent on or derived from the price movements in one or more underlying assets,

    the nature of, and reason for, entering into that transaction, agreement or arrangement and the total value of, and the maximum extent of financial exposure as at the date of the balance sheet resulting from, that transaction, agreement or arrangement;

    (d) a statement as to whether any remuneration or other benefits (together with the amount of such remuneration or, as the case may be, the monetary value of such benefits and the name of the person to whom the remuneration or benefit has been paid or is payable) has been paid or is payable to any person—

        (i) who is a charity trustee of the investment fund;

        (ii) to whom functions in relation to management of the investment fund have been delegated ("manager");

        (iii) connected with such a charity trustee or manager,

    directly or indirectly from the property of the investment fund or from the property of any subsidiary undertaking of the investment fund;

    (e) particulars of any transaction undertaken in the name of or on behalf of the investment fund in which any person referred to in sub-paragraph (d) has a material interest;

    (f) an analysis of the amount and date of any distribution in respect of income and accumulation shares or payment of interest to participating charities;

    (g) a note of any adjustments made in the statement of total return to reflect the amount of income included in the creation or cancellation price of a unit or share in the investment fund;

    (h) the name of any subsidiary undertaking of the investment fund, together with a description of the nature of the investment fund's relationship with that subsidiary

Appendix 1 – The Charities (Accounts and Reports) Regulations 2008

undertaking and of its activities, and, where material, a statement of the turnover and net profit or loss of the subsidiary undertaking for the corresponding financial year and any qualification expressed in an auditor's report on the accounts of the subsidiary undertaking for that financial year;

(i) particulars of any loan or guarantee secured against any of the assets of the investment fund;

(j) an explanation of any amount entered in pursuance of paragraph 2(g)(i) (United Kingdom tax);

(k) an analysis of any entry in the balance sheet relating to—

  (i) tangible fixed assets for use by the investment fund, according to the following categories–

   (aa) freehold interests in land and buildings;

   (bb) any other interest in land and buildings;

   (cc) payments on account and assets in course of construction; and

   (dd) plant, machinery, fixtures, fittings and equipment;

  (ii) debtors, according to the following categories—

   (aa) amounts receivable in respect of securities sold;

   (bb) accrued income;

   (cc) other debtors; and

   (dd) in the case of a common investment fund, amounts receivable in respect of property transferred to the investment fund;

  (iii) creditors, according to the following categories–

   (aa) amounts payable in respect of securities purchased;

   (bb) accrued expenses;

   (cc) other creditors; and

   (dd) in the case of a common investment fund, amounts payable in respect of property withdrawn from the investment fund;

(l) the following particulars of any contingent liability—

  (i) its amount or estimated amount;

  (ii) its legal nature; and

  (iii) whether any valuable security has been provided by the investment fund in connection with that liability and, if so, what;

(m) particulars of any other financial commitments which have not been provided for and are relevant to assessment of the state of affairs of the investment fund;

(n) in the case of—

  (i) any amount required by any of the preceding paragraphs to be disclosed;

  (ii) the percentage of net assets represented by each category of investment required by sub-paragraph (2)(a)(iv) to be disclosed; or

  (iii) the percentage of investment assets represented by each class of investment required by sub-paragraph (2)(a)(v), to be disclosed,

  the corresponding amount or percentage for the financial year immediately preceding the relevant financial year;

(o) a statement as to whether or not the accounts have been prepared in accordance with any applicable accounting standards and statements of recommended practice and particulars of any material departure from those standards and practices and the reasons for such departure;

Appendix 1 – The Charities (Accounts and Reports) Regulations 2008

- (p) where the charity trustees have exercised their powers under regulation 3(4)(b), a statement of their reasons for doing so;
- (q) the information specified—
    - (i) in the case of a common investment fund, in sub-paragraph (2);
    - (ii) in the case of a common deposit fund, in sub-paragraph (3); and
- (r) any other information which is required by these Regulations to be disclosed in a note to the accounts or which may reasonably assist the user to understand the statement of accounts.

(2) In addition to the information specified in sub-paragraph (1), a common investment fund must include in the notes to the accounts the following statements made up to the date of the balance sheet—

- (a) a portfolio statement, specifying—
    - (i) details of each investment held by or on behalf of the investment fund including—
        - (aa) its market value at that date; and
        - (bb) whether the investment in question is listed on a recognised stock exchange;
    - (ii) the category of each such investment determined according to its geographical area or industrial sector;
    - (iii) where the investment fund invests in more than one class of assets, the market value at that date of each class of investment;
    - (iv) the percentage of net assets represented by each investment so held and by each category of investment specified under paragraph (ii);
    - (v) the percentage of investment assets represented by each class of investments specified under paragraph (iii); and
    - (vi) an analysis of the credit rating of any interest-bearing securities held at that date, as may be required by the IMA SORP to be given.
- (b) a statement of major changes in the portfolio, specifying—
    - (i) where—
        - (aa) the relevant financial year is the first financial year of the investment fund and the aggregate value of purchases or sales of a particular investment during the financial year exceeds 2 per cent of net assets at the end of that year; or
        - (bb) the relevant financial year is not the first financial year of the investment fund and the aggregate value of purchases or sales of a particular investment during the relevant financial year exceeds 2 per cent of net assets at the beginning of that year,

        that value;
    - (ii) unless disclosed under paragraph (i), the value of the 20 largest purchases and sales of a particular investment during the relevant financial year; and
    - (iii) the total cost of purchase and net proceeds from sales of investments during the relevant financial year;
- (c) a statement of—
    - (aa) the number of shares issued as at the beginning of the relevant financial year;
    - (bb) the number of shares issued as at the date of the balance sheet;
    - (cc) the value of each income or accumulation share as at each of those dates, calculated by reference to the net asset value of the investment fund; and
- (d) a statement of the amount, if any, in the dividend equalisation reserve.

(3) In addition to the information specified in paragraph (1) a common deposit fund must include in the notes to accounts—

Appendix 1 – The Charities (Accounts and Reports) Regulations 2008

(a) details of sums deposited by participating charities as at the date of the balance sheet, divided into—

    (i) sums repayable on demand; and

    (ii) deposits with agreed maturity dates or periods of notice, divided into—

        (aa) those repayable in not more than three months;

        (bb) those repayable in more than three months but not more than one year;

        (cc) those repayable in more than one year but not more than five years; and

        (dd) those repayable in more than five years;

(b) details as at the date of the balance sheet of–

    (i) sums placed on deposit, divided into—

        (aa) sums repayable on demand; and

        (bb) other deposits, indicating whether they are repayable in not more than 3 months, more than 3 months but not more than 1 year, more than 1 year but not more than 5 years or more than 5 years;

    (ii) investments other than deposits, analysed in accordance with the requirements of paragraph (2)(a).

(4) In this paragraph "corresponding financial year" has the meaning given by regulation 9(3).

PART 6

INTERPRETATION

17.—(1) In this Schedule—

"dividend equalisation reserve" means income withheld from distribution with a view to avoiding fluctuations in the amounts distributed;

"the IMA SORP" means the Statement of Recommended Practice for Financial Statements of Authorised Funds issued by the Investment Management Association in December 2005(a);

"person connected with a charity trustee or manager" has the meaning given by sub-paragraph (2);

"recognised stock exchange" has the meaning given by section 1005 of the Income Tax Act 2007(**b**);

(2) For the purposes of this Schedule, a person ("A") is connected with a charity trustee or a person to whom functions in relation to the management of the investment fund have been delegated if—

    (a) A is the child, parent, grandchild, grandparent, brother or sister of the charity trustee or manager;

    (b) A is the spouse or the civil partner of—

        (i) the charity trustee or manager; or

        (ii) any person connected with a charity trustee or manager by virtue of paragraph (a);

    (c) A is—

        (i) the trustee of any trust—

            (aa) which is not a charity; and

(a) Copies of the IMA SORP are available from the Investment Management Association, 65 Kingsway, London WC2B 6TD.
(b) 2007 c. 3. Section 1005 of the Income Tax Act 2007 was amended by paragraph 1 of Schedule 26 to the Finance Act 2007 (c. 11).

Appendix 1 – The Charities (Accounts and Reports) Regulations 2008

-
  -
    - (bb) the beneficiaries or potential beneficiaries of which include the charity trustee or manager or any person connected with that trustee or manager by virtue of paragraph (a) or (b); and
  - (ii) acting in his capacity as trustee of that trust;
- (d) A is—
  - (i) carrying on a business in partnership with—
    - (aa) the charity trustee or manager; or
    - (bb) any person connected with a trustee or manager by virtue of paragraph (a), (b) or (c); and
  - (ii) acting in his capacity as such a business partner; or
- (e) A is a body corporate—
  - (i) which is not a company which is connected with a charitable institution within the meaning of section 58(5) of the Charities Act 1992(a); but
  - (ii) in which—
    - (aa) the charity trustee or manager has; or
    - (bb) the charity trustee or manager, any other trustee or manager of the investment fund or persons connected with him or them by virtue of paragraphs (a), (b), (c) or (d), taken together, have,

    a substantial interest.

(3) For the purposes of sub-paragraph (2)—
- (a) "child" has the meaning given by paragraph 2 of Schedule 5 to the 1993 Act;
- (b) whether a person controls an institution is to be determined in accordance with paragraph 3 of that Schedule; and
- (c) whether a person has a substantial interest in a body corporate is to be determined in accordance with paragraph 4 of that Schedule.

SCHEDULE 2   Regulation 9

NOTES TO THE STATEMENT OF ACCOUNTS PREPARED BY A CHARITY THAT IS NOT AN INVESTMENT FUND OR SPECIAL CASE CHARITY

1.—(1) Subject to sub-paragraphs (2) and (3) and in so far as it is not provided in the statement of financial activities or in the balance sheet, the information to be provided by way of notes to the accounts is—
- (a) particulars of any material adjustment made under regulation 8(8);
- (b) a description of—
  - (i) each of the accounting policies which—
    - (aa) have been adopted by the charity trustees; and
    - (bb) are material in the context of the accounts of the charity; and
  - (ii) the estimation techniques adopted by the charity trustees which are material to the presentation of the accounts;

(a) 1992 c. 41.

Appendix 1 – The Charities (Accounts and Reports) Regulations 2008

(c) a description of any material change to policies and techniques referred to in paragraph (b), the reason for such change and its effect (if material) on the accounts, in accordance with the methods and principles set out in the SORP;

(d) a description of the nature and purpose of all material funds of the charity in accordance with the methods and principles set out in the SORP;

(e) such particulars of transactions of the charity, or of any subsidiary undertaking of the charity, entered into with a related party as are required to be disclosed by the SORP;

(f) such particulars of the cost to the charity of employing and providing pensions for staff as are required by the SORP to be disclosed;

(g) such particulars of the emoluments of staff employed by the charity as may be required by the SORP to be disclosed;

(h) a description of any incoming resources which represent capital, according to whether or not that capital is permanent endowment;

(i) an itemised analysis of any material movement between any of the restricted funds of the charity, or between a restricted and an unrestricted fund of the charity, together with an explanation of the nature and purpose of each of those funds;

(j) the name of any subsidiary undertaking of the charity, together with a description of the nature of the charity's relationship with that subsidiary undertaking, and of its activities, and, where material, a statement of the turnover and net profit or loss of the subsidiary undertaking for the corresponding financial year and any qualification expressed in an auditor's report on the accounts of the subsidiary undertaking for that financial year;

(k) particulars of any guarantee given by the charity, where any potential liability under the guarantee is outstanding at the date of the balance sheet;

(l) particulars of any loan outstanding at the date of the balance sheet—

   (i) which was made to the charity and which is secured by an express charge on any of the assets of the charity; or

   (ii) which was made by the charity to any subsidiary undertaking of the charity;

(m) particulars of any fund of the charity which is in deficit at the date of the balance sheet;

(n) particulars of any remuneration paid to an auditor or independent examiner in respect of auditing or examining the accounts of the charity and particulars of any remuneration paid to the auditor or independent examiner in respect of any other services rendered to the charity;

(o) subject to paragraph (2), such particulars of any grant made by the charity as may be required by the SORP to be disclosed;

(p) particulars of any ex gratia payment made by the charity;

(q) an analysis of any entry in the statement of financial activities relating to resources expended on charitable activities as may be required by the SORP to be disclosed;

(r) such particulars of any support costs incurred by the charity as may be required by the SORP to be disclosed;

(s) an analysis of any entry in the balance sheet relating to—

   (i) fixed assets;

   (ii) debtors;

   (iii) creditors,

   according to the categories set out in the SORP;

(t) an analysis of all material changes during the financial year in question in the values of fixed assets, in accordance with the methods and principles set out in the SORP;

(u) in the case of any amount required by any of the preceding sub-paragraphs other than sub-paragraph (i), (o) or (t) to be disclosed, the corresponding amount for the financial year immediately preceding the relevant financial year;

Appendix 1 – The Charities (Accounts and Reports) Regulations 2008

   (v) a statement as to whether or not the accounts have been prepared in accordance with any applicable accounting standards and statements of recommended practice and particulars of any material departure from those standards and statements of practice and the reasons for such departure;

   (w) where the charity trustees have exercised their powers under regulation 3(4)(b) so as to determine an accounting reference date earlier or later than 12 months from the beginning of the financial year, a statement of their reasons for doing so;

   (x) if, in accordance with regulation 8(4)(d), the charity trustees have departed from any requirement of regulation 8, particulars of any such departure, the reasons for it, and its effect; and

   (y) any additional information which–

      (i) is required to ensure that the statement of accounts complies with the requirements of regulation 8; or

      (ii) may reasonably assist the user to understand the statement of accounts.

(2) The charity trustees of a charity that is a charitable trust created by any person ("the settler") are not required to disclose under paragraph (o) of sub-paragraph (1) any excepted information if the disclosure of that information would fall to be made at a time when—

   (a) the settlor; or

   (b) the spouse or civil partner of the settlor,

is still alive.

(3) In this Schedule—

   (a) "corresponding financial year" has the meaning given by regulation 9(3);

   (b) "excepted information" means—

      (i) the identities of recipients of grants made out of the funds of the charity;

      (ii) the amounts of individual grants so made.

Appendix 1 — The Charities (Accounts and Reports) Regulations 2008

EXPLANATORY NOTE

(This note is not part of the Regulations)

These Regulations ("the 2008 Regulations"), which extend only to England and Wales, make provision in respect of the preparation and scrutiny of accounts prepared by charities and the preparation of annual reports by charities. These Regulations also make provision for the preparation and scrutiny of group accounts and the preparation of group annual reports by parent charities. These Regulations do not apply to exempt charities.

These Regulations revoke, with savings, the Charities (Accounts and Reports) Regulations 2005 ("the 2005 Regulations") (S.I. 2005/572).

The 2005 Regulations will generally continue to apply to financial years of charities beginning before 1st April 2008. The application of regulation 7(5) of those Regulations is limited however as result of the new whistle-blowing duty in section 44A of the Charities Act 1993 which is expected to come into force on 1st April 2008.

The 2008 Regulations will generally only apply to financial years of charities beginning on or after 1st April 2008. However, the charity trustees may in the circumstances set out in regulation 4 determine that the 2008 Regulations, rather than the 2005 Regulations, apply to a financial year beginning before 1st April 2008. None of the provisions relating to group accounts will apply in respect of a financial year beginning before 1st April 2008.

Part 1 (General) of the 2008 Regulations sets out the definitions that apply for the purposes of the Regulations (regulation 2) and makes provision for the determination of financial years of charities that are not companies (regulation 3). This Part also sets out the application of the 2008 Regulations and various transitional and saving provision.

Part 2 (Form and content of statements of accounts) of and Schedules 1 and 2 to the 2008 Regulations prescribe the form and contents of the statements of account prepared by charity trustees under section 42(1) of the Charities Act 1993 ("the 1993 Act"). This includes the information to be provided by way of notes to the accounts.

Regulation 6 of and Schedule 1 to the 2008 Regulations prescribe the form and content of statements of accounts prepared by charities that are investment funds. Investment fund is defined for the purposes of the 2008 Regulations in regulation 2. Regulation 7 of the 2008 Regulations prescribes the form and content of statements of accounts to be prepared by charitable registered social landlords and certain charities conducting higher education institutions ("special case charity"). Regulation 8 of and Schedule 2 to the 2008 Regulations prescribe the form and content of statements of accounts prepared by other types of charity.

Part 3 (Group Accounts) of the 2008 Regulations makes provision in respect of the preparation of group accounts. This Part of the 2008 Regulations should be read with Schedule 5A to the 1993 Act.

Chapter 1 sets out how aggregate gross income is to be calculated for the purposes of Schedule 5A to the 1993 Act and also how the financial years of subsidiary undertakings are to be determined.

Chapter 2 prescribes the form and content of group accounts including the information to be provided by way of notes to the accounts. Regulations 13 and 16 prescribe the form and content of group accounts prepared by the charity trustees of a parent charity that is an investment fund under paragraph 3(2) of Schedule 5A to the 1993 Act. Regulations 14 and 16 prescribe the form and content of group accounts prepared by the charity trustees of a parent charity that is a special case charity. Regulations 15 and 16 prescribe the form and content of group accounts prepared by the charity trustees of any other parent charity.

Chapter 3 makes provision for various exceptions to the requirement to prepare group accounts.

Appendix 1 – The Charities (Accounts and Reports) Regulations 2008

The requirements of Part 3 apply to a parent charity which is a company where it is not required to prepare group accounts under Part 7 of the Companies Act 1985.

Part 4 of the 2008 Regulations makes provision regarding the duties of auditors carrying out an audit of a charity's accounts and the reports to be made by independent examiners and examiners examining a charity's accounts. Chapter 2 deals with the reports of auditors by reference to the type of entity accounts which they are auditing. Chapter 3 deals with the reports of auditors of group accounts. Chapter 4 deals with the reports of independent examiners and Chapter 5 deals with the reports of examiners of accounts of English and Welsh National Health Service Charities. Chapter 6 makes various supplementary provision including provision for cases in which the Charity Commission may dispense with the requirement for a charity's accounts to be audited or examined.

The requirements of Part 4 apply to a charity that is a company and which is not required to have its accounts audited under Part 7 of the Companies Act 1985.

Part 5 of the 2008 Regulations makes provision regarding the report and information to be contained in the annual report prepared by the charity trustees of a charity under section 45 of the 1993 Act. Regulations 38 and 40 make provision for the preparation of annual reports by the charity trustees of parent charities that are required to prepare group accounts for the financial year in question. Regulations 37 and 39 make provision for the preparation of annual reports by other types of charity.

A full regulatory impact assessment of the effect that these Regulations will have on the costs of business and the voluntary sector is available from the Office of the Third Sector, 35 Great Smith Street, London. SW1P 3BQ (020 7276 6029) and is annexed to the Explanatory Memorandum which is available alongside the Regulations on the OPSI website (http://www.opsi.gov.uk).

© Crown copyright 2008

Printed and published in the UK by The Stationery Office Limited
under the authority and superintendence of Carol Tullo, Controller of Her Majesty's
Stationery Office and Queen's Printer of Acts of Parliament.

E2117 3/2008   182117T   19585

Appendix 2 – Extract from Charities Act 2006: Chapter 6 Audit or Examination of Accounts where Charity is not a Company and Chapter 7 Charitable Companies

CHAPTER 6

AUDIT OR EXAMINATION OF ACCOUNTS WHERE CHARITY IS NOT A COMPANY

28 Annual audit or examination of accounts of charities which are not companies

   (1) Section 43 of the 1993 Act (annual audit or examination of accounts of charities which are not companies) is amended as follows.

Appendix 2 – Extract from Charities Act 2006

(2) For subsection (1) substitute—

"(1) Subsection (2) below applies to a financial year of a charity if—
   (a) the charity's gross income in that year exceeds £500,000; or
   (b) the charity's gross income in that year exceeds the accounts threshold and at the end of the year the aggregate value of its assets (before deduction of liabilities) exceeds £2.8 million.

"The accounts threshold" means £100,000 or such other sum as is for the time being specified in section 42(3) above."

(3) In subsection (2) (accounts required to be audited) for paragraph (a) substitute—

"(a) would be eligible for appointment as auditor of the charity under Part 2 of the Companies Act 1989 if the charity were a company, or".

(4) In subsection (3) (independent examinations instead of audits)—
   (a) for the words from "and its gross income" to "subsection (4) below)" substitute "but its gross income in that year exceeds £10,000,"; and
   (b) at the end insert—
   "This is subject to the requirements of subsection (3A) below where the gross income exceeds £250,000, and to any order under subsection (4) below."

(5) After subsection (3) insert—

"(3A) If subsection (3) above applies to the accounts of a charity for a year and the charity's gross income in that year exceeds £250,000, a person qualifies as an independent examiner for the purposes of paragraph (a) of that subsection if (and only if) he is an independent person who is—
   (a) a member of a body for the time being specified in section 249D(3) of the Companies Act 1985 (reporting accountants);
   (b) a member of the Chartered Institute of Public Finance and Accountancy; or
   (c) a Fellow of the Association of Charity Independent Examiners."

(6) For subsection (8) substitute—

"(8) The Minister may by order—
   (a) amend subsection (1)(a) or (b), (3) or (3A) above by substituting a different sum for any sum for the time being specified there;
   (b) amend subsection (3A) by adding or removing a description of person to or from the list in that subsection or by varying any entry for the time being included in that list."

29 **Duty of auditor etc. of charity which is not a company to report matters to Commission**

(1) After section 44 of the 1993 Act insert—

"**44A Duty of auditors etc. to report matters to Commission**

(1) This section applies to—
   (a) a person acting as an auditor or independent examiner appointed by or in relation to a charity under section 43 above,

Appendix 2 – Extract from Charities Act 2006

Charities Act 2006 (c. 50)
Part 2 – Regulation of charities
Chapter 6 – Audit or examination of accounts where charity is not a company

    (b) a person acting as an auditor or examiner appointed under section 43A(2) or (3) above, and

    (c) the Auditor General for Wales acting under section 43B(2) or (3) above.

(2) If, in the course of acting in the capacity mentioned in subsection (1) above, a person to whom this section applies becomes aware of a matter—

    (a) which relates to the activities or affairs of the charity or of any connected institution or body, and

    (b) which he has reasonable cause to believe is likely to be of material significance for the purposes of the exercise by the Commission of its functions under section 8 or 18 above,

he must immediately make a written report on the matter to the Commission.

(3) If, in the course of acting in the capacity mentioned in subsection (1) above, a person to whom this section applies becomes aware of any matter—

    (a) which does not appear to him to be one that he is required to report under subsection (2) above, but

    (b) which he has reasonable cause to believe is likely to be relevant for the purposes of the exercise by the Commission of any of its functions,

he may make a report on the matter to the Commission.

(4) Where the duty or power under subsection (2) or (3) above has arisen in relation to a person acting in the capacity mentioned in subsection (1), the duty or power is not affected by his subsequently ceasing to act in that capacity.

(5) Where a person makes a report as required or authorised by subsection (2) or (3), no duty to which he is subject is to be regarded as contravened merely because of any information or opinion contained in the report.

(6) In this section "connected institution or body", in relation to a charity, means—

    (a) an institution which is controlled by, or

    (b) a body corporate in which a substantial interest is held by,

the charity or any one or more of the charity trustees acting in his or their capacity as such.

(7) Paragraphs 3 and 4 of Schedule 5 to this Act apply for the purposes of subsection (6) above as they apply for the purposes of provisions of that Schedule."

(2) In section 46 of the 1993 Act (special provisions as respects accounts and annual reports of exempt and excepted charities)—

    (a) in subsection (1) for "sections 41 to 45" substitute "sections 41 to 44 or section 45"; and

    (b) after subsection (2) insert—

    "(2A) Section 44A(2) to (7) above shall apply in relation to a person appointed to audit, or report on, the accounts of an exempt charity which is not a company as they apply in relation to a person such as is mentioned in section 44A(1).

Appendix 2 – Extract from Charities Act 2006

(2B) But section 44A(2) to (7) so apply with the following modifications—

(a) any reference to a person acting in the capacity mentioned in section 44A(1) is to be read as a reference to his acting as a person appointed as mentioned in subsection (2A) above; and

(b) any reference to the Commission or to any of its functions is to be read as a reference to the charity's principal regulator or to any of that person's functions in relation to the charity as such."

30 Group accounts

(1) After section 49 of the 1993 Act insert—

"**49A Group accounts**

The provisions of Schedule 5A to this Act shall have effect with respect to—

(a) the preparation and auditing of accounts in respect of groups consisting of parent charities and their subsidiary undertakings (within the meaning of that Schedule), and

(b) other matters relating to such groups."

(2) Schedule 6 (which inserts the new Schedule 5A into the 1993 Act) has effect.

CHAPTER 7

CHARITABLE COMPANIES

31 Relaxation of restriction on altering memorandum etc. of charitable company

(1) Section 64 of the 1993 Act (alteration of objects clause etc.) is amended as follows.

(2) For subsection (2) substitute—

"(2) Where a charity is a company, any regulated alteration by the company—

(a) requires the prior written consent of the Commission, and

(b) is ineffective if such consent has not been obtained.

(2A) The following are "regulated alterations"—

(a) any alteration of the objects clause in the company's memorandum of association,

(b) any alteration of any provision of its memorandum or articles of association directing the application of property of the company on its dissolution, and

(c) any alteration of any provision of its memorandum or articles of association where the alteration would provide authorisation for any benefit to be obtained by directors or members of the company or persons connected with them.

(2B) For the purposes of subsection (2A) above—

(a) "benefit" means a direct or indirect benefit of any nature, except that it does not include any remuneration (within the meaning of section 73A below) whose receipt may be authorised under that section; and

(b) the same rules apply for determining whether a person is connected with a director or member of the company as apply, in accordance with section 73B(5) and (6) below, for determining whether a person is connected with a charity trustee for the purposes of section 73A."

(3) In subsection (3) (documents required to be delivered to registrar of companies), for "any such alteration" substitute "a regulated alteration".

32 Annual audit or examination of accounts of charitable companies

(1) In section 249A(4) of the Companies Act 1985 (c. 6) (circumstances in which charitable company's accounts may be subject to an accountant's report instead of an audit)—
  (a) in paragraph (b) (gross income between £90,000 and £250,000) for "£250,000" substitute "£500,000"; and
  (b) in paragraph (c) (balance sheet total not more than £1.4 million) for "£1.4 million" substitute "£2.8 million".

(2) In section 249B(1C) of that Act (circumstances in which parent company or subsidiary not disqualified for exemption from auditing requirement), in paragraph (b) (group's aggregate turnover not more than £350,000 net or £420,000 gross in case of charity), for "£350,000 net (or £420,000 gross)" substitute "£700,000 net (or £840,000 gross)".

33 Duty of auditor etc. of charitable company to report matters to Commission

After section 68 of the 1993 Act insert—

"68A Duty of charity's auditors etc. to report matters to Commission

(1) Section 44A(2) to (7) above shall apply in relation to a person acting as—
  (a) an auditor of a charitable company appointed under Chapter 5 of Part 11 of the Companies Act 1985 (auditors), or
  (b) a reporting accountant appointed by a charitable company for the purposes of section 249C of that Act (report required instead of audit),
as they apply in relation to a person such as is mentioned in section 44A(1).

(2) For this purpose any reference in section 44A to a person acting in the capacity mentioned in section 44A(1) is to be read as a reference to his acting in the capacity mentioned in subsection (1) of this section.

(3) In this section "charitable company" means a charity which is a company."

Appendix 3 – Section 505 of the Income and Corporation Taxes Act 1988

505. Charities: general

(1) Subject to subsections (2) and (3) below, the following exemptions shall be granted on a claim in that behalf to the Board –
- [(a) exemption from tax under Schedules A and D in respect of any profits or gains arising in respect of rents or other receipts from an estate, interest or right in or over any land (whether situated in the United Kingdom or elsewhere) to the extent that the profits or gains –
    - (i) arise in respect of rents or receipts from an estate, interest or right vested in any person for charitable purposes; and
    - (ii) are applied to charitable purposes only;][5]
- (b)...[1]
- (c) exemption –
    - (i)...[6]
    - [(ii) from tax under Case IV or V of Schedule D in respect of income eqivalent to income chargeable under Case III of that Schedule but arising from securities or other possessions outside the United Kingdom,
    - [(iia) from tax under Case V of Schedule D in respect of income consisting in any such dividend or other distribution of a company not resident in the United Kiongdom as would be chargeable to tax under Schedule F if the company were so resident, and][5]
    - (iii) from tax under Schedule F in respect of any distribution,

  where the income in question forms part of the income of a charity, or is, according to rules or regulations established by Act of Parliament, charter, decree, deed of trust or will, applicable to charitable purposes only, and so far as it is applied to charitable purposes only;
- [(d) exemption from tax under Schedule D in respect of public revenue dividends on securities which are in the name of trustees, to the extent that the dividends are applicable and applied only for the repair of –
    - (i) any cathedral, college, church of chapel, or
    - (ii) any building used for the purposes of divine worship;][6]
- (e) exemption from tax under Schedule D in respect of the profits of any trade carried on by a charity [(whether in the United Kingdom or elsewhere)][5], if the profits are applied solely to the purposes of the charity and either –

Appendix 3 – Section 505 of the Income and Corporation Taxes Act 1988

        (i)   the trade is exercised in the course of the actual carrying out of a primary purpose of the charity; or

        (ii)   the work in connection with the trade is mainly carried out by beneficiaries of the charity.

[(f)   exemption from tax under Schedule D in respect of profits accruing to a charity from a lottery if –

        (i)   the lottery is promoted and conducted in accordance with section 3 or 5 of the Lotteries and Amusements (Northern Ireland) Order 1985; and

        (ii)   the profits are applied solely to the charity's purposes.]³

[(1A) In subsection (1)(d) above 'public revenue dividends' means –

    (a)   income from securities which is payable out of the public revenue of the United Kingdom or Northern Ireland;

    (b)   income from securities issued by or on behalf of a government or a public or local authority in a country outside the United Kingdom.]⁶

(2)   Any payment which –

    (a)   is received by a charity from another charity; and

    (b)   is not made for full consideration in money or money's worth; and

    (c)   is not chargeable to tax apart from this subsection; and

    (d)   is not, apart from this subsection, of a description which (on a claim) would be eligible for relief from tax by virtue of any provision of subsection (1) above;

shall be chargeable to tax under Case III of Schedule D but shall be eligible for relief from tax under subsection (1)(c) above as if it were an annual payment.

(3)   If in any chargeable period of a charity –

    (a)   its relevant income and gains are not less than £10,000; and

    (b)   its relevant income and gains exceed the amount of its qualifying expenditure; and

    (c)   the charity incurs, or is treated as incurring, non-qualifying expenditure;

relief shall not be available under either subsection (1) above or section [256 of the 1992 Act]² for so much of the excess as does not exceed the non-qualifying expenditure incurred in that period.

(4)   In relation to a chargeable period of less than 12 months, subsection (3) above shall have effect as if the amount specified in paragraph (a) of that subsection were proportionately reduced.

(5)   In subsection (3) above 'relevant income and gains' means –

    (a)   income which apart from subsection (1) above would not be exempt from tax together with any income which is taxable notwithstanding that subsection; and

Appendix 3 – Section 505 of the Income and Corporation Taxes act 1988

    (b) gains which apart from section [256 of the 1992 Act][2] would be chargeable gains together with any gains which are chargeable gains notwithstanding that section.

(6) Where by virtue of subsection (3) above there is an amount of a charity's relevant income and gains for which relief under subsection (1) above and section [256 of the 1992 Act][2] is not available, the charity may, by notice to the Board, specify which items of its relevant income and gains are, in whole or in part, to be attributed to that amount, and if within 30 days of being required to do so by the Board, a charity does not give notice under this subsection, the items of its relevant income and gains which are to be attributed to the amount in question shall be such as the Board may determine.

(7) Where it appears to the Board that two or more charities acting in concert are engaged in transactions of which the main purpose or one of the main purposes is the avoidance of tax (whether by the charities or by any other person), the Board may by notice given to the charities provide that, for such chargeable periods as may be specified in the notice, subsection (3) above shall have effect in relation to them with the omission of paragraph (a).

(8) An appeal may be brought against a notice under subsection (7) above as if it were notice of the decision of the Board on a claim made by the charities concerned.

---

1. Subs(1)(b) repealed by FA 1988 Sch 14Pt V.
2. Words in subss(3), (5)(b), (6) substituted by TCGA 1992 Sch 10 paras 14(1), (31).
3. Subs(1)(f) inserted by FA 1995 s138(1), (2) with effect for chargeable periods beginning, in the case of a company, after 31 March 1995, and in any case, after 5 April 1995.
4. Words in sub-s)96) substituted by FA 1995 s74(2), Sch 17 Pt II, para 7, with effect from the year 1995–96 (and appoy to every settlement, wherever and whenever made or entered into).
5. Sub-s(1)(a) and sub-s(1)(c)(ii), (iia), (iib) substituted (latter for subs(1)(c)(ii) and words in sub-s(1)(e) inserted by FA 1996 s146 with effect for the purposes of income tax from the year 1996–97 and for the purposes of corporation tax for accounting periods after 31 March 1996.
6. Subs(1)(c)(I) repealed, subs(1)(d) is sibstituted and sub-s(1A) inserted by FA 1996 Sch 7 para 19, Sch 41 Pt V(2) with effect as respects income tax from the year 1996–97, and for the purposes of corporation tax, for accounting periods ending after 31 Maqrch 1996.
7. Words in subs (6) repealed by FA 2000 ss41(5), (9), 156, Sch 40 Pt II(1) with effect for covenanted payments falling to be made by individuals after 5 April 2000 or made by companies after 31 March 2000.

Appendix 4 – Section 256 of the Taxation of Chargeable Gains Act 1992

CHARITIES AND GIFTS OF NON-BUSINESS ASSETS ETC.

256 Charities

(1) Subject to section 505(3) of the Taxes Act and subsection (2) below, a gain shall not be a chargeable gain if it accrues to a charity and is applicable and applied for charitable purposes.
(2) If property held on charitable trusts ceases to be subject to charitable trusts –
   (a) the trustees shall be treated as if they had disposed of, and immediately reacquired, the property for a consideration equal to its market value, any gain on the disposal being treated as not accruing to a charity, and
   (b) if and so far as any of that property represents, directly or indirectly, the consideration for the disposal of assets by the trustees, any gain accruing on that disposal shall be treated as not having accrued to a charity,

and an assessment to capital gains tax chargeable by virtue of paragraph (b) above may be made at any time not more than 3 years after the end of the year of assessment in which the property ceases to be subject to charitable trusts.

Appendix 5 – Model Gift Aid declarations

Gift Aid declaration   *giftaid it*

Name of charity or CASC _____

Please treat

- ☐ The enclosed gift of £ _____ as a Gift Aid donation; **OR**
- ☐ All gifts of money that I make today and in the future as Gift Aid donations; **OR**
- ☐ All gifts of money that I have made in the past 6 years and all future gifts of money that I make from the date of this declaration as Gift Aid donations.

✓ *Please tick the appropriate box*

You must pay an amount of income tax and/or capital gains tax in each tax year at least equal to the tax that the charity or Community Amateur Sports Club (CASC) will claim from HM Revenue & Customs on your Gift Aid donation(s).

Donor's details

Title _____ Initial(s) _____ Surname _____

Home address _____

_____

_____

Postcode _____ Date _____

Signature _____

Please notify the charity or CASC if you:
1. Want to cancel this declaration.
2. Change your name or home address.
3. No longer pay sufficient tax on your income and/or capital gains.

Tax claimed by the charity or CASC
- The charity or CASC will reclaim 28p of tax on every £1 you gave up to 5 April 2008.
- The charity or CASC will reclaim 25p of tax on every £1 you give on or after 6 April 2008.
- The Government will pay to the charity or CASC an additional 3p on every £1 you give between 6 April 2008 and 5 April 2011. This transitional relief for the charity or CASC does not affect your personal tax position.

If you pay income tax at the higher rate, you must include all your Gift Aid donations on your Self Assessment tax return if you want to receive the additional tax relief due to you.

Appendix 5 – Model Gift Aid declarations

Sponsorship and Gift Aid declaration form

giftaid it

Please sponsor me _____

To (event) _____

In aid of _____

We, who have given our names and addresses below and have ticked the box headed 'Gift Aid' (✓), want the charity or CASC named above to reclaim tax on the donation detailed below, given on the date shown. We understand that each of us must pay an amount of income tax or capital gains tax at least equal to the tax reclaimed by the charity or CASC on the donation.

Full name (First name and surname)	Home address Not your work address (this is essential for Gift Aid)	Postcode	Amount £	Date paid	Gift Aid? (✓)
			Total donations received £		
			Total Gift Aid donation £		

Remember: Full name + Home address + Postcode + ✓ – *giftaid it*

Appendix 6 – Charity reserves and defined benefit pension schemes

(Version May 2005)

Contents

- Introduction
- Consideration of going concern
- Reserves policy
- Setting a reserve policy
- Risk management
- Role of Regulators
- Appendix A – Reserve Policy Scenarios
- Appendix B – Charity and Pension Trustees: Legal Obligations and Liabilities

1. Introduction

1.1. The implementation of FRS17: Retirement Benefits has brought about (for accounting periods beginning on or after 1st January 2005) the balance sheet recognition of pension assets or liabilities for charities that operate defined benefit pension schemes. The nature of this asset or liability is defined by and calculated in accordance with the methods set out in the Financial Reporting Standard. Detailed accounting guidance is provided in SORP 2005.

Further explanation and background to the SORP's recommendations on the application of FRS 17 in charity accounts can be found in SORP Update Bulletin 1.

1.2. The accounting requirements of the new standard have focused attention on the health of pension schemes generally. For charities with a defined benefit pension scheme, this in turn can influence the stance taken by those parties with whom a sponsoring charity transacts. In addition, the balance sheet disclosure of pension assets or liabilities has raised questions as to how a charity's reserves policy will be affected.

1.3. Whilst the Charity Commission provides detailed guidance on the factors that a charity will consider in setting and explaining its reserves policy, it is recognised that accounting under FRS17 gives rise to a number of particular issues where further guidance may be helpful to charities when setting their

Appendix 6 – Charity reserves and defined benefit pension schemes

policy for reserves. For the SORP definition of reserves please see paragraph 3.3. In some cases a pension liability may exceed the amount of reserves of a charity. This has raised questions as to the impact this may have on the 'going concern' of certain charities.

1.4. The Charity Finance Directors' Group (CFDG) in its publication 'The Charity Pensions Maze' highlighted the need for charities with defined benefit pension schemes to consider the implications and legal liabilities that follow from such schemes. It provided options as to how such risks might be managed with the help of professional advice. This guidance looks at the immediate legal and other implications on a charity having a defined benefit pension scheme.

1.5. The operation of a defined benefit scheme by a charity creates financial risk which in some cases may, if not managed, become a major risk to the charity and its future activities. This guidance also explores how the identification and management of such risk may be addressed in the context of a risk management framework.

2. Consideration of going concern

2.1. The Audit and Assurance Faculty of the Institute of Chartered Accountants in England and Wales has provided guidance in 'Technical Release Audit 1/02' for auditors on how they should approach the question of pension liabilities when assessing the going concern of an entity. Although this guidance is directed at auditors, it does have relevance to charities wishing to understand how pension liabilities may affect solvency. In the view of the Pensions Regulator, and consistent with that of the Audit and Assurance faculty, an FRS17 deficit does not of itself automatically raise an issue over the going concern of the charity.

2.2. FRS17 does not, of itself, affect the cash flows of a charity. The contributions made by an employer charity into a defined benefit pension scheme are usually arrived at in accordance with the terms of the pension scheme, in light of advice from its actuary based on the results of an actuarial valuation of the pension scheme and through statutory requirements. Changes in these statutory requirements mean that pension schemes are likely to be more prudently funded as a result of actuarial valuations occurring on and after 23 September 2005.

2.3. These requirements may involve measuring surpluses or deficits of the pension scheme on a different basis to that required by FRS17. In the context of under funded schemes, increases in contribution rates would arise irrespective of the accounting disclosure provided in the financial accounts.

2.4. Charitable companies are 'legal persons', can incur liabilities, and can become 'insolvent'. Such charities can be deemed insolvent in accordance with s.123 of the Insolvency Act 1986, as amended, for example when it is unable to pay its debts as they fall due. In this context, also see CC12 – Managing Financial Difficulties and Insolvency in Charities.

2.5. When considering the appropriateness of the going concern concept, trustee directors of charitable companies need to consider the cash flow effects of the agreed pension contributions arising under the scheme irrespective of whether any FRS 17 deficit is disclosed on or off balance sheet. The impact of contributions would normally be considered as part of a charity's budgetary process and would focus on the ability of the charity to meet contributions as they fall due, together with consideration of the impact such payments have on the planned programme of charitable activities. In addition trustees/directors will also consider the impact funding deficits may have on existing borrowing arrangements, and compliance with loan covenants, together with the potential impact on the charity's ability to raise funding in the future.

2.6. Unincorporated charities are not 'legal persons' and cannot technically incur liabilities, which are instead incurred by their trustees, acting on behalf of beneficiaries. Unincorporated charities cannot, strictly speaking, become insolvent. However, a charity may reach a financial state where the value of the assets in its trust which are available to the trustees to settle the liabilities of the charity are insufficient. In the context of unincorporated charities the term 'insolvency' is used informally to describe this situation.

2.7. Trustees normally have a right of recourse to the trust assets for reimbursement of liabilities properly incurred. The concern for trustees is that (unless the debts and liabilities have been incurred on the basis that they will only have to be met if there are sufficient funds in the trust to do so) they may have to meet the debts and liabilities personally if there are insufficient funds in the trust. (See section 4 of Appendix B on the contractual liabilities of trustees).

3. Reserves policy

3.1. The Charities SORP recommends that trustees provide a statement of their reserves policy in their trustees' annual report. Trustees will need to consider explaining to the charity's stakeholders the effects of the inclusion of any pension asset or liability on the charity, particularly any impact on its reserves policy; paying particular attention to explaining clearly and simply how the accounting disclosures should be interpreted in the context of the charity's finances. Trustees will also need to consider direct communication with major funders, explaining the impact on cash flows.

3.2. Where material, the reserves policy statement is likely to differentiate the pension asset/liability from other reserves of the charity. It might explain the actuarial valuation resulting in the pension reserve/deficit and that the

Appendix 6 – Charity reserves and defined benefit pension schemes

corresponding asset/liability does not result in an immediate cash flow impact on the charity, i.e. that it is not an asset that can be immediately drawn down or a liability that must be settled immediately. A brief indication of the cash flow effects (i.e. increase or decrease in contributions to the scheme) would put this situation into context.

3.3. The definition of reserves in the SORP is 'that part of a charity's income funds that is freely available for its general purposes.' This definition of reserves therefore normally excludes:

(a) permanent endowment funds;
(b) expendable endowment funds;
(c) restricted income funds and;
(d) any part of unrestricted funds not readily available for spending, specifically: income funds which could only be realised by disposing of fixed assets held for charitable use.

'Reserves' are therefore the resources the charity has or can make available to spend for any or all of the charity's purposes once it has met its commitments and covered its other planned expenditure. More specifically 'reserves' is income which becomes available to the charity and is to be spent at the trustees' discretion in furtherance of any of the charity's objects (sometimes referred to as 'general purpose' income) but which is not yet spent, committed or designated (i.e. is 'free'). Where designations are made as part of a charity's reserves policy, both their purpose and the likely timing of their expenditure should be explained.

3.4. Where, under FRS17, a charity discloses a significant pension fund deficit, this does not mean that an immediate liability for this amount crystallises. Similarly, where a pension surplus is disclosed this does not create an immediately realisable asset that can be released straight away and expended on the purposes of the charity. In particular, the disclosure of a pension liability does not mean that the equivalent amount is already committed and is no longer available to the trustees to further the charity's objectives.

3.5. The funding position of a pension scheme will result in a cash flow effect in terms of an increase or decrease in contributions over a period of years. The charity needs to revisit its business plans and budgets and ascertain how this outflow might impact on future operational plans and budgets. If increased contributions can be met through budgeted inflows then the impact on reserves policy is marginal. In other cases, it might be necessary to set aside resources currently held to help fund anticipated increases in cash flows.

3.6. In looking at cash flow forecasts generally, it is probable that pension contributions are likely to increase at a faster rate than charitable income. Trustees may need to revisit their reserves policy sooner than they might otherwise have done, particularly with the advent of the new statutory scheme specific funding requirement (replacing the minimum funding requirement for defined benefit schemes).

4. Setting a reserves policy

4.1. In so far as an FRS17 calculated pension deficit does not result in an immediate equivalent cash commitment, it would not generally be appropriate for trustees to regard an equivalent amount as a designation of charitable funds. To do so would indicate an intention to apply the amount designated to make good the full amount of any reported pension liability and indicate that such funds were unavailable to expend on the charity's general purposes.

4.2. A good starting point is for a charity to exclude the FRS17 calculated asset or liability when calculating free reserves but then to give careful consideration to the cash flow implications that may arise from the accounting disclosure in terms of increased or reduced contributions.

4.3. Where a charity is confident that it can meet contributions from projected future income without significant impact on its planned levels of charitable activity then it is unlikely that trustees will need to designate any of their existing funds to meet future pension commitments.

4.4. Where contribution increases create uncertainty as to the charity's ability to meet them from projected future income, or would result in a significant curtailment of charitable activities, then urgent consideration by the trustees is required. In such circumstances immediate actuarial and legal advice is likely to be appropriate; it would be prudent to create a designation in so far as it is anticipated that the ability to make future contributions is dependent upon the assets currently held by the charity.

4.5. Additional contributions could result in a situation where designations of currently held resources and future incoming cash flows are insufficient to fund future contributions, or the impact of funding the scheme is such that it would have an unacceptable impact on charitable activities. In such situations issues of viability arise and formal professional advice is essential.

5. Risk management

5.1. The SORP recommends trustees provide a statement within the charity annual report confirming that:

'The major risks to which the charity is exposed, as identified by the trustees, have been reviewed and systems have been established to mitigate those risks.'

Appendix 6 – Charity reserves and defined benefit pension schemes

'Major risks' are those risks which have a high likelihood of occurring and would, if they occurred, have a severe impact on operational performance, achievement of aims and objectives or could damage the reputation of the charity, changing the way trustees, supporters or beneficiaries might deal with the charity.

5.2. In the context of the pension scheme, trustees are encouraged actively to manage any liability by:

- identifying the funding position from the scheme's actuarial valuation;
- using subsequent FRS17 valuations which are updated to reflect changing conditions to monitor trends in the funding position;
- identifying the cash flow requirements;
- identifying how to deal with it: short, medium, or long term;
- reviewing the benefits provided by the existing pension scheme; and
- where circumstances require taking professional advice as to options available to limit the charity's exposure to increasing liabilities accruing under the scheme.

5.3. Risk management should therefore not be seen purely as a compliance issue or as being solely focused on the prevention of a 'disaster'. The process will enable trustees to focus on the mitigation of risks that would prevent the charity achieving its strategic objectives. In so doing, charities will be able to take opportunities and develop them with an understanding of the risks faced, and with confidence that reasonable steps have been taken to mitigate those risks.

5.4. The reputational risk to a sizeable charity from not honouring pension promises, particularly when it is relying on a large number of employees to fulfil its objectives, will not be insubstantial.

5.5. Commission guidance on risk management identifies financial risks: such as accuracy and timeliness of financial information, adequacy of reserves and cash flow.

6. Role of Regulators

6.1. Role of the Charity Commission

The Commission is established by law as the regulator and registrar for charities in England & Wales. We fulfil this role by:

- securing compliance with charity law, and dealing with abuse and poor practice;
- enabling charities to work better within an effective legal, accounting and governance framework, keeping pace with developments in society, the economy and the law; and

- promoting sound governance and accountability.

Our aim is to provide the best possible regulation of charities in England & Wales, in order to increase charities' efficiency and effectiveness and public confidence and trust. We approach our work in a number of ways, including the issuing of information and advice to influence behaviour.

6.2. Role of the Pensions Regulator

The Pensions Regulator is the regulator of work-based pension schemes, and was set up by the Pensions Act 2004. From 6 April 2005 it replaces Opra (the Occupational Pensions Regulatory Authority) and has new powers and a new approach to protecting pension benefits. For example, The Pensions Regulator issues Codes of Practice which Opra did not.

The Pensions Act 2004 gives the Pensions Regulator a set of specific objectives:

- to protect the benefits of members of work-based pension schemes;
- to promote good administration of work-based pension schemes; and
- to reduce the risk of situations arising that may lead to claims for compensation from the Pension Protection Fund.

The Pensions Regulator will be working with trustees, scheme managers and employers to help protect the benefits built up for members.

The Pensions Regulator provides information, education and assistance to everyone involved in running pensions. The aim is to achieve the highest possible standards in the way pension schemes are run. This is the best way to prevent problems from developing – problems which could put members' pensions at risk.

If problems do occur, the Pensions Regulator will have a wide range of powers to help put matters right. In extreme cases, the Regulator will be able to fine trustees or employers, and remove trustees from a scheme.

For further information see: www.thepensionsregulator.gov.uk

6.3. Role of HM Revenue and Customs

IR Savings, Pensions, Share Schemes (Pension Schemes) is a business stream of the Inland Revenue's Capital and Savings Stream. In so far as pensions are concerned, its role is to protect the valuable tax reliefs on offer, through the granting and monitoring of tax approved status for retirement benefit schemes.

Appendix 6 – Charity reserves and defined benefit pension schemes

Appendix A

Reserve Policy Scenarios

This appendix considers a number of possible scenarios setting out how a defined benefit pension scheme funding requirement might impact on a charity's reserves policy. In all cases the assessment necessary in setting a reserves policy goes beyond simply looking at the FRS 17 liability disclosure. It involves looking at the scheme's funding requirements and in particular at the impact of increased contributions on planned activity level and resulting cash flow.

The scenarios presented in this appendix are for illustrative purposes only. As explained in section 4 of the main body of this guidance, actuarial and legal advice is likely to be appropriate where uncertainty exists as to the ability of a charity to meet future contributions to the scheme from projected income or where to do so would result in a significant curtailment of charitable activity.

	Scenario 1 £m	Scenario 2 £m	Scenario 3 £m
Tangible fixed assets	10.0	10.0	10.0
Investments	5.0	5.0	5.0
Net current assets	5.0	5.0	5.0
Net assets excluding pension liability	20.0	20.0	20.0
Pension liability	(10.0)	(17.5)	(22.5)
Net assets/(liabilities) including pension liability	10.0	2.5	(2.5)
Funds of the charity:			
Restricted funds	5.0	5.0	5.0
Unrestricted funds			
General	5.0	2.0	0
Pension	–	3.0	5.0
Property	10.0	10.0	10.0
Unrestricted funds excluding pension liability	15.0	15.0	15.0
Total charity funds excluding pension reserve	20.0	20.0	20.0
Pension reserve	(10.0)	(17.5)	(22.5)
Total charity funds	10.0	2.5	(2.5)

Scenario 1

Financial position

1.1. In this example, the charity's restricted funds of £5m are fully committed to meet a planned project funded by a number of restricted grants. The restricted funds' assets are held as gilt-edged securities within fixed asset investments

Appendix A

pending commencement of the project. The investment would be disclosed as a current asset if expenditure was anticipated in the next accounting period. The accounts disclose unrestricted funds of £15m including tangible fixed assets, used operationally, with a book value of £10m. The remaining unrestricted funds of £5m are held in liquid form as current assets.

1.2. In line with FRS 17 requirements, the charity has obtained an actuarial valuation and recognised a pension liability of £10m in its accounts arising from the pension scheme's actuarial deficit measured using the principles of the accounting standard. The pension liability of £10m reported in the accounts is less than the charity's total unrestricted funds of £15m reported, however, the pension liability does exceed the undesignated general funds of £5m.

Reserves policy

1.3. In setting their reserves policy the charity trustees would identify that restricted funds were fully committed to meet planned expenditure and explain their policy for designating tangible fixed assets. In this example, the charity operates a number of care homes with long term residents. A strategy of freehold ownership is adopted to help ensure long term care commitments are met. The trustees would also give consideration to whether the £5m held as current assets was sufficient to provide for working capital needs and to meet budgeted activity levels.

1.4. In setting a reserves policy, consideration would be given to the pension liability reported in the accounts. Although the reported liability does not exceed the amount held by the charity as unrestricted funds, it will still be necessary to consider the cash flow impact that may arise from the reported pension deficit.

Cash flow impact on reserves policy

1.5. The FRS 17 calculated pension liability does not result in any immediate liability to pay this amount to the pension scheme and hence a designation of unrestricted funds to match the FRS 17 calculated liability will not normally be necessary where any resulting increase in contributions will be met from anticipated future income streams.

1.6. Increased contributions may arise where, for example, the pension scheme's valuation presents a funding deficit. The contribution rate will be arrived at in accordance with the terms of the pension scheme, in the light of advice from its actuary, based on the results of a pension scheme's valuation and through statutory requirements. Both of these will involve measuring surpluses or deficits on a different basis to that required by FRS 17.

1.7. In setting a reserves policy, the charity trustees should give particular attention to the impact any increase in pension contributions will have on cash flow forecasts and planned activity levels. In the case of an open scheme, a

Appendix 6 – Charity reserves and defined benefit pension schemes

designation would normally only be made in the accounts where the cash flow effect of increased contributions is such that it may become necessary to earmark funds held at the balance sheet date in order to meet future contributions.

1.8. In this scenario, it is assumed that the pension scheme actuary undertook a valuation of the pension scheme and discussions were entered into resulting in agreement with the pension scheme trustees to increase employer's contribution to the pension scheme by £1m in each of the next five years. The charity trustees have given consideration to the impact of these additional costs on their planned activity levels and cash flow budgets and have concluded that these additional costs can be absorbed within existing budgets without jeopardising existing activity levels.

1.9. The trustees have therefore concluded that no designation of funds held at the balance sheet date to meet future contributions is necessary, despite the FRS 17 liability disclosed of £10m exceeding undesignated general funds of £5m.

1.10. Had the view been taken that the increase in pension contributions over the next five years could not be fully met from anticipated cash flows, all or part of the £5m held as undesignated general funds could be designated where it is anticipated that the assets of this fund will be needed to meet increased contributions. A charity clearly cannot create a designation in excess of its unrestricted funds; to do so would indicate insufficient funding to deliver planned activities.

Scenario 2

Financial position

2.1. In this example, the charity's restricted funds of £5m are again fully committed to meet a planned project funded by a number of restricted grants. The assets of the restricted fund are again held as investments pending commencement of the project. The accounts again disclose unrestricted funds of £15m including tangible fixed assets, used operationally, with a book value of £10m. The remaining £5m of unrestricted funds are held as liquid current assets. The FRS 17 liability reported, in this scenario, of £17.5m exceeds the unrestricted fund balance of £15m.

2.2. Whilst the pension liability (calculated under FRS 17 principles) exceeds the amount of unrestricted funds of the charity, this should not automatically be interpreted as creating a state of insolvency. It will however act as a trigger for a detailed review of the impact of pension contributions on the charity's cash flow position and ability of the charity to meet its debts as they fall due.

Appendix A

Reserves policy

2.3. The factors identified in scenario 1 relating to restricted funds and property designations would once more be relevant and explained as part of the reserves policy statement. Again, the cash flow implications arising from any pension scheme deficit would impact directly on the reserves policy set by the charity.

Cash flow impact on reserves policy

2.4. In this scenario, it is again assumed that, following a valuation of the pension scheme, agreement was reached with the pension scheme trustees to increase employer's contributions on this occasion by £1.3m in each of the next five years. In addition, in order to meet the scheme's minimum funding requirement (which is to be replaced in relation to actuarial valuations occurring on and after 23 September 2005 by a prudent, statutory scheme specific funding requirement), an additional one-off single payment into the pension scheme of £1.5m is required in the next financial year.

2.5. The charity trustees have taken the view that £1m of the increase in contributions rates is sustainable in the medium term without jeopardising the planned levels of charitable activity. However, the cash flow impact is such that it will be necessary to earmark £0.3m of the increased annual contributions together with the one-off contribution of £1.5m in order to sustain planned activity levels.

2.6. The designation made in the accounts of £3m represents a one off payment of £1.5m to meet the minimum funding requirement and £0.3m of additional contributions over each of the next 5 years which cannot be met from anticipated income streams if planned activity levels are to be maintained. The trustees, in addition to explaining the designation set aside for future pension contribution, would consider the adequacy of the undesignated general fund of £2.0m now reported.

Scenario 3

Financial position

3.1. In this example, the charity's restricted funds of £5m are again fully committed to meet planned project expenditure funded by a number of restricted grants. The accounts again disclose unrestricted funds of £15m including tangible fixed assets, used operationally, with a book value of £10m. The remaining £5m of unrestricted funds are held as liquid current assets. The FRS 17 liability reported of £22.5m exceeds both the unrestricted fund balance of £15m and the total assets of the charity before the pension liability of £20m. The net liability position of the charity including the pension liability is £2.5m.

Appendix 6 – Charity reserves and defined benefit pension schemes

3.2. Whilst the pension liability (calculated under FRS 17 principles) exceeds the net assets of the charity, this should not automatically be interpreted as creating a state of insolvency. It will however act as a trigger for a very detailed review of the impact of pension contributions on the charity's cash flow situation and ability of the charity to meet its debts as they fall due.

Reserves Policy

3.3. Again, in setting a reserves policy, the charity trustees have identified that restricted funds were fully committed to meet planned expenditure and explain their policy for designating tangible fixed assets. The charity trustees have given consideration to whether the £5m held as current assets is sufficient for working capital needs and to meet budgeted future needs. In looking at future budgeted needs, the cash flow impact of any increase in pension contribution would have been particularly relevant.

Cash flow impact on reserves policy

3.4. In this scenario it is again assumed that, following a valuation, the pension scheme trustees have advised the charity that an increase in employer's contributions is necessary to reduce the pension scheme deficit which would result in the charity's contribution increasing by £1.5m in each of the next five years. In addition, in order to meet the scheme's minimum funding requirement (which is to be replaced in relation to valuations occurring on and after 23 September 2005 by a prudent, statutory scheme specific funding requirement), a one-off single payment into the pension scheme of £5m is required in the next financial year.

3.5. The charity trustees have given consideration to the impact of these cash outflows on planned activity levels and the sustainability of these increased payments. In forming their view, the trustees have decided to take legal and actuarial advice on other options available in relation to the pension scheme to reduce its deficit and future contributions.

3.6. For example, the view may be taken that the increased contributions are only sustainable if the terms of the pension scheme are changed to incorporate an increase in employees' contributions to the scheme. It is assumed that, with an increase in employees' contribution, the on-going funding of the scheme is sustainable.

3.7. The cash flow impact is such that the one-off payment of £5m can only be met by a combination of curtailing certain budgeted activities and through earmarking of funds currently held at the balance sheet date. The full amount of the £5m one-off contribution can be designated since undesignated general reserves stand at £5m. This would indicate that no free reserves were held at the balance sheet date. Trustees would therefore review budgets and cash flow forecasts carefully to ensure future income streams were sufficient to meet working capital requirements.

3.8. In this scenario, had it not proved possible to increase employees' contributions to the scheme, the increase in future contributions could only be met from future income streams or by reducing future budgeted expenditure. It would not be possible to increase the pension designation above £5m and create a negative balance on undesignated general funds. The trustees could in such circumstances review the need for other designations if, for example, the policy of retaining freehold property was not central to operational objectives.

3.9. As explained in paragraph 4.5 of the main body of this guidance, where designations of currently held resources and future incoming cash flows are insufficient to fund future contributions, or the impact of funding the scheme is such that it would have an unacceptable impact on charitable activity, then issues of viability arise and formal professional advice is essential.

Appendix B

Role of Charity and Pension Trustees (Legal Obligations & Liabilities)

1. Role of Charity Trustees

1.1. The role and responsibilities of charity trustees generally are set out in the Charity Commission publication CC3 'Responsibilities of Charity Trustees'.

1.2. For trustees of a charity to have set up a defined benefit pension scheme, they will have taken a decision that the scheme in question is expedient in the interests of the charity. Trustees are fiduciaries and can only exercise their powers for the legitimate purposes of the charity and not for any ulterior purposes. Trustees cannot generally make moral or benevolent gestures in the administration of their trusts which are unconnected (directly or indirectly) with the achievement of the charity's objects. Neither can the court or the Commission sanction such gestures (except where the trustees regard themselves as being under a moral obligation such as to bring the matter within the remit of section 27 of the Charities Act 1993).

1.3. It may be the case that salaries in the charitable sector have been lower than in the private sector and that a relatively generous pension scheme has been seen as a way of attracting staff of a suitable calibre and commitment. Alternatively, it may be necessary for a charity's pension scheme to be comparable to the public

Appendix 6 – Charity reserves and defined benefit pension schemes

sector in order to recruit suitable staff from that background. In such a case the scheme may be justified by the benefits to the charity from recruiting and retaining staff.

1.4. The charity trustees will need periodically to consider whether continuing the level of funding required by such a scheme remains in all the circumstances in the interests of the charity.

1.5. The range of options for the charity with regard to the pension scheme will depend on the employment contract, the terms of the pension scheme, the agreed level of contribution by the charity, and any statutory provisions affecting these. In particular, statutory provisions regarding the financial provision to be made on the winding up of a scheme, and other statutory changes, have tended to make the provision of a defined benefit pension scheme a more onerous and expensive option to pursue than previously. Some employers have adopted the policy of closing defined benefit pension schemes to new employees.

1.6. There have also been cases of employers seeking to close defined benefit schemes in relation to the future service of current members. Whether this can be challenged by those members in any particular case will depend on the precise terms of the employment contract, the terms of the pension scheme, and any relevant statutory provisions. The Court of Appeal has held that, where a contract of employment provides for membership of arrangements like a pension scheme, there is an implied obligation upon the employer to discharge their functions in good faith and, so far as lies within their power, to procure the benefits under that arrangement for the employee (*Mihlenstedt v Barclays Bank International* [1989] IRLR 522). Accordingly, charity trustees considering closing a scheme should obtain legal advice before taking any action.

2. Role of Pension Scheme Trustees

2.1. The role of pension scheme trustees is to ensure that the pension scheme is administered in the best way for the members of the scheme and to safeguard their interests. In addition, the pension scheme trustees must understand the employer's financial situation and its commitment to the pension scheme. They must also comprehend the position of the pension scheme and its funding.

3. Legal Obligations of Charity Trustees of Unincorporated Charities with a Defined Benefit Pension Scheme

3.1. This type of pension scheme is usually established by a trust deed and a set of rules. The charity trustees are not necessarily also trustees of the pension scheme but they do have certain obligations in respect of the pension scheme which will vary depending on the exact terms of the pension scheme's trust deed

Appendix B

and rules. The liability of the charity trustees in respect of the pension scheme is likely to be based in trust law and contract but with some overriding statutory requirements.

3.2. The charity trustees will be required to make contributions at a rate to be agreed between the charity trustees and the pension scheme trustees in accordance with the terms of the pension scheme's trust deed and rules. The level of these contributions will be determined in the light of advice from its actuary based on the results of an actuarial valuation of the pension scheme and in accordance with overriding statutory requirements. There is also likely to be a power to reduce or to suspend the contributions to the pension scheme.

3.3. The aim should be to put the pension scheme in the position where it holds sufficient assets to cover its liabilities, both of which are calculated prudently. It is likely that the terms of the pension scheme and the overriding statutory obligations will require the employer to pay sufficient contributions to ensure this. So long as the charity trustees are able to do so out of the funds expendable for that purpose, no difficulty arises.

3.4. Any debt due from the charity trustees for which they are entitled to an indemnity from the charity can usually be paid from the assets of the charity. If the charity trustees are required to transfer an amount to the pension scheme which is more than the value of the assets of the charity, the charity trustees could be personally liable for any shortfall.

3.5. The first call for any debt is on the general funds of the charity (unless incurred in the administration of any restricted fund of the charity). Assets held on special trusts including endowed funds can usually be used to make up any deficiency except where they constitute a distinct charity. Where special trusts are income funds they will be included in SORP compliant accounts as restricted income funds.

3.6. There may be a specific requirement under the pension scheme's trust deed and rules that the rate of contributions must not fall below the minimum required to ensure that, over the lifetime of the pension scheme, the liabilities of the pension scheme do not exceed its assets. Otherwise there will be overriding statutory duties to comply with to ensure that the pension scheme is prudently funded.

3.7. Under new changes to the pensions legislation, if the pension scheme trustees are particularly concerned about the pension scheme's funding position and the ability of its sponsoring employer to resolve the problem, they are able to apply to the Pensions Regulator to see if it can use any of its new powers to help ensure that the pension scheme is being properly supported financially.

3.8. It may also be possible for them to cut back members' future benefits in the pension scheme or even close the pension scheme completely. Ultimately they may need to consider whether to wind it up. A winding up will have the result of crystallising the whole of the pension scheme's liabilities and triggering, as a result of section 75 of the Pensions Act 1995 (as amended by the Pensions Act 2004) a statutory debt due from the pension scheme's sponsoring employer. This will be calculated on the basis of paying all the actual expenses of winding up the pension scheme and securing all members' benefits with annuities purchased from an insurance company. If a pension scheme's sponsoring employer is not able to do this then the trustees of the pension scheme may ultimately be able to approach the new Pension Protection Fund for assistance.

4. Liabilities of charity trustees of an unincorporated charity under a contract

4.1. Liabilities may also arise from contractual arrangements existing between the charity trustees and the trustees of the pension scheme. The contractual liability arising falls on those charity trustees who are parties to the contract. They will be entitled to be reimbursed from the funds of the charity for any liabilities properly incurred under a contract which has been properly entered into. If the assets of the charity are not sufficient to meet the liability, the charity trustees will be personally responsible for the shortfall unless the document imposing the obligation provides that the charity trustees shall only be responsible to the extent of the charity's assets. If there is such a provision, the charity trustees will not be personally liable.

4.2. A person, who has ceased to be a charity trustee but who, as charity trustee, was a party to the contract, is still liable under that contract unless that liability is limited as indicated above or novation occurs. A novation is the substitution of a new contract in place of an old one. It involves an agreement between the original contracting parties and a new contracting party. Thus an agreement between the trustees of the pension scheme, the original charity trustees, and the new charity trustee could substitute the new trustee as one of the contracting parties and release the retiring trustee from future liability under the contract. Such a novation can be express or inferred.

4.3. An inferred novation is where the actions of the parties to the contract and any of their successors indicate that a new contract has been substituted for the old contract and the terms of the old contract do not prevent this. Thus in a partnership case, the acceptance by other parties of payments from the new partners was considered to give rise to a novation of the liabilities of the original partners (*Bilborough v Holmes* (1876) 5 Ch.D 255).

4.4. In any event the former charity trustee will continue to be entitled to an indemnity from the funds of the charity for liabilities properly incurred by him or her.

Appendix B

4.5. It is possible that, after a person has ceased to be a charity trustee, the charity funds are unduly depleted by the actions of the successor charity trustees. If there has been a novation, the former charity trustee will have no liability arising after the date of the novation.

4.6. If the pension trustees were aware of the changes in the charity trustees and have accepted payments made by the new charity trustees, it is likely that there will be an inferred novation of the liabilities of the original trustees (see *Bilborough v Holmes* above).

4.7. If there is no express or inferred novation, and if a former charity trustee has been given an express indemnity from the continuing trustees, s/he will have a claim against those trustees. If no express indemnity has been given, the former charity trustee will have a claim on the charity and not against the continuing trustees.

4.8. If there are insufficient funds to satisfy the indemnity to which the former trustee is entitled from the charity as a result of the continuing trustees having acted in breach of trust, the continuing trustees may be personally liable to the charity to make up the shortfall.

Trustee Liabilities to Employees

4.9. In the case of employment contracts, section 218(5) of the Employment Rights Act 1996 dealing with continuity of employment states 'If there is a change in the partners, personal representatives or trustees who employ any person, the employee's period of employment at the time of the change counts as a period of employment with the partners, personal representatives or trustees after the change, and the change does not break the continuity of the period of employment.'

4.10. Regardless of whether this section in itself means that successor trustees are responsible under the employment contract, a novation is likely to be inferred by the ongoing payment by the trustees of the employees and the work carried out for the benefit of the charity by them.

5. Statutory Requirements

5.1. As explained in paragraph 6.2 in the main body of this guidance, on the Role of the Pensions Regulator, in addition to the contractual responsibilities of the charity trustees under the trust deed and rules of a specific pension scheme, the Pensions Acts impose obligations which may have an impact on charity trustees in certain situations. An example of this would be under section 75 of the Pensions Act 1995 (as amended by the Pensions Act 2004) – see also 3.8 above.

Appendix 6 – Charity reserves and defined benefit pension schemes

5.2. If section 75 of the Pensions Act 1995 (as amended by the Pensions Act 2004) applies, then, a shortfall in the assets of the pension scheme as against the liabilities of the pension scheme is treated as a debt of the employer owed to the trustees of the pension scheme. In such circumstances the debt will fall (in the case of an unincorporated charity) on the charity trustees as the employers at the time of the shortfall rather than at the time the trust deed or any subsequent deed or act of novation is entered into. Whilst the charity trustees would generally be entitled to an indemnity from the assets of the charity, any limitation expressed in the pension scheme rules that sought to limit their liability to the assets of the charity would be ineffective.

6. Conflicts of Interest

6.1. The position regarding conflicts of interest generally is set out in 'A Guide to Conflicts of Interest for Charity Trustees' published by the Charity Commission. A trustee is under a duty not to place themselves in a position where their duty to the charity conflicts with their personal interests unless the conflict is authorised, either expressly or by necessary implication, by the trust instrument (Re Llewellin [1949] Ch 225; *Edge v Pensions Ombudsman* [2000] Ch. 602).

6.2. A pension scheme is usually set up with the trust deed providing for representation among its trustees of various interests, including the employer and the employees. In the Edge case the court took the view that the trustee body as a whole had been set up to take all decisions regarding the pension scheme and that the decisions of that body were not vitiated by the existence of any conflicting interests on the part of a section of the trustees. What mattered was that the decision of the trustees was made properly.

6.3. Even where the existence of a conflict of interest is not authorised by the trust deed it does not in all circumstances vitiate the decision made (The Public *Trustee v Cooper* [2001] WTLR 901). However, where such a conflict exists and cannot be properly managed, charity trustees would be well advised either to apply in advance of any decision for an order of the Charity Commissioners under section 26 of the Charities Act 1993 or to allow any proposed exercise of discretion to be scrutinised in advance by the court.

6.4. A decision by trustees must be reached in accordance with their duties. The duties of the trustees in exercising their discretion are as follows:

- to act within the powers conferred upon them to act reasonably i.e. the decision should be within the range of decisions which a reasonable body of trustees could have made (*Lee v Showmen's Guild of Great Britain* [1952] 1 All ER 1175; *Scott v National Trust* [1998] 2 All ER 705);
- to act within the powers conferred upon them and the established rules and procedures for dealing with issues of the kind under consideration (re Hastings-Bass dec'd (C.A) [1975] Ch 25) ;

Appendix B

- to act in good faith (see re Hastings-Bass above; *Armitage v Nurse* [1997] 2 All ER 705);
- to inform themselves adequately in order to make the decision in question (*R v Charity Commissioners ex parte Baldwin* (2001) 33 HLR 48, QBD; See *Scott v National Trust* above);
- not to take into consideration any factors which it is not proper for them to take into account (*Mettoy Pension Trustees v Evans* (Ch.D.) [1990] 1 WLR 1587; *Dundee General Hospitals Board of Management v Walker and another* [1952] 1 All ER 680; and
- to consider any factors which they should take into account (*Mettoy Pension Trustees v Evans* above; See *Dundee General Hospitals Board of Management v Walker and another* above).

6.5. In case law it is accepted that, provided trustees exercise their discretion in accordance with these duties, the decision in question is not capable of being challenged by the courts.

Index

References are to paragraph number.
Abbreviations:
  Ann – Annex
  App – Appendix
Legal cases and titles of documents referred to in the text, are indicated by italics.

accounting policies
  adoption of   13.2, 16.2.18
  auditing   23.9.7
  disclosures   6.3.9, 13.1–13.4, 13.9, 16.2.18
    examples of   13.3.1, 13.10, 13.11
    fixed assets   13.7.1, 13.7.3
    fund accounting   13.8
    incoming resources   13.5
    investments   13.7.3, 13.7.4
    resources expended   13.6
    small charities   13.11
    stocks   13.7.5
    work in progress   13.7.5
  independent examinations   24.8.8
accounting records
  independent examinations   24.8.4
    accounts comparison   24.8.5
  regulatory framework   3.4.2
accounting reference dates   30.6
  branches   19.4.2
  determination of   3.4.2
  late filing penalties   30.7
accounting requirements 3.4.2
accounting standards
  compliance with   6.3.2, 13.3
accounts disclosure
  exemption for grants   4.13.24
accruals accounting   13.2
  small charities   21.5
acquisition accounting   16.2.6
  fair values in   16.2.7
actuarial valuations   15.3
admission charges
  charity property viewings   28.4.3
advance corporation tax (ACT)
  compensation payments   16.2.16
advertising
  barter transactions   16.3.14
  VAT   27.9.1–27.9.3
affinity card schemes   25.4

agents
  trustees acting as
    disclosure   10.7.1
    incoming resources   9.5.1
analysis of net movement in funds 6.3.6, 14.8
  example of   14.8.1
annual accounts
  preparation of   2.5
  public inspection of   3.4.5, 3.4.7
annual reports *see* trustees' annual report
annual returns
  regulatory framework   3.4.6, 3.4.7
APB *see* Auditing Practices Board
appeals for donations
  right to repayments   5.7
armed services   4.7.3
associates   6.3.11, 16.2.9, 17.8.1, 17.8.2
  audit evidence   23.10.3
  disclosures   17.8.3
Association of Charity Independent Examiners   24.5
audit evidence 23.10
  analytical procedures   23.10.8
  application of funds   23.10.7
  associated operations   23.10.3
  bank reports   23.10.5, 23.Ann.1
  branches   23.10.3
  charitable loans   23.10.6
  completeness of income   23.10.1
  donations   23.10.2
  expenditure   23.10.2
  fixed assets   23.10.4
  internal control system 23.10.1
  investments   23.10.4
  secondary auditors, reliance on   23.10.3
  subsidiaries   23.10.3
auditing   23.1, App2
  accounting policies   23.9.7
  branches   23.3.2, 23.6.6, 23.9.4

699

Index

auditing – *cont'd*
  breaches of trust   23.9.20
  charities' objectives and
    strategies   23.9.10
  Clarity ISAs   23.16.7
  communication with
    client   23.16.4
  company charities   4.10.2
    harmonisation of
      thresholds   4.10.3
  confidentiality   23.3.6
  connected entities   23.9.6
  cost allocations   23.9.11
  engagement letters   23.5
    example of   23.5.1
  entity and environment   23.16.1
  estimates   23.9.9
  Ethical Standards for Auditors *see*
    Ethical Standards for Auditors
    (ESs)
  fraud, detection of   23.9.20
  fundraising services   23.9.8
  going concern   23.11.3
  governance   7.6, 23.3.1
    communication with those
      charged with   23.11.6
  governing documents   23.8.3,
    23.9.10
  HMRC auditing of gift
    aid   28.11.2
  income   23.3.3, 23.9.8, 23.16.3
  internal controls   22.6, 23.9.12–
    23.9.15, 23.9.18, 23.16.2
  knowledge of the charity   23.9.1
  letters of representation   23.11.1
  materiality   23.7
  non-company charities   4.10.1
    harmonisation of
      thresholds   4.10.3
  other information presented with
    financial statements   23.11.5
  overseas operations   23.9.5,
    23.16.3
  performance indicators   23.9.11
  planning   23.6.1
    branches   23.6.6
    groups   23.6.5
    legal structure of
      charity   23.6.4
    materiality   23.7
    overseas operations   23.6.7
    regulatory framework   23.6.2
    reviewing operations of
      charity   23.6.3

  public interest   23.3.6
  regulatory framework   3.4.3, 23.8,
    23.9.2
  related party transactions   23.11.4
  reporting requirements   23.4
  reserves policies   23.9.11
  restricted funds   23.3.4, 23.9.17,
    23.16.3
  review of financial
    statements   23.11.2
  risk register   23.9.16
  risks of material
    misstatement   23.9
    assessment   23.9.19
    fraud   23.9.20
  small charities   21.3
  subsidiaries   23.3.2
  terms of engagement   23.5
  trading activities   23.3.5
  trustees
    education of   23.3.1
    transactions with   23.11.4
  value added exercise   23.14
    whistle blowing   23.8.2, 23.16.5
  see also **audit evidence; audit
    opinion; audit reports;
    auditors**
Auditing Practices Board (APB)
  Practice Notes   23.1, 23.2
audit opinion   23.4, 23.12.1
  examples of   23.12.2, 23.12.3
  qualified opinions   23.12.4
  see also **audit reports**
auditors
  appointment   23.16.6
  ceasing to hold office   23.13.1,
    23.16.6
  discussing matters of material
    significance with
    trustees   23.13.2
  ethical standards *see* **Ethical
    Standards for Auditors
    (ESs)**
  liability limitation   30.9
  payments to   14.6
  reporting to Charity
    Commission   23.13
    duty   23.13.6
    format and contents of
      reports   23.13.7
  rights to information   30.10
  Senior Statutory Auditor
    (SSA)   30.5

700

auditors – *cont'd*
   whistle blowing 4.12, 23.8.2, 23.16.5
   see also **audit evidence; audit opinion; audit reports; auditing**
audit reports 23.12
   addressees 23.12.1
   contents of 23.12.1
   examples of 23.12.2, 23.12.3
   fundamental uncertainties 23.12.4
   receipts and payments accounts 23.12.3
   regulatory framework 3.4.3
   statement of accounts 3.4.3
   summarised financial statements 23.12.5
   see also **audit opinion**
autonomous groups 19.1

balance sheet 6.3.7, 10.1
   charitable companies 18.5, 18.6
   contingent assets and liabilities 10.14
      disclosure 10.14.1
   current assets 10.6
   current liabilities 10.7
   defined benefit pension scheme assets and liabilities 10.9
   fixed assets 10.3
   format 6.Ann.1, 10.2.1
   guarantees 10.13
   heritage assets 10.3.8
      disclosure 10.3.10
   inalienable assets 10.3.9
   intangible fixed assets 10.3.2
   investment assets 10.4
   loan liabilities 10.15
   mixed use of fixed assets 10.3.5
   pension reserve 10.12
   programme-related investments 10.5
   provisions for liabilities and charges 10.8
   revaluation reserve 10.11
   share capital 10.10
   tangible fixed assets 10.3.3, 10.3.4
      depreciation 10.3.6
      disclosure 10.3.7
      revaluation 10.3.11, 10.3.12
bank reports
   audit purposes 23.10.5, 23.Ann.1

beneficiaries
   payments to, PAYE 25.5.4, 26.5
   trades carried on by 25.5.4
benefits in kind
   employees 26.4
borrowing 2.6.4
branches 6.3.4, 19.1
   accounting date 19.4.2
   accounting requirements 19.3
   auditing 19.4.4, 23.3.2, 23.6.6, 23.9.4, 23.10.3
   definition of 19.2
   omission from accounts 13.3, 19.4.3
   restricted funds 19.4.1
   returns 19.4.2
   separate bodies, as 19.4.5
budgeting 2.6.3
business combinations 16.2.6, 16.2.7
business rates 25.11
business review
   company charities 31.2.5

***Carmichael & Anor v National Power plc [1999]* 26.2**
cash flow statements 6.3.8, 12.1, 16.2.1
   acquisitions and disposals 12.3.4
   capital expenditure and financial investment 12.3.3, 12.3.6
   comparatives 12.6
   example of 12.7
   exemptions 12.2
   financing 12.3.6
   format 12.3
   major non-cash transactions 12.4
   management of liquid resources 12.3.5
   operating activities 12.3.1
   reconciliation with balance sheet figures 12.5
   returns on investments and servicing of finance 12.3.2
casual workers 26.2
challenge events
   gift aid 28.4.2
   VAT 27.15.2
Charitable Incorporated Organisation (CIO) 4.9
   Northern Ireland 29.3.1
Charitable Institutions (Fund Raising) Regulations 1994 5
charitable loans 23.10.6

Index

charitable purposes
  definition of 4.3
    Northern Ireland 29.3.1
charities 1.1
  definition of 1.1, 1.3
    previous and new
      requirements 4.3.1
    six 'hallmarks' 1.3.1
  history 1.2
  sectors 1.1
Charities (Accounts and Reports) Regulations 2008 3.1, 3.1.1, App1
  objective of 3.1.1
charities accounts survey 31.3
Charities Act 1960 3.2
Charities Act 1993 3.4
Charities Act 2006 4.1
  amending administrative
    rules 4.13.11
  audit and accounts 4.10, App2
  Charitable Incorporated
    Organisation (CIO) 4.9
  Charity Commission
    authority 14.13.22
    objectives 4.13.23
    public benefit 4.Ann.2
  charity property
    ensuring correct use of 4.13.3
    mortgaging 4.13.21
  Charity Tribunal 4.11
  collections in public places 4.13.8
  company charities 4.13.14
  deciding charity's
    membership 4.13.4
  definition of charitable
    purposes 4.3
  door-to-door collections 4.13.9
  entry and search of premises and
    obtaining documents 4.13.5
  excepted charities 4.7
  exempt charities 4.6
  fundraising solicitation
    statements 4.13.6
  grant making disclosure
    exemption 4.13.24
  group accounts 4.10.4
  flow chart 4.Ann.3
  implementation timetable 4.2.1
    Commencement
      Orders 4.2.2–4.2.6
    ongoing commitments 4.2.7
  local, short-term
    collections 4.13.10
  merger relaxations 4.13.15
  Office of the Third Sector (OTS)
    Thresholds consultation 4.14
  permanent endowments 4.13.13
  public benefit 4.4
    Charity Commission 4.Ann.2
  public collections 4.13.7, 4.13.8
  publicity requirements for
    schemes 4.13.17
  regulatory framework
    comparisons 4.Ann.1
  small charities 4.8
  thresholds for registration 4.5
  transfer of assets of 'failed' appeals
    or trusts 4.13.12
  trustees
    indemnity insurance 4.13.20
    payment 4.13.16
    relief from personal
      liability 4.13.19
    waiver of
      disqualification 4.13.18
  trustees and others
  specific directions for protection of
    charity 4.13.2
  suspension or removal from
    membership of charities 4.13.1
Charities Act (Northern Ireland) 2008 29.3.1
Charities (Northern Ireland) Order 1964 29.3.6
Charities (Northern Ireland) Order 1987 29.3.7
charity auctions
  gift aid 28.4.5
Charity Commission
  accounting guidance 6.1.2
  auditors reporting to *see* **auditors**
  authority 4.13.22
  directions *see* **independent examinations**
  enquiry powers 3.4.7
  guidance, receipts and payments
    accounts 21.4.1
  Northern Ireland 29.3.1
  objectives 4.13.23
  public benefit 4.Ann.2
charity membership
  Charity Commission's
    power 4.13.4
  suspension or removal of trustees
    and others 4.13.1
charity names 1.6

702

Index

charity-owned companies
  payment of profits to
    charity 28.2.6
charity property
  admission charges 28.4.3
  ensuring correct use of 4.13.3
  mortgaging 4.13.21
  protection, specific
    directions 4.13.2
charity shops 25.4
Charity Tribunal 4.11.1
  appeal process 4.11.3
  Northern Ireland 29.3.1
  powers 4.11.2
  process 4.11.2
charity vouchers 28.4.7
Christmas cards 25.4
churches
  excepted church charity
    programme 4.7.1
  registered places of worship 4.7.2
CIFs 6.3.13
Clarity ISAs 23.16.7
commercial participators
  agreements with 5.3
  availability of records 5.4
  definition of 5.2
  identifying benefiting charities 5.6
  method of determining
    consideration 5.6
  revised guidance 5.11
  solicitation statements 4.13.6
  transmissions of money or
    property 5.5
**Common Investment Funds
(CIFs) 6.3.13**
**Community Interest Companies
(CICs) 30.4.1**
  tax reliefs 30.4.3
  unique features 30.4.2
Companies Act 2006 30.1
  auditors
    liability limitation 30.9
    rights to information 30.10
  Community Interest Companies
    (CICs) 30.4.1
    tax reliefs 30.4.3
    unique features 30.4.2
  company charities
    company formation 30.11.4
    company meetings 30.11.2
    company secretary 30.11.3
    directors' age 30.11.5

  directors' service
    addresses 30.11.7
  disclosure on emails and
    websites 30.11.1
  natural person 30.11.6
  directors' duties 30.3.1
    statutory 30.3.2
  filing dates 30.6
  late filing penalties 30.7
  objectives 30.2
  Senior Statutory Auditor
    (SSA) 30.5
  small companies 30.8.1
    exemptions 30.8.3
    qualifying 30.8.2
company charities 3.4.1, 18.1
  auditing 4.10.2
    harmonisation of
      thresholds 4.10.3
  balance sheet 18.5, 18.6
  business review 31.2.5
  company formation 30.11.4
  company meetings 30.11.2
  company secretary 30.11.3
  consolidated financial statements:
    example of 18.8
  directors' age 30.11.5
  directors' report 7.4
  directors' service
    addresses 30.11.7
  disclosure on emails and
    websites 30.11.1
  form and content of
    accounts 6.3.11, 18.2
    group accounts 4.10.4
  income and expenditure
    account 18.3
    example of 18.8
    summary 18.4
  liabilities of 2.9
  Memorandum and Articles of
    Association changes 4.13.14
  natural person 30.11.6
  non-statutory accounts 20.2
  Northern Ireland 29.3.1
  revaluation reserve 18.6
  Statement of Financial
    Activities 18.3, 18.4
    example of 18.8
  statement of total recognised gains
    and losses: example of 18.8
  summary financial
    information 18.7
comparability 13.2

Index

comparative figures 3.4.2, 6.1.1, 12.6
completeness of income 23.10.1
connected charities 19.5
consolidated financial statements 6.3.11, 16.2.2, 16.3.19, 17.1, 17.2, 17.4.2
  disclosures 17.6
  example of 17.8.4
  exclusions 17.6.4
  exemptions 17.4.1, 17.4.2
  filing 17.7
  line-by-line method 17.5
  segmental information 17.5, 17.6.2
  see also **associates; joint arrangements; joint ventures**
construction services
  VAT 27.13.1
contingent assets 10.14, 16.2.12
  disclosure 10.14.1
contingent liabilities 9.13.3, 10.14, 16.2.12
  disclosure 10.14.1
contractual income
  recognition 9.5.1
Control Risk Self Assessment (CRSA) 22.7, 22.8
credit cards
  affinity card schemes 25.4
'credit crunch' *see* **downturn**
creditors
  disclosure 10.7.1
critical risk register 22.2, 22.4, 22.6
CRSA (Control Risk Self Assessment) 22.7, 22.8
current assets 10.6
  disclosure 10.6.1
current liabilities 10.7
custodian trustees 2.2, 7.11

data capture costs 9.16.1
death-in-service benefits 16.3.23
debtors
  disclosures 10.6.1
  long-term 16.3.1
declaration of status 1.5
deeds of covenant 28.3
  taxation 28.3

deferred income
  disclosure 9.5.2
  example 9.5.3
deferred tax 16.2.19
defined benefit pension schemes 6.3.7, 6.3.12, 9.23, 15.1, 15.3, 15.4
  actuarial valuations 15.3
  balance sheet 10.9, 10.12
  death-in-service benefits 16.3.23
  disclosures 15.8
  incapacity benefits 16.3.23
defined contribution pension schemes 15.2
  disclosures 15.8
depreciation
  fixed assets 10.3.6
derivatives 16.2.13
designated funds 6.4, 11.2.2
  see also **funds**
directors
  age 30.11.5
  duties 30.3.1
    statutory 30.3.2
  natural person 30.11.6
  report 7.4
    link with trustees' annual reports 7.3, 7.4
  service addresses 30.11.7
dividends
  compensation for removal of ACT credits 16.2.16
documents
  entry and search of premises to obtain 4.13.5
donations
  audit evidence 23.10.2
  facilities and services 6.3.5, 9.8
    disclosure 9.8.1
  recognition 9.5.1
  services 31.6.4
  VAT 27.6, 27.10, 27.11
door-to-door collections 4.13.9, 5.10
downturn
  key points emerging from survey 32.2
    effective financial management 32.2.2
    fundraising 32.2.1
    investment policy 32.2.6
    management information 32.2.7
    reserves policy 32.2.5

downturn – *cont'd*
  key points emerging from survey – *cont'd*
    risk assessment 32.2.4
    strategic planning 32.2.3
  performance
    management 32.Ann
  priorities during 32.3
  recent survey 32.1

employees
  benefits in kind 26.4
  secondment to charity 28.10
  specific directions for protection of charity 4.13.2
  suspension or removal from membership of charities 4.13.1
employment status 26.2
employment taxes 26.1
  beneficiaries, Schedule E liability 26.5
  benefits in kind 26.4
  casual workers 26.2
  employment status 26.3
  living accommodation 26.4
  Ministers of Religion 26.4
  National Insurance contributions (NIC) 26.6
  non-resident employees of missionary societies 26.4
  temporary workers 26.2
  volunteer workers 26.2
endowment funds 11.2.4
  see also **funds**
engagement letters
  auditing 23.5
  example of 23.5.1
estimation techniques 13.2, 23.9.9
Ethical Standards for Auditors (ESs) 23.15.1
  non-audit services provided to audit clients (ES 5) 23.15.2
  provisions available for Smaller Entities (PASE) 23.15.3
euro 16.3.9
exempt charities 1.4.1, 3.4.1, 4.6
excepted charities 1.4.2, 3.4.1, 4.7
  armed services 4.7.3
  church charity programme 4.7.1
  registered places of worship 4.7.2
exceptional items 9.16.2, 16.2.3

ex-gratia payments 6.3.6
  disclosure 14.7
expenditure
  allocation to activity categories 9.14
    disclosure 9.14.1
  audit evidence 23.10.2
  recognition of 9.13
    contractual arrangements 9.13.1
  see also **resources expended**
***Express and Echo Publications v Tanton [1999]* 26.3**

'failed' appeals or trusts
  transfer of assets 4.13.12
finance leases 16.1.6
financial instruments 16.2.13, 16.2.25, 16.2.26
financial management
  effective, during downturn 32.2.2
Financial Reporting Exposure Draft (FRED) 42 – Heritage Assets 31.7
Financial Reporting Standard for Smaller Entities (FRSSE) 6.Ann.2, 16.2.28, 21.6
  updated 31.4
Financial Reporting Standards (FRSs) 6.3.3, 16.2
financial services
  disclosures 14.6
financial statements
  objective of 31.6.1
financial years
  determination of 3.4.2
fixed assets 10.3
  accounting policies 13.7.1, 13.7.3
  auditing 23.10.4
  depreciation 10.3.6
  gains and losses on 9.2.2
  heritage assets 6.3.7, 10.3.3, 10.3.8
    disclosure 10.3.10
  impairment reviews 10.3.13, 10.3.14, 16.2.11
  inalienable assets 10.3.9
  intangible assets 10.3.2, 16.2.10, 16.3.15
  mixed use of 10.3.5
  tangible fixed assets 10.3.3, 10.3.4, 10.3.6, 10.3.7, 10.3.11, 16.2.15, 16.3.11
    revaluation 10.3.11, 10.3.12

Index

foreign currency translation 16.2.23
fraud
 detection of 23.9.20
friendly societies 3.4.1
FRSs 6.3.3, 16.2
FRSSE 6.Ann.2, 16.2.28, 21.6
fundraising activities
 auditor input 23.14
 dinners 28.4.1
 during downturn 32.2.1
 house-to-house collections 5.10
 Northern Ireland 29.3.1
 professional fundraisers and commercial participators 5.2
  agreements with 5.3
  availability of records 5.4
  identifying benefiting charities 5.6
  method of determining consideration 5.6
  remuneration details 5.6
  revised guidance 5.11
  solicitation statements 4.13.6
  transmissions of money or property 5:5
 promotional ventures 5.6
 public collections 5.9, 5.10
 regulations 5
 resources expended 6.3.5, 9.16.3, 9.16.4
 right to cancel payments 5.7
 street collections 5.9
 tax exemptions, extra-statutory concession 25.7, 25.7.1
 trustees' responsibilities 2.6.5
 types of 25.6.1
 unauthorised fundraising 5.8
 VAT 27.14.1
funds
 accounting policies 13.8
 accounting requirements 6.3.3, 11.1–11.3
 analysis of assets and liabilities 11.4.2
 appropriate form of resources 11.4.3
 definition of 11.2
 disclosures 11.7
 examples of 11.7.1
 'failed', transfer 4.13.12
 nature and purpose of 11.4.5
 overheads 11.6
 realised and unrealised elements 11.4.4
 reconciliation of opening and closing balances 11.4.1
 residual interest and designations 31.6.3
 structure of 11.3
 total return 11.8
 transfers between 11.5
 types of 6.3.3, 8.2.1, 11.2
 see also **Common Deposit Funds; Common Investment Funds; designated funds; permanent endowment funds; restricted funds**
further education institutions 3.4.1

GAYE (give-as-you-earn) 28.5
 statutory references 28.12
gift aid 28.2.1
 benefits received by donors 28.4
  admissions to charity property 28.4.3
  challenge events 28.4.2
  charity auctions 28.4.5
  charity vouchers 28.4.7
  fundraising dinners 28.4.1
  lotteries and raffles 28.4.6
  membership subscriptions 28.4.4
 companies 28.2.6
 consultation, amendments as a result of 28.11.1
 declarations 28.2.2, App5
  linked to sponsored events 28.2.4
  oral 28.2.3
 HMRC auditing 28.11.2
 sale of donated goods 28.2.5
 statutory references 28.12
 tax returns, giving through
  carry back 28.6.1
  self assessment 28.6.2
 transitional reliefs 28.11.1
 see also **deeds of covenant**
gifts in kind 6.3.5, 9.7, 28.2.5
 businesses, from 28.10
 disclosure 9.7.1
 land and buildings 28.9
 shares, securities and other investments 28.8
 statutory references 28.12

give-as-you-earn (GAYE) 28.5
  statutory references 28.12
going concern 13.2
  auditors' consideration of 23.11.3
  consideration: retirement benefits 15.6
  indicators of potential problems 23.11.3
goodwill 16.2.10, 16.2.11, 16.3.15
governance 23.3.1
  auditor input 23.14
  communication with those charged with 23.11.6
governance costs 6.3.5, 9.19, 9.19.1
governing documents 23.8.3
  non-compliance with 23.9.10
government grants 16.1.1
grants
  disclosures 31.2.2
    exemption 4.13.24
  financing of capital projects 31.6.5
  payable
    costs of 9.18
  receivable 16.1.1
    accounting for 31.2.1
    recognition 9.5.1
    VAT 27.5
gross income
  definition of 3.4.2
group accounts 4.10.4
  flow chart 4.Ann.3
groups
  auditing 23.6.5
guarantees
  disclosures 10.13

Hall v Lorimer (1994) 26.3
heritage assets 6.3.7, 10.3.3, 10.3.8, 10.3.10
  Financial Reporting Exposure Draft (FRED) 42 – Heritage Assets 31.7
higher education institutions 3.4.1
higher paid employees 14.5.1, 14.5.2
hire purchase contracts 16.1.6
history of charity 1.2
house-to-house collections 4.13.9, 5.10
housing associations 3.4.1

hyper-inflationery economies 16.2.24

impairment reviews 10.3.13, 10.3.14, 16.2.11
inalienable assets 10.3.9
incapacity benefits 16.3.23
Income and Corporation Taxes Act (ICTA) 1988 App3
income and expenditure account 18.3
  example of 18.8
  summary 18.4
incoming resources
  accounting policies 13.5
  auditing 23.9.8
  subject to restrictions 9.5.1
  see also **Statement of Financial Activities (SOFA)**
incorporated charities *see* **charitable companies**
indemnity insurance 2.9, 4.13.20, 6.3.6
independent examinations 24.1, 24.2
  Commission's directions 24.2, 24.8
    accounting policies 24.8.8
    accounting records 24.8.4
    accounts comparison 24.8.5
    analytical procedures 24.8.6
    documentation 24.8.2
    estimates and judgements 24.8.8
    examination and accounting thresholds 24.8.1
    examiner's report 24.8.10
    form and content of accounts 24.8.7
    reports to Charity Commission 24.8.11
    trustees' annual report 24.8.9
    understanding the charity 24.8.3
  objective of 24.2
  requirement 24.Ann.1.1
  regulatory framework 3.4.3
  summarised accounts 24.9
  see also **independent examiners**
independent examiners
  audit of non-company charities 4.10.1
  competence 24.3, 24.5, 24.Ann.1.4

Index

independent examiners – *cont'd*
   definition of   24.3, 24.4, 24.Ann.1.2
   ethical considerations   24.4
   independent person   24.Ann.1.3
   payments to   14.6, 24.Ann.1.1.3
   preparation of accounts   24.8.5
   relevant practical experience   24.6, 24.Ann.1.5
   reports, examples of   24.Ann.2
   selection of   24.3, 24.7, 24.Ann.1
      procedures   24.Ann.1.6
   whistle blowing   4.12
   see also **independent examinations**
independent living units
   VAT   27.15.4
industrial and provident societies   3.4.1
insurance
   indemnity   2.9, 4.13.20, 6.3.6
   loss to funds resulting from acts and defaults of trustees   2.9
intangible fixed assets   **10.3.2, 16.2.10, 16.3.15**
interest costs   **31.2.4**
inter-fund loans   **10.15**
internal controls   **2.6.1**
   auditing   22.6, 23.9.12–23.9.15, 23.9.18, 23.10.1, 23.16.2
International Standards on Auditing (ISAs)   **23.2**
   see also **Clarity ISAs**
investment properties   **16.1.5**
investments
   accounting policies   13.7.3
      example disclosure   13.7.4
   assets   10.4
      disclosure   10.4.4, 10.4.5
      valuation   10.4.3
   auditing   23.10.4
   classification of investments   10.4.2
   gains and losses   9.22
   income   6.3.5, 9.10
      disclosure   9.10.1, 9.10.2
   management of costs of   6.3.5, 9.16.5, 31.2.3
   policy during downturn   32.2.6
   pooling schemes   6.3.13
   powers of investment   10.4.1
   responsibility for   2.6.2, 2.8
   see also **investment properties; programme-related investments**

ISAs (International Standards on Auditing)   **23.2**
   see also **Clarity ISAs**

joint arrangements   **6.3.11, 16.2.9, 17.8.1, 17.8.2**
   disclosures   17.8.3
joint ventures   **6.3.11, 16.2.9, 17.8.1, 17.8.2**
   disclosures   17.8.3

land and buildings
   gifting
      statutory references   28.12
      tax relief   28.9
      VAT   27.15.1
laws and regulations
   auditor advice   23.14
   giving to charities   28.12
leases   **16.1.6, 16.3.16**
legacies   **6.3.5, 9.6.2, 9.6.4, 21.4.4, 28.7**
   disclosures   9.6.3
      example of   9.6.5
letters of representation   **23.11.1**
liabilities
   recognition of   9.13.2
   trustees   2.6.1, 2.9
      indemnity insurance   4.13.20, 6.3.6
      relief   4.13.19
life assurance   **16.2.27**
linked organisations
   accounting treatment adopted   13.3, 19.4.3
listed buildings
   VAT   27.13.2
living accommodation   **26.4**
loans
   charitable loans   23.10.6
   inter-fund   10.15
   securities on   10.15
   subsidiaries   10.15
local church charities   **4.7.1**
local, short-term collections   **4.13.10**
logo
   payments for use of   25.4
long-term contracts   **16.1.3**
long-term debtors   **16.3.1**
lotteries   **25.4**
   gift aid   28.4.6

MacFarlane and Skivington v Glasgow CC [2000] 26.3
major non-cash transactions 12.4
management information
 during downturn 32.2.7
materiality
 auditing 23.7
medical goods
 VAT 27.12
membership benefits
 VAT 27.8
membership subscriptions
 gift aid 28.4.4
mergers
 accounting 16.2.6
 Northern Ireland 29.3.1
 relaxations 4.13.15
Ministers of Religion 26.4
missionary societies
 non-resident employees 26.4
Monitoring and Control of Charities (Public Accounts Committee) 3.3
multi-employer defined benefit schemes 15.1

National Insurance contributions (NIC) 26.6
National Anti-Vivisection Society v IR Commrs [1948] 1.3
new buildings
 VAT 27.13.1
NHS charitable trusts 3.4.1
non-company charities
 audit and accounts 4.10.1, App2
 harmonisation of thresholds 4.10.3
 group accounts 4.10.4
 trustees, amendment of administrative rules 4.13.11
non-resident employees of missionary societies 26.4
Northern Ireland
 Charities Act (Northern Ireland) 2008 29.3.1
 Charities (Northern Ireland) Order 1964 29.3.6
 Charities (Northern Ireland) Order 1987 29.3.7
 charity accounts 29.3.2
 charity administration 29.3.3
 charity legislation 29.3.5

 Department for Social Development 29.3.4

Office of the Scottish Charity Regulator (OSCR) 29.2
Office of the Third Sector (OTS) Thresholds consultation 4.14
officers
 specific directions for protection of charity 4.13.2
 suspension or removal from membership of charities 4.13.1
operating and financial review (OFR) 31.2.6
operating leases 16.1.6
 incentives 16.3.16
overseas operations
 auditing 23.6.7, 23.9.5, 23.16.3

parent undertakings
 approval of accounts 17.7
 definition of 17.3.1, 17.3.2
 see also **consolidated financial statements**
participators *see* **commercial participators**
payroll giving 28.5
penalties
 late filing of accounts 30.7
pension costs
 allocation of 15.4
 restricted funds 15.5
pension schemes
 tax credits on dividends 16.3.7
 see also **defined benefit pension schemes; defined contribution pension schemes; retirement benefits**
performance management
 during downturn 32.Ann
permanent endowment funds 11.2.4
 effective use of 4.13.13
 see also **funds**
post-balance sheet events 6.3.3, 16.2.21
pre-contract costs 16.3.22
primary purpose trades 25.5
 see also **trading**
professional fundraisers
 agreements with 5.3
 availability of records 5.4
 definition of 5.2

Index

professional fundraisers – *cont'd*
  identifying benefiting charities 5.6
  remuneration 5.6
  revised guidance 5.11
  solicitation statements 4.13.6
  transmissions of money or
    property 5.5
**programme-related
investments 6.3.7, 10.5**
  disclosure 10.5.1
promotional ventures 5.6
property *see* **charity property;
land and buildings**
provisions 10.7, 10.8, 16.2.12
  disclosure 10.8.1, 10.8.2
public benefit
  Charity Commission 4.Ann.2
  concept of 4.4
  Northern Ireland 29.3.1
  reporting 4.4.1
  sub-sector guidance 4.4.2
**public collections 4.13.7,
4.13.8, 5.9, 5.10, 29.3.1**
**public inspection of accounts
and annual reports 3.4.5, 3.4.7**
public interest 23.3.6
publicity for schemes 4.13.17

**quasi-subsidiaries 17.3.2,
19.4.5**

raffles
  gift aid 28.4.6
**receipts and payments
account 21.4.1, 21.4.2, 21.4.4**
  audit reports 3.4.3, 23.12.3
  classification of headings 21.4.3
  donated assets 21.4.4
  external examination of 21.4.1
  features of 21.4.1
recession *see* **downturn**
recreational charities 4.3.1
registration 1.4
  declarations on business
    documents 1.5
  excepted charities 1.4.2, 3.4.1,
    4.7
    armed services 4.7.3
    church charity
      programme 4.7.1
    registered places of
      worship 4.7.2
  exempt charities 1.4.1, 3.4.1
  false representations 5.8

Northern Ireland 29.3.1
  thresholds 4.5
regulatory framework 3.4.1
  comparisons 4.Ann.1
related parties 14.2
  auditing 23.11.4
  disclosures 14.2, 16.2.8
    example of 14.2.1
  transactions 6.3.6, 14.2
  see also **connected charities;
    trustees**
relevance 13.2
reliability 13.2
religious charities
  Northern Ireland 29.3.1
rental income 25.4
reporting accountants
  payments to 14.6
  whistle blowing 4.12
**reporting financial
performance 16.2.3**
representation letters 23.11.1
Republic of Ireland
  adoption of SORP 2005 29.1,
    29.4
  Charities Bill 2007 29.4.1
  move towards common charity
    legislation 29.4.2
reputational risks 22.5
**research and
development 16.1.4**
reserves 8.1, App6
  definition of 8.2.2
  disclosures 8.2.3
  funds of charity 8.2.1
  policy 6.4, 8.2.3, App6
    during downturn 32.2.5
    examples of 8.3
    retirement benefits 15.7, App6
  revaluation reserve 8.4, 10.11,
    18.6
resources expended
  accounting policies 13.6
    example disclosures 13.6.1
  see also **Statement of Financial
    Activities (SOFA)**
restricted funds 11.2.3
  auditing 23.3.4, 23.9.17, 23.16.3
  branches 19.4.1
  misuse of 11.2.3
  overheads 11.6
  pension costs 15.5
  see also **funds**

Index

retirement benefits 16.2.17
  consideration of going
     concern   15.6
  reserves policy   15.7, App6
  see also **defined benefit pension schemes; defined contribution pension schemes**
revaluation
  reserve   8.4, 10.11, 18.6
  tangible fixed assets   10.3.11, 10.3.12
risk management   22.1, 22.2, 22.10, 22.16
  application of strategies to identified risk   22.13
  risk assessment
     auditors   23.16.1
     during downturn   32.2.4
     letter: case study   22.Ann
  charity objectives   22.3
  commitment   22.8
  communication   22.9
  costs and savings   22.11
  critical risk register   22.2, 22.4, 22.6
  CRSA   22.7, 22.8
  cultural issues   22.12
  disclosures   16.2.13
  identification of risks   22.4, 22.15
  internal control system   22.6
  prioritising risks   22.5
  responsibilities, allocation of   22.8
  review process   22.7
  simplicity   22.13
  trustees' responsibilities   2.6.1, 2.7
  types of risk   22.14

Scotland
  Office of the Scottish Charity Regulator (OSCR)   29.2, 29.2.2
     annual monitoring   29.2.1
  Register   29.2.2
  regulatory framework   29.2
secondary auditors
  reliance on   23.10.3
secondment of employees   28.10
segmental reporting 16.1.7, 17.5, 17.6.2
Senior Statutory Auditor (SSA)   30.5
share capital 10.10

shares and securities
  gifting to charities   28.8
     statutory references   28.12
small charities   21.1
  accounting concessions   6.Ann.2, 21.7
  accounting policies   13.11
  accruals accounting   21.5
  audit requirements   21.3
  change of accounting
     basis   21.4.6
  disclosures
     abbreviated accounts   31.5.2
     exemptions   31.5.1
  ethical standards provisions (PASE)   23.15.3
  FRSSE   6.Ann.2, 16.2.28, 21.6
  gift aid   28.11.2
  greater flexibility   4.8
     change of purposes   4.8.2
     transfer of assets   4.8.1
  gross income
     exceeding £100,000   21.2.4
     not exceeding £5,000   21.2.1
     not exceeding £10,000   21.2.2
     not exceeding £100,000   21.2.3
     not exceeding £500,000   21.2.4, 21.7
  receipts and payments
     account   21.3, 21.4.1–21.4.4
  statement of assets and
     liabilities   21.4.1, 21.4.2, 21.4.4, 21.4.5
     legacies   21.4.4
  trustees' annual report   21.2.2, 21.4.6, 21.7
small companies   30.8.1
  exemptions   30.8.3
  qualifying   30.8.2
SOFA *see* Statement of Financial Activities (SOFA)
SORP 2000 *see* Statement of Financial Activities (SOFA)
SORP 2005, *Accounting and Reporting by Charities*   6.1, 7.2, 9.3, 29.1
  accounting for retirement
     benefits   6.3.12
  accounting for small
     charities   6.Ann.2
  aim of   6.2.1
  appendices and tables   6.Ann.3
  areas for further research   31.10.1
  balance sheet   6.3.7

711

Index

SORP 2005, *Accounting and Reporting by Charities* – *cont'd*
branches 6.3.4
cash flow statement 6.3.8
changes in 6.2.4, 7.2
charities accounts survey 31.3
Charity Commission
  guidance 6.1.2
common investment funds 6.3.13
compliance with 13.3
disclosure of accounting
  policies 6.3.9
Financial Reporting Exposure
  Draft (FRED) 42 – Heritage
  Assets 31.7
Financial Reporting Standard for
  Smaller Entities (FRSSE) 31.4
fund accounting 6.3.3
general accounting
  principles 6.3.2
Information Sheet 1 31.2
  accounting for grants
    receivable 31.2.1
  bank interest and other finance
    costs 31.2.4
  business review and company
    charities 31.2.5
  disclosures for grant-making
    charities 31.2.2
  investment management
    costs 31.2.3
  operating and financial review
    (OFR) 31.2.6
Information Sheet 2 31.6
  accounting for business
    combinations 31.6.6
  donated services 31.6.4
  grants for financing capital
    projects 31.6.5
  multi-period liabilities 31.6.2
  objective of financial
    statements 31.6.1
  residual interest and
    designations 31.6.3
international issues 31.10.4
investment pooling
  schemes 6.3.13
overview 6.2.2
practical considerations 6.4
related notes 6.3.6
Republic of Ireland 29.1, 29.4
scope of 6.1.1, 31.1
second edition 6.2.3

small charities 31.10.3
  disclosures 31.5
special sections 6.3.11
stakeholder roundtable
  events 31.10.2
Standard Information Return
  (SIR) 31.9
statement of financial activities
  (SOFA) 6.3.5, 6.Ann.1
summarised financial
  statements 6.3.10
summary financial
  information 6.3.10
trustees' annual report *see*
  trustees' annual report
***Special Commrs of Income Tax
v Pemsel [1891]*** **1.3**
special trusts 19.1, 19.2
sponsored events
  gift aid 28.2.4
sponsorship payments 25.4
  challenge events 28.4.2
  VAT 27.6
sports clubs 4.3.1
SSAPs 16.1
staff costs 6.3.6, 14.5, 14.5.2
  higher-paid staff 14.5.1, 14.5.2
staff hire
  VAT concession 27.15.5
staff numbers 14.5, 14.5.2
**stamp duty land tax
(SDLT) 25.12**
**stamp duty reserve tax
(SDRT) 25.13**
**Standard Information Return
(SIR) 31.9**
start-up costs 9.16.1, 16.3.12
statement of accounts 3.4.2
  audit reports 3.4.3
  regulatory framework 3.4.2
  see also **balance sheet; notes to
    the accounts; Statement of
    Financial Activities (SOFA)**
**statement of assets and
liabilities 21.4.1, 21.4.2,
21.4.4, 21.4.5**
**Statement of Financial
Activities (SOFA) 6.3.5, 6.4, 9.1**
  actuarial gains and losses on
    defined benefit pension
    schemes 9.23
  allocation and apportionment of
    costs 6.3.5
  changes in SORP 2000 9.2

Index

Statement of Financial Activities (SOFA) – *cont'd*
changes in SORP 2005   9.3
charitable companies   18.3, 18.4, 18.8
form and content   6.2.3, 6.Ann.1, 9.4
  example layouts   9.4.1
gains and losses on fixed assets   9.21
gains and losses on investment assets   9.22
incoming resources   6.3.5, 9.5, 9.12
  activities for generating funds   6.3.5, 9.9
  charitable activities   9.11
  disclosure   9.5.2, 9.5.3
  donated services and facilities   9.8
  generated funds   6.3.5
  gifts in kind   9.7
  investment income   6.3.5, 9.10
  recognition of   6.3.5, 9.5.1
  voluntary income   6.3.5, 9.6
notes   6.3.6, 9.4
other recognised gains and losses   6.3.5
resources expended   6.3.5, 9.15
  charitable activities   6.3.5, 9.17, 9.17.1
  costs of generating funds   6.3.5, 9.16
  costs of generating voluntary income   6.3.5, 9.16.1, 9.16.2
  fundraising trading   6.3.5, 9.16.3, 9.16.4
  governance costs   6.3.5, 9.19
  grant making activity   9.18
  investment management costs   6.3.5, 9.16.5
  recognition   6.3.5
  support costs   6.3.5, 9.13.4, 9.13.5
    grant making activity   9.18, 9.18.1
  transfers between funds   6.3.5, 9.20
    disclosure   9.20.1

statement of total recognised gains and losses   18.8

statement of trustees' responsibilities   23.12.1

Statements of Standard Accounting Practice (SSAPs)   16.1
stocks   16.1.3
  accounting policies   13.7.5
strategic planning
  during downturn   32.2.3
street collections   5.9
subscriptions
  gift aid   28.4.4
  VAT 27.8
subsidiaries   17.4.2
  approval of accounts   17.7
  auditing   23.3.2, 23.10.3
  definition of   17.3.2
  disclosures   17.6
  see also **consolidated financial statements**
substance of transactions   16.2.5
substantial donor legislation   28.11.3, 28.12
summarised financial statements   6.3.10, 20.1, 20.1.1, 20.2
  audit reports   23.12.5
  independent examinations   24.9
summary financial information   6.3.10, 18.7, 20.1, 20.1.1, 20.2
  trustees' statement   20.2
support costs   6.3.5, 9.13.4
  disclosure   9.13.5
  grant making   9.18

tangible fixed assets   10.3.3, 10.3.4, 10.3.6, 10.3.7, 10.3.11, 16.2.15, 16.3.11
  see also **fixed assets**
taxation
  administration of tax system   28.11.5
  auditor input   23.14
  deferred   16.2.19
  employment taxes *see* **employment taxes**
  exemptions   25.1, App3
    fundraising events   25.7, 25.7.1
  gifting, relief
    equipment or trading stock   28.10
    land and buildings   28.9
    shares and securities   28.8
  gifts of non-business assets   App4

Index

taxation – *cont'd*
  PAYE 25.5.4, 26.5
  reliefs
    Community Interest
      Companies 30.4.3
    gifting 28.8–28.10
    secondment of
      employees 28.10
    repayments, donation of 28.6.2
  see also **trading; value added tax**
Taxation of Chargeable Gains Act 1992 App4
tax returns
  gift aid payments through
    carry back 28.6.1
    self assessment 28.6.2
    trusts 28.11.5
temporary workers 26.2
terms of engagement *see* **engagement letters**
total expenditure
  definition of 3.4.2
trading activities
  auditing 23.3.5
  flow chart 25.Ann
  primary purpose trades 25.5
    ancillary trading 25.5.1
    mixed trades 25.5.3
    non-primary purpose
      trading 25.5.2
    work carried out by
      beneficiaries 25.5.4
  types of activities 25.4
trading company 25.9
  financing of 25.10
trading income
  business rates 25.11
  categories of trades 25.2
  chargeable periods beginning
    on/after 22 March 2006 25.6
  definition of trade 25.2
  profits, taxation of 25.8
  tax exemptions 25.1, 25.3
    small-scale exemption 25.5.5
  stamp duty land tax
    (SDLT) 25.12
  stamp duty reserve tax
    (SDRT) 25.13
transfers 9.20
  disclosure 9.20.1
true and fair view 3.4.2

trustees 2.1
  agents, as *see* **agents**
  auditors' discussions with 23.13.2
  definition of 2.2
  deliberate or reckless
    misconduct 24.Ann.3
  disqualification from acting as 2.3
    waiver 4.13.18
  expenses 6.3.6
    disclosures 14.4, 14.4.1
  indemnity insurance 2.9, 6.3.6
  non-company charities,
    amendment of administrative
    rules 4.13.11
  Northern Ireland 29.3.1
  payment 4.13.16
  personal liability 2.6.1, 2.9
  relief 4.13.19
  remuneration and benefits 6.3.6,
    14.3, 14.4.1, 14.5.2
  responsibilities 2.4, 2.6
    borrowing 2.6.4
    budgeting 2.6.3
    fundraising activities 2.6.5
    internal controls 2.6.1
    investments 2.6.2, 2.8
    preparation of annual report
      and accounts 2.5, 29.3.1
    risk management 2.7
    statement of 23.12.1
  risk management 22.14
  specific directions for protection of
    charity 4.13.2
  suspension or removal from
    membership of charities 4.13.1
  transactions with 14.4.1
    auditing 23.11.4
  see also **custodian trustees; trustees' annual report**
trustees' annual report 6.3.1, 6.4, 7.1, 31.8.1
  achievements and
    performance 7.8, 31.8.3
  changes in SORP 2005 7.2
  comprehensive examples 7.Ann.1
  content of 6.3.1, 7.4
  custodian trustees, acting as 7.11
  directors' report, link with 7.3, 7.4
  financial review 7.9
  future plans 7.10
  independent examinations 24.8.9
  Northern Ireland 29.3.1
  objectives and activities 7.7

trustees' annual report   6.3.1, 6.4, 7.1, 31.8.1 – *cont'd*
    organisational structure, governance and management   7.6
    preparation   7.3
    public inspection of   3.4.5
    reference and administrative information   7.5
    regulatory framework   3.4.4, 3.4.7
    small charities   21.2.2, 21.4.6, 21.7
    structure and components   7.4
    trustee induction and training   31.8.2
trusts
    tax returns   28.11.4
    see also **NHS charitable trusts; special trusts**

UITF Abstracts   16.3
unauthorised fundraising   5.8
understandability   13.2
unrestricted income funds   11.2.1
    see also **funds**
Urgent Issues Task Force (UITF) Abstracts   16.3

value added tax (VAT)   16.1.2, 27.1
    advertising, zero-rating   27.9.1
        exceptions   27.9.2, 27.9.3
    application   27.2
    business, definition   27.3
    business and non-business activities, examples   27.7
    challenge events   27.15.2

    donations   27.6, 27.10
    goods used to collect donations   27.11
    sale/letting of donated goods   27.10.1
    fundraising events   27.14.1
    grants   27.5
    independent living units   27.15.4
    land and property   27.15.1
    Lennartz regulations   27.15.3
    listed buildings   27.13.2
    medical goods   27.12
    membership benefits   27.8
    new buildings   27.13.1
    recovery of   27.4
    registration   27.2
    sponsorship   27.6
    staff hire concession   27.15.5
    subscriptions   27.8
    voluntary disclosures   27.15.6
voluntary income   6.3.5, 9.6
    costs of generating   6.3.5, 9.16.1
        disclosure   9.16.2
    disclosures   9.6.1, 9.6.3, 9.6.5, 9.16.2
    legacies   9.6.2
        accounting examples   9.6.4
        disclosure   9.6.3, 9.6.5
volunteers
    contribution of   7.7, 9.8
    employment law   26.2

websites   16.3.17
whistle blowing
    duty and protection of whistle blowers   4.12, 23.8.2, 23.16.5
***Woodfield Report*   3.3**
work in progress
    accounting policies   13.7.5